W9-CVO-136

Genealogical & Local History
Books In Print

4th Edition
(Supplement #2)

Volume 5

Complied by
Bette A. Schreiner and Kamm Y. Schreiner

GBIP - New York Branch
Maine, New York
1992

Printed in the United States of America

Library of Congress Catalog Number 75-4225
ISBN 0-89157-136-1 (paper)
ISSN 0146-616X

The Library of Congress cataloged this serial as follows:

Genealogical & local history books in print. 2nd Supplement to 4th ed.
  [Maine, NY] 1976 -
     v.22 cm.

  Continues: Genealogical books in print, ISSN 0147-426X
  Key title: Genealogical & local history books in print,
     ISSN 0146-616X

  1. United States - Genealogy - Bibliography - Periodicals
  2. United States - History, Local - Bibliography - Periodicals
  3. Genealogy - Bibliography - Periodicals

| Z5313.U5G45 | 016.929'1'0973 | 77-648320 |
| [CS47] | [7708] | MARC-S |

This book may be ordered from:

GBIP - New York Branch
PO Box 394
Maine, NY 13802-0394

$19.50 + $2.10 p&h
[*New York residents add sales tax*]

Other books available from this company:
(while supply lasts)

4th edition - *Genealogical & Local History Books in Print* (3 v.) [1985] - $35.00
4th ed. 1st supplement - *Genealogical & Local History Books in Print* [1990] - $19.95

[*Add postage and handling fees - $1.75 for 1st $10.00
plus $.35 for each additional $10.00.*]

Ordering Information

HOW TO USE THIS BOOK

Each of publications listed herein is keyed to a vendor number (located at the extreme right of each listing). The names and addresses of these vendors are given on pages 5 through 14. To order a work, simply fill out an order form and mail to the vendor's address, together with the proper fee. *See notice about sales tax below.*

PLEASE USE ORDER FORMS

The advertisers, authors and publishers of the books listed in this catalog have helped defray the expense, thereby making it possible for you to purchase it at a very nominal price. They will be interested in knowing if this has accrued to their benefit by resulting in orders. An order from you will help assure the continuation of the above policy ONLY if you use the order forms at the back of the book or tell them you saw their work advertised in *Genealogical & Local History Books in Print*.

SALES TAX

You must pay the state sales tax required by the government of the state in which you reside if you order books from vendors operating in your state. **Please do not forget this -- it has not been included in the price.**

General Information

The editors of *Genealogical & Local History Books in Print* have used their best efforts in collecting and preparing material for inclusion in this catalog, but do not assume, and hereby disclaim any liability to any party for loss or damage caused by errors or omissions in *Genealogical & Local History Books in Print - Second Supplement to 4th Edition*, 1992, whether such errors or omissions result from negligence, accident, or any other cause.

GENEALOGICAL CONTENT OF BOOKS NOT GUARANTEED.

The purpose of this work is to provide an inexpensive method of advertising for those who have published genealogical or historical works and to provide the researcher with a knowledge of the publications available in his areas of interest. It is not intended to evaluate any of the publications. Most of the books have not been examined by the editor, and no comment on genealogical value can be made. Some of them are intended merely to provide the historical background helpful to genealogical research rather than to give family names and dates. Many of the vendors have descriptive literature concerning their works which they will provide on request.

HOW TO GET A PUBLICATION LISTED IN THIS WORK

Compilation of the next edition will begin almost as soon as this volume is published. All authors of genealogical/historical books are invited to list their publications. There is a small fee to do so. Write for information.

Table of Contents

RESEARCH SOURCES BY LOCALITY

REGIONAL

Names & Addresses Of Vendors

[F5001] Eleanor G. Tenbarge, 621 E. Iowa St., Evansville, IN 47711

[F5002] Frances W. Waite, 649 S. Chubb Dr., Doylestown, PA 18901

[F5003] Judge Noble K. Littell, 1219 Kat-Ca-Lani Avenue, Sebring, FL 33870-2451

[F5004] Sylvia Fitts Getchell, 51 North Main Street, Newmarket, NH 03857

[F5005] Margaret E./Carol M. Sheaffer, 10 Wexford Drive, Lawrenceville, NJ 08648

[F5006] Shirley A. Weber, N 410 E Fairway Drive, Hoodsport, WA 98548-9745

[F5007] Spencer Butte Press, 84889 Harry Taylor Rd, Eugene, OR 97405

[F5008] The Anundsen Publishing Co., 108 Washington St., Decorah, IA 52101

[F5009] Elwell H. Perry, 2867 Garden St., N Fort Myers, FL 33917

[F5010] James L. Rader, 2633 Gilbert Way, Rancho Cordova, CA 95670-3513

[F5011] Nancie Todd Weber, 514 Eucalyptus Drive, El Segundo, CA 90245

[F5012] COMPU-CHART, 363 South Park Victoria Drive, Milpitas, CA 95035-5708

[F5013] Alan Rumrill, PO Box 244, Stoddard, NH 03464

[F5014] William Rowlands, 1187 Via Mateo, San Jose, CA 95120-2810

[F5015] Monte P. Buzzard, PO Box 353, San Luis Obispo, CA 93406

[F5016] Marjorie W. Nelson, 2315 S E Second Street, Boynton Beach, FL 33435

[F5017] Lee Stockman, PO Box 250, Silver City, NM 88062

[F5018] Dolores Graham Doyle, 765 E Wood Duck Circle, Fresno, CA 93720

[F5019] Joseph C. Hammond, 1702 N Delaware, Roswell, NM 88201

[F5020] Jeanne B. Workman, 26723 Fairfax Lane, North Olmsted, OH 44070

[F5021] Stephen H. Broyles, 71 Neshobe Road, Newton, MA 02168

[F5022] John T. Humphrey, PO Box 15190, Washington, DC 20003

[F5023] Gloria S. Bullock, PO Box 30, Wolfeboro, NH 03894

[F5024] C. R. Stewart, PO Box 3011, Long Beach, CA 90803-0011

[F5025] Gena Walls, 11507 Brookledge Drive, Houston, TX 77099-4138 or 7418 Swanson Drive, Richmond, TX 77469

[F5026] Lorraine Frantz Edwards, PO Box 2076, Lancaster, CA 93539-2076

[F5027] Barbara J. Brown, 6583 South Downing Street, Littleton, CO 80121-2519

[F5028] Greensboro Historical Society, c/o Nancy Hill, Box 1510, Greensboro, VT 05841

[F5029] Silvia Pettem, 3060 15th Street, Boulder, CO 80304

[F5030] Barbary Coast Publications, PO Box 426394, San Francisco, CA 94142-6394

[F5031] Arkansas Research, PO Box 303, Conway, AR 72032

[F5032] La Verne H. McCauley, PO Box 5054, Silver City, NM 88062

[F5033] Arkansas Genealogical Society, 222 McMahan Drive, Hot Springs, AR 71913-6243

[F5034] Nancy Morebeck, 409 Dennis Drive, Vacaville, CA 95688

[F5035] SOLO PRESS, PO Box 507, Keno, OR 97627

[F5036] David A. Helm, 637 Meadow Drive, Macomb, IL 61455

[F5037] Susan Werle, 16830 NW Meadowgrass Ct, Beaverton, OR 97006

[F5038] Bob Lobdell, PO Box 40, Vacherie, LA 70090-0040

[F5039] Ruth Wren, Wren Family Association, 5809 Tautoga, El Paso, TX 79924

[F5040] KINSHIP, 60 Cedar Heights Road, Rhinebeck, NY 12572

[F5041] San Diego Historical Society, PO Box 81825, San Diego, CA 92138

[F5042] Arkansas Ancestors, 222 McMahan Dr, Hot Springs, AR 71913-6243

[F5043] Arlene F. Mansfield, 498 Quartz Street, Los Alamos, NM 87544

[F5044] Debra L. Wiley, 730 Nutwood St, Inglewood, CA 90301

[F5045] James B. Wolfson, 3532 N 3rd St, Fresno, CA 93726

[F5046] South King County Genealogical Society, PO Box 3174, Kent, WA 98032

[F5047] Stowe Historical Society, PO Box 248, Stowe, VT 05672

[F5048] Virginia Cordes, 1085 Powderhorn Dr., Glen Mills, PA 19342-9504

[F5049] Norma Yvonne Garbert, 22009 Liggett Street, Chatsworth, CA 91311-5721

[F5050] Torkwood, Inc., 5 Court of Bucks County, Lincolnshire, IL 60069

[F5051] John C. Abbott, Editor, 1324 Grand Ave, Edwardsville, IL 62025

[F5052] Barbara Smith Buys, Country Mansions Condos #25, 135 Amherst Street, Amherst, NH 03031

[F5053] Marie Strippgen Holtz, 503 Fairview Ave, St. Louis, MO 63119

[F5054] Joan A. Meyers, 871 Peace St., Hazleton, PA 18201

[F5055] Blanche R. Childs, 2115 Payne Street, Evanston, IL 60201-2561

[F5056] Ye Olde Genealogie Shoppe, PO Box 39128, Indianapolis, IN 46239

[F5057] Janis H. Miller, PO Box 2245, Hudson, OH 44236

[F5058] Patricia M. Steele, 10 Cherry Street, Brookville, PA 15825

[F5059] Sycamore Lodge, 7243 North Vandiver, San Antonio, TX 78209

[F5060] MEW Publishing, PO Box 8352, Dallas, TX 75205

[F5061] Iberian Publishing Company, 548 Cedar Creek Drive, Athens, GA 30605-3408
Shipping/Handling: Order totals to $10.00 add $1.50, $10.01 to $25.00 add $2.50, $25.01 to $50.00 add $3.50, over $50.00 add $4.50

[F5062] Dr. Holland D. Warren, 207 Nottingham Circle, Lynchburg, VA 24502

[F5063] E. John Graichen, 2021 Barclay Court, Santa Ana, CA 92701

[F5064] David A. Snyder, 3108 Huntmaster Way, Owings Mills, MD 21117

[F5065] Roger R. Connelly, 5967 Rosinante Run, Columbia, MD 21045

[F5066] Gwendolyn Pryor, 8701 S0. Braeswood #113, Houston, TX 77031-1309

[F5067] Joan E. Murray, 1281 N. Linden Ave, Palatine, IL 60067

[F5068] Ambler Church of the Brethren, 31 East Butler Avenue, Ambler, PA 19002-4319

[F5069] Bell Chimes, P.O. Box 451, Springfield, VT 05156

[F5070] The New York Genealogical and Biographical Society, 122 East 58th Street, New York, NY 10022-1939

[F5071] The Mattanawcook Observer, Alan H. Hawkins, 14 Adelbert Street, South Portland, ME 04106-6512

[F5072] Donald Lewis Osborn, 322 SE Willow Way, Lee's Summit, MO 64063-2928

[F5073] Nan Overton West, 4207 34th Street, Lubbock, TX 79410

[F5074] Margery M. Graham, 13431 Ernst Road, Roanoke, IN 46783

[F5075] Mrs. Carolyn Cell Choppin, 2912 Twelfth St. SE, Puyallup, WA 98374

[F5076] Mrs. Patricia F. Elton, 10012 Penfold Court, Potomac, MD 20854

[F5077] Susan Mortensen, P.O. Box 45184, Boise, ID 83711

[F5078] Priscilla G. DeAngelis, 2921 N Leisure World Blvd #418, Silver Spring, MD 20906

[F5079] Lilac Hill Publications, 6201 Patton Road, Arrington, TN 37014-9116

[F5080] Jo White Linn, C.G., C.G.L., PO Box 1948, Salisbury, NC 28145-1948

[F5081] Primer Publications, PO Box 11894, Salt Lake City, UT 84147

[F5082] Ann Dunkel, 25 Vogt Street, Coldwater, MI 49036

[F5083] HIGH GRASS PUBLICATIONS, 300 W Smith Valley Road, Greenwood, IN 46142

[F5084] Jean M. Rand, 209-07 Whitehall Terrace, Queens Village, NY 11427

[F5085] Seattle Genealogical Society, PO Box 1708, Seattle, WA 98111

[F5086] Donald R. Davis, M.D., Ret, 12131 Goddard, Overland Park, KS 66213

[F5087] Mrs. Ivadelle Dalton Garrison, 3725 W Circle Drive, Fresno, CA 93704

[F5088] Ann Burton, 43779 Valley Road, Decatur, MI 49045

[F5089] Glyndwr Resources, 43779 Valley Road, Decatur, MI 49045

[F5090] Don Jaggi, 3353 S. Main #148, Salt Lake City, UT 84115

[F5091] Crockett A. Harrison, 1327 South Center St Extension, Grove City, PA 16127

[F5092] Virginia Genealogical Society, PO Box 7469, Richmond, VA 23221

[F5093] Wm. Stibal Pettite, PO Box 2127, Fair Oaks, CA 95628

[F5094] Mary McCraw Harland, 1750 Allegro Drive, Richmond, VA 23231

[F5095] Claudette Maerz, PO Box 31010, Bloomington, MN 55431

[F5096] Gordon W. Paul, 4408 Chinlee NE, Albuquerque, NM 87110

[F5097] Family History Educators, PO Box 510606, Salt Lake City, UT 84151-0606

[F5098] Rev. Andrew Eggman, Jr., c/o Suter Rt 10 Box 28, Harrisonburg, VA 22801

[F5099] North Carolina Genealogical Society, PO Box 1492G, Raleigh, NC 27602

[F5100] The Search, Genealogical Consulting & Education, 5634 Caminito Isla, La Jolla, CA 92037-7224

[F5101] Rev. L.A. Glassco, 606 Virginia Ave., Fredericksburg, VA 22401

[F5102] The Pocahontas Foundation, PO Box 431, Berryville, VA 22611
Postage & Handling: one book $2.50;
for each additional book add $1.00

[F5103] McClain County Historical Society, 203 W Washington St., Purcell, OK 73080

[F5104] Ruth B. Powell, 52 Yacht Club Drive #204, N Palm Beach, FL 33408-3909

[F5105] Mrs. Cathryn Dailey Strombo, 140 Mullan Road West, Superior, MT 59872

[F5106] Translation & Interp. Service, 355 W 4th Street, Winona, MN 55987

[F5107] Susan M. Hopfensperger, PO Box 147, Nashotah, WI 53058-0147

[F5108] Research Unlimited, 210 North Main Street, Ames, NE 68621

[F5109] Cora Belle Crane, 426 E Ave R-6, Palmdale, CA 93550

[F5110] Elise Greenup Jourdan, 8624 Asheville Hwy, Knoxville, TN 37924

[F5111] Opal Tillis Flynn, 320 Pine Hills Road, Orlando, FL 32811

[F5112] Russell D. Earnest Associates, 11307 Mountain View Rd, Damascus, MD 20872

[F5113] Lahontan Images, 206 S. Pine St., PO Box 1093, Susanville, CA 96130

[F5114] Association of Blauvelt Descendants, 5 Terra Glen Road, Danbury, CT 06811-3419

[F5115] Hunsaker Publishing Co., 1010 Hunsaker Canyon Road, Lafayette, CA 94549

[F5116] Fair Printing Company, 10417 Long Meadow Rd, Oklahoma City, OK 73162

[F5117] Sherry Harris, 10853 Danube Ave, Granada Hills, CA 91344

[F5118] Patricia L. Haslam, C.G.R.S., PO Box 224, Stowe, VT 05672

[F5119] Dortha Steele, The Genealogy Tree, 721 East 17th South, Salt Lake City, UT 84105

[F5120] Westland Publications, PO Box 117, McNeal, AZ 85617-0117

[F5121] Joan Hackett, 2856 Bingham Drive, Pittsburgh, PA 15241

[F5122] Old Mill Printers, 1104 N Argonne Ave, Sterling, VA 22170-2301

[F5123] Palatine Historical Society, PO Box 134, Palatine, IL 60078

[F5124] Lineages, Inc, 370 East South Temple Street Suite 260, PO Box 417, Salt Lake City, UT 84111

[F5125] Wm E. Wright, PO Box 570368, Houston, TX 77257-0368

[F5126] Dewey Towner, 8108 Sagamore Rd, Leawood, KS 66206

[F5127] Mrs. Elizabeth Walker, 212 Fairlawn Blvd, Zelienople, PA 16063

[F5128] Bettina P. H. Burns, PO Box 325, Cullman, AL 35056-0325

[F5129] Genealogical Publishing Company, Inc, 1001 North Calvert Street, Baltimore, MD 21202
Postage & handling: One book $3.00; each additional book $1.00. Maryland residents add 5% sales tax; Michigan residents add 4% sales tax.

[F5130] Clearfield Company, 200 E. Eager Street, Baltimore, MD 21202
Postage & handling: One book $3.00; each additional book $1.00. Maryland residents add 5% sales tax; Michigan residents add 4% sales tax.

[F5131] Livesay Historical Society, James J. Livesay, Historian, 1290 Breckenridge Drive, Jackson, MS 39204 or Mrs. Virginia Smith, Editor, The Livesay Bulletin, 104 Linden Avenue, Mercersburg, PA 17236

[F5132] Patricia Wilkinson W Balletta, 26 Sunset Road, Bayshore, NY 11706

[F5133] Elisabeth P. Martin, 7204 Rebecca Drive, Alexandria, VA 22307

[F5134] Marcus V. Brewster, PO Box 269, Manning, SC 29102

[F5135] Nancy Gooch, M.L.S., 201 NW 4th Ave, Mineral Wells, TX 76067

[F5136] J. Roberts Harris, 315 Waldheim Drive, Ambler, PA 19002-2425

[F5137] The N.W. Lapin Press, 105 Surrey Road, PO Box 5053, Charlottesville, VA 22905-5053

[F5138] International PAF Users' Group, 2463 Ledgewood Drive, West Jordan, UT 84084

[F5139]   Kusek Genealogical Services, PO Box 32060, Shawnee Mission, KS 66212-2060

[F5140]   TLC Genealogy, PO Box 403369, Miami Beach, FL 33140-1369

[F5141]   AKB Publications, 691 Weavertown Road, Myerstown, PA 17067-2642

[F5142]   GENRESCO, Inc., 7303 18 Ave NW, Bradenton, FL 34209

[F5143]   Margaret B. Kinsey, PO Box 459, LaMesa, TX 79331

[F5144]   Mary Lou C. Mariner, 20 Old Coach Road, Sudbury, MA 01776

[F5145]   Union Cemetery Historical Society, 227 E. 28th Terrace, Kansas City, MO 64108

[F5146]   Timbercreek, LTD., RT 1, Box 242, Miami, OK 74354

[F5147]   Maurice R. Hitt, Jr, C.G., 1400 SW Shorewood Dr., Dunnellon, FL 34431

[F5148]   Genealogy Unlimited, Inc., Dept. GBIP, PO Box 537, Orem, UT 84059-0537

[F5149]   Colorado Genealogical Society, ATTN: Publications, PO Box 9218, Denver, CO 80209

[F5150]   Marietta Publishing Company, 2115 North Denair Avenue, Turlock, CA 95380

[F5151]   Historical Data Services, Box 4293, Queensbury, NY 12804

[F5152]   Roy D. Goold, PO Box 552, Clarkson, NY 14430-0552

[F5153]   Mary Leigh Boisseau, 469 Brightwell Drive, Danville, VA 24540

[F5154]   Anita L. Ockert, 8818 Higdon Drive, Vienna, VA 22182

[F5155]   Margaret K. Fresco, 38 Wynne Rd, Ridge, MD 20680

[F5156]   S. Worrell, PO Box 6016, Falls Church, VA 22040-6016

[F5157]   Neff & Associates, 21 Birchwood Court, PO Box 212, Princeton Junction, NJ 08550-0212

[F5158]   Evelyn C. Lane, 9 Hickory Street - Dept G, Gloucester, MA 01930

[F5159]   Higginson Book Company, 14 Derby Square, PO Box 788, Salem, MA 01970
10% discount on genealogy orders over $100.00 (not applicable on local histories). Postage: $3.00 per book, MC/Visa (508) 745-7170 M-F 10am-7pm EST.

[F5160] Eugene Blood, 9302 Laramie Rd, Philadelphia, PA 19115-2720

[F5161] Dorothy Jane Chance, 18504 Wellesley Court, Sonoma, CA 95476

[F5162] Karen Mann Robuck, 34446 Burdette Road, Franklin, VA 23851

[F5163] Living Roots, Inc, PO Box 24223, Cincinnati, OH 45224

[F5164] Michael Clegg, PO Box 10931, Ft. Wayne, IN 46854

[F5165] Bruce A. Breeding, 8311 Braesview, Houston, TX 77071-1231

[F5166] Debbie Anderson, 7901 Wild Orchid Way, Fairfax Station, VA 22039

[F5167] The Cuban Index, PO Box 11251, San Bernardino, CA 92423

[F5168] Allen Co. Public Library Foundation, PO Box 2270, Ft. Wayne, IN
46801

[F5169] Annette L. Perry, 201 S. 4th Street #625, San Jose, CA 95112

[F5170] Elizabeth S. Lowe, PO Box S, Shepherdstown, WV 25443

[F5171] Clay Co. Landmarks Commission and Historical Society, Box 523, 99
School Street, Clay, WV 25043

[F5172] D.E. Covington, Rte 15 Box 325A, Fayetteville, NC 28306

[F5173] Parrish Family Research Center, PO Box 116, Sheldon, WI 54766

[F5174] Athens County Historical Society & Museum, 65 N. Court Street,
Athens, OH 45701-2506

[F5175] Lorina R. Okamoto, 7685 Danielle Circle, Anaheim, CA 92808-1339

[F5176] Townsend, 5721 Antietam Drive, Sarasota, FL 34231-4903

[F5177] W.S. Dawson Co., PO Box 62823, Virginia Beach, VA 23466
Add $3.00 S&H each order

[F5178] Dockery Family Association Inc., Rt 3, Box 94, Murphy, NC
28906-9313

[F5179] Phelps Family Association of America, 1002 Queen Street, Camden, SC
29020-3113

[F5180] Willis L. Cunning, KTJ (Scot.), 3824 Lanewood Drive, Des Moines, IA
50311

[F5181] South Carolina Historical Society, 100 Meeting Street, Charleston, SC
29401

[F5182] The State Historical Society of Missouri, 1020 Lowry Street, Columbia,
MO 65201-7298

[F5183] 5 County Research, 953 Ridge Rd., Lansing, NY 14882

[F5184] Snackerty Enterprises, RFD 2 Box 668, Center Barnstead, NH 03225

[F5185] Mrs. Doris McAlpin Russell, 8600 Hickory Hill Lane, Huntsville, AL
35802-3552

[F5186] Jann Marie Foster, 4246 32nd Avenue South, Minneapolis, MN 55406

[F5187] Peter Fallone, Mills Terrace, PO Box 223, Fonda, NY 12068

[F5188]   Joyce Hambleton Whitten, RR 1 Box 80, Monette, AR 72447-9726

[F5189]   Vernon County Historical Society, PO Box 444, Viroqua, WI 54665

[F5190]   Carol Cox Bouknecht, 2420 Castletowers Lane, Tallahassee, FL 32301

[F5191]   Henry Rittenhouse, 318 West Reliance Road, Souderton, PA 18964

[F5192]   Centre County Genealogical Society, PO Box 1135, State College, PA 16804

[F5193]   Weynette Parks Haun, 243 Argonne Drive, Durham, NC 27704-1423

[F5194]   First Families of South Carolina, PO Box 21328, Charleston, SC 29413

[F5195]   Judy McPherson, PO Box 432, Linden, CA 95236

[F5196]   Ann S. Bailey, 3960 Five Points Rd, Riner, VA 24149

[F5197]   Wilderness Road Regional Museum, PO Box 373, Newbern, VA 24126

[F5198]   Nancy A Malvesta, PO Box 83, Eaton, NH 03832

[F5199]   Loraine Wallace, 124 N Oak Street, Traverse City, MI 49684

[F5200]   Colonel Thomas Hughart Chapter, NSDAR, c/o Mrs W. E. Bowman, 31 Woodland Drive, Staunton, VA 24401

[F5201]   Katherine G. Bushman, 12 Taylor Street, Staunton, VA 24401

[F5202]   Northwest Arkansas Genealogical Society, PO Box 796, Rogers, AR 72757

[F5203]   Family Genealogical Research Services, 1614 K Avenue NE, Cedar Rapids, IA 52402

[F5204]   Michele C. McNabb, 201 S. Race St, Urbana, IL 61801

[F5205]   Muskogee County Genealogical Society, 801 West Okmulgee, Muskogee, OK 74401

[F5206]   Paulk Genealogy & Research, PO Box 275 - Fish Creek Rd, Salem, FL 32356-0275

[F5207]   Northeast Washington Genealogical Society, c/o Colville Public Library, 195 S Oak, Colville, WA 99114

[F5208]   Howard County Historical Society, PO Box 109, Ellicott City, MD 21041

[F5209]   Data Indexing Services, PO Box 996, Kathleen, FL 33849-0996

[F5210]   Genealogical Society of North Brevard, Inc., PO Box 897, Titusville, FL 32781-0897

[F5211]   William R. Marsh, MD, 2112 Faidley Ave, Grand Island, NE 68803

[F5212]   Mrs. JoAnn DeBoard Touchstone, 815 West Frantz, Enid, OK 73701

[F5213]   Dorothy M. Mercy, 3324 Holly Ct, Falls Church, VA 22042

[F5214]   Lineage Search Associates, 6419 Colts Neck Road, Mechanicsville, VA 23111-4233

[F5215]   Gloucester County Historical Society Library, 17 Hunter Street, PO Box 409, Woodbury, NJ 08096

[F5216] Heritage Books, 1540-E Pointer Ridge Place, Suite 600, Bowie, MD 20716
  Orders Only 1-800-398-7709, Mon-Fri 10am - 4pm EST.
  Postage & Handling $3.00 per order

[F5217] West-Central Kentucky Family Research Association, PO Box 1932, Owensboro, KY 42392

[F5218] Katherine Adamson, 17136 S. Central Ave., Tinley Park, IL 60477

[F5219] Mrs. Albert J. Crull, 29527 Terra Vista, Fair Oaks Ranch, TX 78006

[F5220] Frederick W. Pyne, 7997 Windsail Court, Frederick, MD 21701

[F5221] Skipwith Historical & Genealogical Society Inc., PO Box 1382, Oxford, MS 38655

[F5222] NATMUS, Box 686, Auburn, IN 46706

[F5223] Mrs. Wallace H. Brucker, 5000 Alabama St #21, El Paso, TX 79930-2638

[F5224] J.L.M. Kinkead, 2085 Lakeside Drive, Lexington, KY 40502

[F5225] Jessie M. Jones, 3835 Judy Lane, Visalia, CA 93277

[F5226] William Sheperd West, 1707 Front Street, Beaufort, NC 28516
  or 1432 Altamont Drive, Decatur, GA 30033

[F5227] Florida State Genealogical Society, Inc., PO Box 10249, Tallahasssee, FL 32302

[F5228] The Antient Press, 1320 Mayflower Drive, McLean, VA 22101-3402

[F5229] Mrs. Herbert R. Holden, 430 Greenwood Drive, Petersburg, VA 23805

[F5230] Genealogical Society of Broward Co., Inc, P.O. Box 485, Ft. Lauderdale, FL 33302

[F5231] Platte Co. MO Historical & Genealogical Society, PO Box 103, Platte City, MO 64079-0103

[F5232] Genealogy Publishing Service, 448 Ruby Mine Road, Franklin, NC 28734

[F5233] Norman N. Rudd - Rudd Family Research Association, 461 Emerson Street, Chula Vista, CA 91911

[F5234] Elmer A. Houser, 6601 N.W. 97th Avenue, Tamarac, FL 33321-3349

[F5235] IFR Genealogy, 5721 Antietam Dr., Sarasota, FL 34231-4903

[F5236] Genealogical Books in Print, 6818 Lois Drive, Springfield, VA 22150
  Postage & handling fees on first $10.00 are $1.75;
  plus $.35 for each additional $10.00.

[F5237] Franklin County Genealogical Society, PO Box 2503, Columbus, OH 43216-2503

[F5238] Ancestor Exchange, c/o Tami Kaiser, 455 Essex Avenue, Bloomfield, NJ 07003

[F5239] Phyllis J. Bauer, 3510 W. Turnberry Dr, McHenry, IL 60050

[F5240]   Stanly County Genealogical Society, PO Box 31, Albemarle, NC 28001

[F5241]   Lincoln-Lancaster County Genealogical Society, PO Box 30055, Lincoln, NE 68503-0055

[F5242]   Priscilla Harriss Cabell, Turff & Twigg, PO Box 17091, Richmond, VA 23226

[F5243]   Sierra County Genealogical Society, PO Box 311, Truth or Consequences, NM 87901-0311

[F5244]   Preble County Historical Society, 7693 Swartsel Road, Eaton, OH 45320

General Reference

Abstracts of Family Relationships

A Digest of Family Relationships, Vol. 1, (1720-1750).
Abstracts of Family Relationships found in various Court
Records for the periods shown taken from Antient Press
Virginia Publications. Each entry contains the date and
source of the entry. 15.00 F5228

A Digest of Family Relationships, Vol. II (1750-1763).
Abstracts of Family Relationships found in various Court
Records for the periods shown taken from Antient Press
Virginia Publications. Each entry contains the date and
source of the entry. 15.00 F5228

A Digest of Family Relationships, Vol. III (1764-1775).
Abstracts of Family Relationships found in various Court
Records for the periods shown taken from Antient Press
Virginia Publications. Each entry contains the date and
source of the entry. 15.00 F5228

Bibliographies, Catalogs, and Inventories

Clegg, ed., Michael B. Bibliography of Genealogy and Local
History Periodicals with Union List of Major U.S. Collections.
1990. 528pp.
Bibliography of 5,500+ genealogy, family, and local
history magazines, with publisher addresses. Union list of
holdings of major U.S. genealogical collections. 75.00 .... F5168

Care and Repair of Old Materials

Earnest, Russell D. Grandma's Attic: Making Heirlooms Part of
Your Family History. 1991. 48pp. 11.50 F5112

Cemeteries

Johnson, Robert Foster. Wilderness Road Cemeteries in Kentucky,
Tennessee, and Virginia (312 Cemeteries, Maps). 1981.
300pp. 26.00 20.00 F5217

Colonial Families and Pedigrees

Balletta, Patricia Wilkinson Weaver. The Ancestors & Descendants
of Revolutionary General James Wilkinson of Calvert County,
Maryland Et Ux, Ann Biddle of Philadelphia, Pennsylvania.
1993. 60.00 40.00 F5132

Browning, Charles H. The Magna Charta Barons and Their
American Descendants [1898] Together with the Pedigrees of
the Founders of the Order of Runnemede. (1898) reprint
1991. 463pp.
Illustrated, indexed. 32.50 .... F5130

_____. Magna Charta Barons and Their Descendants [1915].
    (1915) reprint 1991. 366pp.
        Illustrated, indexed.   31.50   ....   F5130

Burke, Arthur Meredyth. The Prominent Families of the United
    States of America. (1908) reprint 1991. 510pp.
        Indexed.   35.00   ....   F5129

Flagg, E. Genealogical Notes on the Founding of New England: My
    Ancestors Part in the Undertaking. (1926) reprint 1991.
    440pp.
        The author was descended from 172 different New
        Englanders who settled in America between 1635-40.
        There are four main groupings: Conn. Valley; eastern
        Mass.; Rhode Island; So. Carolina.   27.00   ....   F5159

Hardy, Stella Pickett. Colonial Families of the Southern States of
    America. (1958) reprint 1991. 643pp.
        A history and genealogy of Colonial Families who settled
        in the Colonies prior to the Revolution. Chief among the
        families covered are: Adams, Alexander, Ambler,
        Armistead, Ball, Bassett, Blackwell, Bolling, Boulding,
        Braxton, Brent, Burwell, Byrd, Carter, Cary, Chilton,
        Clarkson, Collier, Cooke, Corbin, Creel, Downing, Duke,
        Duvall, Ferrill, Fishback, Fitzgerald, Fitzhugh, Green,
        Gwynn, Hammond, Hardy, Harrison, Huddleston,
        Jennings, Johnston, Keith, Langhorne, Lee, Lightfoot,
        Marshall, Martin, Mason, Metcalfe, Murray, Neale,
        Orrick, Parker, Pickett, Raines, Ridgely, Robinson, Scott,
        Shields, Slaughter, Smith, Steptoe, Stewart or Stuart,
        Tayloe, Taylor, Tuberville, Washington, Watts, Wright,
        Wyatt.
        Second Edition, indexed.   35.00   ....   F5129

Hoff, Henry B. English Origins of American Colonists, From The
    New York Genealogical and Biographical Record. 1991.
    287pp.
        Indexed.   28.50   ....   F5129

Holmes, F. Directory of Ancestral Heads of New England Families,
    1620-1700. (1923) reprint 1990. 274pp.
        This contains a list of nearly 15,000 heads of families,
        incl. place of emigration, earliest residence in New
        England, where the emigrant moved in New England,
        occupation, birth & death dates and more. 26.00   F5159

Hutton, Mary Louise M. Seventeeth Century Colonial Ancestors of
    Members of the National Society Colonial Dames XVII
    Century, 1915-1975. (1988) reprint 1991. 468pp.
        3 volumes in a single hardcover book (1976, 1981, 1988)
        consolidated edition 1991. Indexed.   30.00   ....   F5129

Rixford, Elizabeth M. Leach. Three Hundred Colonial Ancestors
    and War Service. (1934, 1938, 1943, 1944) reprint 1991.
    425pp.
        Their Part in Making American History from 495 to
        1934. Bound with Supplement I, Supplement II, and
        Supplement II, Concluded. Illustrated, indexed. 35.00   F5130

Stuart, Roderick W. Foreward by Douglas Richardson. Royalty for
  Commoners. The Complete Known Lineage of John of Gaunt,
  Son of Edward III, King of England, and Queen
  Philippa, 2nd ed. 1992. 412pp.   30.00 .... F5129

Thurtle, Robert Glenn., ed. [Lineage Book of] Hereditary Order of
  Descendants of Colonial Governors. 1980. 405pp.
  Indexed.   25.00 .... F5130

Weis, Frederick Lewis and David Faris. The Magna Charta Sureties,
  1215. 1991. 196pp.
      The Barons Named in the Magna Charta, 1215 and Some
      of Their Descendants Who Settled in America During the
      Early Colonial Years.   Fourth Edition with additions and
      corrections by Walter Lee Sheppard, Jr.   20.00 .... F5129

Weis, Frederick Lewis and Walter Lee Sheppard, Jr. Ancestral Roots
  of Certain American Colonists Who Came to America Before
  1700, 7th Edition. (1950) reprint 1992. 276pp.
      Formerly *"Ancestral Roots of Sixty Colonists Who Came
      to New England Between 1623 and 1650"*.
          The Lineage of Alfred the Great, Charlemagne,
      Malcolm of Scotland, Robert the Strong, and Some of
      Their Descendants. Descent is also traced to the
      following great figures of the Middle Ages: Clovis I,
      Clovis the Riparian, Malcolm II, Isabel de Vermandois,
      William de Warenne, Edward I, Henry II, Henry III,
      Edward III, King Aethelred II, and the early kings of
      Great Britain and Ireland, as well as Norman and Magna
      Charta Barons.   25.00 .... F5129

Computers

Clifford, Karen.   Genealogy and Computers for the Complete
  Beginner. 1992.
          A Step-by-Step Guide to the PAF Computer Program,
      Automated Data Bases, Family History Centers, and
Local Sources.   Indexed. 29.95 F5130

SKY Catalog™

A program for creating a card catalog for your personal library.

★ Have you ever wanted to organize your books?

★ Have you ever wanted to find a book that you knew the author of but couldn't remember the title?

★ Have you ever wanted to print your recipes on 3 x 5 cards?

★ Have you ever found a book you wanted to buy and couldn't remember if you already had it?

If you answered YES to any of these questions you need...

SKY Catalog™

With SKY Catalog you will be able to print a complete list of your books listed alphabetically by Author, Title and Subject. You can print your card catalog on 3 x 5 cards or, standard 8.5" x 11" paper. You can even print your favorite recipes on 3 x 5 cards!

You will be able to create your card catalog in record time because SKY catalog is so easy to use. SKY Catalog is completely menu-driven and the built in on-line help is only a function key press away. SKY Catalog comes to you from the same company that brought you SKY Index and is backed by a 30-day money back guarantee.

Although SKY Catalog is easy to use, it is very powerful! With SKY Catalog you will be able to create individual card catalogs for each family member and then merge the individual catalogs into one household catalog.

You can also use SKY Catalog to assist you in your research. One database could contain all the books you want to research. Then as you find the books you can enter your notes into SKY Catalog and transfer the book information and notes into your database for books that have been researched.

Isn't it time you organized your personal library? How about your favorite recipes? Order SKY Catalog today for only $49.00 plus $4.00 S/H (USA & Canada). Don't miss out on this great opportunity!

SKY Catalog Features

✔Easy to use menu driven system
✔Allows you to create multiple catalog database files
✔Sorts by Author, Title or Subject
✔Search Function
✔Allows up to 8 kilobytes of notes per book
✔Prints 3 x 5" Author, Title or Subject Cards*
✔Prints 8.5"x11" reports sorted by Author, Title and Subject.
✔Browse function
✔Merges multiple databases
✔Copies a single record from one database to another

SKY Catalog System Requirements

IBM Compatible computer with a CGA/EGA/VGA compatible monitor and a printer. *3 x 5 card printouts require tractor feed 3 x 5 cards and a dot matrix printer.

SKY
Software

Dept. B, P.O. Box 394,
Maine, NY 13802-0394
(607) 786-0769 10am - 6pm EST

Only $49.00 + $4.00 S/H (USA & Canada)

Please specify disk size when ordering (3.5" or 5.25"). If no size is specified a 5.25" disk will be sent. NY State residents add sales tax to total - including S/H

Buy both SKY Catalog and SKY Index and the Shipping and Handling is FREE! (Just mention this advertisement).

SKY Catalog and SKY Index are trademarks of SKY Software. Laser Jet is a trademark of Hewlett Packard Company. IBM is a trademark of International Business Machines Corporation.

SKY Index™
Version 3.1

The solution to your indexing needs!

Since 1987, SKY Software has been offering our customers powerful indexing capabilities that are easy to learn and use.

INDEX ANYTHING! - A new book you are publishing. An old one that has no index. Your files. Make a cumulative index for a periodical. SKY Index has virtually no limit; since the page number field of this index program can be up to 99 characters long (and will accept either numbers or characters), and the prime topic and subtopic fields can each be 999 characters long, it can be used for diverse projects.

Takes less than an hour to learn

SKY Index is menu driven and extremely easy to use. The software review editor of The American Society of Indexers stated in his review [ASI Newsletter - Sep/Oct 1991], "SKY Index is actually fun to use . . . a novice computer user should be able to become productive in less than an hour".

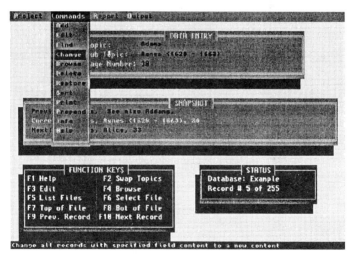

Main SKY Index screen - SKY Index is completely menu-driven. With on-screen status, on-line help, Previous, Current and Next records displayed at all times.

We believe SKY Index is the best and easiest to use Indexing program for your dollar. SKY Index is only $74.95 plus $4.00 S/H USA & Canada and comes with a 30-day money-back guarantee. *(Please specify disk size - 5.25" or 3.5")*.

A demonstration disk is available for $5.00 and comes with a $5.00 coupon towards the purchase of SKY Index.

SKY Software, Dept B, PO Box 394, Maine, NY 13802-0394 (607)786-0769 10am-6pm EST

SKY Index System Reqs: IBM Compatible with 640K RAM, a hard drive and DOS 3.0 or Higher

```
┌─────────────────────────────────────────┐
│  ┌───────────────────────────────────┐  │
│  │                                   │  │
│  │          INTERNATIONAL            │  │
│  │              PAF                  │  │
│  │          USERS' GROUP             │  │
│  │      QUARTERLY  NEWSLETTER        │  │
│  │                                   │  │
│  │           FOR USERS OF            │  │
│  │                                   │  │
│  │     PERSONAL ANCESTRAL FILE™      │  │
│  │                                   │  │
│  │      CURRENT INFORMATION          │  │
│  │       SHARE EXPERIENCES           │  │
│  │        PROBLEM SOLVING            │  │
│  │    FORUM FOR IDEA EXCHANGE        │  │
│  │      DOCUMENTATION HELP           │  │
│  │      LEARN NEW TECHNIQUES         │  │
│  │                                   │  │
│  │      $15.00 PER YEAR              │  │
│  │                                   │  │
│  │      2463 LEDGEWOOD DRIVE         │  │
│  │      WEST JORDAN, UTAH 84084      │  │
│  │                                   │  │
│  └───────────────────────────────────┘  │
└─────────────────────────────────────────┘
```

Nichols, Elizabeth L.   Genealogy in the Computer Age: Understanding FamilySearch™. 1991. 56pp.

This publication explains FamilySearch™ - explanations, illustrations, definitions, and more - all about Ancestral File, International Genealogical Index (IGI), and Social Security Death Index. Family Search™ is a set of genealogical programs and files on compact disc that can be used on a personal computer with a compact disc drive. Published by the Church of Jesus Christ of Latter-day Saints [Mormons - the Genealogical Society of Utah] and being sent to its family history centers in USA and Canada - to go worldwide eventually. this publication explains concepts and gives detailed explanations and illustrations of Ancestral File [pedigree-linked file for sharing genealogies focusing on deceased persons - and tells how you can participate]; IGI [1988 edition contains 147 million names of deceased persons from over 90 countries]; and Social Security Death Index, 1962-88 [39 million names made available by the US government as part of the Freedom of Information Act]; and explains how the Personal Ancestral File (PAF) genealogy software allows you to "download" records from FamilySearch and "upload" them into your own personal computer without rekeying the information.

60 illustrations. 8.95   F5097

DAR Records

Brown, Barbara J. Rx: DAR Records May Be Beneficial to Your
   Genealogical Health. 1990. 80pp.
      A study for genealogists of DAR records, publications,
      and facilities in the centennial year of NSDAR, 1990.   ....   6.50   F5027

Dictionaries, Glossaries, Grammars

Evans, Barbara Jean. The New A to Zax - 2nd Edition, The
   Comprehensive Genealogical Dictionary. (1978) reprint
   1991. 320pp.   23.00   18.00   F5056

Hough, Franklin B. American Biographical Notes. (1875) reprint
      Being short notices of deceased persons, chiefly those not
      included in Allen's or in Drake's biographical dictionaries. 27.50   F5216

Lewis, S. Topographical Dictionary of Ireland, comprising Several
   Counties, Cities, Boroughs, Corporate, Market & Post Towns,
   Parishes & Villages, w/Hist & Stat. (1837) reprint 1992.
   1,412pp.
      Vol. I, A-G, 675pp $65.00
      Vol. II, H-Z. 737pp. $72.00   129.00   ....   F5159

Savage, J. A Gen. Dictionary of the 1st Settlers of New England,
   Showing 3 Generations of Those who Came before May, 1692,
   on the Basis of Farmer's Register. 1986. 2,541pp.
      The basic gen. dictionary of New England settlers, for
      each settler it gives marriage & death dates, birth
      marriage & death dates of children and birthdate & names
      of grandchildren.   4 volumes. (1860-1862)
         Vol. I A-C,
         Vol. II, D-J,
         Vol. III, K-R,
         Vol. IV, S-Z.
         $35.00/Vol.   115.00   ....   F5159

_____. A Genealogical Dictionary of the First Settlers of New
   England. (1860) reprint
      Showing three generations of those who came before
      May, 1692, on the Basis of Farmer's Register. 4 vol.,
      2,541pp. 1860-62.
         Vol. I, A-C;
         Vol. II, D-J;
         Vol. III, K-R;
         Vol. IV, S-Z.
      $35.00/vol. hardcover. **Special Savings:$115.00/set.**   115.00   ....   F5159

Directories of Speakers

Parker, J. Carlyle. Directory of Archivist and Librarian Genealogical
   Instructors. 1990. 39pp. 8.45   F5150

Early American Life

Andrews, Charles M. Narratives of the Insurrections, 1675-1690.
   (1915) reprint 414pp. 27.00   F5216

Earle, Alice Morse. Colonial Dames and Goodwives. (1895) reprint
322pp. 22.00   F5216

_____. Customs and Fashions in Old New England. (1893) reprint
388pp. 25.00   F5216

Field, Edward. The Colonial Tavern: A Glimpse of New England
Town Life in the 17th & 18th Centuries. (1897) reprint
248pp. 18.50   F5216

Fordham, Elias Pym. Edited by Frederic Austin Ogg, A.M. Personal
Narrative of Travels in Virginia, Maryland, Pennsylvania,
Ohio, Indiana, Kentucky; and of a Residence in Illinois
Terr:1817-1818. (1906) reprint 248pp. 18.50   F5216

Kinzie, Juliette A. Wau-Bun: The Early Day in the Northwest.
(1855, 1930) reprint 395pp. 25.00   F5216

Lobdell, editor, Jared C. Recollections of Lewis Bonnett,
Jr.(1778-1850) & Bonnett and Wetzel Families. 1991. 122pp. 18.00   F5216

Rixford, Elizabeth M. Leach. Three Hundred Colonial Ancestors and
War Service - Their Part in Making American History from
495 to 1934. (1934) reprint 1991. 425pp.
Bound with Supplement I (1938), Supplement II (1943)
and Supplement II, Concluded (1944). Illustrated,
indexed. 35.00   F5130

Schouler, James. Americans of 1776: Daily Life in Revolutionary
America. (1906) reprint 317pp. 22.00   F5216

Searight, Thomas B. The Old Pike. A History of the National Road,
with incidents, accidents, and anecdotes thereon. (1894) reprint
404pp. 27.50   F5216

Ethnic

Sullivan Audrey. ed. Index, Vols. 1 and 2, Jos. Besse's A Collection
of Sufferings of People Called Quakers, 1650-1689. 1991.
161pp.
Shows Quaker's resident parish and page reference in Jos.
Besse's original 1753 2-volume publication.   20.00   ....   F5230

Exploration and Travel

Benard, John. Retrospections of America, 1797-1811. (1887)
reprint 380pp. 25.00   F5216

Winship, George Parker, editor. The Journey of Coronado,
1540-1542, from the City of Mexico to the Grand Canyon of
the Colorado and the Buffalo Plains of Texas, Kansas and
Nebraska. (1904) reprint 1992. 251pp. 21.50   F5216

Export/Import Trade

Town History Committee. The China Journal of Amos Porter
1802-1803. 1985. 61pp.
Observations on prominent Vermonters' preparations and
voyage to Canton. Genealogy: Porter-Lincoln. 8.00   F5028

Family Genealogies

Austin, John Osborne. American Authors' Ancestry, Including Some
Others Who Have Influenced Life Wisely--. (1915) reprint
115pp.
    Divines, Diplomats, Jurists, Philanthropists, Reformers,
    and Benefactors 29.00   F5216

Munsell's Sons, Joel. The American Genealogist Being a Catalogue
of Family Histories...Published in America, From 1771 to Date
(1990) 5th Edition. (1900) reprint 1990. 406pp.   25.00   ....   F5130

Pyne, B.S., M.S., Frederick Wallace. The John Pyne Family in
America. 1992. 224pp.
    Includes a full ancestry of John Pyne through the Irish,
    English, and French generations to 754 A.D.! May open
    ancestral clues to DePins, de los Pinos, and the Pynes in
    England. Bibliographic essay contains valuable
    information on sources of research.   22.00   ....   F5220

Games, Humor, Recreation, Fun with Genealogy

Bonsey, Lynn and Lorna Healey. It's All Relative. 1988. 100pp.
           ....   9.50   F5216

Galeener-Moore, Laverne. Collecting Dead Relatives. (1987)
reprint 1992. 155pp.
    4th printing. 8.95   F5129

_____. Further Undertakings of a Dead Relative Collector. (1989)
reprint 1992. 167pp. 9.95   F5129

Heraldry

Elvin, Charles Norton. A Hand-book of Mottoes Borne by the
Nobility, Gentry, Cities, Public Companies, etc. (1860) reprint
1990. 305pp.   22.50   ....   F5130

Matthews, John. Complete American Armoury and Blue Book
Combining 1903, 1907 and 1911-23 Editions. reprint 1991.
544pp. 40.00   F5130

Paul, Sir James Balfour. An Ordinary of Arms Contained in the
Public Register of All Arms and Bearings in Scotland. (1903)
reprint 1991. 452pp.
    Indexed 32.50   F5130

History, Emigration West

Masterson, Martha Gay. Editor: Lois Barton. One Woman's West,
Recollections of the Oregon Trail and Settling the
Northwest Country. 1838-1916. (1886) reprint 1991. 222pp. 9.95   F5007

Immigration, Emigration, Migration

Adams, Raymond D. Ulster Emigrants to Philadelphia, 1803-1850.
1992. 102pp. 14.00   F5130

Banks, C.E. Topographical Dictionary of 2885 English Emigrants to New England, 1620-1650. (1937) reprint 1990. 295pp.
Very useful guide to early settlers, as it lists them by county of origin in England & gives also their parish & where they settled in colonies. Completely indexed. 30.00 F5159

Bolton, C.K. Scotch-Irish Pioneers in Ulster & America. (1910) reprint 1990. 398pp.
A history listing over 250 immigrants who came from Northern Ireland to New England. 40.00 .... F5159

_____. The Founders: Portraits of Persons Born Abroad Who Came to the colonies in North America Before the Year 1701. (1919) reprint 1991. 1,103pp.
3 volumes in 2 85.00 .... F5159

Burgert, Annette K. Eighteenth and Nineteenth Century Emigrants from Lachen-Speyerdorf in the Palatinate. 1989. 42pp. 12.00 F5141

_____. Emigrants from Eppingen to America in the Eighteenth and Nineteenth Centuries. 1987. 46pp. 12.00 F5141

_____. A Century of Emigration from Affoltern Am Albis, Canton Zurich, Switzerland. 1984. 41pp. 10.00 F5141

_____. Eighteenth Century Emigrants from German-Speaking Lands to North America - Volume I: The Northern Kraichgau. 1983. 485pp. 43.00 .... F5141

_____. Eighteenth Century Emigrants from German-Speaking Lands to North America - Volume II: The Western Palatinate. 1985. 421pp. 43.00 .... F5141

_____. Eighteenth Century Emigrants from the Northern Alsace to America. 1992. 700+pp.
Write for price (cloth bound). F5141

Burgert, Annette K and Henry Z. Jones. Westerwald to America - Some 18th Century German Immigrants. 1989. 284pp. 32.45 .... F5141

Coldham, Peter Wilson. Child Apprentices in America From Christ's Hospital, London 1617-1778. 1990. 164pp. 21.50 .... F5129

_____. Emigrants in Chains. 1992. 196pp.
A Social History of forced Emigration to the Americas of Felons, Destitute Children, Political and Religious Non-conformists, Vagabonds, Beggars and other Undesirables, 1607-1776. 19.95 .... F5129

_____. English Adventurers and Emigrants, 1609-1660 Abstracts of Examinations in the High Court of Admiralty with Reference to Colonial America. (1984) reprint 1991. 219pp.
Indexed 22.50 .... F5130

_____. English Estates of American Colonists. American Wills and Administrations in the Prerogative Court of Canterbury, 1700-1799. (1980) reprint 1991. 151pp.
Indexed. 15.00 F5130

_____. The Complete Book of Emigrants, 1607-1660. (1987) reprint 1992. 600pp.
Indexed. 34.95 .... F5129

_____. The Complete Book of Emigrants, 1661 - 1699. 1990. 900pp. 49.95 .... F5129

_____. The Complete Book of Emigrants, 1700-1750. 1992.
748pp.
    Indexed.   44.95 .... F5129

_____. The Complete Book of Emigrants in Bondage, 1614-1775.
1988. 920pp.   60.00 .... F5129

_____. Supplement to The Complete Book of Emigrants in
Bondage, 1614-1775. 1992. 86pp. 9.00 F5129

Faust, Albert Bernhardt and Gaius Marcus Brumbaugh. Lists of
Swiss Emigrants in the Eighteenth Century to the American
Colonies. (1925) reprint 1991. 429pp.
    Two Volumes in one. Reprinted with additions and
    corrections from the National Genealogical Society
    Quarterly (March 1972). Indexed.   30.00 .... F5129

Fothergill, Gerald. Emigrants From England 1773-1776. (1913)
reprint 1992. 206pp.
    Indexed. 21.00   F5130

Goode, Richard U. The Goode Diary: A Personal Journal of the
Northern Transcontinental Survey, 1883. 1990. 120pp. 14.00   F5177

Hargreaves-Mawdsley, R. Bristol and America. A Record of the
First Settlers in the Colonies of North America, 1654-1685.
(1929, 1931) reprint 1992. 198pp.
    Indexed. 20.00   F5130

McDonnell, Frances. Emigrants from Ireland Emigration to
America, 1735-1743, A Transcription of the Report of the Irish
House of Commons into Enforced Emigration to America.
1992. 142pp.
    Indexed.   18.50 .... F5129

Simmendinger, Ulrich. True and Authentic Register of Persons Who
in 1709 Journeyed from Germany to America. (1934) reprint
1991. 20pp. 4.00 F5129

Smith, Clifford Neal. Cumulative Surname Soundex to
German-American Genealogical Research Monographs 14
Through 19 and 21 Through 25. 1990. 42pp. 17.00   F5120

_____. Early Nineteenth-Century German Settlers in Ohio,
Kentucky, and Other States: Part 2. 1988. 58pp. 15.00   F5120

_____. Early Nineteenth-Century German Settlers in Ohio,
Kentucky, and Other States: Part 3. 1988. 71pp. 17.00   F5120

_____. Early Nineteenth-Century German Settlers in Ohio,
Kentucky, and Other States: Part 4A: Surnames A Through J.
1991. 36pp. 15.00   F5120

_____. Early Nineteenth-Century German Settlers in Ohio,
Kentucky, and Other States: Part 4B: Surnames K Through Z.
1991. 40pp. 15.00   F5120

_____. Early Nineteenth-Century German Settlers in Ohio,
Kentucky, and Other States: Part 4C: Appendices. 1991.
28pp. 15.00   F5120

_____. Emigrants from France (Haut-Rhin Department) to
America: Part 2: 1845-1847. 1989. 46pp. 15.00   F5120

_____. From Breman to America in 1850: Some Rare Emigrant
Ship Lists. 1987. 42pp. 15.00   F5120

_____. Gold! German Immigrants to California, 1849-1852.
1988. 50pp. 17.00   F5120

_____. Letters Home: Genealogical and Family-Historical Data on Nineteenth-Century German Settlers in Australia, Bermuda, Brazil, Canada, and the US: Part 1. 1989. 38pp. 17.00 F5120

_____. Passenger Lists (and Fragments Therefrom) from Hamburg and Bremen to Australia and the United States. 1988. 28pp. 15.00 F5120

Smith Jr., C.G., Leonard H. and Norma H. Smith. Nova Scotia Immigrants to 1867. 1992. 560pp. 37.50 .... F5129

Strassburger, Ralph Beaver and William John Hinke. Pennsylvania German Pioneers [:] A publication of the Original Lists of Arrivals In the Port of Philadelphia From 1727 to 1808, Signature Volume. (1934) reprint 1992. 909pp.
This set which is commonly known as "Strassburger & Hinke" is the time-honored reference for arrival of German emigrants to America before 1800. It is one of the basic works for genealogical libraries. Volumes 1 & 3 have been reprinted a number of times, but this is the first time this volume (which shows the actual signatures of the emigrants) has been reprinted. This signature volume is important as it may be used to check signatures on wills, deeds, and other documents to ascertain whether they were written by the same man.
This volume has been printed the same size and with the same cover as the other currently available volumes so that they will make a matching set. It is being sold separately for $55 - for purchase by those who already have the other two volumes. It is necessary to have the other volumes in order to use this one as it does not have a separate index. For those who do not have any of this set, all three volumes are available from us as a set for the very special price of $100.00. The other volumes total 1,564 pages and this one has 909.
All three are printed on acid-free paper and are smythe-sewn with cloth bindings. 55.00 .... F5236

Tepper, Michael. Immigrants to the Middle Colonies. A Consolidation of Ship Passenger Lists from the New York Genealogical and Biographical Record. (1978) reprint 1992. 191pp.
Indexed. 17.50 .... F5129

Indexes to Periodicals

Clegg, Michael B. ed. PERiodical Source Index 1986 - 1987. 900+pp.
Annual subject index to 2,000+ genealogical and local history periodicals. Arranged by place and surname. 45.00 .... F5168

_____. PERiodical Source Index, 1847-1985. 1988. 10,600pp.
Retrospective subject index to 2,000+ genealogical and local history periodicals. Arranged by place and surname. Can be purchased by installments. 1,400.00 .... F5168

Hamrick, David O. Index to the North Carolina Historical and Genealogical Register. 1983. 635pp.
A complete personal index of the three Volumes (11 books) of the "Index to the North Carolina Historical and Genealogical Register" (Hathaway's Register) published from 1900 to 1903. Volume One contains 54,000 names (277 pages), Volume Two - 43,000 names (232 pages), and Volume Three - 24,000 names (126 pages). 42.50 F5142

```
┌─────────────────────────────────────────────┐
│            Immigrants 1851 to 1891           │
│                                              │
│                   Census                     │
│         United States 1850 to 1920          │
│            England 1841 to 1881              │
│            Scotland 1841 to 1891             │
│                                              │
│                Vital Records                 │
│        England 1837-1900 indexed             │
│        Scotland 1855-1900 indexed            │
│                                              │
│               Free estimate                  │
│              GOOD OLD DAYS                    │
│              3353 S. Main #148               │
│          Salt Lake City, UT 84115            │
└─────────────────────────────────────────────┘
```

Indians & Indian Wars

Baker, C. Alice. True Stories of New England Captives Carried to
Canada During the Old French & Indian Wars. (1896) reprint
420pp. 27.50   F5216

Baxter, James P. The Pioneers of New France in New England.
(1894) reprint 450pp. 27.50   F5216

Caverly, Robert B. Heroism of Hannah Duston, together with the
Indian Wars of New England. (1875) reprint 408pp. 26.50   F5216

C'.arch, Esq., Thomas. The History of Philip's War, Commonly
Called the Great Indian War of 1675 & 1676. (1827) reprint
360pp.
Also of the French and Indian Wars at the Eastward in
1689, 1690, 1692, 1696 and 1704.   ....   23.50   F5216

Coleman, Emma Lewis. New England Captives Carried to Canada
Between 1677 & 1760 During the French & Indian Wars,
2 Vols. (1926) reprint 438&452p. 47.50   F5216

Drake, Samuel G. A Particular History of the Five Years French and
Indian War. (1870) reprint 312pp.   25.00   ....   F5216

Geronimo and S.M. Barrett. Geronimo's Story of His Life. (1905)
reprint 244pp. 20.00   F5216

Heckewelder, Rev. John. History, Manners, and Customs of the
Indian Nations who once Inhabited Pennsylvania and
Neighboring States. (1819, 1876) reprint 595pp. 35.00   F5216

Hubbard, Rev. William and Samuel G. Drake. The History of the
Indian Wars in New England from the First Settlement to the
Termination of the War with King Philip in 1677. (1677,
1864) reprint 595pp. 35.00   F5216

Johnson, Mrs. Susanna (Willard). A Narrative of the Captivity of
Mrs. Johnson, together with A Narrative of James Johnson:
Indian captive of Charlestown, NH 1757. (1796, 1814) reprint
232pp. 18.50   F5216

Jordan, Jerry Wright. Cherokee by Blood: Records of Eastern
Cherokee Ancestry in the U.S. Court of Claims, 1906-1910.
Vol 1, Applications 1-1550. 1987. 482pp. 25.00 F5216

_____. Cherokee by Blood: Records of Eastern Cherokee Ancestry
in the U.S. Court of Claims, 1906-1910, Vol 2, Applications
1551-4200. 1988. 485pp. 25.00 F5216

_____. Cherokee by Blood: Records of Eastern Cherokee Ancestry
in the U.S. Court of Claims, 1906-1910, Vol 3, Applications
4201-7250. 1988. 485pp. 25.00 F5216

_____. Cherokee by Blood: Records of Eastern Cherokee Ancestry
in the U.S. Court of Claims, 1906-1910, Vol 4, Applications
7251-10170. 1989. 490pp. 25.00 F5216

_____. Cherokee by Blood: Records of Eastern Cherokee Ancestry
in the U.S. Court of Claims, 1906-1910, Vol 5, Applications
10171-13260. 1990. 489pp. 25.00 F5216

_____. Cherokee by Blood: Records of Eastern Cherokee Ancestry
in the U.S. Court of Claims, 1906-1910, Vol 6, Applications
13261-16745. 1990. 505pp. 25.00 F5216

_____. Cherokee by Blood: Records of Eastern Cherokee Ancestry
in the U.S. Court of Claims, 1906-1910, Vol 7, Applications
16746-20100. 1991. 490pp. 25.00 F5216

_____. Cherokee by Blood: Records of Eastern Cherokee Ancestry
in the U.S. Court of Claims, 1906-10, Vol.8, Applications.
20101-23800. 1992. 489pp. 25.00 F5216

Lantz, Raymond C. Ottawa and Chippewan Indians of Michigan,
1870-1909. 1991. 288pp. 21.00 F5216

Mather, Increase and Samuel G. Drake. The History of King Philip's
War, by the Rev. Increase Mather, D.D., also A History of the
Same War by the Rev. Cotton Mather, D.D. (1676, 1862)
reprint 276pp.
  To which is added An Introduction and Notes by Samuel
  G. Drake 20.00 F5216

Roby, Luther, editor. Reminiscences of the French War with Robert
Roger's Journal and a Memoir of General Stark. (1831) reprint
322pp. 22.50 F5216

Thwaites, LL.D., Rueben Gold and Louise Phelps Kellogg, Ph.D.
Documentary History of Dunmore's War, 1774. (1905) reprint
472pp. 29.00 F5216

Tregillis, Helen Cox. The Indians of Illinois. 1991. 158pp.
.... 22.50 F5216

Indians, Religious & Ethnic groups

Barton, Lois. A Quaker Promise Kept. Philadelphia Friends Work
with the Allegany Senecas. 1795-1960. 1990. 111pp.
  Includes list of staff & students at boarding school, 1851 -
  1938. .... 14.95 F5007

Land Records - Grants

McMullen, Phillip. Grassroots of America: Index to American State
    Papers, Land Grants and Claims 1789-1837. (1972) reprint
    1991. 520pp.
        Covers Alabama, Arkansas, Florida, Georgia, Illinois,
        Indiana, Iowa, Louisiana, Michigan, Minnesota,
        Mississippi, Missouri, Ohio, and Wisconsin.   52.50 .... F5031

Loyalists

Bunnell, Paul J. The New Loyalist Index. 1989. 525pp.
      .... 32.50 F5216

_____. Research Guide to Loyalist Ancestors: Archives,
    Manuscripts and Published Sources. 1990. 146pp. 15.00 F5216

Dwyer, Clifford S. Index to Series I of American Loyalists Claims.
      .... 12.00 F5061

Van Tyne, Claude Halstead. The Loyalists of the American
    Revolution. (1902) reprint 360pp. 24.00 F5216

Manuals and Handbooks

Hartley, William G. Diaries and Personal Journals: Why and How.
    (1978) reprint 1990. 32pp. 2.50 F5081

_____. Preparing a Personal History. (1976) reprint 1990. 32pp.
      .... 2.50 F5081

Shumway, Gary L. and William G. Hartley. An Oral History
    Primer: For Tape-recording Personal and Family Histories.
    (1973) reprint 1991. 32pp. 2.50 F5081

Maps, Atlas, Gazetteers, Place Names

Fanning. Fanning's Illustrated Gazetteer of the United States. (1855)
    reprint 400pp.
        Giving the location, physical aspect, mountains, rivers,
        lakes, climate, productive and manufacturing resources,
        commerce, government, education, general history, etc. of
        the States, Territories, Counties, Cities, Towns, and Post
        Offices in the American Union, with the population and
        other statistics from the census of 1850, illustrated with
        seals and thirty-one state maps in counties, and fourteen
        maps of cities. 26.50 F5216

Mayflower & Pilgrim Histories

Banks, C.E. The English Ancestry & Homes of the Pilgrim Fathers
    who came to Plymouth. (1929) reprint 1990. 187pp.
        In the "*Mayflower*" in 1620, the "*Fortune*" in 1621 & the
        "*Anne*" & "*Little James*" in 1623. .... 19.50 F5159

Hills, Leon Clark. History and Genealogy of the Mayflower
    Planters. (1936) reprint 1990. 461pp.
        2 volumes in 1, indexed. 25.00 .... F5130

Landis, J.T. Mayflower Descendants and Their Marriages for Two
    Generations After the Landing. (1922) reprint 1981. 37pp. 6.00 F5159

_____. Mayflower Descendants and Their Marriages for Two
    Generations After the Landing. (1922) reprint 1990. 37pp. 4.00   F5130

Rixford, Elizabeth M. Leach. Families Directly Descended from
    ALL THE ROYAL FAMILIES IN EUROPE (495-1932) &
    MAYFLOWER DESCENDANTS. (1932) reprint 1992.
    190pp.
        Charts, illustrated, indexed. 28.00   F5130

Roser, Susan E. Mayflower Births & Deaths. From the Files of
    George Ernest Bowman at the Massachusetts Society of
    Mayflower Descendants. 1992. 1,073pp.
        2 volumes 7" x 10". 525 & 548 pp., indexed. 75.00   F5129

_____. Mayflower Increasings (For Three Generations). (1989)
    reprint 1991. 159pp. 18.95   F5129

_____. Mayflower Marriages, From the Files of George Ernest
    Bowman at the Massachusetts Society of Mayflower
    Descendants. 1990. 415pp.
        Contains 10,000 marriages spanning five centuries, with
        names, dates and sources. Indexed. 29.95   F5129

Stoddard, Francis R. The Truth About the Pilgrims. (1952) reprint
    1992. 206pp.
        Indexed. 21.00   F5130

Military - Civil War

Beach, Richard L. Remember Me: the Civil War letters of Lt.
    George Robinson and son, St. James F. Robinson of "The
    Glenn" Hamburg, SC 1861-62. 1991. 92pp. 12.00   F5216

Billings, John D. Hard Tack and Coffee, or the unwritten story of
    Army life. (1887) reprint 414pp. 27.00   F5216

Bradley, James. The Confederate Mail Carrier. (1894) reprint
    281pp.
        Or "From Missouri to Arkansas through Mississippi,
        Alabama, Georgia and Tennessee". Being an Account of
        the Battles, Marches and Hardships of the First and
        Second Brigades, Mo., C.S.A. Together with the Thrilling
        Adventures and Narrow Escapes of Captain Grimes and
        his Fair Accomplice, who Carried the Mail by "the
        Underground Route" from the Brigade to Missouri. 21.50   F5216

Cockrum, Col. William M. History of the Underground Railroad as
    it Was Conducted by the Anti-Slavery League. (1915) reprint
    328pp.
        Including many thrilling encounters between those aiding
        the Slaves to escape and those trying to recapture them. 22.50   F5216

Dooley, Brian. Warriors for the Working Day. 1991. 105pp.
           ....   12.50   F5216

Harris, Gen. T.M. The Assassination of Lincoln: A History of the
    Great Conspiracy, Trial of the Conspirators by a Military
    Commission. (1892) reprint 440pp.
        And a review of the trial of John H. Surratt. 27.00   F5216

_____. Civil War Records "A Useful Tool". 1991. 125pp.
        A step by step guide to the availability and acquisition of
        Civil War Records. Acid-free paper. 17.95   F5117

Herrick, Margaret. A Civil War Soldier's Diary - Peter Funk, 150th
New York Volunteers. 1991. 54pp.   13.50   ....   F5040

Huffstodt, Jim. Hard Dying Men: A History of the 11th Illinois
Infantry. 1991. 360pp. 24.50   F5216

Knibb, Joyce G. and Patricia A. Mehrtens. The Elusive Booths of
Burrillville (R.I.): Investigation of John Wilkes Booth's alleged
wife and daughter. 1991. 266pp. 20.00   F5216

O'Brien, Charles B. 1001 Civil War Trivia. 1991. 150pp.
                                                           .... 12.50   F5216

Oldroyd, Osborn H. The Assassination of Abraham Lincoln: Flight,
Pursuit, Capture, and Punishment of the Conspirators. (1901)
reprint 312pp. 22.50   F5216

Pinkerton, Allan. The Spy of the Rebellion; being a True History of
the Spy System of the U.S. Army during Late Rebellion.
(1883) reprint 700pp.
        Revealing many secrets of the War hitherto not made
        public. Compiled from official reports prepared for
        President Lincoln, General McClellan and the
        Provost-Marshall-General. 35.00   F5216

Steiner, Jane B. Editor & Compiler. George Washington Irwin, The
Civil War Diary of a Pennsylvania Volunteer. 1991. 221pp.
        Additional regimental information in appendixes. Indexed. 15.00   F5115

Taylor, Thomas E. Running the Blockade: A Personal Narrative of
Adventures, Risks, and Escapes During American Civil War.
(1896) reprint 180pp. 17.50   F5216

U.S. Christian Commission. Record of the Federal Dead Buried
from Libby, Bell Isle, Danville & Camp Lawton Prisons & City
Point & in the Field before Petersburg & Richmond. (1866)
reprint 198pp. 17.50   F5216

Military - Frontier Wars

Clark, Murtie June. American Miltia in the Frontier Wars, 1790 -
1796. 1990. 394pp.
        Indexed   30.00   ....   F5129

Military - Mexican War

Frost, LLD, J. The Mexican War and Its Warriors: Comprising a
Complete History of all the Operations of the American Armies
in Mexico. (1850) reprint 342pp.
        With Biographical Sketches & Anecdotes of the Most
        Distinguished Officers in the Regular Army & Volunteer
        Force. 22.50   F5216

Witt, Mary Emily Smith. Index to the Dispatches and to the Names
of United States Soldiers Who Fought in the Final Battles of the
Mexican War. 1991. 35pp.
        Description of War Department dispatches and number of
        pages. 1400 names alphabetized with dispatch numbers.
        Order form for dispatch copies. 6.50   F5060

Military - Pensions and Other Records of Soldiers - All Wars

Clark, Murtie June. Index to U.S. Invalid Pension Records
    1801-1815. 1991. 159pp.   18.50   ....   F5129

_____.   The Pension Lists of 1792-1795, With Other
    Revolutionary War Pension Records. 1991. 216pp.
    Indexed   21.50   ....   F5129

Harris, Sherry. Civil War Records "A Useful Tool". 1991. 125pp.
    A step by step guide to the availability and acquisition of
    Civil War Records. Acid-free paper. 17.95   F5117

The Pension List of 1820. (1820) reprint 1991. 750pp.
    New indexed edition of a major work on Revolutionary War
    Pensioners.   40.00   ....   F5129

The Pension Roll of 1835. reprint 1992. 3,183pp.
    Indexed Edition in four volumes. 185.00   F5129

U.S. Department of the Interior. Rejected or Suspended Applications
    for Revolutionary War Pensions. (1852) reprint 1991. 462pp. 32.50   F5130

U.S. War Department. Revolutionary Pensioners. A Transcript of
    the Pension List of the United States for 1813. (1813) reprint
    1990. 47pp. 5.00   F5130

_____. Revolutionary Pensioners of 1818. (1818) reprint 1991.
    358pp.
    Originally published as "Message from the President of
    the United States, Transmitting a Report of the Secretary
    of War March 28, 1818", United States, War
    Department. 26.50   F5130

Witt, Mary Emily Smith. An Alphabetical List of Navy, Marine &
    Privateer Personnel & Widows from Pension Rolls, Casualty
    Lists, Retirement & Dismission Rolls of the US Navy. 1986.
    92pp.
    Lists and Rolls Dated 1847.   ....   13.50   F5060

Military - Revolutionary War

Balletta, Patricia Wilkinson Weaver. The Ancestors & Descendants
    of Revolutionary General James Wilkinson of Calvert County,
    Maryland Et Ux, Ann Biddle of Philadelphia, Pennsylvania.
    1993.   60.00   40.00   F5132

Benson, Adolph B. Sweden and the American Revolution. (1926)
    reprint 1992. 228pp.
    Indexed. 21.00   F5130

English, William Hayden. Conquest of the Country Northwest of the
    River Ohio, 1778-1783, and Life of Gen. George Rogers
    Clark. (1896) reprint 1,186pp. 60.00   F5216

Gilroy, Marion. Loyalists and Land Settlement in Nova Scotia.
    (1937) reprint 1990. 154pp.   18.00   ....   F5130

Miller, Elizabeth R. The American Revolution as described by
    British Writers and The Morning Chronicle and London
    Advertiser. 1991. 135pp. 14.50   F5216

Peterson, Clarence Stewart. Known Military Dead During the American Revolutionary War, 1775-1783. (1959) reprint 1992. 187pp. 20.00 F5130

Saffell, William T. R. Records of the Revolutionary War, Third Edition. [Bound with:] Index to Saffell's List of Virginia Soldiers in the Revolution. (1894) reprint 1991. 598pp. 32.50 .... F5130

Smith, Clifford Neal. British and German Deserters, Dischargees, and Prisoners of War Who May Have Remained in Canada and the United States, 1774-1783: Part 1. 1988. 24pp. 15.00 F5120

_____. British and German Deserters, Dischargees, and Prisoners of War Who May Have Remained in Canada and the United States, 1774-1783: Part 2. 1989. 18pp. 15.00 F5120

_____. Deserters and Disbanded Soldiers from British, German, and Loyalist Military Units in the South 1782. 1991. .... 15.00 F5120

_____. Some German-American Participants in the American Revolution: The Rattermann Lists. 1990. 49pp. 20.00 F5120

Von Eelking, Max. Trans & abridged by J.D. Rosengarten. The German Allied Troops in the North American War of Independence, 1776-1783. (1893) reprint 369pp. 25.00 F5216

_____. The German Allied Troops in the North American War of Independence 1776-1783. (1893) reprint 1990. 360pp. 25.00 .... F5130

Zall, P.M. The Founding Mothers: Profiles of Ten Wives of America's Founding Fathers. 1991. 212pp. 17.50 F5216

Military - War of 1812

Peterson, Clarence Stewart. Known Military Dead During The War of 1812. (1955) reprint 1991. 74pp. 10.00 F5130

Missionaries

Stone, Rev. Seth Bradley. Transcribed & Indexed by Kay C. Stone Missionary to the Zulus, 1992.
Journal of Captain Jim Stone; descriptions of life in South Africa 1850-187?; genealogical data. 25.00 F5209

Newspapers and Newspaper Indices

Grubb, Farley. Runaway Servants, Convicts, and Apprentices. Advertised in the Pennsylvania Gazette, 1728-1796. 1992. 198pp. 25.00 .... F5129

Passenger Lists

Banks, Charles Edward. The Planters of the Commonwealth. (1930) reprint 1991. 244pp.
A Study of the Emigrants and Emigration in Colonial Times: to which are added lists of passengers to Boston and to the Bay colony; the ships which brought them; their English homes, and the places of their settlement in Massachusetts, 1620-1640. 20.00 .... F5129

Cameron, Viola R. Emigrants From Scotland to America,
1774-1775. (1930) reprint 1990. 117pp.
Indexed · 15.00 .... F5130

Dobson, David. Directory of Scots Banished to the American
Plantations, 1650-1775. (1984) reprint 1990. 239pp. · · · · · 15.00 .... F5130

Hackett, J. Dominick and Charles M. Early. Passengers Lists from
Ireland (Excerpted from "Journal of the American Irish
Historical Society", Volumes 28 and 29). (1931) reprint
1992. 46pp. · 7.50 F5130

Jewson, Charles Boardman. Transcript of Three Registers of
Passengers From Great Yarmouth to Holland and New
England, 1637-1639. (1964) reprint 1990. 98pp.
Indexed · 15.00 .... F5130

Munroe, J.B. A List of Alien Passengers Bonded From January 1,
1847, to January 1, 1851. (1851) reprint 1991. 99pp. · · · · · 12.50 F5130

O'Brien, Michael J. The Irish in America. (1965) reprint 1990.
63pp.
Immigration, Land, Probate, Adminstrations, Birth,
Marriage and Burial Records of the Irish in America in
and about the Eighteenth Century. · · · · · · · · · · · · · · · · · · 5.00 F5130

Passenger Arrivals, 1819-1820. (1821) reprint 1991. 342pp.
Originally published as "Letter from the Secretary of
State, with a Transcript of the List of Passengers Who
Arrived in the United States from the 1st of October,
1819, to the 30th of September, 1820". Indexed. · · · · · · · · 25.00 F5130

Smith, Clifford Neal. From Breman to America in 1850: Some Rare
Emigrant Ship Lists. 1987. 42pp. · · · · · · · · · · · · · · · · · · · 15.00 F5120

_____. Passenger Lists (and Fragments Therefrom) from Hamburg
and Bremen to Australia and the United States. 1988. 28pp. · · 15.00 F5120

Strassburger, Ralph Beaver and William John Hinke. Pennsylvania
German Pioneers [:] A publication of the Original Lists of
Arrivals In the Port of Philadelphia From 1727 to 1808,
Signature Volume. (1934) reprint 1992. 909pp.
This set which is commonly known as "Strassburger &
Hinke" is the time-honored reference for arrival of
German emigrants to America before 1800. It is one of
the basic works for genealogical libraries. Volumes 1 &
3 have been reprinted a number of times, but this is the
first time this volume (which shows the actual signatures
of the emigrants) has been reprinted. This signature
volume is important as it may be used to check signatures
on wills, deeds, and other documents to ascertain whether
they were written by the same man.
This volume has been printed the same size and
with the same cover as the other currently available
volumes so that they will make a matching set. It is being
sold separately for $55 - for purchase by those who
already have the other two volumes. It is necessary to
have the other volumes in order to use this one as it does
not have a separate index. For those who do not have any
of this set, all three volumes are available from us as a set
for the very special price of $100.00. The other volumes
total 1,565 pages and this one has 909.
All three are printed on acid-free paper and are
smythe-sewn with cloth bindings. · · · · · · · · · · · · · · · · · · 55.00 .... F5236

Presidential Genealogy

Henry, R.B. Genealogies of the Families of the Presidents. (1935)
    reprint 1991. 340pp.
        Includes descendants & collateral relations for all U.S.
        presidents through FDR, from their generation on.   37.00 .... F5159

Publishing Your Own Book or Newsletter

Arthur, Stephan and Julia. Your Life & Times,How to Put a Life on
    Tape. An Oral History Handbook. 1990. 50pp.
        8.5" x 11" 2nd Printing. 8.95 F5129

Banks, Keith E. How to Write Your Personal & Family History: A
    Resource Manual. 1988. 240pp. 17.50 F5216

Earnest, Corinne P. The "What Shall I Write" Handbook: For
    Editors of Family and Genealogy Society Newsletters. 1992.
    80pp. 18.00 F5112

Religious

Martin, III, Joseph B. Guide to Presbyterian Ecclesiastical Names
 and Places in South Carolina: 1685-1985. 1989. 212pp.
  List of all Presbyterian churches in South Carolina,
  including locations, variant names, sources of
  information. A special double issue of South Carolina
  Historical Magazine, January-April 1989. .... 11.00 F5181

Tazewell, C.W., ed. Jackson Scrapbook: Called to Serve. 126pp.
  Eight of Family of William Jackson (1757-1812) in four
  generations were ministers. 15.00 F5177

Religious and Ethnic Groups - Afro-Americans

Clayton, Ralph. Black Baltimore, 1820-1870. 1987. 206pp.
  .... 17.50 F5216

_____. Free Blacks of Anne Arundel County, Maryland. 1987.
 66pp. 10.00 F5216

Streets, David H. Slave Genealogy: A Research Guide with Case
 Studies. 1986. 90pp. 15.00 F5216

Turpin, Joan. Register of Black, Mulatto & Poor Persons in Four
 Ohio Counties, 1791-1861. 1985. 50pp. 8.00 F5216

Walker, Barbara D. Index to "The Journal of the Afro-American
 Historical and Genealogical Society Quarterly" Issues
 1980-90. 1992. 171pp. 23.50 F5216

Religious and Ethnic Groups - Cuban

Religious and Ethnic Groups - German

Baxter, Angus. In Search of Your German Roots, A Complete Guide
    to Tracing Your Ancestors in the Germanic Areas of Europe,
    UNITED Germany Edition. 1991. 128pp. 10.95   F5129

Bittinger, Lucy Forney. The Germans in Colonial Times. (1901)
    reprint 314pp. 22.00   F5216

Burgoyne, Bruce E. Waldeck (Germany) Soldiers of The American
    Revolutionary War. 1991. 218pp. 18.00   F5216

Cobb, Sanford H. The Story of the Palatines. (1897) reprint 336pp.
    .... 23.00   F5216

Kuhns, Oscar. The German and Swiss Settlements of Colonial
    Pennsylvania: A study of the so-called Pennsylvania Dutch.
    (1901) reprint 268pp. 20.00   F5216

Thode, Ernest. Address Book for Germanic Genealogy, Fourth
    Edition. 1992. 218pp. 24.95   F5129

_____. German-English Genealogical Dictionary. 1992. 318pp.
    .... 29.95   F5129

Tolzmann, Don Heinrich, editor. Germany and America
    (1450-1700): Julius Freidrich Sachse's "History of the German
    Role in the Discovery, Exploration, and Settlement of the New
    World". 1991. 263pp. 20.00   F5216

_____. The First Germans in America with a biographical
    directory of New York Germans. 1992. 110pp. 13.00   F5216

Religious and Ethnic Groups - German-American

Earnest, Corinne Pattie and Beverly Repass Hoch.
    German-American Family Records in the Fraktur Tradition.
    1991. 254pp. 29.95   F5112

_____. The Genealogist's Guide to Fraktur: For Genealogists
    Researching German-American Families. 1990. 48pp. 14.95   F5112

Tolzmann, Don Heinrich. Ohio Valley German Biographical Index.
    1992. 80pp. 17.00   F5216

Religious and Ethnic Groups - Huguenots

Baird, Charles W. History of the Huguenot Emigration to America.
    (1885) reprint 1991. 802pp.
    2 volumes in 1, 354 and 448 pp., illus., maps, indexed. 45.00 ....   F5129

Lart, Charles Edmund. Huguenot Pedigrees. (1924-28) reprint
    1992. 258pp.
    2 volumes in 1, indexed. 22.50   F5130

Lawton, Mrs. James M. Family Names of Huguenot Refugees to
    America. (1901) reprint 1991. 20pp. 4.00   F5129

Rosengarten, J.G. French Colonists and Exiles in the United States.
    (1907) reprint 234pp. 18.50   F5216

Religious and Ethnic Groups - Irish

McGee, Thomas D'Arcy. A History of the Irish Settlers in North
America from the Earliest Period to the Census of 1850.
(1851) reprint 185pp. 15.50   F5216

Murray, Thomas Hamilton, editor, et al. The Journal of the
American-Irish Historical Society. Volume 1, 1898. reprint
136pp. 15.00   F5216

_____. The Journal of the American-Irish Historical Society,
Volume 2, 1899. reprint 260pp. 20.00   F5216

_____. The Journal of the American-Irish Historical Society,
Volume 3, 1900. reprint 241pp. 19.00   F5216

_____. The Journal of the American-Irish Historical Society,
Volume 4, 1904. reprint 195pp. 17.00   F5216

_____. The Journal of the American-Irish Historical Society,
Volume 5, 1905. reprint 212pp. 18.00   F5216

_____. The Journal of the American-Irish Historical Society,
Volume 6, 1906. reprint 170pp. 15.50   F5216

Religious and Ethnic Groups - Italian

DeAngelis, Priscilla G.   Sources for Italian - American Research.
40+pp.
Records in the U.S. and Italy, including civil and church
records, census and ship passenger lists. Mormon
Library, specialized resources for Italian-American
research. Extensive bibliography and index. Some of the
material appeared previously in genealogical magazines. 9.95   F5078

Religious and Ethnic Groups - Jewish

Cohen, Chester G. Shtetl Finder Gazetteer: Jewish Communities in
the 19th and Early 20th Centuriesin the Pale of Settlement of
Russia and Poland, and in Lithuania, Latvia, Galicia, and
Bukovina, with Names of Residents. (1980) reprint 145pp. 20.00   F5216

Stern, Dr. Malcolm H. First American Jewish Families, 1654-1988,
3rd Edition. 1991. 464pp. 75.00   ....   F5129

Religious and Ethnic Groups - Quakers

Hinshaw, William Wade.   Encyclopedia of American Quaker
Genealogy, Volume I: North Carolina. (1948) reprint 1991.
1,197pp.
With supplement to Volume I by Thomas Worth
Marshall (1948). 8.5 x 11", Indexed. 75.00   F5129

_____. Encyclopedia of American Quaker Genealogy, Volume II:
New Jersey and Pennsylvania. (1938) reprint 1991. 1,126pp.
8.5 x 11", Indexed 75.00   F5129

_____. Encyclopedia of American Quaker Genealogy, Volume III:
New York. (1940) reprint 1991. 540pp.
Containing every item of genealogical value found in all
records and minutes (known to be in existence) of all

meetings of all grades ever organized in New York City and on Long Island (1657 to the Present time). Including both Hicksite and Orthodox Groups of the New York Yearly Meeting of the Society of Friends. 45.00 F5129

Philadelphia Yearly Meeting. A Collection of Memorials Concerning Diverse deceased Ministers and others of the People called Quakers, in Pennsylvania, New Jersey, & Parts adjacent. (1787) reprint 440pp.
From nearly the first Settlement thereof to the Year 1787. .... 27.50 F5216

Sullivan Audrey, Ed. Index, Vols. 1 and 2, Jos. Besse's A Collection of Sufferings of People Called Quakers, 1650-1689. 1991. 161pp.
Shows Quaker's resident parish and page reference in Jos. Besse's original 1753 2-volume publication. 20.00 .... F5230

Religious and Ethnic Groups - Romanian/Germans

Steigerwald, Jacob. Tracing Romania's Heterogeneous German Minority from Its Origins to the Diaspora. 1985. 61pp. 4.95 F5106

Religious and Ethnic Groups - Scotch-Irish

Bolton, Charles Knowles. Scotch Irish Pioneers in Ulster and America. (1910) reprint 398pp. 25.00 F5216

Ford, Henry Jones. The Scotch-Irish in America. (1915) reprint 1992. 607pp.
Indexed. 39.95 F5130

Religious and Ethnic Groups - Scottish

Cory, Kathleen B. Tracing Your Scottish Ancestry. 1990. 195pp.
Indexed. 16.95 F5129

Dobson, David. Scots on the Chesapeake 1607-1830. 1992. 169pp 20.00 .... F5129

_____. Scottish - American Wills, 1650-1900. 1991. 137pp. 20.00 .... F5129

_____. Scottish-American Court Records, 1733-1783. 1991. 105pp.
Indexed. 18.00 .... F5129

_____. Scottish-American Heirs, 1683-1883. (1991) reprint 1992. 165pp. 21.50 .... F5129

_____. The Original Scots Colonists of Early America, 1612 - 1783. 1990. 370pp.
Indexed, 2nd printing. 28.50 .... F5129

MacDougall, Donald, ed. Scots and Scots' Descendants in America. (1917) reprint 1992. 390pp.
Indexed. 29.95 F5130

McLaren, Mike. The Book of Crests of Scottish-American Clans. 1990. 272pp. 20.00 F5216

Whyte, Donald. A Dictionary of Scottish Emigrants to the U.S.A.,
  Volume I. (1972) reprint 1992. 517pp.
    Indexed. 37.50 F5130

```
┌─────────────────────────────────────────────┐
│             COMING to SALT LAKE?             │
│        Let me help you make the most of      │
│                  your time.                  │
│                                              │
│                 Dortha Steele                │
│    721 E 17th So, Salt Lake City, UT 84105   │
└─────────────────────────────────────────────┘
```

Research Aids

Deputy, Marilyn, et al. Register of Federal United States Military
  Records, Vol. 2, The Civil War. 1986. 476pp.
    A Guide to Manuscript Sources Available at the
    Genealogical Library in Salt Lake
    City & the National Archives in Washington. 45.00 F5216

_____. Register of Federal United States Military Records, Volume
  1, 1776-1860. 1986. 265pp.
    A Guide to Manuscript Sources Available at the
    Genealogical Library in Salt Lake City & the National
    Archives in Washington. 30.00 F5216

Gould, Sharry Crofford. Bible Records Index. 1982. 46pp.
    Indexed by Surname. 5.95 F5059

Hamilton, Ann B. Researcher's Guide to United States Census
  Availability, Second Edition, 1790-1920. 1992. 165pp. 26.50 F5216

Jones, Jessie M. Selected Genealogy Hints. 1992. 45pp.
    These Genealogy Hints are selected from those written
    and presented by Jessie M. Jones at Sequoia Genealogical
    Society monthly meetings. They have been included in
    the Society's Newsletter and exchanged with other
    genealogy societies. It is hoped that these "hints" will be
    found as a "light-hearted" approach to serious
    genealogical and family history research. 10.50 F5225

Mellen, Rachael. The Handy Book to English Genealogy, 3rd
  edition. 1990. 228pp. 17.50 F5216

Rogers, Ellen. Genealogical Periodical Annual Index: Key to the
  Genealogical Literature, Vol. 1, 1962. 105pp. 15.00 F5216

_____. Genealogical Periodical Annual Index: Key to the
  Genealogical Literature, Vol. 2, 1963. 130pp. 15.00 F5216

_____. Genealogical Periodical Annual Index: Key to the
  Genealogical Literature, Vol. 3, 1964. 150pp. 15.00 F5216

_____. Genealogical Periodical Annual Index: Key to the
  Genealogical Literature, Vol. 4, 1965. 150pp. 15.00 F5216

Towle, Leslie K. and Laird C. Towle. Genealogical Periodical
  Annual Index: Key to the Genealogical Literature, Vol. 13,
  1974. 56pp. 15.00 F5216

_____. and Laird C. Towle.   Genealogical Periodical Annual Index: Key to the Genealogical Literature, Vol. 14, 1975. 70pp. 15.00   F5216

_____. and Laird C. Towle.   Genealogical Periodical Annual Index: Key to the Genealogical Literature, Vol. 15, 1976. 113pp. 20.00   F5216

_____. and Laird C. Towle.   Genealogical Periodical Annual Index: Key to the Genealogical Literature, Vol. 16, 1977. 175pp. 20.00   F5216

_____. and Laird C. Towle.   Genealogical Periodical Annual Index: Key to the Genealogical Literature, Vol. 17, 1978. 180pp. 20.00   F5216

_____. and Laird C. Towle.   Genealogical Periodical Annual Index: Key to the Genealogical Literature, Vol. 18, 1979. 192pp. 20.00   F5216

_____. and Laird C. Towle.   Genealogical Periodical Annual Index: Key to the Genealogical Literature, Vol. 19, 1980. 178pp. 20.00   F5216

_____. and Laird C. Towle.   Genealogical Periodical Annual Index: Key to the Genealogical Literature, Vol. 20, 1981. 192pp. 20.00   F5216

_____. and Laird C. Towle.   Genealogical Periodical Annual Index: Key to the Genealogical Literature, Vol. 21, 1982. 142pp. 20.00   F5216

_____. and Laird C. Towle.   Genealogical Periodical Annual Index: Key to the Genealogical Literature, Vol. 22, 1983. 240pp. 20.00   F5216

_____. and Laird C. Towle.   Genealogical Periodical Annual Index: Key to the Genealogical Literature, Vol. 23, 1984. 176pp. 20.00   F5216

_____. and Laird C. Towle.   Genealogical Periodical Annual Index: Key to the Genealogical Literature, Vol. 24, 1985. 284pp. 20.00   F5216

_____. and Laird C. Towle.   Genealogical Periodical Annual Index: Key to the Genealogical Literature, Vol. 25, 1986. 286pp. 20.00   F5216

_____. and Laird C. Towle.   Genealogical Periodical Annual Index: Key to the Genealogical Literature, Vol. 26, 1987. 266pp. 20.00   F5216

_____. and Laird C. Towle.   Genealogical Periodical Annual Index: Key to the Genealogical Literature, Vol. 27, 1988. 280pp. 20.00   F5216

_____. and Laird C. Towle.   Genealogical Periodical Annual Index: Key to the Genealogical Literature, Vol. 28, 1989. 270pp. 20.00   F5216

_____. and Laird C. Towle.   Genealogical Periodical Annual Index: Key to the Genealogical Literature, Vol. 29, 1990. 1990. 358pp.   22.50   ....   F5216

Research Aids - Directories and Compendiums

Bentley, Elizabeth Petty. County Courthouse Book. 1990. 400pp.
   Names and addresses of 3,351 county courthouses.
    8.5" x 11" format. 29.92 F5129

_____. Directory of Family Associations. 1991. 405pp.
   Contains information on approximately 5,000 family
   associations across the United States. 29.95 F5129

_____. The Genealogist's Address Book, 1992-93 Edition. 1992.
 568pp. 29.95 F5129

Lainhart, Ann S. State Census Records. 1992. 116pp.
               17.95 .... F5129

Thorndale, William and William Dollarhide. Map Guide to the U.S.
 Federal Censuses, 1790-1920. (1987) reprint 1992. 445pp. 39.95 F5129

Research Aids - Lineage Books, Surname Indices, Ancestor Charts

Franklin County Genealogical Society. Ancestral Surname Indexes.
   These volumes include genealogical information for
   ancestors of members throughtout the United States and
   overseas. Entries list date and place for birth, death, and
   marriage, if known. Name and address of current
   member are included for your correspondence.
     Vol. I, 74pp, 1980, $6.00
     Vol. II, 106pp, 1981, $7.50
     Vol. III, 103pp, 1982, $8.00
     Vol. IV, 109pp, 1984, $8.00
     Vol. V, 130pp, 1986, $8.00
     Vol. VI, 184pp, 1992, $12.00   .... F5237

INTERNATIONAL GENEALOGICAL INDEX
SEARCHES ONLY $3.00

YOU CAN'T BEAT THIS PRICE!

Professional record searchers will search the International Genealogical Index (over 120 million names) for one ancestor for only $3.00! (Minimum order of three ancestors.) Fill in the following details as completely as possible to enable the record searcher to properly identify your ancestors. Estimate dates and offer a place of residence when exact dates and places are unknown. Keep in mind that this collection does not include every person who ever lived and that your ancestor(s) may not be in the collection. You are paying for the time required to do the search!

Ancestor #1
Name: _____
Birthdate: _____
Birthplace: _____
Death Date: _____
Death Place: _____
Name of Spouse: _____
Date of Marriage: _____
Place of Marriage: _____
Names of Bro/Sis: _____
Children's Names:_____

Ancestor #2
Name: _____
Birthdate: _____
Birthplace: _____
Death Date: _____
Death Place: _____
Name of Spouse: _____
Date of Marriage: _____
Place of Marriage: _____
Names of Bro/Sis: _____
Children's Names:_____

Ancestor #3
Name: _____
Birthdate: _____ _____
Birthplace: _____
Death Date: _____
Death Place: _____
Name of Spouse: _____
Date of Marriage: _____
Place of Marriage: _____
Names of Bro/Sis: _____
Children's Names:_____

Please include a check, money order, or charge for $9.00 plus $1.50 postage and handling.
☐ Check or Money Order Enclosed
Charge to my: ☐ American Express ☐ Visa ☐ MasterCard
Card # _____ Expiration: _____
Your Name: _____

Address: _____	**Send to:**
City: _____	Lineages, Inc.
State: _____ Zip: _____	P.O. Box 417
Daytime Telephone: _____	Salt Lake City, UT 84110
Signature: _____	Phone: (801) 531-9297
	Fax: (801) 531-6819

Research Aids - Reference Sources

Anderson, Alloa and Loraine Wallace. Researching Genealogy in Libraries (Revised & Expanded). 1992. 60pp.
With this book genealogists can research public and academic libraries with skill and confidence. Chapters explain card and computer catalogs, Dewey and LC systems, filing rules, record keeping, building your personal library, uses of a variety of reference books, and more. Indexed. 9.50 F5199

Harris, Sherry. Civil War Records "A Useful Tool". 1991. 125pp.
A step by step guide to the availability and acquisition of Civil War Records. Acid-free paper. 17.95 F5117

Nichols, Elizabeth L. Genealogy in the Computer Age: Understanding FamilySearch™. 1991. 56pp.
60 illustrations. See "Computers" for a full definition. 8.95 F5097

Prucha, Francis Paul. Handbook For Research In American History.
1987. 289pp.
The latest sources for bibliographies, biographical
registers, guides and directories, including databases. 11.95   F5108

Weland, Gerald. Last Post. 1989. 288pp.
A guide to the National Cemetary System. 21.50   F5216

Royal Descent

Balletta, Patricia Wilkinson Weaver. The Ancestors & Descendants
of Revolutionary General James Wilkinson of Calvert County,
Maryland Et Ux, Ann Biddle of Philadelphia, Pennsylvania. 1993. 60.00 40.00   F5132

Wurts. The Magna Charta: History & Romance of the Great Charter
and the Baronial Pedigrees. Parts I & II:The Romance of the
Charter & Pedigrees of the Barons. 1939-54. 300+23pp.   31.00   ....   F5159

_____. The Magna Charta: History & Romance of the Great
Charter and the Baronial Pedigrees. Part III: Continuing the
Pedigrees of the Barons. 1944. 319pp.   31.00   ....   F5159

_____. The Magna Charta: History & Romance of the Great
Charter and the Baronial Pedigrees. Part IV: A Collection of
Baronial Pedigrees. 1939-54. 410pp.   41.00   ....   F5159

_____. The Magna Charta: History & Romance of the Great
Charter and the Baronial Pedigrees. Part V: A Collection of
Baronial Pedigrees. 1939-54. 412pp.
Including additions and corrections to Parts I-IV.   41.00   ....   F5159

_____. The Magna Charta: History & Romance of the Great
Charter and the Baronial Pedigrees. Part VI: Families of Royal
Descent. 1939-54. 458pp.   43.00   ....   F5159

_____. The Magna Charta: History & Romance of the Great
Charter and the Baronial Pedigrees. Part VII. 1939-54. 462pp.   45.00   ....   F5159

Settler Lore

Woodstock Series. Recipes and Stories of Early Day Settlers.
The Woodstock Series, Volume I. Its more than just a
cookbook! 15 years of DISCOVERY PUBLICATIONS
RECIPES & STORIES. 8.00   F5231

Weyand, Kenneth C. Steamboat Adventures: Recipes and Stories of
Early Day Settlers.
The Woodstock Series, Volume II. Lots of pictures
depicting the era of steamboat and river travel on both the
Missouri and Mississippi Rivers. Recipes cover a broad
spectrum of time, tradition, and geography. 8.00   F5231

Source Records

Francis, Elisabeth and Ethel Moore. Lost Links. New Recordings of
Old Data from Many States. (1947) reprint 1991. 562pp.
The product of a painstaking search of original
courthouse records and comprises transcriptions of a
bewildering variety of genealogical source records.
Includes information from fifteen states throughout the

South and some of New England. Indentifies more than
15,000 persons in hundreds of miscellaneous courthouse
records.

Indexed.	....	39.95	F5130

Kemp, Thomas Jay. 1989 Physicians' Obituaries, An Obituary Index
to the Journal of American Medical Association. 1990. 96pp. 17.50 F5129

The 1790 Census. Heads of Families at the First Census of the
United States Taken in the Year 1790. reprint 1992. 2,561pp.
Special price offer for the set of twelve volumes
(a $312.00 value). Available individually as follows:

Connecticut,	227pp	$22.50			
Maine,	105pp	$18.50			
Maryland,	189pp	$25.00			
Massachusetts,	363pp	$38.50			
New Hampshire,	146pp	$21.50			
New York,	308pp	$35.00			
North Carolina,	292pp	$32.50			
Pennsylvania,	426pp	$44.50			
Rhode Island,	71pp	$15.00			
South Carolina,	150pp	$21.50			
Vermont,	95pp	$15.00			
Virginia,	189pp	$22.90	250.00	....	F5129

Surnames, Given Names

Ashley, Leonard R. N. What's in a Name? Everything You Wanted
to Know. (1989) reprint 1991. 265pp. 14.95 F5129

Barber, Rev. Henry. British Family Names - Their Origin and
Meaning. (1903) reprint 1990. 298pp. 20.00 .... F5130

Bardsley, Charles Wareing. English Surnames, their Sources and
Significations, 6th Edition. (1898) reprint 612pp. 35.00 F5216

Harrison, Henry. Surnames of the United Kingdom. A Concise
Etymological Dictionary. (1912-18) reprint 1992. 622pp.
2 volumes in 1. .... 39.95 F5130

Long, Henry Alfred. Personal and Family Names: A Popular
Monograph on the Origin and History of the Nomenclature of
the Present and Former Times. (1883) reprint 362pp. 23.50 F5216

Stein, Lou. Clues to Our Family Names. 1986. 196pp.
.... 10.00 F5216

Surnames in the United States Census of 1790. An Analysis of
National Origins of the Population. (1932) reprint 1990.
334pp.
Indexed. 27.50 .... F5130

Textbooks, Manuals and Handbooks

Dollarhide, William. Managing a Genealogical Project, A Complete
Manual for the Management and Organization of Genealogical
Materials, Revised Edition. 1991. .... 14.95 F5129

Donald Jacobus, Jacobus. Genealogy as Pastime and Profession, 2nd
edition. (1968) reprint 1991. 120pp. 7.95 F5129

Hartley, William G. Diaries and Personal Journals: Why and How.
(1978) reprint 1990. 32pp. 2.50 F5081

_____. Preparing a Personal History. (1976) reprint 1990. 32pp.

.... 2.50 F5081

Genealogy Publishing Service. How to Write and Publish Your
Family Book. 1988. 60pp.
This book contains everything the family genealogist
should know about writing and publishing their family
history or other genealogy book. Book contains
examples of margin layouts, indexes, and sample text
pages. Covers questions on organization of data,
footnotes, typesetting, manuscript preparations,
copyrights, text paper, book sizes, etc.

.... 9.95 F5232

Nichols, Elizabeth L. Genealogy in the Computer Age:
Understanding FamilySearch™. 1991. 56pp.
60 illustrations. See "Computers" for a full definition.

.... 8.95 F5097

Shumway, Gary L. and William G. Hartley. An Oral History
Primer: For Tape-recording Personal and Family Histories.
(1973) reprint 1991. 32pp.

.... 2.50 F5081

Textbooks, Manuals and Handbooks for Special Subjects

Arnold, Jackie Smith. KINSHIP: It's All Relative. 1990. 72pp.
In clear, practical terms this book explains everything
there is to know about kinship: about agnate and cognate
kinship, collateral and fictive kinship, degrees of
consanguinity and how to calculate blood relationships,
etc.

.... 6.95 F5129

Hartley, William G. Diaries and Personal Journals: Why and How.
(1978) reprint 1990. 32pp.

.... 2.50 F5081

_____. Preparing a Personal History. (1976) reprint 1990. 32pp.

.... 2.50 F5081

Huberman, Rob and Laura Janis. Video Family Portraits:the User
Friendly Guide to Video Taping Your Family History, Stories
and Memories. 1987. 160pp.

.... 15.00 F5216

Schafer, Louis S. Tombstones of Your Ancestors. 1991. 160pp.

.... 15.00 F5216

Shumway, Gary L. and William G. Hartley. An Oral History
Primer: For Tape-recording Personal and Family Histories.
(1973) reprint 1991. 32pp.

.... 2.50 F5081

Textbooks, Manuals and Handbooks for U.S. Genealogical Research

Harris, Sherry. Civil War Records "A Useful Tool". 1991. 125pp.
A step by step guide to the availability and acquisition of
Civil War Records. Acid-free paper.

.... 17.95 F5117

Western Histories

Montgomery, Donna M. Wojcik. The Brazen Overlanders of 1845.
(1976) reprint 1992. 566pp.

.... 38.50 F5216

Tolzmann, Editor, Don Heinrich. Lives and Exploits of the Daring
Frank and Jesse James: Thaddeus Thorndike's Graphic and
Realistic Description of their Many Deeds. (1909) reprint
1992. 207pp.

.... 19.00 F5216

Alabama

STATEWIDE REFERENCE

	Cloth	Paper	Vendor #
General Reference			
England, Flora D. Alabama Notes. Volumes 1 and 2. (1977) reprint 1990. 240pp.			
2 volumes in 1, indexed.	20.00	....	F5130
Military - Revolutionary War			
Owen, Thomas M. Revolutionary Soldiers in Alabama. (1911) reprint 1990. 131pp.	16.00	....	F5130
West Central Region			
Pettit, Madge. Pioneers and Residents of West Central Alabama. 1988. 400pp.	....	27.50	F5216

CLARKE COUNTY

	Cloth	Paper	Vendor #
Graham, John Simpson. History of Clarke County (Alabama). (1923) reprint 362pp.	....	24.50	F5216

MOBILE COUNTY

	Cloth	Paper	Vendor #
Hamilton, A.M., Peter J. Colonial Mobile: An Historical Study. (1910) reprint 594pp.			
Largely from Original Sources, of the Alabama-Tombigbee Basin and the Old South West from the Discovery to the Spirit Santo in 1519 until the Demolition of Fort Charlotte in 1821.	....	27.50	F5216

Arkansas

STATEWIDE REFERENCE

Family Pedigrees

Published by Northwest Arkansas Genealogical Society. Family
Pedigrees Vol. I. 1991. 143pp.
Member's ancestral charts. 150 pages, over 1150+
families, surnames indexed. Valuable reference for
researcher with roots in Northwest Arkansas. 17.50 F5202

Military

Allen, Desmond Walls. First Arkansas Confederate Mounted Rifles.
1989. 104pp. 17.50 F5031

_____. Index to Arkansas Confederate Pension Applications.
1991. 324pp. 50.50 38.50 F5031

_____. Index to Arkansas Confederate Soldiers: Three Volume
Set. 1990. 618pp. 106.50 70.50 F5031

Turnbo, Silas C. and Desmond Walls Allen - Editor. History of the
Twenty-seventh Arkansas Confederate Infantry. 1988. 280pp. 29.50 F5031

Pioneers

Shinn, Josiah H. Pioneers and Makers of Arkansas. (1908) reprint
1991. 423pp.
Indexed 30.00 .... F5130

BENTON COUNTY

Pearce, Verba Jo and Gail Scott. Marriages of Benton County, AR.
1989. 122pp.
    Book B 1877-1886. Indexed. 17.50   F5202

_____. and Gail Scott. Marriages of Benton County, AR
1860-1877. 1987. 140pp.
    Book A 1860-1877. Oldest existing records. Indexed. 17.50   F5202

Scott, Gail, Compiler. Will Book A, Benton County, AR. 1984.
104pp.
    Estate Records Box #1. Includes wills, April 1837 to
    August 1870 and loose papers 1860-1871. .... 10.50   F5202

FRANKLIN COUNTY

Hanks, Bill. Franklin County, Arkansas, 1870 Census, with
Surname Index. 1990. 139pp. 22.00   F5042

JOHNSON COUNTY

Hanks, Bill. Johnson County, Arkansas, 1860 Census, with
Surname Index. 1989. 157pp. 15.00   F5042

_____. Johnson County, Arkansas, 1870 Census, with Surname
Index. 1989. 133pp. 18.00   F5042

LOGAN COUNTY

Hanks, Bill. Logan County, Arkansas - Marriage Book "B" (1877 -
1884) The Earliest. 1978. 92pp. 15.00   F5042

_____. Logan County, Arkansas - Marriage Records - The First
Fifty Years (1877 - 1924). 1991. 219pp. 28.00   F5042

_____. Logan County, Arkansas, 1880 Census, with Surname
Index (Annotated). 1992. 478pp. 30.00   F5042

_____. Logan County, Arkansas, 1890 Tax Book (Reconstructed
1890 Census). 1987. 118pp. 15.00   F5042

SCOTT COUNTY

Hanks, Bill. Scott County, Arkansas, 1850 Census, with Surname
Index (Annotated). 1992. 91pp. 16.00   F5042

_____. Scott County, Arkansas, 1860 Census, with Surname
Index. 1989. 150pp. 16.00   F5042

_____. Scott County, Arkansas, 1870 Census, with Surname
Index. 1989. 221pp. 22.00   F5042

SEBASTIAN COUNTY

Scott, Transcriber, Gail. 1860 U.S. Census of Sebastian County,
AR. 1979. 121pp.
    Transcribed from microfilm. Includes surname index. 6.50   F5202

SHARP COUNTY

Whitten, Joyce Hambleton. 1870 Census of Sharp County Arkansas.
(1978) reprint 1986. 76pp. 11.75 F5188

_____. 1880 Census of Sharp County Arkansas. (1980) reprint
1986. 164pp. 20.80 F5188

WASHINGTON COUNTY

Published by Northwest Arkansas Genealogical Society. Cemeteries
of Washington County, AR, Volume VI. 1983. 99pp.
Blackburn, Black Oak #1, Brentwood, Coil, Collier also
known as Boston or Yoes), Episcopal (Winslow), Fall
Creek, Funkhouser (Sugar Hill), Ganderville, Hash,
Hutch or Reagan, Kinnibrugh, McGarrah, Mountain
View, Oak Grove, Parks, Sunset, Terry Family, Union
Star, Unknown, West Fork,
Woolsey and Zinnamon.
Indexed. 11.00 F5202

_____. Cemeteries of Washington County, AR, Volume VII.
1984. 99pp.
Fairview Memorial Gardens, Hazel Valley, Nickell,
Salem or Mt. Salem, Smith (at Cincinnati), Stokenbury,
Thomas, Tuttle
and Union Point.
Indexed. 11.00 F5202

_____. Cemeteries of Washington County, AR, Volume VIII.
1985. 90pp.
Campbell, Evergreen, Grave of Revolutionary Soldier,
Highland, Kelton or Winslow, Low Gap, Mineral
Springs, Roberson, Stelle or Shaeffer, Tharp, White
House and
Williford.
Indexed. 11.00 F5202

_____. Cemeteries of Washington County, AR, Volume IX.
126pp.
Academy, Baker, Beaty (at Lincoln), Bethesda,
Billingsley, Boyd, Butler Ford, Carnahan (or Bean), Cox,
Crittenden, Dale Family, Dutch Mills, Edmiston, Harrell,
Hester, Howell (at Hogeye), Lewis (at Evansville),
McDonald, Neale, Old Union, Parks (at Hogeye), Rhea,
St. Joseph (at Tontitown), Scott, Sharp, Stenfield (or
Backbone or Graveyard Point), Summers, (or Missionary
Baptist), Sutton, Vineyard, Walker,
West (or Pool) and White Rock.
Indexed. 11.00 F5202

_____. Cemeteries of Washington County, AR, Volume X. 1987.
121pp.
U.S. National Cemetery at Fayetteville, AR.
Indexed. 11.00 F5202

_____. Cemeteries of Washington County, AR, Volume XI. 123pp.

Abe, Allen or Pettigrew, Allen Graves, Antioch, Barron #2, Bethlehem, Brewster, Burkshed, Burris, Carney, Cheshire, Cloer-Harp, Crawford, Davis, Deen, Dobbs, Dunigan, English, Essex Grave, Flynn Family, Garrett Creek, Gilliland, Goddard, Gollahar-Peerson, Hart, James Son Family, Karnes, Lewis, Mason, Mateer Private, Miller Chapel, Moore Family, Morrow, Morrow #2, Mountain Top, Mt. Pleasant, Norwood or Trident, Old Bethleham, Old Mayfield, Oxford Bend Phillips, Reed Family, Rutherford (Bayless), Sardis or Drake, Shipley, Smith or Smith-Bishop, Temple Hill, Thornsberry, Tramel or Trammel, Wax Family, Weddington, White Oak, Wickwire (also known as Bug Scuffle), Wilson (Benton County), Wilson (Fayetteville) and Woolsey (Farmington).

Indexed. 11.00 F5202

California

STATEWIDE REFERENCE

Bancroft, Hubert H. California Pioneer Register and Index, 1542-1848 Including Inhabitants of California, 1769-1800. (1884) reprint 1990. 392pp.   30.00   ....   F5130

Lorraine Frantz Edwards
Box 2076, Lancaster, CA 93539

specializes in German Baptist
Brethren / Ch. of the Brethren /
"Dunkard" families. Exchange

FRESNO COUNTY

Garrison, Ivadelle D. The History of James' Fresno Ranch. (1991) reprint 1992. 370pp.
> The history of an area of Western Fresno County. Its evolution into first a 175,000 acre cattle ranch,, later into modern farms and two towns. Cross referenced California history, 89 Pioneer Biographies.   95.00   ....   F5087

LASSEN COUNTY

Purdy, Tim I. Big Valley Cemeteries Headstone Enumeration Index 1872-1979. 1986. 53pp. 15.00   F5113

_____. Janesville Cemetery Headstone Enumeration Index 1863-1978. 1986. 74pp. 15.00   F5113

_____. Lassen County Court Index 1864-1931 (Plaintiff). 1986. 109pp. 25.00   F5113

_____. Rural Lassen County Cemetery Index 1858-1979. 1991. 30pp. 15.00   F5113

_____. Susanville Headstone Enumeration Index 1861-1978. 1986. 65pp. 15.00   F5113

_____. Westwood Cemetery Headstone Enumeration Index 1915-1978. 1991. 47pp. 15.00   F5113

LOS ANGELES COUNTY

Edwards, Lorraine Frantz and E. Louise Larick. LaVerne Evergreen Cemetery Tombstone Inscriptions. 1990. 262pp.
> History of the cemetery; section maps; photos; names of Civil War, Spanish War, World Wars One and Two, Korean & Vietnam veterans. 20.00   F5026

SAN DIEGO COUNTY

Crawford, Richard W. Guide to the San Diego Historical Society
    Public Records Collection. 1987. 86pp. 9.95   F5041

SAN FRANCISCO

Crookston, Charles H. and Lawrence E. Burnett, Jr. San Francisco
    Pre-1906 Records. 1992.   ....   F5030

SOLANO COUNTY

Morebeck, Nancy Justus. Index to Property Owners and Township
    List of Historical Atlas Map - Solano County, CA - 1878.
    (1990) reprint 1990. 98pp. 18.00   F5034

Colorado

STATEWIDE REFERENCE

Compiled by Colorado Genealogical Society. Genealogical Index to the Records of the Society of Colorado Pioneers. 1990. 119pp. Information from records of meetings from the 1850's to the 1940's when meetings ceased. 18.00 F5149

Compiled by the Colorado Genealogical Society. Colorado Families: A Territorial Heritage. 1981. 735pp. This fascinating book narrates the stories of more than 130 of Colorado's early pioneer families and their descendants. 20.50 .... F5149

BOULDER COUNTY

Dyni, Anne Quinby. Back to the Basics, The Frontier Schools of Boulder County, Colorado 1860-1960. 1991. 154pp. 17.45 F5029

⊙ **Boulder**

❀ **Denver**

⊙ **Colorado Springs**

⊙ **Pueblo**

Connecticut

STATEWIDE REFERENCE

General Reference

Field, D.D., David D. Centennial Address with Historical Sketches of Cromwell, Portland, Chatham, Middle-Haddam & Middletown in the State of Connecticut. (1853) reprint 318pp. 22.00 F5216

Hinman, Royal R. A Catalogue of the Names of the First Puritan Settlers of the Colony of Connecticut. (1846) reprint 1990. 336pp. 22.50 .... F5130

Knox, Grace and Barbara Ferris. Some Connecticut Nutmeggers Who Migrated. 1988. 210pp. 17.50 F5216

Taylor, John M. The Witchcraft Delusion in Colonial Connecticut, 1647-1697. (1908) reprint 172pp. 16.00 F5216

Census

Heads of Families in the First Census of the U.S. taken in the Year 1790: Connecticut. (1908) reprint 1990. 227pp. 20.00 F5159

The 1790 Census. Heads of Families at the First Census of the United States Taken in the Year 1790 - Connecticut. reprint 1992. 227pp. 22.52 F5129

Maps & Gazetteers

Gannett, H. Geographical Dictionary of Connecticut & R.I. (1894) reprint 1990. 98pp. 18.50 F5159

Pease, John C. and John M. Niles. A Gazetteer of the States of Connecticut and Rhode Island. (1819) reprint 420pp. 27.00 F5216

Pease, J. and J. Niles. Gazetteer of the States of Connecticut & R.I. (1819) reprint 1990. 339pp.
Consisting of Two Parts: I. Geogr. and Statistical Desc. of each State; II. General Geogr. view of each Co. and a Minute and ample Topographical Desc. of each Town, village, etc. 33.00 .... F5159

FAIRFIELD COUNTY

Hill, S.B. History of Danbury, 1684-1896. (1896) reprint 1992. 583pp.
From research by James Montgomery Bailey. 59.50 .... F5159

Hubbard, F.A. Other Days in Greenwich, or Tales & Reminiscences of an Old New England Town. (1913) reprint 1988. 363pp.
A charming & informative history of the town of Greenwich, with many illustrations & photographs. 37.50 .... F5159

Huntington, E.B. History of Stamford from its Settlement in 1641 to 1868, incl. Darien. (1868) reprint 1987. 492pp. 49.75 .... F5159

Hurd, D.H., Compiler. History of Fairfield County, with Illustrations
    & Biogr. Sketches of its Prominent Men & Pioneers. (1881)
    reprint 1987. 847pp.   89.00   ....   F5159

Jacobus, D.L. History & Genealogy of the Families of Old Fairfield,
    2 Volumes. (1930) reprint 1991. 2,051pp.   139.00   ....   F5159

_____. History and Genealogy of the Families of Old Fairfield.
    (1932) reprint 1991. 2,051pp.
        3 Volumes, indexed.   150.00   ....   F5129

Johnson, Jane Eliza. Newtown's History, & Historian Ezra Levan
    Lohnson. With additional material. (1917) reprint 1992.
    365pp.
        Includes genealogies.   41.00   ....   F5159

Majdalany, Jeanne and Edith M. Wicks. The Story of the Early
    Settlers of Stamford, Connecticut, 1641-1700, including
    Genealogies of Principal Families. 1991. 210pp. 17.50   F5216

Orcutt, S. A History of the Old Town of Stratford & the city of
    Bridgeport, Part I. (1886) reprint 1987. 692pp.   69.75   ....   F5159

_____. A History of the Old Town of Stratford & the city of
    Bridgeport, Part II. (1886) reprint 1987. 700pp.   69.75   ....   F5159

The First Planters; The Original Settlers of Stratford. 52pp.
        Extracted from "*A History of the Old Town of Stratford*
        & the City of Bridgeport". 10.00   F5159

Stratford Burying-Places. 131pp.
        Extracted from "*A History of the Old Town of Stratford*
        & the City of Bridgeport". 13.00   F5159

Perry, K.E. The Old Burying Ground of Fairfield. (1882) reprint
    1988. 241pp.
        A memorial of many early settlers, & a transcript of the
        inscriptions & epitaphs on the tombstones found in the
        oldest burying ground in Fairfield.   28.00   ....   F5159

Schenk, Elizabeth H. The History of Fairfield, Genealogies only.
    Vol I. (1889) reprint 103pp. 15.00   F5159

_____. The History of Fairfield, Genealogies only. Vol II. (1905)
    reprint 80pp. 12.00   F5159

_____. The History of Fairfield, Vol I. 1639-1818. (1889) reprint
    423pp.   42.00   ....   F5159

_____. The History of Fairfield, Vol II. 1700-1800. (1905) reprint
    538pp.   53.00   ....   F5159

Sharpe, W.C. Sketches & Records of South Britain. (1898) reprint
    1987. 167pp.   23.00   ....   F5159

Todd, C.B. THe History of Redding, from its 1st Settlement to the
    Present Time, with Notes on the Early Families. (1880) reprint
    1988. 248pp.   32.00   ....   F5159

Waldo, Jr., George C. History of Bridgeport & Vicinity, 2 volumes.
    (1917) reprint 1992. 1,230pp.   109.00   ....   F5159

HARTFORD COUNTY

Andrews, A. Genealogical & Ecclesiastical History of New Britain.
    (1867) reprint 1987. 538pp.   53.00   ....   F5159

_____. The River Towns of Connecticut: a study of Wethersfield, Hartford & Windsor. (1889) reprint 126pp. 13.50 F5216

Bates, ed., Albert C. Hartford, Connecticut, Land Records, 1639-1688, & Births, Marriages & Deaths, 1644-1730. (1912) reprint 716pp. 40.00 F5216

Cemetery Inscriptions in Windsor, Conn. (1929) reprint 1992. 178pp. 18.00 F5159

Dewey and Barbour, Compiled by. Inscriptions from Gravestones in Glastonbury. 101p. 15.00 .... F5159

North, C. History of Berlin. (1916) reprint 1987. 294pp.
38.00 .... F5159

Sheldon, Hezekiah Spencer. Documentary History of Suffield, Conn., in the Colony & Province of Mass. Bay in New England, 1660-1749. (1879) reprint 1992. 342pp. 37.00 .... F5159

Stiles, H.R. The History of Ancient Wethersfield, Vol. II. (1904) reprint 1987. 946pp.
    This volume contains biogr. & gen. info. on hundreds of early Wethersfield families. 94.00 .... F5159

_____. The History & Genealogy of Ancient Windsor, incl E. Windsor, S. Windsor, Bloomfield, Windsor Locks & Ellington, 1635-1891, Vol I Hist & Gen. (1859) reprint 922pp. 91.00 .... F5159

_____. The History & Genealogy of Ancient Windsor, incl E. Windsor, S. Windsor, Bloomfield, Windsor Locks & Ellington, 1635-1891, Vol II Gen. & Biogr. (1859) reprint 867pp. 86.00 .... F5159

Tillotson, Edward Sweetser. Wethersfield Inscriptions: A Complete Record of the Inscriptions in the Five Burial Places in the Ancient Town of Wethersfield. (1899) reprint 372pp.
    Including the Towns of Rocky Hill, Newington, and Beckley Quarter (in Berlin), also a portion of the Inscriptions in the Oldest Cemetery in Glastonbury. 25.00 F5216

Welles, Edwin S. Newington Conn. Census of 1776. (1909) reprint 42pp. 8.00 F5216

Welles, R., Trans & editor. Early Annals of Newington. (1874) reprint 1991. 204pp. 25.00 .... F5159

LITCHFIELD COUNTY

Atwater, F. The History of Plymouth, with an Account of the Centennial Celebration & a Sketch of Plymouth, Ohio, Settled by Local Families. (1895) reprint 1988. 447pp. 47.00 .... F5159

Boswell, G.C. The Litchfield Book of Days: A Collation of the Historical Biographical & Literary Reminiscenses of Litchfield.
(1900) reprint 1992. 221pp. 27.50 .... F5159

Boyd, J. Annuals & Family Records of Winchester, Conn. (1873) reprint 1988. 632pp. 63.50 .... F5159

Chipmn, R. Manning. History of Harwinton. (1862) reprint 1992. 152pp. 22.00 .... F5159

Cothren, W. History of Ancient Woodbury, Conn. (1854) reprint 1990. 833pp. 81.50 .... F5159

_____. The History of Ancient Woodbury, Connecticut, 1659 to 1879. (1879) reprint 708pp.
> Including the present towns of Washington, Southbury, Bethlehem, Roxbury, and part of Oxford and Middlebury, containng the Genealogical Statistics of the same and of Ancient Stratford, from 1639 to 1728. .... 40.00 F5216

Eldridge, J. and T.W. Crissey. History of Norfolk, 1744-1900, Litchfield Co. (1900) reprint 1992. 648pp. 65.00 .... F5159

Goodenough, G.F. Ellsworth. A Gossip about a Country Parish of the Hills, & its People, a Century after its Birth. (1900) reprint 1992. 129pp. 16.00 .... F5159

Goshen Marriages, 1740-1896. Extracted from the History of Goshen. 22pp. 5.50 F5159

Hibbard, A.G. The History of the Town of Goshen, with Genealogies & Biographies, Based upon the Records of Dea. L.M. Norton. (1897) reprint 1988. 602pp. 61.00 .... F5159

Kilbourne, Payne Kenyon. Sketches & Chronicles of the Town of Litchfield. (1859) reprint 1992. 265pp. 32.50 .... F5159

Orcutt, Rev. Samuel. History of Torrington, Connecticut, from Its First Settlement in 1737 with Biographies & Genealogies. (1878) reprint 818pp. 45.00 F5216

_____. History of Torrington, from its first Settlement in 1737 with Biogr. & Gen. (1878) reprint 1988. 817pp. 85.00 .... F5159

_____. History of the Towns of New Milford & Bridgewater, 1703 - 1882. (1882) reprint 1991. 909pp. 90.00 .... F5159

Salisbury Assoc. Historical collections Relating to the Town of Salisbury, Litchfield Co. (1913) reprint 1992. 154pp. 19.00 F5159

Starr, Edward Comfort. A History of Cornwall: a Typical New England Town. (1926) reprint 1992. 547pp. 55.00 .... F5159

White, Alain C. History of the Town of Litchfield, 1720-1920. (1920) reprint 1992. 360pp+. 42.50 .... F5159

MIDDLESEX COUNTY

Adams, M.A,, Charles Collard. Middletown Upper Houses: A History of the North Society of Middletown, Connecticut, from 1650 to 1800. (1908) reprint 848pp.
> With Genealogical and Biographical Chapters on Early Families and a Full Genealogy of the Ranney Family. 45.00 F5216

Fowler, W.C. History of Durham, from its First Grant of Land in 1662 to 1866. (1866) reprint 1991. 460pp. 29.00 .... F5159

NEW HAVEN COUNTY

Atwater, Edward E. History of the Colony of New Haven to its Absorption into Connecticut. (1902) reprint 767pp. 42.50 F5216

Davis, C.H.S. Early families of Wallingford, Conn. (1870) reprint 1990. 363pp. 29.50 .... F5159

_____. History of Wallingford, Conn, from its Settlement in 1670 to the Present, incl. Meriden, which was one of its Parishes until 1806, & Cheshire. (1870) reprint 1988. 956pp. 96.50 .... F5159

_____. Early Families of Wallingford, Conecticut. With a New
Index. (1870) reprint 1992. 363pp. 31.50 F5130

Gillespie, C.B. and G.C. Munson. A Century of Meriden: an
Historic Record & Pictorial Description of the Town of
Meriden. (1906) reprint 1992. 1,226pp. 109.00 .... F5159

Hughes, Sarah E. History of East Haven. (1908) reprint 1992.
324pp. 35.00 .... F5159

Inscriptions from Gravestones of Derby, with additions &
corrections. reprint 1987. 31pp. 6.00 F5159

New Haven Vital Records, 1649-1850. Part I. (1917) reprint
1988. 599pp. 58.00 .... F5159

Orcutt, S. and A. Beardsley. History of the Old Town of Derby,
1642-1880. With biogr. & gen. (1880) reprint 1987. 843pp. 85.00 .... F5159

Prichard, K.A. Ancient Burying-Grounds of the Town of Waterbury,
together with Other Recocrds of Church & town. (1917)
reprint 1988. 338pp.
Incl. cem. inscrp., 1709-1857; various marriage & death
records, taxpayer lists & more. 36.00 .... F5159

_____. Proprietors Records of the Town of Waterbury, 1677-1761.
1988. 260pp.
Contains a hist. of land grants, lotteries, purchases, etc. as
well as notes from public meetingslisting hundreds of
residents. 34.00 .... F5159

Smith, R.D. The History of Guilford from its First Settlement in
1639. (1877) reprint 1988. 219pp. 25.00 .... F5159

Steiner, B.C. History of the Plantation of Menunkatuck, & the
Original Town of Guilford [incl Madison]. (1897) reprint
1992. 54.00 .... F5159

NEW LONDON COUNTY

Avery, Rev J. History of the Town of Ledyard, 1650-1900. (1901)
reprint 1992. 334pp. 35.00 .... F5159

Baker, Henry A. History of Montville, Formerly the N. Parish of
New London, from 1640 to 1896. (1896) reprint 1992.
726pp.
About two-thirds of this book is family sketches. 73.00 .... F5159

Bolles, J.R. and Anna Williams. (New London) The Rogerenes:
Some Hitherto Unpublished Annals Belonging to the Col.
History of Connecticut. (1904) reprint 1990. 396pp.
With appendix of Rogerene writings A fascinating
history of an important but little-known 17th century sect,
this book contains much useful info. on early Conn.
history as well as gen. material on early New London. 41.00 .... F5159

Caulkins, F.M. History of Norwich, from its Possession by Indians
to 1866. (1860) reprint 1991. 704pp. 70.00 .... F5159

_____. The History of New London, from the 1st Survey of the
Coast in 1612, to 1860. (1895) reprint 1988. 714pp. 71.50 .... F5159

First Congregational Church of Preston, 1698-1898, Together with
Statistics of the Church taken from Church Records. (1900)
reprint 1990. 201pp.
Includes sketches of the original members of the church,
and records of admissions, baptisms, deaths & marriages. 21.00 F5159

Hall, Verne M. and Elizabeth B. Plimpton. Vital Records of Lyme,
Connecticut to the End of the Year 1850. (1976) reprint 404pp. 30.00 F5216

Hurd, D.H. History of New London Co., with Biogr. Sketches of
Many of its Pioneers & Prominent Men. (1882) reprint 1990.
768pp. 85.00 .... F5159

Hurd, editor, D. Hamilton. History of New London County,
Connecticut, with Biographical Sketches of Many of Its
Pioneers and Prominent Men. (1882) reprint 768pp. 70.00 F5216

Inscriptions from Gravestones at Old Lyme, Lyme & E. Lyme.
68pp. 10.00 F5159

Perkins, M.E. Old Houses of the Ancient Town Of Norwich,
1660-1800. With Maps. Illus, Portraits & Genealogies. (1895)
reprint 1991. 621pp. 65.00 .... F5159

Prentice, Edw. Ye Ancient Burial Place of New London. (1899)
reprint 1990. 40pp. 8.50 F5159

(New London) Picturesque New London & Environs - Groton -
Mystic - Montville - Waterford. (1901) reprint 1991. 192pp. 30.00 .... F5159

Vital Records of Norwich, 1649-1848, Pts I & II. (1913) reprint
1992. 1,180pp. 108.00 .... F5159

Wheeler, Richard Anson. History of the First Congregational Church
of Stonington, 1647-1874. (1875) reprint 1900. 299pp.
With the report of Bi-Centennial Proceedings, with
appendix containing statistics of the Church. Incls.
thousands of admissions, baptisms, marriages & death
records. 30.00 .... F5159

_____. History of the Town of Stonington, County of New
London, 1649-1900. (1900) reprint 1987. 754pp. 65.00 .... F5159

TOLLAND COUNTY

Cole, J.R. History of Tolland County. (1888) reprint 1992. 992pp.
99.50 .... F5159

WINDHAM COUNTY

Bowen, C.W. History of Woodstock. (1926) reprint 1990.
691pp+. 72.50 .... F5159

WINDSOR COUNTY

Larned, Ellen D. History of Windsor County, 2 vols. (1874) reprint
1992. 1,181pp.
$59.50/Vol. 109.00 .... F5159

Delaware

STATEWIDE REFERENCE

Linn, John B. and William Henry Egle. Lists of Officers of the
  Colonies on the Delaware and the Province of Pennsylvania,
  1614-1776. With a New Index by Robert Barnes. (1880)
  reprint 1992. 221pp. 25.00   F5130

Maddux, Gerald & Dorris.   1800 Census of Delaware.   (1964)
  reprint 1992. 200pp.
        Indexed. 21.00   F5130

Virdin, Donald O.   Delaware Bible Records, Vols. 1 & 2.
  1991&1992. 125&161p.
        Volume 1 - 1991, 125pp $13.50
        Volume 2 - 1992, 161pp $16.50   .... 30.00   F5216

NEW CASTLE COUNTY

Burr, H., Translator. (Wilmington) Records of Holy Trinity (Old
  Swedes) Church from 1697 to 1773, with abstr. of the
  English-language records 1773-1810. 772pp.
        The Old Swedes Church was the first built at what would
        become Wilmington. these records incl. birth, baptism,
        marriage & death records for the early settlers of the area,
        both Swedish & otherwise.   78.00   .... F5159

_____. Index & Errata (Records of Holy Trinity (Old Swedes)
  Church). (1919) reprint 166pp.
        May be ordered bound with the "Records of Holy Trinity
        (Old Swedes) Church". (see above)   17.00   .... F5159

Delaware Society of the Colonial Dames of America. A Calendar of
  Delaware Wills: New Castle County, 1682-1800. (1911)
  reprint 218pp. 18.00   F5216

SUSSEX COUNTY

Turner, C. H. B. Some Records of Sussex County, Delaware.
  (1909) reprint 387pp. 25.00   F5216

District Of Columbia

STATEWIDE REFERENCE

Provine, Dorothy s. Index to District of Columbia Wills, 1801-1920.
1992. 218pp. 25.00   F5129

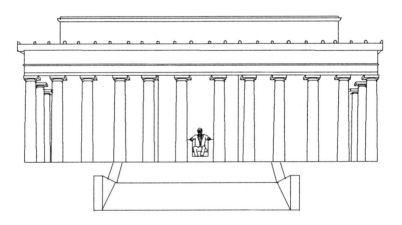

Lincoln Memorial

Florida

STATEWIDE REFERENCE

Government

Florida State Genealogical Society. Delegates to the Saint Joseph
Constitutional Convention 1838-1839. Final Report. 1980.
388pp.
Typescript produced by the Bureau of Historic Sites and
Properties, Division of Archives, History and Records
Management, Dept. of State. No index (delegates are
profiled in alphabetical order). 25.00 F5227

Michaels, Brian E. Florida Voters in Their First Statewide Election,
May 26, 1845. 1987. 114pp.
Florida State Genealogical Society, Special Publication
#1. Indexed. 20.00 .... F5227

Wolfe, William A. and Janet Bingham Wolfe. Names and Abstracts
from the Acts of the Legislative Council of the Territory of
Florida, 1822-1845. 1991. 190pp.
Florida State Genealogical Society, Special Publication
#2. No Index (alphabetical by name of individual). 25.00 .... F5227

Religious

Data Indexing Services. Index to "*History of Methodism in Georgia
and Florida* by Geo G. Smith, Jr.; 1877". 1992. .... 15.00 F5209

**FLORIDA STATE GENEALOGICAL
SOCIETY**

P. O. Box 10249, Tallahassee, FL 32302
Quarterly; *The Florida Genealogist*
Dues $18.00/year.

BREVARD COUNTY

Wooley, Rose (Compiler). Index to Mortuary Records Koon's
Funeral Home North Brevard County Titusville, Florida Nov.
1924-June 1946. 1992. 13pp.
Approximately 700 deaths indexed. Format includes
dates of birth and death and whether kin are listed in
records. Photocopies of actual records indexed are
available from vendor at a nominal cost. Plastic spiral
binding. 5.00 F5210

FRANKLIN COUNTY

Bouknecht, Carol Cox. Florida Juror and Witness Certificates,
Franklin County, 1848, 1850-1860, 1881, 1884. 1991. 49pp.
Names from original certificates; indexed. 9.95 F5190

GADSDEN COUNTY

Bouknecht, Carol Cox. Florida Juror and Witness Certificates,
Gadsden County, 1849-1861. 1991. 32pp.
Names from original certificates; indexed. 9.50 F5190

LEON COUNTY

Bouknecht, Carol Cox. Florida Juror and Witness Certificates, Leon
County, 1847-1862, 1876-1879, 1885. 1991. 57pp.
Names from original certificates; indexed. 9.95 F5190

Davidson, Alvie L. Florida Land: Records of the Tallahassee &
Newnansville General Land Office. 1989. 305pp. 22.50 F5216

POLK COUNTY

Data Indexing Services. Index to *"From Beginning to Boom* by
Bernice More Barber; 1975". 1992.
History of settlement of Polk County to 1920's. 12.00 F5209

WAKULLA COUNTY

Bouknecht, Carol Cox. Florida Juror and Witness Certificates,
Wakulla County, 1849-1862, 1879. 1991. 32pp.
Names from original certificates; indexed. 9.50 F5190

Georgia

STATEWIDE REFERENCE

General Reference

Gilmer, George R. Sketches of Some of the First Settlers of Upper Georgia, of the Cherokees, and the Author. (1926, 1965) reprint 1992. 463pp.
Revised and Corrected Edition with an Added Index. 32.50 F5130

Jones, Jr., Charles C. The Dead Towns of Georgia. (1878) reprint 263pp. 20.00 F5216

Migliazzo, Arlin C. and George F. Jones. Purrysburg. 1991. 38pp. Special section of South Carolina Historical Magazine, October 1991. "Compilation of Lists of German-Speaking Settlers of Purrysburg" by George F. Jones lists all German-named residents with sources. 6.00 F5181

Smith, George Gillman. The Story of Georgia and The Georgia People, 1732-1860. (1901) reprint 1990. 684pp. Second edition, illustrated, indexed. 30.00 .... F5130

Family Genealogies

Rigsby, Lewis Wiley. Historic Georgia Families. (1925-28) reprint 1992. 258pp.
Illustrated, indexed. 22.50 F5130

Land Records

Houston, Martha Lou. Reprint of Official Register of Land Lottery of Georgia 1827. (1928) reprint 1992. 308pp.
Indexed. 25.00 F5130

Mortuary Records

Data Indexing Services. Index to "*Annals of Georgia*, Vol. III, Mortuary Records, Compiled by Carolyn Wilson Price; 1933". 1992. .... 15.00 F5209

Religious

Data Indexing Services. Index to "*History of Methodism in Georgia and Florida* by Geo. G. Smith, Jr.; 1877". 1992. .... 15.00 F5209

CLINCH COUNTY

Data Indexing Services. Index to "*History of Clinch County, Georgia by Folks Huxford*; 1916". 1992. .... 15.00 F5209

EFFINGHAM COUNTY

Jones, George F and Sheryl Exley, Editors. Ebenezer Record Book
1754 - 1781. 1991. 187pp.
>>Births, Baptisms, Marriages and Burials of Jerusalem
Evangelical Lutheran Church of Effingham, Georgia,
More commonly known as Ebenezer Church. Indexed.   25.00   ....   F5129

TIFT COUNTY

Data Indexing Services. Index to "*History of Tift County, (GA)* by
Ida Belle Williams; 1948". 1992.   ....   15.00   F5209

WILKES COUNTY

Smith, Sarah Quinn. Early Georgia Wills and Settlements of Estates:
Wilkes County. (1959) reprint 1992. 81pp.
>>Indexed. 10.00   F5130

Idaho

STATEWIDE REFERENCE

Pettite, Judge Wm. Stibal. Memories of Market Lake, Vol. 4. 1991.
    109pp.
        Perfect bound 8"x11" book covers 1000 pioneers and
        early settlements, with 100's of rare photos from 1870s to
        1930s. Genealogical data is included, along with
        family/town sketches. Farming, business, schools,
        cowboys, music, sports, postal and railroad chapters. Part
        of a series on forgotten people and places and unusual
        events. 34.00   F5093

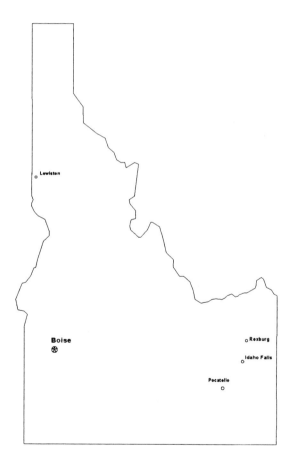

Illinois

STATEWIDE REFERENCE

Boggess, Arthur Clinton Ph.D. The Settlement of Illinois,
1778-1830. (1908) reprint 267pp. 20.00 F5216

Olson, Ernst W. and A. Schon & M.J. Engberg.   History of the
Swedes in Illinois. (1908) reprint 1992. 1,677pp.
2 volume set.
Vol I. History (933pp) \$88.50
Vol II. Biography (684pp) \$66.00 139.00 .... F5159

**CEMETERY RESEARCH
AND TOMBSTONE PHOTOGRAPHY**
Serving: IA, IL, IN, KS, KY,MI, MN, MO, NE, SD, WI
We will also photograph birthplaces,
churches or anything else of genealogical interest.
Long SASE for rates & details
Family Genealogical Research Services
1614 K Avenue NE, Cedar Rapids, IA 52402

**EAST-CENTRAL ILLINOIS
CHAMPAIGN COUNTY
SCANDINAVIAN TRANSLATIONS**

Michele C. McNabb
201 S. Race St, Urbana, IL 61801

COOK COUNTY

Agricultural Censuses of Palatine Township. 1992.
The 1850, 1860, 1870, and 1880 Federal Agricultural
Censuses. F5123

Biographical Directory of the Village of Palatine in 1925.
1992. .... F5123

Directory of Farmers of Palatine Township in 1918. 1992.
.... F5123

125th Anniversary History of Palatine, Illinois. 1991. 154pp.
A 1991 update of the 1950's Centennial Book. 30.00 .... F5123

1900 Census of Palatine Township. 1985. 90pp.
10.00 .... F5123

1910 Census of Palatine Township. 1987. 90pp.
10.00 .... F5123

EDWARDS COUNTY

Flower, G. and E.S. Washburne. History of the English Settlement of
    Edwards Co., Founded in 1817 & 1818. (1882) reprint 1987.
    402pp.   40.00   ....   F5159

IROQUOIS COUNTY

Ely, S.   Centennial History of the Villages of Iroquois &
    Montgomery, & the Twp. of Concord, 1818-1918. (1918)
    reprint 1991. 142pp. 17.00   F5159

STARK COUNTY

Leeson, M.A. Documents & Biography Pertaining to the Settlement
    & Progress of Stark Co., Containing an Authenic Summary of
    records, Documents, Hist. Works & Newspr. (1887) reprint
    1988. 708pp.   72.00   ....   F5159

WINNEBAGO COUNTY

Kett & Co. History & Biography of Winnebago County, Illinois.
    (1877) reprint 490pp. 30.00   F5216

Indiana

STATEWIDE REFERENCE

General Reference

Smith, Hon. O.H. Early Indiana Trials and Sketches. (1858) reprint
640pp. 37.00 F5216

CLARK COUNTY

McCoy, W.H. Pioneer Families of Clark County. (1947) reprint
1987. 15pp. 4.50 F5159

DEKALB COUNTY

Smith, John Martin and Troas May Wise. History of DeKalb
County, Indiana. 1992. 2214pp.
Volumes 1 and 2 contain topical history and Vol. 3
contains family histories. Written and published in an
innovative manner, these books will set the standard for
future county histories. The text is accompanied by
numerous vignettes containing oral history interviews,
excerpts from diaries and similar primary sources which
supplement the text. If any organization is considering
publishing a county history, these books should be
examined to see how DeKalb County, Indiana did it! 89.00 .... F5222

JACKSON COUNTY

Stultz, Carolyne. Jackson County, Indiana, Marriage Index,
1816-1920. 1991. 630pp. 36.00 F5216

MADISON COUNTY

Harden, Samuel. The Pioneers of Madison & Hancock Counties,
Indiana. (1895) reprint 496pp. 30.00 F5216

MARION COUNTY

Sulgrove, B.R. History of Indianapolis & Marion County. (1884)
reprint 665pp. 75.00 .... F5159

MORGAN COUNTY

Littell, Judge Noble K. One Hundred Men, A Legislative History of
Morgan County, Indiana. 1970. 146pp.
Local History and a genealogical-biographical sketch of
the 100 men who represented Morgan County (1822 -
1970) in the State Legislature. 12.50 .... F5003

ST. JOSEPH COUNTY

Ladewski, Lucky and Gene Szymarek. Polish Marriage Applicants
   in St. Joseph County, Indiana, 1905-1915. 1988. 215pp. 17.50   F5216

STARKE COUNTY

Holloway, W.R. A History & Statistical Sketch of the Railroad City;
   A Chronicle of its Social, Municipal, Commercial &
   Manufacturing Progress. (1870) reprint 1987. 390pp.   39.75   ....   F5159

TIPPECANOE COUNTY

Perkins, C.A. Gravestone Records of Sickler Cem. Near Elston.
   (1929) reprint 1987.   ....   3.00   F5159

VANDERBURGH COUNTY

Tenbarge, Eleanor G.   Early Death Records, Evansville,
   Vanderburgh County, Indiana 1818-1883. 1991. 550pp.
      Cemetery Sexton's records from Evansville's oldest and
      largest cemeteries before official death records begin.
      Some early church records.   55.00   ....   F5001

Iowa

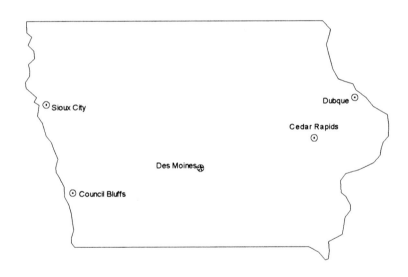

Kansas

STATEWIDE REFERENCE

General Reference

Robertson, Clara Hamlett. Kansas Territorial Settlers of 1860 ...
    Born in TN, VA, NC and SC. (1976) reprint 1990. 215pp.
        Illustrated. 25.00 .... F5130

Cemeteries

Ford, Don L. Abandonded & Semi-Active Cemeteries, Vol I. 1985.
    360pp. 36.00 .... F5159

_____. Abandonded & Semi-Active Cemeteries, Vol II. 1985.
    784pp.
        70.00 .... F5159

_____. Abandonded & Semi-Active Cemeteries, Vol III. 1985.
    399pp.
        39.00 .... F5159

Northeast Region

Kusek, Joan. Federal Naturalizations For the 1st District of Kansas
    (Northeast) 1856-1902. 1990. 192.
        Over 3,000 entries. Many Indian entries. 19.95 F5139

Kusek
  Genealogical
    Services
        Genealogical & Heir Research
            Publisher & Supplier
            City Directory Sales
913-383-2458
P.O. Box 32060 Shawnee Mission, KS 66212-2060

ATCHISON COUNTY

Ford, Don. Atchison Co., Kansas, Cemetery Inscriptions. 1987.
    480pp.
        .... 30.00 F5216

BROWN COUNTY

Ford, D.L. Some Cemeteries of Brown Co., with Supplements.
    1986. 319pp. 36.00 .... F5159

BUTLER COUNTY

Mooney, V.P. History of Butler County. (1916) reprint 1987.
    869pp.   88.00 .... F5159

DONIPHAN COUNTY

Ford, Don L. Doniphan Co. Cemeteries & Burial Sites. 1986.
    194pp.   26.00 .... F5159

DOUGLAS COUNTY

Cordley, R. A History of Lawrence, from 1st Settlement to the Close
    of the Rebellion. (1895) reprint 1987. 269pp.   34.00 .... F5159

Cordley, Richard. A History of Lawrence, Kansas, from the First
    Settlement to the Close of the Rebellion. (1895) reprint
    270pp. 23.50 F5216

JOHNSON COUNTY

Johnson County Genealogical Society. Johnson County Kansas
    Cemetery Index. 1983. 836pp.
        Tombstone inscriptions with nearly 28,000 names.   38.00 .... F5139

WYANDOTTE COUNTY

Kusek, Joan. Index to Wyandotte County, KS Final Naturalizations
    1859-1947. 1991.
        Over 5,000 entries. 29.95 F5139

_____. Index to Wyandotte County, KS Petitions For
    Naturalization 1867-1906. 1990.   ..... 17.95 F5139

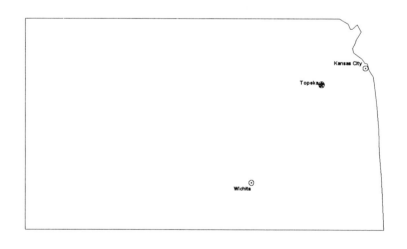

Kentucky

STATEWIDE REFERENCE

Abstracts

King, Junie Estelle Stewart. Abstract of Early Kentucky Wills and
Inventories. Copied from Original and Recorded Wills and
Inventories. (1933) reprint 1992. 298pp.
Indexed. 25.00 F5130

Big Sandy Valley

Ely, William. The Big Sandy Valley: A History of the People and
Country from the Earliest Settlement to the Present. (1887)
reprint 510pp. 30.00 F5216

Census

The 1795 Census of Kentucky. 1991. 195pp.
This is a state-wide tax list constructed from all tax lists
of the Kentucky counties that were in existence in 1795. 18.00 .... F5140

Central Region

Hamilton, Anna. Early Catholic Cemetery Listings of Washington,
Nelson, and Marion Counties, Kentucky. 1984. 86pp. 10.00 F5217

Family/Source Records - 19 West-Central Counties

Morris, Editor, Diane. Kentucky Family Records (Series) Volumes
1-16 (Current issues received with membership). 1970-92.
110pp/ea. 12.00 F5217

Military - Revolutionary War

Quisenberry, Anderson Chenault. Revolutionary Soldiers in
Kentucky. (1896) reprint 1992. 206pp. 21.50 F5130

Quarterly Genealogical Bulletin

Alford, Margaret, Editor. The Bulletin - Quarterly Received with
membership in the West-Central Kentucky Family Research
Association Vol. 1, 1968-Vol. 24, 1992. 1968-92. Varies. F5217

Research Aids

The 1795 Census of Kentucky. 1991. 195pp.
    This is a state-wide tax list constructed from all tax lists
    of the Kentucky counties that were in existence in 1795.   18.00 .... F5140

Taylor, Philip Fall. A Calendar of the Warrants for Land in
    Kentucky, Granted for Service in the French and Indian War.
    (1917) reprint 1991. 76pp. 9.00 F5130

Western Region

Dawson, W.H. The Life Beautiful Diary of W.H. Dawson -
    1866-1908 - Vital Statistics, Daviess, Hancock Counties.
    (1908) reprint 1978. 156pp. 12.00 F5217

**WEST-CENTRAL KENTUCKY
FAMILY RESEARCH ASSOCIATION**
P.O. Box 1932, Owensboro, KY 42302
The Bulletin & Kentucky Family Records
Initial Membership $15.00/year;
Renewal $10.00/year

ADAIR COUNTY

Lawson, Rowena. Kentucky Census Records, Adair County
    1810-40.   .... 12.50 F5216

ALLEN COUNTY

Lawson, Rowena. Kentucky Census Records, Allen County,
    1820-40.   .... 10.00 F5216

ANDERSON COUNTY

Lawson, Rowena. Kentucky Census Records, Anderson County,
    1830-50.   .... 13.50 F5216

BATH COUNTY

Lawson, Rowena. Kentucky Census Records, Bath County,
    1820-40.   .... 12.00 F5216

BOONE COUNTY

Lawson, Rowena. Kentucky Census Records, Boone County,
    1810-40.   .... 12.00 F5216

_____. Kentucky Census Records, Boone County, 1850.
    .... 15.00 F5216

Worrel, S. and A. Fitzgerald.   Boone Co., Kentucky, Marriages,
 1798-1850. 1991. 233pp.
　　　Previously unpublished, and unindexed in the county
　　　archives, these extracts also contain over 700 statements
　　　of relationship in this northern Kentucky county along the
　　　Ohio river, which saw the passage of many early settlers
　　　further west. 2,674 marriages, over 7,500 names -- fully
　　　indexed. Free brochure with list of principal surnames.
　　　$15.00 for fiche.   27.50   ....   F5156

BREATHITT COUNTY

Hayes, Margaret M. Reconstructed Marriage Records for Breathitt
 County, KY, 1839-73, including marriages from Breathitt
 County Marriage Book 1, 1874-1877. 1991. 194pp. 17.00   F5216

BRECKINRIDGE COUNTY

Leftwich, Holly. Breckinridge County, Kentucky 1850 Census
 (Includes early map). 1976. 142pp. 16.00   F5217

BUTLER COUNTY

Leftwich, Holly and Nancy Ford. Butler County, Kentucky 1850
 Census (Includes early map). 1975. 84pp. 10.00   F5217

CLARK COUNTY

Clark County, Kentucky Taxpayers, 1793 thru 1799. 1990.
 84pp.   7.50   ....   F5140

DAVIESS COUNTY

Davis, Albert. Daviess County, Kentucky Cemeteries, Volume 3
 Rose Hill - Owensboro. 147pp. 16.00   F5217

Edgeworth, Mike. Daviess County, Kentucky Order Book "D"
 1837-1846 First Extant. 1978. 138pp. 12.00   F5217

Ford, Nancy and Michael Edgeworth. Daviess County, Kentucky
 1850 Census-Annotated, Indexed, 100's of Notations. 1974.
 161pp. 16.00   F5217

Leftwich, Holly. Daviess County Kentucky Cemeteries, Volume 1,
 Indexed, Eastern Section County. 1977. 110pp. 12.00   F5217

_____. Daviess County, Kentucky Cemeteries, Volume 2, Country
 Cemeteries. 1977. 110pp. 12.00   F5217

Mastin, Emma Dunn. Daviess County, Kentucky Marriages
 1815-1865 From Daviess Co. Courthouse. 1978. 268pp. 22.00   F5217

Sapp, Sue and Lou Hayden, Juanita Lyons, Anna Midkiff. Daviess
 County, Kentucky Cemeteries, Volume 4 Mater
 Dolorosa-Catholic-Owensboro. 1987. 381pp.   27.50   22.50   F5217

EDMONSON COUNTY

Hammers, Marian and Holly Leftwich. Edmonson County,
 Kentucky 1850 Census (Early Map of County). 1978. 84pp. 10.00   F5217

FAYETTE COUNTY

Ranck, George W. History of Lexington, Kentucky: Its Early Annals
and Recent Progress. (1872) reprint 440pp.
Including biographical sketches and personal
reminiscences of the pioneer settlers, notices of prominent
citizens, etc. 27.50 F5216

FRANKLIN COUNTY

Lawson, Rowena. Kentucky Census Records, Franklin Co. 1810-40.
.... 12.50 F5216

GRAYSON COUNTY

Ford, Nancy. Grayson County, Kentucky 1850 Census (Early Map
of County). 1974. 106pp. 12.00 F5217

HANCOCK COUNTY

Ford, Nancy. Hancock County, Kentucky 1850 Census (Early Map
of County). 1974. 60pp. 9.00 F5217

Leftwich, Holly. Hancock County, Kentucky Cemeteries, Volume 1
(Only Volume Printed). 1974. 142pp. 16.00 F5217

HARDIN COUNTY

Jones, Mary Josephine. Hardin County, Kentucky Marriages
1820-1829. 1977. 116pp. 12.00 F5217

HARRISON COUNTY

Harrison County, Kentucky Taxpayers, 1794 thru 1799. 1990.
36pp. 7.50 .... F5140

LOGAN COUNTY

Hammers, Marian and Holly Leftwich. Logan County, Kentucky
1850 Census. 1978. 180pp. 16.00 F5217

MCLEAN COUNTY

Cox, Elizabeth and Holly Leftwich. McLean County, Kentucky
1860 Census, Annotated (First Census, Genealogical
Notations). 1978. 108pp. 12.00 F5217

Cox, Elizabeth and Kathryn Leachman and Holly Leftwich. McLean
County, Kentucky Cemeteries, Volume 1. 1977. 142pp. 15.00 F5217

_____. and Kathryn Leachman and Holly Leftwich. McLean
County, Kentucky Cemeteries, Volume 2. 1977. 112pp. 12.00 F5217

Hill, Willie. McLean County, Kentucky Marriages 1854-1890 From
County Beginning. 1978. 84pp. 10.00 F5217

McManaway, Robert. McLean County, Kentucky 1870 Census
(Second Census of County). 1979. 84pp. 10.00 F5217

MONTGOMERY COUNTY

Lawson, Rowena. Kentucky Census Records, Montgomery Co. 1810-40. .... 12.50 F5216

_____. Kentucky Census Records, Montgomery Co. 1850. .... 12.00 F5216

MORGAN COUNTY

Lawson, Rowena. Kentucky Census Records, Morgan Co. 1830-50. .... 15.00 F5216

NELSON COUNTY

Lawson, Rowena. Kentucky Census Records, Nelson Co. 1850. .... 15.00 F5216

NICHOLAS COUNTY

Lawson, Rowena. Kentucky Census Records, Nicholas Co. 1850. .... 15.00 F5216

OHIO COUNTY

Bennett, J.A. Record of Walton's Creek Baptist Church, Ohio County, Kentucky 1814-1914. 1982. 100pp. 10.00 F5217

Compiled from Microfilm by the Association. Index of Ohio County, Kentucky Circuit Court Equity Records 1798-1900. 1986. 142pp. 26.00 20.00 F5217

Ford, Nancy. Ohio County, Kentucky 1850 Census. 1974. 138pp. 12.00 F5217

Lawson, Rowena. Kentucky Census Records, Ohio Co. 1810-40. .... 9.00 F5216

_____. Kentucky Census Records, Ohio Co. 1850. .... 15.00 F5216

Leftwich, Holly. Ohio County, Kentucky Cemeteries, Volume 1. 1975. 92pp. 10.00 F5217

_____. Ohio County, Kentucky Cemeteries, Volume 2. 1977. 106pp. 10.00 F5217

ROCKCASTLE COUNTY

Bonham, Jeanne Snodgrass and Patricia Heylmann Hiatt. Rockcastle County, Kentucky Cemetery Records. 1986. 856pp.
20,000 names; 400 cemeteries; with complete directions to each; every name index. 52.00 .... F5083

_____. and Patricia Heylmann Hiatt. Rockcastle County, Kentucky Guardians Bonds 1857 - 1899. 1991. 198pp.
Photocopies of all bonds and hand written notes; typed transcript of each; every name index. 20.00 F5083

_____. and Patricia Heylmann Hiatt.   Rockcastle County,
Kentucky Marriages: Court Records 1858 - 1900.   1990.
400pp.
> All official court records; appendix: photocopies of all
> existing hand written notes with typed transcripts; every
> name index. 33.00   F5083

SCOTT COUNTY

Scott County, Kentucky Taxpayers, 1794 thru 1799. 1990.
44pp.   7.50   ....   F5140

WHITLEY COUNTY

Broyles, Stephen H. Whitley County, Kentucky, Tax List Summary,
1819-1850. 1991. 262pp.
> Summary of each taxpayer's entries over the time period,
> giving polls, land holdings, livestock, total valuation, etc. 27.00   F5021

_____.   Whitley County, Kentucky, Will Book 1, 1818-1854.
1991. 120pp.
> Contains wills, appraisals and sales of estates (both
> executed and administered), settlements, and
> miscellaneous entries. 15.00   F5021

WOODFORD COUNTY

Railey, William E. History of Woodford County, KY. (1938)
reprint 1990. 449pp.
> Illustrated, indexed.   27.50   ....   F5130

Woodford County, Kentucky Taxpayers, 1790 thru 1799. 1990.
85pp.   7.50   ....   F5140

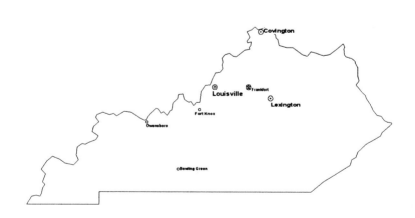

Louisiana

STATEWIDE REFERENCE

Deiler, J. Hanno. Translated and edited by Marie Stella Condon. A
    History of the German Churches in Louisiana (1823-1893).
    (1894, 1983) reprint 1992. 155pp.
        Indexed. 17.50   F5130

Maine

STATEWIDE REFERENCE

Census

The 1790 Census. Heads of Families at the First Census of the United States Taken in the Year 1790 - Maine. reprint 1992. 105pp. 18.50 F5129

Genealogical Dictionaries

Noyes and Libby & Davis. Genealogical Dictionary of Maine & New Hampshire. (1928-1939) reprint 1988. 795pp.
　　　Includes thorough gen. data on every family established before 1699. 45.00 .... F5159

Histories

Drake, Samuel Adams. The Pine-Tree Coast. (1890) reprint 393pp. 25.00 F5216

O'Brien, M.J. The Lost Town of Cork. (1987) reprint 12pp. 4.50 F5159

Scott, Geraldine Tidd. Ties of Common Blood: A History of Maine's Northeast Boundary Dispute with Great Britain, 1783-1842. 1991. 450pp. 32.00 F5216

Williamson, William D. The History of the State of Maine from Its First Discovery, AD 1602, to the Separation, AD 1820, Inclusive, 2 Vols. (1832) reprint 1,400pp. 60.00 F5216

Maps And Gazetteers

Varney, Geo J. A Gazetteer of the State of Maine. (1881) reprint 640pp. 36.50 F5216

Military - Pensions And Other Records Of Soldiers - All Wars

Flagg, Charles Alcott. An Alphabetical Index of Revolutionary Pensioners Living in Maine. (1929) reprint 1992. 91pp. 12.00 F5130

Pioneers

Spencer, W.D. Pioneers on Maine Rivers, with Lists to 1651, Compiled from the Original Sources. (1930) reprint 1992. 414pp. 44.00 .... F5159

_____. Pioneers on Maine Rivers, with Lists to 1651, Compiled from the Original Sources. (1930) reprint 414pp. 26.50 F5216

ANDROSCOGGIN COUNTY

Elder, Janus G. ed. by David & Elizabeth (Keene) Young. A History of Lewiston, Maine, with a Genealogical Register of Early Families. (1882) reprint 1989. 481pp. 30.00 F5216

Merrill, G.D. History of Androscoggin Co. (1891) reprint 1988. 893pp.   94.00 .... F5159

Mower, Walter Lindley. New Preface by David C. & Elizabeth (Keene) Young. Sesquicentennial History of the Town of Greene, Androscoggin County, Maine, 1775-1900, with some matter extending to a later date. (1938) reprint 598pp. 35.00   F5216

Stackpole, E.S. History of Durham, with Genealogical NOtes. (1899) reprint 1987. 314pp.   40.00 .... F5159

Stinchfield, J. History of the Town of Leeds, Androscoggin Co., from its Settlement June 10, 1780. (1901) reprint 1990. 419pp.   44.00 .... F5159

_____. Genealogies only, from the *History of the Town of Leeds*. 227pp.   23.00 .... F5159

AROOSTOOK COUNTY

Ellis, C.H. History of Ft. Fairfield, & Biogr. Sketches with Illustrations. (1894) reprint 1992. 382pp.   41.00 .... F5159

CUMBERLAND COUNTY

Elwell, Edward H. Portland & Vicinity. (1876) reprint 1989. 142pp.   35.00 .... F5159

History of Cumberland County, with Illustrations & Biogr. Sketches of Prominent Men & Pioneers. (1880) reprint 1987. 456pp.   49.00 .... F5159

Jordan, Jr, William B. A History of Cape Elizabeth, Maine. (1965) reprint 385pp. 25.00   F5216

King, Marquis F. and foreward by David C. & Elizabeth (Keene) Young. Baptisms and Admission from the Records of First Church in Falmouth (now Portland, Maine). (1898) reprint 132pp......... 13.50   F5216

Sears, Albert J. Early Families of Standish, Maine. 1991. 375pp. 25.00   F5216

_____. The Founding of Pearsontown (Standish), Maine. 1991. 240pp. 18.50   F5216

Spurr, W.S. History of Otisfield, Cumberland Co., from the Original Grant to the Close of 1944. (1944) reprint 1990. 661pp.   67.00 .... F5159

_____. Otisfield Genealogies Only. 340pp.   34.00 .... F5159

Wheeler, M.D., George Augustus and Henry Warren Wheeler. History of Brunswick, Topsham, and Harpswell, Maine, Including the Ancient Territory Known as Pejepscot, 2 Vols. (1878) reprint 1,014pp. 50.00   F5216

HANCOCK COUNTY

Brooksville Hist. Soc. Traditions & Records of Brooksville. (1936) reprint 1987. 132pp.   18.50 .... F5159

Hosmer, G.L. An Historical Sketch of the Town of Deer Isle, with Notices of its Settlers & Early Inhabitants. (1886) reprint 1988. 292pp.   33.00 .... F5159

Street, G.E. and S.A. Eliot, editor. Mount Desert; A History. (1905) reprint 1988. 386pp.   42.00 .... F5159

KENNEBEC COUNTY

Clark, W.H. The History of Winthrop, 1630-1952. 1952. 313pp.
33.00 .... F5159

Clason, Oliver Barrett and David Colby Young. History of Litchfield (Maine) and an account of its centennial celebration, 1895. (1897) reprint 1992. 568pp.
.... 47.00 F5216

The History of Litchfield, and an Account of its Centennial Celebration in 1895. (1895) reprint 1988. 548pp.
68.00 .... F5159

Kingsbury, H.D. and S.L. Deyo. Illustrated History of Kennebec County, 1625-1892, Vol. I. (1892) reprint 1987. 600pp.
63.00 .... F5159

_____. and S.L. Deyo. Illustrated History of Kennebec County, 1625-1892, Vol. II. (1892) reprint 1987. 637pp.
65.00 .... F5159

Lang, S.D. Winslow Vital Records to the Year 1892: Births, Marriages & Deaths. (1937) reprint 1992. 325pp.
36.00 .... F5159

Whittemore, E.C. The Centennial History of Waterville, Kennebec Co., ME 1802-1902. (1902) reprint 1988. 592pp.
61.00 .... F5159

KNOX COUNTY

Eaton, C. The History of Thomaston, Rockland & South Thomaston, from their First Exploration, A.D. 1605; With Family Genealogies Vol. I. (1865) reprint 1988. 468pp.
47.00 .... F5159

_____. The History of Thomaston, Rockland & South Thomaston, from their First Exploration, A.D. 1605; With Family Genealogies Vol. II. (1865) reprint 1988. 472pp.
COMPLETE SET (Volumes I & II): $90.00
47.00 .... F5159

Locke, J.L. Sketches of the History of the Town of Camden, incl. Incidental References to the Neighbouring Places & Adjacent Waters. (1859) reprint 1988. 267pp.
30.00 .... F5159

LINCOLN COUNTY

Chase, F.S. [History of Wiscasset] Wiscasset in Pownalborough. (1941) reprint 1990. 640pp.
65.00 .... F5159

Cushman, D.Q. History of Ancient Sheepscot & Newscastle, including other Contiguous Places, from Earliest Discovery to the Present Time, with over 400 Gen. (1882) reprint 1992. 458pp.
46.00 .... F5159

Johnston, J. History of the Towns of Bristol & Bremen in the State of Maine, incl. the Pemaquid Settlement. (1873) reprint 1988. 524pp.
52.50 .... F5159

Miller, S.L. History of the Town of Waldoboro. (1910) reprint 1987. 281pp.
34.00 .... F5159

OXFORD COUNTY

Barrows, J.S. Fryeburg, Maine: An Historical Sketch. (1938) reprint 1990. 309pp.
36.00 .... F5159

Bradbury, Dr. Osgood N. Norway in the Forties. (1886-1897) reprint 733+pp.
.... 35.00 F5216

Warren, H.P. and Wm Warren & S. Waarren. HIstory of Waterford, Oxford Co., Comprising Historical Address, Record of Families & Centennial Proceedings. (1879) reprint 1992. 371pp.   38.50   ....   F5159

Whitman, C.F. History of Norway, from Earliest Settlement to 1922. (1924) reprint 1987. 581pp.   59.50   ....   F5159

PENOBSCOT COUNTY

Godfrey, John E. Annals of Bangor, 1769-1882 (Extr. Hist of Penobscot Co. 1882). 1990. 304pp.   38.00   ....   F5159

History of Penobscot Co., 1626-1882, with Illustrations & Biogr. Sketches. (1882) reprint 1990. 922pp.   93.50   ....   F5159

Oak, L. History of Garland. (1911) reprint 1990. 401pp.

    42.00   ....   F5159

SAGADAHOC COUNTY

Vital Records of Topsham, to the Year 1892 Vol. I Births. (1929-30) reprint 1992. 214pp.   27.00   ....   F5159

Vital Records of Topsham, to the Year 1892 Vol. II Marr. & deaths. (1929-30) reprint 1992. 402pp.
    COMPLETE SET (Volumes I & II): $64.50   41.00   ....   F5159

SOMERSET COUNTY

Allen, W. History of Norridgewock. (1849) reprint 1990. 252pp. Compr. Memorials of the Aboriginal Inhabitants & Jesuit Missionaries, Hardships of the Pioneers, Biogr. Notices of the Early Settlers & Ecclesiastical Sketches   31.00   ....   F5159

WALDO COUNTY

Farrow, J.P. The History of Isleborough, 1764-1892. (1893) reprint 1988. 325pp.   36.00   ....   F5159

Morse, T.M. and Mr & Mrs C. White. Genealogical History of the Familes of Morrill. (1957) reprint 1992. 461pp.   46.50   ....   F5159

WASHINGTON COUNTY

Drisko, G.W. Narrative of the Town of Machias; the Old & the New, the Early & the Late. (1904) reprint 1988. 589pp.   62.00   ....   F5159

Kilby, William Henry. Eastport & Passamaquoddy: A Collection of Historical & Biographical Sketches (Incl Weston's "History"). (1834) reprint 1992. 505pp.   49.50   ....   F5159

YORK COUNTY

Bourne, Edward E. The History of Wells and Kennebunk, Maine. (1875) reprint 820pp. 50.00   F5216

Bradbury, Charles.   History of Kennebunkport, from it First Discovery by Bartholomew Gosnold, 1602, to a.d. 1837. (1837) reprint 1992. 338pp.   37.50   ....   F5159

Folsom, George. History of Saco and Biddeford, with Notices of Other Early Settlements and of the Proprietory Governments in Maine. (1830) reprint 352pp.
Including the Provinces of New Somersetshire and Lygonia. 27.50 .... F5216

A History of the First Century of Parsonfield, incorporated Aug. 29, 1785. (1888) reprint 1988. 499pp.
Incl. genealogies. By a committee of the town. 53.00 .... F5159

History of York Co., with Illustrations & Biographical sketches of Prominent Men & Pioneers. (1880) reprint 1987. 441pp. 45.00 .... F5159

Spencer, W.D. Burial Inscriptions of Berwick. (1922) reprint 1987. 133pp. 13.50 F5159

_____. List of Rev. Soldiers of Berwick. (1898) reprint 1987. 18pp. 5.00 F5159

Stackpole, E.S. Old Kittery & Her Families. (1903) reprint 1988. 822pp. 82.00 .... F5159

Taylor, Robert L. Early Families of Limington, Maine. 1991. 438pp. 27.50 F5216

Maryland

STATEWIDE REFERENCE

Census

Heads of Families at the First Census of the U.S. Taken in 1790.
(1907) reprint 1990. 189pp.   19.50   ....   F5159

The 1790 Census. Heads of Families at the First Census of the
United States Taken in the Year 1790 - Maryland. reprint
1992. 189pp. 25.00   F5129

Eastern Shore

Hanson, George A. Old Kent: The Eastern Shore of Maryland.
(1876) reprint 1990. 383pp.
        Indexed.   25.00   ....   F5130

Genealogies

Doliante, Sharon J. Maryland and Virginia Colonials: Genealogies
of Some Colonial Families. 1991. 1,313pp.
        Families of: Bacon, Beall, Beasley, Cheney, Duckett,
        Dunbar, Ellyson, Elmore, Graves, Heydon, Howard,
        Jacob, Morris, Nuthall, Odell, Peerce, Reeder, Ridgley,
        Prather, Sprigg, Wesson, Williams, and Collateral Kin.   87.50   ....   F5129

Spencer, Richard Henry. Genealogical and Memorial Encyclopedia
of the State of Maryland. (1919) reprint 1992. 756pp.
        A Record of the Achievements of Her People in the
        Making of a Commonwealth and the Founding of a
        Nation.
        2 volumes, illustrated, indexed. 59.95   F5130

History

Bozman, John Leeds. The History of Maryland from Its First
Settlement in 1633 to the Restoration in 1660, with a Copious
Introduction and Notes and Illustrations. (1837) reprint
1,050pp.   50.00   ....   F5216

Hall, Clayton Colman. Narratives of Early Maryland, 1633-1684.
(1910) reprint 460pp. 28.00   F5216

Military - Revolutionary War

Brumbaugh, Gaius M. and Margaret R. Hodges. Revolutionary
Records of Maryland. (1924) reprint 1991. 56pp.
        Illustrated, indexed 10.00   F5130

Source Records

Brumbaugh, G.M. Colonial, Revolutionary, County & Church
Records from Originals Sources 2 vols. (1915, 1928) reprint
1985. 513 & 688p.   60.00   ....   F5159

Magruder, Jr., James M. Magruder's Maryland Colonial Abstracts -
Wills, Accounts and Inventories [1772-1777]. (1934-39)
reprint 1991. 682pp.
5 volumes in 1. Indexed. 45.00 F5130

Newman, Harry Wright. To Maryland from Overseas. (1982)
reprint 1991. 190pp. 20.00 .... F5129

ALLEGANY COUNTY

Fair, Patricia Stover. Everyname Index to History of Allegany
County. 1990. 150+pp. 15.00 F5116

ANNE ARUNDEL COUNTY

Ridgely, David. Annals of Annapolis, Comprising Sundry Notices of
that Old City from the First Settlements in 1649 until the War
of 1812. (1841) reprint 1992. 283pp. 32.00 .... F5159

Warfield, J.D. The Founders of Anne Arundel and Howard
Counties, Maryland. (1905) reprint 1991. 599pp.
Indexed 40.00 F5130

BALTIMORE CITY

Cohen, Jerome. Baltimore's Grand Inquisition: 1000 Fascinating
Trivia about Charm City. 1992. 175pp. 18.00 F5216

BALTIMORE COUNTY

Forbes, Marie. Speaking of Our Past: a Narrative History of Owings
Mills, Maryland. 1988. 390pp. 20.00 F5216

Sisco, Louis Dow. With a New Introduction and Index by Robert
Barnes. Baltimore County Land Records, 1665-1687, From
the "Maryland Historical Magazine". (1929-41) reprint 1992.
113pp.
Indexed. 18.00 F5130

CALVERT COUNTY

Balletta, Patricia Wilkinson Weaver. The Ancestors & Descendants
of Revolutionary General James Wilkinson of Calvert County,
Maryland Et Ux, Ann Biddle of Philadelphia, Pennsylvania.
1993. 60.00 40.00 F5132

CHARLES COUNTY

Newman, Harry Wright. Charles County Gentry. (1940) reprint
1990. 321pp.
Includes family histories of: Thomas Dent, John Dent,
Richard Edelen, John Hanson, George Newman and
Humphrey Warren. Coats-of-arms, indexed. 25.00 .... F5130

Wearmouth, Roberta J. Abstracts from the *Port Tobacco Times* and
Charles County Advertiser. Vol. 1, 1844-1854. 1990. 234pp. 20.00 F5216

_____. Abstracts from the *Port Tobacco Times* and *Charles
County Advertiser* Vol. 2, 1855-1869. 1991. 220pp. 18.00 F5216

FREDERICK COUNTY

Moore, Tilden. Abstracts of Marriages and Deaths and Other Articles of Interest in the Newspapers of Frederick & Montgomery Counties, Maryland, 1831-1840. 1991. 415pp. 26.50   F5216

Neff, William . Neff - Naf Family History - A Genealogy. 1991. 480pp.
    Neff, Henry: Descendant of Adam Naf, Zurich, Kappel am Albis; Immigrant, Lancaster Co., PA, Manor Township 1718.
       Neff, Drs. Frances; Hans Heinrich; & Jacob: Lancaster Co., PA, Conestoga Twp., and Frederick Co., MD - 1718.
       See Family History #112.   42.50   ....   F5157

HARFORD COUNTY

Preston, Walter W. History of Harford County, MD. (1901) reprint 1990. 379pp.
    Indexed   25.00   ....   F5130

HOWARD COUNTY

Hopkins, G.M. Atlas of Fifteen Miles Around Baltimore Including Howard Co., Maryland. (1878) reprint 1988. 55pp.
    Includes index. 14.60   F5208

Warfield, J.D. The Founders of Anne Arundel and Howard Counties, Maryland. (1905) reprint 1991. 599pp.
    Indexed 40.00   F5130

MONTGOMERY COUNTY

Omans, Nancy West and Donald James Omans. Marriages of Montgomery County, Maryland. 1987. 293pp. 15.00   F5061

ST. MARY'S COUNTY

Fresco, Margaret K. Doctors of St. Doctors of St. Mary's County 1634-1900. 1992. 325pp.   35.00   ....   F5155

WASHINGTON COUNTY

Williams, Thomas J.C. A History of Washington County, Maryland From the Earliest Settlements to the Present Time. Including a History of Hagerstown. (1906) reprint 1992. 1,347pp.
    2 volumes, illustrated, indexed.   125.00   ....   F5130

Massachusetts

STATEWIDE REFERENCE

General Reference

Barber, John Warner.   Historical Collections, being a General
Collection of Interesting Facts, Traditions, Biographical
Sketches, Anecdotes, Etc.,. (1841) reprint 699pp.
Relating to the History and Antiquities of Every Town in
Massachusetts, with Geographical Descriptions.
2 volumes, new index. 39.50 F5216

Gannett, H. Geographic Dictionary of Mass. (1894) reprint 1991.
126pp. 15.00 F5159

Cape Cod

Smith, Jr., Leonard H.   Cape Cod Library of Local History and
Genealogy, A Facsimile Edition of 108 Phamplets Published in
the Early 20th Century. 1992. 2,066pp.
In Two Volumes. Indexed. 125.00 .... F5129

Census

Bentley, E.P. Index to the 1800 Census of Massachusetts. 1978.
305pp. 28.50 .... F5159

The 1790 Census. Heads of Families at the First Census of the
United States Taken in the Year 1790 - Massachusetts. reprint
1992. 363pp. 38.50 F5129

Family Histories

Hoyt, D.W. Old Families of Salisbury & Amesbury, incl. Towns of
Ipswich, Newbury, Haverhill, Hampton & Coastal New
Hampshire & Coastal York Co., Me., 1897-1919. 1243pp. 55.00 F5159

Massachusetts Bay

Jacobson, Judith. Massachusetts Bay Connections. 1992. 167pp.
Indexed, maps. 20.00 F5130

Military

Bodge, George M. Soldiers in King Philip's War, Containing Lists of
Soldiers of Mass. Colony, who Served in the Indian War of
1675-1677. (1891) reprint 1992. 369pp.
Incl. Sketches of Principal Offices & Copies of Ancient
Documents & Records Relating to the War. 39.00 .... F5159

Stark, James H. The Loyalists of Mass., and the Other Side of the
American Rev. (1910) reprint 509pp. 52.00 .... F5159

_____. The Loyalists of Massachusetts and The Other Side of
the Revolution. (1907) reprint 603pp. 35.00 F5216

Pilgrims

Bacon, Edwin M. Historic Pilgrimages in New England Among
Landmarks of Pilgrim and Puritan Days/Provincial and
Revolutionary Periods. (1898) reprint 1992. 475pp. 30.00 F5216

Shaw, H.K. Families of the Pilgrims. (1956) reprint 1987. 178pp.
Comp. for the Massachusetts Society of Mayflower Desc.
Contains biogr. sketches & genealogies of several
generations of desc. of Mayflower passengers, as well as
an index to their wills & reference information. 19.00 F5159

Pioneers

Flagg, C.A. An Index of Pioneers from Mass. to the West, Esp. to the
State of Michigan. (1915) reprint 1980. 86pp. 10.00 F5159

Pope, C.H. Pioneers of Mass. (1620-1650). (1900) reprint 1990.
550pp. 29.50 F5159

_____. The Pioneers of Massachusetts (1620-1650). A Descriptive
List, Drawn from Records of the Colonies, Towns and
Churches. (1990) reprint 1991. 550pp.
Indexed. 35.00 .... F5129

_____. The Pioneers of Massachusetts, A Descriptive List, Drawn
from Records of the Colonies, Towns, and Churches and Other
Contemporaneous Documents. (1900) reprint 550pp. 27.50 F5216

Plymouth Colony

Shurtleff, Nathaniel B. Records of Plymouth Colony, Births,
Marriages, Deaths, Burials, and Other Records, 1633-1689.
(1857) reprint 1991. 293pp.
Indexed 25.00 .... F5129

Research Aids

Mariner, Mary Lou C. and Patricia Roughan Bellows. A Research
Aid For The Massachusetts 1910 Federal Census. 1988.
115pp.
This book directs you to the volume, roll, ED, and page.
Contains county maps and large 1909 foldout map of
Boston. Indexed by both town and country. 21.00 F5144

Source Records

Bailey, Frederic W. Early Massachusetts Marriages Prior to 1800.
(1914) reprint 1991. 661pp.
With Plymouth County Marriages 1692-1746. Indexed. 38.50 .... F5129

Paige, L. List of Freemen of Massachusetts, 1630-1691. (1849)
reprint 1990. 40p.
Extr. from "New Eng. Hist. & Gen. Reg." During this
period, app. 4,500 men were admitted as freemen; this
complete list also gives the source of the data. 8.00 F5159

BARNSTABLE COUNTY

Bowman, George Ernest (Comp.). Truro Vital Records to the Year
1849. (1933) reprint 480pp. 48.00 .... F5159

Brown, G.E. Gravestone Records in the Ancient Cemetery & the
    Woodside Cemetery in Yarmouth. (1906) reprint 1991. 46pp. 8.50   F5159

Fawsett, Marise. Cape Cod (Massachusetts) Annals. 1990. 218pp.
                                                              ....   15.50   F5216

Ferguson, Edith P. Provincetown, Mass. Census Records,
    1790-1840. 127pp. 15.00   F5216

_____. Provincetown, Mass. Census Records, 1850. 151pp.
                                                              ....   17.50   F5216

_____. Provincetown, Mass. Census Records, 1860. 122pp.
                                                              ....   15.00   F5216

Freeman, F. The History of Cape Cod: Annals of Barnstable Co.,
    Including the district of Mashpee. Vol I. (1858) reprint 1990.
    803pp.   79.00   ....   F5159

_____.   The History of Cape Cod: Annals of Barnstable Co.,
    Including the district of Mashpee. Vol II. (1858) reprint 1990.
    803pp.
        SPECIAL PRICE FOR THE SET: $149.00   79.00   ....   F5159

Hills, L.C. Cape Cod Series. Hist. & Gen of the Mayflower Planters
    & 1st Comers to Ye Olde Colonies, Vol I. (1936-41) reprint
    1989. 177pp.   25.00   ....   F5159

_____. Cape Cod Series. Hist. & Gen of the Mayflower Planters &
    1st Comers to Ye Olde Colonies, Vol II. (1936-41) reprint
    1989. 284pp.   31.00   ....   F5159

Otis, Amos. Genealogical Notes of Barnstable Families. (1890)
    reprint 1991. 827pp.
        2 Volumes originally published in 1888 and 1890
        reprinted in one volume. Indexed.   40.00   ....   F5129

Rich, S. Truro, Cape Cod; Landmarks & Seamarks. (1883) reprint
    1988. 580pp. 58.00   F5159

Swift, C.F. History of Old Yarmouth, Comprising the Present Towns
    of Yarmouth & Dennis. (1884) reprint 1991. 281pp. 35.00   F5159

BERKSHIRE COUNTY

Becket Vital Records to the Year 1850. (1903) reprint 1992.
    98pp.   16.00   ....   F5159

Dalton Vital Records to the Year 1850. (1906) reprint 1992.
    82pp.   16.00   ....   F5159

History of Berkshire County, with Biographical Sketches of its
    Prominent Men, Vol. I. (1885) reprint 1987. 701pp.   72.00   ....   F5159

History of Berkshire County, with Biographical Sketches of its
    Prominent Men, Vol. II. (1885) reprint 1987. 708pp.   72.00   ....   F5159

Hyde (Comp.), C.M. and Alexander Hyde. (Lee) The Centennial
    Celebration & Centennial History of the Town of Lee. (1878)
    reprint 1992. 352pp.   38.50   ....   F5159

Lee Vital Records to the Year 1850. (1903) reprint 1992.
    239pp.   29.50   ....   F5159

New Ashford Vital Records to the Year 1850. (1916) reprint 1992.
    43pp.   15.00   ....   F5159

Otis Vital Records to the Year 1850. (1941) reprint 159pp.
	22.00	....	F5159

Perry, Arthur Latham. Origins of Williamstown. (1896) reprint 1992. 650pp.
	....	65.00	F5159

Peru Vital Records to the Year 1850. (1902) reprint 122pp.
	20.00	....	F5159

Raynor, Ellen M. and Emma L. Peticlerc. History of the Town of Cheshire, Berkshire County. (1885) reprint 1992. 219pp.
	28.00	....	F5159

Richmond Vital Records to the Year 1850. (1913) reprint 113pp.
	19.50	....	F5159

Smith, E.Y. (Comp.). Sandisfield Vital Records to the Year 1850. (1936) reprint 111pp.
	19.50	....	F5159

Taylor, C. History of Great Barrington, Berkshire Co. (1882) reprint 1987. 516pp.
	53.00	....	F5159

_____. and George Edwin McLean. History of Great Barrington, 1676-1882, Extended to 1922. (1928) reprint 1992. 620pp.
	59.95	....	F5159

Tyringham Vital Records to the Year 1850. (1903) reprint 107pp.
	16.00	....	F5159

West Stockbridge Vital Records to the Year 1850. (1907) reprint 115pp.
	18.50	....	F5159

Windsor Vital Records to the Year 1850. (1917) reprint 1992. 153pp.
	22.50	....	F5159

BRISTOL COUNTY

(Bristol Co.) Our County & Its People. Descriptive & Biogr. Record of Bristol Co. (1899) reprint 1991. 799,418p.
	109.00	....	F5159

Ellis, L.B. History of New Bedford & Its Vicinity, 1602-1892. (1892) reprint 1988. 731+175pp.
	....	89.50	F5159

Emery, S.H. History of Taunton. (1893) reprint 1987. 768+110p.
	....	89.50	F5159

Dartmouth Vital Records to the Year 1850. 1992.
    Volume I, Births (1929) 314pp $35.00.
    Volume II, Marriages (1930) 314pp $58.00
    Volume III, Deaths (1930) 82pp $16.00
    The set: $99.50. All volumes hardbound.
	....	....	F5159

History of the Town of Freetown. (1902) reprint 1991. 287pp.
	30.00	....	F5159

Norton Vital Records to the Year 1850. (1906) reprint 404pp.
	41.00	....	F5159

Sanford, E. History of the Town of Berkley. (1872) reprint 1987. 60pp.
	....	10.00	F5159

Thomas, Helen Gurney. Vital Records of the Town of Freetown, Massachusetts, 1686-1890. 1988. 484pp.
	....	30.00	F5216

Westport Vital Records to the Year 1850. (1918) reprint 1992. 296pp.
	34.00	....	F5159

Wright, Otis Olney. History of Swansea, 1667-1917. (1917) reprint 1990. 248pp.
	....	31.00	F5159

Rehobeth

Arnold, James N. Rehobeth Vital Records, 1642-1896. Incl. colonial
    returns; early settlers, purchasers, freemen; inhabitants,
    soldiers. (1897) reprint 926pp.   89.00   ....   F5159

Biogr. Sketches of Rehobeth. 88pp.
                                                        ....   18.00   F5159

Cemeteries of Rehobeth. 30pp.
                                                        ....   6.00   F5159

Tilton, George H. A History of Rehobeth: its History for 275 Years,
    1643-1918. (1918) reprint 1990. 417pp. 45.50   F5159

DUKES COUNTY

Chilmark Vital Records to the Year 1850. (1904) reprint 1992.
    96pp.   16.00   ....   F5159

The History of Martha's Vineyard, Dukes Co., Mass. Vol I.
    General History. (1911) reprint 1988. 535pp.   53.50   ....   F5159

The History of Martha's Vineyard, Dukes Co., Mass. Vol II.
    Town Annuals. (1911) reprint 1988. 645pp.   64.40   ....   F5159

The History of Martha's Vineyard, Dukes Co., Mass. Vol III.
    Genealogies. (1911) reprint 1988. 565pp.
    SPECIAL PRICE FOR THE SET: $159.50   56.50   ....   F5159

New England Historic Genealogical Society.   Vital Records of
    Tisbury, Massachusetts, to the Year 1850. (1910) reprint
    244pp. 19.00   F5216

New England Historic Genealogical Society. and Catherine Merwin
    Mayhew. Vital Records of Chilmark, Massachusetts, to the
    Year 1850 and Addenda. (1904) reprint 1991. 151pp. 16.50   F5216

Tisbury Vital Records to the Year 1850. (1910) reprint 244pp.
                                                        29.50   ....   F5159

ESSEX COUNTY

Allen, M.O. The History of Wenham, Civil & Ecclesiastical, from its
    Settlement in 1639 to 1860. (1860) reprint 1988. 220pp. 26.00   F5159

Amesbury Cemetery Inscriptions prior to 1800, Extr. "*Essex
    Antiquarian*". 27pp. 6.00   F5159

Amesbury First Church Records, Extr. from "*Old Fam. of Salisbury
    & Amesbury*". 18pp. 5.00   F5159

Amesbury Vital Records to the Year 1850. (1913) reprint 1992.
    600pp.   59.50   ....   F5159

Andover Cemetery Inscriptions, Extr. from "*The Essex Antiquarian*".
    13pp. 4.50   F5159

Andover Vital Records to the Year 1850. (1912) reprint 1992.
        Volume I, Births 391pp. $42.00 hardcover.
        Volume II, Marriages & Deaths 575pp. $58.00
        hardcover.
        The set: $95.00.   ....   F5159

Babson, J.J. History of Gloucester, Notes & Additions, First &
    Second Series. (1876&1891) reprint 94+187pp.   34.00   ....   F5159

Bailey, S.L. Historical Sketches of Andover. (1880) reprint 1987. 650pp.   65.00   ....   F5159

Beverly Cemetery Inscriptions prior to 1800., Extr. from "*Essex Antiquarian*". 49pp. 10.00   F5159

Beverly Vital Records to the Year 1850. 1992.
Volume I, Births (1906) 400pp $41.00 hardcover.
Volume II, Marriages & deaths (1907) 627pp $63.00 hardcover.
The set: $97.00.   97.00   ....   F5159

Boxford Cemetery Inscriptions prior to 1800, Extr. from "*Essex Antiquarian*". 23pp. 5.50   F5159

Boxford Vital Records to the Year 1850. (1905) reprint 1992. 274pp.   32.00   ....   F5159

Bradford Cemetery Inscriptions. Extr. from the "*Essex Antiquarian*". 41pp. 8.00   F5159

Byfield Baptisms, 1744-1783. Extr. from "*Essex Antiquarian*". 10pp. 4.00   F5159

Byfield Parish Baptisms, Incl. part of the territory of Newbury, Rowley & Georgetown, 1709-1743 Extr from "*Essex Antiquarian*". 12pp. 4.50   F5159

Byfield Parish Deaths, 1748-1801. Extr. from "*Essex Antiquarian*". 16p. 5.00   F5159

Chelsea Vital Records to the Year 1850. (1916) reprint 1992. 558pp.   56.00   ....   F5159

Chamberlain, M. A Documentary History of Chelsea, incl the Boston Precincts of Wimmisimmet Rumney Marsh & Pullen Point, 1624-1824, Vol I. (1908) reprint 1988. 712pp.   74.00   ....   F5159

_____. A Documentary History of Chelsea, incl the Boston Precincts of Wimmisimmet Rumney Marsh & Pullen Point, 1624-1824, Vol II. (1908) reprint 1988. 793pp.   81.00   ....   F5159

Coffin, J. A Sketch of the History of Newbury, Newburyport & West Newbury, from 1635-1845. (1845) reprint 1987. 416pp. 42.00   F5159

Crowell, R. and D. Choate. History of the Town of Essex from 1634-1868, with Sketches of the Soldiers in the War of the Rebellion. (1868) reprint 1987. 488pp.   49.00   ....   F5159

_____. History of the Town of Essex (Massachusetts) from 1634-1868. (1868) reprint 488pp. 30.00   F5216

Danvers Cemetery Inscriptions Prior to 1800. Extr. from "*Essex Antiquarian*". 10pp. 4.00   F5159

Danvers Vital Records to the Year 1850. 1992.
Volume I, Births (1909) 424pp $44.00 hardcover.
Volume II, Marriages & deaths (1910) 491pp $49.50 hardcover.
The set: $89.00.   89.00   ....   F5159

Dorgan, Maurice B. Lawrence, Yesterday & Today (1845-1918). (1918) reprint 1992. 263pp.   32.50   ....   F5159

Dow, G.F. History of Topsfield. (1940) reprint 1987. 517pp. 52.00   F5159

_____. The Probate Records of Essex County, 1635-1681. (1916) reprint 1990.
      Volume I, 1635-1664;
      Volume II, 1665-1674;
      Volume III, 1675-1681.
      Each vol is indexed.$47.50/Vol or $130.00/Set. 130.00 .... F5159

Essex Cemetery Inscriptions Prior to 1800. Extr. from "*Essex Antiquarian*". 12p. 4.50 F5159

Essex Vital Records to the Year of 1850. (1908) reprint 1992. 86pp. 15.00 .... F5159

Ewell, J.L. The Story of Byfield, A New England Parich. (1904) reprint 1987. 344pp. 38.00 .... F5159

Gloucester Vital Records to the Year 1850. reprint 1992.
      Volume I, Births (1917) 805pp $79.50.
      Volume II, Marriages (1923) 605pp $59.50.
      Volume III, Deaths (1924) 338pp $37.00.
      Complete set: $150.00. All volumes hardcover. 150.00 .... F5159

Gott, L. History of the Town of Rockport. (1888) reprint 1987. 295pp. 35.00 F5159

Hamilton Vital Records to the Year 1850. (1908) reprint 1991. 112pp. 18.00 .... F5159

Hanson, J.W. History of the town of Danvers, from its Early Settlement to 1848. (1848) reprint 1987. 304pp. 36.50 .... F5159

Haverhill Cemetery Inscriptions Prior to 1800. Extr. from "*Essex Antiquarian*". 8.00 F5159

Haverhill Vital Records to the Year 1850. reprint 1992.
      Volume I, Births (1910) 328pp $36.00
      Volume II, Marriages & deaths (1911) 499pp $49.50.
      The set: $80.00. All volumes hardcover. 80.00 .... F5159

History of the Town of Gloucester, Cape Ann, including the Town of Rockport. (1860) reprint 1992. 610pp. 35.00 F5216

Hurd, D.H. History of Essex Co., with Biogr. Sketches of Many Pioneers & Prominent Men Vol. I. (1888) reprint 1987. 957pp. 95.00 .... F5159

_____. History of Essex Co., with Biogr. Sketches of Many Pioneers & Prominent Men Vol. II. (1888) reprint 1987. 1,173pp. 115.00 .... F5159

Johnson, David N. Sketches of Lynn (Mass.). (1880) reprint 490pp. 35.00 .... F5216

Lewis, A. and J.R. Newhall. History of Lynn, Essex Co., incl. Lynnfield, Saugus, Swampscott & Nahant. 1865. 620pp. 62.00 .... F5159

_____. and James R. Newhall. History of Lynn, Essex County, Massachusetts: including Lynnfield, Saugus, Swampscot and Nahant. (1865) reprint 620pp. 35.50 F5216

Lynn Vital Records to the Year 1850. 1992.
      Volume I, births (1905) 429pp $44.00.
      Volume II, Marriages & deaths (1906) 621pp $62.00.
      The set: $99.50. All volumes hardcover. 99.50 .... F5159

Manchester Vital Records, to the end of the Year 1849. (1903)
reprint 1990. 296pp.
    Includes Births, Marriages & Deaths.   29.50 .... F5159

Marblehead Vital Records to the Year 1850. 1992.
    Volume I, Births (1903) 564pp $57.00.
    Volume II, Marriages & deaths (1904) 708pp $71.00.
    Complete set: $118.00. All volumes hardcover.   118.00 .... F5159

Merrill, J. History of Amesbury, incl the first 17 years of Salisbury,
to separation in 1654, & Merrimac from incorp. in 1876.
(1880) reprint 1987. 431pp.   43.50 .... F5159

Methuen Vital Records to the Year 1850. (1909) reprint 1992.
    345pp.   36.00 .... F5159

Middleton Vital Records to the Year 1850. (1904) reprint
1992. 143pp.   20.00 .... F5159

Mirick, Benjamin L. The History of Haverhill, Massachusetts.
(1832) reprint 340pp. 23.00 F5216

Newbury Vital Records to the Year 1850. 1992.
    Volume I, Births 564pp $59.00.
    Volume II, Marriages & deaths 759pp $78.00.
    The set: $125.00. All volumes hardcover.   125.00 .... F5159

Newburyport Vital Records to the Year 1850. reprint 1992.
    Volume I, Births 428pp $43.00.
    Volume II, Marriages & deaths, 845pp $84.50.
    The set: $119.50. All volumes hardcover.   119.50 .... F5159

Perley, S. History of Boxford, from its Settlement to 1875. (1880)
reprint 1987. 418pp.   42.00 .... F5159

Pool, W. Rockport Baptisms, 1755-1808. 21pp.
    Extr. *Essex Antiquarian.* 5.50 F5159

Roads, Jr., S. The History & Traditions of Marblehead, Rev. ed.
(1897) reprint 1987. 595pp.   60.00 .... F5159

Rockport Vital Records to the Year 1850. (1924) reprint
120pp.   20.00 .... F5159

Salisbury Second Church Records. 59pp.
         .... 11.00 F5159

Salisbury Vital Records to the Year 1850. (1915) reprint 1992.
    636pp.   64.00 .... F5159

Saugus Vital Records to the Year 1850. (1907) reprint 1992.
    81pp.   15.00 .... F5159

Stone, Edwin M. History of Beverly, Civil & Ecclesiastical, form its
Settlement in 1639 to 1842. (1843) reprint 1992. 322pp.   36.50 .... F5159

Topsfield Vital Records to the Year 1850. (1912) reprint 1992.
    258pp.   29.50 .... F5159

Wellman, Thomas B. History of Lynnfield, 1635-1895. (1895)
reprint 1990. 283pp.   37.50 .... F5159

Wells, John A. The Peabody Story. (1973) reprint 1992. 530pp.
         .... 49.00 F5159

Wenham Vital Records to the Year 1850. (1904) reprint 1992.
    227pp.   27.00 .... F5159

W. Newbury Vital Records to the Year 1850. (1918) reprint 1992. 122pp.   19.50   ....   F5159

Ipswich

Felt, J.B. History of Ipswich, Essex & Hamilton. (1834) reprint 1987. 304pp.   35.00   ....   F5159

_____. History of Ipswich, Essex, and Hamilton, Massachusetts. 1991. 330pp. 23.00   F5216

Hammatt, Abraham. (Ipswich) The Hammatt Papers: Early Inhbitants of Ipswich, 1633-1700. (1880-1899) reprint 1992. 423pp.   41.00   ....   F5159

_____. The Hammatt Papers: Early Inhabitants of Ipswich, Massachusetts, 1633-1700. (1899) reprint 1991. 448pp.   30.00   ....   F5129

Ipswich Births to 1850. Vol. I, Vital Records. reprint 1991. 404pp.   42.00   ....   F5159

Ipswich Cemetery Inscriptions. Extr. from "The Exxes Antiquarian". 56pp. 9.50   F5159

Ipswich Vital Records to the Year 1850. reprint 1992.
Volume I, Births 404pp $41.00.
Volume II, Marriages & deaths 721pp $72.00.
The set: $105.00. All volumes hardcover.   105.00   ....   F5159

Johnson, A.W. and R.E. Ladd, Jr. (Ipswich cemeteries) Momento More: An Accurate Transcription of the [Memorials] in the Town of Ipswich...from 1634 to [1935]. (1935) reprint 1991. 264pp.   25.00   ....   F5159

Waters, T.F. (Ipswich) Jeffrey's Neck & the Way Leading Thereto, with Notes on Little Neck. (1912) reprint 1987. 94pp. 10.00   F5159

_____. Ipswich in the Massachusetts Bay Colony. Pt. I - Historical, Pt. II - Houses & Lands. (1905) reprint 1987. 586pp.   62.00   ....   F5159

Rowley

Blodgette, George B. Rowley Massachusetts Records:Town, Church and Cemetery. (1900) reprint 480pp.   35.00   ....   F5216

Gage, T. The History of Rowley, Anciently Incl. Bradford, Boxford & Georgetown, from 1639-1840. (1840) reprint 1987. 483pp. 48.50   F5159

Rowley Old Cemetery Inscriptions. 72pp. 11.00   F5159

Rowley Town Records, 1639-1672. Vol. I. 254pp. 32.00   F5159

Rowley Vital Records to the Year 1850. (1928) reprint 1992. 537pp.   54.00   ....   F5159

Rowley. Records of the First Church. 220pp. 31.00   F5159

Salem

Derby, P. Salem Inscriptions from the Charter St. Cemetery. 22pp. 5.00   F5159

Essex Institute. Vital Records of Salem, to the End of the Year 1849.
    (1916) reprint 1991.
        Publ. by Essex Institute.
        Births, A-L   536pp $49.00.
        Births, M-Z   434pp $41.00.
        Marriages, A-L   625pp $59.00.
        Marriages, M-Z   529pp $49.00.
        Deaths, A-L   412pp $39.00.
        Deaths, M-Z   365pp $35.00.
        The Complete Set in 3 Volumes (Births, Marriages &
        Deaths bound together) $225.00.   225.00 .... F5159

Felt, J.B. Annals of Salem. reprint 1988.
    2nd ed. 2 volumes.
    Vol. I 535pp (1845) $54.00.
    Vol. II 563pp (1849) $57.00.   .... F5159

Perley, Sidney. History of Salem. reprint 1987.
    3 volumes.
    Vol. I, 1626-1637 598pp (1924).
    Vol. II, 1638-1670 526pp (1926).
    Vol. III, 1671-1716 (1928).
    Each volume $50.00.   .... F5159

Robinson, Enders A. Salem Witchcraft and Hawthorne's "House of
    the Seven Gables". 1991. 374pp. 29.50 F5216

Salem Vital Records to the Year 1850. reprint 1992.
        Volume I, Births A-L (1916)   536pp $54.00.
        Volume II, Births M-Z (1918)   454pp $46.00.
        Volume III, Marriages A-L (1924)   625pp $63.00.
        Volume IV, Marriages M-Z (1924)   529pp $54.00.
        Volume V, Deaths A-L (1925)   412pp $43.00.
        Volume VI, Deaths M-Z (1925)   365pp $38.00.
        Complete set in 3 Volumes: $250.00. All volumes
        hardcover.   250.00 .... F5159

Yool, George Malcolm. 1692 Witch Hunt: The Layman's Guide to
    the Salem Witchcraft Trials. 1992. 155pp. 15.50 F5216

FRANKLIN COUNTY

Atkins, W.G. History of the Town of Hawley, Franklin Co. from
    1771 to 1887. With fam. records & biogr. sketches. (1887)
    reprint 1987. 132pp.   19.00 .... F5159

Baker and Coleman. Epitaphs in the Old Burying Ground of
    Deerfield. (1924) reprint 1987. 49pp. 9.00 F5159

Buckland, MA, Marriage Intentions, 1793-1820 Extr from "*NEHG*
    Register". 7p. 4.00 F5159

Crafts, J.M. History of the Town of Whately, Incl. Events from the
    1st Planting of Hatfield, 1661-1899. (1899) reprint 1987.
    636pp. 64.00 F5159

Deerfield Vital Records to the Year of 1850. (1920) reprint 1992.
    328pp.   36.00 .... F5159

Gill Vital Records to the Year 1850. (1904) reprint 1992.
    97pp.   18.00 .... F5159

Greenfield Vital Records to the Year 1850. (1915) reprint 1992. 299pp.	34.00	....	F5159
Heath Vital Records to the Year 1850. (1915) reprint 1992. 142pp.	21.00	....	F5159
Howes, F.G. History of the Town of Ashfield, Franklin Co., from Settlement in 1742 to 1910. (1910) reprint 1987. 425pp.	43.00	....	F5159
Inscriptions in the Old Cemetery at Northfield. 18pp.	....	5.50	F5159
Kellogg, Lucy C. History of Greenfield, 1900-1929. (1931) reprint 1991. 629pp. "Vol. 3" of 1904 set "*History of Greenfield*" by F.M. Thompson.	60.00	....	F5159
_____. History of the Town of Bernardston, Franklin Co., 1736-1900, with Genealogies. (1902) reprint 1992. 581pp.	58.50	....	F5159
New Salem Vital Records to the Year 1850. (1927) reprint 1992. 283pp.	33.00	....	F5159
Severance, C.S. History of Greenfield, 1930-1953. (1954) reprint 1991. 551pp. "Vol. 4" of 1904 set "*History of Greenfield*" by F.M. Thompson.	55.00	....	F5159
Shelburne Vital Records to the Year 1850. (1931) reprint 1992. 190pp.	25.00	....	F5159
Smith, J.M. History of the Town of Sunderland, which Originally Embraced within its Limits the Towns of Montague & Leverett. (1899) reprint 1988. 696pp.	....	69.50	F5159
Temple, J.H. and G. Sheldon. History of the Town of Northfield for 150 Years, with Genealogies. (1875) reprint 1987. 636pp.	....	64.00	F5159
Thompson, F.M. History of Greenfield, 1682-1900, 2 vols. (1904) reprint 1991. 1,308pp.	98.00	....	F5159

HAMPDEN COUNTY

Brimfield Vital Records to the Year 1850. (1931) reprint 1992. 336pp.	35.00	....	F5159
Chester Vital Records to the Year 1850. (1911) reprint 1992. 256pp.	29.50	....	F5159
Genealogies extrated from "*Historical Celebration of the Town of Brimfield*". (1879) reprint 1987. 114pp.	....	12.00	F5159
Granville Vital Records to the Year 1850. (1914) reprint 1992. 236pp.	29.00	....	F5159
Historical Celebration of the Town of Brimfield, Hampden Co. (1879) reprint 1987. 487pp.	49.00	....	F5159
Lovering, M. History of the Town of Holland. (1915) reprint 1987. 745pp.	75.00	....	F5159
_____. Holland Military Lists from the French & Indian War through the Civil War. 58pp. Extr. from "*History of the Town of Holland*".	....	12.00	F5159
_____. Holland Vital Statistics, 1767-1848. 37pp. Extr. from "*History of the Town of Holland*".	....	7.50	F5159

Montgomery Vital Records to the Year 1850. (1902) reprint
    1992. 66pp.   15.00   ....   F5159

Noon, A. Ludlow. A Century & a Centennial, Comprising a Sketch
    of the History of the Town of Ludlow. (1875) reprint 1987.
    208pp.   25.00   ....   F5159

_____. The History of Ludlow, with Biogr. Sketches of Leading
    Citizens, Reminiscences, Genealogies, Farm Hist. & an Acct. of
    the Centennial Celebration, 1874. (1912) reprint 1988. 592p.
    2nd Editon, revised & enlarged.   63.00   ....   F5159

Temple, J.H. History of Palmer, Early Known as the Elbow Tract,
    Incl. Records of the Plantation, District & Town, 1716-1889.
    (1889) reprint 1987. 602pp. 67.00   F5159

Wood, S.G. The Taverns & Turnpikes of Blandford, 1733-1833.
    (1908) reprint 1991. 351pp.   39.00   ....   F5159

HAMPSHIRE COUNTY

Barrus, H. History of the Town of Goshen, Hampshire Co., from
    1761-1881, with fam. sketches. (1881) reprint 1987. 262pp.   33.50   ....   F5159

Bicentennial Gen. Comm. History & Genealogy of the Families of
    Chesterfield, 1762-1962. (1962) reprint 1987. 427pp.   48.50   ....   F5159

Boltwood, L.M. Gen. of Hadley Families, Embracing the Early
    Settlers of the Towns of Hatfield, South Hadley, Amherst &
    Granby. (1905) reprint 1990. 205pp.   21.00   ....   F5159

Lyman, P.W. History of Easthampton: Its Settlement & Growth,
    with a Gen. Record of Original Families. (1866) reprint 1987.
    194pp.   32.00   ....   F5159

_____. History of Easthampton, Massachusetts. (1886) reprint
    200pp.
                 27.00   ....   F5216

Middlefield Vital Records to the Year 1850. (1907) reprint
    1992. 138pp.   20.00   ....   F5159

Parmenter, C.O. History of Pelham, from 1738 to 1898, including
    the Early Hist. of Prescott. (1868) reprint 1990. 531pp. 54.00   F5159

Pelham Vital Records to the Year 1850. (1902) reprint 1992.
    177pp.   24.00   ....   F5159

Rice, J.C. The History of the Town of Worthington, from its First
    Settlement to 1874. (1874) reprint 1988. 123pp. 20.00   F5159

Smith, E.C. and P.M. Smith. History of the Town of Middlefield.
    (1924) reprint 1991. 662pp.
        Extensive chapter of genealogy is included. 67.50   F5159

Trumbull, J.R. The History of Northampton, From its Settlement in
    1654. (1989) reprint 1988.
        Vol. I 628pp $64.00;
        Vol. II 699pp $69.00.   ....   F5159

_____. The History of Northampton, from Settlement in 1654.
    (1898) reprint 1992. 628+699p.
        2 Volumes $65.00/vol., $125.00/set. F5159

Wells, D.W. and R.F. Wells. History of Hatfield in 3 Parts, Incl.
    Genealogies of the Families of the 1st Settlers. (1910) reprint
    1987. 536pp.   54.00   ....   F5159

Worthington Vital Records to the Year 1850. (1911) reprint
   1992. 159pp.   22.50   ....   F5159

MIDDLESEX COUNTY

Acton Vital Records to the Year 1850. (1923) reprint 1992.
   311pp.   36.00   ....   F5159

Arlington Vital Records to the Year 1850. (1904) reprint 1992.
   162pp.   22.50   ....   F5159

Bacon, Oliver N. A History of Natick from its First Settlement in
   1651 to the Present Time, with Notices of the First White
   Families. (1856) reprint 1990. 261pp. 32.50   F5159

Baldwin, Thomas W. Vital Records of Natick, Massachusetts to the
   Year 1850. (1910) reprint 249pp. 19.00   F5216

Barry, W. A History of Framingham, Incl. the Plantation, from 1640
   to 1846. Also a Register of Inhabitants before 1800, with Gen.
   Sketches. (1847) reprint 1987. 456pp.   45.50   ....   F5159

_____. A History of Framingham, Massachusetts. (1847) reprint
   456pp.   35.00   ....   F5216

Billerica Vital Records to the Year 1850. (1908) reprint 1992.
   405pp.   41.00   ....   F5159

Bond, Henry. Genealogies of the Families & Descendants of the
   Early Settlers of Watertown,. (1860) reprint 1991. 1094pp.
         Including Waltham & Weston, MA; to which is appended
         the Early History of the Town. 98.00   F5159

Boxboro Vital Records to the Year 1850. (1915) reprint 1991.
   78pp.   15.00   ....   F5159

Brandon, Edward J. The Proprietors Records of Cambridge, Mass.,
   1635-1829. (1896) reprint 414pp. 26.50   F5216

Brooks, C. and rev. by J.M. Usher. History of the Town of Medford,
   Middlesex Co., From its 1st Settlement in 1630 to 1855.
   (1886) reprint 1988. 592pp.   62.00   ....   F5159

Bull, Sidney A. History of the Town of Carlisle, 1754-1920. (1920)
   reprint 1992. 365pp.   39.50   ....   F5159

Burlington Vitaal Records to the Year 1850. (1915) reprint 1992.
   100pp.   18.00   ....   F5159

Cambridge Vital Records to the Year 1850. 1992.
         Volume I, Births (1914) 936pp $91.00 hardcover.
         Volume II, Marriages & deaths 806pp $79.50 hardcover.
         The set: $155.00.   155.00   ....   F5159

Carlisle Vital Records to the Year 1850. (1918) reprint 1992.
   100pp.   20.00   ....   F5159

Chelmsford Cemetery Records. Extr from "*The Hist. of
   Chelmsford*". 40pp. 8.00   F5159

Chelmsford Vital Records to the Year 1850. (1914) reprint 1992.
   460pp.   47.00   ....   F5159

Concord Births, Marriages & Deaths, 1635-1850. (1891) reprint
   1987. 496pp.   50.00   ....   F5159

Concord, Massachusetts, Births, Marriages, and Deaths, 1635-1850.
   (1894) reprint 1992. 496pp. 30.00   F5216

Corey, D.P. History of Malden, Mass., 1633-1785. (1899) reprint
1988. 870pp.   87.00   ....   F5159

_____. The History of Malden, Massachusetts, 1633-1785, 2 Vols.
(1899) reprint 870pp. 50.00   F5216

Cutter, B. & W. History of the Town of Arlington, 1635-1879.
(1880) reprint 1987. 368pp.   37.00   ....   F5159

Dracut Vital Records to the Year 1850. (1907) reprint 1991.
302pp.   32.00   ....   F5159

Dunstable Vital Records to the Year 1850. (1913) reprint 1992.
238pp.   29.50   ....   F5159

Eaton, L. Genealogical History of the Town of Reading. (1874)
reprint 1988. 815pp.
    incl. the present towns of Wakefield, Reading & N.
    Reading, with Chronological & Hist. Sketches, from
    1639 to 1874.   ....   82.00   F5159

Essex Institute. Vital Records of Dunstable Massachusetts to the End
of the Year 1849. (1913) reprint 238pp. 17.50   F5216

_____. Vital Records of Tewksbury, Massachusetts, to the End of
the Year 1849. (1912) reprint 246pp. 19.00   F5216

Fox, Charles J. The History of Old Dunstable. (1846) reprint
293pp.   25.00   ....   F5216

Framingham Vital Records to the Year 1850. (1911) reprint 1992.
474pp.   48.00   ....   F5159

Frothingham, Jr., R. THe History of Charlestown. (1845) reprint
1987. 368pp.   37.00   ....   F5159

Gozzaldi, Mary Isabella. History of Cambridge, Massachusetts,
1630-1877, Index and Supplement. (1930) reprint 860pp.   50.00   ....   F5216

Green, S.A. Groton During during the Indian Wars. (1883) reprint
1987. 214pp.   25.00   ....   F5159

_____. Groton During the Revolution, with an Appendix. (1900)
reprint 1988. 343pp.   34.50   ....   F5159

Groton Vital Records to the Year 1850. reprint 1992.
    Volume I, Births (1926) $32.50.
    Volume II, Marriages & Deaths (1927) $33.50.
    The set: $59.50. All volumes hardcover.   59.50   ....   F5159

Hager, L.C. Boxboro. A New England town & its People, with
Sketches & Illustration. (1891) reprint 1987. 218pp.   29.00   ....   F5159

Hazen, H.A. History of Billerica. (1883) reprint 1987. 513pp.

      51.00   ....   F5159

Hodgman, E.A. History of the Town of Westford in the Co. of
Middlesex, 1659-1993. (1883) reprint 1987. 494pp. 49.75   F5159

Holliston Vital Records to the Year 1850. (1908) reprint 1992.
358pp.   39.00   ....   F5159

Hopkinton Vital Records to the Year 1850. (1911) reprint 1992.
462pp.   47.00   ....   F5159

Hudson, Alfred Sereno. History of Sudbury, 1638-1889. (1889)
reprint 1992. 660pp.   66.00   ....   F5159

_____. History of the Lexington, Middlesex Co., from its 1st Settlement to 1868, with a Gen. Reg. (1868) reprint 1987. 745pp.   74.00   ....   F5159

Jackson, Francis. History of the Early Settlement of Newton County of Middlesex, Mass., from 1639-1800 with a Geneal. Register of its Inhabitants Prior to 1800. (1854) reprint 606pp.   40.00   ....   F5216

Lexington Historical Society and C. Hudson. (Lexington) History of the Town of Lexington, Middlesex Co., from its 1st Settlement to 1868, Rev. & continued to 1912. Genealogies. (1913) reprint 1987. 897pp.   89.75   ....   F5159

_____. and C. Hudson. (Lexington) History of the Town of Lexington, Middlesex Co., from its 1st Settlement to 1868, Rev. & continued to 1912. History. (1913) reprint 1987. 583pp.   59.00   ....   F5159

Lincoln Vital Records to the Year 1850. (1908) reprint 1992. 179pp.   24.00   ....   F5159

Littleton. From the Earliest Records in the Town Books, Begun in 1715.
Births & Deaths; Some Marriages. 542pp.   54.00   ....   F5159

Index to "*Littleton. From the Earliest Records in the Town Books, Begun in 1715. Births & Deaths; Some Marriages*".   18.00   ....   F5159

Lowell Vital Records to the Year 1850. 1992.
    Volume I, Births 404pp $41.00.
    Volume II, Marriages, A-L 543pp $55.00.
    Volume III, Marriages, M-Z 427pp $43.00
    Volume IV, Deaths, 324pp $36.00.
Complete set: $165.00. All volumes hardcover.   165.00   ....   F5159

Malden Vital Records to the Year 1850. (1903) reprint 1991. 393pp.   39.50   ....   F5159

Marlborough Burial Ground Inscriptions: Old Common, Spring Hill & Brigham Cemeteries. (1908) reprint 1987. 218pp.   29.00   ....   F5159

Marlborough Vital Records to the Year 1850. (1908) reprint 1992. 404pp.   41.00   ....   F5159

Medford Vital Records to the Year 1850. (1907) reprint 469pp.   47.00   ....   F5159

Nason, E. A History of the Town of Dunstable, from its Earliest Settlement to the Year 1873. (1877) reprint 1987. 316pp.   37.00   ....   F5159

Natick Vital Records to the Year 1850. (1910) reprint 1992. 249pp.   29.50   ....   F5159

Paige, Lucius R. History of Cambridge, Massachusetts, 1630-1877, with a Genealogical Register. (1877) reprint 732pp.   45.00   ....   F5216

Reading Vital Records to the Year 1850. (1912) reprint 586pp.
                                                                  59.00   ....   F5159

Reading Vital Records to the Year 1850. (1912) reprint 1992. 586pp.   59.00   ....   F5159

Record of Births, Marriages & Deaths to Jan 1, 1898. Pt. I - From Earliest Record to 1853. 213pp.   28.00   ....   F5159

Record of Births, Marriages & Deaths to Jan 1, 1898. Pt. II - From 1854 to 1897. 289pp.   33.00   ....   F5159

Sawtelle, Ithamar B. History of Townsend from the Grant of Hathorn's Farm, 1676-1878. (1878) reprint 1991. 455pp.   45.00 .... F5159

Sewall, Samuel. History of Woburn, Middlesex Co., from the Grant of its Territory to Charlestown in 1640, to the Year 1860. (1868) reprint 1991. 677pp.   65.00 .... F5159

_____. The History of Woburn, Middlesex County, Massachusetts, from the Grant of Its Territory to Charlestown in 1640 to 1860. (1868) reprint 688pp. 39.00   F5216

Shattuck, L. History of the Town of Concord, Middlesex Co., from earliest settlement to 1832, and of the Adjoining Towns Bedford, Acton, Lincoln & Carlisle. (1835) reprint 1987. 412pp.   43.00 .... F5159

Sherborn Vital Records to the Year 1850. (1911) reprint 1992. 229pp.   27.00 .... F5159

Shirley Vital Records to the Year 1850. (1918) reprint 1992. 211pp.   26.00 .... F5159

Stoneham Vital Records to the Year 1850. (1918) reprint 1992. 191pp.   25.00 .... F5159

Stow Vital Records to the Year 1850. (1911) reprint 270pp.   32.00 .... F5159

Sudbury Vital Records to the Year 1850. (1903) reprint 1992. 332pp.   36.00 .... F5159

Temple, J.H. Genealogies extr. from "History of Framingham". 303pp.   36.00 .... F5159

_____. History of Framingham, with a Genealogical Register. (1987) reprint 794pp.   79.50 .... F5159

Tewksbury Vital Records to the Year 1850. (1912) reprint 1992. 246pp.   29.50 .... F5159

Tyngsboro Vital Records to the Year 1850. (1912) reprint 119pp.   18.50 .... F5159

Wakefield Vital Records to the Year 1850. (1912) reprint 1992. 341pp.   36.00 .... F5159

Waltham Vital Records to the Year 1850. (1904) reprint 298pp.   34.00 .... F5159

Waters, W. History of Chelmsford. (1917) reprint 1987. 893pp.   89.50 .... F5159

Winship, J.P.C. Historical Brighton; An Illustrated History of Brighton & its Citizens. (1899, 1902) reprint 1987. 462pp. 2 volumes in 1. 240pp + 222pp.   47.00 .... F5159

Wyman, Thomas Bellows. The Genealogies and Estates of Charlestown, in the County of Middlesex, and the Commonwealth of Massachusetts, 1629-1818. (1879) reprint 1,174pp. 60.00   F5216

NANTUCKET COUNTY

Farnham, Joseph E.C. Fascinating Old Town on the Island in the Sea: Brief Historical Data & Memories of my Boyhood Days in Nantucket (2nd ed). (1923) reprint 1992. 319pp.   36.00 .... F5159

Hinchman, L.S.   Early Settlers of Nantucket; their Associates &
    Descendants. (1901) reprint 1987. 347pp.
        2nd & enlarged edition. 37.00   F5159

Nantucket Vital Records to the Year 1850. 1992.
    Volume I, Births, A-F (1925) 520pp $52.00.
    Volume II, Births, G-Z (1926) 634pp $64.00.
    Volume III, Marriages, A-G (1927) 566pp $57.00.
    Volume IV, Marriages, H-Z (1927) 543pp $55.00.
    Volume V, Deaths (1928) 626pp $63.00.
    Complete set: $250.00. All volumes hardcover. 250.00 .... F5159

Starbuck, Alexander.   The History of Nantucket County, Island &
    Town, Including Genealogies of the First Settlers. (1924)
    reprint 1992. 871pp.   75.00 .... F5159

NORFOLK COUNTY

Bates, Samuel A. Records of the Town of Braintree, 1640-1793.
    (1886) reprint 1988. 939pp.   94.00 .... F5159

_____. Records of the Town of Braintree, 1640-1793, 2
    Vols. (1886) reprint 940pp. 50.00 F5216

Bigelow, E. Victor. A Narrative History of the Town of Cohasset.
    (1898) reprint 1992. 561pp.   56.50 .... F5159

Brookline Vital Records to the Year 1850. (1929) reprint 1992.
    244pp.   29.50 .... F5159

Clark, G.K.   History of Needham, Mass., 1711-1911, incl. West
    Needham, now Wellesley, to its Separation in 1881 with Some
    References to its Affairs to 1911. (1913) reprint 1988. 746pp. 75.00 F5159

Cohasset Vital Records to the Year 1850. (1916) reprint 1992.
    237pp.   29.00 .... F5159

Foxborough Vital Records to the Year 1850. (1911) reprint
    1992. 249pp.   31.00 .... F5159

Hanson, Robert Brand.   Churches of Dedham, Massachusetts:
    Admissions, Dismissions, Adult Baptisms, and Proceedings
    under the Half-Way Covenant, 1638-1844. 1990. 148pp. 15.00 F5216

_____. The Deacon's Book: Records of the First Church, Dedham,
    Massachusetts, 1677-1737. 1990. 336pp. 25.00 F5216

_____. The Vital Records of Dedham, Massachusetts. 1989.
    226pp. 17.50 F5216

History of the Town of Franklin, from its Settlement to the
    Completion of its 1st Century. (1878) reprint 1987. 263pp. 33.00 .... F5159

Hurd, D.H.   The History of Norfolk Co., with Biogr. Sketches of
    Many of its Pioneers & Prominent Men. (1884) reprint 1987.
    1,001pp. 99.00 F5159

Jackson, F.   History of the Early Settlement of Newton from
    1639-1800, with Genealogical Register. (1854) reprint 1987.
    555pp. 58.00 F5159

Jameson, E.O.   Medway. Biographical Sketches of Prominent
    Persons & the Genealogical Records of Many Early & Other
    Families in Medway, 1713-1886. (1886) reprint 1987.
    208pp. 28.00 F5159

Lewis, I.N. A History of Walpole, from its earliest times. (1905) reprint 1987. 217pp. 25.00 F5159

Medfield Vital Records to the Year 1850. (1903) reprint 243pp. 29.50 .... F5159

Medway Vital Records to the Year 1850. (1909) reprint 1992. 345pp. 38.00 .... F5159

Newton Vital Records to the Year 1850. (1905) reprint 1992. 521pp. 53.00 .... F5159

Pattee, W.S. A History of Old Braintree & Quincy, with a Sketch of Randolph & Holbrook. (1878) reprint 1990. 660pp. 66.00 .... F5159

Sharon Vital Records to the Year 1850. (1909) reprint 1992. 193pp. 25.00 .... F5159

Smith, F. A Narrative History of Dover as a Precinct, Parish, District & Town. (1897) reprint 1987. 354pp. 40.00 .... F5159

_____. The Genealogical History of Dover, Tracing 11 Families Previous to 1850 & Many Families that have lived in the Town Since. (1917) reprint 1987. 298pp. 30.00 .... F5159

_____. History of Newton, Town & City, From its Earliest Settlement to the Present Time, 1630-1880. (1880) reprint 1988. 851pp. 86.00 F5159

Tilden, W.S. History of the Town of Medfield, 1650-1886, with Gen. of the Fam. that Held Real Estate or Made any Considerable Stay in the Town During the 1st 2 Cen. (1887) reprint 1987. 556pp. 56.00 .... F5159

Walpole Vital Records to the Year 1850. (1902) reprint 216pp. 26.50 .... F5159

Weymouth Vital Records to the Year 1850. reprint 1992.
Volume I, Births (1910) 359pp $38.00.
Volume II, Marriages & deaths (1910) 376pp $39.50.
The set: $75.00. 75.00 .... F5159

Woods, H.F. Historical Sketches of Brookline. (1874) reprint 1988. 431pp. 43.00 .... F5159

Wrentham Vital Records to the Year 1850. Volume I, Births. (1910) reprint 237p. 28.50 .... F5159

Wrentham Vital Records to the Year 1850. Volume II, Marriages & Deaths. (1910) reprint 518pp. 52.00 .... F5159

PLYMOUTH COUNTY

Abington Vital Records to the Year 1850. Volume I Births. (1912) reprint 251pp. 29.50 .... F5159

Abington Vital Records to the Year 1850. Volume II, Marriages & Deaths. (1912) reprint 381pp. 39.00 .... F5159

Bowman, G.E. Records of Plymouth Colony: Births, Marriages, Deaths, Burials & Other Records 1633-1689. (1857) reprint 1979. 293pp.
A Suppl. from Mayflower Desc. 29.00 F5159

Bradford, Gov. William. Bradford's History "Of Plimoth Plantation" from the Original Manuscript. (1901) reprint 555pp. 32.50 F5216

Briggs, L.V. Hanover. First Congregational Church & Cemetery
Records, 1727-1895. (1895) reprint 1987. 216pp.   23.00   ....   F5159

Brockton Vital Records to the Year 1850. (1911) reprint 1992.
371pp.   39.00   ....   F5159

Carver Vital Records to the Year 1850. (1911) reprint 1992.
179pp.   25.00   ....   F5159

Committee of Town of Mattapoisett. Mattapoisett & Old Rochester,
Being a History of these Towns & also in Part of Marion & a
Portion of Wareham, Third edition. (1907) reprint 1992.
426pp.   44.00   ....   F5159

Davis, W.T. Ancient Landmarks of Plymouth. Pt. 1, Hist. Sketch &
Titles of Estates, Pt. 2, Gen. Register of Plymouth Families.
(1887) reprint 1988. 662pp. 69.00   F5159

_____. Genealogical Register of Plymouth Families. (1899)
reprint 1985. 363pp. 21.50   F5159

Davis, et al, Wm. T. Records of the Town of Plymouth, 1636-1783,
3 Volumes. Reprint from 1889, 1892, 1903, (347, 365 and
481 pp). 60.00   F5216

Dexter, Morton. The Story of the Pilgrims. (1894) reprint 363pp.
   ....   24.50   F5216

Duxbury Vital Records to the Year 1850. (1911) reprint 1992.
446pp.   45.00   ....   F5159

Dwelley and Simmons. The History of the Town of Hanover, with
Family Genealogies, Vol I. History. (1910) reprint 1988.
291pp.   32.00   ....   F5159

_____. and Simmons. The History of the Town of Hanover, with
Family Genealogies, Vol II. Genealogy. (1910) reprint 1988.
474pp.   47.50   ....   F5159

E. Bridgewater Vital Records to the Year 1850. (1917) reprint
1992. 406pp.   42.00   ....   F5159

The English Ancestry & Homes of the Pilgrim Fathers. (1929)
reprint 1990. 187pp.
Who came to Plymouth on the "*Mayflower*" in 1620, the
"*Fortune*" in 1621 and the "*Anne*" and "*Little James*" in
1623.   ....   19.50   F5159

Griffith, Henry S. History of the Town of Carver. (1913) reprint
1991. 366pp.   40.00   ....   F5159

Hanson Vital Records to the Year 1850. (1911) reprint 1992.
110pp.   21.00   ....   F5159

History of the Town of Plymouth from its First Settlement in 1620 to
the Present Time. (1835) reprint 1991. 401pp.
with a Precise History of the Aborigines of New England
& their Wars with the Eng. 40.00   F5159

Hobart, B. History of the Town of Abington, Plymouth Co., from its
1st Settlement. (1866) reprint 1987. 452pp.   47.00   ....   F5159

Hull Vital Records to the Year 1850. (1911) reprint 1992.
75pp.   15.00   ....   F5159

Hurd, D.H. History of Plymouth County, with Biographical
Sketches of Many of its Pioneers & Prominent Men. (1884)
reprint 1987. 1,198pp. 98.00   F5159

Kingman, B. History of North Bridgewater, Plymouth Co. from 1st Settlement to 1866, with Family Register. (1866) reprint 1987. 696pp.   73.00 .... F5159

_____. History of North Bridgewater, Plymouth County, Mass., From its First Settlement to the Present Time, with Family Registers. (1866) reprint 770pp. 43.00 F5216

Kingston Vital Records to the Year 1850. (1911) reprint 1992. 396pp.   41.00 .... F5159

Lazell, T.S. Death Records from the Ancient Burial Ground at Kingston. (1905) reprint 1991. 31pp. 6.50 F5159

Long, E. Waldo. The Story of Duxbury, 1637-1937. (1937) reprint 1992. 237pp.   29.00 .... F5159

Middleboro. Descriptive Catalog of Members of the 1st Congregational Church. (1895) reprint 1991. 16pp. With Index to Surnames. Extr. from "200th Anniversary of 1st Congregational Church". 5.00 F5159

Mitchell, Nahum. History of the Early Settlement of Bridgewater, in Plymouth Co., including an Extensive Family Register. (1840) reprint 1992. 424pp.   44.50 .... F5159

Pembroke Vital Records to the Year 1850. (1911) reprint 1992. 465pp.   47.00 .... F5159

Plympton Vital Records to the Year 1850. (1923) reprint 1992. 540pp.   55.00 .... F5159

Scott, Henry Edwards. Vital Records of Rochester, Massachusetts to the Year 1850, Volume 1, Births. (1914) reprint 318pp. 22.50 F5216

_____. Vital Records of Rochester, Massachusetts to the Year 1850, Volume 2, Marriages and Deaths. (1914) reprint 450pp. 28.50 F5216

Smith Jr., Col. Leonard H. Vital Records of The Town of Plymouth. An Authorized Facsimile Reproduction of Records Published Serially 1901-1935 in *"The Mayflower Descendant"*. (1989) reprint 1992. 327pp. With an Added Index of Persons. 39.95 F5130

West Bridgewater Vital Records to the Year 1850. (1911) reprint 222pp.   27.00 .... F5159

Western, Thomas. History of the Town of Middleboro. (1906) reprint 1992. 724pp. 73.00 F5159

Scituate

Deane, S. History of Scituate from First Settlement to 1831. (1831) reprint 1991. 408pp. 40.00 F5159

Merritt, J.F. A Narrative History of South Scituate/Norwell. (1938) reprint 1987. 203pp. 24.00 F5159

Pratt, H.H. Early Planters of Scituate. A Hist. of the Town of Scituate, from its Establishment to the End of the Rev. War. (1929) reprint 1990. 386pp. 44.00 F5159

Scituate Vital Records to the Year 1850.
    Volume I, Births (1909) 436pp $44.00.
    Volume II, Marriages & Deaths (1926) 473pp $48.00.
    The set: $87.00. All volumes hardcover.   87.00 .... F5159

SUFFOLK COUNTY

Comm. of the Dorchester Antiquarian & Hist. Soc. History of the Town of Dorchester. (1859) reprint 1991. 671pp.	65.00	....	F5159
Drake, F.S. The Town of Roxbury: Its Memorable Persons & Places, Its Hist. & Antiquities, with numerous illus. of its old Landmarks & Noted Personages. (1905) reprint 1987. 475pp.	....	48.00	F5159
Kuhns, Maude P. The "Mary & John": Story of the Founding of Dorchester, 1630. (1943) reprint 1991. 254pp. Authoritative genealogical study on the passengers of the "Mary & John" and their desendants.	32.00	....	F5159
Roxbury Vital Records to the Year 1850. 1992. Volume I, Births (1925) 398pp $43.00. Volume II, Marriages & deaths (1926) 682pp $69.00. **The set: $102.00.** Each volume hardcover.	102.00	....	F5159
Teele, A.K.. The History of Milton, 1640-1887. (1887) reprint 1987. 668pp.	....	68.00	F5159

Boston

Boston Marriages. A Vol. of Records Relating to the Early History of Boston, Containing Boston Marriages, 1752-1809. (1903) reprint 712pp.	71.00	....	F5159
Boston Records: The Statistics of the U.S. Direct Tax of 1798, as Assessed on Boston & the Names of the Inhabitants of Boston in 1790. (1890) reprint 1987. 537pp. As collected for the 1st National Census.	54.00	....	F5159
Bridgman, Thomas. Epitaphs from Copp's Hill Burial Ground, Boston, with Notes. (1851) reprint 252pp.	....	19.00	F5216
Drake, S.G. History & Antiquities of Boston, from its Settlement in 1630 to the Year 1770. (1856) reprint 1987. 840pp. Also, an introducory history of the discovery & settlement of New England.	65.00	....	F5159
Whitmore, W.H. The Graveyards of Boston, First vol: Copp's Hill Epitaphs. (1878) reprint 1987. 116pp.	....	12.50	F5159

WORCESTER COUNTY

Ashburnham Vital Records to the Year 1850. (1909) reprint 1992. 215pp.	27.00	....	F5159
Athol Vital Records to the Year 1850. (1910) reprint 1992. 230pp.	28.00	....	F5159
Bolton Vital Records to the Year 1850. (1910) reprint 1992. 232pp.	27.00	....	F5159
Boylston Vital Records to the Year 1850. (1900) reprint 1991. 124pp.	20.00	....	F5159
Brookfield Vital Records to the Year 1850. (1909) reprint 1992. 549pp.	55.00	....	F5159
Dana Vital Records to the Year 1850. (1925) reprint 1992. 66pp.	15.00	....	F5159

Daniels, G. History of the Town of Oxford. (1892) reprint 1987. 856pp.	....	87.00	F5159
Douglas Vital Records to the Year 1850. (1906) reprint 1992. 192pp.	26.00	....	F5159
Draper, J. History of Spencer, from its Early Settlement to the Year 1860, Incl. a Sketch of Leicester to 1753. (1860) reprint 1987. 276pp.	....	34.00	F5159
Dudley Vital Records to the Year 1850. (1908) reprint 1992. 288pp.	34.00	....	F5159
Emerson, Wm. A. History of the Town of Douglas, From the Earliest Period to the Close of 1878. (1879) reprint 1992. 359pp. With genealogies.	38.50	....	F5159
Ford, Andrew E. History of the Origin of the Town of Clinton, 1653-1865. (1896) reprint 1992. 696pp.	69.50	....	F5159
Grafton Vital Records to the Year 1850. (1906) reprint 1992. 377pp.	42.00	....	F5159
Hardwick Vital Records to the Year 1850. (1917) reprint 1992. 336pp.	36.00	....	F5159
Heywood, W.S. History of Westminster, from 1728 to 1893, with a Biogr. & Gen. Reg. of its Principle Families. (1893) reprint 1987. 963pp.	....	96.00	F5159
History of Worcester County. (1879) reprint 1991. 662+710p. Embracing a Comprehensive History of the Co. from its First Settlement to the Present Time with a History of Cities & Towns. 2 Vols.	....	139.00	F5159
Houghton, William A. History of the town of Berlin, Worcester Co., from 1784 to 1895. (1895) reprint 1992. 584pp. Contains over 200 pages of genealogies.	59.00	....	F5159
Hubbardston Vital Records to the Year 1850. (1907) reprint 1992. 226pp.	27.00	....	F5159
Leominster Vital Records to the Year 1850. (1911) reprint 1992. 369pp.	37.50	....	F5159
Marshall and Cox. Inscriptions from the Burial Grounds of Lunenburg. (1902) reprint 1987. 100pp.	....	11.50	F5159
Marvin, A.P. History of the Town of Lancaster, Mass., from the 1st Settlement to the Present Time, 1643-1879. (1879) reprint 1988. 798pp.	79.00	....	F5159
Mendon Vital Records to the Year 1850. (1920) reprint 1992. 518pp.	52.00	....	F5159
Milford Vital Records to the Year 1850. (1917) reprint 1992. 378pp.	39.50	....	F5159
Millbury Vital Records to the Year 1850. (1903) reprint 1992. 158pp.	21.00	....	F5159
New Braintree Vital Records to the Year 1850. (1904) reprint 163pp.	22.50	....	F5159
Northbridge Vital Records to the Year 1850. (1916) reprint 1992. 202pp.	27.00	....	F5159

Nourse, H.S.   Military Annals of Lancaster, 1740-1865.   (1889)
reprint 1988. 402pp.
    Incl. lists of soldiers who served in the Col. & Rev. Wars
    for Berlin, Bolton, Harvard, Leominster & Sterling.   40.00 .... F5159

Oakham Vital Records to the Year 1850. (1905) reprint 1992.
133pp.   20.00 .... F5159

Oxford Vital Records to the Year 1850. (1905) reprint 1992.
315pp.   35.00 .... F5159

Paige, L.R. The History of Hardwick, Mass., with a gen. register.
(1883) reprint 1988. 555pp.   55.75 .... F5159

Petersham Vital Records to the Year 1850. (1904) reprint 1992.
193pp.   25.00 .... F5159

Phillipston Vital Records to the Year 1850. (1906) reprint 1992.
121pp.   19.00 .... F5159

Pierce, F.C.   History of Grafton, Worcester Co., from Early
Settlement by the Indians in 1647-1879, incl. gen. of 79 Older
Families. (1879) reprint 1987. 623pp.   68.00 .... F5159

Princeton Vital Records to the Year 1850. (1902) reprint 195pp.
    25.00 .... F5159

Records of Oxford, Including Chapters of Nipmuck, Huguenot &
English Hist. from Earliest Date, 1630. (1894) reprint 1991.
429pp. 45.00 F5159

Reed, J. Biographies of the 1st Settlers of Rutland. (1836) reprint
1987. 76pp. 11.00 F5159

_____.   A History of Rutland, Worcester Co., from its Earliest
Settlement, with A Biography of its First Settlers. (1836)
reprint 1992. 168pp.   22.50 .... F5159

Royalston Vital Records to the Year 1850. (1906) reprint
1992. 196pp.   25.00 .... F5159

Rutland Vital Records to the Year 1850. (1905) reprint 1992.
255pp.   28.00 .... F5159

Shrewsbury Vital Records to the Year 1850. (1904) reprint
1992. 282pp.   31.00 .... F5159

Southborough Vital Records to the Year 1850. (1903) reprint
1992. 187pp.   25.00 .... F5159

Spencer Vital Records to the Year 1850. (1909) reprint 1992.
276pp.   31.00 .... F5159

Stackpole, E.S. History of Ashburnham, from 1734-1886, with a
Gen. Register. (1887) reprint 1987. 1,022pp.   92.00 .... F5159

Sturbridge Vital Records to the Year 1850. (1906) reprint
393pp.   41.00 .... F5159

Sutton Vital Records to the Year 1850. (1907) reprint 1992.
478pp.   48.00 .... F5159

Temple, J. History of North Brookfield, with a Genealogical
Register. (1887) reprint 1987. 824pp. 85.00 F5159

Templeton Vital Records to the Year 1850. (1907) reprint
212pp.   26.50 .... F5159

Torrey, R.C. History of the Town of Fitchburg, Comprising also a
History of Lunenburg from its 1st Settlement to the year 1764.
(1865) reprint 1988. 128pp.   21.00   ....   F5159

Upton Vital Records to the Year 1850. (1904) reprint 1992.
190pp.   25.00   ....   F5159

Uxbridge Vital Records to the Year 1850. (1916) reprint 1992.
420pp.   43.00   ....   F5159

Ward, Andrew H. Family Register of the Inhabitants of Shrewsbury,
from its Settlement in 1717 to 1829. (1847) reprint 1991.
294pp. 35.00   F5159

Ward, Esq., Andrew H. History of the Town of Shrewsbury,
Massachusetts From Its Settlement in 1717 to 1829. reprint 530pp.........   32.00   F5216

_____. History of the Town of Shrewsbury, Massachusetts From
Its Settlement in 1717 to 1829. reprint 530pp. 32.00   F5216

Warren Vital Records to the Year 1850. (1910) reprint 1992.
196pp.   25.00   ....   F5159

W. Boylston Vital Records to the Year 1850. (1911) reprint 1992.
153pp.   22.50   ....   F5159

Westborough Vital Records to the Year 1850. (1903) reprint
258pp.   31.00   ....   F5159

Westminster Vital Records to the Year 1850. (1908) reprint 1992.
258pp.   29.50   ....   F5159

Whitcomb and Mayo. Bolton Soldiers & Sailors in the American
Revolution. 1985. 90pp. 16.00   F5216

_____. Inscriptions From Burial Grounds of the Nashaway Towns:
Lancaster, Harvard, Bolton, Leominster, Sterling, Berlin, West
Boylston & Hudson, Mass. 1989. 307pp. 25.00   F5216

Whitney, Peter.   History of the County of Worcester, in the
Commonwealth of Mass. (1793) reprint 1992. 339pp.
with a Particular Account of every Town from its·First
Settlement to the Present Time. 39.00   F5159

Wilder, D. The History of Leominster, or the Northern Half of the
Lancaster New Grant, from 1701 to 1852. (1853) reprint
1987. 263pp.   33.00   ....   F5159

Winchendon Vital Records to the Year 1850. (1909) reprint 1992.
223pp.   27.50   ....   F5159

Michigan

STATEWIDE REFERENCE

Church Records

Burton, Ann and Conrad. Michigan Quakers: Abstracts of 15
    Meetings of the Society of Friends 1831-1960. 1989. 600pp.
        Abstracts of all names, places, locations, events and
        activities found in the known extant records of Friends
        meetings in Michigan.   50.00   ....   F5089

Southwest

Howland, Catherine. A Scrapbook History of Decatur, Michigan.
    1976. 1500pp.
        A compilation of newspaper articles 1829-1976 on
        local/family history of Decatur area including Berrien,
        Cass, Kalamazoo and Van Buren counties and index. 16.00   F5089

ALLEGAN COUNTY

History of Allegan & Barry Counties. (1880) reprint 1990. 521pp.
    With illustrations & biogr. sketches of their prominent
    men & pioneers. 61.50   F5159

CASS COUNTY

Burton, Ann and Conrad. Cass County, Michigan 1870 Census
    Index. 1990. 76pp. 10.00   F5089

GENESEE COUNTY

Powell, Ruth Burr. Fairview Cemetery of Linden, Genesee County,
    Michigan. 1991. 380.
        Tombstone readings of Fairview Cemetery with
        additional data from City Hall records, giving lot and
        grave location, including more complete birth and death
        dates. Family relationships are indicated, where known,
        provided by the Editor. There are 380 pages including
        also an every name index. Soft cover, perfect binding,
        Size, 8.5" x 11. Also, there are 20 pages of historical
        material and seven photos and fifteen maps. 20.00   F5104

Minnesota

DODGE COUNTY

Bowen, Jessie Marsh. A Chronicle of Claremont Township &
   Village. (1937) reprint 1988. 115pp.
      A hist. of Claremont, Dodge Co., MN. 18.50   F5159

WABASHA COUNTY

Lamb, H.E. Gillford. 22pp.
      Biogr. sketch of people buried in the Gillford Cem.,
      Lincoln, Gillford Twp., Wabasha Co., MN. 5.50   F5159

WRIGHT COUNTY

French, C.A. and Frank B. Lamson. Condensed History of Wright
   County, 1851-1935. (1935) reprint 1992. 228pp. 28.00   F5159

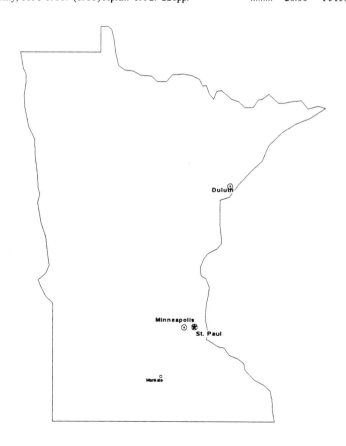

Mississippi

STATEWIDE REFERENCE

King, J. Estelle Stewart. Mississippi Court Records, 1799-1835.
(1936, 1969) reprint 1992. 205pp.
Indexed. 20.00 F5130

Ragland, Mary Lois S. and Vicksburg Genealogical Society.
Spreading the Word: Mississippi Newspaper Abstracts of
Genealogical Interest, 1825-1935. 1991. 249pp. 20.00 F5216

Wiltshire, Betty Couch. Marriages and Deaths from Mississippi
Newspapers. Volume 1, 1837-1863. 1987. 280pp. 20.00 F5216

_____. Marriages and Deaths from Mississippi
Newspapers, Volume 2, 1801-1850. 1988. 330pp. 22.50 F5216

_____. Marriages and Deaths from Mississippi Newspapers,
Volume 3, 1813-1850. 1989. 400pp. 26.00 F5216

_____. Mississippi Confederate Grave Registrations, Names A-L.
1991. 225pp. 18.00 F5216

_____. Mississippi Confederate Grave Registrations, Names M-Z.
1991. 203pp. 17.00 F5216

_____. Mississippi Will Index, 1800-1900. 1989. 212pp.
.... 20.00 F5216

ATTALA COUNTY

Wiltshire, Betty Couch. Attala County, Mississippi Pioneers. 1991.
220pp. 18.00 F5216

CARROLL COUNTY

Wiltshire, Betty Couch. Carroll County, Mississippi, Pioneers: with
Abstracts of Wills, 1834-1875 & Divorces 1857-1875. 1990.
297pp. 22.50 F5216

COPIAH COUNTY

Copiah County, Mississippi Taxpayers, 1825-1841. 1990.
123pp. 12.00 .... F5140

LAFAYETTE COUNTY

Coffey, Walker. Lafayette County (MS) Legacy. 1990. 401pp.
Compilation of the military service records of 1,785 men
who enlisted in the Confederate Army in Lafayette
County. 35.00 F5221

NEWTON COUNTY

Brown, A.J. History of Newton County, Mississippi, from 1834 to
1894. (1894) reprint 500pp. 30.00 F5216

WARREN COUNTY

Ragland, Mary Lois S. Fisher Funeral Home Records, Vicksburg,
  Mississippi, 1854-1867. 1992. 344pp. 27.00   F5216

WILKINSON COUNTY

Wiese, O'Levia Neil Wilson.   The Woodville Republican:
  Mississippi's Oldest Existing Newspaper. Volume 1: Dec. 18,
  1823 - Dec. 17, 1839. 1990. 275pp. 21.50   F5216

_____. The Woodville Republican: Mississippi's Oldest Existing
  Newspaper, Volume 2: Jan. 4, 1840 - Oct. 30, 1847. 1991.
  289pp. 21.00   F5216

YAZOO COUNTY

Roos, Diane Fyans. Yazoo County, Mississippi, 1850 Census &
  Marriages. 1990. 138pp. 20.00   F5216

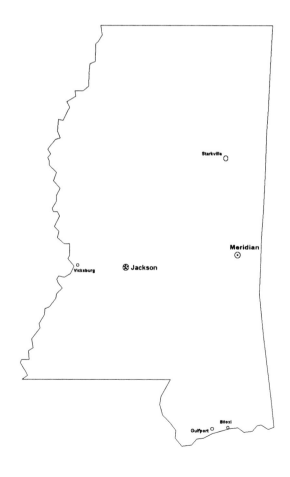

Missouri

STATEWIDE REFERENCE

Directories

The State Historical Society of Missouri. Directory of Local
Historical, Museum and Genealogical Agencies in Missouri.
Biennial. 90+. 6.00 F5182

History

The State Historical Society of Missouri. Historic Missouri: A
Pictorial Narrative. (2nd ed.) reprint 1988. 94pp. 11.45 F5182

Maps & Gazetteers - Bibliographies

1907 Illustrated Historical Atlas. 14x17".
.... 30.00 F5231

The State Historical Society of Missouri and Laurel Boeckman & Pat
B. Weiner (Compilers). Missouri Plat Books in the State
Historical Society of Missouri. Annually. 60+pp.
Bibliography. 5.00 F5182

Military

Bartels, Carolyn. The Civil War in Missouri Day by Day
1861-1865. 8.5x11".
Written in diary style, chronological order, it
encompasses happenings all across Missouri including
Platte County, family names, personal items, names,
places, deaths and burials, citizens caught up in
skirmishes across Missouri. Military units are designated
by name for continuity only. Not a military history but a
record of when and where of people. Great for artifact
hunters. Detailed information on campsites,
crossings, and locations. 17.50 F5231

The State Historical Society of Missouri and Edward Parker,
Compiler. Missouri Union Burials--Missouri Units. 1989.
82pp.
From the U.S. Quartermaster's Department ROLL OF
HONOR lists. 6.00 F5182

_____. and Edward Parker, Compiler. Selected Union
Burials--Missouri Units. 1988. 55pp.
From the U.S. Quartermaster's Department ROLL OF
HONOR lists for states bordering Missouri. 5.00 F5182

Pioneer Families

Bryan, W.S. and R. Rose. A History of the Pioneer Families of
Missouri. (1876) reprint 1984. 569pp.
With numerous sketches, anecdotes, adventures, etc., rel.
to early days in MO. 39.50 F5159

_____. and Robert Rose.   A History of the Pioneer Families of
    Missouri. (1876, 1935) reprint 1992. 586pp.
        Illustrated, indexed. 39.95 F5130

Burgess, Roy.   Early Missourians and Kin: a Genealogical
    Compilation of Inter-related Early Missouri Settlers, their
    Ancestors, Descendants, and Other Kin. (1984) reprint 1987.
    729pp. 40.00 F5216

Campbell, James Brown.   Across the Wide Missouri: the diary of a
    journey from Virginia to Missouri in 1819 and back again in
    1822.   .... 9.95 F5061

Records-Newspapers

Eddlemon, Sherida K. Missouri Genealogical Records & Abstracts,
    Vol. 2, 1752-1839, 40 counties. 1990. 261pp. 20.00 F5216

_____. Missouri Genealogical Records & Abstracts, Vol. 3,
    1787-1839, 43 Counties. 1991. 253pp. 20.00 F5216

The State Historical Society of Missouri. Missouri Newspapers on
    Microfilm at the State Historical Society of Missouri. Annual.
    200+. 12.00 F5182

BATES COUNTY

Christiansen, E. Joyce. Bates County Missouri Births & Deaths
    1883-1886. 1991. 183pp. 19.95 F5139

_____. Bates County, Missouri Cemetery Records. (1980) reprint
    1990. 262pp.
        Re-indexed version. Over 4,500 surnames. 31.95 F5139

_____. Bates County, Missouri Marriages Volume I 1860-1877.
1990. 167pp. 18.95 F5139

_____. Bates County, Missouri Marriages Volume II 1877-1883.
1990. 147pp. 17.95 F5139

_____. Bates County, Missouri Marriages, Volume III 1883-1895.
1990. 278pp. 21.95 F5139

CALLAWAY COUNTY

Eddlemon, Sherida K. Callaway County, Missouri, Marriage
Records: 1821 to 1871. 1991. 154pp. 15.00 F5216

CLAY COUNTY

History Clay-Platte Counties of Missouri, Written & Compiled in
1885 (Incl. biographical & full name index). reprint 1,121pp.
Histories of townships, towns and villages, Pioneer
records, resources, biographical sketches of prominent
citizens. Extended coverage of Civil War in Clay and
Platte Counties. Includes a biographical and full name
index. 50.00 .... F5231

DOUGLAS COUNTY

Weber, Nancie Todd.   1870 Douglas County, Missouri +
Wood-Richland Twp. in Texas County. 1992. 80pp.
1870 census including township temporarily Texas
County jurisdiction. Many spouses, 1860/1880 family
locations, Civil War services cited. Map, indexed. 11.00 F5011

JACKSON COUNTY

Kusek, Joan.   Westport Cumberland Presbyterian Church Records
Volume I (1865-1896). 1989. 198pp.
Births, marriages, deaths, and migratory patterns.
Alexander Majors (Pony Express) and son, John,
mentioned. 19.95 F5139

_____. Westport Cumberland Presbyterian Church Records
Volume II (1897-1908). 1989. 203pp. 19.95 F5139

MORGAN COUNTY

Eddlemon, Sherida K. Morgan County, Missouri, Marriage Records,
1833-1893. 1990. 130pp. 14.00 F5216

NEW MADRID COUNTY

New Madrid County, Missouri Court Orders, 1816-1825. 1990.
89pp.   11.00   ....   F5140

PLATTE CO. MO. HISTORICAL &
GENEALOGICAL SOCIETY
P. O. Box 103, Platte City, MO 64079-0103

Quarterly Magazine *Bulletin*
Dues $12.00/year. No Charge for Research
done at our library for members.

PLATTE COUNTY

1877 Illustrated Historical Atlas of Platte County, Missouri.
14x17". 30.00   F5231

Miller, Gordon. My Heritage & My Life.
A 500 year time-line of history intertwined with Platte
County History and Gordon Miller's family history. 15.00   F5231

Murray, Betty R. 1850 Complete Census Platte County, MO.
400pp. 25.00   F5231

_____. Mortality Schedules 1850-1880 and Register of Deaths as
Filed at the Platte County Clerk's Office 1883-1888.   ....   10.00   F5231

Paxton, W.M.   Annals of Platte County, Missouri, from Its
Exploration Down to June 1, 1897, 2 Vols. (1897) reprint
1,182pp.
With genealogies of its noted families, and sketches of its
pioneers and distinguished people. 70.00   F5216

_____. Annals of Platte County, Missouri (Many Family
Genealogies). (1897) reprint 1,185pp.   48.00   ....   F5231

Platte County Historical Society. Back Issues PCHS "*Bulletin*".
Available for Vol. 37, Spring 1984, #2 through current.
$3.50 each. F5231

Platte County, MO Cemetery Records Volume II.
Send SASE for a list of cemeteries in volume. 15.00   F5231

Welsh, Genrose. Platte County, MO Marriage Records Volume II
1855-1870.   ....   12.00   F5231

_____. Platte County, MO Marriage Records Volume III
1870-1885. 150pp. 12.00   F5231

Welsh, Genrose and Betty Murray and Irma Miller. Platte County,
Missouri Tombstone Inscriptions. 191pp.
As found in cemeteries located in Township 53 North
Range 36 West and Weston Cemetery Sexton Account
1866-1902.   ....   16.00   F5231

Weston Chronicle & Platte City Landmark editors. 1929 Historical
& Genealogical Review of Platte County, MO. 36pp. 6.00   F5231

Whitters, Barbara. 1860 Platte County Census Index.
                                                     ....   12.00   F5231

Woodruff and Hodges. Platte County, MO Marriage Records
     1839-1855. 83pp. 8.00   F5231

TANEY COUNTY

Weber, Nancie Todd. Taney County, Missouri in 1840. 1992-93.
     1840 census included 565 households. Taney's early
     history also Ozark, Christian, Stone, and Douglas
     Counties'. Study aims to identify each citizen, and
     family's residence before 1840, in 1850. Author solicits
     contacts with descendants. F5011

Nebraska

STATEWIDE REFERENCE

History

Lincoln-Lancaster County Genealogical Society. Index for "*A Biographical and Genealogical History of Southeastern Nebraska* - 1904". 1984. 97pp.
> An index to the original two volumes published in 1904 by Lewis Publishing Company. 8.50 F5241

LANCASTER COUNTY

Lincoln-Lancaster County Genealogical Society. An Index to the Early Marriage Records of Lancaster County. Volume I 1866-July 1893. 1986. 296pp.
> The first of projected three volume set which will cover years 1866 through July 1912. .... 16.50 F5241

_____. An Index to the Early Marriage Records of Lancaster County. Volume II July 1893-1906. 1987. 297pp.
> The second of projected three volume set which will cover years 1866 through July 1912. .... 16.50 F5241

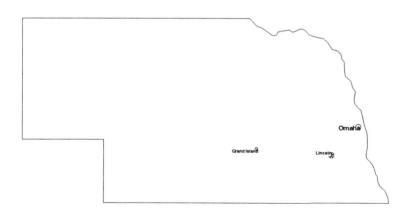

New Hampshire

STATEWIDE REFERENCE

Census

Fipphen, John S. 1798 Direct Tax New Hampshire District #13,.
1989. 106pp.
Consisting of the Towns of Alton, Brookfield, Effingham,
Middleton, New Durham, Ossipee, Tuftonboro,
Wakefield, and Wolfeboro. 17.50 F5216

Threlfall, John Brooks. Heads of Families at the Second Census of
the United States taken in the year 1800:New Hampshire.
(1973) reprint 220pp. 27.50 F5216

The 1790 Census. Heads of Families at the First Census of the
United States Taken in the Year 1790 - New Hampshire.
reprint 1992. 146pp. 21.50 F5129

Genealogies

Tibbetts, Charles W. ed. The New Hampshire Genealogical Record:
An Illustrated Quarterly Magazine Devoted to Genealogy,
History and Biography, 7 Vols. in 4. (1903-1910) reprint
1,400pp. 85.00 F5216

Towle, Gleen C. New Hampshire Genealogical Digest, 1623-1900,
Vol. 1. 1986. 333pp. 22.50 F5216

Towle, Gleen C.and Ann N. Brown. New Hampshire Genealogical
Research Guide. 1983. 98pp. 17.00 F5216

History

Belknap, D.D., Jeremy. The History of New Hampshire, Vol. 1,
Historical Narrative. (1831) reprint 1992. 520pp. 31.50 F5216

Dean, John Ward, Editor and C.W. Tuttle. Captain John Mason,
Founder of New Hampshire. (1887) reprint 1991. 492pp. 49.50 .... F5159

Hammond, Otis G. Hammond's Check List of New Hampshire
History. (1925) reprint 129pp. 15.00 F5216

Maps And Gazetteers

Merrill, Eliphalet and Phinehas Merrill, Esq. Gazetteer of the State
of New Hampshire - 1817. (1817) reprint 251pp. 19.00 F5216

Northern

Dodge, Nancy L. Northern New Hampshire Graveyards &
Cemeteries. 1985. 443pp.
Transcriptions & indexes of burial sites in the towns of
Clarksville, Colebrook, Columbia, Dixville, Pittsburg,
Stewartstown & Stratford. 39.50 F5159

Source Records

Data Indexing Services. Index to "*Colonial Gravestone Inscriptions in State of New Hampshire*; 1913-1942; Compiled by Mrs. Charles Carpenter Goss; 1942". 1992. .... F5209

Hammond, Otis G., et al Probate Records of the Province of New Hampshire, Volumes 1-3.
Vol. 1, 1635-1717, 874pp., $45.00
Vol. 2, 1718-1740, 876pp., $45.00
Vol. 3, 1741-1749, 815pp., $45.00 .... F5216

Oesterlin, Pauline J. New Hampshire Marriage Licenses and Intentions, 1709-1961. 1991. 270pp. 20.00 F5216

White Mountains

Crawford, L. History of the White Mountains from the First Settlement of Upper Coos & Pequaket. (1883) reprint 1991. 230pp. 30.00 .... F5159

Kilbourne, Frederick W. Chronicles of the White Mountains. (1916) reprint 520pp. 20.00 F5216

King, Thomas Starr. The White Hills; Their Legends, Landscape, and Poetry. (1859) reprint 404pp. 25.00 F5216

BELKNAP COUNTY

Hurd, D.H. History of Merrimac & Belknap Counties. (1885) reprint 1987. 915pp. 91.00 F5159

Jewett, J.P. and R.B. Caverly. History of Barnstead, from its First Settlement in 1727 to 1872. (1871) reprint 1990. 271pp. 30.00 F5159

Lancaster, Daniel. History of Gilmanton. (1845) reprint 1990. 304pp.
embracing the...civil, biographical, genealogical & misc. history from the first settlement to the present time, incl. what is now Gilford. 36.50 F5159

Runnels, M.T. History of Sanbornton. (1881) reprint
Vol. I - Annals, 570pp, $57.00;
Vol. II - Genealogies, 1,022pp, $96.00. .... F5159

CARROLL COUNTY

Parker, B.F. History of Wolfeborough. (1901) reprint 1988. 557pp. 57.50 .... F5159

CHESHIRE COUNTY

Bemis, C.A. History of the Town of Marlborough, Cheshire Co. (1881) reprint 726pp.
About one-half this book is a gen. register. 68.00 F5159

Griffin, Gen. Simon G. The History of Keene, NH. (1904) reprint 792pp. 50.00 .... F5216

Hayward, S. The History of the Town of Gilsum, NH, from 1752 to 1879. (1881) reprint 1988. 468pp. 52.00 F5159

History of Dublin, with a Register of Families. reprint 1991. 1,018pp.
The gen. section consists of almost 300 pages. 99.00 F5159

Hurd (Editor), D.H. History of Cheshire & Sullivan Counties. (1886) reprint 1987. 516+409p. 96.00 F5159

Kingsbury, F.B. History of the Town of Surry, Cheshire County. (1925) reprint 1988. 1062pp.
from the Date of Severance from Gilsum & Westmoreland, 1769-1922, with a Gen. Register of the Town. 98.00 F5159

Randall, O.E. History of Chesterfield, Cheshire Co., from 1736 to 1881, with Family Histories. (1882) reprint 1987. 525pp. 53.00 F5159

Read, Benjamin. History of Swanzey, from 1734 to 1890. (1892) reprint 1987. 585pp. 59.50 .... F5159

Rumrill, Alan F. This Silent Marble Weeps: The Cemeteries of Stoddard, New Hampshire. (1990) reprint 1992. 93pp.
Complete gravestone listing with detailed maps, epitaphs, cemetery histories, index. 11.50 F5013

Seward, J.L. A History of the Town of Sullivan, 1777-1917, with Genealogies. (1921) reprint 1987.
Vol. I, 816pp, $80.00.
Vol. II, 800pp, $80.00. .... F5159

Stearns, E.S. History of the Town of Rindge. (1875) reprint 1990. 788pp.
from the Date of the Rowley, Canada or Massachusetts Charter to the Present Time, 1736-1874, with a Genealogical Register. 79.50 F5159

Stone, M.T. Historical Sketch of the Town of Troy & Her Inhabitants, from the 1st Settlement of the Territory Now within the Limits of the Town in 1764-1897. (1897) reprint 1988. 587pp. 59.59 .... F5159

Whitcomb, F.H. A History of the Town of Keene, from 1732 to 1874. (1904) reprint 1987. 792pp. 84.00 F5159

COOS COUNTY

History of Coos County, New Hampshire. (1888) reprint 1992. 956pp. 89.50 .... F5159

Malvesta, Nancy A. Eaton New Hampshire Cemetery Records/With Genealogical Background Material. 1992. 61pp.
Over 800 names most with genealogical background, many compiled from sources other than tombstone readings. Included: brides list and resource listing. 20.00 F519

Somers, A.N. History of Lancaster. (1899) reprint 1987. 652pp.
.... 66.00 F5159

GRAFTON COUNTY

Bittinger, J.Q. The History of Haverhill. (1888) reprint 1988. 443pp. 45.00 F5159

Child, H. Gazetteer of Grafton County, 1709-1886. (1886) reprint
1990.
        Pt. I, History, 644pp, $68.00.
        Pt. II, Business directory, 380pp, $39.50. .... F5159

Downs, C.A. History of Lebanon, 1761-1887. (1908) reprint 1990.
14 + 459pp. 49.50 F5159

Jackson (Editor), James R. History of Littleton, in Three Volumes.
(1905) reprint 1991.
        Vol. I, Annals 771pp $78.00.
        Vol. II, Topical Hist. 733pp $74.00.
        Vol. III, Genealogy (Comp. by G. Furber, ed. by E.
        Stearns, 706pp $71.00.
        Special Price for the Set: $189.00. 189.00 .... F5159

Lord, John King. A History of the Town of Hanover. (1928) reprint
1992. 339pp. 42.50 F5159

Wallace, W.A. and J.B. Wallace (Editor). The History of Canaan.
(1910) reprint 1988. 757pp. 76.00 F5159

HILLSBOROUGH COUNTY

Brown, Ann N. 1850 Hillsborough County, New Hampshire,
Census: Parts 1 and 2. 1992. 625pp. 40.00 F5216

Cochrane, W.R. History of Antrim, from its Earliest Settlement to
1877. (1880) reprint 1987. 791pp. 79.00 F5159

_____. and G.K. Wood. History of Francestown from Earliest
Settlement, 1758-1891. (1895) reprint 1987. 1031pp. 93.00 F5159

Gould, A.A. History of New Ipswich. (1852) reprint 1988. 492pp.
From its First Grant in 1736, with Gen. Notices of the
Principal Families, & the Proceedings of the Centennial
Celebration, Sept. 11, 1850. .... 50.00 F5159

Hayward, W.W. History of Hancock, 1764-1889. (1889) reprint
1987. 1070pp.
        With Gen. Register. 95.00 F5159

Hill, John B. History of the Town of Mason, from its First Grant in
1749 to 1858. (1858) reprint 1992. 324pp.
        Incl. Greenville, NH. 35.00 F5159

The History of Weare, 1735-1888. (1888) reprint 1988.
1,064pp. 106.00 .... F5159

Hurd (Editor), D.H. History of Hillsborough County. (1885) reprint
1989. 748pp. 79.00 F5159

Livermore, A.A. and S. Putnam. History of the Town of Wilton,
Hillsborough Co., with a Gen. Register. (1888) reprint 1988.
575pp. 62.00 .... F5159

Manchester Historic Association. Manchester Historic Association
Collections: Vol. 1, 1896-1899. (1899) reprint 1992. 330pp. 22.50 F5216

_____. Manchester Historic Association Collections: Vol. 2,
1900-1901. (1901) reprint 1992. 310pp. 22.50 F5216

Parker, E.E. The History of Brookline. (1913) reprint 1988.
664pp.
        Formerly Raby, Hillsborough Co., with tables of fam.
        records & genealogies. 71.00 F5159

Ramsdell, G.A. and W.P. Colburn. The History of Milford, with
Family Registers. (1901) reprint 1990. xii+1201. .... 126.50   F5159

Secomb, D.F. History of the Town of Amherst. (1883) reprint
1987. 978pp.
Hillsborough Co., from 1728 to 1882, with Genealogies
of Amherst Families. 95.00   F5159

Smith, Albert. History of the Town of Peterborough, Hillsborough
County. (1876) reprint 1992. 735pp. 74.00   F5159

_____. The History of the Town of Mont Vernon. (1907) reprint
1988. 443pp. 45.00   F5159

Spaulding, C.S. West Dunstable, Monson & Hollis: An acct. of
Some of the Early Settlers. (1915) reprint 1987. 251pp.   34.00   ....   F5159

Webster, K. and G.W. Browne (Editor). The History of Hudson
(1673-1912). (1913) reprint 1988. 648pp.
Formerly a part of Dunstable, Mass., Nottingham, Mass.,
Dist. of Nottingham & Nottingham West. 69.00   F5159

Worcester, S.T. History of the Town of Hollis, from its 1st
Settlement to 1879. (1879) reprint 1987. 394pp. 39.50   F5159

Family Registers. 32pp.
Family Registers only, extr. from "*History of the Town of
Hollis*". Wrprs. F5159

MERRIMACK COUNTY

Bouton, N. History of Concord, from 1725 to 1853. (1856) reprint
1987. 786pp. 79.50   F5159

Cogswell, L.W. History of the Town of Henniker, Merrimac Co.,
NH. (1880) reprint 1988. 807pp.
From the Date of the Canada Grant by the Province of
Mass. in 1735 to 1880, with Gen. Register. 81.00   F5159

Cross, L.H.R. The History of Northfield, 1780-1905, in Two Parts
with Many Biogr. Sketches & Portraits. (1905) reprint 1988.
Pt. I, History, 293pp, $34.00.
Pt. II, Genealogy, 410pp, $45.00. ....   F5159

Dearborn, Adams & Rolfe. The History Salisbury, from Date of
Settlement to 1890. (1890) reprint 1987. 892pp. 89.50   F5159

Eastman, J.R. History of the Town of Andover, 1751-1906, Incl.
Genealogies. (1910) reprint 1987. 450pp. 46.00   F5159

History of the Town of New London, Merrimac Co., 1779-1899.
(1899) reprint 1991. 774pp. 75.00   F5159

Lord, C.C. Life & Times in Hopkinton. (1890) reprint 1992.
583pp.
In three parts: Descriptive & Historical; Personal &
Biographical; Statistical & Documentary. 59.00   F5159

Lyford, J.O. History of the Town of Canterbury, 1727-1912.
(1912) reprint 1990.
Vol. I Narrative xv + 498pp $51.00.
Vol. II Genealogy & Appen. 455pp $47.00. ....   F5159

_____. History of Concord, from the Original Grant in 1725 to the
Opening of the 20th Century. (1903) reprint 1992. 1477pp.
2 volumes. 135.00   F5159

Stark, C. History of the Town of Dunbarton, Merrimack Co., from 1751 to 1860. (1860) reprint 1987. 272pp. 33.00 F5159

Worthen, Mrs. A.H. The History of Sutton, Consisting of the Hist. Collections of Erastus Wadleigh & A.H. Worthen. (1890) reprint 1988.
    2 volumes
    Vol. I, History, 595pp, $59.50.
    Vol. II, Genealogies, 510pp, $53.00. .... F5159

ROCKINGHAM COUNTY

Adams, Nathaniel. Annals of Portsmouth. (1825) reprint 1900. 400pp. 39.00 F5159

_____. Annals of Portsmouth, Comprising a Period of Two Hundred Years from the First Settlement of the Town. (1825) reprint 412pp.
    With biographical sketches of a few of the most respectable inhabitants. 26.50 F5216

Annis, Daniel Gage and George W. Browne. Vital Records of Londonderry, N.H.: A Full and Accurate Transcript of the Births, Marriage Intentions, Marriages and Deaths from Earliest Date to 1910. (1914) reprint 328pp. 23.00 F5216

Bell, Charles H. History of the Town of Exeter, New Hampshire. (1880) reprint 594pp. 40.00 F5216

Brentwood Historical Society. Brentwood's 225 Years, 1742-1967. (1967?) reprint 1990. 120pp. 19.50 F5159

Chase, J.C. History of Chester, Incl. Auburn. Suppl. to History of Old Chester (1869). (1926) reprint 1987. 535pp.
    Genealogies only 110pp wrprs $12.00.
    Cemetery inscrip. only 72pp wrprs $10.00. .... 55.00 F5159

Cogswell, E.C. History of Nottingham, Deerfield & Northwood, Nottingham & Rockingham Cos., with Gen. Sketches. (1878) reprint 1987. 790pp. 79.00 F5159

Eaton, F.B. History of Candia, Once Known as Charmingfare, with Notices of Some of the Early Families. (1852) reprint 1988. 151pp. 21.00 F5159

Fitts, J.H. and N.F. Carter. History of Newfields, 1638-1911. (1912) reprint 1990. 18pp. 5.50 F5159

Getchell, Sylvia Fitts. Tide Turns on the Lamprey - History of Newmarket, NH. 1984. 314pp. 29.00 .... F5004

Gilbert, E. History of Salem, NH. (1907) reprint 1987. 444+160p. 86.00 F5159

Hurd (Editor), D.H. History of Rockingham & Strafford Counties, with Biogr. Sketches of Many of its Prominent Men & Pioneers. (1882) reprint 1987. 889pp. 92.00 F5159

Locke, Arthur. Portsmouth & Newcastle Cemetery Inscriptions: Abstr. from some 2,000 oldest Tombstones. (1907) reprint 1991. 44pp. 9.00 F5159

Mitchell, et al. Exeter and Hampton, NH, 1908 Census and Business Directory. (1908) reprint 290pp. 21.00 F5216

Moore, J.B. History of the Town of Candia, Rockingham Co., from its first settlement to the present time. (1893) reprint 1991.

528pp.	.... 53.00	F5159

Morrison, L.A. The History of Windham, 1719-1883, with the Hist. & Gen. of its 1st Settlers & Desc. (1883) reprint 1987. 862pp.

Includes about 200 families of the 1st settlers.	88.00	F5159

Newfields Marriages & Baptisms, 1717-1909. 18pp.

(From *Hist. of Newfields*, 1912). Wrprs.	.... 5.50	F5159

Noyes, H.E. A Memorial of the Town of Hampstead. Historic & Genealogical Sketches, etc. (1890) reprint 1990. xi+468pp.

	.... 52.00	F5159

_____. Additions & Corrections to the "*Memorial History*". (1903) reprint 1990. 50pp.
    From "Hist. of Congregational Church of Hampstead".

Wrprs., or may be ordered bound with above.	.... 10.00	F5159

Oesterlin, Pauline Johnson. Rockingham County, New Hampshire, Paupers. 1992. 139pp.

	.... 16.50	F5216

Parker, E.L. The History of Londonderry, Comprising the Towns of Derry & Londonderry. (1851) reprint 1988. 418pp.

	.... 43.00	F5159

Parsons, L.B. History of the Town of Rye, 1623-1903. (1905) reprint 1987. 675pp.

	.... 68.00	F5159

STRAFFORD COUNTY

Canney, Robert S. The Early Marriages of Strafford County, New Hampshire, 1630-1850. 1991. 690pp.

	.... 39.50	F5216

Evans, Helen F. Abstracts of the Probate Records of Strafford County, New Hampshire, 1771-1799. 1983. 252pp.

	30.00	F5216

Hardon, Henry Winthrop. Newington, New Hampshire, Families in the Eighteenth Century. 1991. 230pp.

	.... 20.00	F5216

History of Strafford County.
    See under Rockingham. (Hurd).

	.... 92.00	F5159

McDuffee, F. and S. Hayward (Editor). The History of Rochester, from 1722 to 1890. (1892) reprint 1988.
    2 vol. (Index in Vol. II).
    Vol. I 378pp $37.50;

Vol. II 327pp $33.50.	....	F5159

Stackpole, E.S. and L. Thompson. History of the Town of Durham (Oyster River Plantation), with Gen. Notes. (1913) reprint 1990.
    Historical 436pp $45.00.

Genealogical 502pp $52.00.	....	F5159

Dover

Dover Historical Society. Vital Records of Dover, New Hampshire, 1686-1850. (1894) reprint 305pp.

	.... 21.50	F5216

Quint, Rev. Alonzo H. Historical Memoranda Concerning Persons and Places in Old Dover, NH. (1900) reprint 480pp.

	35.00	F5216

Scales, John. Colonial Era History of Dover, NH. (1923) reprint 530pp.

	.... 32.00	F5216

Thompson, Mary P. Landmarks of Ancient Dover, New Hampshire.

(1892) reprint 323pp. 22.50   F5216

SULLIVAN COUNTY

Comm. of the Town. History of Washington, from 1768 to 1886,
    with Gen. (1886) reprint 1987. 696pp.   69.50   ....   F5159

Hist. of Sullivan County.
        See Cheshire County. (Hurd). 96.00   F5159

Merrill, J.L. History of Acworth. (1869) reprint 1988. 306pp.
    With the proceedings of the Centennial Anniversary, Gen.
    Records & Register of Farms. 35.00   F5159

Nelson, W.R. History of Goshen. (1957) reprint 1991. 471pp.
                                                ....   47.00   F5159

Wheeler, Edmund. History of Newport, from 1766 to 1878, with
    Genealogical Register. (1879) reprint 1992. 600pp. 59.50   F5159

New Jersey

STATEWIDE REFERENCE

History & Genealogy

Barber, J.W. and Henry Howe. Historical Collections of the State of
New Jersey. (1844) reprint 1992. 518pp.
Containing a general collection of the most interesting
facts, traditions, biographical sketches, anecdotes, etc.,
relating to its history and antiquities. With a
geographical description of every township. 52.00 .... F5159

_____. Historical Collections of the State of New Jersey. (1845)
reprint 558pp.
Containing a general collection of the most interesting
facts, traditions, biographical sketches, anecdotes, etc.
Relating to the history and antiquities, with geographical
descriptions of every township in the state. Illustrated by
120 engravings. 32.50 F5216

Nelson, William. New Jersey Biographical and Genealogical Notes.
(1916) reprint 1992. 222pp.
Indexed. 21.50 F5130

Nelson (Editor), W. Patents & Deeds & Other Early Records of NJ
1664-1703. (1899) reprint 1982. 770pp. 40.00 .... F5159

Loyalists

Jones, MA, F.R., Alfred. The Loyalists of New Jersey: Their
Memorials, Petitions, Claims, etc. From English Records.
(1927) reprint 346pp. 24.00 F5216

Marriage Records

Nelson (Editor), W. NJ Marriages. Documents Relating to the
Colonial Hist. of NJ: Marriage Records, 1665-1800. (1900)
reprint 1992. 678pp. 55.00 .... F5159

Minisink Valley

New York Genealogical and Biographical Society. Minisink Valley
reformed Dutch Church Records, 1716-1830. (1913) reprint
395pp. 26.00 F5216

Passaic Valley Region

Littell, J. Passaic Valley (And Vicinity) Family Records, or Gen. of
the First Settlers. (1852) reprint 1981. 512pp. 27.50 .... F5159

Whitehead, John. The Passaic Valley in Three Centuries, Past &
Present (2 volumes). 469+528p.
Vol. I History, Vol. II Biography. $49.50/vol. F5159

Religious And Ethnic Groups

Chambers, T.F. Early Germans of NJ, Their History, Churches &
  Gen. (1895) reprint 1991. 667.   39.50   ....   F5159

Haines (Compiler), G. Early Quaker Marriages from Various
  Records in NJ. (1902) reprint 1987. 32pp. 6.50   F5159

Koehler, Albert F. The Huguenots or Early French in New Jersey.
  (1955) reprint 1992. 51pp.
  Indexed. 8.00   F5130

Southern New Jersey

Hoelle, Edith. Genealogical Resources in Southern New Jersey.
  (1980) reprint 1989. 32pp. 4.50   F5215

BERGEN COUNTY

Bergen County, New Jersey Taxpayers, 1777-1797. 1990.
  470pp.   25.00   ....   F5140

Clayton (Ed.), W. Woodford and William Nelson. History of Bergen
  & Passaic Counties, with Biographical Sketches of Many of its
  Pioneers & Prominent Men. (1882) reprint 1992. 570pp.   62.00   ....   F5159

BURLINGTON COUNTY

Woodwrad, E.M. and J.F. Hageman. History of Burlington &
  Mercer Counties, with Biogr. Sketches of its Pioneers &
  Prominent Men. (1887) reprint 1988. 888pp.   97.00   ....   F5159

CAPE MAY COUNTY

Howe, P.S. Cape May Co., NJ, Mayflower Pilgrim Desc. (1921)
  reprint 1977. 464pp.   27.50   ....   F5159

ESSEX COUNTY

Brown, Virginia Alleman. New Jersey Heirs to Estates From
  Partitions and Divisions. Essex County, 1793-1881. 1981.
  168pp.
  Indexed. 16.00   F5130

Shaw (Comp.), William H. History of Essex & Hudson Counties.
  (1884) reprint 1992.
    Vol. I Essex County 678pp $68.00.
    Vol. II Hudson County 734pp $74.00.
    Special price for set $135.00 hardbound.   135.00   ....   F5159

New Jersey Hist. Society. Records of the Town of Newark, New
  Jersey, from Its Settlement in 1666 to Its Incorporation as a
  City in 1836. (1864) reprint 294pp. 21.00   F5216

Wickes, Stephen. History of the Oranges, in Essex County. (1892)
  reprint 1992. 334pp.   36.50   ....   F5159

_____. History of the Oranges in Essex County, NJ from 1666 to
  1806. (1892) reprint 334pp. 22.50   F5216

CUMBERLAND COUNTY

Shourds, Thomas.   History & Genealogy of Fenwick's Colony.
(1876) reprint 1992. 581pp.
    Contains many fam. histories from this colony, which
    comprised one-tenth of western New Jersey.   49.00 .... F5159

GLOUCESTER COUNTY

Baker (Transcriber), Ruthe.   The Diaries of Samuel Mickle
Woodbury, Gloucester County, New Jersey 1792-1829 (2
Volumes). 1991. 481+465p.
    A monumental work of almost four decades of U.S.
    history. Includes thousands of deaths and marriages,
    national events, epidemics, recollections of the revolution,
    War of 1812, hangings, etc. 63.00 F5215

Hammell, Jeanne M.   South Jersey Church Records Baptisms,
Marriages, Deaths 1750-1900 Vol. I. 1990.
    Vital statistics from 17 South Jersey churches in this first
    volume of a planned series. 19.00 F5215

HUDSON COUNTY

Harvey (Comp.), Cornelius B. Genealogical History of Hudson &
Bergen Counties. (1900) reprint 1992. 617pp.   61.50 .... F5159

Shaw, William H. History of Essex & Hudson Counties. Volume II
Hudson County. (1884) reprint 1992. 734pp.
    See Essex County.   74.00 .... F5159

Versteeg, Dingman and Thomas Vermilye, Jr.   BERGEN
RECORDS: Records of the Reformed Protestant Dutch Church
of Bergen in New Jersey, 1666 to 1788. (1913) reprint 1990.
3 volumes (1913-1915) in 1, reprinted 1990. Illustrated,
indexed.   23.50 .... F5130

Winfield, C.H. History of Hudson Co., from Earliest Settlement to
the Present Time. (1874) reprint 1990. 568pp.   62.50 .... F5159

HUNTERDON COUNTY

Cooley, Eli F. and William S. Cooley. Genealogy of Early Settlers in
Trenton and Ewing, "Old Hunterdon County", New Jersey.
(1883) reprint 1992. 336pp.
    Indexed. 29.50 F5130

_____. Gen. of Early Settlers in Trenton & Ewing, "Old Hunterdon
County," NJ. (1883) reprint 1990. 336pp.
    Over 60 family histories are provided.   34.00 .... F5159

Hunterdon County, New Jersey Taxpayers, 1778-1797. 1990.
203pp.   14.00 .... F5140

Snell, James P.   History of Hunterdon & Somerset Cos., with
Illustrations & Biogr. Sketches of its Prominent Men &
Pioneers. (1881) reprint 1992. 864pp.   87.50 .... F5159

MERCER COUNTY

Raum, John O. History of the City of Trenton, Embracing a Period
of Nearly 200 Years. (1871) reprint 1992. 448pp.　　49.50　........　F5159

MIDDLESEX COUNTY

Brown, Virginia Alleman. New Jersey Heirs to Estates From
Partitions and Divisions. Middlesex County, 1780-1870.
1988. 107pp.
Indexed.　　........　16.00　F5130

Whitehead, W.A. Contributions to the Early History of Perth Amboy
& Adjoining Country. (1856) reprint 1991. 428pp.
With sketches of men and events in NJ during the
Provincial Era.　　45.00　........　F5159

MONMOUTH COUNTY

Ellis, Franklin. History of Monmouth County. (1885) reprint 1992.
902pp.　　89.50　........　F5159

Gibson, George and Florence Gibson. Marriages of Monmouth
County, New Jersey, 1795-1843. (1981) reprint 1992.
143pp.
Indexed.　　........　16.50　F5130

Hornor, W.S. This Old Monmouth of Ours: History, Tradition,
Biogr., Gen., Anecdotes rel. to Monmouth Co. (1932) reprint
1991. 444pp.
Genealogical section treats almost 100 early families.　　35.00　........　F5159

_____. This Old Monmouth of Ours. (1932) reprint 1990.
444pp.
Indexed　　35.00　........　F5130

Salter, Edwin. History of Monmouth & Ocean Counties. (1890)
reprint 1990. 510pp.
Includes an 80-page genealogical register.　　52.50　........　F5159

MORRIS COUNTY

Brown, Virginia Alleman. New Jersey Heirs to Estates From
Partitions and Divisions. Morris County, 1785-1900. 1992.
357pp.
Indexed.　　........　28.50　F5130

History of Morris County, with Illustrations & Biographical Sketches
of Prominent Citizens & Pioneers. (1882) reprint 1992.
407pp.　　43.50　........　F5159

Sherman, Andrew M. Historic Morristown, New Jersey: the story of
its first century. (1905) reprint 564pp.　　........　35.00　F5216

Wheeler, William Ogden and Edmund D. Halsey. Inscriptions on the
Tomb Stones and Monuments in the Grave Yards at Whippany
& Hanover, Morris Cty., NJ. (1894) reprint 1992. 93pp.　　........　12.00　F5216

SALEM COUNTY

Baker (Transcriber), Ruthe.   The Diaries of Samuel Mickle
    Woodbury, Gloucester County, New Jersey 1792-1829 (2
    Volumes). 1991. 481+465p.
        See description under Gloucester County. 63.00   F5215

Gibson, Florence H.   Salem County, New Jersey Census 1860.
    1991. 659pp.
        Contains over 19,500 names -- an excellent source of
        South Jersey statistics. 32.50   F5215

Shourds, T. (Salem Co.) Hist. & Genealogy of Fenwick's Colony.
    (1876) reprint 1991. 581pp. 39.50   ....   F5159

_____. History and Genealogy of Fenwick's Colony [N.J.]. (1876)
    reprint 1991. 581pp.
        Illustrated, indexed. 32.50   ....   F5130

SUSSEX COUNTY

Brown, Virginia Alleman.   New Jersey Heirs to Estates From
    Partitions and Divisions. Warren & Sussex Counties,
    1789-1918. 1992. 167pp.
        Indexed. 25.00   F5130

Gibbs, Whitfield. One Hundred Years of the "Sussex Register" and
    County of Sussex, NJ, 1813-1913: Record of Historical,
    Biographical, Industrial, and Statistical Events. (1913) reprint
    108pp. 18.00   F5216

History of Sussex & Warren Cos., with Illustrations & Biographical
    Sketches of Prominent Men & Pioneers. (1881) reprint 1992.
    748pp.
        Illustrations included. 81.00   ....   F5159

UNION COUNTY

Hatfield, Edwin F. History of Elizabeth, incl. the Early History of
    Union Co. (1868) reprint 1990. 701pp. 71.00   ....   F5159

Murray, Rev. Dr. Nicholas.   Notes, Historical and Biographical,
    Concerning Elizabeth-Town, Its Eminent Men, Churches, and
    Ministers. (1844) reprint 180pp. 17.50   F5216

WARREN COUNTY

Brown, Virginia Alleman.   New Jersey Heirs to Estates From
    Partitions and Divisions. Warren & Sussex Counties,
    1789-1918. 1992. 167pp.
        Indexed. 25.00   F5130

New Mexico

SIERRA COUNTY

Sierra County Genealogical Society.   Sierra County New Mexico
   Cemetery Records Vol. I. 1987. 100pp.
   Hot Springs Cemetery, 1907-1980, Truth or
   Consequences, NM. Deaths in Sierra County, Index to
   City Hall Card File, Headstone Recordings. 17.50   F5243

_____. Sierra County New Mexico Marriage Records Vol. I
   1884-1920. 1990. 94pp. 24.00   F5243

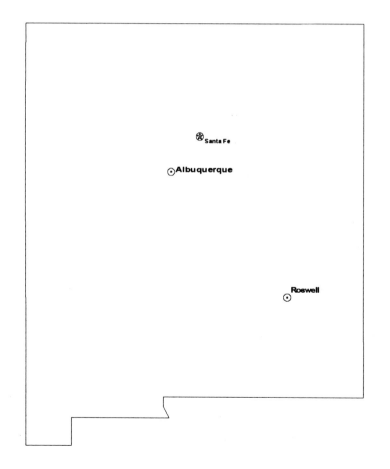

New York

STATEWIDE REFERENCE

General Reference

Evjen, John O. Scandinavian Immigrants in New York, 1630-1674. (1916) reprint 1992. 24+438pp. 45.50 .... F5159

Fernow, Berthold. [New York] Calendar of Wills. (1896) reprint 1991. 672pp.
On File and Recorded in the Office of the Clerk of the Court of Appeals, of the County Clerk at Albany, and of the Secretary of State, 1626-1836. Indexed. 49.95 .... F5130

Haller, Dolores and Marilyn Robinson. Genealogical Gleanings from the Christian Advocate and Journal and Zion's Herald, September 1827-August 1831. 1989. 595pp. 35.00 F5216

Jameson, Ph.D., LL.D. ed., J. Franklin. Narratives of New Netherlands, 1609-1664. (1909) reprint 478pp. 30.00 F5216

Mather, Frederic Gregory. The Refugees of 1776 from Long Island to Connecticut. (1913) reprint 1,204pp. 60.00 F5216

Scott, Kenneth and Rosanne Conway. New York Alien Residents, 1825-1848. (1978) reprint 1991. 122pp. 18.00 .... F5130

Baptismal & Marriage Records

Hoes, R.R. Baptismal & Marriage Registers of the Old Dutch Church of Kingston, Ulster Co., For 150 Years from their Commencement in 1660. (1891) reprint 1988. 797pp. 78.00 .... F5159

Mather, James P. Index to Marriages and Deaths in The New York Herald, Volume I: 1835-1855. 1987. 560pp. 26.50 .... F5130

_____. Index to Marriages and Deaths in The New York Herald, Volume II: 1856-1863. 1991. 685pp. 40.00 .... F5130

Census

Heads of Families at the First Census of the US taken in the Year 1790. (1908) reprint 1990. 308pp. 30.00 F5159

The 1790 Census. Heads of Families at the First Census of the United States Taken in the Year 1790 - New York. reprint 1992. 308pp. 35.00 F5129

Eastern

Bowman, Fred Q. 8,000 More Vital Records of Eastern New York State 1804-1850. 1991. 296pp. 24.00 .... F5040

Hudson Valley

Herrick, Margaret E. Death Notices, Dutchess and Columbia County New York 1859-1918. 1991. 321pp. 56.00 .... F5040

_____. Marriage Notices, Dutchess and Columbia County, New
York 1859-1936. 1991. 206pp.   38.00   ....   F5040

Ptak, Diane Snyder. Cast in Stone: Selected Albany, Rensselaer and
Saratoga County, New York Burials. 1990. 169pp.   35.00   ....   F5040

Specializing in the Mohawk and Hudson Valley Areas
Genealogical and Historical
Research - N.Y.S.
21 Years Experience
Violet Dake Fallone
Box 223, Mills Terrace, Fonda, NY 12068-0223
Phone: (518) 853-4045

Maps, Gazetteers, Place Names

Gordon, T.F. Gazetteer of the State of New York, Comprehending
its Colonial History; General Geogr., Geology, Internal
Improvements; Its Political State;. (1836) reprint 1990.
800pp.
Minute Desc. of its Several Counties, Towns & Villages;
Statistical Tables.   80.00   ....   F5159

Nestler, Harold. A Bibliography of New York State Communities,
third edition. 1990. 301pp. 21.50   F5216

Military

De Lancey, ed., Edward F. Muster Rolls of New York Provincial
Troops, 1755-1764. (1892) reprint 622pp. 36.00   F5216

New York in the Revolution as Colony & State. (1904) reprint
1987. 533pp.   53.50   ....   F5159

Mohawk Valley

Daily, W.N.P. (Mohawk Valley) History of Montgomery Classis, to
which is Added Sketches of Mohawk Val. Men & Events of
Early Days, etc. (1915?) reprint 1991. 198pp.
The "classis" is the regional organisation of the Dutch
Reformed Church. This hist. of the Church and the
region also contains valuable genealogical & biogr.
information about early families. in the area. 22.50   F5159

Penrose, C.G., A.S.I., Maryly B. Compendium of Early Mohawk
Valley Families. 1990. 1,173pp.
2 volume set with a foreward by Henry (Hank) Z.
Jones, Jr. Cross-indexed.   75.00   ....   F5129

Reid, W. Max. The Mohawk Valley: Its Legends and Its History.
(1901) reprint 456pp.   35.00   ....   F5216

Northern New York

Sylvester, Nathaniel B. Historical Sketches of Northern New York
and the Adirondack Wilderness. (1877) reprint 316pp.
Including traditions of the Indians, early explorers,
pioneers settlers, hermit hunters, etc. 22.00   F5216

Ohio Valley Region

Hanna, C.A. Ohio Valley Genealogies. Relating Chiefly to Families in Harrison, Belmont & Jefferson Cos., OH & Washington, Westmoreland & Fayette Cos., PA. (1900) reprint 1990. 172pp. 17.50   F5159

Pioneers

Earle, Alice Morse. Colonial Days in Old New York. (1896) reprint 312pp. 22.00   F5216

Simms, Jeptha R. The Frontiersman of New York, Showing Customs of the Indians, Vicissitudes of Pioneer White Settlers & Border Strife in Two Wars, with a Great Variety of Romantic & Thrilling Stories. (1883) reprint 1992. 712+759p.   135.00   ....   F5159

Source Records

Fernow, Berthold. [NY]Calendar of Wills On File & Recorded in the Offce of the Clerk of the Crt of Appeals, of the Co. Clerk at Albany, & of the Sec of State,1626-1836. (1896) reprint 1991. 672pp.
      Indexed.   49.95   ....   F5130

Southern Tier

Hitt, Jr., C.G., Maurice R. Genealogical Gleanings From Early Broome County, New York Newspapers 1812-1880. 1992. 521pp. 45.00   F5147

Western New York

Livsey, Karen E. Western New York Land Transactions, 1804-1824, Extracted from the Archives of the Holland Land Company. 1991. 472pp.   35.00   ....   F5129

Turner, Orsamus. Pioneer History of the Holland Purchase of Western New York. (1849) reprint 740pp. 40.00   F5216

ALBANY COUNTY

Pearson, J. (Albany) Contributions for the Genealogies of the 1st Settlers of the Ancient Co. of Albany, from 1630 to 1800. (1872) reprint 1987. 182pp.   18.50   ....   F5159

Scott, Kenneth. New York: State Census of Albany County Towns in 1790. (1975) reprint 1991. 68pp. 8.50   F5130

Weise, A.J. History of the City of Albany, from the Discovery of the
Great River in 1524, by Verrazzano, to the Present Time.
(1884) reprint 1988. 528pp.   53.00   ....   F5159

BROOME COUNTY

History of Broome Co. (1885) reprint 1991. 630pp.
          With illustrations & biogr. sketches of some of its
          prominent men & pioneers.   64.50   ....   F5159

BROOKLYN
See New York City

CATTARAUGUS COUNTY

History of Cattaraugus Co., with Illustrations & Biogr. Sketches of
some of its Prominent Men & Pioneers. (1879) reprint 1991.
512pp.
          Includes hundreds of illustrations of landmarks,
          businesses & homes.   61.50   ....   F5159

CAYUGA COUNTY

History of Cayuga Co., with Illustrations & Biogr. Sketches of some
of its Prominent Men & Pioneers. (1879) reprint 1991.
556pp.
          With hundreds of illustrations of landmarks, businesses &
          homes of the county.   65.50   ....   F5159

Monroe, J.H. Historical Records of a Hundred and Twenty Years -
Auburn, NY. (1913) reprint 1992. 278pp.   32.50   ....   F5159

CHAUTAUQUA COUNTY

Hazeltine, G.W. Early History of the Town of Ellicott, (Part of
Johnstown) Chautauqua Co. (1887) reprint 1992. 556pp.   56.00   ....   F5159

Young, Andrew W. History of Chautauqua Co., from its First
Settlement to the Present Time. (1875) reprint 1992. 672pp.   69.00   ....   F5159

_____. History of Chautauqua County, NY, from Its Earliest
Settlement to the Present; with Numerous Biographical and
Family Sketches. (1875) reprint 740pp. 40.00   F5216

**5
County
Research**

**Tompkins, Cortland, Schuyler
Cayuga, Chemung
953 Ridge Rd. Lansing, NY 14882
CGRS**

CHEMUNG COUNTY

History of Tioga, Chemung, Tompkins & Schuyler Counties, with
   Illustrations & Biogr. Sketches of its Prominent Men &
   Pioneers. (1879) reprint 1991. 687pp.
      See "Tioga County".   78.50   ....   F5159

CHENAGO COUNTY

Galpin, Henry J. Annals of Oxford. (1906) reprint 1992. 568pp.
                                                       57.00   ....   F5159

COLUMBIA COUNTY

Divine, A.L. Columbia County, NY Gravestone Inscriptions with
   Guide to Interpretation and Index. 1991.   .... F5040

History of Columbia Co., with Illustrations & Biogr. Sketches of
   Some Prominent Men & Pioneers. (1878) reprint 1990.
   447pp.
      Includes maps & illust. 65.00   F5159

CORTLAND COUNTY

Goodwin, H.C. Pioneer History of Cortland Co., & the Border Wars
   of NY, from the Earliest Period. (1859) reprint 1992. 456pp. 46.00   ....   F5159

DUTCHESS COUNTY

Buck, Clifford M. Dutchess County, New York Tax Lists with
   Rombout Precinct by William W. Reese. 1990. 305pp. 55.00   ....   F5040

Dutchess County Genealogical Society. The 1810 Census, Dutchess
   County, New York. (1978) reprint 1990. 91pp.   20.00   ....   F5040

Hunting, I. Dutchess Co. Hist. of "Little 9 Partners" of the NE
   Precinct & Pine Plains. (1897) reprint 1987. 411pp. 41.00   ....   F5159

ERIE COUNTY

Johnson, Crisfield. Centennial History of Erie County, Being its
   Annals from the Earliest Recorded Events to the Hundreth Year
   of American Independence. (1876) reprint 1992. 512pp. 53.00   ....   F5159

White (Editor), Truman C. Our County & Its People: A Descriptive
   Work on Erie County.
      2 volumes.
      Vol. I History 906pp $91.00;
      Vol.II Biography & "Personal References" 617pp $62.00.
      Complete set $145.00. All hardcover.   145.00   ....   F5159

ESSEX COUNTY

Watson, Winslow C. Military & Civil History of the County of
   Essex. (1869) reprint 1992. 504pp.   51.00   ....   F5159

GREENE COUNTY

History of Greene Co., with Biogr. Sketches of its Prominent
   Men. (1884) reprint 1982. 462pp.   56.00   ....   F5159

JEFFERSON COUNTY

History of Jefferson Co., with Illustrations & Biogr. Sketches of some of its Prominent Men & Pioneers. (1878) reprint 1991. 593pp.   68.50 .... F5159

Hough, F.B. Hist. of Jefferson County from the Earliest Period to the Present Time (1854). (1854) reprint 1988. 601pp.   61.00 .... F5159

Hough, A.M., M.D., Franklin B. A History of Jefferson County in the State of New York from the Earliest Period to the Present Time. (1854) reprint 1992. 602pp. 35.00   F5216

LIVINGSTON COUNTY

History of Livingston County, from its Earliest Traditions to its Part in the War for our Union: with an Acct. of Senena Nation of Indians. (1876) reprint 1991. 685pp.   68.00 .... F5159

MONROE COUNTY

Peck, William F. History of Rochester & Monroe Co., from Earliest Historic Times to the Beginning of 1907. (1908) reprint 1992. 1,434pp.   109.00 .... F5159

MONTGOMERY COUNTY

Davenport, Dr. David Paul. The 1855 Census of Montgomery County, New York, an Index. 1989. 314pp.   38.00 .... F5040

Keefer, Donald A. Records of the First Reformed Protestant Dutch Church of the Town of Glen. 1990. 106pp.   25.00 .... F5040

_____. Records of the First Reformed Protestant Dutch Church, Town of Amsterdam. 1991. 62pp. 13.50   F5040

NASSAU COUNTY

Mallmann, Rev. Jacob E. Historical Papers on Shelter Island (New York) and Its Presbyterian Church with Genealogical Tables. (1899) reprint 350pp. 25.00   F5216

NEW YORK CITY

Evans, Thomas G. and Tobias A. Wright, eds. Baptisms in the Dutch Church, New York, 1639-1800 (2 Vols). (1991) reprint 1968. 1,298pp.   100.00 .... F5070

Riker, James and Rev. by H.P. Toler. Revised History of Harlem (City of NY); Its Origins & Early Annals; Also Sketches of Numerous Families. (1904) reprint 1990. 908pp.   92.50 .... F5159

Scott, Kenneth. Coroner's Reports, New York City, 1843-1849. 1991. 320pp.
Abstracts of inquests on 5,000 unusual deaths.   25.75 .... F5070

_____. Naturalizations in the Marine Court, New York City, 1827-1835. 1990. 192pp.   20.00 .... F5070

_____. Naturalizations in the Marine Court, New York City, 1834-1840. 1991. 192pp.   20.00 .... F5070

Stiles, H.R.   A History of the City of Brooklyn. (1869) reprint
1987.
Including the Old Town & Village of Brooklyn, the
Town of Bushwick & the Village & City of
Williamsburgh.
Vol. I 464pp $49.50;
Vol. II 500pp $49.50;
Vol. III 485pp $49.50.   ....   F5159

_____.   King's Co. Civil, Political, Prof. & Ecclesiastical Hist. &
Commercial & Industrial Record of the Co. of King's & the
City of Brooklyn, 1683-1884. (1884) reprint 1987.
Vol. I   632pp $65.00;
Vol. II 770pp $79.00.   ....   F5159

Long Island

Bunker, M.P.   Long Island Genealogies, Being Kindred Desc. of
Thomas Powell of Bethpage, LI, 1688. (1895) reprint 1988.
350pp.   48.00   ....   F5159

_____.   Long Island Genealogies. (1895) reprint 1990. 350pp.
Indexed   28.50   ....   F5130

Howell, MA, George Rogers. The Early History of Southampton,
L.I., New York, with Genealogies. (1887) reprint 473pp. 29.00   F5216

Jacobson, Judy. Southold Connections, Historical and Biographical
Sketches of Northeastern Long Island. 1991. 113pp.
Maps, indexed. 16.50   F5130

Whitaker, D.D., Rev. Epher. History of Southold, L.I.: Its First
Century. (1881) reprint 362pp. 24.50   F5216

ONEIDA COUNTY

History of Oneida County, with Illustrations & Biographical
Sketches of Some of its Prominent Men & Pioneers. (1878)
reprint 1992. 678pp.   69.50   ....   F5159

Pioneer History of Camden, Oneida County. (1897) reprint
1992. 559pp.   56.00   ....   F5159

Rogers, H.C.   History of the Town of Paris & the Valley of the
Sauquoit: Anecdotes & Reminiscences. (1881) reprint 1992.
398pp.   41.00   ....   F5159

Wager (Ed.), Daniel. Our County & Its People: A Descriptive Work
on Oneida County. (1896) reprint 1991.
Pts. I & II History & Biography 636-215pp $88.00;
Pt. III Family Sketches 411pp $44.00.
Special Price for Set: $125.00 hardcover.   125.00   ....   F5159

ONONDAGA COUNTY

Beauchamp, S.T.D., Rev. W.M. Revolutionary Soldiers Resident or
Dying in Onondaga County, NY, with Supplementary List of
Possible Veterans. (1912) reprint 307pp. 22.00   F5216

ORANGE COUNTY

Coleman, Charles C. The Early Records of the First Presbyterian
    Church at Goshen, New York from 1757 to 1885. (1934)
    reprint 216pp. 17.50 F5216

_____. The Early Records of the First Presbyterian Church at
    Goshen, New York, From 1767 to 1885. (1933) reprint 1990.
    215pp.
        Indexed. 18.00 .... F5130

Ruttenber, E.M. and L.H. Clark. History of Orange County, with
    Illustrations & Biographical Sketches of many of its Pioneers &
    Prominent Men. (1881) reprint 1992. 820pp.
        2 volumes in one. 59.00 .... F5159

ORLEANS COUNTY

Thomas, Arad. Pioneer History of Orleans County. (1871) reprint
    1990. 463pp. 49.00 .... F5159

OSWEGO COUNTY

History of Oswego Co., with Illustrations & Biogr. Sketches of some
    of its Prominent Men & Pioneers. (1877) reprint 1991.
    450pp. 54.50 .... F5159

OTSEGO COUNTY

History of Otsego Co., with Illustrations & Biogr. Sketches of some
    of its Prominent Men & Pioneers. (1878) reprint 1991.
    378pp. 47.50 .... F5159

PUTNAM COUNTY

Buys, B.A., M.A., C.A.L.S., Barbara Smith. Old Gravestones of
    Putnam County, New York. (1975) reprint 369pp.
        11,800 inscriptions of people born through 1850. Maps
        show locations of 79 grounds. Also includes 10 adjacent
        Dutchess County grounds. Smyth sewn. 58.50 .... F5052

Greene, Marilyn Cole. Town Minutes, Town of Carmel, Putnam
    County, New York, 1795-1839. 1990. 183pp. 26.90 .... F5040

QUEENS COUNTY

Hood, Anthony. "Queens County Sentinel", Queens County, New York:Index of Birth, Marriage and Death Announcements, 1858-1878. 1991. 123pp. 13.50 F5216

Riker, James. Annals of Newtown, Queen's County, Containing its History from its Settlement, Together with Many Interesting Facts Concern. Adjacent Towns/Genealog. (1852) reprint 1992. 437pp. 44.50 .... F5159

RENSSELAER COUNTY

Anderson, George Baker. Landmarks of Rensselaer County. (1897) reprint 1992. 570+460p.
Includes over 400 pages of family sketches. 98.50 .... F5159

Sylvester, Nathaniel Bartlett. History of Rensselaer Co., with Illustrations & Biogr. Sketches of its Prominent Men & Pioneers. (1880) reprint 1992. 564pp. 58.00 .... F5159

RICHMOND COUNTY

Clute, J.J. Annals of Staten Island. (1877) reprint 1992. 464pp.
46.50 .... F5159

_____. Old Families of Staten Island. (1877) reprint 1990. 103pp. 15.00 .... F5130

ROCKLAND COUNTY

Cole (Ed.), David. History of Rockland Co., with Biographical Sketches of its Prominent Men. (1908) reprint 1992. 420pp. 49.50 .... F5159

ST. LAWRENCE COUNTY

Sanord, C.E. Early History of the Town of Hopkinton. (1903) reprint 1991. 604pp.
Includes genealogies of 60 pioneer families. 65.00 .... F5159

SARATOGA COUNTY

Cemeteries of the Town of Half Moon, Saratoga Co. (1963) reprint 1990. 74pp. 14.00 F5159

SCHENECTADY COUNTY

Pearson, J. Contrib. for the Gen. of the Desc. of the First Settlers of the Patent & City of Schenectady from 1662-1800. (1873) reprint 1992. 324pp. 29.50 F5159

SCHOHARIE COUNTY

Partridge, Virginia P. and Susan F. Watkins. Transcript of the 1800, 1810 & 1820 Federal Census of Schoharie County, New York. 1991. .... F5040

_____. and Susan F. Watkins. Transcript of the 1830 and 1840 Federal Census of Schoharie County, New York. 1991. 350pp. 69.95 .... F5040

Simms, Jeptha R. History of Schoharie County and the Border Wars
of New York. (1845) reprint 700pp.
Containing also a sketch of the causes which led to the
American Revolution and interesting memoranda of the
Mohawk Valley. 40.00 F5216

STEUBEN COUNTY

Martin, Yvonne E. Marriages & Deaths from Steuben County, New
York, Newspapers, 1797-1868. 1988. 140pp. 14.50 F5216

SULLIVAN COUNTY

Quinlan, J.E. History of Sullivan County, Embracing an Acct. of its
Geology, Settlement, Towns, with Biogr. Sketches of
Prominent Residents, etc. (1873) reprint 1990. 700pp. 69.50 .... F5159

TIOGA COUNTY

History of Tioga, Chemung, Tompkins & Schuyler Counties, with
Illustrations & Biogr. Sketches of some of their Prominent Men
& Pioneers. (1879) reprint 1991. 687pp. 78.50 .... F5159

Gay, W.B. Historical Gazetteer, 1785-1888, and Directory,
1887-1888, of Tioga County, New York. (1887) reprint
820pp. 47.00 F5216

TOMPKINS COUNTY

Lewis, Helen F. New York's Finger Lakes Pioneer Families
Especially Tompkins County, A Genealogical Notebook.
1991. 409pp. 69.95 .... F5040

ULSTER COUNTY

Clearwater (Ed.), Alphonso T. History of Ulster County (With
Illustrations). (1907) reprint 1992. 707pp. 72.50 .... F5159

Klinkenberg, Audrey M. Obituaries, Death Notices, and
Genealogical Gleanings from The Saugerties Telegraph.
1989. 160pp. 16.00 F5216

LeFevre, Ralph. History of New Paltz & its Old Families, from 1678
to 1829. (1903) reprint 1992. 592pp. 59.50 .... F5159

Sylvester, N.B. Hist. of Ulster Co., with Illustrations & Biogr.
Sketches of its Prominent Men & Pioneers. (1880) reprint
1988. 310+340p. 74.50 .... F5159

Versteeg, trans., Dingman. Records of the Reformed Dutch Church
of New Paltz, New York. Containing... Registers of
Consistories, Members, Marriages, and Baptisms. (1896)
reprint 1992. 269pp.
Indexed. 22.50 F5130

WASHINGTON COUNTY

Compiled by Historical Data Services. Cemetery Records of The
Township of Fort Ann, Washington Co., New York. 1992.
120pp.
    Indexed. Add $2.00 postage. 8-1/2 x 11 spiral bound. 17.00   F5151

_____. Cemetery Records of The Township of Hampton,
Washington Co., New York. 1992. 32pp.
    8-1/2 x 11 Spiral Bound Indexed. Add $1.25 postage. 7.50   F5151

_____. Cemetery Records of The Township of Whitehall,
Washington Co., New York. 1992. 208pp.
    Records from all known cemeteries with directions.
    Includes 3 maps. Indexed. Add $2.50 postage. 25.00   F5151

Patten, Jennie M. The Argyle Patent and Accompanying Documents.
(1928) reprint 1991. 68pp. 9.00   F5130

WESTCHESTER COUNTY

Baird, C.W. Rye. Chronicle of a Border Town: History of Rye,
Westchester Co., 1660-1870, Incl. Harrison & White Plains till
1788. (1871) reprint 1987. 570pp.   57.00   ....   F5159

Davis, Norman. Westchester Patriachs: A Genealogical Dictionary
of Westchester County, New York Families. 1988. 337pp. 23.50   F5216

Madden, Joseph P. A Documentary History of Yonkers, New York,
Volume One: The Formative Years, 1820-1852. 1992. 303pp. 24.00   F5216

Shonnard, F. and W. Spooner. History of Westchester County, from
its Earliest Settlement to the Year 1900. (1900) reprint 1990.
638pp.   68.50   ....   F5159

(Tarrytown) Old Dutch Burying Ground of Sleepy Hollow, in N.
Tarrytown. A Record of the Early Gravestones & Inscriptions.
(1953) reprint 1991. 192pp. 19.00   F5159

YATES COUNTY

Stenzel, Dianne. Genealogical Gleanings Abstracted from the Early
Newspapers of Penn Yan, Yates County, NY, 1823-1833 &
1841-1855. 1991. 328pp. 23.00   F5216

North Carolina

STATEWIDE REFERENCE

General Reference

Grimes, J. Bryan. Abstracts of North Carolina Wills [1663-1760]. (1910) reprint 1991. 670pp.
Indexed   40.00 ....   F5130

Haun, Weynette Parks. Morgan District N.C. Superior Court (Loose Papers) "Slave & Misc. Records), 1788-1806, Book III. 1992. 130pp.
Davidson, TN, Wilkes, Burke, Lincoln, Rutherford, Washington, TN, Sullivan TN, & present day Alleghany, Alexander, Catawba, Gaston. 22.50   F5193

_____. North Carolina Revolutionary Army Accounts Vols. III & IV (Part III). 1991. 162pp. 25.00   F5193

Hunter, Cyrus L. Sketches of Western North Carolina Illustrating Principally the Revolutionary Period of Mecklenburg, Rowan, Lincoln and Adjoining Counties. (1877) reprint 1990. 379pp.
Indexed.   22.50 ....   F5130

Olds, Fred A. An Abstract of North Carolina Wills From About 1760 to About 1800, Supplementing Grimes' "Abstract of North Carolina Wills 1663 to 1760". (1925) reprint 1990. 330pp.   21.50 ....   F5130

Reichel, Rev. Levin T. The Moravians in North Carolina. (1857) reprint 1991. 206pp. 20.00   F5130

Census

Heads of Families at the First Census of the United States Taken in the Year 1790 (bicentennial edition)- North Carolina. 1990.   28.50 ....   F5061

The 1790 Census. Heads of Families at the First Census of the United States Taken in the Year 1790 - North Carolina. reprint 1992. 292pp. 32.50   F5129

Bentley, Elizabeth Petty. Index to the 1810 Census of NC. (1978) reprint 1990. 282pp.   22.50   ....   F5130

Family Genealogies

Quattlebaum, Alexander McQueen.   Clergymen and Chiefs: A Genealogy of the MacQueen and Macfarlane Families. 1990. 246pp.
> Families came from Scotland to North Carolina and South Carolina. Extensive information about more than 1,200 families, including the related families of Ellerbe, Holladay, Hudnall, MacDonald, Montgomery, Rogers, White, and more. Includes illustrations, charts, and index.   37.00   ....   F5181

Religious And Ethnic Groups

Bernheim, G.D.   History of the German Settlements and of the Lutheran Church in North and South Carolina. (1872) reprint 550pp.
> From the earliest period of the colonization of the Dutch, German and Swiss settlers to the close of the first half of the present century. 33.00   F5216

Bjorkman, Gwen Boyer. Quaker Marriage Certificates:Perquimans, Pasquotank, Suttons Creek & Piney Woods Monthly Meeting, North Carolina, 1677-1800. 1988. 195pp.
> Perquimans, Pasquotank, Suttons Creek & Piney Woods Monthly Meetings, North Carolina, 1677-1800.   ....   16.50   F5216

Source Records

Broughton, Carrie L.   Marriage and Death Notices in *"Raleigh Register"* and *"North Carolina State Gazette"*, 1826-1845. (1947) reprint 1992. 402pp. 28.00   F5130

_____.   Marriage and Death Notices in *"Raleigh Register"* and *"North Carolina Gazette"*, 1846-1867 [Two Volumes in One]. (1949-50) reprint 1992. 207pp. 20.00   F5130

Mitchell, Thorton W.   North Carolina Wills: A Testator Index, 1665-1900. Corrected and Revised Edition. (1987) reprint 1992. 630pp.
> Originally published in 1987 in 2 volumes, this work has been completely re-formatted, incorporating all corrections and additions noted over the past five years, and it is now published in one comprehensive volume.   49.50   ....   F5129

Ratcliff, Clarence E. North Carolina Taxpayers 1679 - 1790. (1987) reprint 1990. 230pp.   20.00   ....   F5129

ANSON COUNTY

Holcomb, Brent H. Anson County, North Carolina Deed Abstracts 1749-1766, Abstracts of Wills & Estates 1749-1795. (1975) reprint 1991. 170pp.
> Indexed   20.00   ....   F5129

ASHE COUNTY

Waters, Evelyn G. (Comp.). 1880 Federal Census of Ashe County.
    311 + 67pp.   36.00 .... F5159

BUTE COUNTY

Holcomb, Brent H. Marriages of Bute and Warren Counties, North
    Carolina 1764-1868. 1991. 256pp.   27.50 .... F5130

CASWELL COUNTY

Caswell County, North Carolina Tax Lists, 1777, 1780, & 1784.
    1990. 106pp.   10.00 .... F5140

Kendall, Katharine Kerr. Caswell Co., North Carolina, Marriage
    Bonds, 1778-1868. (1981) reprint 1990. 170pp.
        Indexed   20.00 .... F5130

_____. Caswell County, North Carolina Deed Books 1817-1840.
    1992. 368pp.
        This reference book contains a full name index plus a
        slave index. Each abstract includes name of grantor,
        grantee, cost, number of acres of land, location on
        waterway, adjoining landowners, date and witnesses. The
        book contains sales of real and personal property and gifts
        of same. There are many divisions of property to
        legetees, powers of attorney and migrations of owners. 30.00 F5232

CHOWAN COUNTY

Haun, Weynette Parks. Chowan County North Carolina Court
    Minutes 1749-1754, Book III. 1992. 150pp. 25.00 F5193

CRAVEN COUNTY

Haun, Weynette Parks. Craven County N.C. Court Minutes,
    1757-1763, Book V. 1992. 164pp. 25.00 F5193

CURRITUCK COUNTY

Jones, Gordon C. Abstracts of Wills and Other Records, Currituck
    and Dare Counties, North Carolina (1663-1850). (1958)
    reprint 1991. 156pp.
        Indexed. 17.50 F5130

FORSYTH COUNTY

Clewell, John Henry, Ph.D. History of Wachovia in North Carolina,
    1752-1902. (1902) reprint 366pp. 27.50 F5216

JOHNSTON COUNTY

Haun, Weynette Parks. Johnston County N.C. Deed Abstracts, Vol.
    V. 1992. 157pp. 22.50 F5193

MACON COUNTY

McRae, Barbara Sears. Records of Old Macon County, North
    Carolina, 1829-1850. 1991. 212pp.   25.00 .... F5130

MECKLENBURG COUNTY

Holcomb, Brent H. Marriages of Mecklenburg County, North
    Carolina 1783-1868. (1981) reprint 1991. 284pp. 22.50   F5130

NEW HANOVER COUNTY

Waddell, Alfred Moore. A History of New Hanover County (North
    Carolina), and the Cape Fear Region, 1723-1800. (1909)
    reprint 232pp. 20.00   F5216

ORANGE COUNTY

Haun, Weynette Parks. Orange County N.C. Court Minutes,
    1752-1761, Book I. 1992. 156pp. 25.00   F5193

_____. Orange County N.C. Court Minutes, 1762-1766, Book II.
    1992.   ....   25.00   F5193

Orange County, North Carolina Taxpayers 1784-1793. 1991.
    97pp.   12.00   ....   F5140

Shields, Ruth Herndon. Abstracts of Will Recorded in Orange
    County, North Carolina, 1752-1800 and 1800-1850. (1957)
    reprint 1991. 450pp.
        2 volumes in 1 (1957, 1966), indexed.   27.50   ....   F5130

PASQUOTANK COUNTY

Bjorkman, Gwen Boyer. Pasquotank County, North Carolina,
    Record of Deeds, 1700-1751. 1990. 500pp. 35.00   F5216

PERQUIMANS COUNTY

Winslow, Mrs. Watson. History of Perquimans County. (1931)
    reprint 1990. 488pp.
        Indexed.   35.00   ....   F5129

PITT COUNTY

King, Henry T. Sketches of Pitt County (North Carolina): A Brief
    History of the County, 1704-1910. (1911) reprint 274pp. 20.00   F5216

ROWAN COUNTY

Linn, Jo White. 1815 Rowan County, North Carolina, Tax List.
    1987. 64pp. 12.00   F5080

_____. 1850 Census of Rowan County, North Carolina: A
    Genealogical Compilation of All Six Schedules. 1992. 158pp.   28.00   26.00   F5080

_____. Rowan County Register. 1986-1992. Quarterly. 240pp.
    1986-1988, $21.00 per annum.
    1989-1992, $25.00 per annum.
        Tax lists, estates records, petitions, guardian bonds,
        additional wills, deeds, court minutes, methodology,
        queries, reviews, etc. F5080

_____. Rowan County, North Carolina Abstracts of the Minutes of
    the Court of Pleas and Quarter Sessions. 3 vols. 1978-1979.
        Volume I: 1753-1762. 177pp.   30.00   ....   F5080

Volume II: 1763-1774. 210pp.	30.00	.....	F5080
Volume III:1775-1789. 240pp.	28.00	....	F5080

_____. Rowan County, North Carolina, Abstracts of Deeds, 1762-1772. 1974. 197pp. 30.00 F5080

_____. Rowan County, North Carolina, Abstracts of Wills, 1753-1805. 1980.
Revised with additions of tax lists. 25.00 .... F5080

Rumple, Rev. Jethro. A History of Rowan County, North Carolina. (1881) reprint 1990. 434pp.
Illustrated, Indexed. 30.00 .... F5129

Rowan County, North Carolina
Research and Publications

Jo White Linn, C.G., C.G.L.
Box 1948, Salisbury, NC 28145-1948
SASE for brochures, fee schedule

STANLY COUNTY

Stanly County Genealogical Society. Abstracts of the Minutes of the Court of Pleas and Quarter Sessions of Stanly County, NC 1841-1850. 1991. 156pp. 14.00 F5240

SURRY COUNTY

Linn, Jo White. Surry County, North Carolina, Wills 1771-1827. Annotated Genealogical Abstracts. 1992. 215pp.
Indexed. 25.00 .... F5129

WARREN COUNTY

Holcomb, Brent H. Marriages of Bute and Warren Counties, North Carolina 1764-1868. 1991. 256pp. 27.50 .... F5130

Ohio

STATEWIDE REFERENCE

Buchanan, Jim. The Buchanans of Ohio. 1987. 178pp.
.... 16.00   F5216

Hildreth, S.P.   Biographical and Historical Memoirs of the Early
Pioneer Settlers of Ohio, with Narratives of Incidents and
Occurrences in 1775. (1852) reprint 549pp. 32.50   F5216

Moore, Charles. The Northwest Under Three Flags, 1635-1796.
(1900) reprint 402pp. 25.00   F5216

Secretary of State.   Annual Report of the Secretary of State to the
Governor of Ohio, 1852-1955-Jail Reports. (1855) reprint
138pp. 14.00   F5216

_____ . Annual Report of the Secretary of State to the Governor of
Ohio-Return of the Number of Deaf & Dumb, Blind, Insane &
Idiotic Persons, 1856. (1856) reprint 231pp. 18.50   F5216

Slocum, Charles Elihu. The Ohio Country Between the Years
1783-1815. (1910) reprint 321pp. 22.50   F5216

Workman, Jeanne Britton.   1880 Ohio Mortality Records.   1991.
254pp.
Nearly full abstraction of over 17,000 original entries
from only existing Ohio 1880 mortality schedules,
counties Adams-Geauga. Alphabetical by surname.   37.45   ....   F5020

OHIO-KENTUCKY-INDIANA

Genealogical & Lineage Society
RESEARCH
Living Roots, Inc., P.O. Box 24223
Cincinnati, OH 45224

ADAMS COUNTY

Adams County, Ohio Deeds, 1797-1806. 1990. 155pp.
Detailed abstracts of all documents contained in Adams
County Deed Books 1 through 5. In addition to deeds,
mortgages, powers of attorney, and bonds, this volume
also contains the earliest Adams County marriages.
Indexed by surname, place and subject.   12.00   ....   F5140

Adams County, Ohio Deeds, 1806-1812. 1990. 198pp.
Detailed abstracts of all documents in Adams County
Deed Book 6. This is a large deed book with a lot of
information, including Revolutionary War service.
Indexed by surname, place, and subject.   14.00   ....   F5140

ASHTABULA COUNTY

Sargent, M.P. Ashtabula Co. Pioneer Sketches: Scenes & Incidents
of Former Days. (1891) reprint 1992. 512pp.   51.00   ....   F5159

ATHENS COUNTY

Aiken, Nancy and Beverly Schumacher. The Hawk Family of New
Jersey and Athens County, Ohio in the Nineteenth Century.
1984. 97pp. 15.00   F5174

Bowman, Mary L. Abstracts and Extracts of Athens County, Ohio
Newspapers, 1890, Part I. 1992. 354pp. 29.00   F5174

_____. An Index to the Military Grave Registration Card File of
the Athens County Recorders Office. 1988. 51pp. 5.00   F5174

_____. Athens County, Ohio Birth Records, 1867-1881: An
Extract. 1990. 160pp. 20.00   F5174

_____. Civil War Veterans of Athens County, Ohio: Biographical
Sketches. 1989. 141pp. 16.00   F5174

Bowman, Mary L. and Bettsey Stanley. Some Tombstone
Inscriptions of Southwest Athens County, Ohio. 6 Volumes. 21.75   F5174

Davis, Mary Allen. Athens County, Ohio Index to the 1900 Federal
Census. 1988. 95pp. 7.00   F5174

Fletcher, Marvin and Beverly Schumacher. Index to Athens County
Historical Society and Museum Bulletin. Volumes 6-10,
1984-1989. 1986. 82pp. 7.00   F5174

_____. and Beverly Schumacher. Marriage Records, 1805-1866,
Athens County, Ohio. 1985. 273pp. 20.00   F5174

_____. and Beverly Schumacher. Marriage Records, 1906-1913,
Athens Co., Ohio. 1986. 122pp. 10.00   F5174

Flum, Margaret. First Families of Athens County, Ohio, Index to
Applications No. 1-100. 1989.   ....   10.00   F5174

Greiner, Grace Jeffers and Robert & Shirley Harper. Cemetery
Records of Carthage, Lodi and Rome Townships, Book 2.
1989. 57pp. 6.00   F5174

_____. Cemetery Book No. 3: Cemeteries of Troy Township,
Athens Co. 1991. 43pp. 6.00   F5174

_____. Cemetery Book No. 4: Cemeteries of Troy Township,
Athens Co. 1991. 42pp. 6.00   F5174

Harris, Barbara. Death Records of White Funeral Home 1903-1987.
1990. 97pp. 12.00   F5174

_____. Records of Glouster, Ohio Funeral Homes 1953-1989.
1991. 46pp. 6.00   F5174

Levering, Rita. Athens County, Ohio Birth Records, 1883-1891: An
Extract. Vol. 2. 1991. 130pp. 15.00   F5174

_____. Athens County, Ohio Birth Records, 1891-1897: An
    Extract. Vol. 3. 1992. 100pp. 15.00 F5174

_____. Athens County, Ohio Birth Records, 1898-1905: An
    Extract. Vol. 4. 1992. 133pp. 15.00 F5174

_____. Athens County, Ohio Birth Records, 1906-1917: An
    Extract. Vol. 5. 1992. 78pp. 10.00 F5174

McVey, Owen and Faye McVey. Some Tombstone Inscriptions from
    Greenlawn Cemetery, Nelsonville, Ohio. 1987. 200pp. 15.00 F5174

Mitchell, Susan L. The Hewitts of Athens County, Ohio. 1989.
    455pp. 48.00 .... F5174

Schumacher, Beverly. Athens County, Ohio Cemeteries, With
    Township Maps by William E. Peters. 1991. 50pp.
        Cemetery names, locations and availability of tombstone
        inscriptions. 5.00 F5174

_____. Index to Athens County, Ohio Estate Records 1805-1914.
    1988. .... 7.50 F5174

Schumacher, Beverly and Mary L. Bowman. Athens County Family
    History, 1987. 1987. 308pp. 40.00 .... F5174

Schumacher, Beverly and Barbara Harris. Death Records of Hughes
    Funeral Home, Athens, Ohio. 1986. 171pp. 8.00 F5174

Schumacher, Beverly and Rita Levering. Athens County, Ohio Birth
    Records: Delayed Registrations and Corrections, 1867-1977.
    1988. 71pp. 7.00 F5174

_____. and Rita Levering. First Families of Athens County, Ohio,
    Index to Applications No. 101-200. 1992. .... 10.00 F5174

_____. and Rita Levering. Index to Athens County, Ohio Death
    Records 1867-1908. 1989. 241pp. 20.00 F5174

Schumacher, Beverly and Patricia Morrison. Athens County, Ohio
    Ancestor Charts. 1990. 254pp. 15.00 F5174

Tostenson, Kurt. Some Cemeteries of Canaan & Rome Townships,
    Athens County, Ohio. 1990. 51pp. 3.50 F5174

BUTLER COUNTY

McBride, James. Pioneer Biography: Sketches of the Lives of some
    of the Early Settlers of Butler County, Ohio. (1869, 1871)
    reprint 288pp. 37.50 F5216

CHAMPAIGN COUNTY

History of Champaign Co., containing a History of the Co.; its Cities,
    Towns, etc.; General & Local Statistics; Portraits of Early
    Settlers & and prominent men. (1881) reprint 1992. 921pp. 89.50 .... F5159

CUYAHOGA COUNTY

Kennedy, James Harrison. A History of The City of Cleveland: Its
    settlement, rise, and progress, 1796-1896. (1896) reprint
    1992. 585pp. 37.00 F5216

DEFIANCE COUNTY

Broglin, Jana. Defiance, Fulton, Henry, Paulding, Putnam, Williams and Wood Counties Ohio Newspaper Obituary Abstracts, 1838-1870. 1987. 102pp. 15.00 F5164

FAIRFIELD COUNTY

Mercy, Dorothy M. Ohio Eagle, Lancaster, Ohio 1814-1840 Genealogical Abstracts. 1991. .... 12.00 F5213

FRANKLIN COUNTY

Franklin County Genealogical Society. Abstract of Wills, 1805-1831 (and estate settlements) Franklin County Ohio Court Records with Genealogical Notes. 1982. 84pp. 8.00 F5237

_____. Ancestral Surname Indexes.
These volumes include genealogical information for ancestors of members throughtout the United States and overseas. Entries list date and place for birth, death, and marriage, if known. Name and address of current member are included for your correspondence.
Vol. I, 74pp, 1980, $6.00
Vol. II, 106pp, 1981, $7.50
Vol. III, 103pp, 1982, $8.00
Vol. IV, 109pp, 1984, $8.00
Vol. V, 130pp, 1986, $8.00
Vol. VI, 184pp, 1992, $12.00 .... F5237

_____. Confederate Cemeteries in Ohio. 1980. 55pp. 6.00 F5237

_____. Franklin County Cemeteries: Greenlawn Cemetery Records: 20 rolls 16mm microfilm. 1981. 135,000+ names. $20.00 per roll, $300.00 for the set. 300.00 F5237

_____. Franklin County Cemeteries: Vol. I Marion & Mifflin Twps. 1980. 134pp. 8.00 F5237

_____. Franklin County Cemeteries: Vol. II Madison Twp. 1981. 148pp. 10.00 F5237

_____. Franklin County Cemeteries: Vol. III Truro & Jefferson Twps. 1981. 151pp. 10.00 F5237

_____. Franklin County Cemeteries: Vol. IV Blendon & Plain Twps. 1981. 176pp. 10.00 F5237

_____. Franklin County Cemeteries: Vol. V Sharon & Perry Twps. 1983. 142pp. 10.00 F5237

_____. Franklin County Cemeteries: Vol. VI Washinton, Clinton, Montgonery & Brown Twps. 1983. 103pp. 10.00 F5237

_____. Franklin County Cemeteries: Vol. VII Norwich Twp. 1984. 117pp. 10.00 F5237

_____. Franklin County Cemeteries: Vol. VIII Franklin & Prairie Twps. 1984. 158pp. 10.00 F5237

_____. Franklin County Cemeteries: Vol. IX Hamilton Twp. 1987. 178pp.	.... 14.00	F5237
_____. Franklin County Cemeteries: Vol. X Jackson & Pleasant Twps. 1988. 132pp.	.... 14.00	F5237
_____. Genealogical Index to Chancery Books Vol I through IV, 1823-1839. 1987. 173pp. These publications include an everyname index, year and page number of cases and a brief description of the court entry.	.... 17.00	F5237
_____. Genealogical Index to Chancery Books Vol V and VI, 1840-1846. 1992. 72pp. These publications include an everyname index, year and page number of cases and a brief description of the court entry.	.... 14.00	F5237
_____. Genealogical Name Index to Ohio Supreme Court Records, Volumes I-IV 1783-1839. 1983. 84pp.	.... 10.00	F5237
_____. Index to Studer's 1873 History of Columbus and Franklin County, Ohio. 1979. 44pp.	.... 3.50	F5237
_____. Name Index and Genealogical Data Abstracted from "The History of Madison Twp." (Franklin Co.), by George Baries (1902). 1983. 115pp.	.... 10.00	F5237
_____. Name Index to Franklin County Plat Maps: 1842, 1856, 1883. 1982. 174pp. Name of Land Owners as shown on maps.	.... 10.00	F5237
Mollenkamp and Scott. Index and Genealogical Notes to "Sellsville, Circa 1900", by Weisheimer. 1987. 64pp. Headquarters of Sells Bros. Circus	.... 8.00	F5237

FULTON COUNTY

Broglin, Jana. Defiance, Fulton, Henry, Paulding, Putnam, Williams and Wood Counties Ohio Newspaper Obituary Abstracts, 1838-1870. 1987. 102pp.	.... 15.00	F5164

GREENE COUNTY

Patterson, ed., Austin McDowell. Greene County (Ohio), 1803-1908. (1908) reprint 232pp.	.... 20.00	F5216

HAMILTON COUNTY

Hughes, Lois E. Wills Filed in Probate Court Hamilton County, Ohio, 1791-1901. Vol. I, A-K and Vol II. L-Z. 1991. 654pp.	.... 69.50	F5216
University of Cincinnati. Hamilton County, Ohio Citizenship Record Abstracts, 1837-1916. 1991. 435pp.	.... 47.50	F5216

HARRISON COUNTY

Hanna, C.A. Historical Collections of Harrison Co., with Lists of 1st Landowners, Early Marriages to 1841, Will Records to 1861, Burial Records & Numerous Gen. (1900) reprint 1991. 636pp.	62.00	F5159

HENRY COUNTY

Broglin, Jana. Defiance, Fulton, Henry, Paulding, Putnam, Williams
and Wood Counties Ohio Newspaper Obituary Abstracts,
1838-1870. 1987. 102pp. 15.00 F5164

MAHONING COUNTY

Simon, Margaret. Mahoning County Ohio Newspaper Obituary
Abstracts, 1843-1870. 1983. 78pp. 15.00 F5164

MARION COUNTY

Leggett and Conaway & Co. The History of Marion County, Ohio.
(1883) reprint 915pp.
Containing a History of the county; its townships, towns,
churches, schools, etc.; General and Local statistics;
military record; portraits of early settlers and prominent
men. 50.00 F5216

MEIGS COUNTY

Greiner, Grace Jeffers and Jennie Midkiff. Cemetery Records of
Athens and Meigs Counties. 1986. 50pp. 6.00 F5174

Larkin, Stillman Carter. The Pioneer History of Meigs County
(OH). (1908) reprint 224pp. 17.50 F5216

McVey, Owen and Faye McVey. Some Tombstone Inscriptions of
Columbia Township Meigs County, Ohio. 1987. .... 4.50 F5174

MONTGOMERY COUNTY

Mikesell, Shirley Keller. Early Settlers of Montgomery County,
Ohio; Genealogical Abstracts from Land Records, Tax Lists,
and Biographical Sketches. 1991. 292pp. 21.50 F5216

MUSKINGUM COUNTY

Everhart, J.F. History of Muskingum Co., 1794-1882, with
Illustrations and Biographical Sketches of Prominent Men &
Pioneers. (1882) reprint 1992. 481pp. 49.50 .... F5159

OTTAWA COUNTY

Minderman, Edith. Ottawa, Sandusky and Seneca Counties Ohio
Newspaper Obituary Abstracts, 1836-1870. 1985. 92pp. 15.00 F5164

PAULDING COUNTY

Broglin, Jana. Defiance, Fulton, Henry, Paulding, Putnam, Williams
and Wood Counties Ohio Newspaper Obituary Abstracts,
1838-1870. 1987. 102pp. 15.00 F5164

PREBLE COUNTY

Preble County Historical Society. Preble County Ohio. 1992.
686pp.
1808-1991. Over 500 pictures, 589 family histories, All
name index. 70.00 .... F5244

Preble County Historical Society and Seth S. Schlotterbeck.
Cadastral Maps, 1858, 1871, 1887, 1897, 1912, 1940. (1978)
reprint 1983. 302pp.
  Map for each county each year except 1887. Each year
  indexed.   33.15   ....   F5244

Schlotterbeck, Seth S. By Old Mill Streams. 1986. 76pp.
  Commentary on mills, streams, and cemeteries, Preble
  County, Ohio. Many pictures. 30.25   F5244

Short, Anita and Ruth Bowers. Preble County, Ohio Marriage
Records 1808-1840. (1966) reprint 1991. 148pp.
  2 volumes in 1, indexed. 17.50   F5130

PUTNAM COUNTY

Broglin, Jana. Defiance, Fulton, Henry, Paulding, Putnam, Williams
and Wood Counties Ohio Newspaper Obituary Abstracts,
1838-1870. 1987. 102pp. 15.00   F5164

SANDUSKY COUNTY

Minderman, Edith. Ottawa, Sandusky and Seneca Counties Ohio
Newspaper Obituary Abstracts, 1836-1870. 1985. 92pp. 15.00   F5164

SENECA COUNTY

Minderman, Edith. Ottawa, Sandusky and Seneca Counties Ohio
Newspaper Obituary Abstracts, 1836-1870. 1985. 92pp. 15.00   F5164

TRUMBULL COUNTY

Clegg, Michael B. Trumbull County Ohio Newspaper Obituary
Abstracts, 1812-1870. 1981. 146pp. 20.00   F5164

VINTON COUNTY

McVey, Owen and Faye McVey. Some Tombstone Inscriptions of
Vinton County, Ohio Volume 1.   ....   4.00   F5174

Vanover, Vicki. Some Tombstone Inscriptions of Vinton County,
Ohio Volume 2.   ....   9.00   F5174

WARREN COUNTY

Phillips, W. Louis. Warren Co., Ohio, Records of Apprenticeship &
Indenture, 1824-1832 & 1864-1867. 1987. 51pp. 8.00   F5216

WILLIAMS COUNTY

Broglin, Jana. Defiance, Fulton, Henry, Paulding, Putnam, Williams
and Wood Counties Ohio Newspaper Obituary Abstracts,
1838-1870. 1987. 102pp. 15.00   F5164

WOOD COUNTY

Broglin, Jana. Defiance, Fulton, Henry, Paulding, Putnam, Williams
and Wood Counties Ohio Newspaper Obituary Abstracts,
1838-1870. 1987. 102pp. 15.00   F5164

Oklahoma

STATEWIDE REFERENCE

Chickasaw Nation

Rex, Joyce A., Editor.   1890 Census, Chicksaw Nation, Indian Territory (Pontotoc County) Book 1. (1990) reprint 1991.
Now McClain County, portions of Grady, Garvin, Pontotoc, Murray, Johnston and Coal Counties, Oklahoma. 22.25   F5103

_____. 1890 Census, Chickasaw Nation, Indian Territory (Pickens County) Book 2. 1992.
Now Love and Marshall, portions of Grady, Garvin, Stephens, Jefferson, Murray and Johnston Counties, Oklahoma. 22.25   F5103

Research Aids

Koplowitz, Bradford. Guide to the Historical Records of Oklahoma. 1989. 189pp. 20.00   F5216

MCCLAIN COUNTY

Rex, Joyce A., Editor. McClain County, Oklahoma Death Records (1882-1984). 1984. 205pp.
Cemeteries and local records. 22.00   F5103

_____. McClain County, Oklahoma History and Heritage, Books 1, 2, 3. 1986-1991. 225pp ea.   33.10 .... F5103

MUSKOGEE COUNTY

Hagan, Mickey Hooper and Rae Lindsey.   Marriage Records, Muskogee Indian Territory July 1890-March 1893. 1987. 108pp. 11.00   F5205

Penquite, Deone Duncan and Walter Heck Penquite. Cemeteries of Muskogee County, Oklahoma, Vol. I. 1988. 158pp. 11.50   F5205

_____. Cemeteries of Muskogee County, Oklahoma, Vol. II. 1992. 291pp.
5,976 names. 25.00   F5205

Penquite, Walter Heck. Index of Deaths extracted from Muskogee Daily Phoenix, Muskogee OK Janury 16, 1930-May 4, 1935. 1988. 49pp.   5.00 ....   F5205

Siebold, Sheri Sharpnack.   Genealogical Data extracted from Muskogee Weekly Phoenix, Indian Territory 1888-1892. 1985. 56pp. 7.00   F5205

_____. Genealogical Data extracted from Muskogee Weekly Phoenix, Indian Territory, 1898-1902. 1987. 67pp. 9.00   F5205

_____. Genealogical Data extracted from Muskogee Weekly Phoenix, Indian Territory. 1893-1897. 1986. 56pp. 8.00   F5205

Pennsylvania

STATEWIDE REFERENCE

General Reference

Dunn, Dr. Mary. Index to Pennsylvania's Colonial Records Series.
1992. 228pp. · 20.00 .... F5129

McCracken, George E. Penn's Colony: Genealogical and Historical
Materials Relating to the Settlement of PA: Vol. 2 The
Welcome Claimants-Proved, Disproved, and Doubtful. (1970)
reprint 660pp.
With an account of some of their descendants. · · · · · · 40.00 .... F5216

Myers, ed., Albert Cook. Narratives of Early Pennsylvania, West
New Jersey, and Delaware, 1630-1707. (1912) reprint 476pp. 29.00 F5216

Scott, Kenneth. Abstracts (Mainly Deaths) From the *Pennsylvania
Gazette*, 1775-1783. (1976) reprint 1991. 58pp.
Indexed. · 10.00 F5130

_____. Genealogical Abstracts From the *American Weekly
Mercury*, 1719-1746. (1974) reprint 1991. 180pp.
Indexed. · 18.50 F5130

Stapleton, Ammon. Memorials of Huguenots in America, with
Special Reference to their Emigration to Pennsylvania. (1901)
reprint 1992. 164pp. · 17.50 F5159

Virdin, Donald O. Pennsylvania Genealogies and Family Histories:
A Bibliography of Books about Pennsylvania Families. 1992.
269pp. · 33.00 F5216

Westcott, Thompson. Names of Persons Who Took the Oath of
Allegiance to the State of Pennslylvania Between the Years
1777 & 1789, With a History of the "Test Laws" of PA.
(1865) reprint 1992. 192pp.
Indexed. · 19.50 F5130

Baptism, Birth & Burial Records

Fisher, Charles A. Early Pennsylvania Births, 1675-1875. (1947)
reprint 1991. 107pp. · 8.00 F5129

_____. Early Pennsylvania Births, 1675-1875. (1947) reprint
1991. 107pp. · 9.50 F5159

Hildeburn, C.R. Baptisms & Burials from the Records of Christ
Church, Phila., 1709-1760. (1877) reprint 1991. 231pp. 17.50 .... F5159

Buffalo Valley

Linn, John Blair. Annals of Buffalo Valley, Pennsylvania,
1755-1855. (1877) reprint 622pp. · · · · · · · · · · · · · · 35.00 F5216

Census

Heads of Families at The First Census of the US taken in the Year
1790. (1908) reprint 1990. 422pp. · · · · · · · · · · · · · · 42.50 F5159

Heads of Families at the First Census of the United States Taken in
the Year 1790 (bicentennial edition)-Pennsylvania. 1990. 39.95 .... F5061

The 1790 Census. Heads of Families at the First Census of the
United States Taken in the Year 1790 - Pennsylvania. reprint
1992. 426pp. 44.50 F5129

Immigration, Emigration Migration And Naturalization

Burgert, Annette K. Colonial Pennsylvania Immigrants from
Freinsheim in the Palatinate. 1989. 39pp. 12.00 F5141

_____. Pennsylvania Pioneers from Wolfersweiler Parish,
Saarland, Germany. 1983. 46pp. 10.00 F5141

Egle (Ed.), W. H. Foreigners Who Took the Oath of Allegiance to
the Province & State of PA, 1727-1775, with Foreign Arrivals,
1786-1808. (1898) reprint 1991. 787pp. 60.00 .... F5159

Johnson, A. Swedish Settlements on the Delaware. 1638-1664.
(1911) reprint 1990. 879pp.
Gives the background of the immigr. in Sweden & a
detailed early hist. of the Colony in Penn. 88.50 .... F5159

Linn, John B. and William H. Egle. Persons Naturalized in the
Province of Pennsylvania, 1740-1773 With an Added Index.
(1890) reprint 1991. 139pp. 18.50 .... F5130

Tepper, Michael. Emigrants to Pennsylvania. A Consolidation of
Ship Passenger Lists from the Pennsylvania Magazine of
History and Biography. (1975) reprint 1992. 302pp.
Indexed. 20.00 .... F5129

Lebanon Valley

Croll, Rev. P.C. Ancient and Historic Landmarks in the Lebanon
Valley (Pennsylvania). (1895) reprint 340pp. 22.50 F5216

Maps And Gazetters, Place Names

Espenshade, A. Howry. Pennsylvania Place Names. (1925) reprint
1991. 375pp. 27.50 F5130

Gordon, T.F. (Comp.). A Gazetter of the State of Pennsylvania.
(1832) reprint 1989. 63+508pp.
This earliest gazetteer of Pa. is filled with very useful
info. for the genealogist, esp. population surveys &
geographical information. 55.00 .... F5159

Military

Linn, John B. and William Henry Egle. Lists of Officers of the
Colonies on the Delaware and the Province of Pennsylvania,
1614-1776.
With a New Index by Robert Barnes. (1880) reprint
1992. 221pp. 25.00 F5130

Richards, Henry M. M. The Pennsylvania-German in the
Revolutionary War 1775-1783. (1908) reprint 1991. 542pp.
Indexed 35.00 .... F5129

Sypher, J.R. History of the Pennsylvania Reserve Corps: A
Complete Record of the Organization, and of the Different
Companies, Regiments, and Brigades. (1864) reprint 768pp. 43.00 F5216

Religious And Ethnic Groups - German

Strassburger, Ralph Beaver and William John Hinke. Pennsylvania German Pioneers [:] A publication of the Original Lists of Arrivals In the Port of Philadelphia From 1727 to 1808, Signature Volume. (1934) reprint 1992. 909pp.

> This set which is commonly known as "Strassburger & Hinke" is the time-honored reference for arrival of German emigrants to America before 1800. It is one of the basic works for genealogical libraries. Volumes 1 & 3 have been reprinted a number of times, but this is the first time this volume (which shows the actual signatures of the emigrants) has been reprinted. This signature volume is important as it may be used to check signatures on wills, deeds, and other documents to ascertain whether they were written by the same man.
>
> This volume has been printed the same size and with the same cover as the other currently available volumes so that they will make a matching set. It is being sold separately for $55 - for purchase by those who already have the other two volumes. It is necessary to have the other volumes in order to use this one as it does not have a separate index.
>
> For those who do not have any of this set, all three volumes are available from us as a set for the very special price of $100.00. The other volumes total 1,565 pages and this one has 909. All three are printed on acid-free paper and are smythe-sewn with cloth bindings. 55.00 .... F5236

_____. Pennsylvania German Pioneers, A Publication of the Original Lists of Arrivals in the Port of Philadelphia from 1727 to 1808. (1934) reprint 1992. 1,565pp.

> 2 Volumes, indexed. 75.00 .... F5129

VIRGINIA CORDES, C.G.R.S.

1085 Powderhorn Drive
Glen Mills, PA 19342-9504

Quaker & Chester Co., PA Records

Religious And Ethnic Groups - Quakers

Browning, C.H. Welsh Settlement of Pennsylvania: Welsh Quaker Emigr. (1912) reprint 1990. 631pp. 64.50 .... F5159

Glenn, Thomas Allen. Merion in the Welsh. With Sketches of the Townships of Haverford and Radnor. (1896) reprint 1992. 394pp.

> Historical and Genealogical Collections Concerning the Welsh Barony in the Province of Pennsylvania Settled by the Cymric Quakers in 1682.
>
> Illustrated, partially indexed. 32.50 F5130

Hull, William I. William Penn and the Dutch Quaker Migration to PA. (1935) reprint 1990. 460pp.

> Illustrated, indexed. 35.00 .... F5130

Scotch-Irish & German Ancestry

Dunaway, Wayland F. The Scotch-Irish of Pennsylvania. (1944)
 reprint 1992. 273pp.
  Indexed. ... 20.00 .... F5129

Egle, W.H. Pennsylvania Genealogies; Scotch-Irish & German.
 (1886) reprint 1987. 720pp. ... 72.00 .... F5159

Susquehanna Valley

History of that Part of the Susquehanna & Juniata Valleys, Embraced
 in the Counties of Mifflin, Juniata, Perry, Union & Snyder (2
 vols.). (1886) reprint 1992. 1601pp. ... 125.00 .... F5159

Wyoming Valley

Egle, William Henry. Documents Relating to the Connecticut
 Settlement in the Wyoming Valley (of Pennsylvania). (1890)
 reprint 817pp. 45.00 F5216

Miner, Charles. History of Wyoming (Valley, Pennsylvania).
 (1845) reprint 628pp. 35.00 F5216

The Genealogy Tree

Dortha Steele
721 E 17th So,
Salt Lake City, UT 84105
Scotch-Irish pre-1800

ALLEGHENY COUNTY

Indian Reservation

Barton, Lois. A Quaker Promise Kept. Philadelphia Friends Work
 with the Allegany Senecas. 1795-1960. 1990. 111pp.
  Includes list of staff & students at boarding school, 1851 -
  1938. ... . 14.95 F5007

History of Allegheny County, Including its Early Settlement &
 Progress; a Description of its Historical & Interesting
 Localities;. (1889) reprint 1992. 762+786p.
  its cities, towns & villages; portraits of some prominent
  men & biogr. of many citizens. 2 vols. $79/vol. or
  $149/set hardcover. ... 149.00 .... F5159

BEAVER COUNTY

Bausman, J.H. History of Beaver Co. (2 volumes). (1904) reprint
 1989. 612 & 703p. ... 139.00 .... F5159

BEDFORD COUNTY

History of Bedford, Somerset & Fulton Counties (With Illustrations).
 (1884) reprint 1991. 672pp. ... 98.00 .... F5159

BERKS COUNTY

Burgert, Annette K. The Hochstadt Origins of Some of the Early
    Settlers at Host Church, Berks County, PA. 1983. 42pp. 10.00   F5141

Montgomery, M.L. History of Berks County. (1886) reprint 1989.
    1204pp.   129.50   ....   F5159

Montgomery, Morton L.(Comp.). Historical & Biographical Annals
    of Berks Co.: A Concise Hist. of the Co., & a Gen. & Biogr.
    Records of Representative Fams. (1909) reprint 1992. 2 vols. 155.00   ....   F5159

Rupp, I. Daniel. History of the Counties of Berks & Lebanon.
    (1844) reprint 1992. 512pp.   52.50   ....   F5159

BUCKS COUNTY

Bucks County, Pennsylvania Deed Book 5 (1713-1731). 1991.
    89pp.   14.00   ....   F5140

Buck, William J. Local Sketches and Legends pertaining to Bucks
    and Montgomery Counties, Pennsylvania. (1887) reprint
    340pp. 23.00   F5216

Roberts, C.V. Early Friends Families of Upper Bucks Co., with
    Some Account of their Descendants: Hist. & Gen. Info. about
    Early Settlers in Upper Bucks Co., PA. (1925) reprint 1990.
    680pp.   69.50   ....   F5159

PENNSYLVANIA
Bucks, Montgomery, Lehigh &
Northampton Counties

Frances Conley Wise Waite
649 S. Chubb Drive
Doylestown, PA 18901

CENTRE COUNTY

Centre County Genealogical Society. The Cemeteries of Penn
    Township, Centre County, PA. 1988. 95pp. 14.50   F5192

Copper, Ellen. A History of Funeral Directors and Undertakers of
    Centre County, 1813-1989. 1989.   ....   10.00   F5192

CHESTER COUNTY

Bjorkman, Gwen Boyer. Quaker Marriage Certificates: New Garden
    Monthly Meeting, Chester County, PA, 1704-1799. 1990. 317pp.......... 25.00   F5216

Futhey, J.S. and G. Cope. History of Chester Co., with Genealogical
    & Biographical Sketches. (1881) reprint 1990. 782.
    Includes more than 320 illustrations.   91.50   ....   F5159

CLINTON COUNTY

Furey, J. Milton. Past and Present of Clinton County, Pennsylvania.
    (1892) reprint 448pp. 28.50   F5216

CRAWFORD COUNTY

History of Crawford Co., Containing a hist. of the Co., its Twps., Towns, etc., portraits of Early Settlers & Prom. Men, Biogr. (1885) reprint 1990. 1186pp.   119.50   ....   F5159

DAUPHIN COUNTY

Burgert, Annette K.   Early Marriage Evidence from the Court Records of Dauphin County, Pennsylvania (Including Lebanon County). 1986. 68pp. 15.00   F5141

Egle, W.H. History of the Counties of Dauphin & Lebanon in the Commonwealth of PA, Biogr. & Genealogical. (1883) reprint 1990. 616p & 360p.   103.50   ....   F5159

Kelker, Luther Reily. History of Dauphin Co., with Genealogical Memoirs (2 vols.). (1907) reprint 1989.
    Vols. I & II History 1136pp $109.00.
    Vol. III Genealogy 727pp $73.00 all hardcover. F5159

DELAWARE COUNTY

Bjorkman, Gwen Boyer.   Quaker Marriage Certificates: Concord Monthly Meeting, Delaware County, Pennsylvania, 1679-1808. 1991. 246pp. 20.00   F5216

Martin, John Hill. Chester & Its Vicinity, Delaware Co., with Gen. Sketches of Some Old Families. (1877) reprint 1990. 530pp.   55.00   ....   F5159

ERIE COUNTY

Miller, John. A Twentieth Century History of Erie Co.: A Narrative Acct. of its Historical Progress, its People & its Principal Interests (2 volumes). (1909) reprint 1990.
    Vol. I History 897pp $91.00;
    Vol. II Biography 712pp $74.50.   ....   F5159

Sanford, Laura G. History of Erie Co., from its First Settlement. (1894) reprint 1992. 460pp.   46.00   ....   F5159

_____. The History of Erie County, Pennsylvania, from its first settlement. (1861, 1894) reprint 483pp. 31.00   F5216

Whitman, Russell, Weakley & Mansfield.   History of Erie Co., Containing a Hist. of the Co.; its Twps., Towns & Villages; Early Settlers & Biogr., etc. (1884) reprint 1992. 1,006pp & 239pp.   119.00   ....   F5159

FAYETTE COUNTY

Fayette County, Pennsylvania Taxpayers, 1785-1799. 1991. 175pp.   14.00   ....   F5140

A History of Uniontown, the County Seat of Fayette County. (1913) reprint 1992. 824pp.   84.00   ....   F5159

GREENE COUNTY

Bates, Samuel P. History of Greene County. (1888) reprint 1992. 898pp.   89.50   ....   F5159

HUNTINGDON COUNTY

Lytle, M.S. History of Huntingdon Co., from Earliest Times to the Centennial Anniversary of Amer. Independence. (1876) reprint 1989. 360pp.   39.50 .... F5159

Neff, William . Neff - Naf Family History - A Genealogy. 1991. 480pp.
    Neff, Henry: Descendant of Adam Naf, Zurich, Kappel am Albis; Immigrant, Lancaster Co., PA, Manor Township 1718.
        Neff, Drs. Frances; Hans Heinrich; & Jacob: Lancaster Co., PA, Conestoga Twp., and Frederick Co., MD - 1718.
        See Family History #112.   42.50 .... F5157

JEFFERSON COUNTY

McKnight, W.J. A Pioneer Hist. of Jefferson Co., 1755-1844. (1898) reprint 1989. 670pp.   69.50 .... F5159

_____. Jefferson Co., Pennsylvania: Her Pioneers & People, 1800-1915. (1917) reprint 1990.
    Vol. I Historical xxvi+516pp $57.00;
    Vol. II Gen.-Biogr. 701pp $75.00. Hardcover volumes. F5159

Steele, Patricia M. Who, When, and Where, Vol. III. Jefferson County, PA Marriage Licenses 1885 - 1890. 1991. 200.
    Everyname index included.   27.50 .... F5058

JUNIATA COUNTY

    See Susquehanna Valley.

LANCASTER COUNTY

Eshleman, H. Frank. Historic Background and Annals of the Swiss and German Pioneer Settlers of Southeastern Pennsylvania. (1917) reprint 1991. 386pp.
    Indexed.   25.00 .... F5129

Harris, Alex. A Biographical History of Lancaster County (Pennsylvania):Being a History of Early Settlers and Eminent Men of the County. (1872) reprint 640pp. 36.50 F5216

_____. A Biographical History of Lancaster County [Pennsylvania]: Being a History of Eminent Men of the County. (1872) reprint 1992. 638pp. 45.00 F5130

Rupp, I. Daniel. History of Lancaster Co., to Which is Prefixed a Brief Sketch of the Early History of PA. (1844) reprint 1992. 524pp.   53.00 .... F5159

_____. History of Lancaster County,to which is Prefixed a Brief Sketch of the Early History of Pennsylvania. (1844) reprint 568pp. 33.50 F5216

LAWRENCE COUNTY

Hazen, Aaron L. (Ed. & Comp.). Twentieth Century History of New Castle & Lawrence County & Representative Citizens. (1908) reprint 1992. 1015pp.   99.00 .... F5159

LEBANON COUNTY

Burgert, Annette K. Early Marriage Evidence from the Court
  Records of Dauphin County, Pennsylvania (Including Lebanon
  County). 1986. 68pp. 15.00   F5141

Heilman, Robert A. Deaths Reported by Der Libanon Demokrat, a
  German Language Newspaper Published at Lebanon, PA,
  1832-1864. 1990. 130pp. 13.50   F5216

_____. Marriages Reported by Der Libanon Demokrat: A
  German-Language Newspaper Published at Lebanon, PA.
  1990. 126pp. 13.50   F5216

Wolfson, James B. Warrantee Township Map North Annville and
  Annville; Lebanon County, Pennsylvania. 1990.
      Map is 24 x 32 inches, Five page informational index
      included. 12.75   F5045

_____. Warrantee Township Map South Annville; Lebanon
  County, Pennsylvania. 1991.
      Map is 24 x 32 inches, Six page informational index
      included. 12.75   F5045

_____. Warrantee Township Map West Lebanon, Cleona, North
  Cornwall and Lebanon City; Lebanon County, Pennsylvania.
  1990.
      Map is 24 x 32 inches, Four page informational index
      included. 12.75   F5045

LEHIGH COUNTY

Humphrey, John T. Pennsylvania Births, Lehigh County
  1734-1800. 1992. 327pp.   32.50   ....   F5022

LUZERNE COUNTY

Bradsby (Ed.), H.C. History of Luzerne County, with Biographical
  Selections. (1893) reprint 1992. 1509pp.   145.00   ....   F5159

Plumb, H.B. History of Hanover Twp., Incl. Sugar Notch, Ashley &
  Nanticoke Boroughs: also a Hist. of Wyoming Val. in Luzerne
  Co. (1885) reprint 1990. 498pp.
      Incl. gen. tables for 73 Hanover twp. families.   51.00   ....   F5159

Wright, H.B. Hist. Sketches of Plymouth, Luzerne Co. (1873)
  reprint 1988. 404pp.
      Incl. gen. info. on the founding families.   42.00   ....   F5159

MCKEAN COUNTY

History of the Counties of McKean, Elk, Cameron & Potter, with
   Biographical Sketches. (1890) reprint 1989. 1261pp.   126.50   ....   F5159

MERCER COUNTY

History of Mercer Co., its Past & Present. (1888) reprint 1989.
   1,210pp.   119.00   ....   F5159

MONTGOMERY COUNTY

Bean, T.W. History of Montgomery Co. (1884) reprint 1989.
   1197 + 89p.   129.50   ....   F5159

Cramer, Peggy C. Early Records of the Ambler Church of the
   Brethren. 1990. 369pp.
         Founded in 1840 as the Upper Dublin German Baptist
         Church. Covers 1840's through 1940's. Includes photos;
         1,900 every name index.   35.00   ....   F5068

Green, Thomas A. Merion in the Welsh Tract, with Sketches of the
   Twps. of Haverford & Radnor: Hist. & gen. collections
   concerning the Welsh Barony in the Prov. of PA. (1896)
   reprint 1992. 394pp.   39.50   ....   F5159

Roberts, ed., Ellwood. Biographical Annals of Montgomery County,
   Pennsylvania. (1904) reprint 1,104pp.
         Containing genealogical records of representative
         families, including many of the early settlers, and
         biographical sketches of prominent citizens. 60.00   F5216

Weiser, C.Z. and D.D. Goschenhoppen. A Monograph of the New
   Goschenhoppen and Great Swamp Reformed Charge,
   1731-1881. (1882) reprint 170pp. 15.50   F5216

NORTHAMPTON COUNTY

Humphrey, John T. Early Families of Northampton County,
   Pennsylvania - Volume 1. 1991. 424pp.
         Families: Berstler;, Biesecker; Blum; Boemper; Church;
         Ehrenherdt; Eyerly; Frack; Frey; Hoeth; Krebs; Levering;
         Levers; Loesch; Messinger; Miksch; Schweitzer; Stecher;
         Waldborn; Weinland. 38.50   F5022

_____. Early Families of Northampton County, Pennsylvania -
   Volume 2. 1991. 383pp.
         Families: Arnold; Bossard; Dietrich; Erdman; Heil; Hess;
         Huffsmith; Keller; Kurtz; Metzger; Muffley; Ratzel;
         Repsher; Schuck; Smiley; Staples; Weidman. 38.50   F5022

_____. Pennsylvania Births Northhampton County 1733-1800.
   1991. 239pp.   27.50   ....   F5022

Keiffer, J.M. (Trans. & Publ.). (Easton) Some of the 1st Settlers of
   "The Forks of The Delaware" & Their Desc. (1902) reprint
   1991. 404pp.

This is a translation from German of the record books of
the 1st Reformed Church of Easton, 1760-1852. Incls.
settlers, baptisms, marriages & deaths for the twnships
encompassed by Easton.   42.00 .... F5159

Rupp, I.D. History of Northampton, Lehigh, Monroe, Carbon &
Schuylkill Counties. (1845) reprint 1991. 568pp.   59.00 .... F5159

NORTHUMBERLAND COUNTY

Fisher, Charles A. Wills and Administrations of Northumberland
County, Pennsylvania. Including Wills and Administrations of
Union, Mifflin, and Indiana Counties. (1950) reprint 1992.
77pp.
    Indexed. 10.00 F5130

PERRY COUNTY

Hain, H.H. History of Perry Co., Including Descriptions of Indian &
Pioneer Life, from the Time of Earliest Settlement, with
Sketchs of its Noted Men & Women and many professional
men. (1922) reprint 1992. 1088pp.   98.00 .... F5159

PHILADELPHIA RESEARCH
CENSUS, NEWSPAPERS, CITY
DIRECTORIES

EUGENE BLOOD
9302 Laramie Rd. Phila., Pa.19115-2720
$8.00 per hour

PHILADELPHIA COUNTY

Philadelphia City & County, Pennsylvania Taxpayers 1779.
1991. 144pp.   12.00 .... F5140

SNYDER COUNTY

Fisher, Charles A. Probate and Orphans Court Records of Snyder
County, Pennsylvania, 1772-1855. (1940) reprint 1991.
87pp.
    Indexed. 10.00 F5130

_____. Snyder County [Pennsylvania] Pioneers. (1938) reprint
1991. 103pp. 10.00 F5130

SUSQUEHANNA COUNTY

Blackman, Emily C. History of Susquehanna Co, from a Period
Preceding its Settlement to Recent Times. (1873) reprint
1992. 640pp.   65.00 .... F5159

TIOGA COUNTY

History of Tioga County, with Illustrations, Portraits & Sketches of
    Prominent Families & Individuals. (1883) reprint 1992.
    365pp + 35pp.   42.50   ....   F5159

Maginess, Meagher, et al. The Hist. of Tioga County. (1897)
    reprint 1988. 1,186pp.   109.00   ....   F5159

VENANGO COUNTY

History of Venango County: Its Past & Present. (1890) reprint
    1992. 1164pp.
        Including its aboriginal history...its early settlement &
        subsequent growth...its historic & interesting localities,
        family history, etc.   108.50   ....   F5159

WARREN COUNTY

Schenk, J.S. and W.S. Rann (Eds.). History of Warren Co., with
    Illustrations & Biogr. Sketches of Some of its Prominent Men
    & Pioneers. (1887) reprint 1992. 807pp.   79.00   ....   F5159

WASHINGTON COUNTY

Zinsser, Katherine K. and Raymond M. Bell. The 1783 Tax Lists
    and the 1790 Federal Census for Washington County,
    Pennsylvania. 1988. 132pp. 20.00   F5216

YORK COUNTY

Burgert, Annette K. York County Pioneers from Friedelsheim and
    Gonnheim in the Palatinate. 1984. 30pp. 10.00   F5141

Walmer, Margaret B. 100 Years at Warrington: York County, Penn.
    Quaker Marriages, Removals, Births & Deaths. 1989. 323pp. 22.00   F5216

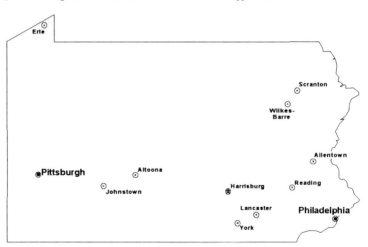

Rhode Island

STATEWIDE REFERENCE

General Reference

Austin, J.O.   Ancestry of 33 Rhodes Islanders, Born in the 18th
Cent.; also 27 Charts of Roger Williams' Desc. to the 5th
Generation. (1889) reprint 1991. 139pp. 14.00   F5159

_____.   One-Hundred & Sixty Allied Families. (1893) reprint
1990. 309pp.
Families of New Eng. settlers, many of whom migrated to
Rhode Island. 29.50   F5159

Hazard, Caroline. (Quakers) The Narragansett Friend's Meeting in
the XVIII Century, with a Chapter on Quaker Beginnings in
R.I. (1899) reprint 1992. 197pp. 19.00   F5159

Weeden, William B. Early Rhode Island: a social history of the
people, 1636-1790. (1910) reprint 407pp. 26.50   F5216

Census

Bartlett, John R. Census of the Inhabitants of the Colony of Rhode
Island and Providence Plantations 1774. (1858) reprint 1990.
359pp.
Indexed 25.00   F5130

Bartlett, John R. (Ed.). Census of the Inhabitants of the Colony of
Rhode Island & Providence Plantations, taken in the Year
1774. (1958) reprint 1990. 238+120p. 35.00   F5159

The 1790 Census. Heads of Families at the First Census of the
United States Taken in the Year 1790 - Rhode Island. reprint
1992. 71pp. 15.00   F5129

Research Aids

Parker, J. Carlyle. Rhode Island Biographical and Genealogical
Sketch Index. 1991. 272pp.   31.95   ....   F5150

BRISTOL COUNTY

Munro, W.H. The History of Bristol: The Story of the Mount Hope
Lands, from the Visit of the Northmen to the Present Time.
(1880) reprint 1988. 396pp.   42.00   ....   F5159

KENT COUNTY

Greene, D.H. History of the Town of East Greenwich & Adjacent
Territory, 1677-1877. (1877) reprint 1987. 263pp.   32.50   ....   F5159

NEWPORT COUNTY

Bayles, Richard M. (Ed.). History of Newport County (Includes
Illustrations). (1888) reprint 1991. 1060pp.   99.00   ....   F5159

Brigham, C.S. (Ed.). Early Records of the Town of Portsmouth.
(1901) reprint 1991. 462pp.   45.00   ....   F5159

Channing, G.G. Early Recollections of Newport, from 1793 to
1811. (1868) reprint 1987. 248pp.   31.00   ....   F5159

Mason, George C. Reminiscences of Newport. (1884) reprint 1990.
407pp.
> A charming history of Newport as a "watering-place",
> from the earliest days as a vacation spot.   42.00   ....   F5159

PROVIDENCE COUNTY

Bayles, Richard M. (Ed.). History of Providence County. (1891)
reprint 1992. 2 vols..
> Vol. I 821 pp $82.00;
> Vol. II 639pp $64.00;
> **Special Price for Set: $135.00.** All volumes hardcover.   135.00   ....   F5159

Keach, Horace A. Burrillville (Rhode Island): As It Was and As It
Is. (1856) reprint 105pp. 12.00   F5216

Kimball, Gertrude S. Providence in Colonial Times (Includes
Illustrations). (1912) reprint 1991. 293pp.   45.00   ....   F5159

Richardson, E. History of Woonsocket. (1876) reprint 1990.
264pp.   32.50   ....   F5159

Steere, T. History of the Town of Smithfield, from its Organization
in 1730 to its Division in 1871. (1881) reprint 1987. 230pp.   29.00   ....   F5159

WASHINGTON COUNTY

Arnold, James N. The Records of the Proprietors of the
Narragansett, Otherwise Called "The Fones Record". (1894)
reprint 1990. 199pp.
> Indexed.   20.00   ....   F5130

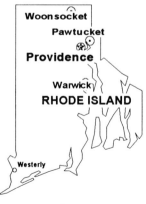

South Carolina

STATEWIDE REFERENCE

General Reference

Hirsch, Ph.D., Arthur Henry. The Huguenots of Colonial South
  Carolina. (1928) reprint 1991. 347pp.
  Indexed. 28.50   F5130

Doyle, J.A. The English in America: Virginia, Maryland and the
  Carolinas. (1882) reprint 556pp. 33.50   F5216

Migliazzo, Arlin C. and George F. Jones. Purrysburg. 1991. 38pp.
  Special section of South Carolina Historical Magazine,
  October 1991. "Compilation of Lists of
  German-Speaking Settlers of Purrysburg" by George F.
  Jones lists all German-named residents with sources. 6.00   N5181

Salley, Jr., Alexander S. Marriage Notices in the South Carolina
  and American General Gazette, 1766 to 1781 and The Royal
  Gazette, 1781-1782. (1914) reprint 1990. 52pp.
  Indexed 5.00   F5130

Abstracts

Moore, Carolina T. (Compl. & Ed.). Abstracts of Wills of the
  State of South Carolina 1670-1740.   30.00   20.00   F5194

_____. Abstracts of Records of the Secretary of the Province, South
  Carolina 1692-1721.   30.00   ....   F5194

_____. Abstracts of Wills of Charleston District, S.C. 1783-1800.
                                                    30.00   ....   F5194

_____. Abstracts of Wills of the State of South Carolina
  1740-1760.   30.00   ....   F5194

_____. Abstracts of Wills of the State of South Carolina
  1760-1784.   30.00   ....   F5194

Census

Heads of Families at the First Census of the United States Taken in
  the Year 1790 (bicentennial edition)- South Carolina. 1990.   21.50   ....   F5061

The 1790 Census. Heads of Families at the First Census of the
  United States Taken in the Year 1790 - South Carolina. reprint
  1992. 150pp. 21.50   F5129

Family Genealogies

Quattlebaum, Alexander McQueen. Clergymen and Chiefs: A
Genealogy of the MacQueen and Macfarlane Families. 1990.
246pp.
Families came from Scotland to North Carolina and
South Carolina. Extensive informtion about more than
1,200 families, including the related families of Ellerbe,
Holladay, Hudnall, MacDonald, Montgomery, Rogers,
White, and more. Includes illustrations, charts, and
index. 37.00 .... F5181

South Carolina Historical Society
100 Meeting Street, Charleston, S.C. 29401
$35 for individual membership/yr.
South Carolina Historical Magazine
Quarterly (scholarly journal) Carologue
Quarterly (popular history)

Military - Revolutionary War

Draper, Lyman C. King's Mountain and Its Heroes. History of the
Battle of King's Mountain, October 7th, 1780. (1881) reprint
1992. 612pp.
Indexed. 30.00 .... F5129

Ervin, Sara Sullivan. South Carolinians in the Revolutions...Also
Abstracts of Wills, Laurens County (Ninety-six District)
1775-1855. (1949) reprint 1991. 230pp.
Illustrated, indexed. 25.00 .... F5130

Revill, Janie. Original Index Book Showing the Revolutionary
Claims Filed in SC Between August 20, 1783 and August 31,
1786. (1941) reprint 1990. 387pp. 30.00 .... F5130

Salley, Alexander S. Records of the Regiments of the South Carolina
Line in the Revolutionary War. (1904-06) reprint 1991.
86pp.
Indexed. 10.00 F5130

Religious And Ethnic Groups

Martin, III, Joseph B. Guide to Presbyterian Ecclesiastical Names
and Places in South Carolina: 1685-1985. 1989. 212pp.
List of all Presbyterian churches in South Carolina,
including locations, variant names, sources of
information. A special double issue of South Carolina
Historical Magazine, January-April 1989. .... 11.00 F5181

Salley, Jr., A.S. Minutes of the Vestry of St. Helena's Parish, South
Carolina, 1726-1812. (1919) reprint 296pp. 21.50 F5216

Townsend, Leah. South Carolina Baptists, 1670-1805. (1935)
reprint 1990. 391pp.
Indexed 26.50 .... F5130

Religious & Ethnic Groups - Huguenots

Hirsch, Arthur Henry. The Huguenots of Colonial South
    Carolina. (1928) reprint 338pp. 25.00 F5216

Ravenel, Daniel. [List of French and Swiss]...Settled in Charleston,
    on the Santee, and at the Orange Quarter in Carolina... (1990)
    reprint 1888. 77pp.
        Indexed. 8.50 F5130

ANDERSON COUNTY

Simpson, R.W. History of Old Pendleton District (SC) with a
    Genealogy of the Leading Families. (1913) reprint 227pp. 18.00 F5216

CHARLESTON COUNTY

Hagy, James W. People and Professions of Charleston, South
    Carolina, 1782-1802. 1992. 112pp. 17.50 F5130

Holcomb, Brent. Marriage and Death Notices from the Charleston
    Observer, 1827-1845. (1980) reprint 283pp. 21.50 F5216

CHESTER COUNTY

Holcomb, Brent H. and Elmer O. Parker. Early Records of Fishing
    Creek Presbyterian Church, Chester County, South Carolina,
    1799-1859. (1980) reprint 191pp.
        With appendices of the visitation list of Rev. John
        Simpson, 1774-1776 and the cemetery roster,
        1762-1979. .... 17.00 F5216

MARION COUNTY

Sellers, W.W. A History of Marion County, From its Earliest Times
    to the Present, 1901. (1902) reprint 1992. 647pp.
        Includes sketches of hundreds of early families. 65.00 .... F5159

NEWBERRY COUNTY

Summer, George Leland. Newberry County, South Carolina:
    Historical and Genealogical Annals. (1950) reprint 1992.
    483pp.
        Indexed. 37.50 F5130

PICKENS COUNTY

Rich, Peggy Burton and Marion Ard Whitehurst. The People's
    Journal: Pickens, South Carolina, 1894-1903, Historical &
    Genealogical Abstracts. 1991. 398pp. 35.00 F5216

SPARTANBURG COUNTY

Landrum, J.B.O. History of Spartanburg County (South Carolina).
    (1900) reprint 770pp.
        Embracing an Account of Many Important Events, and
        Biographical Sketches of Statesmen, Divines, and other
        Public Men, and the Names of Many others worthy of
        record in the History of their county. 43.00 F5216

Tennessee

STATEWIDE REFERENCE

General Reference

Acklen, Jeannette Tillotson et al, Tennessee Records: Bible records
    and Marriage Bonds. (1933) reprint 1992. 521pp.
        Indexed. 36.00 F5130

_____. Tennessee Records: Tombstone Inscriptions and
    Manuscripts. (1933) reprint 1992. 517pp.
        Indexed. 36.00 F5130

Abstracts

Eddlemon, Sherida K. Genealogical Abstracts from Tennessee
    Newspapers Vol 2, 1803-1812. 1989. 248pp. 19.00 F5216

_____. Genealogical Abstracts from Tennessee Newspapers,
    Vol 3, 1821-1828. 1991. 260pp. 20.00 F5216

_____. Genealogical Abstracts from Tennessee Newspapers,
    Vol 1, 1791-1808. 1988. 380pp. 25.00 F5216

Census

Bentley, Elizabeth Petty. Index to the 1820 Census of Tennessee.
    (1981) reprint 1992. 287pp. 25.00 F5130

Foster, Austin P. Counties of Tennessee. (1923) reprint 1992.
    124pp. 14.00 F5130

Cumberland Settlements

Fulcher, Richard C. 1770 - 1790 Census of the Cumberland
    Settlements: Davidson, Sumner and Tennessee Counties.
    1990. 253pp. 22.50 .... F5129

BLOUNT COUNTY

Dockter, Jr., Albert W. Blount County, Tennessee, Chancery Court
    Records, Book 0 and Book 1, 1852-1865. 1992. 180pp. 17.50 F5216

DAVIDSON COUNTY

Eddlemon, Sherida K. Davidson County, Tennessee, County Court
    Minutes. Vol. 2, 1792-1799. 1991. 235pp. 18.50 F5216

_____. Davidson County, Tennessee, County Court Minutes.
    Vol. 3, 1799-1803. 1991. 223pp. 20.00 F5216

Wells, Carol. Davidson County, Tennessee, County Court Minutes.
    Vol. 1, 1783-1792. 1990. 275pp. 20.00 F5216

HENRY COUNTY

Whitley, Edythe. Henry County Tennessee Old Time Stuff. (1968)
    reprint 1991. 123pp.
        Indexed. 14.50   F5130

MORGAN COUNTY

Spurling and Cross. Morgan Co., TN 1850 Census. 1985. 80pp.
    .... 15.00   F5216

PUTNAM COUNTY

McGee, Norman T. and G. Kay McGee. 1870 United States Census
    of Putnam Co., Tennessee. 1989. 164pp. 25.00   F5079

_____. and G. Kay McGee. 1880 United States Census of Putnam
    Co., Tennessee. 1989. 219pp. 30.00   F5079

SULLIVAN COUNTY

Sherman, Karen L. Sullivan County, Tennessee, Cemeteries. 1991.
    219pp. 32.00   F5216

WASHINGTON COUNTY

Grammer, Norma Rutledge and Marion Day Mullins. Marriage
    Record of Washington County, Tennessee 1787-1840. (1940)
    reprint 1991. 68pp.
        Indexed. 6.00   F5129

WHITE COUNTY

Mitchell, Mary F. and J. Sharon Johnson Doliante. White County,
    Tennessee Oldest Marriage Book, 1809-1859. (1976) reprint
    1991. 102pp.
        Indexed 12.00   F5130

Texas

STATEWIDE REFERENCE

Research Aids

Gould, Sharry Crofford. Texas Cemetary Inscriptions: A Source
  Index. 1977. 52pp.
    Indexed by County. 5.95   F5059

Kennedy, Imogene and Leon Kennedy. Genealogical Records in
  Texas. (1987) reprint 1992. 248pp.   35.00   ....   F5129

White, Gifford. Texas Scholastics, 1854-1855: A State Census of
  School Children. 1991. 494pp. 30.00   F5216

ELLIS COUNTY

Kinsey, Margaret B. Ebenezer Baptist of Ellis County, Texas. 1990.
  338pp.
    1880-1892 Church Records. Referenced genealogies of
      members' families.   25.00   ....   F5143

HENDERSON COUNTY

Census Records of Henderson County, Texas, 1870. 1992. 260pp.
                                                ....   35.00   F5216

Vermont

STATEWIDE REFERENCE

General Reference

Dodge, Nancy L. Gravestones of Guildhall, Vermont &
    Northumberland, NH. 185pp.   39.00   ....   F5159

Hayward, John. Gazetteer of Vermont. (1849) reprint 240pp.
    Containing descriptions of all the counties, towns and
    districts in the state, and of its principal mountains, rivers,
    waterfalls, harbors, islands, and curious places. 18.50   F5216

Bibliographical Information

Gilman, M.D. Bibliography of Vermont; or, A List of Books &
    Pamphlets Relating in any way to the State. (1897) reprint
    1991. 349pp.   45.00   ....   F5159

Census

The 1790 Census. Heads of Families at the First Census of the
    United States Taken in the Year 1790 - Vermont. reprint 1992.
    95pp. 15.00   F5129

U.S. Bureau of the Census. Vermont: Heads of Families. At the
    Second Census of the United States Taken in the Year 1800.
    (1938) reprint 1992. 233pp.
        Map, indexed. 30.00   F5130

Military-Revolutionary War

Crockett, Walter H. Soldiers of the Revolutionary War Buried in
    Vermont and Anecdotes and Incidents Relating to Some of
    Them. (1903) reprint 1991. 77pp. 9.00   F5130

Goodrich, John E. (Comp. & Ed.). Rolls of the (Vermont) Soldiers in
    the Revolutionary War, 1775-1783. (1904) reprint 1992.
    927pp.   89.00   ....   F5159

Northeast Region

Dodge, Nancy L. Settlement & Cemeteries in Vermont's Northeast
    Kingdom. 197pp.
        Incl. Indexed Transcr. from Gravesites in Canaan,
        Lemington, Bloomfield, Brunswick & Maidstone, Vt. &
        Hereford, Quebec.   39.00   ....   F5159

ADDISON COUNTY

Smith, H.P. (Ed.). History of Addison County, with Illustrations &
    Biographical Sketches of its Prominent Men & Pioneers.
    (1886) reprint 1992. 774+62pp.   82.50   ....   F5159

CALEDONIA COUNTY

Fairbanks, E.T. The Town of St. Johnsbury: A Review of 125
Years. (1914) reprint 1991. 592pp.   55.00   ....   F5159

Miller, E. and E.P. Wells. History of Ryegate, from its Settlement by
Scotch-American Farmers to 1912. (1913) reprint 1987.
604pp.   61.00   ....   F5159

CHITTENDEN COUNTY

Hayden (Ed.), Chauncey H. History of Jericho. (1916) reprint
1991. 665pp.
    About one-half of this book is family history.   65.00   ....   F5159

FRANKLIN COUNTY

Aldrich (Ed.), L.C. History of Franklin & Grand Isle Counties.
(1891) reprint 1991. 821pp.   80.00   ....   F5159

Dutcher, L.L. History of St. Albans, Civil, Religious, Biogr. &
Statistical (With History of Sheldon). (1872) reprint 1991.
107pp. 16.00   F5159

LAMOILLE COUNTY

Haslam, Patricia L. Historical and Genealogical Data of Stowe,
Vermont. Including Defunct Towns of Sterling and Mansfield.
1987. 94pp.
    Part I: Earmarks, 1850 Census index; School; All known
    church records; Revolutionary War burials; Warnings
    out, to 1816; Overseer of the poor. 20.00   F5118

_____. Historical and Genealogical Data of Stowe, Vermont. Part
II: Old Yard (Center) Cemetery Inscriptions with Historical
Notes. 1989. 124pp.
    Oldest Cemetery, Plot Plan, Index. 18.00   F5118

Bigelow, Walter J. History of Stowe, Vermont 1763-1934. (1934)
reprint 1988. 262pp.
    Indexed.   28.00   ....   F5047

Wilkins, Maria N. History of Stowe, Vermont to 1869. 1987.
84pp.
    From A. M. Hemenway's Vermont Historical Gazetteer.
    Indexed. 12.50   F5047

ORANGE COUNTY

McKeen, S. History of Bradford, Containing Some Account of the
Place from its 1st Settlement in 1765 & the Principle
Improvements & Events to 1874 with genealogical records,
(1875) reprint 1987. 459pp.   46.00   ....   F5159

Wells, F.P. History of Newbury, from the Discovery of Coos Co. to
1902. With Genealogical Records. (1902) reprint 1987.
779pp.   79.00   ....   F5159

ORLEANS COUNTY

Haslam, Patricia L.   Greensboro, Vermont Families Before 1850.
1990. 34pp.
Includes Revolutionary War burials. 12.00   F5118

Town History Committee. The History of Greensboro, VT: The First
Two Hundred Years. 1990. 281pp.
Genealogies to 1850. Index. 28.00   F5028

RUTLAND COUNTY

Adams, Andrew N.   A History of the Town of Fair Haven. (1870)
reprint 1990. 516pp.
Includes over 200 pages of genealogical & biographical
data.   52.00   ....   F5159

Joslin, Frisbie & Ruggles. A History of the Town of Poultney, from
its Settlement to the Year 1875, with Family & Biogr. Sketches
& Incidents. (1875) reprint 1992. 369pp.   41.00   ....   F5159

WASHINGTON COUNTY

Jones, M.B. History of the Town of Waitsfield, 1782-1908, with
Family Genealogies. (1909) reprint 1987. 524pp.   55.00   ....   F5159

WINDSOR COUNTY

Davis, G.A. History of Reading, Windsor Co. (2nd ed.). (1903)
reprint 1987. 375+12pp.   40.00   ....   F5159

Hubbard, C.H. and J. Dartt. Early Marriages of Springfield (Extr.
from "History of the Town of Springfield"). 16pp.   5.00   ....   F5159

_____. and J. Dartt. First Proprietors of Springfield (Extr. from
"History of the Town of Springfield"). 18pp. F5159

_____. and J. Dartt. History of the Town of Springfield, with a
Genealogical Record. (1895) reprint 1990. 618pp.
With over 300 pages of genealogical records.   64.50   ....   F5159

Lovejoy, E.M.W. History of Royalton, with Family Genealogies,
1769-1911. (1911) reprint 1991. 1146pp.   99.50   ....   F5159

Vail, Henry Hobart and Emma Chandler White (Ed.).   Pomfret,
Vermont, In Two Volumes. (1930) reprint 1992.
Vol. I, History 338pp $39.00;
Vol. II, Biogr. & Genealogy 327pp $39.00.
Special Price for Set: $69.50. All hardcover.   69.50   ....   F5159

Virginia

STATEWIDE REFERENCE

Census

Heads of Families at the First Census of the US Taken in the Year 1790: Va. Records of the State's Enumerations 1782-1785. (1908) reprint 1990. 189pp. 19.50 F5159

Heads of Families at the First Census of the United States Taken in the Year 1790 (bicentennial edition)- Virginia (tax enumerations, 1782-1785). 1990. 21.50 .... F5061

The 1790 Census. Heads of Families at the First Census of the United States Taken in the Year 1790 - Virginia. reprint 1992. 189pp. 22.50 F5129

Central Region

Birkett, Joseph. Birkett Diary: Voyage and Visit to America, 1784-5. 1990. 86pp.
New York City, Philadelphia, Baltimore, and mostly Petersburg, Virginia area. 12.00 F5177

County Governments

Chart on the Formation of Virginia Counties. 3.00 F5061

Hiden, Martha W. How Justice Grew. Virginia Counties: An Abstract of Their Formation. (1957) reprint 1992. 101pp. Map, indexed. 12.00 F5130

Robinson, Morgan P. Virginia Counties: Those Resulting from Virginia Legislation. (1916) reprint 1992. 283pp. Indexed. 25.00 .... F5129

THE N.W. LAPIN PRESS
P.O. Box 5053
Charlottesville, VA 22905-5053
•••••••••
Virginia Publications & Research
Joanne Lovelace Nance
- SASE for Details -

Eastern Shore

Turman, Nora Miller. The Eastern Shore of Virginia, 1606-1964. (1964) reprint 316pp. 22.50 F5216

Wise, J.C. Ye Kingdom of Accawmacke, or the New Eastern Shore
of Va. in the 17th Cent. (1911) reprint 1988. 416pp.   42.50   ....   F5159

_____. Ye Kingdome of Accawmacke or the Eastern Shore of
Virginia in the 17th Century. (1911) reprint 1990. 406pp.
Indexed   25.00   ....   F5130

_____. Ye Kingdome of Accawmacke: or the Eastern Shore of
Virginia in the Seventeenth Century. (1911) reprint 406pp. 26.50   F5216

Virginia Genealogical Society
P.O. Box 7469, Richmond, VA 23221

Bi-monthly: VGS Newsletter
Quarterly: *Magazine of Virginia Genealogy*

Membership: $20.00 INDIVIDUAL $22.00 FAMILY

Family Genealogies And Histories

Boddie, John Bennett. Virginia Historical Genealogies. (1954)
reprint 1990. 384pp.
Indexed.   22.50   ....   F5130

Hayden, Horace Edwin. Virginia Genealogies. (1891) reprint
1992. 777pp.
A Genealogy of the Glassell Family of Scotland and
Virginia, Also of the Families of Ball, Brown, Bryan,
Conway, Daniel, Ewell, Holladay, Lewis, Littlepage,
Moncure, Peyton, Robinson, Scott, Taylor, Wallace, and
Others of Virginia and Maryland.
Indexed. 49.95   F5130

Sorley, Merrow Egerton. Lewis of Warner Hall. (1935) reprint
1991. 887pp.
This book covers Col. John Lewis and Frances Fielding
and their descendants; Col. Charles Lewis and Mary
Howell and their descendants, with considerable attention
given to these related families: Ambler, Ball, Barret,
Bowles, Bushrod, Byrd, Carter, Cobbs, Crawford, Eppes,
Fauntleroy, Fielding, Griffin, Howell, Isham, Jefferson,
Kennon, Marshall, Piersey, Ragland, Randolph,
Taliaferro, Taylor, Thompson, Walker, Washington,
Willis, Woodson and Worsham.
Indexed.   45.00   ....   F5129

Stewart, Robert Armistead. Index to Printed Virginia Genealogies Including Key and Bibliography. (1930) reprint 1991. 265pp.   21.50   ....   F5130

Virdin, Donald O. Virginia Genealogies and Family Histories: A Bibliography of Books About Virginia Families. 1990. 210pp. 30.00   F5216

Immigration, Emigration, Migration

Stanard, William G. Some Emigrants to Virginia. 2nd ed. (1915) reprint 1992. 94pp.
     Memoranda in Regard to Several Hundred Emigrants to Virginia During the Colonial Period whose Parentage is Shown or Former Residence Indicated by Authentic Records. 10.00   F5130

Land Grants

Nugent, Nell Marion. Cavaliers and Pioneers, Abstracts of Virginia Land Patents and Grants, 1623-1666, Volume One. (1934) reprint 1991. 767pp.   40.00   ....   F5129

Maps & Gazetteers

Doran, Michael F. Atlas of County Boundary Changes in Virginia, 1634-1895. 1987. 61pp. 17.95   F5061

Military

Bockstruck, Lloyd DeWitt. Virgina's Colonial Soldiers. 1990. 443pp.   30.00   ....   F5129

Butler, Stuart Lee. Virginia Soldiers in the United States Army, 1800-1815. 1986. 188pp. 17.00   F5061

Military - Revolutionary War

McAllister, J.T. Virginia Militia in the Revolutionary War. (1913) reprint 337pp. 23.00   F5216

Wardell, Patrick G. Virginia & West Virginia Genealogical Data from Revolutionary War Pension & Bounty Land Warrant Records. Vol. 1, Aaron-Cyrus. 1988. 342pp. 25.00   F5216

_____. Virginia & West Virginia Genealogical Data from Revolutionary War Pension & Bounty Land Warrant Records. Vol. 2, Dabbs-Hyslop. 1990. 438pp. 30.00   F5216

Military - War Of 1812

Butler, Stuart Lee. A Guide to Virginia Militia Units in the War of 1812. 1988. 340pp. 20.00   F5061

Wardell, Patrick G. War of 1812: Virginia Bounty Land and Pension Applications. 1987. 408pp. 26.50   F5216

New River Valley

Heavener, Rev. Ulysses S. A. German New River Settlement: Virginia. (1929) reprint 1992. 94pp.
     Indexed. 12.50   F5130

Mathews, Geraldine M. Ed., New River Historical Society Journal.
Vols. I, II, III, IV (Published Annually). 1988. 25p +/-.
$2.50/volume. F5197

Newspaper Abstracts

Death Notices from Richmond, Virginia Newspapers 1821-1840.
1987. 347pp.
These notices refer to Virginians throughout the state and
also to Virginians in other states. 20.00 F5092

Marriage Notices from Richmond, Virginia Newspapers, 1821-1840.
1988. 238pp.
These notices refer to Virginians throughout the state and
also to Virginians in other states. 20.00 F5092

Pioneers

Hale, John P. Trans-Allegheny Pioneers: Historical sketches of the
First White Settlers West of the Alleghenies, 1748 and After.
(1886) reprint 340pp. 23.00 F5216

Postal Service

Axelson, Edith F. Virginia Postmasters and Post Offices, 1789-1832.
1991. 350pp. 20.00 F5061

Religious And Ethnic Groups - French

Cabell, Priscilla Harriss. Turff & Twigg, Volume I, The French
Lands. 1988. 468 pp.
Map of individual surveys of Huguenots at
Manakintown. Index of 6,000 names. Generations of
families traced with all references. Much new
information of this part of original shire of Henrico,
beginning in 17th century. Hardcover,
Smythe-sewn binding. 51.50 .... F5242

Religious And Ethnic Groups - German

Schuricht, Herrmann. The German Element in Virginia. (1898)
reprint 1989. 433pp.
2 volumes in 1, indexed. 23.95 .... F5130

Religious And Ethnic Groups - Quakers

Bell, James P. Our Quaker Friends of Ye Olden Time. (1905)
reprint 1991. 287pp.
Being in Part a Transcript of the Minute Books of Cedar
Creek Meeting, Hanover County, and the South River
Meeting, Campbell County, Virginia. Illustrated,
indexed. 25.00 .... F5130

Research Aids

Axelson, Edith F. A Guide to Episcopal Church Records in Virginia.
1988. 136pp. 12.00 F5061

Committee on State Library. Colonial Records of Virginia. (1874)
reprint 1992. 106pp. 17.50 .... F5130

Dorman, John Frederick. Index to the Virginia Genealogist, Volumes 1-20, 1957-1976. 1981. 941pp.   50.00   ....   F5216

_____. The Virginia Genealogist, Vol. 1, 1957. (1957) reprint 235pp. 18.50   F5216

_____. The Virginia Genealogist, Vol. 2, 1958. (1958) reprint 246pp. 18.50   F5216

Vogt, John and T. William Kethley, Jr. Marriage records in the Virginia State Library: A Researcher's guide (2d Edition-1988). 1988. 246pp. 12.00   F5061

_____. and T. William Kethley, Jr. Will and Estate Records in the Virginia State Library: A Researcher's Guide. 1987. 186pp. 10.00   F5061

Wardell, Patrick G. Virginians & West Virginians, 1607-1870. Vol 1, from "History of Virginia" 20,000 entries. 1986. 440pp. 27.50   F5216

_____. Virginians & West Virginians, 1607-1870. Vol. 2, from "Virginia, Rebirth of the Old Dominion" 20,000 entries. 1988. 589pp.   35.00   ....   F5216

_____. Virginians & West Virginians, 1607-1870. Vol. 3, from "History of West Virginia, Old and New, and West Virginia Biography", 32,000 entries. 1992. 1,185pp. 70.00   F5216

Weisiger, III, Benjamin B. Burned County Data, 1809-1848 (As Found in the Virginia Contested Election Files). 100pp. 15.00   F5061

Research Aids - Indices

Wardell, P.G. Timesaving Aid to Virginia-West Virginia Ancestors (A Genealogical Index of Surnames from Published Sources). 1990. 429pp. 36.00   F5061

Shenandoah Valley

Good, Rebecca H. and Rebecca A. Ebert. Finding Your People in the Shenandoah Valley of Virginia. 1988. 104pp. 9.95   F5216

Source Records

Cognets, Jr., Louis des. English Duplicates of Lost Virginia Records. (1958) reprint 1990. 380pp.   25.00   ....   F5129

Fisher, Therese A. Marriage Records of the City of Frederick, and of Orange, Spotsylvania, and Strafford Counties, Virginia, 1722-1850. 1990. 267pp. 21.50   F5216

Torrence, Clayton. Virginia Wills and Administrations 1632 - 1800. (1931) reprint 1990. 483pp.   25.00   ....   F5129

Southside Region

Watson, Walter A. Notes on Southside Virginia. (1925) reprint 1990. 346pp.
Indexed   23.50   ....   F5130

Southwest

Worrell, Anne Lowry. Over the Mountain Men, Their Early Court Records in Southwest Virginia. (1934) reprint 1991. 69pp. 6.00   F5129

```
SOUTHEASTERN VIRGINIA PUBLICATIONS
        W.  S.  DAWSON  CO.
           P. O. BOX 62823
       VIRGINIA BEACH, VA 23466

       Catalog and fliers available
```

Tidewater Region

Boddie, John Bennett.   Southside Virginia Families Volume I.
    (1955) reprint 1991. 380pp.
        Contains lineages of more than fifty families from the
        early counties of Isle of Wight, Prince George, and Surry.
        Illustrated, indexed.   27.50   ....   F5130

_____. Southside Virginia Families Volume II.   (1956) reprint
    1991. 304pp.
        Contains lineages of more than forty families from the
        early counties of Isle of Wight, Surry, and Sussex.
        Illustrated, indexed.   24.50   ....   F5130

Western

Doddridge, Rev. Dr. Joseph.   Notes on the Settlement and Indian
    Wars of the Western Parts of Virginia and Pennsylvania from
    1763-1783. (1912) reprint 320pp. 22.50   F5216

McWhorter, Lucullus V.   The Border Settlers of Northwestern
    Virginia, From 1768 to 1795. (1915) reprint 1991. 509pp.
        Embracing the Life of Jesse Hughes and Other Noted
        Scouts of the Great Woods of the Trans-Allegheny.
        Illustrated. 34.00   F5130

ACCOMACK COUNTY

Abercrombie, Janice Luck and Richard Slatten.   Accomack County,
    Virginia Publick Claims. 1991. 6pp. 5.00   F5061

Mihalyka, Jean Merritt and Faye Downing Wilson.   Graven Stones:
    Inscriptions from Lower Accomack County, Virginia, including
    Liberty and Parksley Cemeteries - 2nd ed. (1987) reprint
    1992. 324pp. 28.50   F5216

Nottingham, Stratton.   Certificates and Rights, Accomack County,
    Virginia, 1663-1709. (1929) reprint 1992. 91pp.
        Indexed. 11.00   F5130

_____.   The Marriage License Bonds of Accomack County,
    Virginia, From 1774 to 1806. (1927) reprint 1991. 49pp.
        Indexed 8.50   F5130

_____. Wills and Administrations of Accomack County, Virginia,
    1663-1800. (1931) reprint 1990. 575.   ....   33.50   F5216

_____. and Miles Barnes.   Accomack Land Causes, 1728-1825.
    (1930) reprint 1989. 178pp. 17.50   F5216

ALBEMARLE COUNTY

Abercrombie, Janice Luck and Richard Slatten. Albemarle County,
Virginia Publick Claims. 1991. 70pp. 8.75 F5061

Deed & Will Abstracts of Albemarle County, Virginia (1748-1752).
.... 23.00 F5228

Deed Abstracts of Albemarle County, Virginia (1758-1761).
.... 18.00 F5228

Deed Abstracts of Albemarle County, Virginia (1764-1768).
.... 21.00 F5228

Deed Abstracts of Albemarle County, Virginia (1768-1770).
.... 21.00 F5228

Deed Abstracts of Albemarle County, Virginia (1771-1772).
.... 18.00 F5228

Deed Abstracts of Albemarle County, Virginia (1772-1776).
.... 23.00 F5228

Deed Abstracts of Albemarle County, Virginia (1861-1764).
.... 21.00 F5228

Vogt, John and T. William Kethley, Jr. Albemarle County, Virginia
Marriages, 1780-1853 (3 volume set). 1991. 862pp. 44.95 F5061

Weisiger, III, Benjamin B. Albemarle County, VA Court Papers,
1744-1783. 1987. 86pp. 10.00 F5061

Woods, Rev. Edgar. Albemarle County in Virginia. (1901) reprint
1990. 412pp.
Indexed 27.50 .... F5130

_____. New index by Roger L. Goodman. Albemarle County
in Virginia. (1901) reprint 450pp. 27.50 F5216

ALEXANDRIA COUNTY

Tallichet, Margorie D. Alexandria, Virginia City and County 1850
Census. 1986. 219pp. 27.50 F5216

ALLEGHANY COUNTY

Martin, Nora B. The Federal Census of 1830, 1840 and 1850 for
Alleghany County, Virginia. 118pp. 11.00 F5061

_____. The Federal Census of 1870 for Alleghany County,
Virginia. 122pp. 11.00 F5061

AMELIA COUNTY

Abercrombie, Janice Luck and Richard Slatten. Amelia County,
Virginia Publick Claims. 1991. 107pp. 14.00 F5061

Amelia County, Virginia Deeds, 1759-1765. 1990. 178pp.
12.00 .... F5140

Amelia County, Virginia Deeds, 1765-1768. 1990. 71pp.
10.00 .... F5140

Williams, Kathleen Booth. Marriages of Amelia County, Virginia
1735-1815. (1961) reprint 1992. 165pp.
Indexed. 18.50 F5130

AMHERST COUNTY

Abercrombie, Janice Luck and Richard Slatten. Amherst County, Virginia Publick Claims. 1991. 50pp. 6.75 F5061

Sweeny, William Montgomery. Marriage Bonds and Other Marriage Records of Amherst County, Virginia 1763-1800. (1937) reprint 1991. 102pp.
Indexed 17.50 .... F5130

ARLINGTON COUNTY

Miller, T. Michael. Alexandria and Alexandria (Arlington) County, Virginia Minister Returns & Marriage Bonds 1801-1852. 1987. 195pp. 16.50 F5216

_____. Artisans and Merchants of Alexandria, Virginia 1780-1820, Vol. 1. 1991. 275pp. 20.00 F5216

_____. Pen Portraits: Alexandria, Virginia, 1739-1900. 1987. 413pp. 26.50 F5216

Munson, James D. Alexandria, Virginia: Alexandria Hustings Court Deeds Vol. 2, 1797-1801. 1991. 287pp. 21.50 F5216

Munson, Ph.D., James D. Alexandria, Virginia: Alexandria Hustings Court Deeds. Vol. 1, 1783-1797. 1990. 272pp. 20.00 F5216

AUGUSTA COUNTY

Abercrombie, Janice Luck and Richard Slatten. Augusta County, Virginia Publick Claims. 1991. 5pp. 5.00 F5061

Burials in Augusta Glebe Cemetery.
.... 3.00 F5200

Bushman, Compiler, Katherine G. Naturalization Records, Augusta County, Virginia, 1753-1906. 1992. 36pp. 12.00 F5201

_____. Register of Free Blacks of Augusta County & City of Staunton, Virginia, 1810-1864. 1989. 146pp. 12.00 F5201

Cleek, George Washington. Early Western Augusta Pioneers. (1957) reprint 1992. 492pp.
Including the Families of Cleek, Gwin, Lightner and Warwick and Related Families of Bratton, Campbell, Carlile, Craig, Crawford, Dyer, Gay, Givens, Graham, Harper, Henderson, Hull, Keister, Lockridge, McFarland and Moore. Indexed. 37.50 F5130

Kaylor, Peter C. Abstract of Land Grant surveys of Augusta and Rockingham Counties, Virginia, 1761-1791. (1930) reprint 1991. 150pp.
Indexed 21.50 .... F5130

Marriage Records of Augusta County, Virginia 1785-1813 (4th Reprint). (1930) reprint 1985. 75pp. 10.00 F5200

Marriage Records of Augusta County, Virginia 1813-1850. (1972) reprint 1981. 139pp. 12.00 F5200

Peyton, J. Lewis. History of Augusta County, Virginia. (1882) reprint 420pp. 32.50 .... F5216

Reese, Margaret C. Abstract of Augusta County, Virginia Death Registers, 1853-1896. 1983. 236pp. 12.50 F5061

Vogt, John and T. William Kethley, Jr. Augusta County, Virginia Marriages, 1748-1850. 1986. 414pp.	.... 17.00	F5061
Waddell, Jos. A. Annals of Augusta County, Virginia, From 1726 to 1871. (1901) reprint 1991. 555pp. Second edition, fldg. map, indexed.	.... 35.00	F5130
Weaver, Dorothy Lee. The Federal Census of 1850 for Augusta County, Virginia. 1991. TBD.	....	F5061

BATH COUNTY

Morton, Oren F. Annals of Bath County, Virginia. (1917) reprint 1990. 208pp. Indexed	25.00	F5130

BEDFORD COUNTY

Abercrombie, Janice Luck and Richard Slatten. Bedford County, Virginia Publick Claims. 1991. 64pp.	.... 7.75	F5061
Bedford County, Virginia Deeds, 1761-1766. 1991. 92pp.	11.00	F5140

BOTETOURT COUNTY

Abercrombie, Janice Luck and Richard Slatten. Botetourt County, Virginia Publick Claims. 1991. 49pp.	.... 6.75	F5061
Vogt, John and T. William Kethley, Jr. Botetourt County Marriages, 1770-1853. 1987. 600pp.	.... 21.95	F5061

BRUNSWICK COUNTY

Abercrombie, Janice Luck and Richard Slatten. Brunswick County, Virginia Publick Claims. 1991. 58pp.	.... 7.50	F5061
Brunswick County, Virginia Court Orders, 1732-1741. 1992. Abstracts of Brunswick Order Book 1. Publication date February 1992. Write for information.	....	F5140
Brunswick County, Virginia Deeds, 1740-1744. 1991. 75pp.	11.00	F5140
Brunswick County, Virginia Deeds, 1745-1749. 1991. 96pp.	11.00	F5140
Brunswick County, Virginia Wills, 1739-1750. 1991. 76pp.	14.00	F5140
Fothergill, Augusta B. Marriage Records of Brunswick Co. Virginia, 1730-1852. (1953) reprint 1989. 153pp. Indexed	18.00	F5130
Vogt, John and T. William Kethley, Jr. Brunswick County Marriages, 1750-1853. 1988. 296pp.	.... 15.00	F5061

BUCKINGHAM COUNTY

Abercrombie, Janice Luck and Richard Slatten. Buckingham County, Virginia Publick Claims. 1991. 37pp.	.... 5.00	F5061
Weisiger, III, Benjamin B. Buckingham County, Virginia 1850 U.S. Census. 1984. 151pp.	.... 10.00	F5061

CAMPBELL COUNTY

Abercrombie, Janice Luck and Richard Slatten. Campbell County, Virginia Publick Cliams. 1991. 28pp. 5.00 F5061

Campbell County, Virginia Deeds, 1782-1784. 1991. 52pp. 9.00 .... F5140

Campbell County, Virginia Deeds, 1784-1790. 1991. 112pp. 14.00 .... F5140

Campbell County, Virginia Deeds, 1790-1796. 1991. 141pp. 15.00 .... F5140

Campbell County, Virginia Wills, 1782-1800. 1991. 129pp. 14.00 .... F5140

CAROLINE COUNTY

Abercrombie, Janice Luck and Richard Slatten. Caroline County, Virginia Publick Cliams. 1991. 100pp. 13.00 F5061

Caroline County, Virginia Chancery Court Deeds, 1758-1845. 1990. 79pp. 12.00 .... F5140

Caroline County, Virginia Land Tax Lists, 1787-1799. 1991. 167pp. 14.00 .... F5140

Order Book Abstracts of Caroline County, Virginia (1765). 20.00 F5228

Order Book Abstracts of Caroline County, Virginia (1765-1767). 18.00 F5228

Order Book Abstracts of Caroline County, Virginia (1767-1768). 18.00 F5228

Order Book Abstracts of Caroline County, Virginia (1768-1770). 18.00 F5228

Order Book Abstracts of Caroline County, Virginia (1770-1771). 18.00 F5228

Wingfield, Marshall. A History of Caroline County, Virginia From Its Formation in 1727 to 1924 To Which is Appended "A Discourse of Virginia" by Edward Maria Wingfield. (1924) reprint 1991. 528pp.
Indexed 30.00 .... F5130

CHARLES CITY COUNTY

Abercrombie, Janice Luck and Richard Slatten. Charles City County, Virginia Publick Cliams. 1991. 30pp. 5.00 F5061

Foley, Louise Pledge Heath. Early Virginia Families Along the James River, Charles City County - Prince George County. (1978) reprint 1990. 211pp.
Maps, Indexed. 25.00 .... F5129

Weisiger, III, Benjamin B. Charles City County, Virginia 1725-1731. 1984. 63pp. 10.00 F5061

_____. Charles City County, Virginia Court Orders, 1687-1695. 1980. 249pp. 22.95 F5061

_____. Charles City County, Virginia, Records, 1737-1774. 1986. 201pp. 20.00 F5061

CHARLOTTE COUNTY

Abercrombie, Janice Luck and Richard Slatten. Charlotte County,
  Virginia Publick Claims. 1991. 33pp. 5.00 F5061

Charlotte County, Virginia Deeds, 1771-1777. 1990. 120pp.
  12.00 .... F5140

Charlotte County, Virginia Wills, 1765-1791. 1991. 218pp.
  Detailed abstracts of all the documents in Charlotte Will
  Book No. 1. This large will book is rich in family
  relationships and has many references to court cases and
  military service. Refers to about 7,000 individuals. Why
  pay more when you can get the best for less?
  Map, index, soundex index. 19.00 .... F5140

Nance, Joanne Lovelace. Charlotte County, Virginia 1765-1771
  Deed Books 1 and 2. 1990. 110pp. 20.00 F5137

CHESTERFIELD COUNTY

Abercrombie, Janice Luck and Richard Slatten. Chesterfield County,
  Virginia Publick Claims. 1991. 57pp. 7.50 F5061

Chesterfield Co., Virginia Court Orders, 1749-1752. 1991.
  140pp. 15.00 .... F5140

Weisiger, III, Benjamin B. Chesterfield County, Virginia 1850 U.S.
  Census. 1988. 204pp. 15.00 F5061

_____. Chesterfield County, Virginia Deeds, 1749-1756. 1986.
  95pp. 10.00 F5061

_____. Chesterfield County, Virginia Deeds, 1756-1764. 1989.
  91pp. 10.00 F5061

_____. Chesterfield County, Virginia Deeds, 1764-1768. 1991.
  74pp. 10.00 F5061

_____. Chesterfield County, Virginia Marriages, 1816-1853.
  1981. 201pp. 17.00 F5061

_____. Chesterfield County, Virginia Wills, 1749-1774. 1979.
  213pp. 17.00 F5061

_____. Chesterfield County, Virginia Wills, 1774-1802. 1982.
  327pp. 27.95 F5061

CITY OF RICHMOND

Weisiger, III, Benjamin B. City of Richmond, Virginia Wills
  1782-1810. 1983. 55pp. 10.00 F5061

CLARKE COUNTY

Vogt, John and T. Willliam Kethley, Jr. Clarke County Marriages,
  1836-1850. 1983. 62pp. 5.00 F5061

CULPEPER COUNTY

Abercrombie, Janice Luck and Richard Slatten. Culpeper County,
  Virginia Publick Claims. 1991. 82pp. 11.00 F5061

Deed Abstracts of Culpeper County, Virginia (1769-1773).
  .... 21.00 F5228

Deed Abstracts of Culpeper County, Virginia (1773-1775).
.... 17.00 F5228

Deed Abstracts of Culpeper County, Virginia (1775-1778).
.... 22.00 F5228

Deed Abstracts of Culpeper County, Virginia (1778-1779).
.... 16.00 F5228

Deed Abstracts of Culpeper County, Virginia (1779-1781).
.... 18.00 F5228

Deed Abstracts of Culpeper County, Virginia (1781-1783).
.... 18.00 F5228

Deed Abstracts of Culpeper County, Virginia (1783-1785).
.... 23.00 F5228

Slaughter, D.D., Rev. Philip. A History of St. Mark's Parish, Culpeper County, Virginia. (1877) reprint 216pp. With notes of old churches and old families, and illustrations of the manners and customs of the olden time.
.... 18.50 F5216

Vogt, John and T. William Kethley, Jr. Culpeper County Marriages, 1780-1853. 1986. 257pp.
.... 15.00 F5061

Will Abstracts of Culpeper County, Virginia (1749-1770).
.... 21.00 F5228

Will Abstracts of Culpeper County, Virginia (1791-1803).
.... 22.00 F5228

Will Abstracts of Culpeper County, Virginia (1803-1809).
.... 21.00 F5228

CUMBERLAND COUNTY

Abercrombie, Janice Luck and Richard Slatten. Cumberland County, Virginia Publick Claims. 1991. 71pp.
.... 8.75 F5061

Cumberland County, Virginia Deeds, 1749-1752. 1991. 60pp.
9.00 .... F5140

DINWIDDIE COUNTY

Abercrombie, Janice Luck and Richard Slatten. Dinwiddie County, Virginia Publick Claims. 1991. 51pp.
.... 6.75 F5061

ELIZABETH CITY COUNTY

Abercrombie, Janice Luck and Richard Slatten. Elizabeth City County, Virginia Publick Claims. 1991. 17pp.
.... 5.00 F5061

Neal, C.G., Rosemary Corley. Elizabeth City County, Virginia: Deeds, Wills, Court Orders, Etc. 1986. 330pp.
.... 22.50 F5216

ESSEX COUNTY

Abercrombie, Janice Luck and Richard Slatten. Essex County, Virginia Publick Claims. 1991. 31pp.
.... 5.00 F5061

Abstracts of Land Causes of Essex County, Virginia (1711-1741).Contains Essex County Land Cause Books 1711-1716 and 1715-1741.
.... 19.00 F5228

Deed & Will Abstracts of Essex County, Virginia (1695-1697).
.... 20.00 F5228

Deed & Will Abstracts of Essex County, Virginia (1697-1699).
.... 20.00 F5228

Deed & Will Abstracts of Essex County, Virginia (1699-1701).
.... 20.00 F5228

Deed & Will Abstracts of Essex County, Virginia (1701-1703).
.... 20.00 F5228

Deed Abstracts of Essex County, Virginia (1721-1724).
.... 18.00 F5228

Deed Abstracts of Essex County, Virginia (1724-1728).
.... 21.00 F5228

Deed Abstracts of Essex County, Virginia (1728-1733).
.... 18.00 F5228

Deed Abstracts of Essex County, Virginia (1733-1738).
.... 22.00 F5228

Deed Abstracts of Essex County, Virginia (1738-1742).
.... 21.00 F5228

Deed Abstracts of Essex County, Virginia (1742-1745).
.... 22.00 F5228

Order Book Abstracts of Essex County, Virginia (1695-1699).
.... 21.00 F5228

Order Book Abstracts of Essex County, Virginia (1699-1702).
.... 23.00 F5228

Order Book Abstracts of Essex County, Virginia (1716-1723)
Part I.
.... 22.00 F5228

Order Book Abstracts of Essex County, Virginia (1716-1723)
Part II.
.... 22.00 F5228

Order Book Abstracts of Essex County, Virginia (1716-1723)
Part III.
.... 22.00 F5228

Order Book Abstracts of Essex County, Virginia (1716-1723)
Part IV.
.... 22.00 F5228

Order Book Abstracts of Essex County, Virginia (1723-1725)
Part I.
.... 20.00 F5228

Order Book Abstracts of Essex County, Virginia (1723-1725)
Part II.
.... 20.00 F5228

Order Book Abstracts of Essex County, Virginia (1725-1729)
Part I.
.... 20.00 F5228

Order Book Abstracts of Essex County, Virginia (1725-1729)
Part II.
.... 20.00 F5228

Record Abstracts of Essex County, Virginia (1692-1693).
Contains Deeds, Wills, and Orders.
.... 21.00 F5228

Record Abstracts of Essex County, Virginia (1693-1694).
Contains Deeds, Wills and Orders.
.... 21.00 F5228

Record Abstracts of Essex County, Virginia (1694-1695).
Contains Deeds, Wills, and Orders.
.... 21.00 F5228

Will Abstracts of Essex County, Virginia (1730-1735).
.... 21.00 F5228

Will Abstracts of Essex County, Virginia (1735-1743).

.... 23.00 F5228

Will Abstracts of Essex County, Virginia (1743-1745).

.... 19.00 F5228

Will Abstracts of Essex County, Virginia (1745-1748).

.... 22.00 F5228

FAIRFAX COUNTY

Abercrombie, Janice Luck and Richard Slatten. Fairfax County,
Virginia Publick Claims. 1991. 23pp. 5.00 F5061

Deed Abstracts of Fairfax County, Virginia (1742-1750).

.... 21.00 F5228

Deed Abstracts of Fairfax County, Virginia (1750-1761).

.... 21.00 F5228

Deed Abstracts of Fairfax County, Virginia (1761-1768).

.... 21.00 F5228

Deed Abstracts of Fairfax County, Virginia (1772-1774).

.... 21.00 F5228

Deed Abstracts of Fairfax County, Virginia (1774-1777).

.... 16.00 F5228

Deed Abstracts of Fairfax County, Virginia (1783-1784).

.... 20.00 F5228

Deed Abstracts of Fairfax County, Virginia (1784-1785).

.... 20.00 F5228

Deed Abstracts of Fairfax County, Virginia (1785-1788).

.... 23.00 F5228

Deed Abstracts of Fairfax County, Virginia (1788-1789).

.... 20.00 F5228

Index Missing Deed Book N, Fairfax County, Virginia (1778-1783).

.... 16.00 F5228

Indexes to Missing Deed Books, Fairfax County, Virginia
(1750-1770). 18.00 F5228

Land Records of Long Standing, Fairfax County, Virginia
(1742-1770). 21.00 F5228

Will Abstracts of Fairfax County, Virginia (1767-1783).

.... 18.00 F5228

Will Abstracts of Fairfax County, Virginia (1784-1791).

.... 18.00 F5228

Will Abstracts of Fairfax County, Virginia (1791-1794).

.... 16.00 F5228

FAUQUIER COUNTY

Abercrombie, Janice Luck and Richard Slatten. Fauquier County,
Virginia Publick Claims. 1991. 49pp. 6.75 F5061

Gott, John K. Fauquier County, Virginia Deed Abstracts,
1759-1778. 1988. 218pp. 17.50 F5216

_____. Fauquier County, Virginia, Guardian Bonds, 1759-1871. 1989. 139pp. 13.50 F5216

_____. Fauquier County, Virginia, Marriage Bonds (1759-1854), and Marriage Returns (1785-1848). 1989. 296pp. 21.50 F5216

Gott, John K. and T. Triplett Russell. The Dixon Valley, Its First 250 Years. 1991. 160pp. 17.50 F5216

Peters, Joan W. Abstracts of Fauquier County, Virginia Birth Records, 1853-1896. 1989. 270pp. 25.00 F5216

FLOYD COUNTY

Wood, Amos D. and Ann S. Bailey, Editor. Floyd County: A History of Its People and Places. (1981) reprint 1986. 510pp. 22.25 F5196

FLUVANNA COUNTY

Abercrombie, Janice Luck and Richard Slatten. Fluvanna County, Virginia Publick Claims. 1991. 34pp. 5.00 F5061

Fluvanna County, Virginia Deeds, 1777-1783. 1991. 77pp.
10.00 .... F5140

Vogt, John and T. William Kethley, Jr. Fluvanna County Marriages, 1781-1849. 1984. 103pp. 9.00 F5061

FRANKLIN COUNTY

Franklin County, Virginia Wills, 1786-1812. 1991. 162pp.
18.00 .... F5140

Mann Robuck, Karen. Franklin County, Virginia 1850 and 1860 Censuses. 1990. 402pp. 42.50 .... F5162

Wingfield, Marshall. Marriage Bonds of Franklin County, Virginia 1786-1858. (1939) reprint 1991. 299pp.
With a new index of Brides, Parents and Sureties. 21.50 F5130

FREDERICK COUNTY

Abercrombie, Janice Luck and Richard Slatten. Frederick County, Virginia Publick Claims. 1991. 45pp. 6.25 F5061

Cartmell, T.K. Shenandoah Valley Pioneers and Their Descendants: A History of Frederick Cty., VA from formation in 1738 to 1908. (1909) reprint 588pp. 60.00 F5216

Hutton, Jr, James V. Tell Me of a Land That's Fair. 1987. 52pp.
.... 5.00 F5061

_____. The Federal Census of 1850 for Frederick Co., VA. 1987. 369pp. 15.00 F5061

Kangas, M.N. and D.E. Payne. Frederick County, Virginia, Wills & Administrations, 1795-1816. (1983) reprint 1992. 144pp. Indexed. 16.50 F5130

Kerns, Wilmer L. Historical Records of Old Frederick and Hampshire Counties, Virginia (Revised). (1988) reprint 1992. 430pp. 32.00 F5216

Tylor, Dola S. City of Winchester, Virginia, Register of Births, 1853-1891 Vol. 2, 1865-1891. 1991. 310pp. 35.00 F5216

_____. City of Winchester, Virginia, Register of Births,
1853-1891. Vol. 1, 1853-1860. 1991. 115pp. 20.00 F5216

_____. Winchester, Virginia, Register of Deaths, 1871-1891.
1991. 204pp. 26.00 F5216

_____. Winchester, Virginia, Will Abstracts, 1794-1894. 1990.
118pp. 20.00 F5216

Vogt, John and T. William Kethley, Jr. Frederick County Marriages,
1738-1850. 1984. 461pp. 17.00 F5061

FREDERICKSBURG CITY

Deed Abstracts of Fredericksburg City, Va. Hustings Court
(1782-1787). 19.00 F5228

Deed Abstracts of Fredericksburg City, Va. Hustings Court
(1787-1794). 19.00 F5228

Deed Abstracts of Fredericksburg City, Va. Hustings Court
(1794-1804). 19.00 F5228

Hodge, Robert A. Fredericksburg, Virginia Death Records,
1853-1895. 1991. 136pp. 20.00 F5216

Quinn, S.J. The History of the City of Fredericksburg, Virginia,
from its settlement to the present time. (1908) reprint 349pp. 27.00 F5216

GILES COUNTY

Vogt, John and T. William Kethley, Jr. Giles County Marriages,
1806-1850. 1985. 147pp. 11.00 F5061

GLOUCESTER COUNTY

Abercrombie, Janice Luck and Richard Slatten. Gloucester County,
Virginia Publick Claims. 1991. 35pp. 5.00 F5061

Matheny, Emma R. and Helen K. Yates. Kingston Parish Register,
Gloucester and Mathews Counties, Virginia, 1749-1827.
(1963) reprint 1991. 167pp.
Indexed. 17.50 F5130

GOOCHLAND COUNTY

Abercrombie, Janice Luck and Richard Slatten. Goochland County,
Virginia Publick Claims. 1991. 52pp. 6.75 F5061

Goochland County, Virginia Court Orders, 1735-1737. 1991.
134pp. 15.00 .... F5140

Goochland County, Virginia Deeds, 1741-1745. 1990. 104pp.
Detailed abstracts of all documents in Goochland County
Deed Book 4. Not available elsewhere. 12.00 .... F5140

Weisiger, III, Benjamin B. Goochland County, Virginia, Wills &
Deeds, 1728-1736. 1983. 105pp. 10.00 F5061

_____. Goochland County, Virginia, Wills & Deeds, 1730-1742.
1984. 76pp. 10.00 F5061

GREENBRIER COUNTY

Shuck, Larry.   Greenbrier County Records, Volume 1.   1988.
457pp.
Early Survey Records, 1780-1799;
Early Court Minutes, 1780-1801 [1811];
Magistrate's Memoranda, 1817-1819;
Court Record Books, 1828-1835;
District Court Records, 1792-1797;
Deeds, Sweet Springs Courthouse, 1789-1808 .... 22.00   F5061

_____.   Greenbrier County Records, Volume 2: Personal property
tax lists: 1782/83, 1786/88, 1792, 1796, 1799, 1805, 1815.
1989. 302pp. 22.00   F5061

_____.   Greenbrier County Records, Volume 3: U.S, Federal
Population Schedules: 1820; 1830; 1840; & 1850. 1990.
421pp. 22.00   F5061

_____.   Greenbrier County Records, Volume 4: Marriages of
Greenbrier County, [W.] Virginia, 1782-1900 (3v. set). 1991.
997pp. 49.95   F5061

GREENE COUNTY

Vogt, John and T. William Kethley, Jr. Greene County Marriages,
1838-1850. 1984. 44pp. 5.00   F5061

GREENSVILLE COUNTY

Abercrombie, Janice Luck and Richard Slatten. Greensville County,
Virginia Publick Cliams. 1991. 21pp. 5.00   F5061

Vogt, John and T. William Kethley, Jr. Greensville County
Marriages, 1781-1853. 1989. 156pp. 15.00   F5061

HALIFAX COUNTY

Abercrombie, Janice Luck and Richard Slatten. Halifax County,
Virginia Publick Cliams. 1991. 61pp. 7.75   F5061

Boisseau, Mary Leigh (Abstracter). Abstractions of Military
Exemptions, 1863, A Record of Halifax Co., VA. 1980. .... 6.00   F5153

Carrington, Wirt Johnson. History of Halifax County [Virginia].
(1924) reprint 1991. 525pp.
Indexed 37.50   F5130

Halifax County, Virginia Deed Book 9 (1773-1775). 1991. 98pp.
10.00   ....   F5140

Halifax County, Virginia Deed Book 10 (1775-1778). 1991. 94pp.
10.00   ....   F5140

Halifax County, Virginia Deeds, 1767-1772. 1989. 117pp.
12.00   ....   F5140

Halifax County, Virginia Tithables and Voters, 1755-1780. 1990.
44pp. 7.50   F5061

Halifax County, Virginia Wills, 1792-1797. 1991. 131pp.
16.00   ....   F5140

HAMPTON

Hayes, Jr., Francis W. Elizabeth City Parish, Hampton, Virginia, 19th Century Parish Registers. 1986. 390pp. 40.00 F5216

McClellan, Phyllis I. The Artillerymen of Historic Fort Monroe, Virginia. 1991. 270pp. 20.00 F5216

HANOVER COUNTY

Abercrombie, Janice Luck and Richard Slatten. Hanover County, Virginia Publick Claims. 1991. 116pp. 14.50 F5061

_____. and Richard Slatten. Hanover County, Virginia Superior Court Records Vol. 1: Superior Court of Law, 1809-1826; 1815-1826. 1987. 257pp. 20.00 F5061

_____. and Richard Slatten. Hanover County, Virginia Superior Court Records Vol. 2: Superior Court of Law and Chancery, 1831-1838. 1987. 172pp. 20.00 F5061

Cocke, William Ronald. Hanover County Chancery Wills and Notes. (1940) reprint 1992. 215pp.
  A Compendium of Genealogical, Biographical andHistorical Material as Contained in Cases of the Chancery Suits of Hanover County, Virginia.
  Indexed. 21.50 F5130

_____. Hanover County Taxpayers (St. Paul's Parish), 1782-1815. (1956) reprint 1990. 158pp.
  Indexed 20.00 .... F5130

HENRICO COUNTY

Abercrombie, Janice Luck and Richard Slatten. Henrico County, Virginia Publick Claims. 1991. 23pp. 5.00 F5061

Brock, Dr. R. A. The Vestry Book of Henrico Parish, Virginia, 1730-1773, from the Original Manuscript, with Notes and Appendix. (1904) reprint 221pp. 18.00 F5216

Chamberlayne, Churchill Gibson. Births From the Bristol Parish Register of Henrico, Prince George and Dinwiddie Counties, Virginia 1720-1798. (1898) reprint 1990. 133pp.
  Indexed 15.00 F5130

Foley, Louise Pledge Heath. Early Virginia Families Along the James River. Volume I: Henrico County - Goochland County. (1974) reprint 1992. 162pp.
  Maps, indexed. 18.50 F5130

Henrico County, Virginia Court Order Book, 1737-1746: An Every-Name Index. 1992. 101pp. 12.00 .... F5140

Weisiger, III, Benjamin B. Colonial Wills of Henrico County, Virginia 1677-1737. 1976. 214pp. 20.00 F5061

_____. Colonial Wills of Henrico County, Virginia 1737-1781 with addenda. (1977) reprint 1985. 185pp. 20.00 F5061

_____. Henrico County, Virginia Deeds, 1677-1705. 1986. 188pp. 20.00 F5061

_____. Henrico County, Virginia Deeds, 1706-1737. 1985. 216pp. 17.00 F5061

_____. Henrico County, Virginia Deeds, 1767-1750. 1985.
124pp. 17.00 F5061

HENRY COUNTY

Abercrombie, Janice Luck and Richard Slatten. Henry County,
Virginia Public Claims. 1991. 53pp. 7.25 F5061

Miller, Anne V. 1850 Federal Census of Henry County, Virginia.
1991. 112p.
Revised Edition. 376 footnotes and slave index. 20.00 F5122

_____. Death Records of Henry County, Virginia. Vol. I,
1853-1874. 1992. 120pp.
Glossary of causes of death. Indexed. 20.00 F5122

_____. Death Records of Henry County, Virginia. Vol. II
1875-1896.
In preparation. Write for details. F5122

Pedigo, Virginia G. and Lewis G. Pedigo. History of Patrick and
Henry Counties, Virginia. (1933) reprint 1990. 400pp.
Illustrated, Indexed. 35.00 .... F5129

ISLE OF WIGHT COUNTY

Abercrombie, Janice Luck and Richard Slatten. Isle of Wight
County, Virginia Public Claims. 1991. 33pp. 5.00 F5061

JAMES CITY COUNTY

Abercrombie, Janice Luck and Richard Slatten. James City County,
Virginia Public Claims. 1991. 26pp. 5.00 F5061

Blackmon, Jean E. James City County, Virginia Land Tax Records,
1782-1813. 1991. 330pp. 34.95 F5061

KING AND QUEEN COUNTY

Abercrombie, Janice Luck and Richard Slatten. King & Queen
County, Virginia Publick Claims. 1991. 66pp. 8.25 F5061

Bagby, Rev. Alfred. King and Queen County, Virginia. (1908)
reprint 1990. 402pp.
County history, includes genealogical sketches and family
records. Indexed, illustrated. 27.50 .... F5130

KING GEORGE COUNTY

Abercrombie, Janice Luck and Richard Slatten. King George
County, Virginia Publick Claims. 1991. 27pp. 5.00 F5061

Deed Abstracts of King George County, Virginia (1721-1735).
.... 22.00 F5228

Deed Abstracts of King George County, Virginia (1735-1752).
.... 22.00 F5228

Deed Abstracts of King George County, Virginia (1753-1773).
.... 22.00 F5228

Nicklin, John B. C. St. Paul's Parish Register (Stafford-King George
   Counties, Virginia) 1715-1798. (1962) reprint 1990. 78pp. 7.50   F5130

Order Book Abstracts of King George County, Virginia
   (1721-1723).
         Part of King George County Order Book 1721-1735.   .... 19.00   F5228

Order Book Abstracts of King George County, Virginia
   (1723-1725).
         Part of King George County Order Book 1721-1735.   .... 19.00   F5228

Order Book Abstracts of King George County, Virginia
   (1725-1728).
         Part of King George County Order Book 1721-1735.   .... 19.00   F5228

Will Abstracts of King George County, Virginia (1752-1780).
                                                            .... 21.00   F5228

KING WILLIAM COUNTY

Abercrombie, Janice Luck and Richard Slatten. King William
   County, Virginia Publick Claims. 1991. 58pp. 7.50   F5061

LANCASTER COUNTY

Abercrombie, Janice Luck and Richard Slatten. Lancaster County,
   Virginia Publick Claims. 1991. 30pp. 5.00   F5061

Deed & Will Abstracts of Lancaster County, Virginia (1652-1657).
                                                            .... 25.00   F5228

Deed & Will Abstracts of Lancaster County, Virginia (1654-1661).
                                                            .... 24.00   F5228

Deed & Will Abstracts of Lancaster County, Virginia (1661-1666 &
   1700-1702). 24.00   F5228

Nottingham, Stratton. The Marriage License Bonds of Lancaster
   County, Virginia From 1701 to 1848. (1927) reprint 1992.
   106pp.
         Indexed. 13.50   F5130

Nottingham, Stratton. and Miles Barnes. Virginia Land Causes:
   Lancaster County, 1795-1848 & Northampton County,
   1731-1868. (1931) reprint 1991. 150pp. 15.00   F5216

LEE COUNTY

Vogt, John and T. William Kethley, Jr. Lee County Marriages,
   1830-1836. 1984. 28pp. 5.00   F5061

LOUDOUN COUNTY

Abercrombie, Janice Luck. Loudoun County, Virginia Publick
   Claims. 1991. 64pp. 7.75   F5061

Deed Abstracts of Loudoun County, Virginia (1757-1762).
                                                            .... 21.00   F5228

Deed Abstracts of Loudoun County, Virginia (1762-1765).
                                                            .... 21.00   F5228

Deed Abstracts of Loudoun County, Virginia (1766-1770).
                                                            .... 21.00   F5228

Deed Abstracts of Loudoun County, Virginia (1770-1772).

.... 23.00 F5228

Deed Abstracts of Loudoun County, Virginia (1771-1773).

.... 18.00 F5228

Deed Abstracts of Loudoun County, Virginia (1774-1775).

.... 18.00 F5228

Deed Abstracts of Loudoun County, Virginia (1775-1778).

.... 18.00 F5228

Deed Abstracts of Loudoun County, Virginia (1779-1782).

.... 18.00 F5228

Deed Abstracts of Loudoun County, Virginia (1782-1784).

.... 19.00 F5228

Deed Abstracts of Loudoun County, Virginia (1784-1785).

.... 18.00 F5228

Deed Abstracts of Loudoun County, Virginia (1785-1786).

.... 21.00 F5228

Deed Abstracts of Loudoun County, Virginia (1787-1788).

.... 21.00 F5228

Deed Abstracts of Loudoun County, Virginia (1788-1789).

.... 20.00 F5228

Deed Abstracts of Loudoun County, Virginia (1789-1790).

.... 20.00 F5228

Fee Books of Loudoun County, Virginia (1762, 1764 & 1765).

.... 10.00 F5228

Hopkins, Margaret Lail. Index to the Tithables of Loudoun County,
Virginia and to Slaveholders and Slaves 1758-1786. 1991.   20.00 .... F5129

Loudoun County, Virginia Minute Book, 1780-1783. 1990. 183pp.
This volume includes hundreds of claims paid by the
County Court of Loudoun for material assistance given
during the Revolutionary War. These claims can be used
to prove patriotic service. Indexed by surname, place,
and subject.   12.00 .... F5140

Tithables of Loudoun County, Virginia, Vol. 1; (1758-1769).

.... 19.00 F5228

Loudoun County Virginia Tithables, Vol. II, (1770-1774).

.... 20.00 F5228

Vogt, John and T. William Kethley, Jr. Loudoun County Marriages,
1760-1850. 1985. 462pp. 17.00 F5061

Wertz, Mary Alice. Marriages of Loudoun County, Virginia 1757 -
1853. 1990. 231pp.
Indexed, 2nd printing.   22.50 .... F5129

Will Abstracts of Loudoun County, Virginia (1757-1771).

.... 18.00 F5228

Will Abstracts of Loudoun County, Virginia (1772-1782).

.... 21.00 F5228

Will Abstracts of Loudoun County, Virginia (1783-1788).

.... 16.00 F5228

Will Abstracts of Loudoun County, Virginia (1788-1793).

.... 16.00 F5228

LOUISA COUNTY

Abercrombie, Janice Luck. Louisa County, Virginia Publick Claims.
1991. 73pp. 7.75 F5061

Kiblinger, William H. and Janice L. Abercrombie (comps.).
Marriages of Louisa County, Virginia, 1815-1861. 1989. 188pp. 18.50 F5061

Maps of Louisa County, Virginia (1863). 23"x29".
.... 6.00 F5061

LUNENBURG COUNTY

Bell, Landon C. SUNLIGHT ON THE SOUTHSIDE Lists of
Tithes, Lunenburg County, Virginia, 1748-1783. (1931)
reprint 1991. 503pp.
Illustrated, indexed. 37.50 .... F5130

Lunenburg County, Virginia Court Orders, 1746-1748. 1990.
219pp.
Detailed abstracts of order book #1. Indices, map. 15.00 .... F5140

Lunenburg County, Virginia Deeds, 1746-1752. 1990. 86pp.
Why pay more when you can get the best for less?
Detailed abstracts of deed books #1 and #2. Indices,
map. 12.00 .... F5140

Lunenburg County, Virginia Deeds, 1752-1757. 1990. 137pp.
Detailed abstracts of deed books #3 and #4. Index, map. 12.00 .... F5140

Lunenburg County, Virginia Deeds, 1757-1761. 1990. 143pp.
Detailed abstracts of deed books #5 and #6. Indices,
map. 12.00 .... F5140

Lunenburg County, Virginia Deed Books #7 & #8 (1761-1764).
1990. 134pp.
Why pay more when you can get the best for less?
Detailed abstracts. Indices, map. 12.00 .... F5140

Lunenburg County, Virginia Deed Book #9 (1763-1764). 1990.
66pp.
Why pay more when you can get the best for less?
Detailed abstracts. Indices, map. 9.00 .... F5140

Lunenburg County, Virginia Deeds, 1764-1771. 1990. 126pp.
Why pay more when you can get the best for less?
Detailed abstracts of deed books #10 and #11. Indices,
map. 12.00 .... F5140

Lunenburg County, Virginia Deeds, 1771-1777. 1990. 114pp.
Detailed abstracts of deed book #12. Indices, map. 12.00 .... F5140

Lunenburg County, Virginia Deeds, 1777-1784. 1991. 142pp.
Detailed abstracts of deed book #13. Indices, map. 12.00 .... F5140

Lunenburg County, Virginia Deeds, 1784-1787. 1990. 79pp.
Detailed abstracts of deed book #14. Indices, map. 10.00 .... F5140

Lunenburg County, Virginia Deeds, 1787-1790. 1991. 78pp.
Why pay more when you can get the best for less?
Detailed abstracts of deed book #15. Indices, map. 9.00 .... F5140

Lunenburg County, Virginia Land Patents, 1746-1916. 1990.
169pp.
Has separate indices of patentees, neighbors, geographical
names, and map. 12.00 .... F5140

Lunenburg County, Virginia Will Book 2 (1760-1778).   1991.
145pp.
Detailed abstracts of the entire Lunenburg Will Book 2,
covering all the years 1760-1778 (other versions are
incomplete and missing many names). Indices, map.   16.00   ....   F5140

Matheny, Emma R. and Helen K. Yates. Marriages of Lunenburg
County, Virginia, 1746-1853. (1967) reprint 1990. 177pp.
Illustrated, fldg. map, indexed.   24.50   ....   F5130

Vogt, John and T. William Kethley, Jr. Lunenburg County
Marriages, 1750-1853. 1988. 174pp. 12.00   F5061

LYNCHBURG

Cabell, Margaret Couch. Sketches and Recollections of Lynchburg
(VA) by the Oldest Inhabitant. (1858) reprint 372pp. 25.00   F5216

MADISON COUNTY

Deed Abstracts of Madison County, Virginia (1793-1804).
     ....   22.00   F5228

Vogt, John and T. William Kethley, Jr. Madison County Marriages,
1792-1850. 1984. 156pp. 10.00   F5061

Will Abstracts of Madison County, Virginia (1793-1813).
Contains Marriage Bonds 1793-1800.   ....   22.00   F5228

MECKLENBURG COUNTY

Mecklenburg County, Virginia Deeds, 1765-1771. 1990.
157pp.   12.00   ....   F5140

Mecklenburg County, Virginia Deeds, 1771-1776. 1991.
171pp.   14.00   ....   F5140

Mecklenburg County, Virginia Deeds, 1779-1786. 1991.
165pp.   14.00   ....   F5140

Nottingham, Stratton. Marriages of Mecklenburg County [Virginia]
From 1765 to 1810. (1928) reprint 1992. 71pp.
Indexed. 9.00   F5130

Vogt, John and T. William Kethley, Jr. Mecklenburg County
Marriages, 1765-1853. 1989. 302pp. 15.00   F5061

MIDDLESEX COUNTY

Deed Abstracts of Middlesex County, Virginia (1679-1688).
     ....   18.00   F5228

Deed Abstracts of Middlesex County, Virginia (1688-1694).
     ....   18.00   F5228

Deed Abstracts of Middlesex County, Virginia (1694-1703).
     ....   25.00   F5228

Deed Abstracts of Middlesex County, Virginia (1703-1709).
     ....   18.00   F5228

Deed Abstracts of Middlesex County, Virginia (1709-1720).
     ....   18.00   F5228

Order Book Abstracts of Middlesex County, Virginia (1673-1678).

.... 18.00 F5228

Order Book Abstracts of Middlesex County, Virginia (1677-1680).

.... 18.00 F5228

The Parish Register of Christ Church, Middlesex County, Virginia
From 1653 to 1812. (1897) reprint 1990. 341pp.
Indexed 22.50 .... F5130

MONTGOMERY COUNTY

Fisher, Therese A. Marriages in the New River Valley, Virginia:
Montgomery, Floyd, Pulaski, and Giles Counties. 1991.
319pp. 22.50 F5216

NELSON COUNTY

Vogt, John and T. William Kethley, Jr. Nelson County Marriages,
1808-1850. 1985. 129pp. 9.50 F5061

NORFOLK CITY

Grigsby, H.B. Oration: All Power Resides in the People. (1831)
reprint 1991. 77pp.
"Greatest of all Fourth of July celebrations," 1831,
Norfolk, Va. 9.00 F5177

Tazewell, Editor, C.W. Vignettes From the Shadows: Glimpses of
Norfolk's Past. 1992. 124pp.
Previously unknown info. 14.00 F5177

Tucker, George H. Norfolk Highlights 1584-1881. 1972. 134pp.
"The interesting and the offbeat" 18.00 .... F5177

Wing, Frank and William G. Wing. Ye Hysterical Historie of Ye
Norfolk Towne: With Master of Mirth. (1931) reprint 1990.
76pp.
Humorous history to 1931. .... 9.00 F5177

NORFOLK COUNTY

Wingo, Mrs. William B. Norfolk County, Virginia Will Book I,
1755-1772. 155pp. 20.50 F5061

Wingo, Elizabeth B. Compiler. Marriages of Norfolk County,
Virginia: 1805, 1818-1840. (Vol. III). (1988) reprint 1989.
173pp. 21.00 F5177

NORTHAMPTON COUNTY

Abercrombie, Janice Luck. Northampton County, Virginia Publick
Claims. 1991. 11pp. 5.00 F5061

Mihalyka, Jean M. Marriages: Northampton County, Virginia,
1660/1-1854. 1991. 165pp. 16.50 F5216

Nottingham, Stratton. The Marriage License Bonds of Northampton
County, Virginia From 1706 to 1854. (1929) reprint 1991.
135pp.
Indexed 15.00 F5130

NORTHUMBERLAND CO.

Abercrombie, Janice Luck. Northumberland County, Virginia
Publick Claims. 1991. 22pp. 5.00 F5061

ORANGE COUNTY

Abercrombie, Janice Luck. Orange County, Virginia Publick
Claims. 1991. 68pp. 8.25 F5061

Chancery Suits of Orange County, Virginia (1831-1845).
.... 20.00 F5228

Deed Abstracts of Orange County, Virginia (1743-1759).
.... 23.00 F5228

Deed Abstracts of Orange County, Virginia (1759-1778).
.... 25.00 F5228

Deed Abstracts of Orange County, Virginia (1778-1786).
.... 17.00 F5228

Deed Abstracts of Orange County, Virginia (1786-1791).
.... 21.00 F5228

Deed Abstracts of Orange County, Virginia (1791-1795).
.... 22.00 F5228

A Digest of Orange County, Virginia, Will Books (1734-1838).
This book is not indexed but arranged alphabetically by
decedent. 20.00 F5228

Klein, Margaret C. Tombstone Inscriptions of Orange County,
Virginia. (1979) reprint 1992. 132pp.
Indexed. 14.50 F5130

Little, Barbara Vines. Orange County, Virginia Order Book One,
1734-1739: Part One, 1734-1736. 1990. 114pp. 15.00 F5061

Pamunkey Neighbors of Orange County, Virginia.
Compiled by using transcripts and abstracts of County
Court Records of Virginia, Kentucky & Missouri
Counties, personal letters, Bible records & c., as well as
Family Lines emphasizing the Lindsay, Mills, Mountague
& Stevens families. 30.00 .... F5228

Scott, William W. A History of Orange Co. VA. (1907) reprint
1990. 292pp.
Illustrated, indexed. 25.00 .... F5130

Vogt, John and T. William Kethley, Jr. Orange County Marriages,
1747-1850. 1991. 320pp. 15.00 F5061

Will Abstracts of Orange County, Virginia (1778-1821).
.... 23.00 F5228

Will Abstracts of Orange County, Virginia (1821-1838).
.... 23.00 F5228

PAGE COUNTY

Miller, Anne V. 1850 Federal Census of Page County, Virginia.
1991. 130pp.
Revised edition (data analysis). Indexed. 20.00 F5122

_____. Genealogical Abstract of Rev. John N. Stirewalt's Pastoral
Record. 1869-1906, Page County, Virginia. 1991. 140pp.
Indexed. 19.50 F5122

Vogt, John and T. William Kethley, Jr. Page County Marriage
Bonds, 1831-1850. 1983. 57pp. 5.50 F5061

PATRICK COUNTY

Pedigo, Virginia G. and Lewis G. Pedigo. History of Patrick and
Henry Counties, Virginia. (1933) reprint 1990. 400pp.
Illustrated, Indexed. 35.00 .... F5129

PITTSYLVANIA COUNTY

Abercrombie, Janice Luck. Pittsylvania County, Virginia Publick
Claims. 1991. 43pp. 6.25 F5061

Boisseau (Transcriber), Mary Leigh. Vestry Book of Camden
Parish, Pittsylvania Co, VA 1767-1820. 1986. .... 21.50 F5153

Pittsylvania County, Virginia Deed Book 4 (1774-1778). 1991.
103pp.
Detailed abstracts of all 389 documents, other than wills,
that were recorded in Pittsylvania Deed Book 4. 12.00 .... F5140

Pittsylvania County, Virginia Deeds, 1791-1794. 1991. 114pp.
Detailed abstracts of all 438 documents, other than wills,
that were recorded in Pittsylvania County Deed and Will
Book 9. 12.00 .... F5140

PORTSMOUTH

Hallahan, John M. The Battle of Craney Island: A Matter of Credit.
1986. 124pp.
First enemy missile attack in Virginia (in War of 1812). 17.00 .... F5177

POWHATAN COUNTY

Abercrombie, Janice Luck. Powhatan County, Virginia Publick
Claims. 1991. 40pp. 6.00 F5061

Vogt, John and T. William Kethley, Jr. Powhatan County
Marriages,1777-1850. 1985. 143pp. 11.00 F5061

Weisiger, III, Benjamin B. Powhatan County, Virginia Wills,
1777-1795. 1986. 66pp. 10.00 F5061

PRINCE EDWARD COUNTY

Abercrombie, Janice Luck. Prince Edward County, Virginia Publick
Claims. 1991. 43pp. 6.25 F5061

Prince Edward County, Virginia Deed Book 1 (1754-1759). 1990.
71pp. 10.00 .... F5140

Prince Edward County, Virginia Deed Book 2 (1759-1765).
1990. 74pp. 10.00 .... F5140

Prince Edward County, Virginia Wills, 1754-1776. 1991.
91pp. 14.00 .... F5140

Warren, Mary Bondurant and Eve B. Weeks.   Virginia's District
    Courts, 1789-1809: Records of The Prince Edward District:
    Buckingham, Charlotte, Cumberland, Halifax, and Prince
    Edward Counties. 1991. 497pp.   25.00   ....   F5061

PRINCE GEORGE COUNTY

Abercrombie, Janice Luck. Prince George County, Virginia Publick
    Claims. 1991. 18pp. 5.00   F5061

Foley, Louise Pledge Heath.   Early Virginia Families Along the
    James River, Charles City County - Prince George County.
    (1978) reprint 1990. 211pp.
    Maps, Indexed.   25.00   ....   F5129

Weisiger, III, Benjamin B. Prince George County, Virginia
    Miscellany, 1711-1814. 1986. 121pp. 17.00   F5061

_____. Prince George County, Virginia Records, 1733-1792.
    1975. 228pp. 17.00   F5061

_____. Prince George County, Virginia Wills & Deeds,
    1713-1728. 1973. 184pp. 17.00   F5061

PRINCE WILLIAM CO.

Abstracts of Prince William County Land Causes (1789-1790).
    Although this book (abstracted from Prince William
    County Land Causes 1789-1793) is described as Prince
    William County Records; the contents of the two books
    are for trials held at the District Court in Dumfries, Prince
    William County, for dispute about lands to be found in
    Fairfax, Fauquier and Loudoun Counties, which suits
    contains Deeds, Wills and Depositions relating to the
    Causes. 22.00   F5228

Abstracts of Prince William County Land Causes (1790-1793).
    Although this book (abstracted from Prince William
    County Land Causes 1789-1793) is described as Prince
    William County Records; the contents of this book are for
    trials held at the District Court in Dumfries, Prince
    William County, for dispute about lands to be found in
    Fairfax, Fauquier and Loudoun Counties, which suits
    contains Deeds, Wills and Depositions relating to the
    Causes. 22.00   F5228

Deed Abstracts of Prince William County, Virginia
    (1763-1767). 22.00   F5228

Deed Abstracts of Prince William Co., Virginia
    (1745-1746/1748-1749). 18.00   F5228

Deed Abstracts of Prince William Co., Virginia
    (1749-1752/1761-1764). 22.00   F5228

Deed Abstracts of Prince William County, Virginia
    (1740-1741). 19.00   F5228

Deed Abstracts of Prince William County, Virginia (1767-1771).
                                                               ....   22.00   F5228

Deed Abstracts of Prince William County, Virginia (1774-1779).
                                                               ....   19.00   F5228

Deed Abstracts of Prince William County, Virginia (1779-1784).	22.00	F5228
Deed Abstracts of Prince William County, Virginia (1784-1787).	19.00	F5228
Deed Abstracts of Prince William County, Virginia (1787-1791).	25.00	F5228
Order Book Abstracts of Prince William County, Virginia (1752-1753).	20.00	F5228
Order Book Abstracts of Prince William County, Virginia (1753-1757).	22.00	F5228

PRINCESS ANNE COUNTY

Abercrombie, Janice Luck. Princess Anne County, Virginia Publick Claims. 1991. 20pp.	5.00	F5061
Green, Laurie Boush and Virginia Bonney West. Old Churches, Their Cemeteries and Family Graveyards of Princess Anne County, Virginia. 1985. 295pp.	25.00	F5177
Kight, John R. The Cape Henry Threshold. 1990. 33pp. Local history of Princess Anne County and Cape Henry, Virginia.	5.00	F5177
Tazewell, Editor, C.W. Where The Wild Goose Goes: B.D. White, Preservationist. 1992. 64pp. Includes "Gleanings in The History of Princess Anne County".	8.00	F5177
Turner, Florence Kimberly. Gateway to the New World: A History of Princess Anne County, Virginia 1607-1824. (1984) reprint 1992. 308pp. 20.00		F5177

PULASKI COUNTY

Vogt, John and T. William Kethley, Jr. Pulaski County Marriages, 1839-1857. 1984. 36pp.	5.00	F5061

RAPPAHANNOCK COUNTY

Deed & Will Abstracts of (Old) Rappahannock Co., VA., (1677-1682) Part I.	23.00	F5228
Deed & Will Abstracts of (Old) Rappahannock Co., VA., (1677-1682) Part II.	23.00	F5228
Deed & Will Abstracts of (Old) Rappahannock Co., Virginia (1665-1677).	16.00	F5228
Deed Abstracts of (Old) Rappahannock County, Virginia (1656-1664) Part I.	23.00	F5228
Deed Abstracts of (Old) Rappahannock County, Virginia (1656-1664) Part II.	23.00	F5228
Deed Abstracts of (Old) Rappahannock County, Virginia (1663-1668).	22.00	F5228
Deed Abstracts of (Old) Rappahannock County, Virginia (1668-1670).	18.00	F5228

Deed Abstracts of (Old) Rappahannock County, Virginia (1670-1672).	.... 18.00	F5228
Deed Abstracts of (Old) Rappahannock County, Virginia (1672-1676) Part I.	.... 18.00	F5228
Deed Abstracts of (Old) Rappahannock County, Virginia (1672-1676) Part II.	.... 19.00	F5228
Deed Abstracts of (Old) Rappahannock County, Virginia (1682-1686).	.... 22.00	F5228
Deed Abstracts of (Old) Rappahannock County, Virginia (1686-1688).	.... 21.00	F5228
Deed Abstracts of (Old) Rappahannock County, Virginia (1688-1692).	.... 23.00	F5228
Order Book Abstracts of (Old) Rappahannock County, Virginia (1683-1685).	.... 21.00	F5228
Order Book Abstracts of (Old) Rappahannock County, Virginia (1685-1687).	.... 21.00	F5228
Order Book Abstracts of (Old) Rappahannock County, Virginia (1687-1689).	.... 21.00	F5228
Order Book Abstracts of (Old) Rappahannock County, Virginia (1689-1692).	.... 21.00	F5228
Vogt, John and T. William Kethley, Jr. Rappahannock County Marriages, 1833-1850. 1984. 75pp.	.... 5.00	F5061
Will Abstracts of (Old) Rappahannock County, Virginia (1682-1687).	.... 18.00	F5228

RICHMOND COUNTY

Abercrombie, Janice Luck. Richmond County, Virginia Publick Claims. 1991. 20pp.	.... 5.00	F5061
Account Book Abstracts of Richmond County, Virginia (1724-1751).	.... 23.00	F5228
Account Book Abstracts of Richmond County, Virginia (1751-1783).	.... 22.00	F5228
Deed Abstracts of Richmond County, Virginia (1692-1695).	.... 19.00	F5228
Deed Abstracts of Richmond County, Virginia (1695-1701).	.... 19.00	F5228
Deed Abstracts of Richmond County, Virginia (1701-1704).	.... 19.00	F5228
Deed Abstracts of Richmond County, Virginia (1705-1708).	.... 20.00	F5228
Deed Abstracts of Richmond County, Virginia (1708-1711).	.... 20.00	F5228
Order Book Abstracts of Richmond County, Virginia (1692-1694).	.... 19.00	F5228
Order Book Abstracts of Richmond County, Virginia (1694-1697).	.... 23.00	F5228
Order Book Abstracts of Richmond County, Virginia (1697-1699).	.... 23.00	F5228

Order Book Abstracts of Richmond County, Virginia (1699-1701).
.... 19.00 F5228

Order Book Abstracts of Richmond County, Virginia (1702-1704).
.... 23.00 F5228

Richmond County, Virginia Deeds, 1734-1741. 1991. 101pp.
14.00 .... F5140

Richmond County, Virginia, Deeds and Bonds, 1721-1734.
1991. 155pp. 14.00 .... F5140

ROANOKE COUNTY

Vogt, John and T. William Kethley, Jr. Roanoke County Marriages,
1838-1850. 1984. 54pp. 5.00 F5061

ROCKBRIDGE COUNTY

Kirkpatrick, Dorthie and Edwin. Rockbridge County Births,
1853-1877 (2 Vol set). 1988. 734pp. 23.50 F5061

_____. Rockbridge County Marriages, 1778-1850. (1985) reprint
1992. 443pp. 15.00 F5061

Ruley, Angela M. Rockbridge County, Virginia Cemeteries, Volume
1: Kerr's Creek District. 158pp. 19.95 F5061

_____. Rockbridge County, Virginia Death Registers, 1853-1870,
1912-1917. 504pp. 29.95 F5061

ROCKINGHAM COUNTY

Abercrombie, Janice Luck. Rockingham County, Virginia Publick
Claims. 1991. 45pp. 6.25 F5061

Ritchie, Patricia Turner. Index to the 1880 Rockingham County,
Virginia Census. 178pp. 14.00 F5061

Vogt, John and T. William Kethley, Jr. Rockingham County
Marriages, 1778-1850. 1984. 433pp. 15.00 F5061

Wayland, Ph.D., John W. A History of Rockingham County,
Virginia. (1912) reprint 554pp. 32.50 F5216

RUSSELL COUNTY

Fugate, Mary D. Implied Marriages of Russell County, Virginia:.
112pp.
Maiden names of wives mentioned in the wills and deeds
of Russell County Prior to 1860, and in the earliest
records of Lee and Scott counties, formed from Russell in
1793 and 1814 respectively. 14.00 F5061

SCOTT COUNTY

Fugate, C.G.R.S., Mary D. Scott County Marriages, 1815-1853.
1989. 109pp. 12.00 F5061

SHENANDOAH COUNTY

Abercrombie, Janice Luck. Shenandoah County, Virginia Publick
Claims. 1991. 26pp. 5.00 F5061

Vogt, John and T. William Kethley, Jr. Shenandoah County
Marriage Bonds, 1772-1850. 1984. 417pp. 15.00 F5061

SMYTH COUNTY

Vogt, John and T. William Kethley, Jr. Smyth County Marriages,
1832-1850. 1984. 89pp. 5.50 F5061

SOUTHAMPTON COUNTY

Abercrombie, Janice Luck. Southampton County, Virginia Publick
Claims. 1991. 25pp. 5.00 F5061

SPOTSYLVANIA COUNTY

Abercrombie, Janice Luck. Spotsylvania County, Virginia Publick
Claims. 1991. 52pp. 7.25 F5061

Crozier, William Armstrong. Spotsylvania County Records [Vol. 1
of Virginia County Records]. (1905) reprint 1990. 576pp. 35.00 .... F5129

Fisher, Therese. Marriages in Virginia: Spotsylvania County,
1851-1900 and Orange County, 1851-1867. 1992. 421pp. 31.00 F5216

Order Book Abstracts of Spotsylvania County, Virginia
(1724-1730) Part I. 19.00 F5228

Order Book Abstracts of Spotsylvania County, Virginia
(1724-1730) Part II. 19.00 F5228

Order Book Abstracts of Spotsylvania County, Virginia
(1724-1730) Part III. 19.00 F5228

Order Book Abstracts of Spotsylvania County, Virginia
(1724-1730) Part IV. 19.00 F5228

Order Book Abstracts of Spotsylvania County, Virginia
(1730-1732). 19.00 F5228

Order Book Abstracts of Spotsylvania County, Virginia
(1732-1734). 19.00 F5228

Order Book Abstracts of Spotsylvania County, Virginia
(1734-1735). 19.00 F5228

Order Book Abstracts of Spotsylvania County, Virginia
(1735-1738). 19.00 F5228

STAFFORD COUNTY

Abercrombie, Janice Luck. Stafford County, Virginia Publick
Claims. 1991. 45pp.
    Maiden names of wives mentioned in the wills and deeds
    of Russell County Prior to 1860, and in the earliest
    records of Lee and Scott counties, formed from Russell in
    1793 and 1814 respectively. 6.25 F5061

Deed & Will Abstracts of Stafford County, Virginia (1686-1689).
.... 25.00 F5228

Deed & Will Abstracts of Stafford County, Virginia (1689-1693).

.... 25.00   F5228

Deed & Will Abstracts of Stafford County, Virginia (1699-1709).

.... 25.00   F5228

Deed & Will Abstracts of Stafford County, Virginia (1780-1786).
     Also contains Stafford County Order Book, 1790-1793. .... 25.00   F5228

Deed Abstracts of Stafford County, Virginia
     (1722-1728/1755-1765). 25.00   F5228

Order Book Abstracts of Stafford County, Virginia (1664-1668/
     1689-1690) 25.00   F5228

Order Book Abstracts of Stafford County, Virginia (1691-1692).

.... 22.00   F5228

Order Book Abstracts of Stafford County, Virginia (1692-1693).

.... 22.00   F5228

Will Abstracts of Stafford County, Virginia (1729-1748).

.... 25.00   F5228

Will Abstracts of Stafford County, Virginia (1748-1767).

.... 25.00   F5228

Vogt, John and T. William Kethley, Jr. Stafford County, Virginia
     Tithables: Quit Rents, Personal Property Taxes and related lists
     and petitions, 1723-1790 (2 Vol. set). 1990. 612pp.
         Maiden names of wives mentioned in the wills and deeds
         of Russell County Prior to 1860, and in the earliest
         records of Lee and Scott counties, formed from Russell in
         1793 and 1814 respectively. 30.00   F5061

SURRY COUNTY

Abercrombie, Janice Luck. Surry County, Virginia Publick Claims.
     1991. 19pp. 5.00   F5061

Boddie, John Bennett. Colonial Surry [Virginia]. (1948) reprint
     1992. 249pp.
         Indexed.   25.00 ....   F5130

_____. The Albemarle Parish Register of Surry and Sussex
     Counties, Virginia Births, Deaths and Sponsors, 1717-1778.
     (1958) reprint 1992. 167pp.
         Indexed.   22.00 ....   F5130

Surry County, Virginia Deed Book 4 (1742-1747). 1991. 95pp.
         The loss of court records of several adjoining counties
         makes these records all the more important.
             Map, index, soundex index.   15.00 ....   F5140

SUSSEX COUNTY

Sussex County, Virginia Wills, 1754-1764. 1991. 131pp.
         This book consists of detailed abstracts of all 290
         documents (wills, inventories, accounts, estate sales) that
         were recorded in Sussex Will Book A.
             Map, index, soundex index.   15.00 ....   F5140

TAZEWELL COUNTY

McIntosh, Francis W. and Elise G. Jourdan. 1840-1850 Federal
Census, Tazewell County, Virginia. 1989. 198pp.
Two indexes, acid-free paper. 15.00 F5110

_____. and Elise G. Jourdan. 1860 Federal Census, Tazewell
County, Virginia. 1990. 171pp.
Surname index, acid-free paper. 18.00 F5110

_____. and Elise G. Jourdan. 1870 Federal Census, Tazewell
County, Virginia. 1990. 216pp.
Surname Index, acid-free paper. 20.00 F5110

VIRGINIA BEACH CITY

Tazewell, Editor, C.W. Virginia Beach Vibes: More People and
Hogs. 1991. 176pp.
Anthology of over 400 years. 19.00 F5177

WARREN COUNTY

Vogt, John and T. William Kethley, Jr. Warren County Marriages,
1836-1850. 1983. 48pp. 5.00 F5061

WASHINGTON COUNTY

Slaughter, D.D., Rev. Philip. A History of Bristol Parish, VA., with
Genealogies of Families. (1879) reprint 258pp. 19.50 F5216

WESTMORELAND COUNTY

Fothergill, Augusta B. Wills of Westmoreland County, Virginia
1654-1800. (1925) reprint 1990. 229pp.
Indexed 20.00 .... F5130

WYTHE COUNTY

Vogt, John and T. William Kethley, Jr. Wythe County Marriages,
1790-1850. 1985. 224pp. 12.50 F5061

YORK COUNTY

Weisiger, III, Benjamin B. York County, Virginia Records,
1659-1662. 1989. 180pp. 15.00 F5061

_____. York County, Virginia Records, 1665-1672. 1987.
281pp. 20.00 F5061

_____. York County, Virginia Records, 1672-1676. 1991.
216pp. 22.00 F5061

Washington

STATEWIDE REFERENCE

Land Claims

Seattle Genealogical Society - Project Committee. Washington
Territory Donation Land Claims (before 1850). 1980. 372pp. 16.00   F5085

FERRY COUNTY

Ferry County, Washington Birth & Death Records 1899-1911.
1990. 26pp. 6.00   F5207

Ferry County, Washington Index to Marriage Returns November
1900-July 1932. 1991. 80pp. 10.00   F5207

KING COUNTY

South King County Genealoical Society. Kent Area Obituaries From
Early Kent, Washington Newspapers - Volume I - 1893-1910.
1988. 216pp. 11.00   F5046

_____. Kent Area Obituaries From Early Kent, Washington
Newspapers - Volume II - 1911-1920. 1988. 277pp. 12.00   F5046

_____. Kent Area Obituaries From Early Kent, Washington
Newspapers - Volume III - 1921-1931. 1989. 444pp. 18.75   F5046

_____. Kent Area Obituaries From Early Kent, Washington
Newspapers - Volume IV - 1932-1934. 1991. 169pp. 11.00   F5046

_____. Memorial Records of South King County, Washington
Volume I. 1981. 89pp.
     Records of St. Patrick, Saar, and Mess Cemeteries. 7.00   F5046

_____. Memorial Records of South King County, Washington
Volume II. 1983. 344pp.
     Records of Hillcrest Cemetery, Kent, Washington. 18.50   F5046

_____. Obituaries Extracted From The Renton, Washington
Record Chronical Newspaper - Volume I - 1927-1932. 1991.
222pp. 11.00   F5046

West Virginia

STATEWIDE REFERENCE

Family Genealogies

Genealogies of West Virginia Families. From "The West Virginia
Historical Magazine Quarterly". (1901-05) reprint 1992.
286pp.
Indexed. 29.50 F5130

Kanawha Valley

Dayton, Ruths Woods. Pioneers and Their Homes on Upper
Kanawha. (1947) reprint 320pp. 22.00 F5216

Military

Johnston, Ross B. West Virginians in the American Revolution.
(1939) reprint 1990. 320pp. 23.50 .... F5130

Lewis, Virgil A. The Soldiery of West Virginia. (1911) reprint
1991. 227pp.
In the French and Indian War; Lord Dunmore's War; the
Revolution; the Later Indian Wars; the Whiskey
Insurrection; the Second War with England; the War with
Mexico. And Addenda Relating to West Virginians in the
Civil War. 21.50 F5130

Panhandle

Newton, J.H. and G.G. Nichols and A.G. Sprankle. History of the
Pan-handle, being Historical Collections of the Counties of
Ohio, Brooke, Marshall, and Hancock, West Virginia. (1879)
reprint 550pp. 50.00 F5216

Source Records

Sims, Edgar B. Sims West Virginia Land Grants. (1952) reprint
1992. 1,024pp.
Contains all land grants for West Virginia territory
including those conferred while a part of Virginia.
Furnishes name of grantee, year, number of acres,county
in which land was located, and description (usually the
watercourse on which it was located). The earliest grants
were in the 1740s and 1750s in Augusta and Frederick
Counties, Virginia. The bulk of the grants were between
1760 and 1870, but a few are recorded after 1870.
Approximately 52,000 tracts are citied. Includes material
in a supplement subsequently issued by the author; also
grants in the panhandle area which were omitted by Sims.

This work is to West Virginia what Nugent's "Cavaliers and Pioneers" is to Virginia; and what Jillson's "Kentucky Land Grants" and "Old Kentucky Entries & Deeds" are to Kentucky - a work which is basic to the study of the entire state.
A new every-name index has been added.   65.00 .... F5236

BERKELEY COUNTY

Abercrombie, Janice Luck and Richard Slatten. Berkeley County, Virginia Publick Claims. 1991. 30pp. 5.00 F5061

Lowe, Elizabeth S. The Folks of Swan Pond. 1989. 734pp. History - Families of Berkeley Co., W.Va. 1753-1988. Includes Folks (Foulke, Fulk, Volch) Billmyer, Byers, Hill, Hollida, Lemen, Marshall, Turner, Whiting. Wills, deeds, maps, inventories, illustrations, photos.
Indexed.   60.00 .... F5170

BROOKE COUNTY

Sherman, Renee Britt. Brooke County, Virginia/West Virginia, Licenses and Marriages, 1797-1874. 1991. 339pp. 28.00 F5216

CLAY COUNTY

Clay County Historical Society. Clay County History Volume II. 1992. 390pp.
Early history of County, Schools, Churches, Businesses; over 800 family histories and genealogies. Census, Marriage records, Cemeteries, Military history, and Elk River history. Elk River Coal and Lumber Company, BC&G history. Surname index. Leather binding.
Price does not include shipping.   55.00 .... F5171

_____. and Eloise Boggs, Editor. Now and Then, Historical Society Quarterly Newsletter. 16-18pp.
Features Genealogical articles, Queries, County History and current preservation activities.
Subscription $10.00/yr, Seniors $8.00/year. 10.00 F5171

Clay County History Book Committee. Clay County History 1989. 1990. 390pp.
Early history of County, Schools, Churches, Businesses; over 800 family histories and genealogies. Census, Marriage records, Cemeteries, Military history, and Elk River history. Elk River Coal and Lumber Company, BC&G history. Surname index. Leather binding.
Price does not include shipping.   55.00 .... F5171

FAYETTE COUNTY

Shuck, Jarry G. The Federal Census of 1850 for Fayette County [West] Virginia. 1991. 127pp. 10.00 F5061

_____. The Federal Census of 1870 for Fayette County [West] Virginia. 1991. 224pp. 15.00 F5061

HAMPSHIRE COUNTY

Abercrombie, Janice Luck and Richard Slatten. Hampshire County,
    Virginia Publick Claims. 1991. 37pp. 5.00 F5061

Hampshire County, (West) Virginia Personal Property Tax Lists,
    1782-1799. 1990. 308pp. 16.00 .... F5140

Sage, Clara McCormack and Laura Sage Jones. Early Records,
    Hampshire County, Virginia (Now West Virginia). (1939)
    reprint 1990. 170pp.
        7 x 10", Indexed. 25.00 .... F5129

HARRISION COUNTY

Hickman, Patrica B. Harrison County, West Virginia, Death
    Records: 1853-1903. 1991. 210pp. 18.00 F5216

MONONGALIA COUNTY

Zinn, Melba Pender. Monongalia County, (West) Virginia: Records
    of the District, Superior, and County Courts. Vol. 1,
    1776-1799. 1990. 333pp. 25.00 F5216

_____. Monongalia County, (West) Virginia: Records of the
    District, Superior, and County Courts. Vol. 2,
    1800-1803. 1990. 325pp. 25.00 F5216

_____. Monongalia County, (West) Virginia: Records of the
    District, Superior, and County Courts. Vol. 3, 1804-1810.
    1991. 329pp. 22.50 F5216

_____. Monongalia County, (West) Virginia: Records of the
    District, Superior, and County Courts. Vol. 4, 1800-1802 &
    1810. 1992. 359pp. 24.00 F5216

PENDLETON COUNTY

Morton, Oren F. A History of Pendleton Co. WV. (1910) reprint
    1990. 493pp.
        Illustrated 35.00 .... F5130

POCAHONTAS COUNTY

Price, William T. Historical Sketches of Pocahontas County, West
    Virginia. (1901) reprint 660pp. 37.50 F5216

Wisconsin

MILWAUKEE COUNTY

Milwaukee County, Wisconsin Censuses of 1846 & 1847. 1991. 104pp.

	12.00	....	F5140

Wheeler, A.C. The Chronicles of Milwaukee (Wisconsin): being a narrative history of the town from its earliest period to the present. (1861) reprint 303pp.

	....	22.50	F5216

VERNON COUNTY

1884 History of Vernon County. (1884) reprint 1990. 826pp. Lists over 10,000 names, some pictures, comprehensive history; indexed.

	65.00	....	F5189

Regional

Mid-Atlantic States

Rehr, Sherry Shopp. Compiler.   Ancestors from the Eastern
Heartland Pennsylvania, New Jersey, Maryland and Delaware.
1990. 291+pp.
    One event before 1880. .... 15.00 F5085

Richardson, Ralph W. Historic Districts of America, The
Mid-Atlantic. 1991. 283pp. 20.00 F5216

Van Voorhis, John S.   The Old and New Monongahela. (1893)
reprint 1990. 504pp.
    Indexed 30.00 .... F5130

Weis, Frederick Lewis. The Colonial Clergy of Maryland, Delaware
and Georgia. (1950) reprint 1991. 104pp. 12.50 F5130

_____. The Colonial Clergy of the Middle Colonies NY, NJ, and
PA 1628-1776. (1957) reprint 1991. 184pp. .... 18.50 F51⌃⌃

New England

Brown, D.D., John. The Pilgrim Fathers of New England and their Puritan Successors. (1896) reprint 368pp. 25.00 F5216

Drake, Samuel Adams. Nooks and Corners of the New England Coast. (1875) reprint 460pp. 25.00 F5216

Flagg, Ernest. Genealogical Notes on the Founding of New England. (1926) reprint 1990. 440pp. 27.50 .... F5130

Howells, John Mead. Architectural Heritage of the Piscataqua:Early Houses & Gardens of the Portsmouth District in Maine and New Hampshire. (1937) reprint 250pp. 34.50 .... F5216

New England Historic Genealogical Society The New England Historical and Genealogical Register. Vol 1, 1847. (1992) reprint 1847. 400pp. 25.00 F5216

._____. The New England Historical and Genealogical Register, Vol 2, 1848. (1848) reprint 1992. 418pp. 25.00 F5216

Noyes, Sybil and Charles T. Libby and Walter G. Davis. Genealogical Dictionary of Maine and New Hampshire. (1939) reprint 1991. 795pp.
     5 parts in 1 (1928-39). 35.00 .... F5129

O'Brien, Michael J. Pioneer Irish in New England. (1937) reprint 325pp. 22.50 F5216

Pope, Charles Henry. The Pioneers of Maine and New Hampshire, 1623-1660: A Descriptive List drawn from Records of the Colonies, Towns, Churches Courts, and Other Sources. (1908) reprint 252pp. 20.00 F5216

Richardson, Ralph W. Historic Districts of America, New England. 1988. 182pp. 17.00 F5216

Sanborn, Melinde Lutz. Supplement to Torrey's New England Marriages Prior to 1700. 1991. 80pp.
     Indexed 12.50 .... F5129

Savage, James. A Genealogical Dictionary of the First Settlers of New England. 1990. 2,541pp.
     4 volumes, Indexed. 125.00 .... F5129

Sperry, Kip. New England Genealogical Research: A Guide to Sources. 1988. 140pp. 20.00 F5216

Torrey, Clarence Almon. New England Marriages Prior to 1700. 1992. 1,009pp.
    The book contains
    (1) the names of virtually every married couple living in New England before 1700;
    (2) the date of their marriage or the birth year of a first child;
    (3) the maiden names of 70% of the Wives;
    (4) the birth and death years of both partners;
    (5) mention of earlier or later marriages;
    (6) the residences of every couple, so that the geographical spread of any surname can be easily surmised; and
    (7) an index of names. 50.00 .... F5129

Towle, Laird C. New England Annals: History & Genealogy, Vol. 1.
1980. 510pp.   35.00   ....   F5216

Weis, Frederick Lewis. The Colonial Clergy and the Colonial
Churches of New England. (1936) reprint 1991. 280pp. 24.00   F5130

Mayflower Histories

Roser, Susan E. Mayflower Births & Deaths. From the Files of
George Ernest Bowman at the Massachusetts Society of
Mayflower Descendants. 1992. 1,073pp.
    2 volumes 7" x 10". 525 & 548 pp., indexed. 75.00   F5129

_____. Mayflower Increasings (For Three Generations). (1989)
reprint 1991. 159pp. 18.95   F5129

_____. Mayflower Marriages, From the Files of George Ernest
Bowman at the Massachusetts Society of Mayflower
Descendants. 1990. 415pp.
    Contains 10,000 marriages spanning five centuries, with
    names, dates and sources. Indexed. 29.95   F5129

Southeastern U.S.

Coates, Robert M. The Outlaw Years: the history of the land pirates
of the Natchez Trace. (1930) reprint 308pp. 23.00   F5216

Feldman, Lawrence H. Anglo-Americans in Spanish Archives, Lists
of Anglo-American Settlers in the Spanish Colonies of
America. 1991. 349pp. 30.00 .... F5129

Jillson, Willard Rouse. THE BIG SANDY VALLEY. A Regional
History Prior to the Year 1850. (1923) reprint 1970. 183pp.
This is the standard history of the Big Sandy Valley
region of Eastern Kentucky. Illustrated, indexed. 20.00 .... F5130

Lester, Memory Aldridge.   Old Southern Bible Records.
Transcriptions of Births, Deaths and Marriages from Family
Bibles, Chiefly of the 18th and 19th Centuries. (1974) reprint
1990. 378pp.
Indexed. 25.00 .... F5130

Richardson, Ralph W. Historic Districts of America, The South.
1987. 239pp. 18.50   F5216

Weis, Frederick Lewis. The Colonial Clergy of VA, NC and SC.
(1955) reprint 1990. 100pp. 16.00 .... F5130

Western States

Bowles, Samuel. Our New West: records of travel between the
Mississippi River and the Pacific Ocean. (1869) reprint 524pp. 31.50 F5216

Inman, Col. Henry and Preface by Buffalo Bill Cody. The Old Santa
Fe Trail: The Story of a Great Highway. (1897) reprint
528pp. 32.00 F5216

Montgomery, Donna M. Wojcik. The Brazen Overlanders of 1845.
(1976) reprint 1992. 566pp. 38.50 F5216

Remington, Frederic. Crooked Trails. (1898) reprint 153pp.
.... 18.00 F5216

Tolzmann, Editor, Don Heinrich. Lives and Exploits of the Daring
Frank and Jesse James: Thaddeus Thorndike's Graphic and
Realistic Description of their Many Deeds. (1909) reprint
1992. 207pp. 19.00 F5216

Localities Other Than The United States

Bahamas

Bethell, A. Talbot. The Early Settlers of the Bahamas and Colonists
of North America, 3rd ed. revised. (1937) reprint 1992.
218pp. 19.95 F5130

Bermuda

Mercer, Julia E. Bermuda Settlers of the 17th Century.
(1942-1947) reprint 1992. 276pp.
Many of the early settlers of Bermuda, or their
descendants, removed to the mainland and were among
the pioneer settlers of the Carolinas, Georgia, and
Virginia. About 5,000 of the earliest settlers in the New
World are identified for the first time in this important
work. 20.00 .... F5129

Smith, Clifford Neal. Letters Home: Genealogical and
Family-Historical Data on Nineteenth-Century German Settlers
in Australia, Bermuda, Brazil, Canada, and the US: Part 1.
1989. 38pp. 17.00 F5120

Canada

COUNTRYWIDE REFERENCE

Desaulniers, F.L.   Les Vieilles Familles D'Yamachiche.   (1898)
   reprint 1987.
    Vol. I. Dix Gen.: Les Blais, Lacerte, Lamy, Loranger,
    Vaillancourt, Gerin-Lajoie, Boucher, Carbonneau, Caron,
    Comeau. 242pp $31.00 hardcover.
    Vol. II. Trois Gen.: Les Desaulniers, Bellemare, Galinas.
    303pp $36.00 hardcover.
    Both volumes bound together for a **Special Low Price $54.00**.......... ....   F5159

_____.   Notes Historiques Sur La Paroisse De St. Guillaume
   D'Upton. (1905) reprint 1991. 143pp.
    In French. 16.00   F5159

Herbin, John Frederic. The History of Grand-Pre, the Home of
   Longfellow's "Evangeline". (1907) reprint 168pp. 16.50   F5216

The Old United Empire Loyalists List. (Centennial of the Settlement
   of Uppper Canada by United Emp. Loyalists, 1885). (1885)
   reprint 1990. 334pp.
    Lists over 7,000 Loyalists with data. 20.00   F5159

Smith,   Clifford   Neal.   Letters   Home: Genealogical   and
   Family-Historical Data on Nineteenth-Century German Settlers
   in Australia, Bermuda, Brazil, Canada, and the US: Part 1.
   1989. 38pp. 17.00   F5120

NEW BRUNSWICK

Hale, R. Wallace. Early New Brunswick (Canada) Probate Records,
   1785-1835. 1989. 558pp. 35.00   F5216

NOVA SCOTIA

Allison, David. History of Nova Scotia (3 volumes). (1914) reprint
   1987.
    Vol. I & II 940pp $94.00;
    Vol. III 700pp $70.00.   ....   F5159

Calnek, W.A. and A.W. Savary (Ed.).   Hist. of the County of
   Annapolis, Incl. Old Port Royal & Acadia, with Gen. Sketches
   of its Early English Settlers & Their Fams. (1897) reprint
   1988. 682pp.   69.50   ....   F5159

Savary, A.W. Supplement to "History of the County of Annapolis".
   (1913) reprint 1988. 142pp.
    Bound with "History of the County of Annapolis" $14.00.
    Ordered separately $21.00.
    Genealogies only 185pp $18.50 paper. 21.00   F5159

Crowell, E. A History of Barrington Twp. & Vicinity, Shelburne
   Co., Nova Scotia, 1604-1870, with a Biogr. & Gen. Appendix.
   (1870) reprint 1987. 610pp.   61.00   ....   F5159

Gilroy, M. and D.C. Harvey. Loyalists & Land Settlements in Nova
    Scotia. (1937) reprint 1992. 154pp.   15.00   ....   F5159

ONTARIO

Chadwick, Edward M.   Ontarian Families: Genealogies of
    United-Empire Loyalist & other Pioneer Families of Upper
    Canada. (1895) reprint 1990. 2 vols..
        Vol. I 203pp $22.50;
        Vol. II 194pp $21.50. Paperback.
        Compiled using a wide variety of sources, this is an
        invaluable resource for Canadian researchers. The set
        contains chapters on more than 100 different families,
        with info. on over 1,000 surnames. F5159

QUEBEC

Desaulniers, F.L.   (Quebec) Recherches Genealogique Sur les
    Families Gravel, Cloutier, Bruneau, et al. (1902) reprint
    1991. 197pp.
        In French. Genealogies of 21 prominent Quebec families. 21.00   F5159

Hubbard, B.F.   The History of Stanstead County, Province of
    Quebec, Sketches of More than 500 Families. (1874) reprint
    367pp. 25.00   F5216

Parker, Gilbert and Clause G. Bryan. Old Quebec: The Fortress of
    New France. (1903) reprint 1992. 486pp. 30.00   F5216

Thomas, C. Contributions to the History of the Eastern Townships:
    St. Armand, Dunham, Sutton, Broome, Potton & Bolton.
    (1866) reprint 1989. 387pp.   19.95   ....   F5040

Cuba

Carr, Peter E. Guide to Cuban Genealogical Research. 1991.
103pp. 21.50 F5167

Germany

Staudt, Ricardo W. Palatine Church Visitations, 1609. Deanery of Kusel. (1930) reprint 1990. 147pp.
Indexed   18.00   ....   F5130

Tribbeko, John and Geroge Ruperti. List of Germans from the Palatinate Who Came to England in 1709. (1965) reprint 1990. 44pp. 5.00   F5130

Italy

Italian-American

DeAngelis, Priscilla G.   Sources for Italian - American Research.
   40+pp.
   See Religious and Ethnic Groups - Italian, for a full
   description. 9.95   F5078

Jamaica

Livingston, Noel B. Sketch Pedigress of Some of the Early Settlers
   in Jamaica. reprint 1992. 139pp.
      Compiled from the Records of the Court of Chancery
      ofthe Island with a List of the Inhabitants in 1670 and
      Other Matter.
         Indexed 14.50   F5130

United Kingdom

ENGLAND

Baxter, Angus. In Search of Your British & Irish Roots. (1982)
reprint 1992. 310pp. 14.95 F5129

Burke, B. Burke's Dormant, Abeyant, Forfeited & Extinct Peerages
of the British Empire. (1883) reprint 1990. 642pp. 39.50 .... F5159

_____. Roll of Battle Abbey. (1848) reprint 1989. 127pp.
A list of several hundred noble companions of William
the Conqueror, with biog. & gen. details. 14.50 F5159

Christian, M.A., Anne Hait. The Setchfield and Holmes Families of
Whittlesey Cambridgeshire England: A Social and Family
History 1660-1990. 1991. 225pp.
See Family Number 76 in Family Genealogies &
Newsletters Section. 33.00 .... F5100

Coldham, Peter Wilson. American Wills Proved in London,
1611-1775. 1992. 325pp. 30.00 .... F5129

Fairbairn (Comp.), J. and L. Butters & J. McLaren (Rev. & Ed.).
Fairbairn's Crests of the Leading Families in Great Britain &
Ireland & their Kindred in other Lands (2 volumes in 1).
(1911) reprint 1990. 137+605p. 75.00 .... F5159

Gibson, J.S.W. Bishops' Transcripts and Marriage Licenses in
England, Wales, and Ireland. 3rd ed. 1991. 40pp. 6.00 F5129

_____. Quarter Sessions Records in England and Wales. A Select
List. 3rd ed. 1992. 47pp. 6.50 F5129

_____. The Hearth Tax, Other Later Stuart Tax Lists, and the
Association Oath Rolls. 1990. 60pp. 7.50 F5129

Gibson, J.S.W. and Colin Rogers. Electoral Registers Since 1832;
and Burgess Rolls. 1990. 60pp. 7.50 F5129

_____. and Colin Rogers. Poll Books c. 1696 - 1872, A Directory
to Holdings in Great Britain. 1990. 60pp. 7.50 F5129

Gibson, J.S.W. and Elizabeth Hampson. Marriage, Census and
Other Indexes in Great Britain. 4th ed. 1992. 60pp. 7.50 F5129

Gibson, J.S.W. and Mervyn Medlycott. Local Census Listing
1522-1930. Holdings in the British Isles. 1992. 60pp. 7.50 F5129

_____. and Mervyn Medlycott. Militia Lists and Musters 1757 -
1876, A Directory of Holding in the British Isles. 1990. 42pp. 6.50 F5129

Gibson, J.S.W. and Pamela Peskett. Record Offices in England and
Wales. How to Find Them. 5th ed. 1991. 60pp. 7.50 F5129

Saul, Pauline and F.C. Markwell. The A-Z Guide to Tracing
Ancestors in Britain, 4th ed. 1991. .... 17.95 F5129

IRELAND

Eustace, P. Beryl and Olive C. Goodbody. Quaker Records, Dublin,
Abstracts of Wills. (1957) reprint 1992. 136pp.
Indexed. 16.50 F5130

Farrar, Henry. Irish Marriages Being an Index to the Marriages in "Walker's Hibernian Magazine", 1771-1812, With an Appendix from the Notes of Sir Arthur Vicars. (1897) reprint 1992. 532pp.
    2 volumes in 1. .... 36.50 F5130

General Alphabetical Index to the Townlands and Towns, Parishes and Baronies of Ireland, Based on the Census of Ireland for the Year 1851. (1861) reprint 1992. 968pp. 45.00 .... F5129

Mitchell, Brian. A New Genealogical Atlas of Ireland. (1986) reprint 1992. 123pp.
    3rd Printing. 7" x 10". 18.95 F5129

_____. Pocket Guide to Irish Genealogy. 1991. 63pp.
    Maps 9.95 F5130

O'Hart, J. Irish Pedigrees, or the Origin & Stem of the Irish Nation. (1915) reprint 1987. 912 & 948p.
    $89.00/vol.
        Vol. I contains gen. from the 3rd ed. of Irish Pedigrees & also Irish Landed Gentry when Cromwell Came to Ireland.
        Vol. II gives families in Ireland from the 12th to the end of the 16th Cent., settlers under the "Plantation of Ulster", adventurers who came to Ireland with the Cromwellian Settlement, of Huguenot & Palatine families settled in Ireland, the gen. of Anglo-Irish & other families who settled in Ireland since the Eng. invasion, & Irish Brigades in the service of foreign nations. 89.00 .... F5159

Schlegel, Donald M. Irish Genealogical Abstracts From the Londonderry Journal, 1772-1784. 1990. 189pp. 25.00 .... F5130

White, P. History of Clare & the Dalcassian Clans of Tipperary, Limerick & Galway, with an Ancient & a Modern Map. (1893) reprint 1992. 398pp.
    Contains not only a history of the County of Clare that will be fascinating reading to anyone with ancestral ties to Clare, but also a chapter on Clare in the 1890's, and a map and appendix that will help the genealogist researching the county. 41.00 .... F5159

Yurdan, Marilyn. Irish Family History. 1990. 207pp.
.... 19.95 F5129

SCOTLAND

Ferguson, J.P.S. Scottish Family Histories Held in Scottish Libraries. (1960) reprint 1987. 194pp.
    This catalog records the whereabouts of some 2,000 Scottish family histories held in 76 libraries around Scotland. 25.00 .... F5159

Paul, Sir James Balfour. An Ordinary of Arms Contained in the Public Register of All Arms and Bearings in Scotland. (1903) reprint 1991. 452pp.
    Indexed 32.50 F5130

Smith, Jr., Philip D. Tartan For Me! Suggested Tartans for Scottish, Scotch-Irish, Irish, and North American Surnames with Lists of Clan, Family, and District Tartans. 1992. 140pp. 22.50 .... F5216

WALES

Nicholas, Thomas.   Annals and Antiquities of the Counties and
   County Families of Wales. (1875) reprint 1991. 964pp.
      2 Volumes, illus., indexed.   75.00   ....   F5129

Anglesey

Rowlands, William A. ANGLESEY, WALES A Research
   Reference. 1991. 285pp. 25.00   F5014

The Genealogy Tree

Dortha Steele
721 E 17th So,
Salt Lake City, UT 84105
over 20 years experience

Family Genealogies & Newsletters

6   - SCOTTISH KIN OF MY GRANDCHILDREN, **SUTHERLAND - DONALDSON**, by Judge Noble K. Littell. 1992.
         IN PROCESS - James (Jaime the Scot) **Sutherland** and Robert **Donaldson** were born in Scotland, Jaime came to Virginia, Robert to Kentucky, their progeny intermarried in Indiana.   Each line is traced as well as Scot descendant James **Seaton** (c1690, Virginia).
         Collateral families include **Kiser, LaForce, Littell, McGinnis, Shake, Whitaker**, and many more.
         Will contain over 350 pages, 6x9, indexed, cloth. Includes a brief history of Clan **Sutherland** and Clan **Donald** (approximately 275 pages in computer now). Publication in Fall of 1992. Volume IV in a series. Write for more details.
         .... F5003

7   - **MARDEN** FAMILY GENEALOGY, by Sylvia Fitts Getchell. 1974.
         Cloth--$34.00--656pp F5004

8   - **FITTS** FAMILIES (**FITTS/FITZ/FITTZ**), A GENEALOGY, by Sylvia Fitts Getchell. 1989.
         Cloth--$60.00--704pp F5004

9   - **BERRYS** BY THE BEACH - ONE OF NEW HAMPSHIRE'S FIRST FAMILIES, by Sylvia Fitts Getchell. 1980.
         Cloth--$6.00---41pp F5004

10   - GENEALOGY OF THE **FITTS** OR **FITZ** FAMILY, by James Hill Fitts. Repr. of 1869 ed. 1970.
         Cloth--$13.00--91pp F5004

11   - BEGINNING AT A PINE TREE: THE **YEARLING/EARLING/EARLIN** LINE, by Margaret E. Sheaffer and Carol M. Sheaffer, MD. 1987.
         BEGINNING AT A PINE TREE: **THE YEARLING/EARLING/EARLLIN** LINE is a genealogical history of an early southern New Jersey family covering a time frame of 1700's to present.   Related family lines are traced and include: **Malsbury, Webb, Glenn, Garroute, Howell, Horner, Meyer, Murphy, Tweed** and many others.
         Cloth--$20.00--145pp F5005

12   - **SCHAEFFER/ SHAEFFER/ SHEAFFER** SEARCH, by Carol M. Sheaffer, MD and Margaret E. Sheaffer. 1991.
         Contains the history and genealogy of the Levi and Mary (**Knox**) **Shaeffer** Family. Information on the **Shaeffer** Surname and 244 **Shaeffer** immigrants to Colonial America.   Surname and descendant charts of thirty-one **Shaeffer** Families of Lancaster, Dauphin, Berks, Chester, Bucks, York and Lebanon Counties, Pennsylvania.
         Cloth--$32.00--158pp F5005

13   - FITHIAN **STRATTON** 1738-1817; PATRIOT AND PREACHER, by Margaret E. Sheaffer and Carol M. Sheaffer, MD. 1985.
         Biographical Sketch, Fithian **Stratton's** Bible Records, **Glenn** Family Genealogy
         Paper--$6.00--20pp F5005

14   - A **JENNINGS** FAMILY GENEALOGY, by Shirley A. Jennings Weber. 1989.
         As Descended from Charles Lawson **Jinings** of Maryland and North Carolina, to the seventh generation of Samual B. **Jinings** in America - 1774-1985.
         Book includes all spellings of **Jennings**, many photographs, family bibles, wills, history of **Jennings** estate left in England, complete documentation and index.   Early descendants located in Arkansas, Illinois, Kansas, Kentucky, Missouri, Nebraska,

Tennessee, Texas. Major allied lines: **Allen, Bonafield, Hays, Killman, Long, McCord, McMurtry, Mabery, Miller, Richardson, Robeson, Wriston.**
Cloth--$40.50--602pp F5006

15   - PERRY - LONG GENEALOGY, by Elwell H. Perry. Repr. of 1976 ed. 1976.
       Ezra **Perry** & 11 generations of descendants. Joel **Long** & 6 generations of descendants.
       Paper--$15.00--286pp F5009

16   - THE DESCENDANTS OF CASPER **RADER** (1732-1812), by James Rader. Every year.
       From Pennsylvania Dutch 1750 thru Virginia and Tennessee 1800. Nine generations, Every person index, over 200 pages. Updated version published every 6 months.
       Cloth--$45.00--Paper--$35.00--200+pp F5010

17   - **RADER** RAMBLINGS, by James Rader. .
       Quarterly newsletter dedicated to finding ALL **Rader/Röder/Roeder** immigrant ancestor's history and genealogy. $15 per year.
       Subscription $15.00/yr F5010

18   - ELIZABETH **TODD** (BORN 1760S) OF LAWRENCE COUNTY, INDIANA IN 1820: HER DESCENDANTS, by Nancie Todd Weber. 1991.
       Circumstantial family reconstruction (11 children), theorizing marriage, Elizabeth **Seip** to **Andrew Todd** 1782 Frederick County, Maryland. Surnames include **Bales, Brooks, Dayton, Fields, Fleetwood, Hays, Helton, Newton, Pritchett, Renick, Ragsdale, Rogers.** Traditional link to Mary Lincoln's **Todds**, alternative ancestry discussed. Maps, charts, indexed.
       Paper--$22.00--206pp F5011

19   - **PERKINS** FAMILY NEWSLETTER, by Paula Perkins Mortensen. Since 1986.
       Quarterly newsletter. Covers all **PERKINS** lines. Free queries
       Subscription--$10.00/yr--12pp F5012

20   - **MASON** FAMILY NEWSLETTER, by Paula Perkins Mortensen. Since 1987.
       Quarterly Newsletter. Covers all **MASON** Lines. Free queries.
       Subscription--$10.00/yr--12pp F5012

21   - **BUCK** SURNAME BOOKLETS, by Paula Perkins Mortensen. Since 1988.
       Issued periodically. Covers all **BUCK** lines. Free submission of any **BUCK** material and/or queries.
       Paper--$6.00--35-40pp F5012

22   - **BUZZARD** AND **ALT** FAMILIES, by Monte P. Buzzard. 1991.
       The descendants of Henry **Buzzard** and Elizabeth **Alt** are mentioned in this book. Henry and Elizabeth were married about 1760 and spent their lives in Virginia and what is now West Virginia. This book also contains a great amount of information on **Buzzards** and **Alts** that are not descendants of Henry and Elizabeth **Buzzard**. This means that the book would be a valuable resource for anyone who is researching the **Buzzard** and **Alt** surnames.
       Some collateral families: **Ault, Arbogast, Chestnut, Grimes, Hull, Radabaugh** and **Zickafoose.**
       Indexed; documented.
       Paper--$15.00--207pp F5015

23   - ROBERT **PALMATARY** OF DUCK CREEK DELAWARE AND HIS DESCENDANTS, by Marjorie Watts Nelson. 1991.

Starting with Robert **Palmatary**, who received a grant of 500 acres of land on Duck Creek, Delaware, from William Penn in 1684, his descendants are traced down to the present day. This is a collection of biographical sketches of every descendant located. Present day descendants are in many states and Canada but mostly in Philadelphia, Baltimore, Delmarva Peninsula and Missouri.

Indexed, with some photographs and documents.

Cloth--$30.00--576pp F5016

24   - **STOCKMAN** FAMILY NEWSLETTER, by Lee Stockman. Repr. of 1986 ed. .

Quarterly newsletter - All U.S. **Stockman** families. Specializing in Southern **Stockmans** and related families.

Subscription--$10.00/yr--80pp F5017

25   - THREE HUNDRED YEARS IN AMERICA WITH THE **MERCERS**, by Dolores Graham Doyle. 1991.

2300 descendants of: Edward **Mercer**, Virginia, 1704- 1763; John **Dickerson**, Pennsylvania, 1721-1785; Morris **Matson**, Pennsylvania, 1716-1776. Related families include: **Cecil, Dawson, Dunlap, Eastlick, Graham, Knox, McCallister, Peringer, Prentice, Russell, Smith, Stetzel, Van Blaricom, Vaughan, Witten** and more. Early pioneers: Ohio, Illinois, Indiana, Oregon, Washington.

Cloth--$30.00--200pp F5018

26   - CHRISTIAN **FEERO**, LOYALIST OF NEW BRUNSWICK AND HIS DESCENDANTS, by Gloria Spaulding Bullock. 1983.

Traces seven generations **Feero** family in N.B., N.E., mid-West, Alaska. Over 75 individual biographies, 100 early photographs, maps, documents, family letters, index, ancestral chart. **Way, Cronkite, Adams, Birmingham, Carr, Cochrane, Eastman, Grant, Marney, McLaughlin, Nason, Nicholson, Ritchie, Spaulding, Wright,** others.

Cloth--$35.00--261pp F5023

27   - GENEALOGICAL CLASSIFICATION BY FAMILY GROUP CODING FOR DESCENT FROM COMMON ANCESTORS, by Cameron Ralph Stewart. 1986.

Ancestors and descendants of:

(1) **Stewart**, John son of James, b. Perthshire, Scotland, d. Ontario, 1858;

(2) **McAlester-McMaster**, Arran, Scotland; **Cook-McMaster** to Canada, 1832/33;

(3) **Sarles**, NY to Ontario CA 1808; **Sharrard**, England to NY, 1760 to Canada 1789;

(4) **Bentl(e)y**, Ampthill, Bedfordshire, England, to RI 1670s; **Scranton-Shippee**, Warwick RI, m. 1664; **Lichfield-Shippee**, MA-RI, m. 1702;

(5) **Badgerow**, NY to Ontario, 1798;

(6) **Gjer(d)e-Trodo** and **Afdal**, Voss, Norway, 1860 to WI-IA (Miltzow, 16th C. Pomerania, Germany and Norway);

(7) **Osmundsdatter-Knutson**, Setesdal, Norway (incl. **Kvale**, 1434), to WI 1859 to MN, 1880.

Separate volumes available, Indexed.

Cloth--$189.00--2349pp F5024

28   - THE **NETHERLAND, LEATHERLIN** LEGACY WITH ALLIED **CRANE** AND **WALLS** FAMILIES, by Gena **Ayers** Walls. 1991.

Netherland, Neatherlin, Leatherlin: Richmond County, GA-1789; Greensburg Dist., LA-1804; Amite, Lawrence, and Lincoln Counties, MS-1811; Williamson and Frio Counties, TX-1860.

Crane, Crain: SC-1783; KY-1802; Washington Par., LA-1810; Rankin, Lawrence, and Lincoln Counties, MS-1820.

Walls: PA-1834; St. Louis County, MO-1850; Smith, Jasper, Lawrence and Lincoln Counties, MS-1820.

Related families include **Bingham, Champion, Cummins, Domingoes, Dow, Duke, Fore, Fretwell, Fuller, Givens, Harrell, Hayhurst, Hedgepeth, Hoover, Killbrew, King, Lambert, Landrum, Mansfield, Massey, Melton, Neal, Newton, Peavy, Pennington, Pinholster, Pomes, Saul, Seago, Sego, Takewell Taylor, Thames, Tidwell, Vickers, Walker, Ward, Watts, Wilson, Winter.**

Descendants can be found in almost every state and several countries. Vital statistics include cause of death, place of burial, epitaph, and personality profiles. It contains 175 documents and photographs, with more than 10,000 indexed names representing 1,800 surnames.

Cloth--$60.00--600pp F5025

29   - FRANTZ FAMILIES - KITH & KIN, by Dore M. Frantz, Sr., Lowell Beachler, Hazel Frantz Turner, and Lorraine Frantz Edwards, et al. 1993.

Descendants of Swiss/German immigrant Michael **Frantz** (1687-1748) from 1700's to the present, including female lines. These Mennonite/German Baptist Brethren/Church of the Brethren/"Dunkard" families live(d) in PA, VA, OH, IL, IN, KS, ND, CA, WA. Substantial data on collateral families: **Barnhart, Brubaker, Cripe, Crist, Filbrun, Flora/Flory, Garst, Grisso, Hamm, Heck, Landes/Landis, Naff/Neff, Neher, Ohmart, Royer, Shoup, Showalter, Trout, Wertz, Wolf/Wolfe, Ziegler/Zigler, Zug.**

Over eleven thousand names in Roots 3 computer genealogy database. All information is footnoted and indexed. Dozens of **Frantz**-family researchers have contributed to this book that will exceed one-thousand pages. There is still time to submit your line. Send data and inquires to Lorraine, vendor #F5026.

1000+pp F5026

30   - PIONEER FAMILIES OF GRANT COUNTY, NEW MEXICO - A HISTORY OF THE **HOOKER-SHELLEY** FAMILIES AND THE 916 RANCH, by La Verne Mccauley and Terrell T. Shelley. 1987.

Six generations descended from John Metcalf **Shackleford** and Amelia Jane **Hickman**, Peter McKindree **Shelley** and Emily Jane **York**. John M. **Shackleford** and family moved west to St. Joseph, Missouri from Lexington, Kentucky. After the gold rush he moved his family to Red Bluff, California. In 1875 they arrived in Grant County on New Years Day. Peter McKindree **Shelley** left Glascow, Kentucky in 1861 at the age of ten with his parents, John **Shelley** and Sally Ann **Davis** and family settling in Fannin County, Texas.

Both parents died there within a day of each other in 1863. Peter McKindree **Shelley** married Emily Jane **York**, June 25, 1874. In 1884, Peter McKindree **Shelley** left Edwards County, Texas with his family and a herd of cattle for New Mexico where he settled on Mogollon Creek building the "916" Ranch with the brand and cattle he brought from Texas.

Some collateral families: **Hooker, York, Grimes, Hollimon, McClain, Shaw, Cook, Lewis, Burgess, Rice, Moss, Metcalf, Williams, Sixby.**

Cloth--$40.00--499pp F5032

31   - DESCENDANTS OF HENRY **TUTHILL** 1612-1650, by Gwen Campbell, Editor. 1991.

Henry was born in Tharston, Norfolk County, England. He came, prior to 1637 to Hingham, MA. In 1644 he went to Southold, LI. His descendants settled on Long Island until after the Revolution when they began to disperse; some changed the spelling to **TUTTLE**. He and his descendants are listed on Family Group sheets.

Paper--$35.00--434pp F5035

32   - PIONEER ILLINOIS FAMILIES BEFORE 1820: **BRICKEY, RALLS, CRISLER,**
        STRAIT, THOMPSON, ARMSTRONG, CONWAY, by David A. Helm. 1992.
            Ancestry and descendants of Jarrett **Brickey** of Botetourt County, VA; Rawleigh
        Ralls of Stafford County, VA; Silas **Crisler** (1788-1851) of Boone County, KY; Israel
        Strait (1776-1836) of Wake County, NC; John **Thompson** (1759-1843) of Botetourt
        County, VA; George **Armstrong** (1780-1860) of Muhlenberg County, KY; Jesse
        Conway (1761-1840) of Bourbon County, KY. All located in Illinois before 1820.
        Paper--$19.00--130pp F5036

33   - **HELMS** OF GERMANY AND PENNSYLVANIA, by David A. Helm. 1992.
            Three **Helm** cousins came from Beerfelden Parish to America: Johann Nicolaus,
        1750; Johann Jacob, 1754; Johann Friederich, 1766.   Bedford, Somerset, and
        Cumberland Counties, PA. Extensive information about ancestors of these **Helms** in
        Germany, from 1570. Nine generations of descendants in America.
        Cloth--$29.00--360pp F5036

34   - ISRAEL FOOTE **HALE** (1804-1891) AND VERONICA **KEEPERS**: THEIR
        ANCESTORS AND DESCENDANTS, by David A. Helm. 1992.
            Letters of I.F. **Hale**, Randolph County, MO, and also his California Gold rush
        diary.   His ancestry includes **Foote, Otis, Welles**, from Connecticut. Her ancestry
        includes **Elder, Mills, Livers**, Frederick County, Maryland. Numerous descendants
        identified from their seven children.
        Paper--$21.00--160pp F5036

35   - ANCESTORS & DESCENDANTS OF JONATHAN **SMITH** (1789), by Susan
        Farrell Werle. 1991.
            Includes his wife Thirzah **Eastman** (1800), & children Thirzah (Smith) **Proctor**,
        Joseph **Smith**, Josiah Bissell **Smith**, Tilton Eastman **Smith** & Charles Finney **Smith**.
        Paper--$18.95--145pp F5037

36   - **LOBDELL** LINES NEWSLETTER, by Bob Lobdell, Editor. Repr. of 1988 ed. .
            Genealogical and general information exchange. For **Lobdell's** and their related
        families everywhere!
        Subscription--$6/year-- F5038

37   - **WREN** KIN NEWSLETTER, by Ruth Wren, Editor. 1990/91.
            The **Wren** Kin Newsletter was started in January, 1990, as an official publication
        of the **Wren** Family Association, to provide a gathering place for **Wren** Kin research
        material.   Research indicates several spellings of **Wren (Wren, Ren, Rhen)**, and all
        spellings are represented, including some information on collateral families (too
        numerous to name).
            The **Wren** Family Association is trying to put together an accurate portrait of the
        Wren family. Documented and supported evidence is solicited and published, as space
        permits. Cost: $10.00 a year (No Cost for Queries) Issued Quarterly.
        Subscription--$10/year--4-12pp F5039

38   - DESCENDANTS OF CONRAD **BOWER**, MARTIN **EASTERDAY** II, JOHN
        HOOVER SR. AND GABRIEL **SWINEHART** FAMILIES: FROM COLONIAL
        MARYLAND TO OHIO IN THE 1800'S, by Arlene F. Mansfield. 1992.
            Part I and II includes eleven generations descended from Conrad **Bower** and Martin
        Easterday II.   Three of Martin **Easterday's** sons married three of Conrad **Bower's**
        daughters. Part III and IV is a compiling of the descendants of John **Hoover** Sr. and
        Gabriel **Swinehart**.   Several of their descendants intermarried with the **Bower** and
        Easterday families. Some Collateral lines, **Dague, Grimm, Long, Minnich, Tope,**
        Swickard.

Indexed; illustrated; documented.
Paper--$29.50--270pp F5043

39   - DESCENDANTS AND FOREBEARS OF JAMES KUYKENDALL **BYERS** AND
        ARY ANN **BURCH**, by Norma Y. (Harris) Garbert. 1989.
            James K. **Byers** of Alabama, Seminole War veteran, was son of 19th-century Baptist
        minister Joseph J. **Byers** and 1st wife Mary **Kuykendall**, whose father won bounty land
        in Georgia for his Revolutionary War Service. Ary Ann **Burch** was daughter of Jarrett
        Burch of Georgia and Milly **Pinson**, whose father and grandfather were Revolutionary
        War patriots in North Carolina. Other forebears include New York Dutch families: **Cole**,
        Tack, and **Westfall**. Byers descendants, some to 8th generation, are arranged in chapters
        headed by 4 sons and 4 daughters of James K. **Byers**, with the last chapter: "Other
        Descendants of Elder Joseph J. **Byers**." Descendants of female lines include: **Falkner**,
        Gardner, **Gilbert**, **Harris**, **Jones**, **Martin**, and **Moore**.
            Documented with references, photos, maps, charts, and 6,000 name index.
        Cloth--$35.00--464pp F5049

40   - **WOODS** - **PEDEN** GENEALOGY, by John L. Woods. 1991.
            Ancestry of James **Woods**, WV Darke Co. Ohio, b. 1767, 1st of line in America,
        traced 8 generations to 16th century England; mar. (2) Rebecca **Peden**, WV.
            Adds 70 **Woods**; & 400 **Pedens** to those in *Ancestry of John L. Woods*. Thomas
        Peden, b. 1792 in Darke Co., Ohio and his descendants in Ohio and Indiana are covered
        here and are not known to be covered elsewhere.
            Also covers the Lucius Chambers **Smith** and Lewis **Shedrick** Families.
        Cloth--$35.00--282pp F5050

41   - ANCESTRY OF JOHN L. **WOODS**, by John L. Woods. 1988.
            Ancestral Families: **WOODS**, **CLARKE**, **MORTON**, **SMITH**, **PEDEN**,
        ORCHARD.   Some documented more than 20 generations.   100 pictures; narrative
        information; family group sheets.
        Cloth--$35.00--688pp F5050

42   - ANCESTRY OF JOHN L. **WOODS** & **WOODS** - **PEDEN** GENEALOGY, by
        John L. Woods. .
            The above two items ordered together are $50.00.
        Cloth--$50.00-- F5050

43   - **CORDES** AND **SANDAU** FAMILIES, by Marie Strippgen Holtz. 1992.
            Ancestors of Heinrich **Hoeft**, Pr Hannover, Germany. His descendants in Germany
        and United States.
        Cloth--$25.00-- F5053

44   - A **ROYSE-FARRINGTON** TRILOGY: MEMOIR OF LIEUTENANT VERE
        ROYSE; THE **FARRINGTONS** IN AMERICA; DESCENDANTS OF JOHN
        FARRINGTON, by W.E. Decrow (I & II) and E.C. Farrington III. Repr. of 1896 ed.
        1971.
            Royse and John **Farrington** settled in Fryeburg, Maine in 18th Century.
        Cloth--$40.00--91pp F5051

45   - **STRIPPGEN** FAMILY ANCESTORS AND DESCENDANTS, by Marie Strippgen
        Holtz. 1991.
            Carl Emil **Strippgen** married Emma Marie **Holtfort**, 1887, Mülheim/Rughr,
        Germany.   Their ancestors in Germany, descendants in America.   History of name
        Strippgen from 1407.
        Cloth--$20.00--128pp F5053

46   - A **REARDON** FAMILY HISTORY, WILLIAM J. **REARDON** AND BRIDGET **MURRAY** FROM COUNTY TIPPERARY TO ST. CROIX COUNTY WISCONSIN., by Blanche Reardon Childs. 1991.

         Six generations traced from Ireland (1830's) through Ohio, Kentucky, Illinois (1860's) to Minnesota and Wisconsin (1870's to the present). Describes activities of the families and surrounding local history and events.

         Descendant families: **Kelly, Kilty, McMahon, O'Keeffe, Stapleton**.

         Every-name index; illustrated; documented.

         Cloth--$17.50--245pp F5055

47   - **KITTRELLS** IN AMERICA. A BRIEF SURVEY AND CLUES TO THEIR WHEREABOUTS, by Mary Emily Smith Witt. 1991.

         Over 650 people from 1600s to present who were born to or acquired the **Kittrell** name. Appendices of surnames of **Kittrell** wives and husbands.

         Paper--$17.50--104pp F5060

48   - **WARRENS** AND RELATED FAMILIES OF NORTH CAROLINA AND VIRGINIA, by Dr. Holland D. Warren. 1990.

         Here are the descendants of John and Rachel **Warren**, who lived in Old Rappahannock County, Virginia in the seventeenth century. In Virginia, Dr. Warren tracks the family through Spotsylvania, Orange and Halifax counties; in North Carolina, the trail leads through Caswell, Person, Wilkes and Ashe counties. Much attention is focused on the associated families: **West, Hawkins, Williams, Parker, Hackley, Rogers, Burgess, Hamm, Farish, Askew, Goodloe, Lucas, Holt, Brooks, Stone, Murdoch, Brown, Shaver, McKaughan, DeBorde** and **Wall**.

         Cloth--$48.50--442pp F5062

49   - CONNELLY CONNECTIONS, A **CONNELLY** FAMILY NEWSLETTER, VOLS 1 THRU 7, by Roger R. Connelly. 1980-86.

         Two brothers of Scotch-Irish origin, Thomas and Arthur **Connelly**, raised large families in Augusta County, Virginia, during the late 1700's. Over 4,300 of their descendants (male and female lines) are identified, primarily residents of Kentucky (Boone, Gallatin, Grant, Kenton, and Montgomery Counties), Indiana (Carroll, Clay, Putnam, and Tippecanoe Counties), Kansas (Atchison, Leavenworth, and Thomas Counties), Missouri (Cass, Jasper, and Shelby Counties), and Louisiana (East Baton Rouge and Terrebonne Parishes).

         Some collateral lines: **Adams, Atha, Baker, Barton, Bates, Black, Bobbitt, Browning, Burke, Calvert, Castleman, Clearwater, Clements, Cloake, Cooper, Crouch, Feaster, Felker, Garner, Gowdy, Graham, Gros, Hall, Hoard, Hollis, Hood, Howlett, Hume, Idenden, Lemmon, Logan, Lowry, McHaffie, McMains, Marsh, Miers, Moody, Moore, Morehouse, Nye, Oldaker, Ostheimer, Pearson, Plunkett, Pratt, Ridlen, Riley, Rothrock, Sands, Shrewsbury, Steele, Tisdale, Waller, Warrington**, and **Yockey**.

         Paper--$20.00--184pp F5065

50   - THE SWISS CONNECTION: HANS CASPAR **KUHN** (1713-1792) OF SOUTH CAROLINA AND HIS DESCENDANTS WITH RELATED FAMILIES OF **KINSLER, NETTLES**, AND **WYRICK**, by Gwendolyn Pryor. 1991.

         Hans Caspar **KUHN**, his wife, and two children were part of a group of Swiss-German immigrants who landed at Charles Town (now Charleston) in the British colony of South Carolina in January 1749/50 on board the ship *Greenwich*. Like so many of the British settlers who came to America, he came seeking a better life for himself and his family.

         This book spans thirteen generations of **KUHNS/COONS/KOONS** from the baptism of Hans Caspars's great grandfather in 1608 in Switzerland, to the births of his seventh great grandchildren (the 10th generation in America). It also contains brief biographies on the families and descendants of Conrad **KINSLER**, Robert **NETTLES**, and Nicholas **WYRICK**; whose descendants intermarried with descendants Hans Caspar **KUHN**.

Some of the families named in the book include: **BUSER, COATS, CRISP, DAVIS, DEMOSS, DUFFIE, EDWARDS, FAUST, FRIDAY, GEIGER, GRADICK, HAVARD, HORNSBY, HUMPHREYS, LINDSAY, LOMAS, MCDONALD, MCKINSTRY, MARLER, MOSS, RAWLS, ROBERTS, ROLLINS, SCUDDER, SESSIONS, SHERRARD, SIMPKINS, WHITE** and many others.

Descendants included in the book lived chiefly in the States of South Carolina, Mississippi, Louisiana, and Tennessee.

Indexed, Illustrated, Documented.

Cloth--$33.00--463pp F5066

51   - THE **BANTAS** OF PLEASANT HILL, KENTUCKY, THEIR ANCESTORS AND DESCENDANTS, by Joan England Murray. 1985.

Follows descent of the emigrant, Epke Jacob **Banta**, from Holland to New York, New Jersey, Pennsylvania, and Kentucky. Centers on role of the **Bantas** in formation of the Shaker Society at Pleasant Hill. Indexed, documented, and illustrated.

Cloth--$20.00--128pp F5067

52   - BUNNELL AND ALLIED FAMILIES, by Joan England Murray. 1990.

Follows nine generations of descent from the emigrant, William **Bunnell**. Includes collateral lines of **Barkeloo, Haldron, Jayne, Mallory, Plumb, Wilmot** and many more. Indexed, documented, illustrated.

Cloth--$44.00--Paper--$38.00--382pp F5067

53   - BELL CHIMES, PUBLISHED BIMONTHLY FOR ALL DESCENDED FROM A **BELL** OR VARIANT.

Subscription--$11.50/yr-- F5069

54   - THE **JIPSON-JEPSON-GIPSON** FAMILY OF MAINE, by Alan H. Hawkins. 1991.

Nine generations descended from William **Jepson** and Elizabeth **Boothby** of Moywater, Co. Mayo, Ireland, who came to Wells, Maine about 1719. He was killed by the Indians in 1723.

Indexed; illustrations; documented.

Cloth--$43.25--Paper--$26.50--328pp F5071

55   - JOSEPH **BRUNNER** OF ROTHENSTEIN, SCHIFFERSTADT, AND FREDERICK, by Donald Lewis Osborn. 1991.

Ancestry (back to 1400's) and five descending generations of Frederick, Maryland immigrant Joseph **Brunner**, born 1678 (died 1753?), son of Heinrich and Maria (**Braun**) **Brunner** of Rothenstein near Groenenbach, Germany. (Companion volume to *Knowing the Bruners* [1968] with minimum repetition.) Sources documented; abundant footnotes. Two marriages, descendants of Jacob **Sturm/Storm** (1701-1757).

Other families: **Bruner, Gah, Saur, Strihl, Briggs, Jeffries, Thomas, Sinn, Zimmerman, Ramsburg/Remsberg, Getzendanner**.

Ancestry chart insert. Illustrations (57). Relics brought on ships. Gold Rush and other letters. California minister's 1846-1872 journal.

Cloth--$155.00--600pp F5072

56   - THE **WESTS** AND THE **RAYS** AND ALLIED FAMILIES: SOUTHERN FAMILIES FROM THE COLONIES TO TEXAS, by Nan Overton West. 1991.

A genealogical history of families who came to America between 1619 and 1800. Related lines: **Swain, Boatner, Norris, Smith, Sanford, Wyatt, Culver, Egner, Dean, Richards, Culpepper, Gillespie, Young, Lee** (Hugh **Lee** of VA).
1991 Grand Prize Winner, Texas State Genealogical Society.
Cloth--$42.50--495pp F5073

57   - THE **OVERTON** AND **JENNINGS** FAMILIES AND THEIR ALLIES: FROM SOUTHERN COLONIES TO TEXAS, by Nan Overton West. 1992.
A genealogical history, tracing 300-600 years in America and British Isles. Related lines: **Lawson, Crook, Garnett, Poindexter, Whitworth, Clough, Dunlap, Humphries, Harkness, Pettigrew, Alsup, Appling**, and others.
Cloth--$45.00--500+pp F5073

58   - **WERTZ** RELATIONS: FOR **WERTS, WIRT, WUERTZ**, ETC. FAMILIES OF PENNSYLVANIA, by Carolyn Cell Choppin, Editor. Repr. of 1990 ed. .
Subscription: $2.00/yr or $5.00 for three years.
Quarterly newsletter for all descendants of Pennsylvania **Wertz, Wirts, Wurts**, etc. families.
Subscription $2.00/yr--8p/issue F5075

59   - THE HISTORY AND GENEALOGY OF JOHN YANCEY **FOSTER** OF HAT CREEK, CAMPBELL COUNTY,, VIRGINIA, by Patricia Foster Elton. 1990.
Six generations, 1,059 names, indexed, 33 pictures, old documents, bibliography and charts. Printed on acid-free paper.
Cloth--$30.00--140pp F5076

60   - **BURGESS** BULLETIN, by Susan Mortensen. Repr. of 1991 ed. 1992.
A newsletter and clearinghouse for all **Burgess** researchers. Free Queries.
Subscription--$15.00/yr--88pp F5077

61   - THE **BATER** BOOK AND ALLIED FAMILIES: **SHORE, ENSLEY, GRANGER, THOMAS**, by A.L. Bowerman. 1987.
The **Bater** family history is traced from Devon, England in the sixteenth century. Twelve chapters delineate the family of William **Bater** (1797-1866) in Devon and America. Ten chapters describe other **Bater/Batter** families.
Cloth--$35.00--613pp F5082

62   - SOME DESCENDANTS OF JAN AERTSEN **VANDERBILT**, by Jean M. Rand. 1991.
Traces lines mostly in New York, New Jersey, Pennsylvania, Indiana, Arkansas, and Texas. Includes all **Vanderbilts** in the U.S. 1850 and earlier censuses.
Some related surnames: **Acker, Ackerson, Brinkerhoff, Britten, Cole, Deal, Egbert, Elliman, Fosnot, Garrison, Griffith, Grove, Hagood, Higginbotham, Johnson, Kimsey, Lacy, LaRue, Pate, Pitts, Polhemus, Remsen, Rightmire, Stevens, Stockton, Stumbaugh, Tuers, Van Cleef, Van Duzer, Van Liew, Van Syckel, Waer, Winner, Woodrow, Wyckoff**, others.
7 x 10" acid-free paper, citation of sources, index, bibliography, illustrations,
Cloth--$37.50--328pp F5084

63   - A FAMILY HIERARCHY IN CANADA AND THE UNITED STATES OF AMERICA 1619 - 1971 **CAMERON** ALLIED **KINZE** AND **WARTH** FAMILIES, by C.E. Cameron, Resident of Kent, WA (Deceased). 1972.
Includes: **Cook, Dixon, Freeman, Green, Hardy, Ivey, Johnson, Kinze, McLeod, Miller, Murphy, Thompson, Walsh**, and **Warth** surnames.
Cloth--$12.00--320pp F5085

64   - "THE **WILDER** CONNECTION": ELIAS **WILDER**, HIS DESCENDANTS AND ANTECEDENT LINEAGE (THOMAS LINE), by Donald R. Davis, M.D.. 1992.

A contribution by extension of Rev. Moses Hale Wilder's *Book of the Wilders* and also connecting to Justin E. Wilder's *The Descendants of Harvey Wilder*. This pioneer, Elias **Wilder**, elusive and unlinked until now, was born April 2, 1765 at Killingly, Connecticut, married in 1791 in Massachusetts, farmed and started his family near Stowe, Vermont, migrated in 1808 to Ontario County, New York and thence to Ashtabaula County, Ohio. Moving ever deeper into the wilderness, his sons settled in Ogle County, Illinois and from there, their descendants disseminated throughout western United States, Canada and Australia. Eighteen generations of lineal descent are compiled from Nicholas, the first **Wilder** known in history we can trace, and who was the military Chieftain for the Earl of Richmond in the battle of Bosworth at Leicestershire, England, 1485.

Indexed; documented; 30 photographs; Coat-of-Arms. 7 x 10 Hardcover.
Cloth--$35.00--376pp F5086

65   - ROOTS & BRANCHES OF OUR **GARRISON** FAMILY TREE, by Ivadelle D. Garrison. 1987.

Includes information on these families: **Boyd, Frazier, Garrison, Garrisson, Jackson, Kyle, Neal, Pearce, Reynolds, Thomas**. Indexed, Cross reference California history.
Cloth--$45.00--116pp F5087

66   - ROOTS AND BRANCHES OF OUR **DALTON** FAMILY TREE, by Ivadella D. Garrison. Repr. of 1987 ed. 1989.

Includes information on **Chaillet, Cheney, Childers, Covington, Dalton, Damm, Duralde, Janes, Kidwell, Lee, McBurney, Roberts, Weber, Wood**. Cross reference California history.
Cloth--$45.00--272pp F5087

67   - **CRAIG** - LINKS, by Ann Burton, Editor. .

A family name quarterly (**Craig** any spelling) with end-of-year index. 12th year of publication. Free queries.
Subscription--$15.50/yr-- F5088

68   - DESCENDANTS OF ABRAHAM ORWIG **BURTON** AND ELIZABETH ELECTA PAYNE **BURTON** OF SENECA COUNTY, OHIO AND KOSCUISKO & WABASH COUNTIES, INDIANA, by Conrad L. Burton. 1991.

Contains families from 1840 down to 1990. Everyname index.
Paper--$10.00-- F5089

69   - THOMAS **SEAVEY** AND ROBERT **IRWIN** - DESCENDANTS AND CONNECTING LINES, by Crockett A. Harrison. 1988.

Old English records tell of Devon County fishing vessels coming to the general area of Newfoundland as early as the fourteenth century.

The book picks up William **Seavey** (1601-1686) who settled on the Isles of Shoals off the coast of New Hampshire in 1632. His line is followed for several generations and then the book concentrates on Thomas **Seavey**, his nephew. One branch of this line is followed to the present with connecting lines. Included are early Quakers of Salem, Massachusetts who were persecuted, also a Plymouth Mayflower line, other early Plymouth settlers. More early **Seavey** family information is included than has appeared elsewhere to date.

Several generations of **Irwins** and connecting lines who arrived from Ireland about 1820 are also included.

The principal families other than **Seavey** and **Irwin** are; **Berry, Foss, Pearce, Emerson, Fuller, Buffum, Pope, Buxton, Osborne, Cooke, Washburn, Mitchell, Packard** and **Leonard**.
Cloth--$75.00--452pp F5091

70   - THE **WOODSON** WATCHER PLUS ALLIED LINES, by Felix Earle Luck, co-editor and Mary McCraw Harland, co-editor. 1992.
This quarterly was started in 1982 and has been growing steadily. Queries are free. Many lost **Woodson** lines have been discovered and cousins have been reunited.
Census materials, cemeteries, marriages, tax records are some of the subjects which have been printed. We are interested in the allied lines, too.
Subscription--$15.00/yr--144+/yr F5094

71   - HISTORICAL GENEALOGY OF THE **WOODSONS** AND THEIR CONNECTIONS, by Henry Morton Woodson. Repr. of 1915 ed. 1992.
This book was out of print for years. It begins with John and Sarah **Woodson** who arrived in Virginia in 1619 on the ship, *George*, and continues with their descendants. Many allied lines are carried down also. It is a must for **Woodsons** everywhere.
Paper--$50.00--760pp F5095

72   - JOHN **BOYD** OF BERKELEY COUNTY, WEST VIRGINIA, by Gordon W. Paul. 1991.
The book contains the names of over 3,500 descendants of John and Sarah Griffith **Boyd** and some 1,500 names of in-laws and their parents, together with (in most cases) dates and places, and in some instances additional personal information about the individual. It also includes maps, including those of John **Boyd's** property in Berkeley County, photographs of earlier family members, wills of John and Sarah **Boyd**, and the partition of the slaves of General Elisha **Boyd**, the youngest son, upon his death. There are more than 50 photographs of **Boyd** descendants produced on glossy paper, many of which were taken before 1900.
A full name index completes this excellent record.
Cloth--$50.00--520pp F5096

73   - **EGGMAN** AND **ECKMAN** FAMILY, HISTORY OF PENNSYLVANIA, OHIO, NEW JERSEY, by Andrew Eggman, Jr.. Repr. of 1979 ed. 1986.
260pp F5098

74   - **ROSEBERRY** AND **ADAMSON** FAMILY, HISTORY OF PENNSYLVANIA AND CALIFORNIA, by Andrew Eggman, Jr.. 1988.
30pp F5098

75   - **ROUDABUSH** AND **RUEBUSH** FAMILY HISTORY OF VIRGINIA, by Andrew Eggman, Jr.. 1988.
25pp F5098

76   - THE **SETCHFIELD** AND **HOLMES** FAMILIES OF WHITTLESEY CAMBRIDGESHIRE ENGLAND: A SOCIAL AND FAMILY HISTORY 1660-1990, by Anne Hait Christian, M.A.. 1991.
Fully researched, documented and indexed 225-page history of two families in the Whittlesey, Coates and Wisbech areas for over 300 years. Includes geography and history and reproductions of 35 documents, 25 maps, 14 drawings, 60 photographs and 44 Family Charts. The story of these 13 families who emigrated from Whittlesey to Michigan, USA between 1840-1860 will be published soon.
Perfect bound, colored cover with photographs.
Cloth--$33.00--225pp F5100

77   - THE **GLAS(S)COCK - GLASSCO** SAGA, by Lawrence a. Glassco. Repr. of 1974
        ed. 1990.
                The first five generations of **Glas(s)cocks** in America. From 1643 into the mid 19th
        century.
        Paper--$15.00--136pp F5101

78   - THE **GLAS(S)COCKS** OF ENGLAND AND AMERICA, by Lawrence A. Glassco.
        1984.
                Glas(s)cocks of England prior to 1643 and of America after 1643.
        Cloth--$20.00--290pp F5101

79   - **POCAHONTAS'** DESCENDANTS, by Stuart E. Brown, Jr. and Lorraine F. Myers
        and Eileen M. Chappel. 1985.
                A revision, enlargement and extension of the list as set out by Wyndham Robertson
        in his book *POCAHONTAS, ALIAS MATOAKA, AND HER DESCENDANTS* (1887).
                Indexed, Illustrated.
        Cloth--$49.50--451pp F5102

80   - CORRECTIONS AND ADDITIONS TO **POCAHONTAS'** DESCENDANTS, by
        Stuart E. Brown, Jr. and Lorraine F. Myers and Eileen M. Chappel. 1992.
                This supplement adds to and corrects the book *POCAHONTAS' DESCENDANTS*
        (1985).
                Indexed.
        Cloth--$18.50--192pp F5102

81   - HAROLD FREDERIC **POWELL** GENEALOGY, by Harold F. Powell. 1991.
                The ancestors of Harold Frederic **Powell's** grandchildren, Robert James **Hendry** and
        Elizabeth Jean **Hendry** and Alan Ramon **Barbuzano**, came from England, Scotland,
        Wales and Ireland and France, Germany, Spain and Switzerland.
                They also arrived from 1620 to 1960 and lived in Massachusetts and Maine,
        Connecticut, New Hampshire and Vermont. They were also from New York State,
        Pennsylvania and New Jersey. Some lived in Maryland and Virginia and West Virginia.
        Several families went west to Michigan and settled there for several generations.
                Many of their descendants have gone west, east and south. Now, these three
        grandchildren live in Georgia and Florida.
                It is a hard cover book, indexed for 1200 personal names, in 240 families, citations
        for sources, 35 photos, narratives, and an appendix of pedigree charts, also indexed, 450
        pages.
                The families include: **Allen, Baker, Bonnell, Bunnell, Bowles, Burr, Compton,
        Crane, Doty, Elliott, Fairbanks, Ford, Gray, Hatch, Hendry, Hull, Lanspeary,
        MacGregor, Manning, McDonald, McGarvah, McGuire, McWilliams, Miller,
        Powell, Richardson, Stevens, Tallman, Thompson, Wilder, Willard** and **Wotring**.
        The families are arranged from the earliest ancestors down to the present generation.
                The Book was prepared on a computer using Roots III software and was published
        by Gateway Press of Baltimore, Maryland.
        Cloth--$30.00--390pp F5104

82   - **EASTMAN** FAMILY HISTORY AND GENEALOGY WITH INFORMATION
        ON RELATED FAMILIES, by Susan Marie Schultz Hopfensperger. 1982.
                Descendants of Johanis (John) **Eastman**, Wiltshire, England (d. 1565) through John,
        born in Salisbury, Massachusetts (1640-1720), whose grandson, Thomas (1755-1839)
        fought in the American Revolution. Primarily descendants of Aquilla **Eastman** who
        settled in Wisconsin, Kansas and California. Photos, Military records.
                Related families: **Bohm, Brooks, Brown, Flaherty, Giersch, Hazelton, Schultz**.
        Cloth--$55.00--300pp F5107

83   - **WALBORN (WALBURN)** GENEALOGICAL HISTORY OF AMERICAN
      DESCENDANTS (SINCE 1709), by Herman W. Walborn. Repr. of 1975 ed. 1985.
      Includes some data on allied families and similar names. Immigrant family in New
      York, then Pennsylvania.
      Cloth--$32.00--414pp F5109

84   - FLINN PLACE, by Opal Tillis Flynn. 1991.
      A record of **Flinn/Flynn** ancestry and history covering South Carolina, Georgia, and
      Florida, from 1730-1991.
      Indexed, detailed biographies, maps, charts, group sheets, pictures and documents.
      Related families covering 13 generations: **Acosta, Allen, Backus, Barkowski,
      Beardin, Barr, Beckett, Bovis, Bowden, Curry, Clayton, Flinn/Flynn, Forman,
      Gardner, Hagin, Harris, Hartley, Higginbotham, Hodges, Hudnall, James, Jaster,
      Jones, Keating, Linton, Llabres, McLean, McDowell, McLenden, Macy, Petty,
      Pickett, Sheargold, Spearing, Tate, Turner, Williams** and others.
      Cloth--$29.00-- F5111

85   - REPASS FAMILY NEWSLETTER: DESCENDANTS OF HANS JACOB **RIPPAS**
      AND ANNA **GERBER**, by Beverly Repass Hoch, Editor. 1991+.
      12pp/issue F5112

86   - THE **BLAUVELT** FAMILY GENEALOGY REVISED EDITION, VOLUME I, by
      Dorothy Moos. 1987.
      The first six generations, male and female lines, of Gerrit Hendrickszen (**Blauvelt**)
      who arrived in Nieuw Amsterdam in 1638 and married Marretje Lamberts **Moll**.
      Indexed; illustrated.
      Cloth--$33.00--461pp F5114

87   - THE **BLAUVELT** NEWS, THE QUARTERLY NEWSLETTER OF THE A.B.D.,
      by Jean C. Anderson, Editor. .
      The official newsletter of the Association of **Blauvelt** Descendants. Includes
      activities, news, historical and genealogical information, queries.
      Free to members.
      Subscription--$4.00/yr-- F5114

88   - THE **SEALOCK STORY**, by Kendrick Grant Jackson (1921-1990). 1990.
      Thomas and Susannah (**Cooper**) **Sealock** moved from Chester County,
      Pennsylvania to Loudoun County, Virginia, between 1771 and 1774. Descendants of 6
      of their children - John, William, Thomas, Samuel, Robert and Mary - are traced.
      Some collateral families: **Fox, Eiler, Powell, Garrett, Kidwell, Grant, John**.
      Indexed.
      Paper--$20.00--194pp F5121

89   - THE DESCENDANTS OF JOHN **SEGAR** OF SOUTH KINGSTOWN, RI.
      INCLUDING THE DESCENDANTS OF WILLIAM **BROWNING** AND MARY
      HOXIE (**LEWIS**) **GREENE** OF CHARLESTOWN, RI, by Willam E. Wright. 1992.
      Twelve generations descended from John **Segar** born about 1655 in Connecticut
      including female lines. William Browning **Greene** (1803-1884) is a descendant of John
      Greene of Quidnessett. Mary Hoxsie **Lewis** is the third great granddaughter of John
      Segar.
      Allied families include: **Arnold, Babcock, Brightman, Buffum, Card, Champlin,
      Clarke, Hazard, Kenyon, Money, Peary, Perry, Potter, Rathbun, Sheffer, Sheldon,
      Wright**.
      Complete Index and Documentation.
      Cloth--$19.00--100pp F5125

90   - A GENEALOGY OF THE **TOWNER** FAMILY, by Dolores (Jackie) Towner and
        Dewey Towner. Repr. of 1910 ed. 1990.
            The descendants of Richard **Towner** who came from Sussex County, England to
        Guilford, Connecticut before 1685.
        Cloth--$30.00--303pp F5126

91   - THE **ROSEBAUGH** LINE AND RELATED BRANCHES, by Elizabeth Walker.
        1985.
            George **Rosebaugh** Family of Butler County, Pennsylvania.   Related branches:
        Lowe, Dunn, Myres, Kennedy, Bolton, O'Neil.
            Indexed, Illustrated, Documented.
        Paper--$18.00--182pp F5127

92   - THE **RENISONS**, THE **KENNEDYS** AND RELATED FAMILIES, by Elizabeth
        Walker. 1985.
            John **Renison** Family, Samuel Anderson **Kennedy** family.
            Indexed, Illustrated, Documented.
        Paper--$18.00--129pp F5127

93   - SEEK AND YE SHALL FIND: **PEARSON** (ALL SPELLINGS) VOLS I, II, III, by
        Bettina Pearson Higdon Burns. 1979, 1985, 1990.
            3 Vol set $130.00, 1,263 pages including indexes.
            Vol III $60.00, 425 pages including index. Other names.
        Paper--$130.00--1263pp F5128

94   - **PEARSON**, PLACES & THINGS, by Bettina Pearson Higdon Burns, Editor.
            Quarterly newsletter with free queries for **Pearson** (All spellings). Indexed.
        $12.00/year.
        Subscription--$12.00/yr-- F5128

95   - MARYLAND AND VIRGINIA COLONIALS: GENEALOGIES OF SOME
        COLONIAL FAMILIES, by Sharon J. Doliante. 1991.
            Families of: **Bacon, Beall, Beasley, Cheney, Duckett, Dunbar, Ellyson, Elmore,
        Graves, Heydon, Howard, Jacob, Morris, Nuthall, Odell, Peerce, Reeder, Ridgley,
        Prather, Sprigg, Wesson, Williams,** and Collateral Kin.
        Cloth--$87.50--1,313pp F5129

96   - **LEWIS** OF WARNER HALL, by Merrow Egerton Sorley. Repr. of 1935 ed. 1991.
            This book covers Col. John **Lewis** and Frances **Fielding** and their descendants; Col.
        Charles **Lewis** and Mary **Howell** and their descendants, with considerable attention given
        to these related families: **Ambler, Ball, Barret, Bowles, Bushrod, Byrd, Carter,
        Cobbs, Crawford, Eppes, Fauntleroy, Fielding, Griffin, Howell, Isham, Jefferson,
        Kennon, Marshall, Piersey, Ragland, Randolph, Taliaferro, Taylor, Thompson,
        Walker, Washington, Willis, Woodson** and **Worsham.**
            Indexed.
        Cloth--$45.00--887pp F5129

97   - FAMILY HISTORIES - **CARTER**, by J. Montgomery Seaver. .
        Paper--$7.50--54pp F5130

98   - FAMILY HISTORIES - **MARTIN**, by J. Montgomery Seaver. .
        Paper--$7.50--60pp F5130

99   - FAMILY HISTORIES - **STEWART**, by J. Montgomery Seaver. .
        Paper--$8.50--65pp F5130

100   - FAMILY HISTORIES - **LEE**, by J. Montgomery Seaver. .
        Paper--$7.50--61pp F5130

101   - FAMILY HISTORIES - **DAVIS**, by J. Montgomery Seaver. .
        illustrated
        Paper--$8.50--81pp F5130

102   - FAMILY HISTORIES - **MACDONALD**, by J. Montgomery Seaver. .
        illustrated
        Paper--$7.50--54pp F5130

103   - THE **LIVESAY** FAMILY, USA, by compiled by members of the **Livesay** Historical
        Society. 1979.
              This publication is an overview of the history of the **Livesay** (and other spellings)
        family in the U.S. with charts and other explanatory information. There is also data on
        the family in England. Covers 17th Century to the 20th Century.
              Price does not include postage.
        Paper--$10.00--45pp F5131

104   - **LIVESAYS** IN THE UNITED STATES, THE JOSEPH LINE, by Mrs. Arkie
        (Livesay) Longmire, Talbott, TN., (deceased) and Mrs Ann (Livesay) Harrison,
        Dandridge, TN. 1974.
              History of Joseph and Lavina **Hurley Livesay** and their descendants who came to
        Hawkins (later Hancock) County, Tennessee, between 1817 and 1819. Born in Grayson
        County, Virginia, on May 19, 1802, Joseph was the son of George and Nancy **Anderson**
        Livesay. George **Livesay** was a Revolutionary War soldier who came to Wythe County,
        Virginia, from Franklin County, Virginia circa 1788. Wythe County became part of
        Grayson County. The history deals with the descendants of Joseph and Lavina Livesay
        from the 1820's through the early 1970's.
        Paper--$12.00--95pp F5131

105   - THE **LIVESAY** BULLETIN, by Mrs Virginia Smith, Editor, Mercersburg, PA., and
        Mrs Betty McCarthy, Asst. Editor, Media, PA. .
              A quarterly newsletter containing genealogical information about Livesays (and
        other spellings of the surname) in the United States, England and other countries. There
        is no charge for receipt of the publication. Those on the mailing list are invited to
        contribute to the **Livesay** Historical Society to help with the expenses.
        No Charge - donations accepted -- 4-8pp F5131

106   - THE ANCESTORS & DESCENDANTS OF REVOLUTIONARY GENERAL
        JAMES **WILKINSON** OF CALVERT COUNTY, MARYLAND ET UX, ANN
        BIDDLE OF PHILADELPHIA, PENNSYLVANIA, by Patricia Wilkinson Weaver
        Balletta. 1993.
              Part I: Twenty generations of ancestors from James **Wilkinson** to Edward III
        through Henry **Morgan** of Wales and Kent Island, Maryland with fully cited sources in
        Maryland Hall of Records for **Wilkinson, Skinner, Mackall, Heighe, Holdsworth,
        Smith** and **Morgan**. British sources cited. Ancestral Charts.
              Part II: Twenty generations of ancestors from Ann **Biddle** to King John through
        Owen **Owen** of the Welsh Tract. Pennsylvania sources cited. British Sources cited.
        Ancestral Charts.
              Part III: Nine generations of Descendants from General **James** through son, Joseph
        Biddle **Wilkinson** and wife Catherine **Andrews** of Pointe Celeste Plantation,
        Plaquemines Parish, Louisiana.
              Illustrated, Indexed, Full Documentation plus Bibliography.
        Cloth--$60.00--Paper--$40.00-- F5132

107   - DEACON JOHN **BURNHAM** OF IPSWICH AND EBENEZER **MARTIN** OF REHOBOTH, MASSACHUSETTS, WITH SOME OF THEIR DESCENDANTS, by Elisabeth Puckett Martin. 1987.

      A thorough study of the 1637 immigrant John **Burnham**, later Deacon of Chebacco Parish. His line includes Ebenezer of Windham, Connecticut, Revolutionary soldier Joseph from Ashford, Connecticut, Alba an innkeeper in Batavia, New York.

      Ebenezer **Martin** joined the Revolution from Berkshire County, Massachusetts; son Jarvis was a canal contractor in New York. Jarvis' children settled in western New York and Ashtabula County, Ohio.

      Martin family charts to present. Allied lines are **Andrews, Varney, Holt, Durkee, Byles, Snow, Mason, Waters, Montgomery, Bieder.**

      Indexed.

Cloth--$25.00--305pp F5133

108   - MARK **BREWSTER** OF HULL, ENGLAND AND ALLIED FAMILIES IN AMERICA, by Marcus V. Brewster. 1991.

      Starting in the mid-1700s with **Brewster** origins in Lincolnshire, England, and **ATKEY** and **YELF** families in the Isle of Wight, this book also records partial genealogies to present day of some families surnamed **CARPENTER, DARE, DARNELL, FOWLER, HEWITT, HISCOCK, PIERCE, POTTER** AND **SWINGLY.**

      Several of these families emigrated to the U.S. and then migrated from Rhode Island, Connecticut and New York to Illinois and western states. Hardcover, acid-free paper, over 100 photos plus maps, illustrations, and uniquely designed charts and a complete every name index.

Cloth--$42.50--352pp F5134

109   - **ROBERTS** FAMILY TREE - JOHN & SARAH **BURLINGTON,** WEST JERSEY 1677 "KENT", by Rebecca H. Roberts. Repr. of 1852 ed. 1980.

      Allen, Ballinger, Barr, Borton, Burr, Burroughs, Busby, Cadwallader, Cattel, Clement, Clothier, Coles, Collins, Core, Cowperthwait, Crispin, Darlington, Darnell, Dudley, Eldridge, Elkinton, Ely, Evans, Eves, Foster, French, Gardiner, Haines, Harlan, Heulings, Hunt, Lamb, Lippincott, Logue, Mattlack, Middleton, Newbold, Paul, Pierson, Pine, Reeves, Saunders, Sebrell, Shreve, Stiles, Stockton, Stokes, Warrick, Warrington, Wills, Wister, Woodward, Woolman, Zane.

      36" x 45" actual tree size 24.5" x 35".

Paper--$20.00--1p F5136

110   - OUR JAMES **CROW,** by E. Joyce Christiansen. 1984.

      Descendants of James **Crow** (Revolutionary War Veteran - VA).

Paper--$17.95--180pp F5139

111   - THE **CLYMER** CLAN OF MARYLAND, DELAWARE AND POINTS WEST, by Anita L. Ockert. 1987.

      The American ancestry and descendants of Charles Fountain **Clymer.** Historical background, documents, maps, etc. Indexed.

Cloth--$28.00--320pp F5154

112   - NEFF - NAF FAMILY HISTORY - A GENEALOGY, by William A. Neff. 1991.

      Neff, Henry: Descendant of Adam **Naf,** Zurich, Kappel am Albis; Immigrant, Lancaster Co., PA, Manor Township 1718.

      Neff, Drs. Frances; Hans Heinrich; & Jacob: Lancaster Co., PA, Conestoga Twp., and Frederick Co., MD - 1718

      Related families include **Brubaker, Brenneman, Charles, Erb, Heistand, Herr, Harnish, Huyette, Kauffman, Landis, Miller, Musselman, Rohrer, Senher, Swarr,**

Stoner. Extensive study of migration to Huntington Co., PA, and Ohio counties. Over 2700 individuals, 800 **Neffs**, 900 marriages, and cemetery locations in great detail; 39 photographs and examples of **Neff** fractur and vorschriften; 2 fold out maps. **Neffs** and related families were Swiss Anabaptist (Mennonite) immigrants.
Printed by Princeton University Press.
Cloth--$42.50--480pp F5157

113   - **BISHOP** AND **BURROUGHS** FAMILIES IN EARLY MASSACHUSETTS, VITAL RECORDS FROM PRINTED SOURCES, by Evelyn C. Lane. 1992.
Records are by towns and are completely indexed; taken from Massachusetts vital record books, which contain records through 1850.
Paper--$20.75--122pp F5158

114   - **CARRIER/CURRIER** FAMILIES IN EARLY MASSACHUSETTS, VITAL RECORDS FROM PRINTED SOURCES, by Evelyn C. Lane. 1992.
Records are by towns and are completely indexed; taken from Massachusetts vital record books, which contain records through 1850.
Paper--$20.50--117pp F5158

115   - **PROCTOR** FAMILY IN EARLY MASSACHUSETTS, VITAL RECORDS FROM PRINTED SOURCES, by Evelyn C. Lane. 1991.
Records are by towns and are completely indexed; taken from Massachusetts vital record books, which contain records through 1850.
Paper--$20.75--129pp F5158

116   - **NURSE** AND **ESTY** FAMILIES IN EARLY MASSACHUSETTS, VITAL RECORDS FROM PRINTED SOURCES, by Evelyn C. Lane. 1991.
Records are by towns and are completely indexed; taken from Massachusetts vital record books, which contain records through 1850.
Paper--$23.50--150 .... F5158

117   - **TOWNE** FAMILY IN EARLY MASSACHUSETTS, VITAL RECORDS FROM PRINTED SOURCES, by Evelyn C. Lane. 1990.
Records are by towns and are completely indexed; taken from Massachusetts vital record books, which contain records through 1850.
Paper--$17.00--100pp F5158

118   - MEM OF CAPT. THOMAS **ABBEY**; ANC. & DESC. OF THE **ABBEY** FAM.: PATHFINDERS, SOLDIERS, PIONEERS OF CT., ITS WESTERN RESERVE IN OHIO & THE GREAT WEST., by . Repr. of 1917 ed. .
Cloth--$36.50--Paper--$26.50--175pp F5159

119   - ANC. & DESC. OF JONATHAN **ABELL**, WHO CAME FROM CONN. & SETTLED IN SCHENECTADY CO., NY, ABOUT 1812., by H.A. Abell. Repr. of 1933 ed. .
Paper--$12.00--61pp F5159

120   - **ADAIR** HISTORY & GENEALOGY., by J.B. Adair. Repr. of 1924 ed.
Paper--$51.50--330pp F5159

121   - **ADAMS**. FAM. RECORDS, A GEN. AND VIOGR. HIST.: VOL. I, NO. 1., by J.T. Adams. Repr. of 1929 ed.
Paper--$19.50--108pp F5159

122 - GEN. & HIST. OF PART OF THE NEWBURY **ADAMS** FAM., FORMERLY OF DEVONSHIRE, ENG., DESC. OF ROBERT **ADAMS** & WIFE ELEANOR., by S. Adams. Repr. of 1895 ed.
Paper--$12.50--61pp F5159

123 - A RECORD OF THE **AGEE** FAMILY., by P.M. Agee. Repr. of 1937 ed.
Cloth--$62.50--Paper--$52.50--330pp F5159

124 - THE BOOK OF THE **AGNEWS**. JAMES **AGNEW** OF PA.; HIS RACE, ANC. & DESC., by M.V. Agnew. Repr. of 1926 ed.
Cloth--$99.50--Paper--$89.50--607pp F5159

125 - **ALBEE** FAMILY RECORDS., by R.S. Albee. Repr. of 1920 ed. .
Cloth--$40.00--Paper--$30.00--221pp F5159

126 - GEN. OF FOURTEEN FAMS. OF THE EARLY SETTLERS OF NEW ENGLAND, OF THE NAMES OF **ALDEN, ADAMS, ARNOLD, BASS, BILLINGS, CAPEN** ET AL., by E. Thayer. Repr. of 1835 ed. .
Cloth--$38.00--Paper--$28.00--180pp F5159

127 - "HI, COUSIN": THE MASON J. **ALDRICH** FAM. HIST., by M.M. Aldrich. Repr. of 1967 ed. .
Paper--$21.00--125pp F5159

128 - EARLIER GEN. OF THE **ALEXANDER** FAM. OF VA., by S.M. Culbertson. Repr. of 1934 ed.
Paper--$9.50--46pp F5159

129 - MEMORIAL, 2ND SERIES. DESC. OF SAMUEL **ALLEN** OF WINDSOR, CT., 1640-1907., by O.P. Allen. Repr. of 1907 ed.
Cloth--$49.50--Paper--$39.50--303pp F5159

130 - A BRIEF HIST. OF LEWIS **ALLEN** OF FISHER'S IS. & NEW LONDON, CONN., & HIS DESC., FROM 1699-1954., by M.A. Phinney. Repr. of 1954 ed.
Cloth--$44.50--Paper--$34.50--207pp F5159

131 - SKETCH OF MATTHEW **ALLYN** OF CAMBRIDGE, MASS., by J. Allyn. Repr. of 1884 ed.
Paper--$7.50--37pp F5159

132 - **ALSTONS** OF N. & S. CARO., COMP. FROM ENG., COL. & FAM. REC., WITH PERSONAL REMINISCENCES & NOTES OF SOME ALLIED FAMS., by J.A. Groves. Repr. of 1901 ed.
Cloth--$68.50--Paper--$58.50--367pp F5159

133 **ANDERSON - OVERTON** GENEALOGY. A CONTINUATION OF *"ANDERSON FAM. RECORDS"* (1936) & *"EARLY DESC. OF WM. OVERTON & ELIZABETH WATERS OF VA."* (1938)., by W.P. Anderson. Repr. of 1938 ed.
Cloth--$69.50--Paper--$59.50--376pp F5159

134 **ANDERSON - KROGH** GENEALOGY: ANC. LINES & DESC., by L.W. Hansen. Repr. of 1956 ed.
Cloth--$61.50--Paper--$51.50--323pp F5159

135   - THOMAS **ANDREW**, IMMIGRANT. A GEN. OF THE POSTERITY OF THOMAS **ANDREW**, ONE OF THE EARLY SETTLERS OF NEW ENGLAND., by L.C. Andrew. Repr. of 1971 ed.
Cloth--$36.00--Paper--$26.50--166pp F5159

136   - WM. **ANDREWS** OF HARTFORD, CT. & HIS DESC. IN THE DIRECT LINE TO ASA **ANDREWS** OF HARTLAND, CT. & HARTFORD, OHIO, by F. Andrews. Repr. of 1938 ed.
Paper--$14.00--69pp F5159

137   - "POSTMARKED HUDSON": LETTERS OF SARAH **ANDREWS** TO HER BROTHER JAMES A. **ANDREWS**, 1864-5, WITH GEN. OF THE **ANDREWS** FAM., by W. Miller. Repr. of 1955 ed.
Paper--$15.00--76pp F5159

138   - RICHARD **AREY** OF MARTHA'S VINEYARD & SOME OF HIS DESC., by R.V. Chamberlin. Repr. of 1932 ed.
Paper--$10.00--51pp F5159

139   - CHRONICLES OF THE **ARMSTRONGS**, by J.L. Armstrong. Repr. of 1903 ed.
Cloth--$62.00--Paper--$52.00--407pp F5159

140   - THE STORY OF THE **ARNDTS**. THE LIFE, ANTECEDANTS & DESC. OF BERNHARD **ARNDT**, WHO EMIGR. TO PA. IN 1731, by J.S. Arndt. Repr. of 1922 ed.
Cloth--$77.50--Paper--$67.50--428pp F5159

141   - **ARNOLD-LUCKEY** FAMILY TIES: AUTHORIZED HIST. & GEN., COMPLETE., by L.W. Arnold and E.Z. Luckey. Repr. of 1931 ed.
Paper--$25.00--168pp F5159

142   - **ASHBY-TURNER** RECORDS; **ASHBY** OF FAUQUIER CO., VA., Repr. of 1952 ed.
Paper--$5.00--18pp F5159

143   - JOHN & ELIZABETH **AUCHINCLOSS**; THEIR ANC. & DESC., by J.R. Auchincloss and C.A. Fowler. Repr. of 1957 ed.
Paper--$13.50--67pp F5159

144   - **AULL** AND **MARTIN** GENEALOGY, by W.F. Aull. Repr. of 1920 ed.
Paper--$39.00--189pp F5159

145   - THE DESC. OF RICHARD **AUSTIN** OF CHARLESTOWN, MASS., 1638., by E.A. Moore and W.A. Day. Repr. of 1951 ed.
Cloth--$99.50--Paper--$89.50--608pp F5159

146   - FAM. & DESC. OF CAPT. JOHN **AUTRY**, by M.B. Autry. Repr. of 1964 ed.
Paper--$31.00--209pp F5159

147   - **AVERELL-AVERY** FAM. A RECORD OF DESC. OF WM. & ABIGAIL **AVERELL** OF IPSWICH, MA., by C.A. Avery. Repr. of 1906 ed.
Cloth--$159.00--Paper--$149.00--1094pp F5159

148   - THE **AVERYS** OF GROTON, CT., GEN. & BIOGR., by H.D. Sweet. Repr. of 1894 ed.
Cloth--$98.00--Paper--$88.00--698pp F5159

149   - **AYMAR** FAM. OF N.Y. (EXTR. FROM "HUGUENOT SOC. OF AMER."), by B. Aymar. Repr. of 1903 ed.
Paper--$13.00--63pp F5159

150   - ISAIAH **BABCOCK**, SR., & DESC., by A.E. Babcock. Repr. of 1903 ed.
Paper--$19.50--119pp F5159

151   - **BAILEY**. GEN. JAMES, JOHN & THOMAS & THEIR DESC., IN THREE PARTS, by H.R. Bailey. Repr. of 1899 ed.
Cloth--$71.00--Paper--$61.00--479pp F5159

152   - ACCTS. OF 2ND, 3RD AND 12TH ANNUAL GATHERINGS OF THE **BAILEY-BAYLEY** FAM. ASSOC., by . Repr. of 1894 ed.
Paper--$18.75--123pp F5159

153   - **BAKER** FAMILY GEN.: DESC. OF JOHN NICHOLAS **BAKER**, 1701-63 (NATIVE OF GERMANY; CAME TO U.S. IN 1754) WITH SOME CONNECTING LINES., by R.H. Baker. Repr. of 1955 ed.
Cloth--$48.50--Paper--$38.50--233pp F5159

154   - **BALCH** LEAFLETS. VOL. I, # 1-12, by E. Putnam. Repr. of 1897 ed.
Paper--$15.00--75pp F5159

155   - DESC. OF JOHN **BALL**, WATERTOWN, MASS., 1630-1635, by F.D. Warren and G.H. Ball. Repr. of 1932 ed.
Cloth--$36.00--Paper--$26.00--161pp F5159

156   - THE GEN. REC. OF THE **BANKS** FAM. OF ELBERT CO., GA., COLL., by G.B. Young and S.B. Franklin. Repr. of 1934 ed.
Cloth--$42.50--Paper--$32.50--215pp F5159

157   - GEN. OF DESC. OF LYMAN **BARBER** OF NEWARK VALLEY, N.Y., by L.B. Barber. Repr. of 1944 ed.
Paper--$12.00--60pp F5159

158   - ROBERT **BARNARD** OF ANDOVER, MASS., AND HIS DESC., by R.M. Barnard. Repr. of 1899 ed.
Paper--$9.00--40pp F5159

159   - MANY INTERESTING FACTS CONNECTED WITH THE LIFE OF COMMODORE JOSHUA **BARNEY**, HERO OF U.S. NAVY, 1776- 1812; ALSO A COMP. OF GEN. MATERIAL REL. TO HIS., by W.F. Adams. Repr. of 1912 ed.
Cloth--$46.00--Paper--$36.00--228pp F5159

160   - **BASSETT-PRESTON** ANCESTORS: HISTORY OF ANCESTORS IN AMERICA OF THE CHILDREN OF EDWARD M. & ANNIE **PRESTON** **BASSETT**, by B. Preston. Repr. of 1930 ed.
Cloth--$59.00--Paper--$49.00--359pp F5159

161   - ONE **BASSETT** FAM. IN AMERICA WITH ALL CONNECTIONS IN AMERICA AND MANY IN GREAT BRITAIN AND FRANCE, by B.B. Bassette. Repr. of 1926. Paper--$119.00--867pp F5159

162   - **BATES** BULLETIN, SERIES 1 THROUGH 5., by . Repr. of 1907 ed. Cloth--$81.00--Paper--$71.00--574pp F5159

163   - **BAXTER** FAMILY: DESC. OF GEARGE & THOMAS **BAXTER** OF WESTCHESTER CO., NY, AS WELL AS SOME WV & SC LINES, by F. Baxter. Repr. of 1913 ed. Paper--$25.00--157pp F5159

164   - MEMORIAL OF THE **BAXTER** FAMILY, by J.N. Baxter. Repr. of 1879 ed. Paper--$19.00--114pp F5159

165   - SOME MARYLAND **BAXTERS** & THEIR DESC., INCLUDING FAMS. WITH SURNAMES **ANDERSON, BAKER, BONNER, BROWN, BUTLER**, ET AL., by A.S. Humphreys. Repr. of 1948 ed. Paper--$22.50--139pp F5159

166   - HIST. GEN. OF THE FAM. OF **BAYNE** OF NIDDERDALE, SHOWING ALSO HOW **BAYEUX** BECAME **BAYNES**., by J. Lucat. Repr. of 1896 ed. Cloth--$90.00--Paper--$80.00--635pp F5159

167   - REV. JOHN **BEACH** & DESC., WITH HIST. & BIOGR. SKETCHES, & ANC. & DESC. OF JOHN **SANFORD** OF REDDING, CONN., by Beach & Gibbons. Repr. of 1898 ed. Cloth--$71.00--Paper--$61.00--397pp F5159

168   - THE **BEALES** OF CHESTER CO., PA., by M.B. Hitchens. Repr. of 1957 ed. Paper--$12.00--58pp F5159

169   - **BEAMAN & CLARK** GEN.: A HIST. OF THE DESC. OF GAMALIEL **BEAMAN** & SARAH **CLARK** OF DORCHESTER & LANCASTER, MASS., 1635-1909, by E.B. Wooden. Repr. of 1909 ed. Cloth--$45.00--Paper--$35.00--219pp F5159

170   - GEN. HIST. OF **BEARDSLEY-LEE** FAMILY IN AMER., 1635-1902, by I.H. Beardsley. Repr. of 1902 ed. Cloth--$79.50--Paper--$69.50--453pp F5159

171   - **BEATH** FAMILY OF SCOTLAND & AMERICA, by K.G. Stone. Repr. of 1898 ed.

      Paper--$5.50--20pp F5159

172   - THE **BEATH-PELHAM** FAMILIES, by M.R.B. Potter. Repr. of 1870 ed. Paper--$4.50--13pp F5159

173   - DESC. OF RICHARD **BECKLEY** OF WETHERSFIELD, CONN., by C.B. Sheppard. Repr. of 1948 ed. Cloth--$71.50--Paper--$61.50--406pp F5159

174   - **BEDON** FAMILY OF SOUTH CAROLINA. Cloth--$42.50--Paper--$32.50--4pp F5159

175   - GENEALOGY OF THE FAMILY OF **BEEBE**, FROM THE EARLIEST KNOWN
        IMMIGRANT, JOHN **BEEBE** OF BROUGHTON, ENGLAND, 1650., by Clifford
        Beebe. Repr. of 1991 ed.
        Cloth--$41.00--Paper--$31.00--217pp F5159

176   - **BELCHER** FAM. IN ENG. & AMER., COMPREHENDING A PERIOD OF 765
        YEARS WITH PART. REF. TO DESC. OF ADAM **BELCHER** OF SOUTHFIELDS,
        ORANGE CO., N.Y., by W. Belcher and J. Belcher. Repr. of 1941 ed.
        Cloth--$85.00--Paper--$75.00--481pp F5159

177   - **BELSER** FAM. OF SO. CAROLINA, by W.G. Belser. Repr. of 1941 ed.
        Paper--$13.50--67pp F5159

178   - **BENNETT** FAM. OF SUSSEX CO., DELAWARE, 1680-1860, WITH
        BRANCHES INTO THE **WARREN, SHOCKLEY** & OTHER FAMS., by J.B. Hill.
        Repr. of 1970 ed.
        Paper--$14.00--71pp F5159

179   - **BERGEY**. GEN.; A RECORD OF THE DESC. OF JOHN ULRICH **BERGEY** &
        HIS WIFE MARY, by D. Bergey. Repr. of 1925 ed.
        Cloth--$178.00--Paper--$168.00--1166pp F5159

180   - GENEALOGICAL HIST. OF THE **BERTOLET** FAM.; DESCENDANTS OF
        JEAN **BERTOLET**, by D.H. Bertolet. Repr. of 1914 ed.
        Cloth--$51.00--Paper--$41.00--260pp F5159

181   - **BIDDLE**. A SKETCH OF OWEN **BIDDLE**, TO WHICH IS ADDED A SHORT
        ACCT. OF THE **PARKE** FAM., WITH A LIST OF HIS DESC., by H.D. Biddle. Repr.
        of 1927 ed.
        Paper--$21.00--111pp F5159

182   - **BIGELOW**. GEN. OF THE **BIGELOW** FAM. OF AMER., FROM THE MARR.
        IN 1642 OF JOHN **BIGELOW** & MARY **WARREN** TO THE YEAR 1890., by G.B.
        Howe. Repr. of 1890 ed.
        Cloth--$75.00--Paper--$65.00--517pp F5159

183   - **BILL**. HIST. OF THE **BILL** FAM., by L. Bill. Repr. of 1867 ed.
        Cloth--$57.50--Paper--$47.50--368pp F5159

184   - **BINGHAM**. THE **BINGHAM** FAM. IN THE U.S., ESP. OF THE STATE OF
        CONN., by T.A. Bingham. Repr. of 1927 ed.
            Incl. notes on the **Binghams** of Phila. & of Irish desc.: mediaeval records; arm.
        bearings, etc. 473, 434, 447pp. 3 volumes, 1927- 30.
            Special price for the set: $205.00 hardcover; $175.00 paper.
        Cloth--$75.00/volume--Paper--$69.00/volume-- F5159

185   - **BISHOP** FAMILIES IN AMER., BOOK III: RICHARD OF SALEM, by I.E.
        Bishop. Repr. of 1966 ed.
        Paper--$16.00--80pp F5159

186   - **BISHOP** FAMILIES OF AMERICA, BOOK VIII: EDWARD **BISHOP** OF
        SALEM, by I.E. Bishop. Repr. of 1967 ed.
        Paper--$21.00--115pp F5159

187   - BISHOP. FAM. HIST. OF JOHN **BISHOP** OF WHITBURN, SCOT. & SOME AMER. DESC., by Scott & Montgomery.
Paper--$25.00--148pp F5159

188   - **BISHOP** FAMILIES IN MAINE, by C.N. Sinnett. Repr. of 1922 ed.
Paper--$4.50--13pp F5159

189   - BISHOP. RECORD OF DESC. OF JOHN **BISHOP**, ONE OF THE FOUNDERS OF GUILFORD, CT., IN 1639, by W.W. Cone and G.A. Root. Repr. of 1951 ed.
Cloth--$52.50--Paper--$42.50--277pp F5159

190   - **BISSELL** FAM. EXTR. FROM HIST. OF WINDSOR, CONN., Repr. of 1892 ed.
Paper--$7.00--34pp F5159

191   - BIXBY. GEN. OF THE DESC. OF JOSEPH **BIXBY**, 1621-1701, OF IPSWICH & BOXFORD, MASS., by W.G. Bixby. Repr. of 1914 ed.
    Who spell the name **Bigsby, Byxbee**, etc., & of the **Bixby** fam. in Eng., desc. of Walter **Bekesby** (1427) of Thorpe Morieux, Suffolk, Pts. I-III.
Cloth--$109.00--Paper--$99.00--707pp F5159

192   - **BLACKMAN** & ALLIED FAM., by A.L. Holman. Repr. of 1928 ed.
Cloth--$49.00--Paper--$39.00--258pp F5159

193   - **BLATCHFORD** MEMORIAL II: A GEN. REC. OF THE FAM. OF REV. SAMUEL **BLATCHFORD**, D.D., WITH SOME MENTION OF ALLIED FAMS., by E.W. Blatchford. Repr. of 1912 ed.
Paper--$21.00--123pp F5159

194   - **BLISH** FAMILY GEN., 1637-1905, by J.K. Blish. Repr. of 1905 ed.
Cloth--$68.50--Paper--$58.50--10+366pp F5159

195   - BLODGETT. ASAHEL **BLODGETT** OF HUDSON & DORCHESTER, N.H., HIS AMER. ANC. & DESC., by I.D. Blodgett. Repr. of 1906 ed.
Paper--$23.00--144pp F5159

196   - BLOOD. THE STORY OF THE **BLOODS**, INCL. AN ACCT. OF THE EARLY GEN. OF THE FAM. IN AMERICA, by R.D. Harris. Repr. of 1960 ed.
    In geneal. lines from Robt. **Blood** of Concord & Richard **Blood** of Groton (Mass.)
Cloth--$42.50--Paper--$32.50--201pp F5159

197   - BOGARDUS. GEN. HIST. OF THE ANC. & DESC. OF GEN. ROBERT **BOGARDUS**, by M. Gray. Repr. of 1927 ed.
Cloth--$55.00--Paper--$45.00--281pp F5159

198   - **BOGART** FAM., EXTR. FROM GEN. NOTES OF N.Y. & NEW ENG. FAMS., by S.V. Talcott. Repr. of 1883 ed.
Paper--$9.50--47pp F5159

199   - BOGART. THE **BOGART** FAM.: TUNIS GYSBERT **BOGAERT** & HIS DESC., by J.A. Bogart. Repr. of 1959 ed.
Cloth--$54.00--Paper--$44.00--280pp F5159

200   - **BOGUE** & ALLIED FAMS., by V.T. Bogue. Repr. of 1947 ed.
Cloth--$85.00--Paper--$75.50--439+49pp F5159

201   - **BOIT**. CHRONICLES OF THE **BOIT** FAM. & THEIR DESC., & OTHER
        ALLIED FAMS., by R.A. Boit. Repr. of 1915 ed.
        Cloth--$49.00--Paper--$39.00--260pp F5159

202   - **BOONE** FAMILY. GEN. HIST. OF DESC. OF GEORGE & MARY **BOONE**,
        WHO CAME TO AMERICA IN 1717, by H. Spraker. Repr. of 1922 ed.
        Cloth--$119.00--Paper--$109.00--707pp F5159

203   - **BORDEN**. RICHARD **BORDEN** OF PORTSMOUTH, R.I. & DESC., by H.F.
        Johnston.
        Paper--$11.00--56pp F5159

204   - **BOSWORTH**. HIST. OF THE DESC. OF EDWARD **BOSWORTH**, WHO
        ARRIVED IN AMER. IN 1634, WITH APPENDIX CONTAINING OTHER LINES
        OF AMER. **BOSWORTHS**, by M.B. Clarke. Repr. of 1926 ed.
        Cloth--$91.50--Paper--$81.50--551pp F5159

205   - **BOSWORTH**. HIST. OF THE DESC. OF EDWARD **BOSWORTH**, WHO
        ARRIVED IN AMERICA IN 1634 PTS. 5 & 6, by M.B. Clarke. Repr. of 1936 ed.
            Special price for Pts. 1-6 $145.00/hardcover; $137.50 paper.
        Cloth--$79.50--Paper--$69.50--464pp ....,................ F5159

206   - **BOUTON**. THE **BOUTON-BOUGHTON** FAM. DESC. OF JOHN **BOUTON** OF
        FRANCE, WHO LANDED AT BOSTON, 1635, AND SETTLED AT NORWALK,
        CONN., BY J. **BOUGHTON**., by J. Boughton. Repr. of 1890 ed.
        Cloth--$100.00--Paper--$90.00--684pp F5159

207   - **BOWDEN**. HIST. & BIOGR. SKETCH OF **BOWDEN, BODINE, BEAUDOIN,
        BODEN, BOWDOIN** FAM.
        Paper--$6.50--32pp F5159

208   - **BOWDEN**. MICHAEL **BOWDEN** & SOME DESC., by W. Bowden. Repr. of
        1960 ed.
        Paper--$11.00--54pp F5159

209   - **BOWEN**. MEM. OF THE **BOWEN** FAM., by E.C. Bowen. Repr. of 1884 ed.
        Paper--$19.50--102pp F5159

210   - **BOWIE**. THE **BOWIES** & THEIR KINDRED: A GEN. & BIOGR. HIST., by
        W.W. Bowie. Repr. of 1899 ed.
        Cloth--$88.50--Paper--$78.50--523pp F5159

11   - **BRADBURY** MEMORIAL. RECORDS OF SOME OF THE DESC. OF THOMAS
        BRADBURY OF AGAMENTICUS (YORK) IN 1634 AND OF SALISBURY, MA. IN
        1638, by W.B. Lapham. Repr. of 1890 ed.
            With a brief sketch of the **Bradburys** of Eng.
        Cloth--$51.00--Paper--$41.00--320pp F5159

12   - **BRADLEY** OF ESSEX COUNTY (MA.): EARLY RECORDS, 1643- 1746, by E.B.
        Peters. Repr. of 1915 ed.
        Cloth--$45.00--Paper--$35.00--8+213pp F5159

213   - **BRADLEY**. ANCESTORS & DESC. OF MORRIS A. **BRADLEY**, by Mrs. G. Rideout. Repr. of 1948 ed.
Paper--$28.00--176pp F5159

214   - **BRAINERD**. GEN. OF THE **BRAINERD-BRAINARD** FAM. HIST., 1649-1908; DESC. OF DANIEL, THE EMIGR. ANC., by L.A. Brainard. Repr. of 1908 ed.
        3 Vols. 1908. Vol. I or II $99.00/ea.; Vol. III (Index) $49.00.
Special price for the set: $230.00 hardcover; $205.00 paper. F5159

215   - **BRATTLE**. AN ACCT. OF SOME OF THE DESC. OF CAPT. THOMAS **BRATTLE**, by E.D. Harris. Repr. of 1867 ed.
Paper--$18.00--90pp F5159

216   - **BRAY**. SEVEN GENERATIONS OF **BRAYS**, OF MASS., ME., WISC. & MINN., by W.M. Bray. Repr. of 1956 ed.
Paper--$9.00--43pp F5159

217   - **BREWER**. HIST. OF THE **BREWER** FAM. OF N.C., TENN., IND., & ILL., Repr. of 1936 ed.
Paper--$15.00--75pp F5159

218   - **BRIDGE**. GEN. OF THE JOHN **BRIDGE** FAM. IN AMER., 1632- 1924, REV. ED., by W.D. Bridge. Repr. of 1924 ed.
Cloth--$91.50--Paper--$81.50--547pp F5159

219   - **BRIGGS**. WE & OUR KINFOLK: EPHRAIM & REBEKA **WATERMAN BRIGGS**, THEIR DESC. & ANC., by M.B. Briggs. Repr. of 1887 ed.
Paper--$23.00--150pp F5159

220   - **BRIGHAM**. THE HIST. OF THE **BRIGHAM** FAM., VOL. II, WITH ENG. ORIG. OF THOMAS **BRIGHAM**, THE EMIGRANT, 1603-35, by E.E. Brigham. Repr. of 1927 ed.
Cloth--$55.00--Paper--$45.00--300pp F5159

221   - **BRILLHART**. A PICTORIAL HIST. OF THE **BRILLHARTS** OF AMER., by J.A. Brillhart. Repr. of 1926 ed.
Cloth--$52.00--Paper--$42.00--268pp F5159

222   - **BRINKMAN**. DESC. OF OTTO HENRICH WILHELM **BRINKMAN**, by I.H. DeLong. Repr. of 1925 ed.
Paper--$10.00--55pp F5159

223   - **BRISTOL** GEN., by W.E. Bristol. Repr. of 1967 ed.
Cloth--$96.00--Paper--$86.00--561pp F5159

224   - **BRISTOL**. THE FAM. OF HENRY **BRISTOL**, by D. Jacobus. Repr. of 1905 ed.
Paper--$4.00--7pp F5159

225   - **BRITT** FAM. IN MAINE, by C.N. Cinnett. Repr. of 1923 ed.
Paper--$4.00--7pp F5159

226   - **BRITTAIN-BRITTEN** FAM. OF N.Y., VA. & PA., by Purcel, Brand & Mathews.
Paper--$4.50--12pp F5159

227   - **BRITTON**. GENEALOGY **BRITTON**, by E.E. Britton. Repr. of 1901 ed.
Paper--$10.00--50pp F5159

228   - **BROOKFIELD**. TWELVE GEN. IN AMER. LIN. OF W.L. **BROOKFIELD**,
H.M. **BROOKFIELD**, & S.L. **BROOKFIELD**, by H.M. Brookfield. Repr. of 1937
ed.
Cloth--$59.00--Paper--$49.00--310pp F5159

229   - **BROWN** GEN.; DESC. OF THOMAS, JOHN & ELEAZOR **BROWN**, SONS OF
THOMAS & MARY (**NEWHALL**) **BROWN** OF LYNN, MA., 1629-1915, by C.H.
Brown. Repr. of 1907 ed.
618 + 611pp., 2 Volumes.
Special price for the set: $172.00 hardcover; $152.00 paper.
Cloth--$91.50/volume--Paper--$81.50/volume--618&611p F5159

230   - GENEALOGY OF THE **BROWN** FAM. OF PRINCE WILLIAM CO., VA., &
ALLIED FAMILIES **BLAND, BUCKNER, BYRNE, FAIRFAX, MORGAN,
TEBBS, WATSON, ZIMMS** & OTHERS, by J.E. Brown. Repr. of 1930 ed.
Cloth--$127.50--Paper--$117.50--874pp F5159

231   - **BROWNE**. CHAD **BROWNE** MEMORIAL, CONSISTING OF GEN. MEMOIRS
OF A PORTION OF THE DESC. OF CHAD & ELIZABETH **BROWNE**, 1638-1888,
by A.I. Bulkley. Repr. of 1888 ed.
Paper--$25.50--173pp F5159

232   - **BRUBACHER** GENEALOGY IN AMER., by J.N. Brubacher. Repr. of 1882 ed.
Cloth--$54.00--Paper--$44.00--344pp F5159

233   - **BRUCE**. FAMILY REC. OF THE **BRUCES** & THE **CUMYNS**, WITH AN HIST.
INTRO. & APPENDIX, by M.E.C. Bruce. Repr. of 1870 ed.
Cloth--$109.00--Paper--$99.00--692pp F5159

234   - **BRUCE**. BOOK OF **BRUCE**. ANC. & DESC. OF KING ROBERT OF
SCOTLAND, by L.H. Weeks. Repr. of 1907 ed.
Cloth--$55.00--Paper--$45.00--352pp F5159

235   - **BRUMBACH**. GENEALOGY OF THE **BRUMBACH** FAM., INCL. THOSE
USING...VARIATIONS OF THE ORIGINAL NAME & MANY OTHER
CONNECTED FAMS., by G.M. Brumbaugh. Repr. of 1915 ed.
Cloth--$125.00--Paper--$115.00--850pp F5159

236   - **BRUMFIELD**. DESC. OF THOMAS **BRUMFIELD** OF BERKS CO., PA. GEN.
& FAM. HIST. 1720 TO 1960, by R.C. Brumfield. Repr. of 1962 ed.
Cloth--$86.00--Paper--$76.00--493pp F5159

237   - **BUCHANAN** ANCESTRY, by M.G. Buchanan. Repr. of 1962 ed.
Paper--$18.00--93pp F5159

238   - **BUCHANAN**. FIRST GATHERING OF THE **BUCHANAN** CLAN, TROTTERS
CREEK, MIAMI CO., OHIO, WITH GEN. NOTES, 10/01/1892., Repr. of 1892 ed.
Paper--$10.00--55pp F5159

239   - **BUELL**. HIST. OF THE **BUELL** FAM. IN ENGL., FROM REMOTEST TIES...& IN AMER., FROM TOWN, PARISH, CHURCH & FAM. RECORDS, by A. Welles. Repr. of 1881 ed.
Cloth--$71.50--Paper--$61.50--384+xixp F5159

240   - **BULKELEY**. REV. PETER **BULKELEY**; AN ACCT. OF HIS CAREER, HIS ANC. & ANC. OF HIS TWO WIVES, & HIS DESC., by D.L. Jacobus. Repr. of 1933 ed.
Cloth--$149.00--Paper--$139.00--1073pp F5159

241   - **BULLEN**. ANC. & DESC. OF PHILLIP OF JERSEY, ENG. & CHARLESTOWN, MASS., by M.L. Holman and W.L. Holman. Repr. of 1930 ed.
Paper--$25.00--170pp F5159

242   - **BULLOCH**. HIST. & GEN. OF THE FAMS. OF **BULLOCH, STOBO, IRVING & CULTS**, by J.G.B. Bulloch. Repr. of 1911 ed.
Paper--$17.00--102pp F5159

243   - **BUNKER** GEN. DESC. OF JAMES **BUNKER** OF DOVER, NH, by E.C. Moran, Jr.. Repr. of 1961 ed.
Cloth--$73.50--Paper--$63.50--405pp F5159

244   - **BUNTING** FAMILY. OUR PEOPLE & OUR SELVES, by A.M. Bunting. Repr. of 1909 ed.
Cloth--$49.50--Paper--$39.50--245pp F5159

245   - **BURBANK**. GEN. OF THE **BURBANK** FAM. & THE FAM. OF **BRAN, WELLCOME, SEDGLEY & WELCH**, by G. Sedgley. Repr. of 1928 ed.
Cloth--$97.00--Paper--$87.00--586pp F5159

246   - **BURGNER**. HIST. & GEN. OF THE **BURGNER** FAM. IN THE U.S., AS DESC. FROM PETER **BURGNER**, A SWISS EMIGR. OF 1734, by J. Burgner. Repr. of 1890 ed.
Paper--$23.00--171pp F5159

247   - **BURNETT** FAM. WITH COLL. BRANCHES, by C. Burnett. Repr. of 1950 ed.
Cloth--$58.00--Paper--$48.00--316pp F5159

248   - **BURNHAM**. GEN. RECORDS OF THOMAS **BURNHAM**, THE EMIGR., WHO WAS AMONG THE EARLY SETTLERS AT HARTFORD, CT., & HIS DESC., by R.H. Burnham. Repr. of 1884 ed.
Paper--$45.50--292pp F5159

249   - **BURR**. **BURES** OF SUFFOLK, ENG. & **BURR** OF MASS. BAY COLONY, NEW ENGL, by C.R. Burr. Repr. of 1926 ed.
Paper--$19.50--131pp F5159

250   - **BURTON**. DESC. OF JOSIAH **BURTON** OF MANCHESTER, VT., by W.L. Holman. Repr. of 1926 ed.
Cloth--$59.00--Paper--$49.00--310pp F5159

251   - **BUSHNELL** FAM. GEN.; ANC. & POSTERITY OF FRANCIS **BUSHNELL** (1580-1646) OF HORSHAM, ENGLAND, & GUILFORD, CONN., INCL. GEN NOTES OF OTHER **BUSHNELL** FAM., by G.E. Bushnell. Repr. of 1948 ed.

(print size in orig. book is quite small)
Cloth--$51.50--Paper--$41.50--276pp F5159

252   - **BUTLER**. THOMAS **BUTLER** & HIS DESC., 1674-1886, by G.H. Butler. Repr. of 1886 ed.
Paper--$26.50--199pp F5159

253   - **BYE**. HIST. OF THE **BYE** FAM. & SOME ALLIED FAMS., by A.E. Bye. Repr. of 1956 ed.
Cloth--$79.00--Paper--$69.00--450pp F5159

254   - **CABELL**. THE **CABELLS** & THEIR KIN: A MEMORIAL VOL. OF HISTORY, BIOGR. & GENEALOGY, by A. Brown. Repr. of 1939 ed.
Cloth--$109.00--Paper--$99.00--708pp F5159

255   - **CADLE**. LIST OF 115 COLONIAL ANC. OF CORNELIUS **CADLE** OF MUSCATINE, IOWA, by C.F. Cadle.
Paper--$4.50--12pp F5159

256   - **CALVIN**. THE **CALVIN** FAMS.: ORIGIN & HIST. OF THE AMER. **CALVINS** WITH A PARTIAL GEN., by C.W. Calvin. Repr. of 1945 ed.
Cloth--$72.00--Paper--$62.00--405pp F5159

257   - **CAMPBELL** CLAN IN VA., by L.L. Campbell. Repr. of 1954 ed.
Paper--$27.00--154pp F5159

258   - HIST SKETCHES OF THE **CAMPBELL, PILCHER** & KINDRED FAMS., INCL. THE **BOWEN, RUSSELL, OWEN, GRANT, GOODWIN, AMIS, CAROTHERS, HOPE, TALIAFERRO** & **POWELL** FAM, by M.C. Pilcher. Repr. of 1911 ed.
Cloth--$78.50--Paper--$68.50--444pp F5159

259   - GEN. OF THE **CAMPBELL, NOBLE, GORTON, SHELTON, GILMOUR** & **BYRD** FAMS., & NUMEROUS OTHER FAMS. OF PROMINENCE IN AMER., WITH WHOM THEY HAVE INTERMARRIED, by M.C. Whitaker. Repr. of 1927 ed.
Cloth--$48.50--Paper--$36.50--230pp F5159

260   - **CANTRILL-CANTRELL** GEN. REC. OF THE DESC. OF RICHARD **CANTRILL** WHO WAS A RESIDENT OF PHILADELPHIA PRIOR TO 1689, & OF EARLIER **CANTRILLS** IN ENG. & AMER., by S.C. Christie. Repr. of 1908 ed.
Cloth--$45.00--Paper--$35.00--271pp F5159

261   - **CAPEN** FAM.; DESC. OF BERNARD **CAPEN** OF DORCHESTER, MASS., BY C. Hayden, revised by J. Tuttle. Repr. of 1929 ed.
Cloth--$59.00--Paper--$49.00--312pp F5159

262   - **CARRELL**. THE DESC. OF JAMES **CARRELL** & SARAH **DUNGAN** HIS WIFE, by E.P. Carrell. Repr. of 1928 ed.
Cloth--$109.00--Paper--$99.00--708pp F5159

263   - **CARROLL**. HIST. OF THE WM. **CARROLL** FAM. OF ALLEGHANY CO., NY, by K. Stevenson. Repr. of 1929 ed.
Cloth--$29.00--Paper--$19.00--100pp F5159

264   - **CARTER**. THE **CARTER** TREE, TABULATED & INDEXED, by R.R. Carter and R.I. Randolph. Repr. of 1951 ed.
Cloth--$48.00--Paper--$38.00--241pp F5159

265   - **CARVER** FAMILY OF NEW ENGLAND: ROBERT **CARVER** OF MARSHFIELD & HIS DESC., by C.N. Carver. Repr. of 1935 ed.
Cloth--$41.00--Paper--$31.00--204pp F5159

266   - **CARVER**. ROBERT **CARVER** OF MARSHFIELD, MA., & SOME DESC., by W. Jones. Repr. of 1934 ed.
Paper--$10.00--49pp F5159

267   - **CASE**. DESC. OF STEPHEN **CASE** OF MARLBORO, NY, INCLUDING ALLIED FAMILIES, by Lynn M. Case. Repr. of 1971 ed.
Paper--$17.00--82pp F5159

268   - **CHADBOURNE-CHADBOURN** GENEALOGY, by W.M. Emery. Repr. of 1904 ed.
Paper--$13.00--66pp F5159

269   - **CHADWICK**. NOTES ON DESCENDANTS OF JOHN & JOAN **CHADWICK** & RELATED FAMS., by A.D. Kilham. Repr. of 1966 ed.
Paper--$19.50--120pp F5159

270   - **CHAFEE & LEBOSQUET** FAMS.: INFORMAL GEN. OF OLIVIA K. **CHAFFEE**, HUSBAND MAURICE **LEBOSQUET** & THEIR CHILDREN, by O.K. LeBosquet. Repr. of 1955 ed.
Paper--$23.00--228pp F5159

271   - **CHAFFEE**. THE BERKSHIRE, VT., **CHAFFEES** & THEIR DESC., 1801-1911, by A.J. Elliot. Repr. of 1911 ed.
Cloth--$67.50--Paper--$57.50--356pp F5159

272   - **CHANCELLOR** FAMILY, by J.C. Chancellor. Repr. of 1963 ed.
Paper--$13.50--69pp F5159

273   - **CHANDLER**. DESC. OF ROGER **CHANDLER** OF CONCORD, MA, 1658, by C.H. Chandler. Repr. of 1949 ed.
Paper--$24.50--152pp F5159

274   - **CHAPIN** GEN., CONTAINING A VERY LARGE PROPORTION OF THE DESC. OF DEA. SAM'L **CHAPIN**, WHO SETTLED IN SPRINGFIELD, MA., 1642, by O. Chapin. Repr. of 1862 ed.
Cloth--$68.50--Paper--$58.50--376pp F5159

275   - **CHAPIN** BOOK OF GEN. DATA, WITH BRIEF BIOGR. SKETCHES OF THE DESC. OF DEA. SAMUEL **CHAPIN**, VOL. I., by G.W. Chapin. Repr. of 1924 ed.
Cloth--$163.00--Paper--$153.00--1320pp F5159

276   - **CHAPLIN**. JOHN **CHAPLIN** (1758-1837) OF ROWLEY, MA. & BRIDGTON ME., HIS ANC. & DESC., by M. Ellis and L. Ellis. Repr. of 1949 ed.
Paper--$21.00--139pp F515

277   - **CHASE.** SEVEN GEN. OF THE DESC. OF AQUILA & THOMAS **CHASE,** by
J.C. Chase and G.W. Chamberlain. Repr. of 1928 ed.
Cloth--$103.50--Paper--$93.50--624pp F5159

278   - **CHENEY.** JOHN **CHENEY** OF PLAISTOW, NH, ORANGE CO., VT, &
MONROE CO., NY & HIS DESC., by E. Gundry. Repr. of 1959 ed.
Paper--$11.00--55pp F5159

279   - **CHESEBROUGH.** BIOGR. SKETCH OF WM. **CHESEBROUGH,** 1ST
SETTLER OF STONINGTON, CT., by A. Chesebrough. Repr. of 1893 ed.
Paper--$5.00--25pp F5159

280   - **CHESEBROUGH.** GEN. OF THE DESC. OF WILLIAM **CHESEBROUGH** OF
BOSTON, REHOBETH, MA., THE FOUNDER & FIRST SETTLER OF
STONINGTON, CT., by A.C. Wildey. Repr. of 1903 ed.
Cloth--$96.00--Paper--$86.00--688pp F5159

281   - **CHIPP** FAMILY, IN ENG. & AMER., WITH GEN. TREE; ALSO, HIST. & GEN.
NOTES ON ALLIED FAMS., by C.H. Burnett. Repr. of 1933 ed.
Cloth--$39.50--Paper--$29.50--182pp F5159

282   - **CHUTE.** GEN. & HIST. OF THE **CHUTE** FAM. IN AMER., WITH SOME
ACCT. OF THE FAM. IN GT. BRIT. & IRELAND, & AN ACCT. OF 40 ALLIED
FAMS., by W.E. Chute. Repr. of 1894 ed.
Cloth--$73.00--Paper--$63.00--493pp F5159

283   - **CLAFLIN.** GEN. OF THE **CLAFLIN** FAM., BEING A REC. OF ROBT.
MACKCLOTHLAN, OF WENHAM, MA., & HIS DESC., 1661-1898, by C.H.
Wight. Repr. of 1903 ed.
Cloth--$70.00--Paper--$60.00--473pp F5159

284   - **CLAGHORN.** THE BARONY OF **CLEGHORNE,** A.D. 1203, LANARKSHORE,
SCOTLAND, TO THE FAM. OF **CLAGHORN,** A.D. 1912, USA, by W.C. Claghorn.
Repr. of 1912 ed.
Paper--$24.00--132pp F5159

285   - **CLARK.** DEACON GEORGE **CLARK(E),** & SOME OF HIS DESC., by G.C.
Bryant. Repr. of 1949 ed.
Cloth--$51.00--Paper--$41.00--258pp F5159

286   - **CLARK.** LOYALIST **CLARKS, BADGLEYS** & ALLIED FAMILIES, by E.
Watson. Repr. of 1954 ed.
     Pt. 1, Anc. & desc. of Matthias & Rachel **Abbott Badgley;** Pt. 2, Robt. & Isabel
Ketchum Clarke, UE Loyalists & their desc., by E. Watson.
Cloth--$64.00--Paper--$54.00--338pp F5159

287   - **CLARKE-CLARK** GEN.; REC. OF THE DESC. OF THOMAS **CLARKE**
(1623-1697) OF PLYMOUTH., by . Repr. of 1884 ed.
Paper--$23.50--192pp F5159

288   - **CLARKE** FAMS. OF R.I., by G.A. Morrison, Jr.. Repr. of 1902 ed.
Cloth--$53.50--Paper--$43.50--337pp F5159

289   - **CLEVELAND**. GEN. OF THE **CLEVELAND-CLEAVELAND** FAMS., DESC.
       OF MOSES FROM WOBURN, MA. & ALEXANDER FROM VA.; & EDW. WINN
       FROM WOBURN, by E.J. Cleveland and H.G. Cleveland. Repr. of 1899 ed. .
          2,900 pp, 3 vols. Special price for the set: $325.00 hardcover; $295.00 paper.
       Cloth--$129.00--Paper--$119.00--2,900pp F5159

290   - **CLOUGH**. THE GEN. & DESC. OF JOHN **CLOUGH** OF SALISBURY, MASS.,
       Ed. by E.C. Speare. Pub. by The John Clough Soc., Repr. of 1952 ed.
       Cloth--$85.00--Paper--$75.00--511pp F5159

291   - **CLOUGH**. VOLUME II OF ABOVE., Repr. of 1966 ed.
       Cloth--$53.00--Paper--$43.50--286pp F5159

292   - **COATES**. GEN. OF MOSES & SUSANNA **COATES**, WHO SETTLED IN
       PENN. IN 1717, & THEIR DESC., by T. Coates. Repr. of 1906 ed.
       Cloth--$54.00--Paper--$44.00--319pp F5159

293   - **COCHRANE**. THE **COCHRANES** OF RENFREWSHIRE, SCOTLAND. THE
       ANC. OF ALEXANDER **COCHRANE** OF BILLERICA & MALDEN, MA., by W.K.
       Watkins. Repr. of 1904 ed.
       Paper--$11.00--53pp F5159

294   - **CODY** FAMILY IN AMER., 1698: DESC. OF PHILIP & MARTHA OF MASS.,
       BIOGR. & GEN., by Compiled by **Cody** Fam. Assoc.. Repr. of 1954 ed.
       Cloth--$51.00--Paper--$41.00--257pp F5159

295   - **COGGESHALLS** IN AMER.; GEN. OF THE DESC. OF JOHN **COGGESHALL**
       OF NEWPORT, WITH A BRIEF NOTICE OF THEIR ENG. ANC., by C.P
       Coggeshall and T.R. Coggeshall. Repr. of 1930 ed.
       Cloth--$72.50--Paper--$62.50--395pp F5159

296   - **COGSWELL**. THE **COGSWELLS** IN AMER., by E.O. Jameson. Repr. of 1884
       ed.
       Cloth--$98.00--Paper--$88.00--707pp F5159

297   - **COLCORD**. DESC. OF EDWARD **COLCORD** OF N.H., by D.B. Colcord. Repr.
       of 1908 ed.
       Paper--$24.00--166pp F5159

298   - **COLGATE**. ROBERT **COLGATE**, THE IMMIGRANT: A GEN. OF THE N.Y.
       COLGATES & SOME ASSOC. LINES, by T. Abbe and H.A. Howson. Repr. of 1941
       ed.
       Cloth--$83.00--Paper--$73.00--464pp F5159

299   - DESC. OF JOHN **COLLIN**: CYCLOPEDIA OF BIOGR., CONTAINING A HIST.
       OF THE FAM. & DESC. OF JOHN **COLLIN**, FORMER RESIDENT OF MILFORD,
       CT., by J.F. Collin. Repr. of 1872 ed.
       Paper--$18.00--124pp F5159

300   - **COLLINS**. REMINISC. OF ISAAC & RACHEL **BUDD COLLINS**, WITH
       ACCT. OF SOME DESC. & HIST. OF A REUNION HELD AT PHILA., 1892, by J.
       Collins. Repr. of 1893 ed.
       Paper--$24.50--164pp F5159

301   - **COLLINS**. THE **COLLINS** FAM.: A REC. OF THE DESC. OF WM. **COLLINS** & ESTHER **MORRIS** FROM 1760 TO 1897, by W.H. Collins. Repr. of 1897 ed. Paper--$26.50--188pp F5159

302   - **COMLY** FAM. IN AMER.; DESC. OF HENRY & JOAN **COMLY** WHO CAME TO AMER. IN 1682 FROM BEAMINSTER, SOMERSETSHIRE, ENG., by G.N. Comly. Repr. of 1939 ed.
With short accts. of the anc. of Chas. & Debby Ann (**Newbold**) **Comly**
Cloth--$180.00--Paper--$170.00--1148pp F5159

303   - **COMLY**. SUPPL. TO **COMLY** FAMILY IN AMERICA, BEING ADD. & CORR., by G.N. Comly. Repr. of 1952 ed.
Paper--$22.00--142pp F5159

304   - **COMSTOCK - THOMAS** ANCE. OF RICHARD WILMOT **COMSTOCK**, by H.M. Pitman. Repr. of 1964 ed.
Cloth--$79.50--Paper--$69.50--452pp F5159

305   - **COMSTOCK**. HISTORY & GEN. OF THE **COMSTOCK** FAM. IN AMERICA, by J.A. Comstock. Repr. of 1949 ed.
Cloth--$109.50--Paper--$99.50--715pp F5159

306   - **CONGER**. A REC. OF BIRTHS, MARR. & DEATHS OF THE DESC. OF JOHN **CONGER** OF WOODBRIDGE, NJ, by C.G.B. Conger. Repr. of 1903 ed.
Paper--$25.50--165pp F5159

307   - **CONVERSE**. FAM. RECORDS OF DEACONS J.W. **CONVERSE** & E. **CONVERSE**, by W.G. Hill. Repr. of 1887 ed.
Cloth--$47.00--Paper--$37.00--246pp F5159

308   - DESC. OF MORDECAI **COOKE** OF "MORDECAI'S MOUNT", GOUCESTER CO., VA, 1650, & THOMAS **BOOTH** OF WARE NECK, GLOUCESTER CO., VA, 1685, by Dr. & Mrs. W.C. Stubbs. Repr. of 1923 ed.
Cloth--$59.50--Paper--$49.50--286+35pp F5159

309   - **COOKE**. THE **COOKE** ANC., by Van Dycke & Cooke. Repr. of 1960 ed.
Paper--$27.50--162pp F5159

310   - **COOLEY** GENEALOGY: DESC. OF ENSIGN BENJ. **COOLEY**, EARLY SETTLER OF SPRINGFIELD & LONGMEADOW, MA., & OTHER MEMBERS OF THE FAM. IN AMERICA, by M.E. Cooley and Compiled by V.B. Keatley. Repr. of 1941 ed.
Cloth--$159.00--Paper--$149.00--1199pp F5159

311   - **COOLEY**. DESCENDANTS OF DR. ASAHEL & SALLY **WILBUR COOLEY** (SUPPL. TO "COOLEY GEN."), by A.S. Cooley and Edited by L.A.C. Cooley. Repr. of 1952 ed.
Paper--$23.00--153pp F5159

312   - **COOLIDGE**. DESC. OF JOHN & MARY **COOLIDGE** OF WATERTOWN, MASS., 1630, by E.D. Coolidge. Repr. of 1930 ed.
Cloth--$68.00--Paper--$58.00--418pp F5159

313   - **COOLIDGE**. ONE BRANCH OF THE **COOLIDGE** FAM. 1427-1963, by F.C.
       Crawford. Repr. of 1964 ed.
       Paper--$17.50--91pp F5159

314   - THE **KOON-COONS** FAMS. OF EASTERN NY: HIST. OF THE DESC. OF
       MATTHAIES **KUNTZ** & SAMUEL **KUHN**, by W.S. Coons. Repr. of 1937 ed.
            Two distinct families which came with the Palatine immigr. & settled in the Hudson
       River in 1710
       Cloth--$88.50--Paper--$78.50--502pp F5159

315   - **COPELAND** FAMILY: A **COPELAND** GEN., by W.T. Copeland. Repr. of 1937.
       Cloth--$124.50--Paper--$114.50--821pp F5159

316   - **COPPAGE-COPPEDGE** FAMILY 1542-1955, by Monahan & Coppage. Repr. of
       1955 ed.
       Paper--$25.00--126pp F5159

317   - **CORNELIUS**. HISTORY OF THE **CORNELIUS** FAMILY IN AMERICA:
       HISTORICAL, GENEALOGICAL & BIOGRAPHICAL, by C.S. Cornelius and S.F.
       Cornelius. Repr. of 1926 ed.
       Cloth--$56.00--Paper--$46.00--292pp F5159

318   - **CORNELL**. GEN. OF THE **CORNELL** FAM., BEING AN ACCT. OF THE
       DESC. OF THOMAS **CORNELL** OF PORTSMOUTH, RI, by J. Cornell. Repr. of
       1902 ed.
       Cloth--$69.50--Paper--$59.50--468pp F5159

319   - **CORNWALL**. WM. **CORNWALL** & HIS DESC.; A GEN. HIST. OF THE FAM.
       OF WM. **CORNWALL**, WHO CAME TO AMER. IN 1633 & DIED IN
       MIDDLETON, CONN. IN 1678, by E. Cornwall. Repr. of 1901 ed.
       Paper--$28.00--185pp F5159

320   - THREE HUNDRED YEARS WITH THE **CORSON** FAMILIES IN AMERICA, by
       O. Corson. Repr. of 1939 ed.
            Incl. Staten Isl.-Penn. Corsons; NJ **Corsons**; Dumfriesshire, Scotland, **Corsons**;
       New Eng. **Corsons**; Canadian **Corsons**.
            303 + 336pp. 2 volumes.
            Special price for the set: $109.00/hardcover; $92.00/paper.
       Cloth--$58.50/volume--Paper--$48.50/volume--303+336p F5159

321   - **COTTON**. A SHORT BIOGR. OF REV. JOHN **COTTON** OF BOSTON & GEN.
       OF HIS **COTTON** DESC., by L. Cooley. Repr. of 1945 ed.
       Paper--$24.00--125pp F5159

322   - **COWDEN-GILLILAND**. ILLUSTRATED HIST. & BIOGR. SKETCH OF THE
       DESC. OF WILLIAM **COWDEN**, WHO MIGRATED FROM IRELAND TO
       AMERICA ABOUT 1730, by R. Cowden. Repr. of 1915 ed.
            And of James **Gilliland**, which came from the same land & about the same time
       (with charts)
       Paper--$27.50--179pp F5159

323   - **COWLES**. GEN. OF THE **COWLES** FAMS. IN AMER., by C.D. Cowles. Repr.
       of 1929 ed.
            2 volumes.
       Cloth--$208.00--Paper--$198.00--1510pp F5159

324   - **CRANDALL**. ELDER JOHN **CRANDALL** OF RHODE ISLAND & HIS DESC., by J.C. Crandall. Repr. of 1949 ed.
Cloth--$119.00--Paper--$109.00--797pp F5159

325   - **CROCKETT** FAMILY & CONNECTING LINES, by French & Armstrong. Repr. of 1928 ed.
       Vol. V, "Notable Southern Fams."
Cloth--$101.00--Paper--$91.00--611pp F5159

326   - HISTORY OF THE **CRONE, PENCE, SWITZER, WEAVER, HEATWOLE, STOUT, STEEL & FISSELL** FAMILIES, FROM WHICH ARE DESCENDED JOHN S. **CRONE** & ELLA **WEAVER CRONE**, by F.L. Crone. Repr. of 1916 ed.
Paper--$10.00--50pp F5159

327   - **CROWE**. JOHN **CROWE** & HIS DESC., by L. Crowell. Repr. of 1903 ed.
Paper--$19.00--109pp F5159

328   - **CULBERTSON**. GEN. OF THE **CULBERTSON-CULBERSON** FAM. WHO CAME TO AMER. BEFORE THE YEAR 1800, & SEVERAL FAM. THAT HAVE COME SINCE THEN, by L. Culbertson. Repr. of 1923 ed.
Cloth--$84.50--Paper--$74.50--477pp F5159

329   - **CURTISS**. A GEN. OF THE **CURTISS-CURTIS** FAM. OF STRATFORD, CONN.; A SUPPL. TO THE 1903 ED., by H.D. Curtis. Repr. of 1953 ed.
Cloth--$97.00--Paper--$87.00--585pp F5159

330   - A HIST. OF THE ANCIENT HOUSE OF **CURWEN**, OF WORKINGTON IN CUMBERLAND & ITS VARIOUS BRANCHES, by J.F. Curwen. Repr. of 1928 ed.
       Being a collection of extracts from (many) available sources
Cloth--$67.50--Paper--$57.50--363pp F5159

331   - **CUSHMAN** GENEALOGY & GENERAL HIST., INCL. THE DESC. OF THE FAYETTE CO., PA. & MONONGALIA CO., VA, FAMILIES, by A.W. Burt. Repr. of 1942 ed.
Cloth--$77.00--Paper--$67.00--432pp F5159

332   - **CUTTER**. A HIST. OF THE **CUTTER** FAM. OF NEW ENGLAND, by B. Cutter and R.W. Cutter. Repr. of 1923 ed.
Cloth--$64.00--Paper--$54.00--432pp F5159

333   - **DAKIN**. DESC. OF THOMAS **DAKIN** OF CONCORD, MASS., by A.H. Dakin. Repr. of 1938 ed.
Cloth--$109.00--Paper--$99.00--716pp F5159

334   - **DARE** FAMILY HISTORY, by W.H. Montgomery and N.L. Montgomery. Repr. of 1939 ed.
Cloth--$64.00--Paper--$54.00--340pp F5159

335   - **DARLING** FAM. IN AMER.: EARLY SETTLERS PRIOR TO 1800, by W.M. Clemens. Repr. of 1913 ed.
Paper--$6.00--31pp F5159

336   - **DARLINGTON**. GEN. OF THE **DARLINGTON** FAM.: REC. OF THE DESC.
OF ABRAHAM **DARLINGTON** OF BIRMINGHAM, CHESTER CO., PA., & SOME
OTHER FAMS. OF THE NAME, by G. Cope. Repr. of 1900 ed.
Cloth--$97.00--Paper--$87.00--693pp F5159

337   - **DAVIS** FAMS. OF EARLY ROXBURY & BOSTON, by S.F. Rockwell. Repr. of
1932 ed.
Cloth--$58.50--Paper--$48.50--314pp F5159

338   - **DAVIS**. SAM'L **DAVIS** OF OXFORD, MA. & JOS. **DAVIS** OF DUDLEY, MASS.,
& THEIR DESC., by G. Davis. Repr. of 1884 ed.
Cloth--$87.00--Paper--$77.00--618pp F5159

339   - **DAVIS** FAM. OF EARLY ROXBURY & BOSTON, by S.F. Rockwell. Repr. of
1932 ed.
Cloth--$59.00--Paper--$49.00--326pp F5159

340   - **DAWES-GATES** ANCESTRAL LINES: A MEM'L VOL. CONTAINING THE
AMER. ANCESTRY OF RUFUS R. **DAWES**.   VOL. I: **DAWES** & ALLIED
FAMILIES, by M.W. Ferris. Repr. of 1943 ed.
Cloth--$115.00--Paper--$105.00--758pp F5159

341   - **DEAN**. DESC. OF JOHN **DEAN** (1650-1727) OF DEDHAM, MASS., by M.D.
Cooper. Repr. of 1957 ed.
Paper--$33.00--217pp F5159

342   - **DEANE**. BRIEF MEM. OF JOHN & WALTER **DEANE**, TWO OF THE 1ST
SETTLERS OF TAUNTON, MA., & THE EARLY GEN. OF THEIR DESC., by W.R.
Dean(e) and J.W. Dean(e). Repr. of 1849 ed.
Paper--$5.00--16pp F5159

343   - **DECAMP**.   RECORD OF THE DESC. OF EZEKIAL & MARY **BAKER
DECAMP** OF BUTLER CO., OHIO, by J.M. DeCamp. Repr. of 1896 ed.
Paper--$24.00--177pp F5159

344   - **DECARPENTIER** ALLIED ANCESTRY OF MARIA **DE CARPENTIER**, WIFE
OF JEAN PAUL **JAQUET** OF NEW NETHERLAND, by E.J. Sellers. Repr. of 1928
ed.
Cloth--$47.50--Paper--$37.50--235pp F5159

345   - **DECKARD**. GEN. OF THE **DECKARD** FAM. SHOWING ALSO THOSE DESC.
FROM **DECKER, DECKERT, DECHER, DECHERT, DECHERD**, ETC., by P.E.
Deckard. Repr. of 1932 ed.
Cloth--$143.00--Paper--$133.00--893pp F5159

346   - **DECOU**. GEN. OF THE **DE COU** FAM., SHOWING THE DESC. FROM
LEOREN **DES COU**, by S.E. de Cou and J.A. de Cou. Repr. of 1910 ed.
Cloth--$47.00--Paper--$37.00--219pp F5159

347   - **DEERING-DEARING**. ABSTR. OF ENGLISH RECORDS, GATHERED
PRINCIPALLY IN DEVONSHIRE & ESSEX IN A SEARCH FOR THE ANC. OF
ROGER **DARING**, 1624-76 AND MATTHEW **WHIPPLE**, 1560-1618, by M.L.
Holman and G.R. Marvin. Repr. of 1929 ed.
Cloth--$106.50--Paper--$96.50--647pp F5159

348   - **DEGRAFFENRIED**. HISTORY OF THE **DEGRAFFENRIED** FAMILY, FROM 1191 TO 1925, by T.P. DeGraffenried. Repr. of 1925 ed.
Cloth--$54.50--Paper--$44.50--282pp F5159

349   - **DELAND** FAMILY IN AMER.ICA; A BIOGR. GEN., by F. Leete. Repr. of 1943 ed.
Cloth--$76.00--Paper--$66.00--414pp F5159

350   - GEN., HIST. & ALLIANCES OF THE AMER. HOUSE OF **DELANO**, 1621-1899, WITH HIST. & HERALDRY OF MAISON **DE FRANCHIMONT & DE LANNOY** TO **DELANO**, 1096-1621, by J.A. Deland and M.D. de Lannoy. Repr. of 1899 ed.
Cloth--$81.00--Paper--$71.00--561pp F5159

351   - **DEMAREST**. DAVID **DES MAREST** OF THE FRENCH PATENT ON THE HACKENSACK & HIS DESC., by W. & M. Demarest. Repr. of 1938 ed.
      Suppl. I 57 pp. 1942 $10.00
      Suppl. II 24pp 1944 $5.50
      Suppl. III 20pp 1947 $5.00
Cloth--$99.00--Paper--$89.00--576pp F5159

352   - **DENIO**. GENEALOGY OF AARON **DENIO** OF DEERFIELD, MA., 1704-1925, by F.B. Denio and H.W. Denio. Repr. of 1926 ed.
Cloth--$63.00--Paper--$53.00--345pp F5159

353   - **DENISON** MEM., IPSWICH, MA., 1882. 200TH ANNIV. OF THE DEATH OF MAJ.-GEN. DANIEL **DENISON**. BIOGR. SKETCH OF D.D. **SLADE**; HIST. SKETCH, by A. Caldwell. Repr. of 1871 ed.
Paper--$10.00--52pp F5159

354   - **DIBBLE** FAMILY OF CONN., by V. Lamb. Repr. of 1949 ed.
Paper--$25.00--124pp F5159

355   - **DICKEY**. GEN. HIST. OF THE **DICKEY** FAM., by R.S. Currier. Repr. of 1935.
Cloth--$64.00--Paper--$54.00--340pp F5159

356   - **DILLE** FAMILY. THREE HUNDRED YEARS IN AMER., by G.E. Dille and J.K & E.K. Dille. Repr. of 1965 ed.
Paper--$21.00--138pp F5159

357   - **DIXON**. KITH & KIN, GEN. DATA OF **DIXON** & COLLATERAL LINES, by W.M. Dixon. Repr. of 1922 ed.
Paper--$16.50--83pp F5159

358   - **DODD**. GEN. & HIST. OF THE DANIEL **DODD** FAM. IN AMER., 1646-1940, by A. Dodd and J.F. Folsom. Repr. of 1940 ed.
Cloth--$78.50--Paper--$68.50--442pp F5159

359   - **DOMMERICH**. OUR COL. & CONTINENTAL ANC. ANC. OF MR. & MRS. LOUIS WM. **DOMMERICH**, by I. de Forest. Repr. of 1930 ed.
Cloth--$59.25--Paper--$49.25--328pp F5159

360   - **DONALD** FAM. WITH NOTES ON REL. FAM., by D. Gordon. Repr. of 1906 ed.
Paper--$16.00--79pp F5159

361   - **DORMAN**. SOME DESCENDANTS OF JABEZ **DORMAN** OF ARUNDEL (1678-1765): TEN GENERATIONS OF DORMANS IN MAINE, by Franklin A. Dorman. Repr. of 1992 ed.
Paper--$16.50--112pp F5159

362   - **DORSEY** FAMILY. DESC. OF EDWARD **DARCY-DORSEY** OF VA. & MD. FOR FIVE GENERATIONS, by Dorsey & Nimmo. Repr. of 1947 ed.
Cloth--$53.00--Paper--$43.00--270pp F5159

363   - **DOUGLAS**. A COLL. OF FAM. RECORDS, WITH BIOGR. SKETCHES & OTHER MEMORANDA OF VARIOUS FAMS. & INDIVIDUALS OF THE NAME **DOUGLAS**, by C.H.J. Douglas. Repr. of 1879 ed.
Cloth--$84.00--Paper--$74.00--563pp F5159

364   - **DOWSE**. LAWRENCE **DOWSE** OF LEGBOURNE, ENG.; HIS ANC., DESC., & CONNECTIONS IN ENG., MASS. & IRELAND, by W.B.H. Dowse. Repr. of 1926 ed.
Cloth--$66.50--Paper--$56.50--359pp F5159

365   - DESC. OF JOHN **DRAKE** OF WINDSOR, CT., by F.B. Gay. Repr. of 1933 ed.
Cloth--$69.00--Paper--$59.00--380pp F5159

366   - **DRYER**. ANCESTRY OF RUFUS K. **DRYER**, WITH NOTES ON WILLIAM **DRYER** OF REHOBETH & SOME OF HIS DESC., by J.F. Dryer. Repr. of 1942 ed.
Cloth--$53.50--Paper--$43.50--280pp F5159

367   - **DUDLEY**. HIST. OF THE **DUDLEY** FAM. 2 VOLS., by D. Dudley. Repr. of 1894 ed.
Cloth--$168.00--Paper--$158.00--1253pp F5159

368   - **DUDLEY**. YEARBOOK OF GOV. THOMAS **DUDLEY** FAM. ASSOC., by Repr. of 1930 ed.
Cloth--$48.00--Paper--$38.00--252pp F5159

369   - **DUFOUR**. THE **DUFOUR** SAGA: STORY OF 8 **DUFOURS** WHO CAME FROM SWITZERLAND & FOUNDED VEVAY, SWITZERLAND CO., IND., by J.L. Knox. Repr. of 1942 ed.
Paper--$29.00--167pp F5159

370   - **DUKE**. A GEN. OF THE **DUKE-SHEPARD-VAN METRE** FAM., FROM CIVIL, MILITARY, CHURCH RECS. & DOCUMENTS, by S.G. Smyth. Repr. of 1902 ed.
Cloth--$68.00--Paper--$58.00--454pp F5159

371   - **DUNAWAY**. THE **DUNAWAYS** OF VA., by A.E. Clendening. Repr. of 1959 ed.
Paper--$25.00--156pp F5159

372   - **DUNHAM**. JACOB **DUNHAM** OF LEBANON, CONN., & MAYFIELD, NY, HIS ANC. & DESC., by S.D. Moore. Repr. of 1933 ed.
Paper--$10.00--51pp F5159

373   - **DUNWOODY**. GEN. OF THE **DUNWOODY** & **HOOD** FAMS. & COLL. BRANCHES; THEIR HIST. & BIOGR., by G. Cope. Repr. of 1899 ed.
Paper--$26.00--172pp F5159

374   - **DUPUY**. THE HUGUENOT BARTHOLOMEW **DUPUY** & HIS DESC., by B.H. Dupuy. Repr. of 1908 ed.
Cloth--$68.00--Paper--$58.00--455pp F5159

375   - **DUPUY**. A GEN. HIST. OF THE **DUPUY** FAM., by C.M. Dupuy and H. Dupuy. Repr. of 1910 ed.
Cloth--$40.00--Paper--$30.00--175pp F5159

376   - **DUSTON-DUSTIN** FAM. GEN. 1937-1960, by Kilgore & Curtis. Repr. of 1937 ed.
Cloth--$49.00--Paper--$39.00--247pp F5159

377   - **DUYCKINCK** & ALLIED FAMS., BEING A RECORD OF THE DESC. OF EVERT **DUYCKINCK** WHO SETTLED IN NEW AMSTERDAM, NOW NY, IN 1638, by Duyckinck & Cornell. Repr. of 1908 ed.
Cloth--$41.00--Paper--$31.00--256pp F5159

378   - **DWIGHT**. THE HIST. OF THE DESC. OF JOHN **DWIGHT** OF DEDHAM, MASS., by B.W. Dwight. Repr. of 1874 ed.
2 vol. 1,173pp.
Cloth--$164.50--Paper--$154.50--1,173pp F5159

379   - **EAGER**. HIST. OF THE **EAGER** FAM., FROM THE COMING OF THE 1ST IMMIGRANT, WILLIAM **EAGER**, IN 1630 TO 1952,, by S.E. Trotter. Repr. of 1952
Cloth--$53.00--Paper--$43.00--251pp F5159

380   - **EARLE**. HIST. & GEN. OF THE **EARLES** OF SECAUCUS, WITH AN ACCOUNT OF OTHER ENGLISH & AMER. BRANCHES, by I.N. Earle. Repr. of 1924 ed.
Cloth--$119.00--Paper--$109.00--828pp F5159

381   - **EARLY**. THE FAM. OF **EARLY** WHICH SETTLED UPON THE EASTERN SHORE OF VA., by R.H. Early. Repr. of 1920 ed.
Cloth--$64.50--Paper--$54.50--343pp F5159

382   - **EATON**. HISTORY, GEN. & BIOGR., OF THE **EATON** FAMILY, by N.Z.R. Molyneux. Repr. of 1911 ed.
Cloth--$109.00--Paper--$99.00--782pp F5159

383   - **EBERHART**. HIST. OF THE **EBERHARTS** IN GERMANY & THE U.S., FROM 1265-1890, WITH AN AUTOBIOGR. OF THE AUTHOR, by Rev. U. Eberhart. Repr. of 1891 ed.
Cloth--$49.50--Paper--$39.50--263pp F5159

384   - **ECK**. ZACHARIAS **ECK** FAM. RECORD, by L.E. Cooper. Repr. of 1959 ed.
Paper--$19.50--126pp F5159

385   - **EDDY**. ANCESTORS & DESC. OF ZACHARIAH **EDDY** OF **WARREN**, PA., by B.B. Horton. Repr. of 1930 ed.
Cloth--$61.00--Paper--$51.00--332pp F5159

386   - **EDGERLY**. REC. OF THE **EDGERLY** FAM., DESC. OF THOMAS **EDGERLY** OF DURHAM, NH, 1630, by E. Edgerly.
Paper--$9.00--43pp F5159

387   - **EDWARDS**. A GEN. REC. OF THE DESC. OF JOHN **EDWARDS**, 168(?) - 1915, by L.N. Edwards. Repr. of 1916 ed.
Cloth--$71.00--Paper--$61.00--395pp F5159

388   - **EDWARDS**. RICHARD **EDWARDS** & HIS WIFE CATHERINE POND **MAY**; THEIR ANC., LIVES & DESC., by M. Edwards. Repr. of 1931 ed.
Cloth--$41.50--Paper--$31.50--209pp F5159

389   - **ELIOT**. THE FAM. OF WM. GREENLEAF **ELIOT** & ABBY **ADAMS ELIOT** OF ST. LOUIS, MO., 3RD ED., 1811-1943., by Repr. of 1943 ed.
Paper--$24.00--157pp F5159

390   - **ELKINTON**.   THE ANC. & DESC. OF GEORGE **ELKINTON** OF BURLINGTON CO., NJ, by A. Adams. Repr. of 1945 ed.
Paper--$10.00--48pp F5159

391   - **ELLER**. GEORGE MICHAEL **ELLER** & HIS DESC. IN AMERICA, INCL. INFO. ON RELATED FAMS. OF **VANNOY-VAN NOY, MCNEIL, STOKER, WELKER** & OTHERS, by J.W. Hook. Repr. of 1957 ed.
Cloth--$85.00--Paper--$75.00--485pp F5159

392   - **ELLIOT**. THE JOHN **ELLIOT** FAM. OF BOSCAWEN, NH, by H.A. Kimball. Repr. of 1918 ed.
Paper--$19.50--132pp F5159

393   - **ELLIS**. HIST. OF THE **ELLIS** FAM., & DESC. OF WILLIAM **ELLIS** OF BIDEFORD, P.E.I., by P. Ellis. Repr. of 1950 ed.
Cloth--$68.50--Paper--$58.50--368pp F5159

394   - **ELSTON** FAMILY IN AMER., by J.S. Elston. Repr. of 1942 ed.
Cloth--$104.50--Paper--$94.50--632pp F5159

395   - **EMERSON**. THE ENG. **EMERSONS**: A GEN. HIST. SKETCH OF THE FAM. FROM EARLIEST TIMES TO THE END OF THE 17TH CENT., INCL. VARIOUS MODERN PEDIGREES, by P.H. Emerson. Repr. of 1898 ed.
Cloth--$51.00--Paper--$41.00--320pp F5159

396   - **EVANS-JACKSON**.   THE **JONES** & **EVANS** FAM. OF PORTAGE & MAHONING COS., OHIO; & THE **JACKSON** & **SOMERS** FAM. OF PORTSMOUTH, NH & BUFFALO, NY, by O.O. Evans and A.J. Evans. Repr. of 1954 ed.
Paper--$15.00--74pp F5159

397   - **EWING**. REC. OF THE FAM. OF THOMAS **EWING**, WHO EMIGR. FROM IRELAND TO AMER. IN 1718, by R.P. DuBois. Repr. of 1858 ed.
Paper--$7.50--38pp F5159

398   - THE ANC. OF MARGUERITE **EYERMAN**: A STUDY IN GEN.: **OSTER, SCHAEFFER, ROESSEL, SCHNEIDER, BLACK, HELLER, WAGENER, KACHLEIN, BUTZ, SEWITS, BAHL, DETWILLER**, by J. Eyerman. Repr. of 1898 ed.
Paper--$10.00--48pp F5159

399 - **EYERMAN**. THE ANC. OF MARGUERITE & JOHN **EYERMAN**, by J. Eyerman. Repr. of 1899 ed.
  Suppl. to 1898 ed.
  Paper--$7.00--35pp F5159

400 - **FAHNESTOCK** GENEALOGY. ANC. & DESC. OF JOHANN DIEDRICH **FAHNESTOCK**, by H.M. Pinot. Repr. of 1945 ed.
  Paper--$67.50--442pp F5159

401 - **FAHNESTOCK**. FAM. MEM. OF THE **FAHNESTOCKS** IN THE U.S., by A.K. Fahnestock and W.F. Fahnestock. Repr. of 1879 ed.
  Paper--$14.00--69pp F5159

402 - **FAIRFAX**. THE **FAIRFAXES** OF ENG. & AMER. IN THE 17TH & 18TH CENT., INCL. LETTERS FROM & TO HON. WM. **FAIRFAX** OF VA. & HIS SONS, by E.D. Neill. Repr. of 1868 ed.
  Cloth--$44.50--Paper--$34.50--234pp F5159

403 - **FANCHER** FAMILY, by W.H. Fancer. Repr. of 1947 ed.
  Paper--$24.00--144pp F5159

404 - **FARLEY**. 12 GEN. OF **FARLEYS**., by J. Farley, Jr.. Repr. of 1943 ed.
  Cloth--$49.00--Paper--$39.00--260pp F5159

405 - **FARWELL** FAM. A HIST. OF HENRY **FARWELL** & HIS WIFE OLIVE **(WELBY) FARWELL** OF BOSTON, ENG., & CONCORD & CHELMSFORD, MA., 1605-1927, by Farwell, Abbott & Wilson. Repr. of 1929 ed.
  With 12 gen. of their desc. & lin. of many allied fam. 2 vols. 941pp.
  Cloth--$149.00--Paper--$139.00--941pp F5159

406 - **FEATHERSTONE**. **FEATHERSTONES** & **HALLS**; GLEANINGS FROM OLD FAM. LETTERS & MSS., by M. Irwin. Repr. of 1890 ed.
  Paper--$18.00--99pp F5159

407 - **FELCH**. MEMORIAL HIST. OF **FELCH** FAM. IN AMERICA & WALES, by W.F. Felch. Repr. of 1881 ed.
  Paper--$16.50--98pp F5159

408 - GEN. HIST. OF THE **FELTON** FAM.: ANC. & DESC. OF LT. NATHANIEL **FELTON**, WHO CAME TO SALEM, MASS. FROM GT. YARMOUTH, ENG., IN 1633, by W.R. Felton. Repr. of 1935 ed.
  With brief hist. of some fams. that intermarried with **Feltons** during the 1st 150 years
  Cloth--$82.00--Paper--$72.00--467pp F5159

409 - **FELTON**. THE **FELTON** FAM.: DESC. OF LT. NATHANIEL **FELTON**, WHO CAME TO SALEM, MASS., IN 1633, (EXTENSION OF 1886 & 1935 BOOKS)., by N.F. Koster. Repr. of 1963 ed.
  Cloth--$48.50--Paper--$38.50--251pp F5159

410 - **FERGUSON**. GEN. OF DESC. OF JOHN **FERGUSON** OF SCOTLAND & U.S., by A.B. Ferguson. Repr. of 1911 ed.
  Paper--$22.50--112pp F5159

411   - FIELD. FIELDS OF SOWERBY NEAR HALIFAX, ENG. & FLUSHING, NY,
WITH SOME NOTICES OF THE FAM. OF UNDERHILL, BOWNE, BURLING,
HAZARD & OSGOOD, by O. Field. Repr. of 1895 ed.
Paper--$21.00--138pp F5159

412   - FILLMORE. MEM. OF CAPT. JOHN FILLMORE, by A. Woodward. Repr. of
1857 ed.
Paper--$4.50--13pp F5159

413   - FILLOW, PHILO & PHILEO GEN.: A REC. OF THE DESC. OF JOHN
FILLOW, HUGUENOT REFUGEE FROM FRANCE., by D.H. Van Hoosear. Repr. of
1888 ed.
Cloth--$53.50--Paper--$43.50--274pp F5159

414   - FISCHER. JACOB FISCHER, THE IMMIGR. EARLY SETTLER IN THE
PERKIOMAN VAL., by Dotterer & Strassburger. Repr. of 1927 ed.
Paper--$8.00--39pp F5159

415   - FISH. THE GEN. & DESC. OF LUKE FISH, SR., IN CHRONOLOGICAL
ORDER FROM 1760-1904., by D. Fish. Repr. of 1904 ed.
Paper--$16.00--80pp F5159

416   - FISHBACK FAM. IN AMER. DESC. OF JOHN FISHBACK, THE EMIGR.,
WITH HIST. SKETCH OF HIS FAM. & THE COL. AT GERMANNA &
GERMANTOWN, VA., by W.M. Kemper. Repr. of 1914 ed.
Cloth--$66.50--Paper--$56.50--356pp F5159

417   - FISHER. LIFE OF GEORGE FISHER (1795-1873) & THE HIST. OF THE
FISHER FAM. IN MISSISSIPPI, by Parmenter, Fisher & Mallette. Repr. of 1959 ed.
Cloth--$57.00--Paper--$47.00--299pp F5159

418   - FITCH. HIST. OF THE FITCH FAM., 1400-1930, by R.C. Fitch. Repr. of 1930
ed.
        2 volumes.
Cloth--$99.00--Paper--$89.00--557pp F5159

419   - FITE. THE BIOGRAPHICAL & GENEALOGICAL RECORDS OF THE FITE
FAMILIES IN THE U.S., by E.M.S. Fite. Repr. of 1907 ed.
Paper--$28.00--175pp F5159

420   - FITTS. GEN. OF THE FITTS OF FITZ FAM. IN AMER., by J.H. Fitts. Repr. of
1869 ed.
Paper--$18.00--91pp F5159

421   - FLAGG. GEN. NOTES ON THE FOUNDING OF NEW ENG.; MY ANC. PART
IN THAT UNDERTAKING., by E. Flagg. Repr. of 1926 ed.
Cloth--$78.50--Paper--$68.50--440pp F5159

422   - FLANDERS FAM. FROM EUROPE TO AMER.: BEING A HIST. OF THE
FLANDERS FAM. IN AMER. & ITS PROBALE ORIGIN IN EUROPE., by E.F.
Dunbar. Repr. of 1935 ed.
Cloth--$149.00--Paper--$139.00--1032pp F5159

423   - FLEMING. FAMILY RECORDS., by J.M. Seaver. Repr. of 1929 ed.
Paper--$8.00--40pp F5159

424   - **FLICKINGER** FAMILY HIST., by R.E. Flickinger. Repr. of 1927 ed.
Cloth--$119.00--Paper--$109.00--820pp F5159

425   - **FLINT**. THOMAS **FLINT** & WM. **FLINT** OF SALEM, MA. & THEIR DESC., by A.M. Smith. Repr. of 1931 ed.
        Also the probably unrelated lines of Lt. Robt. **Flint** of Sproutbrook, Montgomery Co., NY, & Robt. **Flint** of Va. & Trenton.
Paper--$30.00--232pp F5159

426   - **FOLSOM**. GEN. OF THE **FOLSOM** FAM., 1638-1938. REV. & EXT. ED. INCL. ENG. RECORDS. 2 VOL., by E. Folsom. Repr. of 1938 ed.
Cloth--$169.00--Paper--$159.00--1135pp F5159

427   - **FOOTE** FAMILY, COMPR. THE GEN. & HIST. OF NATHANIEL **FOOTE**, OF WETHERSFIELD, CT., & HIS DESC., by A.W. Foote. Repr. of 1907 ed.
        607 pp. Vol I, 1907.
Cloth--$99.00--Paper--$89.00--607pp F5159

428   - **FOOTE** FAMILY, VOL. 2 (2ND ED.), by   Repr. of 1932 ed.
Cloth--$109.00--Paper--$99.00--723pp F5159

429   - **FORBES**. THE HOUSE OF **FORBES**, by A. Thayer and H. Thayer. Repr. of 1937
Cloth--$86.50--Paper--$76.50--494pp F5159

430   - **FORD**. THE VALLEY OF THE SHADOW; A GEN. STUDY OF THE ANC. & DESC. OF CAPT. PAUL **FORD** OF LYMAN, MAINE, 1577-1952., by P.G. Ford. Repr. of 1953 ed.
Paper--$11.50--59pp F5159

431   - **FOSTER**. PEDIGREE OF JESSE W. FOSTER: THE LINES OF **FOSTER**, **COGGIN**, **FARLEY**, **PHELPS**, **BURRITT**, **CURTISS**, **LORD**, **SMITH**, **WEBSTER**, & ALLIED FAMS., by G.E. Foster. Repr. of 1897 ed.
Paper--$30.00--253pp F5159

432   - **FOWLE**. IMMIGRANT ANC. OF THE VARIOUS **FOWLE** FAM. OF AMER. & HIST. FACTS PERTAINING TO THEM & THEIR DESC., by E.P. Pierce. Repr. of 1912 ed.
Paper--$5.50--22pp F5159

433   - **FOWLER**. WIVES OF THE **FOWLERS**, IN ONE LINE FROM WM. THE MAGISTRATE., by W.C. Fowler.
Paper--$5.50--24pp F5159

434   - HIST. OF THE **FRASERS** OF LOVAT, WITH GEN. OF THE PRINCIPAL FAMS. OF THE NAME; TO WHICH IS ADDED THOSE OF **DUNBALLOCH** & **PHOPACHY**, by A. Mackenzie. Repr. of 1906 ed.
        Published in Scotland.
Cloth--$115.00--Paper--$105.00--871pp F5159

435   - **FREESE** GEN., by C.N. Sinnett. Repr. of 1929 ed.
Paper--$14.00--68pp F5159

436   - **FRENCH**. AMER. ANC. OF CHARLES E. **FRENCH** & HIS WIFE ANNA RICHMOND **WARNER**., by A.R.W. French. Repr. of 1894 ed.
Paper--$25.00--187pp F5159

437 - **FRENCH**. A GEN. HIST. OF THE **FRENCH** & ALLIED FAMILIES., by M.Q. Beyer. Repr. of 1912 ed.
Cloth--$68.50--Paper--$58.50--373pp F5159

438 - **FRISBEE-FRISBIE**. EDWARD **FRISBYE** OF BRANFORD, CT., & HIS DESC., WITH AN APPENDIX WITH BRIEF LINE. OF **FISKES, HASKELLS, MABVIES & PARKES**., by E.S. Frisbee. Repr. of 1926 ed.
Cloth--$119.00--Paper--$109.00--778pp F5159

439 - **FROST** GENEALOGY; DESC. OF WM. **FROST** OF OYSTER BAY, NY, SHOWING CONNECTIONS WITH THE **WINTHROP, UNDERHILL, FEKE, BROWN & WICKES** FAMS., by J.C. Frost. Repr. of 1912 ed.
Cloth--$67.00--Paper--$57.00--458pp F5159

440 - **FROST**. THE NICHOLAS **FROST** FAM., INCL. SUPPL., by J.E. Frost. Repr. of 1943 ed.
Paper--$25.50--170pp F5159

441 - **FULLER**. GEN. OF SOME DESC. OF EDWARD **FULLER** OF THE MAYFLOWER., by W.H. Fuller. Repr. of 1908 ed.
Cloth--$50.00--Paper--$40.00--306pp F5159

442 - GEN. OF SOME DESC. OF DR. SAMUEL **FULLER** OF THE MAYFLOWER. TO WHICH IS ADDED A SUPPL. TO THE GEN. OF SOME DESC. OF EDW. **FULLER** OF THE MAYFLOWER, by W.H. Fuller. Repr. of 1910 ed.
Cloth--$44.00--Paper--$34.00--263pp F5159

443 - **GALE**. GEN. OF THE DESC. OF DAVID **GALE** OF SUTTON, MASS., by L.A.E. Gale. Repr. of 1909 ed.
Paper--$11.50--57pp F5159

444 - **GARDNER**. A BIOGR. & GEN. REC. OF THE DESC. OF THOM. **GARDNER**, PLANTER. OF CAPE ANN SALEM (MASS.), THROUGH HIS SON, LIEUT. GEO. **GARDNER**., by F.A. Gardner. Repr. of 1933 ed.
Cloth--$54.00--Paper--$44.00--295pp F5159

445 - **GARRETT**. HIST. OF WELCOME **GARRETT** & HIS DESC., by S.B. Garrett. Repr. of 1909 ed.
Paper--$24.50--141pp F5159

446 - **GATES**. **DAWES-GATES** ANCESTRAL LINES: A MEM'L. VOL. CONTAINING THE AMER. ANC. OF RUFUS R. **DAWES**. VOL. II: **GATES** & ALLIED FAMILIES., by M.W. Ferris. Repr. of 1931 ed.
Cloth--$127.50--Paper--$117.50--918pp F5159

447 - **GEIB**. JOHN **GEIB** & HIS 7 CHILDREN., by A.C. Gildersleeve. Repr. of 1945 ed.
Paper--$5.50--23pp F5159

448 - **GIBBS**. A GOLDEN LEGACY TO THE **GIBBS** IN AMERICA., by M.B. Gibbs. Repr. of 1893 ed.
Paper--$15.50--77pp F5159

449 - **GILDERSLEEVE** PIONEERS., by W.H. Gildersleeve. Repr. of 1941 ed.
Cloth--$64.00--Paper--$54.00--337pp F5159

450   - **GILFILLAN**. SKETCHES, OUR LANDS & PEOPLE, **GILFILLAN** FAM., by
        J.B. Gilfillan. Repr. of 1918 ed.
        Paper--$5.50--25pp F5159

451   - **GILMAN**. THE **GILMAN** FAM. TRACED IN THE LINE OF HON. JOHN
        GILMAN OF EXETER, NH, & AN ACCT. OF MANY OTHER **GILMANS** IN ENG.
        & AMER., by A. Gilman. Repr. of 1869 ed.
        Cloth--$62.50--Paper--$52.50--337pp F5159

452   - **GILPIN**. GEN. OF THE FAMILY OF GIDEON **GILPIN**, GRANDSON OF JOS.
        GILPIN OF DORCHESTER, CO. OF OXFORD, ENG., WHO SETTLED IN
        CHESTER CO., PA., IN 1696., by J.E. Gilpin. Repr. of 1897 ed.
        Paper--$5.50--23pp F5159

453   - **GLEN**. HISTORY OF THE **GLEN** FAM. OF S. C. & GEORGIA., by J.G.B.
        Bulloch. Repr. of 1923 ed.
        Paper--$22.00--134pp F5159

454   - **GLIDDEN**. DESCENDANTS OF CHARLES **GLIDDEN** OF PORTSMOUTH &
        EXETER, N.H., by G.W. Chamberlain and L.G. Strong. Repr. of 1925 ed.
        Cloth--$75.00--Paper--$65.00--420pp F5159

455   - **GOLDTHWAIT**. GEN. NOTES BEARING UPON THE NEW ENG. ANC. OF
        THE CHILDREN OF WILLIAM JOHNSON **GOLDTHWAIT** & MARY LYDIA
        PITMAN-GOLDTHWAIT OF MARBLEHEAD, MA, by H. Tutt. Repr. of ed.
        Paper--$8.00--39pp F5159

456   - **GOODWIN** FAMILY. VARIOUS ANCESTRAL LINES OF JAMES **GOODWIN**
        & LUCY **MORGAN GOODWIN** OF HARTFORD, CT., by F.F. Starr. Repr. of 1915
        ed.
        Cloth--$59.50--Paper--$49.50--317pp F5159

457   - **GOODWIN**. VOL. II. , by F.F. Starr. Repr. of ed.
        Cloth--$85.00--Paper--$75.00--481pp F5159

SPECIAL PRICE FOR THE SET(#456 & #457): $135.00 HARDCOVER; $115.00 PAPER.

458   - ENGLISH **GOODWIN** FAM. PAPERS, BEING MATERIAL COLL. IN THE
        SEARCH FOR THE ANC. OF WILLIAM & OZIAS **GOODWIN**, EMIGR. OF 1632
        & RESIDENTS OF HARTFORD, CT, by Repr. of 1921 ed. Vols. I & II.
        Cloth--$154.50--Paper--$144.50--1196pp F5159

459   - **GORDON-MACY**. ALLIED FAMILIES: **GORDON-MACY** & **HIDDLESTON** -
        CURTIS ET AL., by M.G. Carman and J.G. Flack. Repr. of 1967 ed.
        Cloth--$55.00--Paper--$45.00--293pp F5159

460   - **GORTON**. THE LIFE & TIMES OF SAMUEL **GORTON**: THE FOUNDERS &
        FOUNDING OF THE REPUBLIC & A HIST. OF THE COL. OF PROVIDENCE &
        R.I., WITH A GEN. OF SAMUEL., by Gorton. Repr. of 1907 ed.
        Cloth--$131.50--Paper--$121.50--966pp F5159

461   - **GOULD**. THE FAM. OF ZACCHEUS **GOULD** OF TOPSFIELD., by B.A. Gould.
        Repr. of 1895 ed.
        Cloth--$55.50--Paper--$45.50--360pp F5159

462 - **GOULDS** OF RHODE ISLAND., by R.G. Mitchell. Repr. of 1875 ed.
Paper--$18.00--99pp F5159

463 - **GOURLAY**. MEM. OF THE SCOTTISH HOUSE OF **GOURLAY**., by C. Rogers.
Repr. of 1888 ed.
Cloth--$52.75--Paper--$42.75--285pp F5159

464 - **GOWDY**. FAMILY HIST. COMPRISING THE SURNAMES OF **GADE,
GAUDIE, GAWDY, GOWDY, GAUDERN** & VARIANT FORMS, FROM A.D.
800-A.D. 1919., by M.M. **Gowdy** and G.T. Ridlon. Repr. of 1919 ed.
Cloth--$99.50--Paper--$89.50--xx+628pp F5159

465 - **GRAHAM**. THE REV. JOHN **GRAHAM** OF WOODBURY, CONN., & HIS
DESC., by H.G. Carpenter. Repr. of 1942 ed.
Cloth--$94.50--Paper--$84.50--550pp F5159

466 - **GRANNIS**. HIST. OF **GRANNIS** FAM. IN AMER. 1630-1901., by S.S. Grannis.
Repr. of 1901 ed.
Paper--$10.00--49pp F5159

467 - **GREELY**. GEN. OF THE **GREELY-GREELEY** FAM., by G.H. Greeley. Repr. of
1905 ed.
Cloth--$124.50--Paper--$114.50--915pp F5159

468 - **GREEN**. GEN. OF THE FAM. OF TIMOTHY & EUNICE **ELLSWORTH
GREEN**., by J.M. Green. Repr. of 1904 ed.
Cloth--$44.50--Paper--$34.50--227pp F5159

469 - **GREENE**. THE **GREENE** FAM. OF R.I., WITH HIST. REC. OF ENG. ANC.,
1534-1902. 2 VOLUMES IN 1., by L.B. Clarke. Repr. of 1903 ed.
Cloth--$129.00--Paper--$119.00--892pp F5159

470 - **GREENWOOD** GEN., 1154-1914; THE ANC. & DESC. OF THOMAS OF
NEWTON, MASS., NATHANIEL & SAMUEL OF BOSTON, JOHN OF VA. &
MANY LATER ARRIVALS IN AMERICA, by F. Greenwood. Repr. of 1914 ed.
Also the early hist. of the **Greenwoods** in Eng.
Cloth--$94.50--Paper--$84.50--548pp F5159

471 - **GREENWOOD** FAM. OF NORWICH, ENG. IN AMER., by H.M. Pitman and
M.M. Greenwood. Repr. of 1934 ed.
Paper--$61.00--396pp F5159

472 - **GRIFFING**. GEN. OF THE DESC. OF JASPER **GRIFFING**., by C.J. Stone. Repr.
of 1881 ed.
Paper--$30.00--194pp F5159

473 - **GRIMES** FAMILY, by E.B. Grimes. Repr. of 1946 ed.
Paper--$14.00--70pp F5159

474 - **GRISWOLD**. THE **GRISWOLD** FAM. OF ENG. & AMER.: EDWARD OF
WINDSOR, MATTHEW OF LYME, MICHAEL OF WETHERSFIELD (ALL
CONN.)., by G.E. Griswold. Repr. of 1943 ed.
Cloth--$71.00--Paper--$61.00--391pp F5159

475   - **GROUT**. "A FAMILY AFFAIR" CONCERNING CERTAIN DESC. OF CAPT. JOHN **GROUT**, WHO CAME FROM ENG. TO NEW ENG. EARLY IN THE 17TH CENT., by H.S.B. Osgood. Repr. of 1949 ed.
Paper--$19.50--116pp F5159

476   - **GUSTINE**. THE **GUSTINE** COMPENDIUM., by G.C. Weaver. Repr. of 1929 ed.
Cloth--$64.00--Paper--$54.00--339pp F5159

477   - **HAINES**. "THE CLOVERCROFT CHRONICLES", 1314-1893., by M.R. Haines. Repr. of 1893 ed.
Cloth--$63.50--Paper--$53.50--347pp F5159

478   - **HALE** HOUSE & REL. FAMILIES, MAINLY OF THE CONN. RIVER VALLEY., by Jacobus & Waterman. Repr. of 1952 ed.
Cloth--$119.00--Paper--$109.00--914pp F5159

479   - **HALEY**. THE ANC. OF CHARITY **HALEY**, 1755-1800, WIFE OF MAJ. NICHOLAS **DAVIS** OF LIMINGTON, MAINE., by W.G. Davis, Jr.. Repr. of 1916 ed.
Paper--$18.00--91pp F5159

480   - **HALL**. MEMORANDA REL. TO THE ANC. & FAM. OF SOPHIA FIDELIA **HALL**., by S.F.H. Coe. Repr. of 1902 ed.
Paper--$30.00--231pp F5159

481   - **HALLOCK**. THE DESC. OF PETER **HALLOCK**, WHO LANDED AT SOUTHOLD, LI, 1640., by L. Hallock. Repr. of 1926 ed.
Cloth--$119.00--Paper--$109.00--749pp F5159

482   - **HAMLIN**. HIST. OF THE **HAMLIN** FAM., WITH GEN. OF EARLY SETTLERS OF THE NAME IN AMER., 1629-1894., by H.F. Andrews. Repr. of 1894 ed.
Paper--$21.00--130pp F5159

483   - **HAMLIN**. A GEN. OF JAMES **HAMLIN** OF BARNSTABLE, MASS., ELDEST SON OF JAMES **HAMLIN**, THE IMMIGR., 1639-1902., by H.A. Andrews. Repr. of 1902 ed.
Cloth--$208.50--Paper--$198.50--1411pp F5159

484   - **HAMLINS** OF NEW ENG., DESC. OF JAMES & ANNA **HAMLIN**., by S.M. Hamlin. Repr. of 1936 ed.
Paper--$13.00--65pp F5159

485   - **HAMPTON**. JOSEPH **HAMPTON** & THE PENN. QUAKERS., by V.B. Hampton. Repr. of 1940 ed.
Paper--$22.50--116pp F5159

486   - **HANAFORD**. FAM. RECORDS OF BRANCHES OF THE **HANAFORD**, **THOMPSON**, **HUCKINS**, **PRESCOTT** & ALLIED FAM., by M.E.N. Hanaford. Repr. of 1915 ed.
Cloth--$65.00--Paper--$55.00--345pp F5159

487   - **HANEY** FAMILY, by J.L. Haney. Repr. of 1930 ed.
Paper--$9.00--46pp F5159

488   - HANNUM. WILLIAM HANNUM OF NEW ENGLAND, & SOME DESC., by
W.H. Hannum. Repr. of 1936 ed.
Paper--$13.50--67pp F5159

489   - HARBAUGH HISTORY. A DIRECTORY, GEN. & SOURCE BOOK OF FAM.
RECORDS., by C.B. Cooprider and J.L. Cooprider. Repr. of 1947 ed.
Cloth--$78.50--Paper--$68.50--441pp F5159

490   - THE DESC. OF LEWIS HART & ANNE ELLIOTT WITH ADD. GEN. & HIST.
DATA ON THE FAMS. OF HART, WARNER, CURTISS, MCCOLLEY,
THOMPSON, TORRANCE & VOSBURGH, by J.S. Torrance. Repr. of 1923 ed.
Cloth--$69.50--Paper--$59.50--380pp F5159

491   - HARVARD. JOHN HARVARD & HIS ANC., by H.F. Waters. Repr. of 1885 ed.
Paper--$9.00--46pp F5159

492   - A GEN. HIST. OF THE HARWOOD FAM., DESC. FROM ANDREW
HARWOOD, WHOSE ENG HOME WAS IN DARTMOUTH, DEVENSHIRE, &
WHO EMIGR. TO AMER. & RESIDED IN BOSTON, MA, by W.H. Harwood. Repr.
of 1911 ed.
Paper--$21.00--155pp F5159

493   - HASKELL. CHRON. OF THE HASKELL FAM., by I. Haskell. Repr. of 1943 ed.
Cloth--$54.00--Paper--$44.00--294pp F5159

494   - HATCH. GENEALOGY & HIST OF THE HATCH FAMILY: DESC. OF
THOMAS & GRACE HATCH OF DORCHESTER, YARMOUTH &
BARNSTABLE, MASS., by Compiled by Hatch Gen. Society. Repr. of 1925 ed.
Cloth--$88.00--Paper--$78.00--776pp F5159

495   - THE HATFIELDS OF WESTCHESTER: A GEN. OF THE DESC. OF THOMAS
HATFIELD, OF NEW AMSTERDAM & MAMARONECK, WHOSE SONS
SETTLED IN WHITE PLAINS,NY, by A. Hatfield. Repr. of 1935 ed.
Cloth--$44.50--Paper--$34.50--222pp F5159

496   - DESC. OF SIMEON HATHAWAY, ALSO CONTAINING SOME LIN. OF
BRECKENRIDGE, BINGHAM, CASS, HINSDILL, LYMAN, MARTIN,
MCCOY, SMITH, SHEPARD, & WARNER, by E.H. Parks. Repr. of 1957 ed.
Paper--$13.50--68pp F5159

497   - HAWLEY & NASON ANC., by E.H. Everett. Repr. of 1929 ed.
Paper--$12.50--78pp F5159

498   - HAY. A HIST. OF THE PROGENITORS & SOME SO. CAROLINA DESC. OF
COL. ANN HAWKES HAY, WITH COLLATERAL GEN., 500-1908., by C.J.
Colcock. Repr. of 1908 ed.
Paper--$36.00--216pp F5159

499   - HAYDEN FAM. MAG., VOL. III, INCL. HIST., BIOGR., & FAM. RECORDS.,
Repr. of 1931 ed.
Cloth--$40.00--Paper--$30.00--202pp F5159

500   - HAYDEN. ABOVE, VOL IV., by Repr. of 1932 ed.
Cloth--$41.00--Paper--$31.00--206pp F5159

501   - **HAYDEN**. ABOVE, VOL V., by Repr. of 1933 ed.
        Cloth--$30.00--Paper--$20.00--133pp F5159

502   - **HAYES**. GEORGE **HAYES** OF WINDSOR & HIS DESC., by C.W. Hayes. Repr.
        of 1883 ed.
        Cloth--$55.00--Paper--$45.00--354pp F5159

503   - **HAYES**. JOHN **HAYES** OF DOVER, N.H.: A BOOK OF HIS FAMILY., by K.F.
        Richmond. Repr. of 1936 ed.
        Cloth--$139.50--Paper--$129.50--911pp F5159

504   - HIST. OF THE **HAYFORD** FAM., 1100-1900, ITS CONNECTIONS BY THE
        BONNEY, **FULLER** & **PHINNEY** FAM. WITH THE MAYFLOWER 1620
        CHICKERING FAM., 1356-1900, by O. Hayford. Repr. of 1901 ed.
        Cloth--$51.00--Paper--$41.00--253pp F5159

505   - **HAYNIE** FAM. OF NORTHUMBERLAND CO., VA., by G. Torrence. Repr. of
        1949 ed.
        Paper--$8.00--41pp F5159

506   - **HAZEN** FAMILY IN AMERICA; A GENEALOGY., by T.E. Hazen. Repr. of 1947
        Cloth--$159.00--Paper--$149.00--1175pp F5159

507   - **HELMER** FAMILY. PHILIP **HELMER**, THE PIONEER, & HIS DESC., by P.W.
        Williams. Repr. of 1931 ed.
        Paper--$27.50--183pp F5159

508   - **HEMENWAY**. GEN. RECORD OF ONE BRANCH OF THE **HEMENWAY**
        FAM. 1634-1880., by A. Hemenway. Repr. of 1880 ed.
        Paper--$18.00--92pp F5159

509   - **HEMENWAY**. RALPH **HEMENWAY** OF ROXBURY, MASS., 1634, & HIS
        DESC., WITH **DIETZ** GEN., by C.A. Newton. Repr. of 1943 ed.
        Paper--$28.50--152pp F5159

510   - **HENCH**. RECORDS OF THE ANNUAL **HENCH** & **DROMGOLD** REUNIONS,
        HELD IN PERRY CO., PENN., 1897-1912., by L.D. Emig. Repr. of 1913 ed.
        Paper--$28.50--191pp F5159

511   - **HENDERSHOT**. GENEALOGY OF THE **HENDERSHOT** FAMILY IN
        AMERICA., by A.E. Hendershot. Repr. of 1961 ed.
        Cloth--$43.00--Paper--$33.00--213pp F5159

512   - **HENRY**. THE DESC. OF SAMUEL **HENRY** OF HADLEY & AMHERST,
        MASS., 1734-1790, & LURANA **CADY** HIS WIFE., by W.H. Eldridge. Repr. of 1915
        ed.
        Cloth--$46.00--Paper--$36.00--240pp F5159

513   - **HERRICK** GENEALOGY. ONE LINE OF DESC. FROM JAMES **HERRICK**,
        WHO SETTLES AT SOUTHAMPTON, L.I., ABOUT 1653, by H.C. Brown. Repr. of
        1950 ed.
            With particular attention to desc. of Rev. Claudius **Herrick** (Yale, 1798) & his wife
        Hannah **Pierpont**.
        Paper--$18.50--95pp F5159

514   - HESTER. HISTORY & GENEALOGY OF THE DESCENDANTS OF JOHN
LAWRENCE HESTER & GODFREY STOUGH, 1752-1905 (WITH ADDENDUM
TO 1908)., by M.M. Hester. Repr. of 1905 ed.
Cloth--$68.00--Paper--$58.00--323+43pp F5159

515   - HIGBY. EDWARD HIGBY & HIS DESC., by C.D. Higby. Repr. of 1927 ed.
Cloth--$79.75--Paper--$69.75--467pp F5159

516   - HIGGINS. RICHARD HIGGINS, A RESIDENT & PIONEER SETTLER AT
PLYMOUTH & EASTHAM, MASS., & AT PISCATAWAY, N.J., & HIS DESC., by
K.C. Higgins. Repr. of 1918 ed.
Cloth--$109.00--Paper--$99.00--799pp F5159

517   - HIGGINS. SUPPL. TO ABOVE., by K.C. Higgins. Repr. of 1924 ed.
Cloth--$42.00--Paper--$32.00--216pp F5159

518   - JESSE HIGGINS & DAVID HIGGINS, COLONIAL RESIDENTS AT
EASTHAM, MASS. & PIONEER SETTLERS AT WEST EDEN, ME, by Harvard
DeLorraine Higgins. Repr. of 1990 ed.
     Their ancestors in Amer. & their desc. on Mt. Desert Island.
Paper--$29.50--200pp F5159

519   - HILL. GEN. OF THE HILL, DEAN, PINCKNEY, AUSTIN, BARKER,
ANDERSON, RHOADES & FINCH FAMS., by F. Couch. Repr. of 1907 ed.
Paper--$22.00--124pp F5159

520   - HILLHOUSE. HIST. & GEN. COLL. REL. TO THE DESC. OF REV. JAMES
HILLHOUSE, by M.P. Hillhouse. Repr. of 1924 ed.
Cloth--$109.00--Paper--$99.00--694pp F5159

521   - HILLMAN. ANC. CHRONOLOGICAL RECORD OF THE HILLMAN FAM.,
1550-1905., by H.W. Hillman. Repr. of 1905 ed.
Paper--$27.00--203pp F5159

522   - HINSDALE GEN.: DESC. OF ROBT. HINSDALE OF DEDHAM, MEDFIELD,
HADLEY & DEERFIELD, MA, WITH ACCT. OF THE FRENCH FAM. OF DE
HINNIDAL, by H. Andrews. Repr. of 1906 ed.
Cloth--$86.50--Paper--$76.50--508pp F5159

523   - HOAGLAND. HIST. & GEN. OF THE HOAGLAND FAM. IN AMER.,
1638-1891., by D.H. Carpenter. Repr. of 1891 ed.
Cloth--$52.00--Paper--$42.00--276pp F5159

524   - HOBART. DESC. OF EDMUND HOBART OF NORFOLK, ENG., &
HINGHAM, MASS., by Repr. of ed.
Paper--$6.50--32pp F5159

525   - HODGES. GENEALOGICAL RECORDS OF THE HODGES FAM. OF NEW
ENG., TO DEC. 31, 1894., by A.D. Hodges, Jr.. Repr. of 1896 ed.
Cloth--$96.50--Paper--$86.50--566pp F5159

526   - HOFFMAN. GEN. OF THE HOFFMAN FAM.; DESC. OF MARTIN
HOFFMAN, WITH BIOGR. NOTES, COMP., by E.A. Hoffman. Repr. of 1899 ed.
Cloth--$80.00--Paper--$70.00--545pp F5159

527 - **HOLCOMB(E)** GENEALOGY. A GEN., HIST. & DIRECTORY OF THE **HOLCOMB(E)S** OF THE WORLD, INCL. THE ANCIENT & MODERN ENG. BRANCH, THE AMER. BRANCHES & OTHERS., by J. Seaver. Repr. of 1925 ed. Cloth--$52.00--Paper--$42.00--283pp F5159

528 - **HOLCOMBE**. THE **HOLCOMBES**: NATION BUILDERS., by E.W. McPherson. Repr. of 1947 ed. Cloth--$152.50--Paper--$142.50--1346pp F5159

529 - **HOLLEMAN** FAM., A GEN. & HIST. REC. OF THE DESC. OF CHRISTOPHER **HOLLYMAN** OF ISLE OF WIGHT CO., VA. & REL. FAM., by G. Holleman. Repr. of 1953 ed. Cloth--$51.00--Paper--$41.00--275pp F5159

530 - **HOLLINGSWORTH**. DESC. OF VALENTINE **HOLLINGSWORTH**, SR., by J.A. Stewart. Repr. of 1925 ed. Cloth--$42.00--Paper--$32.00--214pp F5159

531 - **HOLLON**. GEN. OF **HOLLON** & REL. FAM., EARLY SETTLERS OF E. KY. & THEIR DESC., by C. Hollon. Repr. of 1958 ed. Paper--$18.00--108pp F5159

532 - **HOLMAN**. THE **HOLMANS** IN AMERICA, CONCERNING THE DESC. OF SOLAMAN **HOLMAN** WHO SETTLED IN W. NEWBURY, MASS., IN 1692-3, ONE OF WHOM IS WM. HOWARD **TAFT**., by D.E. Holman. Repr. of 1909 ed. Cloth--$64.50--Paper--$54.50--45+295pp F5159

533 - **HOOD**. THE TUNIS **HOOD** FAMILY: ITS LINEAGES & TRADITIONS., by D.O. Hood. Repr. of 1960 ed. Cloth--$97.50--Paper--$87.50--602pp F5159

534 - **HOOK**. JAMES **HOOK** & VIRGINIA ELLER; FAMILY HIST. & GEN., by J.W. Hook. Repr. of 1925 ed. Paper--$29.00--171pp F5159

535 - **HOTTEL**. HIST. OF THE DESC. OF JOHN **HOTTEL** (IMMIGR. FROM SWITZERLAND) & AN AUTHENTIC GEN. FAM. REG. OF TEN GEN. FROM 1732 TO 1929., by W.D. Huddle and L.M. Huddle. Repr. of 1930 ed. Cloth--$175.00--Paper--$165.00--1182pp F5159

536 - **HOUSTON** FAMILY IN VA., by L.L. Campbell. Repr. of 1956 ed. Paper--$16.00--77pp F5159

537 - **HOUSTON**. BRIEF BIOGRAPHICAL ACCOUNTS OF MANY MEMBERS OF THE **HOUSTON** FAMILY, WITH GENEALOGICAL TABLE., by S.R. Houston. Repr. of 1882 ed. Cloth--$75.50--Paper--$65.50--420pp F5159

538 - **HOVEY**. THE **HOVEY** BOOK, DESCRIBING ENG. ANC. & AMER. DESC. OF DANIEL **HOVEY** OF IPSWICH, MA., by Compiled by the Daniel Hovey Assoc.. Repr. of 1914 ed. Cloth--$84.50--Paper--$74.50--487pp F5159

539   - HOWARD LIN. ANC. OF IDA **BOYDSTUN WELCH** THROUGH HER MOTHER, EOLINE F. **HOWARD** BOYDSTUN., by G. Weaver. Repr. of 1929 ed. Cloth--$44.50--Paper--$34.50--230pp F5159

540   - HOWARD. ABRAHAM **HOWARD** OF MARBLEHEAD, MA., & HIS DESC., by Howard, Holden & Howard. Repr. of 1897 ed. Paper--$14.00--71pp F5159

541   - HOWARD. DESC. OF JOHN **HOWARD** OF BRIDGEWATER, MASS., 1643-1903., by H. Howard. Repr. of 1903 ed. Cloth--$62.50--Paper--$52.50--330pp F5159

542   - HOWE. GEN. OF ABRAHAM OF ROXBURY, JAMES OF IPSWICH, ABRAHAM OF MARLBOROUGH & EDWARD OF LYNN, MA., WITH APPENDIX., by D.W. Howe and G.B. Howe. Repr. of 1929 ed. Cloth--$107.50--Paper--$97.50--655pp F5159

543   - HOWES. DESC. OF JOHN & MARY **HOWES** OF MONTGOMERY CO., MD., by J.J.W. Howes. Repr. of 1946 ed. Paper--$10.50--53pp F5159

544   - HOYLE. GEN. OF PEITER **HEYL** (HOYLE) & HIS DESC., 1100-1936, WITH INTERMARRIED FAMILIES OF **ARNOLD, BESS, BYRD, CANSLER**, ET AL., by E.H. Rucker. Repr. of 1938 ed. Cloth--$208.00--Paper--$198.00--1539pp F5159

545   - **HUFFORD** FAMILY HISTORY, 1729-1909., by F.P. Hoffert. Repr. of 1909 ed. Cloth--$51.00--Paper--$41.00--269pp F5159

546   - **HUGHES** & ALLIED FAM., by D.D. Hughes and W.H. Hughes. Repr. of 1879 ed. Cloth--$51.00--Paper--$41.00--253pp F5159

547   - HUME. EARLY AMER. HIST. **HUME** & ALLIED FAM., by W.E. Brockman. Repr. of 1926 ed. Cloth--$47.00--Paper--$37.00--217pp F5159

548   - HUNGERFORD. THOMAS **HUNGERFORD** OF HARTFORD & NEW LONDON, CONN., & SOME OF HIS DESC., WITH THEIR ENG. ANC., by F.P. Leach. Repr. of 1924 ed. Paper--$7.00--34pp F5159

549   - HUNGERFORD. ADD. & CORR. FOR ABOVE., by F.P. Leach. Repr. of 1932 ed. Paper--$12.00--60pp F5159

550   - HUNSICKER. GEN. HIST. OF THE **HUNSICKER** FAMILY., by H.A. Hunsicker. Repr. of 1911 ed. Cloth--$66.50--Paper--$56.50--358pp F5159

551   - HUNT. A GEN. HIST. OF THE ROBERT & ABIGAIL **PANCOAST HUNT** FAMS., by C.C. Hunt. Repr. of 1906 ed. Cloth--$37.00--Paper--$27.00--202pp F5159

552   - HUNTER. JOSEPH **HUNTER** & RELATED FAMILIES **BECKWITH, BIRD,
        MEDLEY, PHILLIPS, RILEY & SIKES** OF S.E. MISSOURI., by S.B. Hunter and
        M.A.M. Hunter & F.E. Snider. Repr. of 1959 ed.
        Cloth--$68.50--Paper--$58.50--374pp F5159

553   - HURD. HIST. & GEN. OF THE FAM. OF **HURD** IN THE U.S.; ALSO A
        PARTIAL HIST. OF THE NEW ENGLAND FAMILIES. OF **HEARD & HORD,** by
        D.D. Hurd. Repr. of 1910 ed.
        Cloth--$54.00--Paper--$44.00--339pp F5159

554   - HUTCHINSON. THE BOOK OF BROTHERS; THE HIST. OF THE
        HUTCHINSON FAM., by   Repr. of 1852 ed.
        Paper--$9.50--48pp F5159

555   - HUTCHINSON. NOTES UPON THE ANC. OF WILLIAM **HUTCHINSON** &
        ANNE **MARBURY.**, by J.L. Chester. Repr. of 1866 ed.
        Paper--$10.00--48pp F5159

556   - HYNES. OUR PIONEER ANCESTORS, by Riggs & Riggs. Repr. of 1941 ed.
            Record of available info. as to the **Hynes, Chenault, Dunn, McKee, Anderson,
        Talylor, Finley, Letcher & Houston** fams. in the direct line of anc. of Samuel B. &
        Ellen M. **Anderson Hynes.**
        Cloth--$42.00--Paper--$32.00--207pp F5159

557   - HYNES. OUR HERITAGE: REC. OF INFO. ABOUT THE **HYNES, WAIT,
        POWERS, CHENAULT, MAXET, BREWSTER, STARR & MCINTOSH**
        FAMILIES., by L.P. Hynes. Repr. of 1957 ed.
        Paper--$18.00--93pp F5159

558   - IDE. SIMON **IDE,** WITH A GEN. OF THE **IDE** FAM., by Flanders. Repr. of
        1931 ed.
        Cloth--$65.00--Paper--$55.00--347pp F5159

559   - INGALLS. THE **INGALLS** FAM. IN ENG. & AMER., IN COMM. OF THE
        300TH ANNIVERSARY OF THE SETTLEMENT OF LYNN, MASS., by E. Ingalls
        and F. Ingalls. Repr. of 1930 ed.
        Paper--$16.50--84pp F5159

560   - INGHAM FAMILY: OR **JOSEPH INGHAM** & HIS DESC., 1639- 1871., by
        Repr. of 1871 ed.
        Paper--$12.00--59pp F5159

561   - INGPEN. AN ANCIENT FAMILY: A GENEALOGICAL STUDY SHOWING
        THE SAXON ORIGIN OF THE FAMILY OF **INGPEN,** by A.R. Ingpen. Repr. of
        1916 ed.
        Cloth--$43.50--Paper--$33.50--208pp F5159

562   - INGRAHAM. TO THE DESCENDANTS OF TIMOTHY **INGRAHAM:**
        INFORMATION RESPECTING THE GREAT **INGRAHAM** ESTATE, IN GREAT
        BRITAIN., by G.R. Gladding. Repr. of 1859 ed.
        Paper--$16.00--80pp F5159

563   - INNES. AN ACCT. OF THE FAMILY OF **INNES**, COMP. BY DUNCAN
       FORBES OF CULLODEN (1698), WITH AN APPENDIX OF CHARTERS &
       NOTES., by C. Innes. Repr. of 1864 ed.
       Cloth--$55.00--Paper--$45.00--286pp F5159

564   - IRVINE.   THE **IRVINES** & THEIR KIN: A HISTORY OF THE **IRVINE**
       FAMILY & THEIR DESCENDANTS., by L. Boyd. Repr. of 1898 ed.
       Paper--$18.00--115pp F5159

565   - IRVINE. THE **IRVINES** & THEIR KIN. HISTORY OF THE **IRVINE** FAM. &
       THEIR DESCENDANTS; ALSO, SKETCHES OF THEIR KINDRED., by L. Boyd.
       Repr. of 1908 ed.
       Cloth--$77.50--Paper--$67.50--432pp F5159

566   - IRWIN. GEN. OF THAT BRANCH OF THE **IRWIN** FAM. IN N.Y., FOUNDED
       IN THE HUDSON RIVER VALLEY BY WM. **IRWIN**, 1700-1787., by R.S. Hosmer
       and M.T. Fielder. Repr. of 1938 ed.
       Cloth--$49.50--Paper--$39.50--258pp F5159

567   - ISAAC. ANCESTRY OF MARY **ISAAC**, C.1549-1613, WIFE OF THOMAS
       APPLETON OF LITTLE WALDINFIELD, CO. SUFFOLK, & MOTHER OF
       SAMUEL **APPLETON** OF IPSWICH, MASS., by W.G. Davis. Repr. of 1955 ed.
       Cloth--$71.00--Paper--$61.00--400pp F5159

568   - ISHAM GENEALOGY: BRIEF HIST. OF JIRAH **ISHAM** OF NEW LONDON,
       CT., & HIS DESC., FROM 1670 TO 1940., by M.A. Phinney. Repr. of 1940 ed.
       Paper--$27.00--179pp F5159

569   - ISHAM. THE **ISHAMS** IN ENGLAND & AMER.: 850 YEARS OF HIST. &
       GEN., by H.W. Brainard. Repr. of 1938 ed.
       Cloth--$108.50--Paper--$98.50--672pp F5159

570   - IVES.   GEN. OF THE **IVES** FAM., INCL. A HIST. OF THE EARLY
       SETTLEMENTS., by A.C. Ives. Repr. of 1932 ed.
       Cloth--$58.50--Paper--$48.50--321pp F5159

571   - PROCEEDINGS OF THE SESQUICENT. GATHERING OF THE DESC. OF
       ISAAC & ANN **JACKSON** AT HARMONY GROVE, CHESTER CO., PA. (AUG.,
       1875), TOGETHER WITH FAM. GEN., by Compiled by the Publ. Comm.. Repr. of
       1878 ed.
       Cloth--$68.50--Paper--$58.50--372pp F5159

572   - JACKSON. HON. JONATHAN **JACKSON** & HANNAH **TRACY JACKSON**:
       THEIR ANCESTORS & DESCENDANTS., by E.C. Putnam and J.J. Putnam. Repr. of
       1907 ed.
       Paper--$14.00--70pp F5159

573   - JACOBY FAM. GEN.; REC. OF THE DESC. OF THE PIONEER PETER
       JACOBY OF BUCKS CO., PA., by H.S. Jacoby. Repr. of 1930 ed.
       Cloth--$108.00--Paper--$98.00--680pp F5159

574   - JARVIS FAMILY, OR, THE DESC. OF THE 1ST SETTLERS OF THE NAME IN
       MA & LONG ISLAND & THOSE WHO HAVE RECENTLY SETTLED IN OTHER
       PARTS OF THE US & BRIT AMR, by Jarvis, Jarvis & Wetmore. Repr. of 1879 ed.
       Cloth--$66.50--Paper--$56.50--347pp F5159

575   - **JENKS** FAM. OF AMER., by W.B. Browne. Repr. of 1952 ed.
Cloth--$120.00--Paper--$110.00--739pp F5159

576   - **JEWETT.** HIST. & GEN. OF THE **JEWETTS** OF AMER.; REC. OF EDWARD **JEWETT** OF BRADFORD, ENG., & OF HIS SONS, SETTLERS OF ROWLEY, MASS., IN 1639. 2 VOLUMES., by F. Jewett. Repr. of 1908 ed.
Cloth--$169.00--Paper--$159.00--1216pp F5159

577   - **JOHNSON-STEBBINS.** ONE LINE OF DESC. FROM JOHN **JOHNSON** OF ROXBURY, MASS. TO LYDIA **STEBBINS.** MANUSCRIPT., by F.Z. Rossiter. Repr. of 1907 ed.
Paper--$15.00--75pp F5159

578   - **JOHNSON** & ALLIED FAM. OF LINCS., ENG., BEING THE ANC. & POSTERITY OF LAWRENCE **JOHNSON** OF PHILA., PENN., by R.W. Johnson, Sr. and L.J. Morris. Repr. of 1934 ed.
Cloth--$80.50--Paper--$70.50--478pp F5159

579   - **JOHNSON.** GEN. OF CAPT. JOHN **JOHNSON** OF ROXBURY, MASS., GENERATIONS I TO XIV. Edited By P.F. JOHNSON & A.J. MODERN., by F.L. Johnson. Repr. of 1951 ed.
Cloth--$86.50--Paper--$76.50--499pp F5159

580   - **JOHNSON.** THE JOHNSONS & THEIR KIN, OF RANDOLPH, N.C., by J.O. Shaw. Repr. of 1955 ed.
Cloth--$43.50--Paper--$33.50--214pp F5159

581   - **JOHNSON.** THE **JOHNSTONS** OF SALISBURY, WITH A BRIEF SUPPL. CONCERNING THE **HANCOCK, STROTHER, & PRESTON** FAM., by W.P. Johnston. Repr. of 1897 ed.
Cloth--$39.50--Paper--$29.50--216pp F5159

582   - **JONES** FAM. OF LONG ISLAND, DESC. OF MAJ. THOMAS **JONES** (1665-1726) & ALLIED FAM., by J.H. Jones. Repr. of 1907 ed.
Cloth--$78.00--Paper--$68.00--435pp F5159

583   - **JONES** & RELATED FAMILIES: A GEN. COMP. & HISTORY, INCL. **STUBBS, GIFFORD, JOHNSON, HAWKINS, SMALL, HOBSON, GREEN** & OTHERS., by C.B. Jones. Repr. of 1951 ed.
Cloth--$77.50--Paper--$67.50--436pp F5159

584   - **JONES.** PETER & RICHARD **JONES** GENEALOGIES, by A.B. Fothergill. Repr. of 1924 ed.
Cloth--$67.00--Paper--$57.00--363pp F5159

585   - DESC. OF JOEL **JONES,** OF MASS. & PA., 1764-1845. ALSO AN ACCT. OF HIS ANC. BACK TO LEWIS & ANN OF WATERTOWN, MA, by E. Smith. Repr. of 1925 ed.
          Also desc. of Lemuel **Smith** of Ma. & Pa., 1770-1817.
Cloth--$75.00--Paper--$65.00--414pp F5159

586   - **JUNKINS.** THE DESC. OF ROBERT **JUNKINS** OF YORK CO., MAINE., by H.A. Davis. Repr. of 1938 ed.
Cloth--$40.00--Paper--$30.00--197pp F5159

587   - **KAGY**. A HIST. OF THE **KAGY** REL. IN AMER., FROM 1715 TO 1900., by F. Keagy. Repr. of 1899 ed.
Cloth--$95.50--Paper--$85.50--675pp F5159

588   - **KEEN-KYN**. THE DESC. OF JORAM **KYN**, FOUNDER OF "UPLAND-NEW SWEDEN" (NOW CHESTER, PA) & WHOSE DESC. WERE SOME OF THE EARLIEST SETTLERS OF WABASH CO., IL, From "Pa. Mag. Hist. & Biogr.", Repr. of 1878 ed.
Cloth--$49.50--Paper--$39.50--243pp F5159

589   - **KEEN**. GEN. OF THE **KEEN** FAMILY OF WAYNE CO., IL., by H.T. Keen. Repr. of 1965 ed.
Paper--$19.00--132pp F5159

590   - **KELLER**. HISTORY OF THE **KELLER** FAMILY., by Eli Keller. Repr. of 1905 ed.
Cloth--$39.50--Paper--$29.50--192pp F5159

591   - **KELLOGG**. THE **KELLOGGS** IN THE OLD WORLD & THE NEW, by T. Hopkins. Repr. of 1903 ed.
       3 Vols. 897, 848, & 321pp.
Cloth--$285.00--Paper--$255.00-- F5159

592   - **KELLY**. A GENEALOGICAL ACCOUNT OF THE DESCENDANTS OF JOHN **KELLY** OF NEWBURY, MASS., by G.M. Kelly. Repr. of 1886 ed.
Paper--$28.50--178pp F5159

593   - **KELLY**.   THE   ANC.   &   DESC.   OF   SETH   **KELLY**,   1762-1850,   OF BLACKSTONE, MASS., by W.P. Kelly. Repr. of 1937 ed.
Paper--$14.00--71pp F5159

594   - **KELSEY**. GENEALOGY OF THE DESC. OF WM. **KELSEY**, WHO SETTLED AT CAMBRIDGE, MA., IN 1632; AT HARTFORD, CT. IN 1636; & AT KILLINGSWORTH, CT., IN 1663., by Claypool, Clizbee & Kelsey. Repr. of 1928 ed.
Cloth--$57.00--Paper--$47.00--295pp F5159

595   - **KELSEY**. VOL. II.,   Repr. of 1929 ed.
Cloth--$76.50--Paper--$66.50--424pp F5159

596   - **KELSEY**. VOL. III.   Repr. of 1947 ed.
       SPECIAL PRICE FOR THE SET: $219.00 HARDCOVER; $189.00 PAPER.,
Cloth--$149.00--Paper--$139.00-- F5159

597   - **KENNEDY**. HIST. & GEN. ACCT. OF THE PRINCIPAL FAMS. OF THE NAME OF **KENNEDY**, WITH NOTES & ILLUS., by R. Pitcairn. Repr. of 1830 ed.
Cloth--$44.50--Paper--$34.50--218pp F5159

598   - **KENNEDY**. EARLY AMER. HIST.; **KENNEDY** & ALLIED FAM., by W.E. Brockman. Repr. of 1926 ed.
Paper--$14.00--71pp F5159

599   - AMERICAN **KENYONS**: HIST. OF **KENYONS** & ENGLISH CONNECTIONS OF AMERICAN **KENYONS**; GEN. OF THE AMERICAN **KENYONS** OF RHODE ISL.; MISC. **KENYON** MATERIAL, by H.N. Kenyon. Repr. of 1935 ed.
Cloth--$54.50--Paper--$44.50--285pp F5159

600   - HIST. OF THE **KIDDER** FAM., 1320-1676, INCL. THE BIOGR. OF OUR EMIGR. ANC. JAMES **KIDDER** & A GEN. OF HIS DESC. THROUGH HIS SON, JOHN, by F. Kidder. Repr. of 1886 ed.
       John settled in Chelmsford, Ma., 1681.
Paper--$26.50--174pp F5159

601   - **KIDDER**. A GEN. OF THE **KIDDER** FAM., COMPRISING THE DESC. IN THE MALE LINE OF ENSIGN JAMES **KIDDER**, 1626- 1676, OF CAMBRIDGE & BILLERICA, MA., by M.H. Stafford. Repr. of 1941 ed.
Cloth--$119.00--Paper--$109.00--750pp F5159

602   - **KILLAM**. GEN. OF THE **KILLAM** FAM. OF ESSEX CO., MASS., by S. Perley. Repr. of 1913 ed.
Paper--$6.00--29pp F5159

603   - **KILMER**. HIST. OF THE **KILMER** FAM. IN AMER., by C.H. Kilmer. Repr. of 1897 ed.
Paper--$28.00--214pp F5159

604   - **KIMBALL**. REC. OF THE FAM. OF LEVI **KIMBALL** & SOME OF HIS DESC., by L. Darbee. Repr. of 1861 ed. 1913.
Paper--$25.75--173pp F5159

605   - **KIMBALL**. HIST. OF THE **KIMBALL** FAM. IN AMER., 1634- 1897; ALSO ANC. OF THE **KIMBALLS** OR **KEMBOLDES** OF ENG., WITH ACCT. OF THE **KEMBLES** OF BOSTON., by L.A. Morrison and S.P. Sharples. Repr. of 1897 ed.
Cloth--$161.00--Paper--$151.00--1278pp F5159

606   - **KIMBALL**. THE LT. MOSES & JEMIMA **CLEMENT KIMBALL** FAM., by P.K. Skinner. Repr. of 1941 ed.
Paper--$20.50--138pp F5159

607   - DESC. OF RICHARD **KIMBER**: GEN. HIST OF THE DESC. OF RICHARD **KIMBER** OF GROVE, BERKS., ENG., CONTAINING THE FAMS. IN THE U.S. FROM SETTLEMENTS IN PA & NY, by S.A. Kimber. Repr. of 1894 ed.
       Families in Eng. & desc. in Australia.
Paper--$17.50--91pp F5159

608   - **KINGMAN**. DESC. OF HENRY **KINGMAN**. SOME EARLY GEN. OF THE **KINGMAN** FAM., by B. Kingman. Repr. of 1912 ed.
Paper--$15.00--102pp F5159

609   - **KINGSBURY**. GEN. REC. OF THE EARLY ENG. ANC. TO AMER., & LINES OF DESC. TO NATHANIEL **KINGSBURY** OF KEENE, N.H., by F.B. Kingsbury. Repr. of 1904 ed.
       And desc. of three daughters: Abigail **Kingsbury White**, Hannah **Kingsbury White**, Cloe **Kingsbury Sumner**.
Paper--$12.50--63pp F5159

610   - **KINGSBURY**. GEN. OF THE DESC. OF HENRY **KINGSBURY** OF IPSWICH
       & HAVERHILL, MASS., by F.J. Kingsbury and M.K. Talcott. Repr. of 1905 ed.
       Cloth--$102.00--Paper--$92.00--732pp F5159

611   - **KINSMAN**.   GEN. RECORD OF THE DESC. OF ROBT. **KINSMAN** OF
       IPSWICH, MASS., 1624-1875., by L.W. Stickney. Repr. of 1876 ed.
       Cloth--$49.50--Paper--$39.50--258pp F5159

612   - **KIP**.   HIST. OF THE **KIP** FAMILY IN AMER., by Kip & Hawley. Repr. of 1928
       ed.
       Cloth--$81.00--Paper--$71.00--462pp F5159

613   - **KISTLER** FAM., DESC. FROM GEORGE **KISTLER**, JR. OF BERKS CO.,
       PENN., by F.K. Sprague. Repr. of 1944 ed.
       Paper--$10.00--47pp F5159

614   - **KITE** FAM., by V.A. Kite. Repr. of ed.
       Paper--$23.50--122pp F5159

615   - **KNICKERBACKER-VIELE**. SKETCHES OF ALLIED FAMILIES, TO WHICH
       IS ADDED AN APPENDIX CONTAINING FAM. DATA., by K.K. Viele. Repr. of
       1916 ed.
       Paper--$22.50--134pp F5159

616   - **KNOWLES** FAM. OF EASTHAM, MASS., by C.T. Libby. Reprint
       Paper--$14.00--72pp F5159

617   - **KNOX**.   WILLIAM **KNOX** OF BLANDFORD, MA.; A RECORD OF THE
       BIRTHS, MARRIAGES & DEATHS OF SOME OF HIS DESC., by N. Foote. Repr. of
       1926 ed.
       Cloth--$58.50--Paper--$48.50--302pp F5159

618   - **KOINER**. HIST. SKETCH OF MICHAEL **KEINADT** & MARGARET **DILLER**,
       HIS WIFE. HIST. & GEN. OF THEIR NUMEROUS POSTERITY IN THE AMER.
       STATES UP TO 1893, Repr. of 1893 ed.
       Paper--$27.00--177pp F5159

619   - **KOLLOCK**. GEN. OF THE **KOOLOCK** FAM. OF SUSSEX CO., DELAWARE,
       1657-1897., by E.J. Sellers. Repr. of 1897 ed.
       Paper--$15.00--76pp F5159

620   - **KREKLER** AND RELATED FAMILIES., by Bessie K. Schafer. Repr. of 1963 ed.
       Paper--$7.00--35pp F5159

621   - **LAMB**. THE **LAMBS** OF MINNESOTA., by Harold E. Lamb. Reprint
       Paper--$5.50--24pp F5159

622   - **LAMB**. NATHAN **LAMB** OF LEICESTER, MASS., HIS ANC. & DESC., by C.F.
       Lamb. Repr. of 1930 ed.
       Paper--$19.00--96pp F5159

623   - **LAMBERT**. ROGER **LAMBERT** & HIS DESC., by I. Lambert. Repr. of 1933 ed.
       Paper--$12.50--61pp F5159

624   - **LANTZ** FAMILY RECORD, BEING A BRIEF ACCT. OF THE **LANTZ** FAM. IN
        THE U.S., by Jacob W. Lantz. Repr. of 1931 ed.
        Cloth--$51.50--Paper--$41.50--265pp F5159

625   - **LAPHAM** FAMILY IN AMERICA, by B.B.B. Aldridge. Repr. of 1853 ed.
            13,000 descendants, incl. desc. of John (Devonshire, Eng. to Providence, RI, 1673),
            & Thomas (Kent, Eng. to Scituate, Mass., 1634), also genealogical notes of other
            Lapham fams.
        Cloth--$95.00--Paper--$85.00--552pp F5159

626   - **LAUDER**. NOTES ON HIST. REFERENCES TO THE SCOTTISH FAM. OF
        LAUDER., by J. Young. Repr. of 1884 ed.
        Paper--$21.00--154pp F5159

627   - **LAWRENCE**. HIST. GEN. OF THE **LAWRENCE** FAM., 1635- 1858., by T.
        Lawrence. Repr. of 1858 ed.
        Cloth--$42.00--Paper--$32.00--240pp F5159

628   - **LAWRENCE**. HIST. SKETCHES OF SOME MEMBERS OF THE **LAWRENCE**
        FAMILY, by R.M. Lawrence. Repr. of 1888 ed.
        Cloth--$42.00--Paper--$32.00--215pp F5159

629   - **LAWRENCE**. MEM. OF ROBT. **LAWRENCE**, ROBT. **BARTLETT**, & THEIR
        DESC., by H.B. Lawrence. Repr. of 1888 ed.
        Paper--$29.00--223pp F5159

630   - **LEADBETTER** RECORDS., by J.E. Ames. Repr. of 1917 ed.
        Cloth--$59.50--Paper--$49.50--317pp F5159

631   - **LEAVITT**. THE **LEAVITTS** OF AMER.: A COMP. OF FIVE BRANCHES &
        GLEANINGS FROM NEW ENG. TO CALIF. & CANADA., by C.G. Steer. Repr. of
        1924 ed.
        Cloth--$49.50--Paper--$39.50--254pp F5159

632   - **LEE** OF VIRGINIA, 1642-1892; BIOGR. & GEN. SKETCHES OF THE DESC.
        OF COL. RICHARD **LEE**, WITH BRIEF NOTICES OF REL. FAMS. OF
        ALLERTON, ARMISTEAD, ETC., by E.J. Lee. Repr. of 1895 ed.
        Cloth--$84.00--Paper--$74.00--586pp F5159

633   - **LEETE**. THE FAM. OF WILLIAM **LEETE**, ONE OF THE FIRST SETTLERS
        OF GUILFORD, CT. & GOV. OF THE NEW HAVEN & CONN. COLONIES., by E.
        Leete. Repr. of 1884 ed.
        Cloth--$36.00--Paper--$26.00--168pp F5159

634   - **LEETE**. DESC. OF WILLIAM **LEETE**, ONE OF THE FOUNDERS OF
        GUILFORD, CT., PRES. OF THE FED. OF COLONIES, & GOV. OF NEW HAVEN
        & CONN. COLONIES. 2ND ED., by E. Leete. Repr. of 1934 ed.
        Cloth--$73.50--Paper--$63.50--408pp F5159

635   - **LEFFERTS**. GEN. OF THE **LEFFERTS** FAM., 1650-1878., by T.G. Bergen.
        Repr. of 1878 ed.
        Paper--$26.50--172pp F5159

636   - **LEFTWICH-TURNER** FAMILIES OF VA. & THEIR CONNECTIONS., by W.L. Hopkins. Repr. of 1931 ed.
Cloth--$68.50--Paper--$58.50--368pp F5159

637   - **LEGARE**. BIOGR. SKETCHES OF HUGUENOT SOLOMON **LEGARE**; ALSO HIS FAMILY EXTENDING TO THE 4TH GEN. OF HIS DESC., by E.C.K. Fludd. Repr. of 1886 ed.
Paper--$21.50--144pp F5159

638   - **LEIGHTON**. GEN. SKETCH OF DOVER, N.H., BRANCH OF **LEIGHTON** FAM., by W.L. Leighton. Repr. of 1940 ed.
Paper--$6.50--31pp F5159

639   - **LENT**. HIST. OF THE **LENT (VAN LENT)** FAM. IN THE U.S., GEN. & BIOGR., 1638-1902., by N.B. Lent. Repr. of 1903 ed.
Paper--$23.50--171pp F5159

640   - **LEONARD**. STEPHEN BANKS **LEONARD** OF OWEGO, TIOGA CO., N.Y., by W.A. Leonard. Repr. of 1909 ed.
Cloth--$64.50--Paper--$54.50--342pp F5159

641   - **LEONARD**. ANNALS OF THE **LEONARD** FAMILY, by F. Koster. Repr. of 1911 ed.
Cloth--$44.00--Paper--$34.00--226pp F5159

642   - **LEONARD**. MEM. OF THE **LEONARD, THOMPSON & HASKELL** FAMS., WITH COLL. FAMS., by C. Goodenough. Repr. of 1928 ed.
Cloth--$64.50--Paper--$54.50--344pp F5159

643   - **LESLIE**. HISTORICAL RECORDS OF THE FAMILY OF **LESLIE**, FROM 1067 TO 1869, COLLECTED FROM PUBLIC RECORDS & AUTHENTIC PRIVATE SOURCES, by Col. Leslie. Repr. of 1869 ed.
        3 vols. in 2.
Cloth--$144.50--Paper--$134.50--430pp, & 681pp F5159

644   - **LEVERING** FAMILY, OR A GEN. ACCT. OF WIGARD & GERHARD **LEVERING**, TWO OF THE PIONEER SETTLERS OF ROXBOROUGH TWP., PHILA. CO., (PA.) & THEIR DESC., by H.G. Jones. Repr. of 1858 ed.
Cloth--$41.00--Paper--$31.00--203pp F5159

645   - **LEWIS** OF WARNER HALL: THE HIST. OF A FAM. INCL. THE GEN. OF THE MALE & FEMALE LINES, BIOGR. SKETCHES OF ITS MEMBERS AND THEIR DESC. FROM OTHER EARLY VA. FAM., by M.E. Sorley. Repr. of 1935 ed.
Cloth--$142.50--Paper--$132.50--887pp F5159

646   - **LEWIS**. GEN. OF THE **LEWIS** & KINDRED FAM., by J.M. McAllister and L.B. Tandy. Repr. of 1906 ed.
Cloth--$75.00--Paper--$65.00--416pp F5159

647   - **LEWIS**. WM. **LEWIS** OF STOKE-BY-NAYLAND, ENG., & SOME OF HIS ANC. & DESC., by I. Lewis. Repr. of 1932 ed.
Paper--$20.00--106pp F5159

648   - **LIBBY** FAMILY IN AMERICA, 1602-1881., by C.T. Libby. Repr. of 1882 ed.
Cloth--$89.50--Paper--$79.50--628pp F5159

649   - **LIGON** FAM. & CONNECTIONS. VOL. I., by W.D. Ligon, Jr.. Repr. of 1947 ed.
Cloth--$144.50--Paper--$134.50--943pp F5159

650   - **LIGON** FAMILY & CONNECTIONS, VOL. II., by Repr. of 1957 ed.
Cloth--$44.50--Paper--$34.50--232pp F5159

651   - **LINCOLN**. STEPHEN **LINCOLN** OF OAKHAM, MASS., HIS ANC. & DESC.,
by J.E. Morris. Repr. of 1895 ed.
Paper--$18.00--109pp F5159

652   - **LINCOLN**. THE ANCESTRY OF ABRAHAM **LINCOLN**., by J.H. Lea and J.R.
Hutchinson. Repr. of 1909 ed.
Cloth--$50.00--Paper--$40.00--310pp F5159

653   - **LITTLEFIELD**. MEM. REL. TO THE **LITTLEFIELDS**, ESP. TO THE DESC.
OF EDMUND WHO FOUNDED THE MASS. BRANCH OF THE FAM. IN 1690 AT
BRAINTREE., by G. Littlefield. Repr. of 1897 ed.
Paper--$16.00--80pp F5159

654   - **LLOYD**. A REC. OF THE DESC. OF ROBERT **LLOYD**, WHO CAME FROM
WALES & SETTLED IN THE WELSH TRACT AT MERION, PA., ABOUT 1684.,
by R.L. Lloyd. Repr. of 1947 ed.
Paper--$18.00--119pp F5159

655   - BOOK OF THE **LOCKES**: A GEN. & HIST. RECORD OF DESC. OF WM.
LOCKE OF WORBURN, WITH APPENDIX CONTAINING A HIST. OF THE
LOCKES IN ENGLAND, by J.G. Locke. Repr. of 1853 ed.
     Also incl. fam. of John **Locke** of Hampton, NH & kindred fams. & individuals.
Cloth--$62.00--Paper--$52.00--406pp F5159

656   - **LONGS** OF CHARLESTOWN & NANTUCKET, MASSACHUSSETTS, by H. P.
Long. Reprint of 1926 ed.
Paper--$6.00--28pp F5159

657   - **LONGACRE**. HIST. OF THE **LONACRE-LANGAKER-LONGENECKER**
FAM. PUBL. FOR THE COMMITTEE, Repr. of 1902 ed.
Cloth--$50.00--Paper--$40.00--310pp F5159

658   - **LOOMIS**. DESC. OF JOSEPH **LOOMIS** IN AMER. & HIS ANTECEDENTS IN
THE OLD WORLD., by E.S. Loomis. Repr. of 1908 ed.
Cloth--$145.00--Paper--$135.00--859pp F5159

659   - **LOOS** FAMILY GENEALOGY, 1535-1958., by S.L. Bast. Repr. of 1959 ed.
Cloth--$47.00--Paper--$37.00--245pp F5159

660   - **LORD**. ANC. & DESC. OF LT. TOBIAS **LORD**., by C.E. Lord. Repr. of 1913 ed.
Cloth--$52.00--Paper--$42.00--263pp F5159

661   - **LORING** GEN., by C.H. Pope and K.P. Loring. Repr. of 1917 ed.
Cloth--$78.50--Paper--$68.50--443pp F5159

662   - **LOTT** FAM. IN AMER., INCL. ALLIED FAM. **CASSELL, DAVIS, GRAYBEAL, HARING, HEGEMAN, HOGG, KERLEY, PHILLIPS, THOMPSON** & OTHERS., by A. Phillips. Repr. of 1942 ed.
Paper--$29.00--179pp F5159

663   - GENEALOGY OF THE **LOUCKS** FAMILY, BEGINNING WITH JOHANN DIETRICH **LOUCKS** & HIS DESCENDANTS IN DIRECT LINE TO JOSEPH **LOUCK**, & ALL HIS KNOWN DESC. TO DATE, by E.M. McBrier. Repr. of 1940 ed.
Cloth--$58.50--Paper--$48.50--22+295pp F5159

664   - **LOUD**. GEN. REC. OF THE DESC. OF CALEB **LOUD**, CHILD OF FRANCIS **LOUD** & ONNER PRINCE **LOUD**., by W. Loud. Repr. of 1889 ed.
Paper--$14.50--83pp F5159

665   - **LOVE**. GEN. OF THOMAS **LOVE** OF NO. CAROLINA & TENN. & HIS BROTHERS, ROBERT & JAMES., by R.A. Love. Repr. of 1955 ed.
Paper--$10.00--47pp F5159

666   - THE **LOWRYS**; ROBERT & MARY **LOWRY** & CHILDREN (6 GEN.)., by L. Lowry and H. Lowry. Repr. of 1921 ed.
Paper--$20.00--118pp F5159

667   - **LUCAS** GENEALOGY., by A. Kemp. Repr. of 1964 ed.
Cloth--$85.50--Paper--$75.50--495pp F5159

668   - **LUKIN**. GEN. NOTES & PEDIGREES OF THE **LOVEKYN-LUCKYN-LUKIN** FAM. IN ENG., by A.T. Tudor-Craig. Repr. of 1932 ed.
Paper--$11.50--58pp F5159

669   - **LUNT**. ANCESTRY OF ABEL **LUNT**, 1769-1806, OF NEWBURY, MA., by W.G. Davis. Repr. of 1963 ed.
Cloth--$52.00--Paper--$42.00--269pp F5159

670   - **LYNDE**. THE DIARIES OF BENJ. **LUNDE** & OF BENJ. **LYNDE**, JR., WITH AN APPENDIX, ED. BY F. OLIVER., by   Repr. of 1880 ed.
Cloth--$50.00--Paper--$40.00--267pp F5159

671   - **LYON** MEM.: FAMS. OF CONN. & N.J., INCL. RECS. OF THE IMMIGR. RICHARD **LYON** OF FAIRFIELD, HENRY **LYON** OF FAIRFIELD., by   Lyon, Johnson & Lyons. Repr. of 1907 ed.
Cloth--$68.00--Paper--$58.00--453pp F5159

672   - **MACK** GEN.; THE DESC. OF JOHN **MACK** OF LYME, CONN., WITH APPENDIX CONTAINING GEN. OF ALLIED FAM., ETC., by S. Martin. Repr. of 1903 ed.
Cloth--$229.00--Paper--$219.00--1788pp F5159

673   - **MACKENZIE**. HIST. OF THE **MACKENZIES**, WITH GEN. OF THE PRINCIPAL FAMS. OF THE NAME. REV. ED., by A. MacKenzie. Repr. of 1904 ed.
Cloth--$93.00--Paper--$83.00--663pp F5159

674   - **MACLAY** MEMORIAL, SKETCHING THE LIN., LIFE & OBSEQUIES OF HON. WM. B. **MACLAY**, by O.B. Judd. Repr. of 1884 ed.
Paper--$28.75--192pp F5159

675   - **MACOMBER**. THE **MACOMBER** GEN., by E.S. Stackpole. Repr. of ed.
        Cloth--$48.00--Paper--$38.00--252pp F5159

676   - GEN. OF THE **MACY** FAMILY, 1635-1868., by S. Macy. Repr. of 1868 ed.
        Cloth--$68.00--Paper--$58.00--457pp F5159

677   - **MAGILL-MCGILL** GENEALOGY, FROM THE 1700'S., by Eunice Parr McGill.
        Repr. of 1963 ed.
        Paper--$11.50--57pp F5159

678   - **MAIN-MAINE** FAM. OF STONINGTON, CONN., by A. Aspinall. Repr. of 1911
        ed.
        Paper--$12.00--57pp F5159

679   - **MAKEPEACE**. THE GEN. OF THE **MAKEPEACE** FAMS. IN THE U.S.,
        1637-1857., by W. Makepeace. Repr. of 1858 ed.
        Paper--$15.00--107pp F5159

680   - **MALBONE**. GODFREY **MALBONE'S** ARM. SILVER, DATA ON THE
        MALBONE FAM. OF NEWPORT, RI., by R. Bowen. Repr. of 1950 ed.
        Paper--$6.00--27pp F5159

681   - **MALLINSON**. TWO FOUNDERS OF ROWLEY, MASS., **JEWETT** &
        MALLINSON., by T.E. Hazen. Repr. of 1940 ed.
        Paper--$4.50--15pp F5159

682   - THE DESC. OF RICHARD & GILLIAN **MANSFIELD**, WHO SETTLED IN NEW
        HAVEN, 1639, WITH SKETCHES OF SOME OF THE MOST DISTINGUISHED &
        CONNECTIONS OF OTHER NAMES, by H. Mansfield. Repr. of 1885 ed.
        Paper--$28.00--198pp F5159

683   - **MARGESON** AND RELATED FAMS., by H.M. Spinney. Repr. of ed.
        Paper--$18.00--95pp F5159

684   - **MARIS** FAM. IN THE U.S. REC. OF THE DESC. OF GEO. & ALICE **MARIS**,
        1683-1885., by G. Maris and A.M. Maris. Repr. of 1885 ed.
        Cloth--$46.00--Paper--$36.00--279+33pp F5159

685   - **MARSH**. GEN. OF THE FAM. OF GEO. **MARSH**, WHO CAME FROM ENG. IN
        1635 & SETTLED IN HINGHAM, MA., by E.J. Marsh. Repr. of 1887 ed.
        Cloth--$40.00--Paper--$30.00--229pp F5159

686   - **MARSHALL**. FAM. RECORD, WITH **HASKELL, BOUTWELL, BARRETT**,
        & ALLIED FAM., by F.B. Kingsbury. Repr. of 1913 ed.
        Paper--$15.00--103pp F5159

687   - **MARTIN** GENEALOGY. DESC. OF LT. SAMUEL **MARTIN** OF
        WETHERSFIELD, CT., SHOWING DESC. FROM ROYALTY, by T.A. Hay. Repr. of
        1911 ed.
        Also giving brief hist. of, & desc. from, related col. fams. Vol. I of 1.
        Cloth--$56.50--Paper--$46.50--291pp F5159

688   - **MARVIN** FAM., EXTR. FROM GEN. NOTES OF N.Y. & NEW ENG. FAM., by S.V. Talcott. Repr. of 1883 ed.
Paper--$6.00--23pp F5159

689   - **MARVIN**. ENG. ANC. OF REINOLD & MATTHEW **MARVIN** OF HARTFORD, CONN., 1638., by W.T.R. Marvin. Repr. of 1900 ed.
Paper--$27.50--184pp F5159

690   - **MASON**. CAPT. JOHN **MASON**, FOUNDER OF NEW HAMPSHIRE...WITH LETTERS & OTHER HIST. DOCUMENTS, WITH A MEMOIR BY C.W. TUTTLE. Ed. by J.W. Dean, Repr. of 1887 ed.
Cloth--$84.50--Paper--$74.50--491pp F5159

691   - **MASON**. GEN. OF THE SAMPSON **MASON** FAM., by A.H. Mason. Repr. of 1902 ed.
Cloth--$47.00--Paper--$37.00--288pp F5159

692   - **MATHER**. LIN. OF REV. RICHARD **MATHER**., by H. Mather. Repr. of 1890 ed.
Cloth--$78.00--Paper--$68.00--540pp F5159

693   - **MATHESON**. HIST. OF THE **MATHESONS**, WITH GEN. OF THE VAR. BRANCHES (IN SCOTLAND)., by A. MacKenzie. Repr. of 1882 ed.
Paper--$15.00--72pp F5159

694   - **MATTESONS** IN AMER.: ORIG. RECORDS OF EARLY **MATTESON** PIONEERS., by P. Matteson. Repr. of 1960 ed.
Paper--$8.50--42pp F5159

695   - JOHN **MAULL** (1714-1753) OF LEWES, DELA.: A GEN. OF HIS DESC. IN ALL BRANCHES., by R.F. Bailey. Repr. of 1941 ed.
Cloth--$53.50--Paper--$43.50--241+39pp F5159

696   - **MAULSBY**. GEN. OF THE **MAULSBY** FAM. FOR FIVE GENERATIONS, 1699-1902., by C.M. Payne. Repr. of 1902 ed.
Paper--$20.00--147pp F5159

697   - **MAVERICK**. REMARKS ON THE **MAVERICK** FAM. & THE ANC. OF GOV. SIMON BRADSTREET., by I.J. Greenwood. Repr. of 1894 ed.
Paper--$4.00--8pp F5159

698   - **MAXSON** FAMILY OF R.I., by Johnson & Jones. Reprint.
Paper--$13.50--68pp F5159

699   - **MAXWELL** HISTORY & GENEALOGY, INCLUDING ALLIED FAMILIES., by Houston, Blaine & Mellette. Repr. of 1916 ed.
Cloth--$106.50--Paper--$96.50--642pp F5159

700   - **MAYER**. MEMOIR & GEN. OF THE MARYLAND & PENN. FAM. OF **MAYER**., by B. Mayer. Reprint.
Paper--$27.00--179pp F5159

701   - **MAYHUGH** OF VA. & KY., & ALLIED FAM., by M. Thompson. Repr. of 1957 ed.
Paper--$19.50--100pp F5159

702   - **MCCALL-TIDWELL** & ALLIED FAM., by E.T. McCall. Repr. of 1931 ed.
        Cloth--$109.00--Paper--$99.00--672pp F5159

703   - **MCCALLUM.** DAVID **MCCALLUM** & ISABEL SELLARS: THEIR
        ANTECEDENTS, DESCENDANTS & COLLATERAL RELATIVES., by L. Farrell
        and F.J.H. Hooker. Repr. of 1949 ed.
        Cloth--$47.50--Paper--$37.50--234pp F5159

704   -THOMAS **MCCARTY** OF NORTHAMPTON CO., PA. & SOME DESC. (IN
        LANCASTER FAM.)., by H. Lancaster. Repr. of 1902 ed.
        Paper--$12.50--63pp F5159

705   - **MCCLAUGHRY.** GEN. OF THE **MACCLAUGHRY** FAMILY: A SCOT- IRISH
        FAMILY FROM GALLOWAY, SCOTLAND, APPEARING IN IRELAND ABOUT
        1600, & EMIGR. TO N.Y. IN 1765., by C.C. McClaughry. Repr. of 1913 ed.
        Cloth--$81.00--Paper--$71.00--459pp F5159

706   - **MCCLUNG** GEN.; A GEN. & BIOGR. RECORD OF THE **MCCLUNG** FAM.
        FROM THE TIME OF THEIR EMIGRATION TO THE YEAR 1904., by W.
        McClung. Repr. of 1904 ed.
        Paper--$44.00--296pp F5159

707   - **MCCOY.** WM. **MCCOY** & HIS DESC. ALSO A HIST. OF THE FAM. OF
        ALEXANDER **MCCOY**, by L. McCoy. Repr. of 1904 ed.
        Cloth--$41.50--Paper--$31.50--204pp F5159

708   - **MCCUTCHEON (CUTCHEON)** FAM. RECORDS. ALLIED FAM. OF
        MCCLARY, TRIPP, BROWN & CRITCHETT, by F. McKee. Repr. of 1931 ed.
        Cloth--$65.00--Paper--$55.00--352pp F5159

709   - **MCFARLAN.** OUR KINDRED: **MACFARLAN & STERN** FAMS. OF
        CHESTER CO., PA. & NEW CASTLE CO., DELAWARE., by C. Stern. Repr. of 1885
        Paper--$24.00--179pp F5159

710   - GEN. HIST. OF THE **MCGAFFEY** FAM. INCL. ALSO THE **FELLOWS,
        ETHRIDGE & SHERMAN** FAMILIES., by G.W. McGaffey. Repr. of 1904 ed.
        Paper--$23.50--145pp F5159

711   - **MCGAVOCK** FAMILY. GEN. HIST. OF JAMES **MCGAVOCK** & HIS DESC.
        FROM 1760 TO 1903., by R. Gray. Repr. of 1903 ed.
        Paper--$24.00--180pp F5159

712   - **MCGUIRE** FAMILY IN VA. (IRISH ANC.)., by W.G. Stannard. Repr. of 1926 ed.
        Paper--$25.00--126pp F5159

713   - **MCINTIRE.** THE **MCINTIRE** FAM., DESC. OF MICUM **MECANTIRE** OF
        YORK CO., MAINE., by H.A. Davis. Repr. of 1939 ed.
        Cloth--$49.50--Paper--$39.50--251pp F5159

714   - DESC. OF MICUM **MCINTIRE**, A SCOTTISH HIGHLANDER DEPORTED BY
        CROMWELL & SETTLED AT YORK, ME. ABOUT 1668, by R.H. McIntire. Repr. of
        1940 ed.
        Paper--$23.50 .... F5159

715   - DESC. OF PHILIP **MCINTIRE**, A SCOTTISH HIGHLANDER DEPORTED BY CROMWELL & SETTLED AT READING, MA., ABOUT 1660., by R. McIntire. Repr. of 1941 ed.
Cloth--$42.50--Paper--$32.50--218pp F5159

716   - **MCKEAN**. GEN. OF THE **MCKEAN** FAM. OF PA., WITH BIOGR. OF THE HON. THOMAS **MCKEAN**, by R. Buchanan. Repr. of 1890 ed.
Paper--$37.00--288pp F5159

717   - **MCNAIR-MCNEAR & MCNEIR** GEN., by J.B. McNair. Repr. of 1923 ed.
Cloth--$58.50--Paper--$48.50--322pp F5159

718   - **MCNAIR** SUPPLEMENT TO ABOVE., by J.B. McNair. Repr. of 1928 ed.
Cloth--$62.25--Paper--$52.25--349pp F5159

719   - **MCNAIR-MCNEAR & MCNEIR** GEN., by J.B. McNair. Repr. of 1955 ed.
Cloth--$81.00--Paper--$71.00--457pp F5159

720   - **MCNAIR** SUPPLEMENT TO ABOVE., by J.B. McNair. Repr. of 1960 ed.
Cloth--$56.50--Paper--$46.50--314pp F5159

721   - **MCNARY** FAMILY, WITH FAMILY TREES & HIST., by Repr. of 1907 ed.
Cloth--$41.00--Paper--$31.00--236pp F5159

722   - **MCQUISTON - MCCUISTON - MCQUESTEN** FAMILIES, 1620-1937., by L.B. McQuiston. Repr. of 1937 ed.
Cloth--$119.00--Paper--$109.00--750pp F5159

723   - **MEAD**. HIST. & GEN. OF THE **MEAD** FAM., OF FAIRFIELD CO., CONN., EASTERN N.Y., WESTERN VT. & WESTERN PENN., FROM 1180-1900., by S.P. Mead. Repr. of 1901 ed.
Cloth--$85.00--Paper--$75.00--480pp F5159

724   - **MEAD**. INDEX TO ABOVE. (MAY BE ORDERED BOUND WITH ABOVE)., by Repr. of 1907 ed.
Paper--$12.00--73pp F5159

725   - **MEARS**. SOME DESC. OF JOHN & LUCY **(ROCKWELL) MEARS** OF WINDSOR, CONN., by H. Healy. Repr. of 1960 ed.
Paper--$22.50--116pp F5159

726   - **MERIVALE** FAMILY MEMORIALS., by A.W. Merivale. Repr. of 1884 ed.
Cloth--$62.00--Paper--$52.00--404pp F5159

727   - **MERIWETHER**. THE **MERIWETHERS** & THEIR CONNECTIONS. A FAMILY RECORD GIVING THE GEN. OF THE **MERIWETHERS** IN AMERICA., by L.H.A. Minor. Repr. of 1892 ed.
Paper--$24.00--180pp F5159

728   - **MERRILL**. JAMES **MERRILL** OF NEW GLOUCESTER & LEE, MAINE., by C.N. Sinnett. Repr. of ed.
Paper--$5.50--21pp F5159

729 - **MERRILL**. GEN. PUBL. IN 1864, AS APPENDIX TO HIS BOOK, *"MY WIFE & MY MOTHER; ANC. OF FRANCES E. **MERRILL** & NAOMI **HUMPHREY**"*., by H. Barbour. Repr. of 1885 ed.
Paper--$16.00--84pp F5159

730 - **MERRITT**. REVISED **MERRITT** REC., by D. Merritt. Repr. of 1916 ed.
Paper--$33.50--204pp F5159

731 - **MERROW**. HENRY **MERROW** OF READING, MASS. & HIS DESC. NAMED **MARROW, MARROW & MERRY**, by O.E. Merrow. Repr. of 1954 ed.
Cloth--$108.00--Paper--$98.00--659pp F5159

732 - MILES **MERWIN**, 1772-1859; HIS ANC. & DESC., by C.G. Newton. Repr. of 1903 ed.
Paper--$17.50--87pp F5159

733 - MILES **MERWIN**, 1623-1697, & ONE BRANCH OF HIS DESC., by C.G. Newton. Repr. of 1909 ed.
Paper--$19.00--105pp F5159

734 - **MESICK** GEN., by J.F. Mesick. Reprint.
Paper--$10.00--46pp F5159

735 - **MEYER-MOYER**. GEN. OF THE DESC. OF CHRISTIAN & HANS **MEYER** (**MOYER**) & OTHER PIONEERS., by A.J. Fretz. Repr. of 1896 ed.
Cloth--$115.00--Paper--$105.00--739pp F5159

736 - **MEYER**. GEN. OF THE **MEYER** FAMILY, by H. Meyer. Repr. of 1890 ed.
Paper--$19.50--131pp F5159

737 - GEN. OF THE **MICKLEY** FAMILY OF AMER., WITH BRIEF GEN. REC. OF THE **MICHELET** FAM. OF METZ, by M. Mickley. Repr. of 1893 ed.
     And some interesting & valuable correspondence, biogr. sketches, obits. & hist. memorabilia.
Paper--$27.50--182pp F5159

738 - **MIEDEMA**, HET **MIEDEMA**-BOEK ("THE **MIEDEMA** BOOK"); GENEALOGISH OVERZICHT VAN ALLE FRIESE GESLCHTEN **MIEDEMA**, DEEL I., by W.T. Vleer. Repr. of 1955 ed.
Paper--$15.00--96pp F5159

739 - **MILES**. ANNALS OF **MILES** ANC. IN PA. & STORY OF A FORGED WILL., by C.H. Banes. Repr. of 1895 ed.
Paper--$25.00--182pp F5159

740 - **MILLER** FAMILY: DESC. OF FRANK **MILLER**, WHO SETTLED IN WALDOBOROUGH, MASS. (NOW MAINE) IN 1753., by F.B. Miller. Repr. of 1934 ed.
Cloth--$47.00--Paper--$37.00--174pp F5159

741 - **MILLER**. THE **MILLERS** OF MILLERBURG & THEIR DESC., by J.B. Nicklin, Jr.. Repr. of 1923 ed.
Cloth--$89.50--Paper--$79.50--514pp F5159

742   - **MILLER**. ANC. OF SARAH **MILLER** OF ME., by W. Davis. Repr. of 1939 ed.
Paper--$17.50--93pp F5159

743   - **MILLIS** & ALLIED FAMILIES, by F. Millis. Repr. of 1944 ed.
Paper--$12.50--64pp F5159

744   - **MILLS**. FAM. OF CAPT. JOHN **MILLS** OF MEDWAY & SHERBURN, MA., &
AMHERST, NH., by W.C. Hill. Repr. of 1942 ed.
Paper--$21.00--136pp F5159

745   - **MINER**. ONE BRANCH OF THE **MINER** FAM., WITH EXTENSIVE NOTES
ON THE **WOOD, LOUNSBERRY, ROGERS** & 50 OTHER ALLIED FAM. OF
CONN. & L.I., by L.M. Selleck. Repr. of 1928 ed.
Cloth--$51.00--Paper--$41.00--275pp F5159

746   - **MOLYNEUX**. HIST., GEN., & BIOGR. OF THE **MOLYNEUX** FAM., by N.Z.
Molyneux. Repr. of 1904 ed.
Cloth--$68.00--Paper--$58.00--370pp F5159

747   - ORIGIN & HIST. OF THE **MONTGOMERYS**: COMTES DE **MONTGOMERY**,
PONTHIEU, ALENCON & LAMARCHE; EARLS OF **ARUNDEL**,
CHICHESTER, SHREWSBURY, ET AL., by B.G. de Montgomery. Repr. of ed.
    About fam. in Europe.
Cloth--$57.50--Paper--$47.50--303pp F5159

748   - **MONTGOMERY**. A GEN. HISTORY OF THE **MONTGOMERYS** & THEIR
DESCENDANTS., by D.B. Montgomery. Repr. of 1903 ed.
Cloth--$77.50--Paper--$67.50--436pp F5159

749   - **MONTGOMERY**. THE **MONTGOMERY** GEN. (DESC. OF ELIAS)., by C.G.
Hurlburt. Repr. of 1926 ed.
Paper--$13.50--66pp F5159

750   - **MOORE** AND ALLIED FAMS.: ANC. OF WM. HENRY **MOORE**., by L.E. de
Forst and A.L. de Forst. Repr. of 1938 ed.
Cloth--$103.00--Paper--$93.00--744pp F5159

751   - **MOORE**. ANCESTORS & DESCENDANTS OF ANDREW **MOORE**,
1612-1897., by J.A.M. Passmore. Repr. of 1897 ed.
Cloth--$189.00--Paper--$179.00--1599pp F5159

752   - **MOORE**. MEMORIAL OF RANSOM BALDWIN **MOORE** & ALLIED FAM., by
W.B. Towne. Repr. of 1920 ed.
Paper--$22.50--138pp F5159

753   - **MOORE**. ANCESTRY OF SHARPLESS & RACHEL **(ROBERTS) MOORE**,
WITH THEIR DIRECT ANC., TO & INCL. 36 FIRST OR IMMIGRANT ANC., by
B.M. Haines. Repr. of 1937 ed.
    With some old world pedigrees & origins & direct desc.
Cloth--$43.50--Paper--$33.50--214pp F5159

754   - **MORAN** FAMILY: 200 YEARS IN DETROIT., by J.B. Moran. Repr. of 1949 ed.
Paper--$28.00--152+32pp F5159

755   - MOREHOUSE.   ANC. & DESC. OF GERSHOM MOREHOUSE, JR., OF
REDDING, CONN., A CAPT. IN THE AMER. REV., by C. Morehouse. Repr. of ed.
Paper--$8.00--40pp F5159

756   - MORGAN. "LIMBUS PATRUM MORGANIAE AT GLAMORGANIAE": GEN.
OF THE OLDER FAMS. OF LORDSHIPS MORGAN & GLARMORGAN., by G.T.
Clark. Repr. of 1886 ed.
Cloth--$89.00--Paper--$79.00--620pp F5159

757   - A HIST. OF THAT BRANCH OF THE MORGAN FAM. BEGINNING WITH
JAMES OF NEW LONDON, THROUGH LINE OF COL. SAM'L & SYBIL
HUNTINGTON MORGAN OF WEATHERSFIELD,VT TO 1911. by C.W. Morgan.
Repr. of 1911 ed.
Paper--$15.00--93+7pp F5159

758   - MORRIS.   A GEN. & HIST. REG. OF THE DESC. OF EDW. MORRIS OF
ROXBURY, MASS., & WOODSTOCK, CONN., by J.F. Morris. Repr. of 1887 ed.
Cloth--$76.50--Paper--$66.50--423pp F5159

759   - MORRIS.   EPHRAIM & PAMELA (CONVERSE) MORRIS, THEIR ANC. &
DESC., by T.S. Morris. Repr. of 1894 ed.
Cloth--$41.00--Paper--$31.00--207pp F5159

760   - HIST. OF THE MORISON OR MORRISON FAMILY, by L.A. Morrison. Repr.
of 1880 ed.
    A complete hist. of most settlers of Londonderry, NH, of 1719 & their desc., with
gen. sketches, (also other N.H. Morisons), & branches of Morisons of Del., Pa., Va. &
Nova Scotia.
Cloth--$69.50--Paper--$59.50--468pp F5159

761   - MORTON.   MEM. RELATING TO THE ANC. & FAM. OF HON. LEVI
PARSONS MORTON, V.P. OF THE U.S. (1889-1893)., by J.G. Leach. Repr. of 1894
ed.
Cloth--$41.50--Paper--$31.50--198pp F5159

762   - MOUNT. HISTORY & GEN. RECORD OF THE MOUNT & FLIPPIN FAMS.,
by J.A. Mount. Reprint.
Paper--$21.00--120pp F5159

763   - MULFORD. GEN. OF FAM. OF MULFORD, by W.R. Mulford. Reprint.
Paper--$4.50--10pp F5159

764   - MUMFORD MEM.: BEING THE STORY OF THE NEW ENG. MUMFORDS
FROM THE YEAR 1655 TO THE PRESENT TIME., by J.G. Mumford. Repr. of 1900
ed.
Cloth--$52.00--Paper--$42.00--279pp F5159

765   - MUNDY. NICHOLAS MUNDY & DESC. WHO SETTLED IN N.J. IN 1665., by
E.F. Mundy. Repr. of 1907 ed.
Paper--$24.50--160pp F5159

766   - MUNSELL.   A GEN. OF THE MUNSELL FAM. (MUNSILL, MONSELL,
MAUNSELL) IN AMERICA., by F. Munsell. Repr. of 1884 ed.
Paper--$21.50--130pp F5159

767 - **MUNSEY-HOPKINS** GEN., BEING THE ANC. OF ANDREW CHAUNCEY **MUNSEY** & MARY JANE **MERRILL HOPKINS.**, by D.O.S. Lowell. Repr. of 1920 ed.
Cloth--$46.00--Paper--$36.00--233pp F5159

768 - **MURPHY** FAM.; GEN., HISTORY & BIOGRAPHY, by M.W. Downes. Repr. of 1909 ed.
With official stats. of the part played by members of this numerous fam. in the making & maintenance of this great Amer. republic.
Cloth--$67.50--Paper--$57.50--363pp F5159

769 - **MURRAY.** JONATHAN **MURRAY** OF E. GUILFORD, CONN., & SOME OF HIS DESC., by W.B. Murray. Repr. of 1948 ed.
Paper--$4.00--8pp F5159

770 - **MURRAY.** THE DESC. OF JONATHAN **MURRAY** OF E. GUILFORD, CONN., by W.B. Murray. Repr. of 1956 ed.
Cloth--$71.50--Paper--$61.50--385pp F5159

771 - **NASH.** FIFTY PURITAN ANC., 1628-1660; GEN. NOTES, 1560-1900., by E.T. Nash. Repr. of 1902 ed.
Paper--$23.00--194pp F5159

772 - **NAVARRE.** OR, RESEARCHES AFTER THE DESC. OF ROBERT **NAVARRE,** WHOSE ANC. ARE THE NOBLE BOURBONS OF FRANCE, by C. Denissen. Repr. of 1897 ed.
And some hist. notes on fams. intermarried with Navarres.
Cloth--$76.00--Paper--$66.00--418pp F5159

773 - ANC. OF JOSEPH **NEAL,** 1769-C.1835, OF LITCHFIELD, ME, INCL. **HALL, WHITE, ROGERS, TILDEN, TWISDEN, CLAPP, WRIGHT, FORD, HATCH & HOLBROOK** LINES FROM MA, by W.G. Davis. Repr. of 1945 ed.
Paper--$23.50--145pp F5159

774 - **NEEDHAM.** DESC. OF JOHN **NEEDHAM** OF BRAINTREE, MASS. & BOSTON 1669-75, 1675-89., by R.F. Needham. Repr. of 1934 ed.
Paper--$5.00--18pp F5159

775 - **NEEDHAM. NEEDHAMS** OF WALES, MASS., & STAFFORD, CONN., by G.O. Chapman. Repr. of 1942 ed.
Paper--$20.00--93pp F5159

776 - **NEFF** ADDENDA., by Repr. of 1899 ed.
Paper--$7.00--35pp F5159

777 - **NEFF.** A CHRONICLE, TOGETHER WITH A LITTLE ROMANCE, REGARDING RUDOLF & JACOB **NAF,** OF FRANKFORD, PENN., & THEIR DESC., by E.C. Neff. Repr. of 1886 ed.
Incl. an acct. of the **Neffs** in Switzerland & America.
Cloth--$65.50--Paper--$55.50--352pp F5159

778 - **NESBIT.** A GEN. OF THE **NESBIT, ROSS, PORTER, TAGGART** FAM. OF PENN., by B.T. Hartman. Repr. of 1929 ed.
Cloth--$46.00--Paper--$36.00--242pp F5159

779   - **NEVIUS.** JOANNES **NEVIUS**, SCHEPEN & 3RD SECRETARY OF NEW AMSTERDAM, & HIS DESC., 1627-1900, by A. Van Doren Honeyman. Repr. of 1900 ed.
Cloth--$109.00--Paper--$99.00--732pp F5159

780   - **NEWCOMB.** ANDREW **NEWCOMB**, 1618-1686, & HIS DESC.: A REV. ED. OF "GEN. MEM." OF THE **NEWCOMB** FAM. (1874)., by B.M. Newcomb. Repr. of 1923 ed.
Cloth--$154.50--Paper--$144.50--1021pp F5159

781   - **NORRIS.** LIN. & BIOGR. OF THE **NORRIS** FAM. IN AMER., FROM 1640 TO 1892., by L.A. Morrison. Repr. of 1892 ed.
Cloth--$41.00--Paper--$31.00--207pp F5159

782   - **NOURSE.** JAMES **NOURSE** & HIS DESC., by M.C.N. Lyle. Repr. of 1897 ed.
Paper--$22.50--167pp F5159

783   - **NOYES.** DESC. OF REV. WM. **NOYES**, B. ENG. 1568, IN DIRECT LINE TO LAVERNE **NOYES GIFFEM** & FRANCES **NOYES GIFFEN**, by Repr. of 1900 ed. Incl. allied families. **Stanton, Sanford, Thompson, Holdredge,** etc.
Paper--$16.50--115pp F5159

784   - GEN. OF THE **NYE** FAMILY, by G. Nye and F. Best, Ed. by D.F. Nye, Repr. of 1907 ed.
Cloth--$99.00--Paper--$89.00--704pp F5159

785   - **OBERHOLTZER.**   GEN.   REC.   OF   THE   DESC.   OF   MARTON **OBERHOLTZER,** WITH HIST. & BIOGR. SKETCHES., by A.J. Fretz. Repr. of 1903 ed.
Cloth--$43.00--Paper--$33.00--254pp F5159

786   - **ODELL** GENEALOGY IN THE US & CANADA (1635-1935); TEN GEN. IN AMER. IN DIRECT LINE., by M.A.L. Pool. Repr. of 1935 ed.
Paper--$21.00--123pp F5159

787   - **ODIORNE.** GEN. OF THE **ODIORNE** FAM., WITH NOTICES OF OTHER FAM. CONNECTED THEREWITH., by J.C. Odiorne. Repr. of 1875 ed.
Cloth--$43.00--Paper--$33.00--232pp F5159

788   - OGDEN. THE **OGDEN** FAM. IN AMER. (ELIZABETHTOWN BRANCH) & THEIR ENG. ANC. JOHN **OGDEN,** THE PILGRIM, & HIS DESC., 1640-1906; THEIR HIST., BIOGR. & GEN., by W.O. Wheeler. Repr. of 1907 ed.
Cloth--$89.50--Paper--$79.50--526pp F5159

789   - **OGLE.** THE ENGLISH ORIGIN OF JOHN **OGLE,** FIRST OF THE NAME IN DELAWARE., by F.H. Hibbard and S. Parks. Repr. of 1967 ed.
Paper--$9.50--47pp F5159

790   - **OPDYKE** GENEALOGY, CONTAINING THE **OPDYCK-OPDYCKE- UPDIKE** AMER. DESCENDANTS OF THE **WESEL & HOLLAND** FAMS., by C.W. Opdyke. Repr. of 1889 ed.
Cloth--$87.50--Paper--$77.50--499pp F5159

791 - **OSBORN**. GEN. OF **OSBORN** FAM., 1755-1891., by H. Runyan. Repr. of 1891 ed.
Paper--$4.50--11pp F5159

792 - **OTIS**. SOME OF THE DESC. OF EPHRAIM **OTIS** & RACHEL (**HERSEY**) **OTIS** OF SCITUATE, MASS., by R.L. Weis. Repr. of 1943 ed.
Paper--$15.00--74pp F5159

793 - **OWEN**. JOHN **OWEN** OF WINDSOR, CONN., & SOME DESC., by   Repr. of ed.
Paper--$6.50--31pp F5159

794 - **OWEN**. DESC. OF JOHN **OWEN** OF WINDSOR, CONN. (1622- 1699)., by R.D. Owen. Repr. of 1941 ed.
Cloth--$93.00--Paper--$83.00--535pp F5159

795 - GEN. OF THE **PAGE** FAM. IN VA.; ALSO A CONDENSED ACCT. OF THE **NELSON, WALKER, PENDLETON & RANDOLPH** FAM., WITH REF. TO...OTHER DISTINGUISHED FAMS. IN VA., by R.C.M. Page. Repr. of 1893 ed.
Cloth--$46.00--Paper--$36.00--275pp F5159

796 - **PAGE**. WISCONSIN **PAGE** PIONEERS & KINFOLK., by   Turner, Turner & Sayre. Repr. of 1953 ed.
Cloth--$84.50--Paper--$74.50--485pp F5159

797 - **PAGE**.   THE FAMILY OF JOHN **PAGE** OF HAVERHILL, MASS.: A COMPREHENSIVE GEN. FROM 1614 TO 1977, by Lynn Case and Page Sanderson. Repr. of 1978 ed.
Paper--$37.50--250pp F5159

798 - **PAINE**. HIST. OF SAMUEL **PAINE**, JR., 1778-1861, & HIS WIFE, PAMELA **CHASE PAINE**, 1780-1856, RANDOLPH, VT., & THEIR ANC. & DESC., by A. Paine. Repr. of 1923 ed.
Cloth--$45.00--Paper--$35.00--218pp F5159

799 - **PALMER-TRIMBLE**. GEN. RECORD OF THE DESC. OF JOHN & MARY **PALMER** OF CONCORD, CHESTER (NOW DELAWARE) CO., PA., by L. Palmer. Repr. of 1910 ed.
In two divisions. **PALMER** div., embracing also the surnames **Almond, Arment, Baker**...& others. **TRIMBLE** div.: A gen. rec. of desc. of Wm. & Ann **Trimble** of Concord Co., & James & Mary **Trimble** of Chester Co., & others. 725p + 398p.
Palmer Div.: $117.00 hardcover; $107.00 paper.
Trimble Div.: $69.50 hardcover; $59.50 paper.
Special Price for Complete book: Cloth--$159.50 --Paper--$149.50 . ... F5159

800 - BRIEF GEN. HIST. OF THE ANC. & DESC. OF DEA. STEPHEN **PALMER** OF CANDIA, NH, by F. Palmer. Repr. of 1886 ed.
With some acct. of other lines of desc. from Thomas **Palmer**, a founder of Rowley, Ma., 1635.
Paper--$20.00--106pp F5159

801 - **PARDEE**. THE **PARDEE** GEN., by D.L. Jacobus. Repr. of 1927 ed.
Cloth--$115.00--Paper--$105.00--701pp F5159

802   - **PARKE**. SUPPL. TO THE **PARKE** FAMS. OF CONN., by F.S. Parks. Repr. of 1934 ed.
Paper--$19.00--97pp F5159

803   - GEN. & BIOGR. NOTES OF JOHN **PARKER** OF LEXINGTON & HIS DESC., SHOWING HIS EARLIER ANC. IN AMER. FROM DEA. THOMAS **OARKER** OF READING, MA, FROM 1635-1893, by T. Parker. Repr. of 1893 ed.
Cloth--$78.00--Paper--$68.00--528pp F5159

804   - **PARKER**. HISTORY OF PETER **PARKER** & SARAH **RUGGLES** OF ROXBURY, MASS., & THEIR ANC. & DES., by J.W. Linzee. Repr. of 1913 ed.
Cloth--$99.50--Paper--$89.50--609pp F5159

805   - **PARLEE** & RELATED FAMILIES., by Helen Spinney. Repr. of ed.
Paper--$15.00--69+34pp F5159

806   - **PARRISH** FAMILY, INCL. THE ALLIED FAMILIES OF **BELT, BOYD, COLE-MALONE, CLOKEY, GARRETT, MERRYMAN, PARSONS, PRICE & TIPTON**, by Boyd & Gottschalk. Repr. of 1935 ed.
Cloth--$73.00--Paper--$63.00--413pp F5159

807   - **PARRISH**. A COMP. OF THE AVAILABLE RECORDS COVERING DIRECT DESC. OF HENRY, JOEL, ANSEL & ABSOLOM, SONS OF HENRY **PARRISH** (1740), by J.T. Parrish. Repr. of 1948 ed.
     And grandsons of Joel **Parrish** (1700); also desc. of Henry Jackson **Parrish**.
Cloth--$74.00--Paper--$64.00--410pp F5159

808   - **PARSHALL**. HIST. OF THE **PARSHALL** FAM., 1066 TO THE CLOSE OF THE 19TH CENT., by J.C. Parshall. Repr. of 1903 ed.
Cloth--$51.00--Paper--$41.00--309pp F5159

809   - **PATTEN**. ANC. OF JAMES **PATTEN** OF KENNEBUNKPORT, MAINE., by W.G. Davis. Repr. of 1941 ed.
Paper--$22.50--113pp F5159

810   - **PATTERSON**. GEN. OF THE **PATTERSON, WHEAT & HEARN** FAMS., by R.E.H. Randle. Repr. of 1926 ed.
Cloth--$51.00--Paper--$41.00--261pp F5159

811   - **PAUL**. ANC. OF KATHARINE **CHOATE PAUL**, by E.J. Paul. Repr. of 1914 ed.
Cloth--$70.00--Paper--$60.00--386pp F5159

812   - **PAXTON**. THE **PAXTONS**: THEIR ORIGIN IN SCOTLAND & MIGR. THROUGH ENG. & IRELAND TO THE COL. OF PA., WHENCE THEY MOVED SOUTH & WEST., by W. Paxton. Repr. of 1903 ed.
Paper--$76.50--485pp F5159

813   - **PAYNE**. THE **PAYNES** OF HAMILTON: A GEN. & BIOGR. RECORD., by A.F.P. White. Repr. of 1912 ed.
Cloth--$49.50--Paper--$39.50--245pp F5159

814   - **PAYNE**. THOMAS **PAYNE** OF SALEM & HIS DESC., THE SALEM BRANCH OF THE **PAINE** FAM., by N.E. Paine. Repr. of 1928 ed.
Paper--$27.50--184pp F5159

815   - PEARSALL. HIST. & GEN. OF THE PEARSALL FAM. IN ENG. & AMER. , by
        C.E. Pearsall. Repr. of 1928 ed.
            3 Vols. SPECIAL PRICE FOR THE SET: $275.00 HARDCOVER; $250.00
        PAPER.
        Cloth--$99.00/Vol.--Paper--$89.00/Vol.--1806pp F5159

816   - PEARSON. CRISPIN PEARSON OF BUCKS CO., PA., 1748- 1806, by A.P.
        Darrow D. Ed. by W.C. Armstrong, Repr. of 1932 ed.
        Paper--$25.00--166pp F5159

817   - PEASE. GEN.-HIST. REC. OF DESC. OF JOHN PEASE, SR., LAST OF
        ENFIELD, CT., by Fiske & Pease. Repr. of 1869 ed.
        Cloth--$72.50--Paper--$62.50--401pp F5159

818   - PEASE. THE EARLY HIST. OF THE PEASE FAM. IN AMER., by A.S. Pease.
        Repr. of 1869 ed.
        Paper--$18.50--96pp F5159

819   - PECKHAM GENEALOGY.   ENG. ANC. & AMER. DESC. OF JOHN
        PECKHAM OF NEWPORT, RI, 1630., by S. Peckham. Repr. of 1922 ed.
        Cloth--$101.00--Paper--$91.00--602pp F5159

820   - PEIRCE. SOLOMON PIERCE FAM. GEN., WITH A REC. OF HIS DESC.,
        ALSO AN APP. WITH THE ANC. OF SOLOMON & HIS WIFE, AMITY
        FESSENDEN, by M Bailey. Repr. of 1912 ed.
        Paper--$28.50--190pp F5159

821   - PENGRY. A GEN. RECORD OF THE DESC. OF MOSES PENGRY OF
        IPSWICH, MASS., by W.M. Pingry. Repr. of 1881 ed.
        Paper--$28.00--186pp F5159

822   - PEPPERRELL IN AMERICA, by C.H.C. Howard. Repr. of 1906 ed.
        Paper--$20.50--110pp F5159

823   - PERKINS FAM. OF CONN., by F.B. Perkins. Repr. of 1860 ed.
        Paper--$4.00--8pp F5159

824   - PERKINS. THE DESC. OF EDWARD PERKINS OF NEW HAVEN, CONN., by
        C.E. Perkins. Repr. of 1914 ed.
        Paper--$21.00--135pp F5159

825   - PERRY. OUR PERRY FAM. IN MAINE; ITS ANC. & DESC., by C.N. Sinnett.
        Repr. of 1911 ed.
        Paper--$19.00--127pp F5159

826   - PERRYS OF R.I. & TALES OF SILVER CREEK, THE BOSWORTH-PERRY
        HOMESTEAD., by C.B. Perry. Repr. of 1913 ed.
        Paper--$23.00--115pp F5159

827   - PERRY. INCOMPLETE HIST. OF THE DESC. OF JOHN PERRY OF
        LONDON, 1604-1955., by Bertram Adams. Repr. of 1955 ed.
        Cloth--$115.00--Paper--$105.00--738pp F5159

828   - **PETERS.**   CONRAD **PETERS** & WIFE, CLARA **SNIDOW**: THEIR DESCENDANTS & ANCESTRY., by O.E. Peters. Repr. of ed.
Cloth--$45.00--Paper--$35.00--229pp F5159

829   - HIST. & GEN. ACCT. OF THE **PETERSON** FAMILY, by W.H. Peterson and S.J. & C.E. Peterson. Repr. of 1926 ed.
     Gen. rec. & sketches of the desc. of Lawrens **Peterson** & Nancy **Jones-Peterson**, who planted the fam. tree in Amer. before the Rev. War.
Cloth--$69.00--Paper--$59.00--372pp F5159

830   - **PFEIFFER.**   GEN. OF DR. FRANCIS J. **PFEIFFER**, PHILA., PA. & DESC., 1734-1899., by E. Sellers. Repr. of 1899 ed.
Paper--$14.00--67pp F5159

831   - **PHINNEY** GEN.; BRIEF HIST. OF EBENEZER **PHINNEY** OF CAPE COD & HIS DESC., 1637-1947., by M.A. Phinney. Repr. of 1948 ed.
Paper--$22.00--146pp F5159

832   - **PICKERING** GEN.; ACCT. OF THE 1ST THREE GENERATIONS OF THE **PICKERING** FAM. OF SALEM, MA, & THE DESC. OF JOHN & SARAH (**BURRILL**) **PICKERING** OF THE 3RD GEN., by Ellery & Bowditch. Repr. of 1897 ed.
Cloth--$186.00--Paper--$176.00--1284pp F5159

833   - SEVEN **PIERCE** FAMILIES: RECORD OF BIRTHS, DEATHS & MARRIAGES OF THE FIRST SEVEN GENERATIONS OF **PIERCES** IN AMERICA, by H.C. Pierce. Repr. of 1936 ed.
     Including descendants of Abial **Peirce**.
Cloth--$67.50--Paper--$57.50--48+324pp F5159

834   - **PIERPONT** GEN. & CONNECTING LINES.   PARTICULARLY REV. JOHN **PIERPONT** OF HOLLIS ST. CHURCH, BOSTON., by M.P. Barnum and A.E. Boardman. Repr. of 1928 ed.
Paper--$8.50--42pp F5159

835   - **PILLSBURY.**   ANC. OF CHAS. STINSON **PILLSBURY** & JOHN SARGENT **PILLSBURY**., by M.L. Holman. Repr. of 1938 ed.
Cloth--$192.00--Paper--$182.00--1212pp F5159

836   - GEN. OF ELISHA **PIPER**, OF PARSONFIELD, ME., & HIS DESC., INCL. PORTIONS OF OTHER REL. FAM. & AN APPENDIX CONT. THE GEN. OF ASA **PIPER** OF BOSTON, by H. Piper. Repr. of 1889 ed.
     An appendix cont. the gen. of Stephen **Piper** of Newfield, Me. & their immediate desc., from 1630 to 1889.
Paper--$17.50--121pp F5159

837   - **PLANT.** THE HOUSE OF **PLANT** OF MACON, GA., WITH GENEALOGIES & HIST. NOTES., by G.S. Dickerman. Repr. of 1900 ed.
Cloth--$43.50--Paper--$33.50--259pp F5159

838   - **PLATT** LIN. A GEN. RESEARCH & RECORD., by G. Platt. Repr. of 1891 ed.
Cloth--$61.50--Paper--$51.50--398pp F5159

839   - **PLIMPTON**. A GEN. & HIST. NOTICES OF THE FAM. OF **PLIMPTON** OR
       PLYMPTON IN AMER., & OF **PLUMPTON** IN ENG., by L.B. Chase. Repr. of
       1884 ed.
       Cloth--$42.00--Paper--$32.00--240pp F5159

840   - **PLOWMAN**. REGISTER OF **PLOWMANS** IN AMER....& EXTR. FROM ENG.
       & AMER. RECORDS., by B.H.F. Plowman. Repr. of 1901 ed.
       Paper--$17.50--90pp F5159

841   - **PLUMER**. GEN. FRANCIS **PLUMER**, WHO SETTLED AT NEWBURY,
       MASS., & SOME DESC., by S. Perley. Repr. of 1917 ed.
       Cloth--$49.00--Paper--$39.00--259pp F5159

842   - **PLUMMER**. GEN. RECORD OF COMPILER'S BRANCH OF **PLUMMER**
       FAM., by J.P. Thurston. Repr. of 1885 ed.
       Paper--$5.00--22pp F5159

843   - ORIGIN OF THE EARLY HIST. OF THE FAMS. OF **POE**, WITH FULL
       PEDIGREES OF THE IRISH BRANCH OF THE FAMS. & A DISCUSSION OF THE
       TRUE ANC. OF EDGAR ALLEN **POE**, by E.T. Bewley. Repr. of 1906 ed.
       Paper--$16.00--102pp F5159

844   - **POPE**. NOTICE OF SOME OF THE DESC. OF JOSEPH **POPE** OF SALEM., by
       H. Wheatland. Reprint.
       Paper--$4.50--14pp F5159

845   - **PORTER**. DESC. OF JOHN **PORTER** OF WINDSOR, CT., 1635-9,   by H.P.
       Andrews. Repr. of 1893 ed.
          2 Vol. SPECIAL PRICE FOR THE SET: $125.00 HARDCOVER; $105.00
       PAPER.
       Cloth--$66.00/Vol.--Paper--$56.00/Vol.--436 & 451p F5159

846   - **PORTER**. THE DESC. OF MOSES & SARAH **KILHAM PORTER** OF
       PAWLET, VT., WITH SOME NOTICE OF THEIR ANC., by J.S. Lawrence. Repr. of
       1910 ed.
       Paper--$26.50--203pp F5159

847   - **POTTER**. GEN. OF THE **POTTER** FAMS. & THEIR DESC. IN AMER., WITH
       HIST. & BIOGR SKETCHES., by C.W. Potter. Repr. of 1888 ed.
       Cloth--$48.00--Paper--$38.00--300pp F5159

848   - **POTTS**. OUR FAMILY RECORD., by T.M. Potts. Repr. of 1895 ed.
       Cloth--$64.00--Paper--$54.00--434pp F5159

849   - HIST. COLL. RELATING TO THE **POTTS** FAM. IN GT. BRIT. & AMER.,
       WITH AN HIST-GEN. OF THE DESC. OF DAVID **POTTS**, AN EARLY
       ANGLO-WELSH SETTLER OF PA., by T.M. Potts. Repr. of 1901 ed.
       Cloth--$104.50--Paper--$94.50--735pp F5159

850   - **POUND & KESTER** FAM. AN ACCT. OF THE ANC. OF JOHN **POUND** (B.
       1735) & WM. **KESTER** (B. 1733) & A GEN. RECORD OF ALL THEIR DESC., by
       J.E. Hunt. Repr. of 1904 ed.
       Cloth--$104.00--Paper--$94.00--628pp F5159

851 - **POWELL**. AUTHENTIC GEN. MEM'L. HIST. OF PHILIP **POWELL** OF MIFFLIN CO., PA. & HIS DESC. & OTHERS., by J. Powell. Repr. of 1880 ed. Cloth--$67.00--Paper--$57.00--447pp F5159

852 - **POWERS-BANKS** ANC. CHARLES **POWERS**, 1819-1871, & HIS WIFE, LYDIA ANN **BANKS**, 1829-1919., by W. Powers. Repr. of 1921 ed. Cloth--$58.75--Paper--$48.75--325pp F5159

853 - **PRATT**. A COLL. OF SOME FACTS ABOUT SOME OF THE DESC. OF JOHN **PRATT** OF DORCHESTER, MA., T.S. N.D., by Repr. of ed. Paper--$7.50--37pp F5159

854 - **PRESBREY**. WM. **PRESBREY** OF LONDON, ENG., & TAUNTON, MASS., & HIS DESC., 1690-1918., by J.W. Presby. Repr. of 1918 ed. Paper--$22.50--151pp F5159

855 - **PRESTON**. MEM. OF THE **PRESTON** FAM., by O. Brown. Repr. of 1842 ed. Paper--$5.00--16pp F5159

856 - **PRESTON**. MEM. OF THE **PRESTON** FAM., by O. Brown. Repr. of 1864 ed. Paper--$5.50--26pp F5159

857 - **PRESTON**. DESCENDANTS OF ROGER **PRESTON** OF IPSWICH & SALEM VILLAGE., by C.H. Preston. Repr. of 1931 ed. Cloth--$66.00--Paper--$56.00--355pp F5159

858 - **PRICE**. A GEN. OF THE DESC. OF REV. JACOB **PRICE**, EVANGELIST-PIONEER., by G.F.P. Wanger. Repr. of 1926 ed. Cloth--$134.50--Paper--$124.50--832pp F5159

859 - **PRINCE**. THE GEN. OF THE **PRINCE** FAM. FROM 1660 TO 1899., by F.A. Prince. Repr. of 1899 ed. Paper--$23.00--153pp F5159

860 - **PRIOR**. A LITTLE INFO. ON THE **PRIOR-PRYOR** FAM., by H.E. Pryor. Reprint. Paper--$12.50--58pp F5159

861 - **PROCTOR**. A GEN. OF THE DESC. OF ROBERT **PROCTOR** OF CONCORD & CHELMSFORD, MA., WITH NOTES OF SOME CONNECTED FAM., by Mr. & Mrs. W.L. Proctor. Repr. of 1898 ed. Cloth--$56.50--Paper--$46.50--315pp F5159

862 - **PROUTY (PROUTE)** GEN., by C.H. Pope. Repr. of 1910 ed. Paper--$32.00--247pp F5159

863 - **PROVOST**. BIOGR. & GEN. NOTES OF THE **PROVOST** FAM. FROM 1545-1895., by A.J. Provost. Repr. of 1895 ed. Paper--$20.00--147pp F5159

864 - **PRUDDEN**. PETER **PRUDDEN**: A STORY OF HIS LIFE AT NEW HAVEN & MILFORD, CONN., WITH THE GEN. OF SOME OF HIS DESC., by L.E. Prudden. Repr. of 1901 ed. Paper--$25.00--169pp F5159

865   - **PUCKETT.   PUCKETT** POINTS: FAM. OF RICHARD **PUCKETT** OF
       LUNENBURG CO., VA., by J.D. Gallaway. Repr. of 1931 ed.
       Paper--$8.00--39pp F5159

866   - A TRIBUTE TO THE MEM. OF JOHN **PUNCHARD**; A SERMON PREACHED
       AT HIS FUNERAL, FEB. 16, 1857, & AN APPENDIX CONTAINING THE GEN. OF
       THE **PUNCHARD** FAMILY, by S.M. Worcester. Repr. of 1857 ed.
       Paper--$14.00--69pp F5159

867   - **PURDY.   ALLIED FAMS. OF PURDY, FAUCONNIER (FALCONER),
       ARCHER & PERRIN,** by A.F. Perrin and M.F.P. Meeker. Repr. of 1911 ed.
       Paper--$16.50--114pp F5159

868   - **PUTNAM.** COLONIAL **PUTNAM** FAMS. OF THE PROVINCE OF S. CAROL.,
       by C.P. Mehringer. Repr. of ed.
       Paper--$4.00--7pp F5159

869   - THE **PUTNAM** LINEAGE, by E. Putnam. Repr. of 1907 ed.
          Hist.- gen. notes concerning the **Puttenham** fam. in Eng., with lines of royal desc., &
       the anc. of John **Putnam** of Salem & desc. through five gen., with some acct. of other
       Putnam fams. & the **Putnams** of the Mohawk Val.
       Cloth--$61.00--Paper--$51.00--400pp F5159

870   - **PUTNAM.** HIST. OF THE **PUTNAM** FAM. IN ENG. & AMER. (INCL.
       "*PUTNAM LEAFLETS*")., by E. Putnam. Repr. of 1891 ed.
       Cloth--$109.00--Paper--$99.00--720pp F5159

871   - **QUACKENBUSH** FAM., EXTR. FROM GEN. NOTES OF N.Y. & NEW ENG.
       FAM., by S.V. Talcott. Repr. of 1883 ed.
       Paper--$6.00--28pp F5159

872   - **QUICK.** GEN. OF THE **QUICK** FAM. IN AMERICA (1625- 1924)., by A.C.
       Quick. Repr. of 1942 ed.
       Cloth--$87.50--Paper--$77.50--507pp F5159

873   - **RANKIN.** THE **RANKIN & WHARTON** FAM. & THEIR GEN., by S.M. Rankin.
       Repr. of 1931 ed.
       Cloth--$54.00--Paper--$44.00--295pp F5159

874   - **RATHBONE** GEN. A COMPLETE HIST. OF THE **RATHBONE** FAM., FROM
       1574 TO DATE., by J.C. Cooley. Repr. of 1898 ed.
       Cloth--$114.00--Paper--$104.00--827pp F5159

875   - **RAVENEL** RECORDS.   HIST. & GEN. OF THE HUGUENOT FAM. OF
       RAVENEL, OF S.C., by H.E. Ravanel. Repr. of 1898 ed.
          With some incidental acct. of the Parish of St Johns Berkeley, their principal
       location.
       Cloth--$46.00--Paper--$36.00--279pp F5159

876   - **RAWLE.** RECORDS OF THE **RAWLE** FAM., COLL. FROM THE NAT'L.
       ARCHIVES, PARISH REG. & OTHER SOURCES., by E.J. Rawle. Repr. of 1898 ed.
       Cloth--$53.00--Paper--$43.00--336pp F5159

877 - **RAYMOND** GEN. DESC. OF JOHN & WM. **RAYMOND.**, by S.E. **Raymond** and
L.H. Raymond. Repr. of 1972 ed.
Cloth--$139.00--Paper--$129.00--886pp F5159

878 - **READ.** RECORD OF THE **READES** OF BARTON COURT, BERKSHIRE,
WITH A SHORT PRECIS OF OTHER LINES OF THE NAME., by C. Reade. Repr. of
1899 ed.
Paper--$23.50--148pp F5159

879 - **READ.** ALLIED FAMILIES OF **READ, CORBIN, LUTTRELL, & BYWATERS**
OF CULPEPER CO., VA., by A.M. Prichard. Repr. of 1930 ed.
Cloth--$56.00--Paper--$46.00--292pp F5159

880 - **REED** GENEALOGY., by J.M. Seaver. Repr. of ed.
Paper--$13.00--62pp F5159

881 - **REED** DESC. 13 GEN., INCL. THE ANC. & DESC. OF PAUL **REED**, 1605-1955.
ALSO OTHER DESC. OF HIS IMMIG. ANC. WM. **READE**, B. 1609, ENG., by B.B.
Aldridge. Repr. of 1955 ed.
Paper--$23.50--139pp F5159

882 - HIST. & GEN. OF THE **REED** FAM.: JOHANN PHILIB **RIED, RIETH, RITT,
RUDT**, ETC., IN EUROPE & AMERICA, by W.H. Reed. Repr. of 1929 ed.
      An early settler of Salford Twp., (New Goshenhoppen, Phila. Co., Pa.).
Cloth--$91.50--Paper--$81.50--529pp F5159

883 - **REMICK.** GEN. COMP. FROM THE MSS. OF LT. OLIVER **PHILBRICK
REMICK** FOR THE MAINE HIST. SOC., by W.L. Holman. Repr. of 1933 ed.
Cloth--$44.50--Paper--$34.50--211pp F5159

884 - **REQUA.** THE FAM. OF **REQUA**, 1678-1898., by A.C. Requa. Repr. of 1898 ed.
Paper--$15.00--102pp F5159

885 - **RESSEGUIE** FAMILY. A HIST. & GEN. REC. OF ALEXANDER **RESSEGUIE**
OF NORWALK, CT., & FOUR GEN. OF HIS DESC., by J.E. Morris. Repr. of 1888
ed.
Paper--$19.50--99pp F5159

886 - **REX.** GEORGE **REX** GEN. ANC. & DESC. OF GEORGE **REX**, FIRST OF
ENG. TO PENNA. IN 1771., by L.F. Rex. Repr. of 1933 ed.
Cloth--$41.50--Paper--$31.50--192pp F5159

887 - THE **RENNOLDS-REYNOLDS** FAM. OF ENG. & VIRGINIA, 1530-1948,
BEING THE HIST. OF CHRISTOPHER **REYNOLDS** OF CO. KENT, ENG. & HIS
DESC. IN VA., ETC, by S.F. Tillman. Repr. of 1948 ed.
Cloth--$49.50--Paper--$39.50--255pp F5159

888 - **REYNOLDS.** REPORTS OF **REYNOLDS** FAM. ASSOC., INCL. GEN. NOTES.,
by   Repr. of 1923 ed.
Paper--$16.00--117pp F5159

889 - **RICE.** "WE SOUGHT THE WILDERNESS" (MEMOIR OF SOME DESC. OF
DEA. EDMUND **RICE**)., by C.S. Rice. Repr. of 1949 ed.
Cloth--$49.50--Paper--$39.50--257pp F5159

890   - **RICH.** GEN. DESC. OF JONATHAN **RICH.**, by G. Rich. Repr. of 1892 ed.
Paper--$8.00--39pp F5159

891   - **RICHARDS.** DESC. OF THOMAS **RICHARDS** OF DORCHESTER, MASS., B.
CA. 1590. V. III OF "GEN. REG. OF SEVERAL ANCIENT PURITANS"., by A.
Morse. Repr. of 1861 ed.
Cloth--$48.50--Paper--$38.50--243pp F5159

892   - **RICHARDSON** MEM. SUPPL., by I. Richardson and F. Richardson. Repr. of 1898
ed.
Paper--$7.00--34pp F5159

893   - **RICHARDSON.** THOMAS **RICHARDSON** OF S. SHIELDS, DURHAM CO.,
ENG. & DESC. IN THE USA., by M. Seaman. Repr. of 1929 ed.
Cloth--$46.00--Paper--$36.00--241pp F5159

894   - **RICKETSON.** WILLIAM **RICKETSON** & HIS DESC., VOL. 2., by G.W. Edes.
Repr. of 1932 ed.
Cloth--$107.50--Paper--$97.50--658pp F5159

895   - **RING.** THE GEN. OF THE DESC. OF JERE FOSTER **RING** & PHEBE **ELLIS**
OF WELD, MAINE., by H.P. Ring. Repr. of 1931 ed.
Paper--$8.50--43pp F5159

896   - **RISLEY** FAM. HIST., INCL. RECORDS OF SOME OF THE EARLY ENG.
RISLEYS; A GEN. OF THE DESC. OF RICHARD **RISLEY** (1633) & (1636)., by
E.H. Risley. Repr. of 1909 ed.
Cloth--$50.00--Paper--$40.00--318pp F5159

897   - **RIVES.** RELIQUES OF THE **RIVES (RYVES)**, BEING HIST. & GEN. NOTES
OF THE ANCIENT FAM. OF **RYVES** OF CO. DORSET & THE **RIVES** OF VA., by
J.R. Childs. Repr. of 1929 ed.
Cloth--$119.00--Paper--$109.00--780pp F5159

898   - **RIXEY** GEN., WITH REF. TO THE **MOREHEAD, HUNTON, GIBBS, HALL,
THOMAS, JONES, LEWIS, CHANCELLOR, PENDLETON** & OTHER ALLIED
FAM., by R. Rixey. Repr. of 1933 ed.
Cloth--$78.00--Paper--$68.00--436pp F5159

899   - **ROACH, ROBERTS, RIDGEWAY** & ALLIED FAMILIES., by M.R. Fair. Repr.
of 1951 ed.
Paper--$41.50--258pp F5159

900   - **ROARKS** OF IRELAND & PEDIGREE OF NATHAN **ROARK** FAM. IN U.S., by
M.I. Roark. Repr. of 1950 ed.
Paper--$13.00--64pp F5159

901   - **ROBARDS.** HIST. OF THE **ROBARDS** FAM., by B. Farrior. Repr. of 1959 ed.
Paper--$15.00--74pp F5159

902   - **ROBBINS.** HIST. OF THE **ROBBINS** FAM. OF WALPOLE, MASS.: DESC. OF
WILLIAM & PRISCILLA **ROBBINS.**, by D.W. Robbins. Repr. of 1949 ed.
Cloth--$53.50--Paper--$43.50--60+221pp F5159

903   - THOMAS **ROBERTS** FAMILY OF MARATHON, IOWA., by Repr. of 1960 ed.
Paper--$25.00--110pp F5159

904   - **ROBERTS**. DESC. OF JOHN **ROBERTS** OF SIMSBURY & BLOOMFIELD,
CONN., by L.A. Roberts. Repr. of 1888 ed.
Paper--$4.00--7pp F5159

905   - **ROBERTSON**. GEN. OF THE **ROBERTSON, SMALL** & RELATED FAM., by
A.R. Small. Repr. of 1907 ed.
Cloth--$49.00--Paper--$39.00--258pp F5159

906   - **ROBINSON** FAM. GEN. & HIST. ASSOC. (THE **ROBINSONS** & THEIR KIN
FOLK, 1ST SERIES), by Repr. of 1902 ed.
     Officers, constitution & by-laws, hist. sketches of early **Robinson** emigr. to Amer.
Paper--$19.50--104pp F5159

907   - **ROBINSON** FAM. GEN. & HIST. ASSOC., 2ND SERIES., by Repr. of 1904 ed.
Paper--$16.00--80pp F5159

908   - **ROCKWELL** FAMILY IN AMER.: GEN. REC., FROM 1630 TO 1873., by H.E.
Rockwell. Repr. of 1873 ed.
Cloth--$40.00--Paper--$30.00--224pp F5159

909   - **ROCKWELL**. GEN. OF THE FAMS. OF JOHN **ROCKWELL** OF STAMFORD,
CT., 1641, & RALPH **KEELER** OF HARTFORD, 1639., by J. Boughton. Repr. of
1903 ed.
Cloth--$87.00--Paper--$77.00--615pp F5159

910   - **ROCKWOOD**. HIST. & GEN. RECORD OF THE DESC. OF TIMOTHY
ROCKWOOD, 1727-1806., by E.L. Rockwood. Repr. of 1856 ed.
Paper--$24.50--152pp F5159

911   - **RODMAN**. NOTES ON **RODMAN** GEN., by W.W. Rodman. Repr. of 1887 ed.
Paper--$5.50--27pp F5159

912   - **ROGERS**. JAMES **ROGERS** OF LONDONDERRY, & JAMES **ROGERS** OF
DUMBARTON., by J.H. Drummond. Repr. of 1897 ed.
Paper--$4.50--12pp F5159

913   - **ROGERS**. JOHN **ROGERS** OF MARSHFIELD (MA) & SOME OF HIS DESC.,
by J.H. Drummond. Repr. of 1898 ed.
Paper--$29.50--221pp F5159

914   - **ROGERS**. HOPE **ROGERS** & HIS DESC., by J.S. Rogers. Repr. of 1901 ed.
Paper--$4.00--7pp F5159

915   - **ROGERS**. THE ANC. & DESC. OF LUKE **ROGERS** & SARAH WRIGHT
BROWN., by E.B. Leatherbee. Repr. of 1907 ed.
Paper--$14.00--71pp F5159

916   - **ROLLINS**. RECORD OF FAM. OF THE NAME OF **RAWLINS** OR **ROLLINS**
IN THE U.S., by J.R. Rollins. Repr. of 1874 ed.
Cloth--$56.00--Paper--$46.00--362pp F5159

917   - **ROMER**. HIST. SKETCHES OF THE **ROMER, VAN TASSEL,** & ALLIED
       FAM., by J.L. Romer. Repr. of 1917 ed.
       Paper--$24.00--159pp F5159

918   - **ROOSEVELT** GENEALOGY, 1649-1902., by C.B. Whittlesey. Repr. of 1902 ed.
       Paper--$18.00--121pp F5159

919   - **ROSS**. DR. SAMUEL **ROSS** OF COLERAIN, MASS., HIS ANC. & DESC., by
       D.C. MacBryde. Repr. of 1934 ed.
       Paper--$5.50--22pp F5159

920   - **ROSSON**. THE **ROSSON** STORY., by S. Jackson. Repr. of ed.
       Paper--$5.50--24pp F5159

921   - **ROTCH**. THE **ROTCHES** (BIOGRAPHY & GENEALOGY OF THE **ROTCH**
       FAMILY OF NANTUCKET & NEW BEDFORD, MASS.)., by J.M. Bullard. Repr. of
       1947 ed.
       Cloth--$99.00--Paper--$89.00--583pp F5159

922   - **ROUND-ROUNDS** GEN. DESC. OF JOHN **ROUND** OF SWANSEA, MASS.,
       WHO DIED 1716, AND **ROUNDS** FAMS. OF UNDETERMINED RELATIONSHIP.,
       by N.R. Nichols. Repr. of 1928 ed.
       Cloth--$49.00--Paper--$39.00--259pp F5159

923   - **ROUSE**. **ROUSE, ZIMMERMAN, TANNER, HENDERSON, MCCLURE,
       PORTER** & ALLIED FAM., by E.R. Lloyd. Repr. of 1932 ed.
       Cloth--$40.00--Paper--$30.00--228pp F5159

924   - **ROY**. THE **ROY** FAM. OF VA. & KY., by N.R. Roy. Repr. of 1935 ed.
       Paper--$28.50--190pp F5159

925   - **RUCKER**.   THE **RUCKER** FAM. GEN., WITH ANC., DESC., &
       CONNECTIONS., by S.R. Wood. Repr. of 1932 ed.
       Cloth--$97.50--Paper--$87.50--585pp F5159

926   - **RULISON**. GEN. OF THE **RULISON, RULIFSON** & ALLIED FAMS. IN
       AMER., 1689-1918., by H.F. Rulison. Repr. of 1919 ed.
       Cloth--$44.50--Paper--$34.50--216pp F5159

927   - **RUSLING** FAMILY., by J.F. Rusling. Repr. of 1907 ed.
       Paper--$24.00--160pp F5159

928   - **RUSSELL**. DESC. OF WM. **RUSSELL**, CAMBRIDGE, MA., ABT. 1640., by
       H.S. Russell. Repr. of 1900 ed.
       Paper--$10.00--52pp F5159

929   - **RUTLEDGE** FAM. OF THE SOUTH., by J.T. Cupit. Repr. of 1954 ed.
       Paper--$9.00--45pp F5159

930   - **SAGE**. GEN. RECORD OF DESC. OF DAVID **SAGE** OF MIDDLETOWN,
       CONN., by E.L. **Sage** and C.H. Sage. Repr. of 1919 ed.
       Paper--$25.00--128pp F5159

931   - SAGE. SAGE NOTES., by M.L. Holman. Repr. of 1932 ed.
Paper--$4.50--13pp F5159

932   - SAGE. DESC. OF DAVID SAGE OF MIDDLETOWN, CONN., SECOND
BRANCH., by H.K. Sage. Repr. of 1951 ed.
Paper--$18.50--94pp F5159

933   - SAMPSON FAM. (OF PENN. & OHIO)., by L.B. Sampson. Repr. of 1914 ed.
Cloth--$45.50--Paper--$35.50--238pp F5159

934   - SANDFORD.   ROBERT SANDFORD & HIS WIFE, ANN (ADAMS)
SANDFORD, WITH SOME OF THEIR DESC., 1650-1930., by J.S. Ware. Repr. of
1930 ed.
Paper--$17.50--85pp F5159

935   - SANDS. JAMES SANDS OF BLOCK ISL., RI & SOME DESC., by Repr. of 1912
ed.
Paper--$3.50--4pp F5159

936   - SANFORD. JOHN SANFORD & HIS DESC. OF R.I. COLONY., by R.F. Pierce.
Repr. of ed.
Paper--$4.50--12pp F5159

937   - SANFORD. THOMAS SANFORD, EMIGR. TO NEW ENG.: ANC., LIFE &
DESC., 1632-4; ALSO SKETCHES OF FOUR OTHER PIONEER SANFORDS &
SOME DESC., by C.E. Sanford. Repr. of 1911 ed.
Cloth--$108.00--Paper--$98.00--768pp F5159

938   - SANTEE. GEN. OF THE SANTEE FAM. IN AMER., by E.M. Santee. Repr. of
1927 ed.
Cloth--$43.50--Paper--$33.50--211pp F5159

939   - SARGEANT. GEN. OF THE SARGEANT FAM: THE DESC. OF WM. OF
MALDEN, MASS., by A. Sargent. Repr. of 1858 ed.
Paper--$19.00--108pp F5159

940   - SAUNDERS. FOUNDERS OF THE MASS. BAY COLONY., by S.S. Smith. Repr.
of 1897 ed.
Cloth--$58.00--Paper--$48.00--372pp F5159

941   - SAVARY. A GEN. & BIOGR. RECORD OF THE SAVERY FAM. (SAVORY,
SAVARY), & OF THE SEVERY FAM., (SEVERIT, SAVERY, SAVORY), by A.
Savary. Repr. of 1893 ed.
       Desc. from early immigr. to New Eng. & Phila.
Cloth--$53.00--Paper--$43.00--286pp F5159

942   - SAVERY SUPPLEMENT., by A.W. Savary. Repr. of 1905 ed.
Paper--$11.00--58pp F5159

943   - SAWYER. GENEALOGICAL INDEX OF THE SAWYER FAMILIES OF NEW
ENGLAND PRIOR TO 1900., by Fred E. Sawyer. Repr. of 1983 ed.
Cloth--$49.50--Paper--$39.50--394pp F5159

944   - **SAYLER**. A HIST. OF THE **SAYLER** FAM., BEING A COLL. OF GEN. NOTES RELATIVE TO DANIEL OF FREDERICK CO., MD., WHO CAME TO AMER. 1725-1730, & HIS DESC., by J.L. Sayler. Repr. of 1898 ed.
Paper--$28.00--164pp F5159

945   - **SAYWARD** FAM.; BEING THE HIST. & GEN. OF HENRY **SAYWARD** OF YORK, ME. & HIS DESC., by C. Sayward. Repr. of 1890 ed.
Paper--$26.50--183pp F5159

946   - **SCARRITT**. GEN. HIST. OF THE **SCARRITT** CLAN IN AMERICA. 2 VOL. IN 1., by R.E. Pearson. Repr. of 1938 ed.
Cloth--$50.00--Paper--$40.00--265pp F5159

947   - **SCHALL**. A HIST. ACCT. OF THE **SCHALL/SHAULL** FAM., by J.L.S. Lutz. Repr. of 1968 ed.
Cloth--$83.50--Paper--$73.50--468pp F5159

948   - **SCHOFF**. THE DESC. OF JACOB **SCHOFF**, WHO CAME TO BOSTON IN 1752 & SETTLED IN ASHBURNHAM IN 1757., by W.H. Schoff. Repr. of 1910 ed.
Paper--$24.50--163pp F5159

949   - **SCHOLL-SHOLL-SHULL** GEN., THE COL. BRANCHES., by J.W. Scholl. Repr. of 1930 ed.
Cloth--$137.50--Paper--$127.50--910pp F5159

950   - **SCHOPPE** FAMILY GENEALOGY, 1782-1932., by M.C. Schoppe. Repr. of 1932 ed.
Cloth--$41.00--Paper--$31.00--208pp F5159

951   - **SCHRAMM** FAM. IN GERMANY & U.S., by A. Schramm. Repr. of 1938 ed.
Paper--$5.00--18pp F5159

952   - **SCHUREMAN** OF N.J. 2ND ED., by R. Wynkoop. Repr. of 1902 ed.
Paper--$22.00--144pp F5159

953   - **SCHWENK**. GENEALOGY OF THE **SCHWENK** FAMILY., by E.S. & J.K. Schwenk and R.B. Strassburger. Repr. of 1929 ed.
Cloth--$54.50--Paper--$44.50--282pp F5159

954   - **SCHWENKFELDER**. GEN. REC. OF THE **SCHWENKFELDER** FAMS., SEEKERS OF RELIGIOUS LIBERTY WHO FLED FROM SILESIA TO SAXONY, & THENCE TO PA. IN 1731 TO 1737., by S.K. Brecht. Repr. of 1923 ed. 2 vols.
Cloth--$235.00--Paper--$215.00--1752pp F5159

955   - **SCOTT** FAM. OF SCOTLAND & STAFFORD CO., by   Repr. of ed.
Paper--$17.00--86pp F5159

956   - **SCOTT**. HUGH **SCOTT**, AN IMMIGR. OF 1670, AND HIS DESC., by J. Scott. Repr. of 1895 ed.
Cloth--$57.50--Paper--$47.50--314pp F5159

957   - **SCOTT**. DESC. OF WILLIAM **SCOTT** OF HATFIELD, MASS., 1668-1906, & OF JOHN **SCOTT** OF SPRINGFIELD, MASS., 1659-1906., by O.P. Allen. Repr. of 1906 ed.
Cloth--$43.00--Paper--$33.00--220pp F5159

958   - **SCOTT**. THE **SCOTT** FAM. OF SHREWSBURY, N.J., BEING THE DESC. OF WM. **SCOTT** & ABIGAIL **TILTON WARNER**, WITH SKETCHES OF REL. FAM., by A. Cole. Repr. of 1908 ed.
Paper--$14.00--73pp F5159

959   - **SCOTT**. THE SCOTCH-IRISH & CHARLES **SCOTT'S** DESC. & RELATED FAM., by O.C. Scott. Repr. of 1917 ed.
Paper--$23.50--115pp F5159

960   - **SCOTT**. HIST. OF THE **SCOTT** FAM., by H. Lee. Repr. of 1919 ed.
Paper--$20.00--117pp F5159

961   - **SCOTT**. THE **SCOTT** GEN., by M.L. Holman. Repr. of 1919 ed.
Cloth--$73.50--Paper--$63.50--410pp F5159

962   - **SCOVELL**. ARTHUR **SCOVELL** & HIS DESCENDANTS IN AMERICA, 1660-1900., by J.M. Holley and H.W. Brainard. Repr. of 1941 ed.
Cloth--$55.50--Paper--$45.50--285pp F5159

963   - **SCOVILLE**. SCOVILLE FAM. RECORDS., by C.R. Eastman. Repr. of 1910 ed.
Paper--$15.00--75pp F5159

964   - **SEAMAN**. HISTORY OF THE **SEAMAN** FAMILY IN PA., WITH GENEALOGICAL TABLES., by G.S. Seaman. Repr. of 1911 ed.
Paper--$22.00--135pp F5159

965   - **SEAMANS** FAM. IN AMER. AS DESC. FROM THOMAS **SEAMANS** OF SWANSEA, MASS., 1687., by Lawton & Brown. Repr. of 1933 ed.
Cloth--$54.50--Paper--$44.50--299pp F5159

966   - **SEARS**. GEN. & BIOGR. SKETCHES OF THE ANC. & DESC. OF RICHARD **SEARS**, THE PILGRIM., by E.H. Sears. Repr. of 1857 ed.
Paper--$17.50--96pp F5159

967   - **SEATON**. **SEATONS** OF WESTERN PENN., by J.S. Crosby. Repr. of 1945 ed.
Paper--$12.50--63pp F5159

968   - **SEBOR**. THE DESC. OF JACOB **SEBOR**, 1709-1793, OF MIDDLETOWN, CONN., by H. Beach. Repr. of 1923 ed.
Paper--$19.00--109pp F5159

969   - **SEELY**. ANC. OF DANIEL JAMES **SEELY** & CHARLOTTE LOUISA **VAIL**, WITH DESC., by W.P. Bacon. Repr. of 1914 ed.
Paper--$29.50--185pp F5159

970   - **SELDEN**. **SELDENS** OF VA. & ALLIED FAM., by M. Kennedy. Repr. of 1911 ed.
Cloth--$191.00--Paper--$171.00--1363pp F5159

971 - SEMPLE. GEN. HIST. OF THE FAM. SEMPLE FROM 1214 TO 1888., by W.A. Semple. Repr. of 1888 ed.
Paper--$12.00--60pp F5159

972 - SENSINEY. SENSINEYS OF AMER. (INCL. SENSENY, SENSENIG, ETC.)., by B. Sensening. Repr. of 1943 ed.
Paper--$24.00--159pp F5159

973 - SESSIONS. MATERIALS FOR A HIST. OF THE SESSIONS FAM. IN AMER., THE DESC. OF ALEXANDER SESSIONS OF ANDOVER, MASS., 1669., by F.C. Sessions. Repr. of 1890 ed.
Cloth--$47.50--Paper--$37.50--252pp F5159

974 - SEVERANS GEN. HIST., by J.L. Severance. Repr. of 1893 ed.
Paper--$15.00--97pp F5159

975 - SEWALL FAM. OF ENG. & AMER., 1624-1857., by E. Salisbury. Repr. of 1885 ed.
Paper--$15.00--75pp F5159

976 - SEWALL. THOMAS SEWALL; SOME OF HIS ANC. & ALL OF HIS DESC.: A GEN., by H.S. Webster. Repr. of 1904 ed.
Paper--$5.00--20pp F5159

977 - SEWARD. OBADIAH SEWARD OF LONG ISL., N.Y., & HIS DESC., by F.W. Seward, Jr.. Repr. of 1948 ed.
Cloth--$54.00--Paper--$44.00--288pp F5159

978 - THE SEWELLS IN THE NEW WORLD, by Sir H.L. Duff. Repr. of 1924 ed.
Paper--$22.00--122pp F5159

979 - SEYMOUR. A RECORD OF THE SEYMOUR FAM. IN THE REV., by M.W. Seymour. Repr. of 1912 ed.
Paper--$8.00--40pp F5159

980 - HIST. OF THE SEYMOUR FAM. DESC. OF RICHARD OF HARTFORD, CONN., FOR 6 GEN. WITH AMPLIFICATION OF THE LINES DERIVING FROM HIS SON, JOHN OF HARTFORD, by D. Jacobus. Repr. of 1939 ed.
Cloth--$109.50--Paper--$99.50--662pp F5159

981 - SHAKSPEARE. "SHAKESPEAREANA GENEALOGICA": PT. I, IDENTIFICATION OF THE DRAMATIS PERSONAE IN THE HIST. PLAYS, FROM KING JOHN TO HENRY VIII, by G.R. French. Repr. of 1869 ed.
Notes on characters in MacBeth & Hamlet, persons & places alluded to in several plays; Pt. II, Shakespeare & Arden fams. & their connections.
Cloth--$91.00--Paper--$81.00--546pp F5159

982 - SHANKS. SOME ANC. & DESC. OF JAMES SHANKS OF HURON CO., OHIO., by H.S. Blaine. Repr. of 1951 ed.
Paper--$16.00--82pp F5159

983 - SHANNON. SHANNON GEN., GEN. RECORD & MEMORIALS OF ONE BRANCH IN AMERICA., by G. Hodgdon. Repr. of 1905 ed.
Cloth--$83.00--Paper--$73.00--609pp F5159

984   - SHARPE. RECORDS OF THE **SHARPE** FAM. IN ENG. & AMER. FROM 1580
TO 1870., by W.C. Sharpe. Repr. of 1874 ed.
Paper--$7.00--34pp F5159

985   - SHARPE. MARY ALICE **SHARPE YALDEN THOMSON** & ALEXANDER
BEATTY **SHARPE**, JR.: **CARTER, SHARPE** & ALLIED FAMS., by E.E.B. Jones.
Repr. of 1940 ed.
Cloth--$58.50--Paper--$48.50--311pp F5159

986   - SHEDD. DANIEL **SHED** GEN.; APPENDIX, 1921-1931., by Repr. of 1931 ed.
Paper--$6.50--29pp F5159

987   - SHELDON. **SHELDONS** OF DERBYSHIRE, ENG. & ISRAEL **SHELDON** OF
NEW ENG., by J.G. Bartlett. Repr. of ed.
Paper--$5.50--24pp F5159

988   - SHEPARD. RALPH **SHEPARD**, PURITAN., by R.H. Shepard. Repr. of 1893 ed.
Paper--$10.00--50pp F5159

989   - SHERMAN. ANC. OF REV. JOHN **SHERMAN** & CAPT. JOHN **SHERMAN.**,
by C.A. White. Repr. of 1897 ed.
Paper--$4.00--9pp F5159

990   - SHERWOOD. THOMAS **SHERWOOD** OF FAIRFIELD, CONN. & DESC., by
M.B. Carlson. Repr. of 1950 ed.
Paper--$19.00--92pp F5159

991   - SHILLABER. REC. OF PROCEEDINGS AT THE 1ST GATHERING OF DESC.
OF JOHN **SHILLABER** AT THE OLD HOMESTEAD, PEABODY, MA, 1877., by
Repr. of 1877 ed.
Paper--$9.50--48pp F5159

992   - SHIPLEY-SHEPLEY. OUR FAMILY (**ALLEN, HITCHCOCK, RUTLEDGE,
SHEPLEY**). N.D., by Shepley, shepley & Allen. Repr. of ed.
Paper--$18.00--89pp F5159

993   - SHOBE. GENEALOGY OF THE **SHOBE, KIRKPATRICK & DILLING**
FAMS., REV. 1950 ED., by F.D. Shobe. Repr. of 1919 ed. 1950.
Cloth--$41.00--Paper--$31.00--182+19pp F5159

994   - SHOEMAKER FAMILY., by t.H. Shoemaker. Repr. of 1893 ed.
Paper--$21.00--112pp F5159

995   - SHOTWELL. ANNALS OF OUR COL. ANC. & THEIR DESC.; OR, OUR
QUAKER FOREBEARS & THEIR POSTERITY, by A.M. Shotwell. Repr. of 1895 ed.
       Embracing a gen. & biogr. reg. of nine gen. of the **Shotwell** fam. in Amer.
Cloth--$54.00--Paper--$44.00--291pp F5159

996   - SHRECK. THE **SHRECK** GEN., THE FAM. OF PAUL & BETHANY **SHRECK**,
1771-1954., by C. May. Repr. of 1954 ed.
Paper--$11.00--56pp F5159

997   - **SHRIVER**. ANC. OF SUSANNAH **SHRIVER GORDON**., by D. Gordon. Repr. of ed.
Paper--$4.00--9pp F5159

998   - **SHUEY**. HIST. OF THE **SHUEY** FAM. IN AMER., FROM 1732 TO 1876., by D.B. Shuey. Repr. of 1876 ed.
Cloth--$45.50--Paper--$35.50--279pp F5159

999   - **SHUFORD**. A HIST. SKETCH OF THE **SHUFORD** FAM., by J.H. Shuford. Repr. of 1902 ed.
Paper--$27.50--156pp F5159

1000   - **SILL** FAMILY. OLD SILLTOWN: SOMETHING OF ITS HIST. & PEOPLE, BEING PRINCIPALLY A BRIEF ACCT. OF THE EARLY GENERATIONS OF THE **SILL** FAMILY., by S.S.W. Burt. Repr. of 1912 ed.
Paper--$22.00--148pp F5159

1001   - GEN. OF DESC. OF JOHN **SILL** OF CAMBRIDGE., by G.G. Sill. Repr. of 1859 ed.
Paper--$17.50--108pp F5159

1002   - **SIMMONDS**. JOHN & SUSAN **SIMMONDS** & SOME OF THEIR DESC. WITH RELATED ANC. LINES., by F.W. Simmonds. Repr. of 1940 ed.
Cloth--$43.00--Paper--$33.00--222pp F5159

1003   - **SIMMONS**. HIST. OF THE **SIMMONS** FAM., FROM MOSES **SIMMONS** (**SYMONSON**), SHIP FORTUNE, 1621., by L. Simmons. Repr. of 1930 ed.
Cloth--$59.00--Paper--$49.00--315pp F5159

1004   - **SIMS**. GEN. OF THE **SIMS** FAM., by McClure & Nichols. Repr. of ed.
Paper--$4.00--16pp F5159

1005   - **SINCLAIR**. THE **SINCLAIRS** OF ENGLAND., by Repr. of 1887 ed.
Cloth--$71.00--Paper--$61.00--414pp F5159

1006   - **SINGLETARY**. GEN. OF THE **SINGLETARY-CURTIS** FAM. (COMP. FROM REC. FROM MASS., N.Y., S.C. & OTHERS)., by L. Singletary-Bedford. Repr. of 1907 ed.
Paper--$19.50--115pp F5159

1007   - **SINNOTT, ROGERS, COFFIN, CORLIES, REEVES, BODINE** & ALLIED FAMS., by M.E. Sinnott. Repr. of 1905 ed.
Cloth--$46.00--Paper--$36.00--278pp F5159

1008   - **SLADE**. WM. **SLADE** OF WINDSOR, CONN. & HIS DESC., by T.B. Peck. Repr. of 1910 ed.
Cloth--$40.50--Paper--$30.50--205pp F5159

1009   - **SLATE**. WM. **SLATE** OF WINDHAM & **MANSFIELD**, CONN., & SOME DESC., by G.O. Chapman. Repr. of 1941 ed.
Paper--$7.00--33pp F5159

1010   - **SLAUGHTER**. DESC. OF ROBERT **SLAUGHTER** & FRANCES ANN **JONES**, by I.P. DuBellet. Repr. of 1907 ed.
Paper--$5.00--19pp F5159

1011   - **SLOSSON**. A GEN. MEMOIR OF NATHANIEL **SLOSSON** OF KENT, CONN. & HIS DESC., 1696-1872, WITH NATHAN **SLOSSON'S** DESC. TO 1896., by D.W. Patterson. Repr. of 1896 ed.
Paper--$8.00--38pp F5159

1012   - **SMALL**. DESC. OF EDW. **SMALL** OF NEW ENG. & ALLIED FAM., & TRACINGS OF ENG. ANC., by L. Underhill. Repr. of 1934 ed.
Cloth--$269.00--Paper--$259.00--1835pp F5159

1013   - **SMITH** FAMILY, BEING A POPULAR ACCT. OF MOST BRANCHES OF THE NAMES - HOWEVER SPELT - FROM THE 14TH CENT., WITH NUMEROUS PEDIGREES. (PUBL. IN ENGLAND)., by C. Reade. Repr. of 1904 ed.
Cloth--$59.50--Paper--$49.50--324pp F5159

1014   - **SMITH** FAM. OF PA. JOHANN FRIEDERICH **SCHMIDT**, 1746- 1812., by J.B. Nolan. Repr. of 1932 ed.
Cloth--$45.00--Paper--$35.00--203pp F5159

1015   - **SMITH**. GEN. OF FAM. OF WM. **SMITH** OF PETERSBOROUGH, N.H., by Leonard & Smith. Repr. of 1852 ed.
Paper--$5.50--24pp F5159

1016   - **SMITH**. GEN. & REMINISCENCES OF WM. **SMITH** & FAM., by M.T. Smith. Repr. of 1884 ed.
Paper--$15.00--86pp F5159

1017   - **SMITH**. A GEN. HIST. OF THE DESC. OF THE REV. NEHEMIAH **SMITH** OF NEW LONDON CO., CONN., WITH MENTION OF HIS BROTHER, JOHN, & NEPHEW, EDWARD, 1638-1888., by H.A. Smith. Repr. of 1889 ed.
Cloth--$59.00--Paper--$49.00--320pp F5159

1018   - **SMITH**. A MEM'L. OF REV. THOMAS **SMITH** & HIS DESC.: A FULL GEN. RECORD, 1707-1895., by S.A. Smith. Repr. of 1895 ed.
Paper--$23.00--146pp F5159

1019   - **SMITH**. WILLS OF THE **SMITH** FAMILIES OF N.Y. & LONG ISL., 1664-1794, WITH GEN. & HIST. NOTES., by W.S. Pelletreau. Repr. of 1898 ed.
Paper--$27.50--151pp F5159

1020   - **SMITH**. JESSE **SMITH**, HIS ANC. & DESC., by L. Smith. Repr. of 1909 ed.
Cloth--$40.00--Paper--$30.00--187pp F5159

1021   - **SMITH**. COLLATERAL LINES & MAYFLOWER CONNECTIONS., by H.S.L. Barnes. Repr. of 1910 ed.
Paper--$10.00--51pp F5159

1022   - **SMITH**. NOTES & ILLUSTRATIONS CONCERNING THE FAM. HIST. OF JAMES **SMITH** OF COVENTRY (ENGLAND), (1731- 1794), & HIS DESC., by Lady Durning-Lawrence. Repr. of 1912 ed.
Paper--$24.00--156pp F5159

1023   - SMITH. GEN. OF CONSIDER SMITH OF NEW BEDFORD, WITH ALLIED
        FAM. OF MASON & THWING., by L.T. Smith. Repr. of 1915 ed.
        Paper--$5.00--26pp F5159

1024   - SMITH. MATTHEW SMITH OF MARTHA'S VINEYARD & READFIELD,
        ME., & DESC., by F.M. Ames. Repr. of 1925 ed.
        Paper--$4.00--8pp F5159

1025   - SMITH. ANC. OF HIRAM SMITH & HIS WIFE, SARAH JANE BULL, by J.G.
        Frost.
        Paper--$6.00--30pp F5159

1026   - SMITH. HIST. & GEN. OF THE SMITHS OF "BIG SPRING PLANTATION",
        FREDERICK CO., VA., WITH A CHRON. OF THE DRUGAN & CARNAHAN
        FAMS. OF PA. & OHIO., by B.T. Hartman. Repr. of 1929 ed.
        Paper--$18.00--101pp F5159

1027   - SMITH. JOHN SMITH OF ALABAMA, HIS ANC. & DESC., by M.O. McDavid.
        Repr. of 1948 ed.
        Paper--$23.00--189pp F5159

1028   - SMITH. LT. SAMUEL SMITH; HIS CHILDREN & ONE LINE OF DESC. &
        RELATED FAMS., by J.W. Hook. Repr. of 1953 ed.
        Cloth--$69.50--Paper--$59.50--381pp F5159

1029   - SNELL. THOMAS SNELL (1625-1725) OF BRIDGEWATER, MASS. & SOME
        DESC., by H.P. Long. Repr. of 1958 ed.
        Paper--$4.00--8pp F5159

1030   - SNIDER. SOLOMON SNIDER (1778-1845) & DESC. FROM BURRIS DIAL
        BOOK, by W.A. Dial. Repr. of ed.
        Paper--$4.50--15pp F5159

1031   - SNIDER. DESC. OF JONAS SNIDER & ANNA HOSTUTTER SNIDER,
        SHELBY & SPENCER CO., KY., by J. Franklin. Repr. of 1950 ed.
        Paper--$5.00--18pp F5159

1032   - SNODDY. FAM. HIST. & GEN. OF JAS. SNODDY OF PENN., by Sanders &
        Walton. Repr. of 1959 ed.
        Paper--$6.00--28pp F5159

1033   - SNODGRASS FAMILY, by S.C. Scott. Repr. of 1928 ed.
        Paper--$19.00--95pp F5159

1034   - SNOW-ESTES ANCESTRY., by N.E. Snow and M. Jillson. Repr. of 1939 ed.
        Vol. I, The Snow Family. 667p. $107.00 hardcover; $97.00 paper.
        Vol. II, The Estes Family. 436p. $78.00 hardcover; $68.00 paper.
        Special Price for the Set: $165.00 hardcover; $149.00 paper. F5159

1035   - SNOW. HIST. OF THE FAM. OF BENJ. SNOW, A DESC. OF RICHARD SNOW
        OF WOBURN, MASS., by O. Wilcox. Repr. of 1907 ed.
        Cloth--$71.50--Paper--$61.50--385pp F515

1036   - **SOLLEY**. THOMAS **SOLLEY** & HIS DESC., by G.W. Solley. Repr. of 1911 ed. Paper--$32.50--217pp F5159

1037   - **SOULE**. A CONTRIBUTION TO THE HIST., BIOGR. & GEN. OF THE FAM. NAMED **SOLE, SOLLY, SOULE, SOWLE, SOULIS**. 2 VOLS., by G.T. Ridlon, Sr.. Repr. of 1926 ed. Cloth--$187.00--Paper--$177.00--1180pp F5159

1038   - **SPAID** GEN.; FROM THE FIRST OF THE NAME IN THIS COUNTRY TO THE PRESENT TIME, WITH A NUMBER OF ALLIED FAMS. & MANY HIST. FACTS., by A.T. Secrest. Repr. of 1922 ed. Cloth--$72.50--Paper--$62.50--403pp F5159

1039   - **SPARE**. THE **SPARE** FAM. LEONARD **SPARE** & HIS DESC., by The Spare Fam. Assoc.. Repr. of 1931 ed. Cloth--$58.50--Paper--$48.50--323pp F5159

1040   - **SPEAR**. THE ANC. OF ANNIS **SPEAR**, 1775-1858, OF LITCHFIELD, ME., by W.G. Davis. Repr. of 1945 ed. Paper--$25.50--170pp F5159

1041   - **SPENCER**. GENEALOGICAL SKETCH OF DESC. OF SAMUEL **SPENCER** OF PA., by H.M. Jenkins. Repr. of 1904 ed. Cloth--$49.00--Paper--$39.00--253pp F5159

1042   - **SPOONER**. RECORDS OF WM. **SPOONER** OF PLYMOUTH, MASS., & OF HIS DESC. VOL. I., by T. Spooner. Repr. of 1883 ed. Cloth--$98.00--Paper--$88.00--694pp F5159

1043   - **SPOONER**. MEM. OF WM. **SPOONER**, 1637, & OF HIS DESC. TO THE 3RD GEN., OF HIS GR-GRANDSON, ELNATHAN **SPOONER**, & OF HIS DESC. TO 1871., by T. Spooner. Repr. of 1871 ed. Cloth--$46.00--Paper--$36.00--242pp F5159

1044   - **SPOONER**. BRIEF SKETCH OF THE ANC. OF ALDEN **SPOONER**, LATE OF BROOKLYN, NY, WITH RECORD OF HIS DESC. TO AUG. 1909., by A.S. Huling. Repr. of 1909 ed. Paper--$6.00--28pp F5159

1045   - **SPOOR**. THE **SPOOR** FAM. (ALIAS **WYBESSE**) OF N.Y. STATE., by H.F. Johnston. Repr. of ed. Paper--$10.00--54pp F5159

1046   - **SPRINGER**. A GEN. TABLE & HIST. OF THE **SPRINGER** FAM. IN EUROPE & N. AMER. Rev. by E. Scribner. Vol. I., by M. Springer. Repr. of 1917 ed. Paper--$25.00--154pp F5159

1047   - **STANTON**. OUR ANCESTORS, THE **STANTONS**, by W.H. Stanton. Repr. of 1912 ed. Cloth--$104.50--Paper--$94.50--649pp F5159

1048   - **STARKIE** FAM. OF ENG., by J.P. Rylands. Repr. of 1880 ed. Paper--$5.00--18pp F5159

1049   - **STARR**. HIST. OF THE **STARR** FAM. OF NEW ENG., FROM COMFORT **STARR** OF ASHFORD, CO. KENT, ENG., WHO EMIGR. TO BOSTON (1635)., by B. Starr. Repr. of 1879 ed.
Cloth--$99.00--Paper--$89.00--587pp F5159

1050   - **STEBBINS**. GENEALOGY & HIST. OF SOME **STEBBINS** LINES TO 1953., by J.A. Stebbins. Repr. of 1957 ed.
Cloth--$39.00--Paper--$29.00--190pp F5159

1051   - **STEIN**. THE **STEINS** OF MUSCATINE (IA.): A FAM. CHRONICLE., by S.G. Stein. Repr. of 1961 ed.
Paper--$11.00--53pp F5159

1052   - **STEPHENS**. AMER. GEN. RECORD, VOL. I. **STEPHENS** FAM. WITH COLL. BRANCHES., by E. Clark. Repr. of 1892 ed.
Paper--$27.30--185pp F5159

1053   - **STEVENS** GEN. SOME DESC. OF THE FITZ **STEVENS** FAM. IN ENG. & NEW ENG., by C.E. Stevens. Repr. of 1904 ed.
Paper--$17.00--93pp F5159

1054   - **STEVENS** GEN.; BRANCHES OF THE FAM. DESC. FROM PURITAN ANC., 1650 TO PRESENT., by E. Barney. Repr. of 1907 ed.
Cloth--$51.50--Paper--$41.50--319pp F5159

1055   - **STEVENS**. A GEN. OF THE LIN. DESC. OF JOHN **STEEVENS**, WHO SETTLED IN GUILFORD, CONN. IN 1645., by C.S. **Holmes** and C.W. Holmes. Repr. of 1906 ed.
Paper--$26.00--162pp F5159

1056   - **STEWART**. THE **STEWARTS** OF COITSVILLE: HIST. OF ROBERT & SARAH **STEWART** OF ADAMS CO., PA., & THEIR DESC., by Repr. of 1899 ed.
Paper--$27.50--198pp F5159

1057   - **STEWART**. COL. GEORGE **STEUART** & HIS WIFE, MARGARET **HARRIS**: THEIR ANC. & DESC., WITH APPENDIXES OF REL. FAMS., by R. Stewart. Repr. of 1907 ed.
Cloth--$89.50--Paper--$79.50--522pp F5159

1058   - **STICHTER**. GEN. OF THE **STICHTER** FAM., 1189-1902., by J. Stichter and J.L. Stichter. Repr. of 1902 ed.
Paper--$8.50--42pp F5159

1059   - **STILLWELL**. HIST. OF CAPT. RICHARD **STILLWELL**, SON OF LT. NICHOLAS **STILLWELL** & HIS DESC., by J. Stillwell. Repr. of 1930 ed.
Cloth--$56.00--Paper--$46.00--285pp F5159

1060   - **STOCKWELL**. THE **STOCKWELL** FAM., by Brown & Chestnut. Repr. of 1956 ed.
Paper--$5.50--17pp F5159

1061   - **STONE**. SOUVENIR OF A PART OF THE DESC. OF GREGORY & LYDIA **COOPER STONE**, 1634-1892., by J.L. Stone. Repr. of 1892 ed.
Paper--$14.50--78pp F5159

1062 - **STONE**. SIMON & JOAN **CLARKE STONE** OF WATERTOWN, MA., & THREE GEN. OF THEIR DESC., by D. Brown. Repr. of 1899 ed.
Paper--$4.00--8pp F5159

1063 - **STONE**. ANC. OF SARAH **STONE**, WIFE OF JAMES **PATTEN** OF ARUNDEL (KENNEBUNKPORT) ME., by W. Davis. Repr. of 1930 ed.
Paper--$23.50--158pp F5159

1064 - **STORER**. ANNALS OF THE **STORER** FAM., TOGETHER WITH NOTES ON THE **AYRAULT** FAM., by M. Storer. Repr. of 1927 ed.
Paper--$18.50--107pp F5159

1065 - **STORKES**. ENGLISH **STORKES** IN AMERICA., by C.A. Storke. Repr. of 1935 ed.
Cloth--$44.00--Paper--$34.00--224pp F5159

1066 - **STORY**. ELISHA **STORY** OF BOSTON & SOME OF HIS DESC., by P. Derby and F.A. Gardner. Repr. of 1915 ed.
Paper--$6.00--28pp F5159

1067 - **STOVER** GENEALOGY, BIOGRAPHY & HISTORY: A GENEALOGICAL RECORD OF THE DESC. OF WILLIAM **STOVER**, PIONEER, & OTHER **STOVERS**., by B.E. Hughey. Repr. of 1936 ed.
Cloth--$49.50--Paper--$39.50--249pp F5159

1068 - **STOWELL**. A RECORD OF THE DESC. OF SAM'L. **STOWELL** OF HINGHAM, MASS., by W.H.H. Stowell. Repr. of 1922 ed.
Cloth--$149.00--Paper--$139.00--980pp F5159

1069 - **STRICKLER**. FORERUNNERS. A HIST. OR GEN. OF THE **STRICKLER** FAM., by H.M. Strickler. Repr. of 1925 ed.
Cloth--$78.50--Paper--$68.50--440pp F5159

1070 - **STRONG**. THE HIST. OF THE DESC. OF ELDER JOHN **STRONG** OF NORTHAMPTON, MASS. 2 VOLS., by B.W. Dwight. Repr. of 1871 ed.
Cloth--$209.50--Paper--$199.50--1649pp F5159

1071 - **STROUD** FAM. HIST., DESC. OF CAPT. RICHARD **STROUD** OF NEW LONDON, CONN., by H.D. Lowell. Repr. of 1934 ed.
Paper--$8.50--40pp F5159

1072 - **STUKEY**. GENEALOGY OF THE **STUKEY, REAM, GROVE, CLEM & DENNISTON** FAMILIES., by E.L. Denniston. Repr. of 1939 ed.
Cloth--$99.50--Paper--$89.50--591pp F5159

1073 - **STURGEON**. A GENEALOGICAL HISTORY OF THE **STURGEONS** OF N. AMER., by C.T. McCoy. Repr. of 1926 ed.
Cloth--$48.00--Paper--$38.00--239pp F5159

1074 - **SULLIVAN**. MATERIALS FOR A HIST. OF THE FAM. OF JOHN **SULLIVAN** OF BERWICK, NEW ENG., & OF THE **O'SULLIVANS** OF ARDEA, IRELAND., by T.C. Amory. Repr. of 1893 ed.
Paper--$26.00--151pp F5159

1075 - **SUMNER**. REC. OF THE DESC. OF WM. **SUMNER** OF DORCHESTER, MASS., 1636., by W.S. Appleton. Repr. of 1879 ed.
Cloth--$41.50--Paper--$31.50--209pp F5159

1076 - A HIST. OF THE AMER. & PURITANICAL FAM. OF **SUTCLIFF** OR **SUTLIFFE**, SPELLED **SUTCLIFFE** IN ENG., & A GEN. OF ALL THE DESC. THROUGH NATHANIEL **SUTLIFF**, JR., by S.M. Sutcliff, Jr.. Repr. of 1909 ed.
Cloth--$40.00--Paper--$30.00--198pp F5159

1077 - **SUTCLIFFE**. A GEN. OF THE **SUTCLIFFE-SUTLIFFE** FAM. IN AMER. FROM BEFORE 1661 TO 1903., by B.H. Sutcliffe. Repr. of ed.
The desc. of Nathaniel **Sutcliffe**, with a brief account of their Eng. anc. back to 1500.
Cloth--$46.50--Paper--$36.50--242pp F5159

1078 - **SWAN**. ANC. OF ALDEN SMITH **SWAN** & HIS WIFE, MARY ALTHEA **FARWELL**., by J.C. Frost. Repr. of 1923 ed.
Cloth--$49.50--Paper--$39.50--264pp F5159

1079 - **SWEET**. SILAS **SWEET** OF NEW BEDFORD, MASS. & BRADFORD, VT. & HIS DESC., by C. Johnson. Repr. of 1898 ed.
Paper--$5.00--21pp F5159

1080 - **SWIFT** FAMILY: HIST. NOTES, COMP., by K.W. Swift. Repr. of 1955 ed.
Paper--$28.00--170pp F5159

1081 - **SWING**. EVENTS IN THE LIFE & HIST. OF THE **SWING** FAMILY, by G.S. Swing. Repr. of 1889 ed.
Cloth--$71.00--Paper--$61.00--398pp F5159

1082 - **SYLVESTER** FAMILY IN MAINE., by C.N. Sinnett. Repr. of 1922 ed.
Paper--$5.00--19pp F5159

1083 - **TAFT** FAM. GATHERING: PROCEEDINGS AT THE MEETING OF THE **TAFT** FAM. AT UXBRIDGE, MA., 1874., by Repr. of 1874 ed.
Paper--$19.00--103pp F5159

1084 - **TAINTER**. HIST. & GEN. OF THE DESC. OF JOSPEH **TAYNTER**, WHO SAILED FROM ENGLAND, APR. 1638, & SETTLED IN WATERTOWN, MA., by D.W. Tainter. Repr. of 1859 ed.
Paper--$18.00--94pp F5159

1085 - **TALLMAN**. THE HON. PELEG **TALLMAN**, 1764-1841. HIS ANC. & DESC., by W.M. Emery. Repr. of 1935 ed.
Cloth--$49.00--Paper--$39.00--260pp F5159

1086 - **TAPPAN**. A SKETCH OF THE LIFE OF REV. DANIEL DANA **TAPPAN**, WITH AN ACCT. OF THE **TAPPAN** FAM., BY HIS CHILDREN., by Repr. of 1890 ed.
Paper--$6.00--28pp F5159

1087 - DESC. OF JOHN **TAYLOR** OF HADLEY., by F.L. Taylor. Repr. of 1922 ed.
Paper--$8.00--40pp F5159

1088   - **TAYLOR**. FAMILY HIST. OF ANTHONY **TAYLOR** OF HAMPTON, N.H., & SOME DESC., 1635-1935., by H.M. Taylor. Repr. of 1935 ed.
Cloth--$89.50--Paper--$79.50--530pp F5159

1089   - **TAYLOR**. ANTHONY **TAYLOR** OF HAMPTON, N.H., by H.M. Taylor. Repr. of 1945 ed.
Paper--$23.50--134pp F5159

1090   - SOME ACCT. OF THE **TEMPLE** FAMILY, by Temple Prime. Repr. of 1887 ed.
Paper--$18.00--100pp F5159

1091   - **TEMPLE**. ABOVE, SECOND EDITION., by Repr. of 1894 ed.
Paper--$19.50--111pp F5159

1092   - **TEMPLE**. ABOVE, THIRD EDITION., by Repr. of 1896 ed.
Paper--$22.00--146pp F5159

1093   - **TEMPLE**. ABOVE, FOURTH EDITION., by Repr. of 1899 ed.
Paper--$16.00--77pp F5159

1094   - **TEMPLE**. SOME **TEMPLE** PEDIGREES: GEN. OF THE KNOWN DESC. OF ABRAHAM **TEMPLE**, WHO SETTLED IN SALEM, MA., IN 1636 (& SOME CONNECTED FAMS.)., by L. Temple. Repr. of 1900 ed.
Paper--$47.50--316pp F5159

1095   - **TEMPLETON** & ALLIED FAM. A GEN. HIST. & FAM. RECORD., by Y.T. Clague. Repr. of 1936 ed.
Paper--$25.50--169pp F5159

1096   - **TENNANT**. GEN. OF THE **TENNANT** FAM.: ANC. & DESC. THROUGH MANY GENERATIONS., by A.M. Tennant. Repr. of 1915 ed.
Cloth--$54.00--Paper--$44.00--356pp F5159

1097   - **TERRELL**. RICHMOND, WILLIAM & TIMOTHY **TERRELL**, COL. VIRGINIANS., by C.J.T. Barnhill. Repr. of 1934 ed.
Cloth--$64.00--Paper--$54.00--339pp F5159

1098   - **THORNBURG** FAMILY OF RANDOLPH CO., IND., by Thornburg & Weiss. Repr. of 1959 ed.
Paper--$12.00--60pp F5159

1099   - **THORNDIKE**. DESCENDANTS OF JOHN **THORNDIKE** OF ESSEX CO., MASS., by M.H. Staffod. Repr. of 1960 ed.
Cloth--$64.00--Paper--$54.00--349pp F5159

1100   - **THORNTON**. FAM. OF JAMES **THORNTON**., by C.T. Adams. Repr. of 1905 ed.
Paper--$7.50--34pp F5159

1101   - **THORNTON**. THE DOZIER **THORNTON** LINE., by J. Thornton. Repr. of 1957 ed.
Paper--$10.00--52pp F5159

1102   - **TIBBETTS.** HENRY **TIBBETTS** OF DOVER, NH & SOME OF HIS DESCENDANTS., by M.T. Jarvis. Repr. of 1937 ed.
Cloth--$127.00--Paper--$117.00--821pp F5159

1103   - **TICE** FAMILIES IN AMER.: **THEIS, THYSSEN, TYSSEN, DEIS.** VOL. I., by J.S. Elson. Repr. of 1947 ed.
Cloth--$59.50--Paper--$49.50--320pp F5159

1104   - **TIERNAN** FAMILY IN MARYLAND., by C.B. Tiernan. Repr. of 1898 ed.
Cloth--$43.50--Paper--$33.50--222pp F5159

1105   - **TIERNAN** & OTHER FAMS., by C.B. Tiernan. Repr. of 1901 ed.
Cloth--$79.50--Paper--$69.50--466pp F5159

1106   - **TILTON.** ANC. OF PHOEBE **TILTON,** 1775-1847, WIFE OF CAPT. ABEL LUNT OF NEWBURYPORT, MA., by W. Davis. Repr. of 1947 ed.
Cloth--$48.50--Paper--$38.50--257pp F5159

1107   - **TIPPIN.** ANC. OF **TIPPIN** FAM. OF KY., WITH MAYFIELD ANC., by J.J. Tippin. Repr. of 1940 ed.
Paper--$8.00--38pp F5159

1108   - **TOMKINS-TOMPKINS** GENEALOGY., by R.A. Tompkins and C.F. Tompkins. Repr. of 1942 ed.
Cloth--$109.50--Paper--$99.50--720pp F5159

1109   - **TORREY** FAMS. & THEIR CHILDREN IN AMER. VOL. I., by F.C. Torrey. Repr. of 1924 ed.
Cloth--$68.50--Paper--$58.50--396pp F5159

1110   - **TORREY** FAMS. & THEIR CHILDREN IN AMER. VOL. II., by   Repr. of 1929 ed.
Cloth--$86.50--Paper--$76.50--488pp F5159

1111   - **TOUSEY** FAM. IN AMER., by T.C. Rose. Repr. of 1916 ed.
Paper--$27.50--137pp F5157

1112   - **TOWNER.** A GEN. OF THE **TOWNER** FAM. THE DESC. OF RICHARD **TOWNER** WHO CAME FROM SUSSEX CO., ENG. TO GUILFORD, CT., BEFORE 1685., by J.W. Towner. Repr. of 1910 ed.
Cloth--$53.00--Paper--$43.00--269pp F5159

1113   - **TOWNSEND.** A MEMORIAL OF JOHN, HENRY & RICHARD **TOWNSEND** & THEIR DESCENDANTS (WITH 1969 INDEX)., by W.A. Townsend. Repr. of 1865 ed.
Cloth--$57.00--Paper--$47.00--233+60pp F5159

1114   - **TOWNSEND.** ENGLISH **TOWNSENDS;** TANCRED CRUSADERS; **TOWNSENDS** OF WATERTOWN, MA.; **TOWNSENDS** OF HEBRON, CT. & HANCOCK, MA., by M.I. Townsend. Repr. of 1899 ed.
Paper--$7.50--37pp F5159

1115   - **TRAYNE**. JOHN **TRAYNE** AND SOME DESC., ESPECIALLY CHARLES JACKSON **TRAIN**, USN., by S.T. Hand. Repr. of 1933 ed.
Paper--$29.50--198pp F5159

1116   - **TREMAN-TRUMAN**. HIST. OF THE **TREMAN, TRMAINE, TRUMAN** FAM. IN AMER., WITH THE REL. FAMS. OF **MACK, DEY, BOARD & AYERS**., by Treman & Poole. Repr. of 1901 ed.
Being a hist. of Joseph **Truman** of New London, Ct., (1666); Richard **Dey** of N.Y.C. (1641); Cornelius **Board** of Boardville, N.J. (1730); John **Ayer** of Newbury, Ma. (1635); & their desc. 2,129pp. 2 vols.
Special Price for the Set: $280.00 hardcover; $260.00 paper.
Cloth--$145.00/Vol.--Paper--$135.00/Vol.--2,129pp F5159

1117   - **TRICKEY**. GEN. OF THE **TRICKEY** FAM., by W.D. Trickey. Repr. of 1930 ed.
Paper--$5.50--22pp F5159

1118   - **TRIPP** WILLS, DEEDS & WAYS, WITH KEY TO **TRIPP** DESC. VIA NEW ENGLAND & ALSO NEW YORK., by Valentine Research Bureau. Repr. of 1932 ed.
Paper--$29.50--196pp F5159

1119   - **TRIPP**. GEN. RECORD OF AUGUSTUS **TRIPP** OF LANESBORO, MASS., by G.A. Tripp. Repr. of 1914 ed.
Paper--$4.50--11pp F5159

1120   - **TRIPP** GEN.; DESC. OF JAMES, SON OF JOHN **TRIPP**., by G.L. Randall. Repr. of 1924 ed.
Cloth--$49.50--Paper--$39.50--264pp F5159

1121   - **TROWBRIDGE** FAM.; OR, THE DESC. OF THOMAS **TROWBRIDGE**, ONE OF THE FIRST SETTLERS OF NEW HAVEN, CONN., by F.W. Chapman. Repr. of 1872 ed.
Cloth--$81.00--Paper--$71.00--461pp F5159

1122   - THE **TROWBRIDGE** GEN., HIST. OF THE **TROWBRIDGE** FAMILY IN AMERICA, by F.B. Trowbridge. Repr. of 1908 ed.
Cloth--$160.00--Paper--$150.00--848pp F5159

1123   - **TUCKER**. ANC. & DESC. OF JIREH **TUCKER** OF ROYALTON, VT., by E.a. Bliefling. Repr. of 1927 ed.
Paper--$5.00--24pp F5159

1124   - **TUDOR** GENEALOGY., by W. Tudor. Repr. of 1896 ed.
Paper--$5.00--17pp F5159

1125   - **TUPPER**. THOMAS **TUPPER** & HIS DESC., by F.W. Tupper. Repr. of 1945 ed.
Paper--$14.00--71pp F5159

1126   - **TURNLEY**. THE **TURNLEYS**: A BRIEF RECORD, BIOGRAPHIC & NARRATIVE, OF SOME **TURNLEYS** IN THE U.S. & EUROPE., by P.T. Turnley. Repr. of 1905 ed.
Cloth--$56.00--Paper--$46.50--298pp F5159

1127   - **TWINING** FAM. DESC. OF WM. **TWINING**, SR., OF EASTHAM, MASS., WITH NOTES OF ENG., WELSH, & NOVA SCOTIA FAM. OF THE NAME. REV. ED., by T.J. Twining. Repr. of 1905 ed.
Cloth--$43.50--Paper--$33.50--264pp F5159

1128   - **TYLER** GEN. THE DESC. OF JOB **TYLER** OF ANDOVER, MASS., 1619-1700. 2 VOLS., by W.I.T. Brigham. Repr. of 1912 ed.
Cloth--$134.00--Paper--$124.00--891pp F5159

1129   - **UNDERHILL** BURYING GROUND: ACCT. OF A PARCEL OF LAND...AT LOCUST VAL., LONG ISLAND...KNOWN AS THE **UNDERHILL** BURYING GROUND., by D.H. Underhill and F.J. Underhill. Repr. of 1924 ed.
Paper--$16.00--79pp F5159

1130   - **UNDERWOOD**. THE **UNDERWOOD** FAMILIES OF AMERICA. ED. BY H.J. BANKER., by L.M. Underwood. Repr. of 1913 ed.
Cloth--$117.50--Paper--$107.50--809pp F5159

1131   - **UPTON** MEM. A GEN. REC. OF THE DESC. OF JOHN **UPTON**, OF N. READING, MA., WITH SHORT GEN. OF THE **PUTNAM**, **STONE** & **BRUCE** FAM., by J.A. Vinton. Repr. of 1874 ed.
Cloth--$79.50--Paper--$69.50--556pp F5159

1132   - **UPTON** FAM. RECORDS: BEING GEN. COLLECTIONS FOR AN **UPTON** FAM. HIST., by W.H. Upton. Repr. of 1893 ed.
Cloth--$93.00--Paper--$83.00--534pp F5159

1133   - **VAIL**. GEN. OF THE **VAIL** FAM., DESC. FROM JEREMIAH **VAIL**, AT SALEM, MASS., 1639., by H.H. Vail. Repr. of 1902 ed.
Cloth--$68.00--Paper--$58.00--371pp F5159

1134   - **VAN BENTHUYSEN** GENEALOGY. DESC. OF PAULUS MARTENSE **VAN BENTHUYSEN**, WHO SETTLED IN ALBANY, N.Y., MALE & FEMALE LINES, by A.S. Van Benthuysen and E.M. Hall. Repr. of 1953 ed.
        Also gen. of certain branches of..other fams. of Dutch & Huguenot origin in N.Y.
Cloth--$99.50--Paper--$89.50--592pp F5159

1135   - **VAN BUREN**. HIST. OF CORNELIS MAESSEN **VAN BUREN**, WHO CAME FROM HOLLAND TO THE NEW NETHERLANDS IN 1631, & HIS DESC., by H.C. Peckham. Repr. of 1913 ed.
        Incl. the gen. of the fams. of Bloomingdale.
Cloth--$77.50--Paper--$67.50--431pp F5159

1136   - **VAN DOORN** FAMILY (**VAN DORN**, **VAN DOREN**, ETC.) IN HOLLAND & AMER., 1088-1908)., by A.V.D. Honeyman. Repr. of 1909 ed.
Cloth--$119.00--Paper--$109.00--765pp F5159

1137   - **VAN VOORHIS**. NOTES ON THE ANC. OF MAJ. WM. ROE **VAN VOORHIS** OF FISHKILL, DUCHESS CO., N.Y., by E.W. Van Voorhis. Repr. of 1881 ed.
Cloth--$41.00--Paper--$31.00--239pp F5159

1138   - **VANDERLIP, VAN DERLIP, VANDER LIPPE** FAM. IN AMER., WITH ACCT. OF **VON DER LIPPE** FAM. OF LIPPE, GER., by C. Booth. Repr. of 1914 ed.
Cloth--$50.00--Paper--$40.00--194pp F5159

1139   - VAUGHAN. THE VAUGHANS IN WALES & AMERICA: A SEARCH FOR THE WELSH ANC. OF WILLIAM VAUGHAN (1750-1840)., by James E. Vaughan. Repr. of 1990 ed.
Cloth--$53.00--Paper--$43.00--270pp F5159

1140   - VIALL. JOHN VIALL OF SWANSEY, MASS., & SOME OF HIS DESC., by D. Jillson. Repr. of ed.
Paper--$7.50--37pp F5159

1141   - VROOMAN FAMILY IN AMER.: DESC. OF HENDRICK MEESE VROOMAN, WHO CAME FROM HOLLAND TO AMER. IN 1664., by G.V. Wickersham and E.B. Comstock. Repr. of 1949 ed.
Cloth--$63.00--Paper--$53.00--341pp F5159

1142   - WAIT. A GEN. SKETCH OF A BRANCH OF THE WAIT OR WAITE FAM. OF AMER., by D.B. Waite. Repr. of 1893 ed.
Paper--$5.50--28pp F5159

1143   - WALDRON. JOHN WALDRON OF DOVER, N.H., & HIS DESC., by A.H. Quint. Repr. of 1879 ed.
Paper--$4.00--10pp F5159

1144   - WALSH, THE NAME & THE ARMS., by Frankford. Repr. of 1910 ed.
Paper--$4.00--9pp F5159

1145   - WALTON FAM., by J.C. Martindale. Repr. of 1911 ed.
Paper--$4.00--12pp F5159

1146   - WARD FAM. DESC. OF WM. WARD, WHO SETTLED IN SUDBURY, MA. IN 1639, WITH AN APP. OF THE NAMES OF FAM. THAT HAVE INTERMARRIED WITH THEM., by A.H. Ward. Repr. of 1851 ed.
Cloth--$45.00--Paper--$35.00--265pp F5159

1147   - WARE GEN.: ROBERT WARE OF DEDHAM, MA., & HIS LINEAL DESC., by E. Ware. Repr. of 1901 ed.
Cloth--$63.50--Paper--$53.50--335pp F5159

1148   - WARNER. DESC. OF ANDREW WARNER, by L.C. Warner and J.G. Nichols. Repr. of 1919 ed.
Cloth--$125.00--Paper--$115.00--804pp F5159

1149   - WARNER. SIR THOMAS WARNER, PIONEER OF THE WEST INDIES: A CHRONICLE OF HIS FAMILY., by A. Warner. Repr. of 1933 ed.
Paper--$26.00--174pp F5159

1150   - WARREN. A GEN. OF THE DESC. OF JAMES WARREN, WHO WAS IN KITTERY, MAINE, 1652-1656., by O. Warren. Repr. of 1902 ed.
Paper--$20.50--138pp F5159

1151   - GEN. NOTES OF THE WASHBURN FAM. WITH A BRIEF SKETCH OF THE FAM. IN ENG., CONTAINING A FULL REC. OF THE DESC. OF ISRAEL WASHBURN OF RAYNHAM, 1755-1841, by J.C. Washburn. Repr. of 1898 ed.
Paper--$18.00--104pp F5159

1152   - **WASHBURN**. EBENEZER **WASHBURN**; HIS ANC. & DESC., WITH SOME CONNECTED FAM. A FAM. STORY OF 700 YEARS., by G.T. Washburn. Repr. of 1913 ed.
Cloth--$43.50--Paper--$33.50--224pp F5159

1153   - **WATERHOUSE**. ANCESTRY OF JOSEPH **WATERHOUSE**, 1754- 1837, OF STANDISH, ME., by W.G. Davis. Repr. of 1949 ed.
Paper--$21.00--144pp F5159

1154   - **WATERMAN**. DESC. OF ROBERT **WATERMAN** OF MARSHFIELD, MA., THROUGH SEVEN GENERATIONS. VOL. I., by D.L. Jacobus. Repr. of 1939 ed.
Cloth--$119.00--Paper--$109.00--818pp F5159

1155   - **WATERMAN**. DESCENDANTS OF ROBERT **WATERMAN** OF MARSHFIELD, MA., FROM 7TH GENERATION. VOL. II., by Waterman & Jacobus. Repr. of 1942 ed.
Cloth--$119.00--Paper--$109.00--784pp F5159

1156   - **WATERMAN**. DESC. OF RICHARD **WATERMAN** OF PROVIDENCE, R.I., WITH RECORDS OF MANY OTHER FAMILY GROUPS OF THE **WATERMAN** NAME. VOL. III., by D.L. Jacobus and E.F. Waterman. Repr. of 1954 ed.
Cloth--$119.00--Paper--$109.00--808pp F5159

1157   - **WATERS**. GEN. HIST. OF ABEL **WATERS** OF SUTTON, MASS., by M. Waters and E. Waters. Repr. of ed.
Paper--$5.00--15pp F5159

1158   - **WATKINS**. **WATKINS** FAM. OF N.C., DESC. OF LEVIN **WATKINS** (TO ALA. & MISS.)., by W.B. Watkins. Repr. of ed.
Paper--$17.50--85pp F5159

1159   - **WEAVER** FAM. OF N.Y. CITY., by I.J. Greenwood. Repr. of 1893 ed.
Paper--$4.50--13pp F5159

1160   - **WEAVER**. THE NAME & FAM. OF **WEAVER**, by Media Research Bureau. Reprint.
Paper--$5.00--16pp F5159

1161   - **WEAVER**. RECORD OF WM. **WEAVER** & HIS DESC. OF ILLINOIS., by R.I. Weaver. Repr. of 1925 ed.
Paper--$20.00--106pp F5159

1162   - **WEBSTER**. HIST. & GEN. OF THE GOV. JOHN **WEBSTER** FAM. OF CONN. 2 VOLS., by W.H. Webster and M.R. Webster. Repr. of 1915 ed.
      SPECIAL PRICE FOR THE SET: $223.00 HARDCOVER; $209.00 PAPER
Cloth--$119.00/Vol.--Paper/Vol.--$109.00--833 & 827p F5159

1163   - **WELCH**. **WELCH** & ALLIED FAMILIES, by G.C. Weaver. Repr. of 1932 ed.
Cloth--$58.00--Paper--$48.00--312pp F5159

1164   - **WELCH**. PHILIP **WELCH** OF IPSWICH, MASS., & HIS DESC., by A.M. Welch. Repr. of 1947 ed.
Cloth--$66.00--Paper--$56.00--354pp F5159

1165   - HIST. OF THE **WELD** FAM., FROM 1632 TO 1878., by C.W. Fowler. Repr. of
1879 ed.
Paper--$13.50--64pp F5159

1166   - **WELLES**. HIST. OF THE **WELLES** FAM. IN ENGLAND, WITH THEIR
DERIVATION IN THIS COUNTRY FROM GOV. THOMAS **WELLES** OF CONN.,
by Welles & Clements. Repr. of 1874 ed.
Paper--$21.50--127pp F5159

1167   - **WELLS**. THOMAS & ABIGAIL **WELLS**, IPSWICH, MASS., & SOME OF
THEIR DESC., by A. Caldwell. Reprint.
Paper--$4.00--8pp F5159

1168   - **WELLS**. ANC. & DESC. OF COL. DANIEL **WELLS** (1760-1815) OF
GREENFIELD, MASS., by S.C. Wells. Reprint.
Paper--$13.00--65pp F5159

1169   - **WELLS**. WM. **WELLS** OF SOUTHOLD & HIS DESC., 1638-1878., by C.W.
Hayes. Repr. of 1878 ed.
Cloth--$59.50--Paper--$49.50--300pp F5159

1170   - **WELLS**. GEN. OF THE **WELLS** FAM. & FAMS. RELATED., by G.W.
Wells-Cushing. Repr. of 1903 ed.
Cloth--$42.00--Paper--$32.00--205pp F5159

1171   - **WELLS**. THE **WELLS** FAMILY, by Norris & Feldman. Repr. of 1942 ed.
Cloth--$75.00--Paper--$65.00--417pp F5159

1172   - **WEST** FAM. REG.; IMPORTANT LINES TRACES, 1326-1928., by L.B. Stone.
Repr. of 1928 ed.
Cloth--$87.00--Paper--$77.00--493pp F5159

1173   - **WESTCOTT**. HIST. & GEN. OF THE ANC. & DESC. OF STUKELY
WESTCOTT, ONE OF THIRTEEN ORIG. PROPS. OF PROVIDENCE
PLANTATION & COL. OF R.I., by R.L. Whitman. Repr. of 1932 ed.
Cloth--$76.50--Paper--$66.50--435pp F5159

1174   - **WHALEY**. ENGLISH RECORDS OF THE **WHALEY** FAMILY & ITS
BRANCHES IN AMER., by S. Whaley. Repr. of 1901 ed.
Cloth--$46.50--Paper--$36.50--234pp F5159

1175   - **WHEAT** GEN. A HIST. OF THE **WHEAT** FAM. IN AMER., WITH A BRIEF
ACCT. OF THE NAME & FAM. IN ENG. & NORMANDY. VOL. I., by S.C. Wheat.
Repr. of 1902 ed.
Paper--$22.00--122pp F5159

1176   - **WHEELER**. GEN. OF A BRANCH OF THE **WHEELERS**., by G. Wheeler. Repr.
of 1908 ed.
Paper--$12.00--61pp F5159

1177   - **WHITE**. ANC. CHRONOLOGICAL RECORD OF THE WM. **WHITE** FAM.,
FROM 1607-8 TO 1895., by T. White and S. White. Reprint.
Cloth--$71.00--Paper--$61.00--393pp F5159

1178   - **WHITE**. GENEALOGY OF DESCENDANTS OF JOHN **WHITE** OF WENHAM
        & LANCASTER, MASS., 1638-1900. VOL. I., by A.L. White. Repr. of 1900 ed.
        Cloth--$125.00--Paper--$115.00--931pp F5159

1179   - THE NICHOLAS **WHITE** FAMILY, 1643-1900., by T.J. Lothrop. Repr. of 1902
        ed.
        Cloth--$73.00--Paper--$63.00--493pp F5159

1180   - **WHITE**. GENEALOGY OF DESCENDANTS OF JOHN **WHITE** OF WENHAM
        & LANCASTER, MASS., 1638-1903. VOL. II., by A.L. White. Repr. of 1903 ed.
        Cloth--$123.00--Paper--$113.00--924pp F5159

1181   - **WHITE**. GENEALOGY OF DESCENDANTS OF JOHN **WHITE** OF WENHAM
        & LANCASTER, MASS., 1638-1903. VOL. III., by A.L. White. Repr. of 1905 ed.
        Cloth--$115.00--Paper--$105.00--754pp F5159

1182   - **WHITE**. GENEALOGY OF DESCENDANTS OF JOHN **WHITE** OF WENHAM
        & LANCASTER, MASS., 1638-1909. VOL. IV., by A.L. White. Repr. of 1909 ed.
        Cloth--$42.00--Paper--$32.00--210pp F5159

1183   - **WHITE**. ANC. OF JOHN BARBER **WHITE** & OF HIS DESC., by A.L. White.
        Repr. of 1913 ed.
        Cloth--$66.00--Paper--$56.00--355pp F5159

1184   - GENESIS OF THE **WHITE** FAMILY, by E.S. White. Repr. of 1920 ed.
        A rec. of the **White** family beginning in 900 at the time of its Welsh origin when the
        name was **Wynn**, & tracing the fam. into Ireland & Eng. Also Scotts of Scot's Hall, Kent,
        England.
        Cloth--$65.00--Paper--$55.00--346pp F5159

1185   - **WHITE**. YOUR FAM.: AN INFORMAL ACCT. OF THE ANC. OF ALLEN
        KIRBY **WHITE** & EMMA **CHAMBERS WHITE** (INCL. **WHITE, ALLEN,
        CHAMBERS, HAYES** FAM.)., by E. White. Repr. of 1941 ed.
        Cloth--$42.00--Paper--$32.00--196pp F5159

1186   - **WHITE**. DESCENDANTS OF THOMAS **WHITE**, SUDBURY, MASS., 1638., by
        E.W. Ford. Repr. of 1952 ed.
        Paper--$17.00--93pp F5159

1187   - THE **WHITE** GENEALOGY. A HIST. OF THE DESC. OF MATTHEW &
        ELIZABETH **(GIVEN) WHITE** OF CO. TYRONE, IRELAND, & ALBANY NY, by
        Harold Putnam White, Jr.. Repr. of 1988 ed.
        Origin. comp. in 1908; updated in 1951 & 1987. VOL II: The line of William &
        Laura **(Putnam) White**.
        Cloth--$45.50--Paper--$35.50--234pp F5159

1188   - **WHITE**. ABOVE, VOL. III: THE LINE OF JOHN G. & HANNAH **(PUTNAM)
        WHITE**, by Repr. of 1989 ed.
        Cloth--$63.50--Paper--$53.50--370pp F5159

1189   - THE **WHITE** GENEALOGY. A HISTORY OF THE DESCENDANTS OF
        MATTHEW & ELIZABETH **(GIVEN) WHITE** OF CO. TYRONE, IRELAND, &
        ALBANY, N.Y., by Harold Putnam White, Jr.. Repr. of 1991 ed.

Orig. comp. in 1908, updated in 1951 & 1987. VOL. I: The line of Joseph & Elizabeth (**White**) **Strain**.
Cloth--$45.00--Paper--$35.00--236pp F5159

1190   - **WHITIN** FAMILY HIST. NOTES., by K.W. Swift. Repr. of 1955 ed.
Cloth--$41.00--Paper--$31.00--216pp F5159

1191   - **WHITING**. MEM. OF REV. SAM'L. **WHITING** & HIS WIFE, ELIZABETH **ST. JOHN**; WITH REF. TO SOME OF THEIR ENG. ANC. & AMER. DESC. 2ND ED., by W. Whiting. Repr. of 1873 ed.
Cloth--$63.00--Paper--$53.00--334pp F5159

1192   - **WHITING**. NATHANIEL **WHITING** OF DEDHAM, MA., 1641, & FIVE GENERATIONS OF HIS DESC., by T.S. Lazell. Repr. of 1902 ed.
Paper--$16.00--80pp F5159

1193   - **WHITON**. **WHITON** FAM. IN AMER. THE DESC. OF THOMAS **WHITON** (1635)., by A.S. Whiton. Repr. of 1932 ed.
Cloth--$49.00--Paper--$39.00--258pp F5159

1194   - **WHITTEMORE**. ANC. OF REV. WM. HOWE **WHITTEMORE**, BOLTON, CONN., 1800 - RYE, N.Y., 1885, & OF HIS WIFE, MARIE **CLARK**, N.Y., 1803 - BROOKLYN, 1886., by W.P. Bacon. Repr. of 1907 ed.
Paper--$22.50--124pp F5159

1195   - **WHITTEMORE**. **WHITTEMORE** FAMILY OF FITZWILLIAM, N.H., by L.W. Rhodes. Repr. of 1923 ed.
Paper--$4.00--9pp F5159

1196   - **WHITTIER**. GEN. OF TWO BRANCHES OF THE **WHITTIER** FAM., FROM 1620 TO 1873., by D.B. Whittier. Repr. of 1873 ed.
Paper--$5.50--22pp F5159

1197   - **WHITTIER**. NOTES ON THE ENG. ANC. OF THE **WHITTIER & ROLFE** FAM. OF NEW ENG., by C. Whittier. Repr. of 1912 ed.
Paper--$4.50--14pp F5159

1198   - **WHITTIER**. DESC. OF THOMAS **WHITTIER** & RUTH **GREEN** OF SALISBURY & HAVERHILL, MA., by C. Whittier. Repr. of 1937 ed.
Cloth--$99.00--Paper--$89.00--594pp F5159

1199   - GENEALOGY OF THE **WICKWARE** FAMILY, by A.M. Wickwire. Repr. of 1909 ed.
Containing an acct. of the origin & early hist. of the name & fam. in England; the rec. of John **Wickware**, who emigr. to New London, Conn., in 1675, & his desc. in Amer.
Cloth--$47.50--Paper--$37.50--283pp F5159

1200   - **WIGHT**. MEM. OF **THOMAS WIGHT** OF DEDHAM, WITH GEN. NOTICES OF HIS DESC., 1637-1840., by D.P. Wight. Repr. of 1848 ed.
Paper--$27.50--119pp F5159

1201   - **WIGHTMAN**. GEORGE **WIGHTMAN** OF QUIDNESSETT, R.I. (1632-1721/2) & DESC., INCL. **WAITMAN, WEIGHTMAN, WHITEMAN, WHITMAN**, by M.R. Whitman. Repr. of 1939 ed.
Cloth--$83.50--Paper--$73.50--486pp F5159

1202   - **WILBUR**. THE **WILDBORES** IN AMER: A FAMILY TREE, COMP. REV. ED. 5 VOLS. 1933-8, by J.R. Wilbor and B.F. Wilbour. Repr. of 1933 ed.
        SPECIAL PRICE FOR THE SET: $249.00 HARDCOVER; $199.00 PAPER
        Cloth--$54.00/Vol.--Paper--$44.00/Vol.-- F5159

1203   - DANIEL **WILCOX** OF PORTSMOUTH, R.I. & DESC., by H.F. Johnston. Reprint.
        Paper--$7.50--36pp F5159

1204   - WILLIAM **WILCOX** OF STRATFORD, CONN. & DESC., by H.F. Johnston. Reprint.
        Paper--$26.00--138pp F5159

1205   - **WILCOX**. DESC. OF WILLIAM **WILCOXSON**, VINCENT **MEIGS** & RICHARD **WEBB**, by R.W. Wilcox. Repr. of 1893 ed.
        Paper--$12.50 .... F5159

1206   - **WILCOX**. JOHN **WILCOX** OF HARTFORD, CONN. & DESC., by H.F. Johnston. Repr. of 1948 ed.
        Paper--$10.00--52pp F5159

1207   - **WILKINS**. FAM. OF BRAY **WILKINS**, PATRIARCH OF WILL'S HILL OF SALEM (MIDDLETON), MA., by W. Hill. Repr. of 1943 ed.
        Cloth--$42.00--Paper--$32.00--213pp F5159

1208   - **WILKINSON**. GEN. OF **WILKINSON** & KINDRED FAMS. (SOUTHERN BRANCH)., by M.M. Wilkinson. Repr. of 1949 ed.
        Paper--$82.50--546pp F5159

1209   - **WILLIAMS** CHRONICLE. DESC. OF THOMAS **WILLIAMS** OF SULLIVAN CO., N.Y., & JEFFERSON CO., PA., INCL. REL. FAMS., by F.H. Ehrig. Repr. of 1969 ed.
        Paper--$29.50--198pp F5159

1210   - **WILLIAMS**. ROGER **WILLIAMS** OF PROVIDENCE, R.I. (& DESC.). 2 VOL., by B.W. Anthony and H.W. Weeden. Repr. of 1949 ed. 1966.
        Cloth--$74.00--Paper--$64.00--220+213p F5159

1211   - **WILLIAMS**. ANC. OF LAWRENCE **WILLIAMS**. PT. I, ANC. OF HIS FATHER, SIMON BREED **WILLIAMS**; PT. II, ANC. OF HIS MOTHER, CORNELIA **JOHNSTON**, by C. Williams. Repr. of 1915 ed.
        Cloth--$53.50--Paper--$43.50--291pp F5159

1212   - **WILLIAMS**. DESC. OF JOHN **WILLIAMS**, OF NEWBURY & HAVERHILL, MA., 1600-1674, by C. Williams and A. Williams. Repr. of 1925 ed.
        Paper--$28.50--179pp F5159

1213   - **WILLIAMS**. LIFE, ANC. & DESC. OF ROBERT **WILLIAMS** OF ROXBURY, MASS., 1607-1693, WITH BIOGR. SKETCHES., by H. Williams. Repr. of 1934 ed.
        Cloth--$43.00--Paper--$33.00--216pp F5159

1214   - **WILLIS**. RECORDS OF THE **WILLIS** FAM. OF HAVERHILL, PORTLAND & BOSTON. 2ND ED., by P. Willis. Repr. of 1908 ed.
        Paper--$22.50--130pp F5159

1215   - WINSLOW. GEN. OF EDW. **WINSLOW** OF THE MAYFLOWER & HIS
DESC., FROM 1620 TO 1865., by M.W. Bryant. Repr. of 1915 ed.
Cloth--$49.00--Paper--$39.00--243pp F5159

1216   - **WINTERMUTE** FAMILY HISTORY., by J.B. Wintermute. Repr. of 1900 ed.
Cloth--$63.00--Paper--$53.00--335pp F5159

1217   - **WISDOM** FAMILY., by G.W. Wisdom. Repr. of 1910 ed.
Cloth--$40.00--Paper--$30.00--231pp F5159

1218   - **WISE.** COL. JOHN **WISE** OF ENGLAND & VA., 1617-1695: HIS ANC. &
DESC., by J.C. Wise. Repr. of 1918 ed.
Cloth--$66.00--Paper--$56.00--355pp F5159

1219   - **WOOD** GEN. & OTHER FAM. SKETCHES. GEN. MEMORANDA OF A
BRANCH OF THE **WOOD** FAM. IN ENG. & AMER. ALSO SKETCHES OF REL
FAMS., by L.N. Wood. Repr. of 1937 ed.
Paper--$25.00--130pp F5159

1220   - **WOOD.** THE ANC. & DESC. OF EBENEZER **WOOD** OF W.
GOULDSBOROUGH, MAINE, by E. Wood. Repr. of ed.
Paper--$18.00--90pp F5159

1221   - **WOOD.** DESC. OF THE BROTHERS JEREMIAH & JOHN **WOOD,** by W.S.
Wood. Repr. of 1885 ed.
Cloth--$48.50--Paper--$38.50--292pp F5159

1222   - **WOOD.** YORKSHIRE TO WESTCHESTER: CHRONICLE OF THE **WOOD**
FAMILY, by H.B. Howe. Repr. of 1948 ed.
Cloth--$55.00--Paper--$45.00--290pp F5159

1223   - **WOODBRIDGE** RECORDS: AN ACCT. OF THE DESC. OF THE REV. JOHN
WOODBRIDGE OF NEWBURY, MASS., by L. Mitchell. Repr. of 1883 ed.
Cloth--$45.00--Paper--$35.00--272pp F5159

1224   - **WOODBURY.** ANNALS OF THE CLAN: A STORY FOR DESC. OF FRANCIS
WOODBURY., by A.K. Woodbury. Repr. of 1932 ed.
Paper--$19.00--102pp F5159

1225   - **WOODCOCK.** HIST. OF THE **WOODCOCK** FAM. 1692-1912., by W.L.
Woodcock. Repr. of 1913 ed.
Paper--$12.00--62pp F5159

1226   - **WOOLSEY.** FAM. RECORDS, BEING SOME ACCT. OF THE ANC. OF MY
FATHER & MOTHER, CHARLES W. **WOOLSEY** & JANE ELIZA **NEWTON,** by
E.W. Howland. Repr. of 1900 ed.
Cloth--$50.00--Paper--$40.00--270pp F5159

1227   - **WORCESTER.** THE DESC. OF REV. WM. **WORCESTER,** WITH A BRIEF
NOTICE OF THE CONN. **WOOSTER** FAM., PUB. IN 1856, by J.F. Worcester and
S.A. Worcester. Repr. of 1914 ed.
Cloth--$53.50--Paper--$43.50--292pp F5159

1228　　- **WORDEN**. SOME RECORDS OF PERSONS BY THE NAME OF **WORDEN**., by O.N. Worden. Repr. of 1868 ed.
Paper--$24.00--160pp F5159

1229　　- **WORK** FAMILY HISTORY: TWELVE GEN. OF **WORKS** IN AMER., 1690-1969., by V.G. Hamilton. Repr. of 1969 ed.
Cloth--$99.50--Paper--$89.50--613pp F5159

1230　　- **WORTHINGTON**. THE GEN. OF THE **WORTHINGTON** FAMILY, by G. Worthington. Repr. of 1894 ed.
Cloth--$86.00--Paper--$76.00--489pp F5159

1231　　- **WRIGHT**. COLONIAL FAM. & THEIR DESC.; **WRIGHT** & OTHERS., by M.B. Emory. Repr. of 1900 ed.
Cloth--$52.00--Paper--$42.00--255pp F5159

1232　　- **WRIGHT**. THE **WRIGHT** ANCESTRY OF CAROLINE, DORCHESTER, SOMERSET & WICOMICO COS., MD., by C.W. Wright. Repr. of 1907 ed.
Cloth--$44.00--Paper--$34.00--218pp F5159

1233　　- **WYNKOOP**. **WYNKOOP** GEN. IN THE U.S.A., by R. Wynkoop. Repr. of 1904 ed.
Cloth--$51.50--Paper--$41.50--254pp F5159

1234　　- **YATES**. MEMORIALS OF A FAM. IN ENG. & VA., 1771-1851: **YATES, ORFEUR, AGLIONBY, MUSGRAVE** FAMS., by A.E. Terrill. Repr. of 1887 ed.
Cloth--$69.00--Paper--$59.00--383pp F5159

1235　　- **YEAGER**. BRIEF HIST. OF THE **YEAGER, BUFFINGTON, CREIGHTON, JACOBS, LEMON, HOFFMAN & WOODSIDE** FAM. & THEIR COLL. KINDRED OF PA., by J. Yeager. Repr. of 1912 ed.
Cloth--$53.00--Paper--$43.00--278pp F5159

1236　　- **YEAMANS-YEAOMANS-YOUMANS** GEN., by G.S. Youmans. Repr. of 1946 ed.
Paper--$25.00--127pp F5159

1237　　- **YODER**. DESC. OF JACOB **YODER**., by D.A. Hostetler. Repr. of 1951 ed.
Paper--$19.00--105pp F5159

1238　　- **YORK**. THE **YORK** FAMILY, by W.M. Sargent. Repr. of ed.
Paper--$5.50--22pp F5159

1239　　- **YOUNG**. ROBERT JOHN **YOUNG** & DAISIE FRANCES **DENTON**; ANCESTRAL NOTES & SOME DESCENDANTS., by R.M. Young Widdifield. Repr. of 1961 ed.
Cloth--$41.00--Paper--$31.00--160+34pp F5159

1240　　- **ZIMMERMAN, WATERS** AND ALLIED FAMILIES, by D.E.Z. Allen. Repr. of ed.
Paper--$26.00--162pp F5159

1241 - **ZINK** FAMILIES IN AMERICA, INCL. MANY OF THE **ARCHER, COLGLAZIER, MARSHAL, MARTIN, PERISHO, SEATON & ZIMMERLY** FAMILIES, by D.Z. Kellogg. Repr. of 1933 ed.
Cloth--$71.00--Paper--$61.00--385pp F5159

1242 - THE **KETCHAM-KETCHUM** FAMILY IN AMERICA, by Dorothy Jane Chance. 1991.
Descendants of Edward **Ketcham**, born c.1590, England; to Ipswich, Massachusetts 1635, are followed through the families of his grandsons, Nathaniel **Ketcham** of Huntington, Long Island and Nathaniel **Ketchum** of Norwalk, Connecticut to the 13th generation.
Index, Bibliography.
Cloth--$19.95--196pp F5161

1243 - THE **BREEDING/BREEDEN** GENEALOGICAL EXCHANGE, by
Published semi-annually. Each issue is indexed.
Subscription--$15.00/yr-- F5165

1244 - THE **BLIZZARD** FAMILY, by Debbie Anderson. 1988.
Follows descendants of John **Blizzard** of Pendleton County, West Virginia from mid-1700's. Locations include Virginia, West Virginia, Maryland, Ohio and Indiana.
Cloth--$22.50--163pp F5166

1245 - **COVINGTONS** REMEMBERED FROM GRAVESTONES, WILLS, DEEDS, AND OTHER RECORDS, by DaCosta E. Covington. 1991.
Traces five immigrant **Covingtons**. John and William to Va., Thomas & Nehemiah to Md. and Henry of The Will of 1744 Md. This history has 3 generations of Henry in Bedfordshire England and is mostly his descendants that all researched that came to N.C.
Cloth--$58.00--544pp F5172

1246 - THE **PARRISH** FAMILY UPDATE, by Rev. Brent L. Parrish, Editor.
Monthly Newsletter.
Subscription--$12.00/yr--4-6pp F5173

1247 - THE **PARRISH** FAMILY, by Rev. Brent L. Parrish, Compiler. 1991.
The descendants of Captain Edward **Parrish**.
Cloth--$25.00--386pp F5173

1248 - THE **PARRISH** FAMILY ENCYCLOPEDIA, by Rev. Brent L. Parrish, Editor.
A collection of **Parrish** Genealogical data from over 280 contributors.
Paper--$15.00--150pp F5173

1249 - THE **HEWITTS** OF ATHENS COUNTY, OHIO, by Susan L. Mitchell. 1989.
Cloth--$48.00--455pp F5174

1250 - HELEN **CARRIS HUFF**: HARVEST MOON MEMOIRS, by Helen Estelle Carris Huff and Lorina R. Okamoto. 1990.
Carris, Farnum, Huff, Storer, Sweeting, VanWickle, Westbrook families.
Areas: Wayne County, New York, coastal New York and New Jersey, and Florida.
Indexed, photos.
Cloth--$12.00--100pp F5175

1251   - **TOWNSEND** MISSING LINKS, by Charles D. Townsend, Editor.
Magazine for all who have **TOWNSEND** missing Ancestry prior 1850. Write for details.
Subscription--$15.00/yr-- F5176

1252   - ROTA-GENE INTERNATIONAL GENEALOGY MAGAZINE, by Charles D. Townsend, Editor.
Genealogical magazine for Rotarians & Non-Rotarians. FREE Queries to Subscribers.
Subscription--$15.00/yr-- F5235

1253   - DISCOURSE ON THE LIFE AND CHARACTER OF GOV. **TAZEWELL**, by H.B. Grigsby. Repr. of 1860 ed. 1990.
Eulogy on L.W. **Tazewell** (1774-1860).
Paper--$13.00--116pp F5177

1254   - MEET THE **TAZEWELLS**: TOO MUCH BIRTHDAY WINE, by C.W. Tazewell, Editor. 1990.
Tazewells of Virginia, England, and others.
Paper--$8.00--60pp F5177

1255   - **WALLER** SCRAPBOOK: HERO OR BUTCHER OF SAMAR?, by C.W. Tazewell, Editor. 1990.
Waller Family of Virginia and England.
Paper--$11.00--88pp F5177

1256   - **HAWKES** SCRAPBOOK: A NEW TASTE IN LITERATURE, by John Hawkes.
(Auto)biographical anthology: "I want to try to create a world, not represent it."
Paper--$10.00--74pp F5177

1257   - THE **TAZEWELL** QUANDARY, by C.W. Tazewell, Editor. 1991.
Periodic newsletter of world-wide **Tazewells** (**Taswell, Tanswell, Tasswell, Tazwell** and **Tarzwell**).
Paper--$2.00--12pp F5177

1258   - **DOCKERYS** OF DIXIE, by William G. Allen. 1991.
Connecting families include: **ALLEN; ASHE; BEAVER; CHAMBERS; CORNWELL; DAVIS; DAVIDSON; DOCKERY; FARMER; FREEMAN; FRICKS; GARRETT; GRAVES; HEMBREE; JOHNSON; KEPHART; KILLIAN; LOVINGOOD; LUNSFORD; MARCUS; McDONALD; MILLS; PALMER; PANTHER; PEEBLES; POSTELL; ROBERTS; RADFORD; ROSE; SNEED; WEEKS** and **WOODY**. Oldest generations resided in Rutherford, Burke, Buncombe and Cherokee Counties, N.C. Today, major pockets live in Cherokee and Gaston Counties, N.C.; North and Central GA; East TN; Eastern OK; Central TX; Akron, OH; Detroit, MI and Cottage Grove area of OR. 107 page index, 700 photographs and ten generation genealogy.
Cloth--$56.00--1136pp F5178

1259   - "THE **CLENCONNAN**": CLAN **CUNNING** - ANCIENT CLAN OF THE **DAL CAIS** PEOPLE IN IRELAND AND SCOTLAND, by Willis L. Cunning. 1991.
Reconstructs history of a "buried clan". 1350, David II's Great Seal of Scotland named a "Captain of **Clenconnan**", from original Scotti tuath/tribe (**Dalcassians** of Keltic transEuropean migration). Tells Viking contact in Ireland, royal Ulster and Scottish Dalriada, Iona and highlands. Loss of lands, barons, knights in Highland wars--Patrick, 6th Earl Atholl, murdered 1242. Last Baron, John **Cuningson** of

Eddradour, murdered 1510 by Struan Robertson clan. A few early Colonial mentions (Flora **MacDonald** connection in No. Carolina). Clan surnames in ancient Irish and Scottish charters: **Cunning, Gunning, Conings, Conning, Conynges, Coningus, Cuninges, Cunien, Cunnein, Cunnin, MacCuning, MacConing, McChoning, Mahoning, MacConich** (the prop- Gaelic case-ending for Mac--) **MacCanich, McCanish, MacConochie, McConkie, MacConquchar, MacConochar, MacCunneain** (Englished in Ireland as **Kenyon**) **MacGunyon, Conan, Connan, Conand, Conant, Cunnane, Canine, Kenning, Kinning, Cunningson, Cunnieson, Gunnison, Kennison, Kinnison**. History, not genealogy, but all named should start with this clan history to clear up many old fallacies on origins. Favorably reviewed by academics and authorities in U.S. and Scotland. These proven findings never previously published. Full documentation footnotes, appendices, bibliography, maps, photos of ancient clan castles, manor houses, original manuscripts.
Gold imprinted cover, im. leather; $35 + $4 p.&h. (+ 4% for Iowa orders) 102pp . F5180

1260 - CLERGYMEN AND CHIEFS: A GENEALOGY OF THE **MACQUEEN** AND **MACFARLANE** FAMILIES, by Alexander McQueen Quattlebaum. 1990.
Families came from Scotland to North Carolina and South Carolina. Extensive information about more than 1,200 families, including the related families of **Ellerbe, Holladay, Hudnall, MacDonald, Montgomery, Rogers, White**, and more. Includes illustrations, charts, and index.
Cloth--$37.00--246pp F5181

1261 - A **BUCKNAM-BUCKMAN** GENEALOGY, by Ann Theopold Chaplin. 1988.
Some descs. of William **Bucknam** of Charlestown and Malden, Mass. and John **Bucknam** of Boston. "...the basis for all **Bucknam/Buckman** research for years to come," says the NEHGS Register of Jan. 1989. Every- name Index, other names include: **Brown, Green, Merrill, Pratt, Stone, Wilson**.
Cloth--$37.50--325pp F5184

1262 - DESCENDANTS OF ROBERT **DUNBAR** OF HINGHAM, MASSACHUSETTS, by Ann Theopold Chaplin, C.G.. 1992.
Settled at Hingham by 1655. Known desc., in some instances to the 12th generation and spread from Mass. to Calif., Mich. to Texas. Fully documented and includes an every-name index.
Cloth--$42.50--514pp F5184

1263 - MCALPIN(E) GENEALOGIES 1730-1990, ALEXANDER **MCALPIN** OF SOUTH CAROLINA AND GEORGIA AND HIS DESCENDANTS PLUS OTHER **MCALPIN(E)** FAMILIES IN NORTH AMERICA, by Doris McAlpin Russell. 1990.
Comprehensive genealogies of **McAlpin(e)** families (variant spellings) covering almost every state and Canada.
Cloth--$65.00--750pp F5185

1264 - THE **WICKENBURG** FAMILY: IN SEARCH OF MEMORIES, by Jann Marie Foster. 1988.
The author has traced her ancestors in Sweden to the 1600's when the records began. Documentation is thorough. Individual sections include biographies, photographs and documents. Some of the surnames which appear most frequently: **Abrahamsson, Bjorklund, Johannesdotter, Nilsdotter, Pehrsson** and **Svennsson**.
Paper--$26.95--122pp F5186

1265   - **RITTENHOUSE** FAMILY ASSOCIATION ANNUAL NEWSLETTERS, by Carl
Shuster and Mark Haacke, Editor. 1992.
        These professionally published newsletters contain historical and family information
on **Rittenhouse** families. The focus is on the descendants of Wilhelm **Rittenhouse** (b.
1644 in Mulheim) the first paper maker in the US in 1688. Other information about
German families **Rittinghausen, Rittinghaus, Rettinghausen** and **Rettinghaus** also
appears. Cost is $15 per year. Back issues available.
Subscription--$15.00/yr--24-32pp/yr F5191

1266   - DANIEL **MCPHERSON** OF CHESTER COUNTY, PENNSYLVANIA, HIS
CHILDREN & GRANDCHILDREN, by Judy McPherson Bender. 1990.
        Daniel **McPherson** ca. 1682 to 1755. Children: Ann, John, Daniel, Jr., William &
Stephen. Majority of research data from Virginia.
Cloth--$32.50--269pp F5195

1267   - DESCENDANTS OF ROBERT **BARTLETT** (1603-1676) OF PLYMOUTH,
MASSACHUSETTS, by L. Reichert. 1992.
        Descendants through five generations.
Paper--$5.00--30pp F5203

1268   - DESCENDANTS OF WILLIAM **SPRAGUE** (1609-1675) OF HINGHAM,
MASSACHUSETTS, by L. Reichert. 1992.
        Descendants through five generations, includes two generations of ancestors.
Paper--$5.00--30pp F5203

1269   - DESCENDANTS OF CLEMENT **KING** (?-1669) OF MARSHFIELD,
MASSACHUSETTS, by L. Reichert. 1992.
        Descendants through three generations.
Paper--$2.50--5pp F5203

1270   - DESCENDANTS OF ANTHONY **EAMES** (1595/6-1686) OF CHARLESTOWN
AND MARSHFIELD, MASSACHUSETTS, by L. Reichert. 1992.
        Descendants through five generations, includes his father and brothers.
Paper--$3.00--10pp F5203

1271   - DESCENDANTS OF THOMAS **HARRIS** (1600-1686) OF PROVIDENCE,
RHODE ISLAND, by L. Reichert. 1992.
        Descendants through five generations and some select lines through eight
generations, includes information on his brother, William, through two generations.
Paper--$5.00--30pp F5203

1272   - DESCENDANTS OF RICHARD **TEW** (?-1673/4) OF NEWPORT, RHODE
ISLAND, by L. Reichert. 1992.
        Descendants through four generations.
Paper--$3.50--15pp F5203

1273   - DESCENDANTS OF NATHANIEL **TILDEN** (1583-1641) OF SCITUATE,
MASSACHUSETTS, by L. Reichert. 1992.
        Descendants through four generations, with several generations of ancestors.
Paper--$4.00--20pp F5203

1274   - THE **PAULKS** OF AMERICA, by Jessie H. Paulk and Delma Wilson Paulk. 1990.
        Ancestors and descendants of Samuel **PALK/PAULK** of Concord, MA and Tolland,
CT., with related families.

Related families included are: ABBOTT, BARROWS, BRANCH, CHAPMAN, CLEMENTS, COBB, DANIEL(S), DORMINY, FLETCHER, GASKINS, GIBBS, GRANT, GRIFFIN, HARPER, HENDERSON, HOBBY, KIRKLAND, LOTT, MCMILLAN, MERRITT, PARSONS, RICKETSON, ROBERTS, SEARS, STEARNS, STEEL, STIMSON, SUMNER, TUCKER, VICKERS, WHIDDON, and WILLS.

This handsome, hardbound volume is in descendant order and includes over 10,000 names. It is clear, thorough, exhaustively documented, fully indexed, and printed on archival paper. Several pages of photos are also included.
Cloth--$43.00--704pp F5206

1275   - WILEY **VICKERS** - PIONEER OF COFFEE COUNTY, GA, by Jessie H. Paulk and Delma Wilson Paulk. 1992.
Ancestors and descendants of WILEY & BEADY **(PURVIS) VICKERS** of Coffee County, Ga and NC/SC and related families.
This handsome, hardbound volume is in family descendant order and includes over 10,000 names. It is clear, thorough, exhaustively documented, fully indexed, and printed on archival paper. It includes over 50 photos of the older **Vickers**.
Cloth--$43.00--704pp F5206

1276   - **LOTT(S)** OF GEORGIA, by Jessie H. Paulk and Delma Wilson Paulk. 1992.
Ancestors and descendants of John & Elizabeth **(Joyner)** Lott of NC/SC/GA with emphasis on those who settled the Wiregrass area of South Georgia. Hardbound, in descendant order, fully indexed, printed on archival paper and includes over 100 photos of **Lott** and related families.
Cloth--$55.00--896pp F5206

1277   - ANCESTORS AND DESCENDANTS OF F.A. **MARSH** AND IVY **CRITES**, by William R. Marsh, M.D.. 1990.
The Marsh-Montgomery lines were New York Loyalists. The **Crites-Saxton** lines include three Mayflower ancestors. Indexed.
The geographical areas most heavily emphasized are: Plymouth Colony; Puritan communities of Massachusetts and Connecticut, Little Compton, Rhode Island; The Loyalist of New Brunswick and Toronto; Ridgetown, Ontario; western New York; Hardy and Grant Counties, West Virginia; southern Ohio; western Illinois; Merrick County, Nebraska.
At least two generations of the following families are outlined: **Alden, Bigelow, Birchard, Biscoe, Bond, Brooks, Caulkin(s), Church, Conrad, Crites, Doggett (Daggett), Eddy, Ferris, Flagg, Hart, Heath, Heller, Horsewell, Hyde, Janes, Judd, Linnell, Lockwood, Lombard, Long, Lord, Marsh, Montgomery, Moody, Mullins, Myers, Newcomb, P(e)abodie, Parker, Pearce (Pierce), Potter, Pratt, Pyles, Rogers, Rossiter, Rouse, Savery, Saxton, Searles, Shaw, Simmons, Skinner, Spencer, Steele, Stonard, Sunderland, Talcott, Tallman, Tonge, Tucker, Warren, Wickwire, Wilbore, and Woolson.**
Cloth--$25.00--331pp F5211

1278   - **ELLIOTT**, by Mrs. Joann DeBoard Touchstone. 1991.
Johnston **Elliott** b.1748 & wife, Rebecca **Mayes**. Related families **White, McFarland, Rutherford, Findlay, Duffield, Vest, Hatter, Weber, Kohler.** Geographically involves PA, KY & OK. Photographs, indexed, documented.
Hardback--$35.00--280pp F5212

1279   - **POLLOCK** POTPOURRI, by Michael E. Pollock.
Quarterly   for   researcers   of   **Pollock**/all   variants,   including **POAGUE/POLK/PAULK**, whether Scottish/other national/ethnic origin. Original

source material (largely abstracted) stressed, including European. (Documented) submissions welcomed. Full name/place index.
Subscription--$10.00/vl--20pp/vol F5214

1280   - FLANINGAM FAMILY HISTORY, by Ora L. Flaningam. 1991.
        Contains all the known descendants of Patrick **Flaningham** (168?-1713). Includes female lines of descent, 120 allied families, photographs, charts, illustrations and an 11,000 name index. A monumental work!
        Paper--$41.00--740pp F5215

1281   - EMIGRANT FATHERS, NATIVE SONS, SHANE FAMILY OF PRESCOTT COUNTY, ONTARIO, CANADA 1817-1990, by Katherine Madden Adamson. 1990.
        Documents the family of Maurice **Shane** c.1760 and Anne **Byrnes** 1769 and their six children who emigrated from Co. Wexford, Ireland to settle in Plantagenet township in 1817. Descendants of three of the sons are traced to the present. Related families include **Byrnes, Bradley, Brown, Darragh, Furlong, Hamilton, Landrigan, Lalonde, MacGregor, Madden, McCrank, McDonald, McKinley, McPhee, Moore, Ryan, Sequin, Shea, Shehan, Stewart, Terry**. 52 photos. Includes a listing of all land owners from 1862, 1881 plat maps of Plantagenet townships.
        Cloth--$40.00--362pp F5218

1282   - DR. AMANDUS **CRULL** OF JEFFERSON COUNTY MISSOURI: HIS ANCESTORS, LIFE AND TIMES AND DESCENDANTS, by Albert J. Crull. 1992.
        A genealogical study of the **CRULL** family from 1410 to 1992 with emphasis on Dr. Amandus **Crull** from Mecklenberg, Germany who came to the U.S. in 1840 at the age of 20 and eventually settled in Jefferson County Missouri.
        Cloth--$32.50--279pp F5219

1283   - THE JOHN **PYNE** FAMILY IN AMERICA BEING THE COMPREHENSIVE GENEALOGICAL RECORD OF THE DESCENDANTS OF JOHN **PYNE** (1766-1813) OF CHARLESTON, SOUTH CAROLINA, by Frederick Wallace Pyne, B.S., M.S.. 1992.
        All 177 descendants of John **Pyne**, including a full comprehensive (all the female lines) genealogy of his related descendants in the **Adams, Bankhead, Barretto, Cary, Cowley, Crow, DiGiacomo, Edwards, Guest, Hutchinson, Kennedy, Lundie, March, Marr, Morris, Mulford, Neilson, Newhall, Oliver, Ostrander, Parker, Patterson, Roberts, Shadduck, Schreiber, Smelser, Way,** and **Whitelock** lines. 67 photographs, 22 descendant charts. Full of biographical and genealogical history, printed by Gateway Press, Baltimore, Maryland. A very handsome book at a very reasonable price.
        Cloth--$22.00--224pp F5220

1284   - JOHANN ADAM **BRUCKER** AND HIS AMERICAN DESCENDANTS, by Wallace Hawn Brucker, Brigadier General, U.S. Army, Retired. 1978.
        In addition to the text, this book contains 117 photographs, 2 maps, 82 family charts and full name index. Sources used include church and civil documents, family chronicles, and oral and written recollections obtained by author. Earliest documented **Brucker**, Joseph, was born circa 1680. Johann Adam was born in Hesse-Darmstadt 1787, went to Austria where he married, reared a family and had career as architect and builder. Three children, Ferdinand in 1849, followed by Anna and Karl migrated to Michigan. Text includes biographical sketches of Adam's descendants through successive generations to present. Related families include **Carmichael, Eberly, Elliott, Green, Gump, Kerr, Lehman, Lever, McNally, Parker, Robertson, Rossiter, Simmons, Sinclair, Wagner, Wernert**. Though mainly in Michigan, Ohio and California, these families also live in twenty other states.
        Cloth--$20.00--264pp F5223

1285   - OUR KENTUCKY PIONEER ANCESTRY: A HISTORY OF THE **KINKEAD** AND **MCDOWELL** FAMILIES OF KENTUCKY AND THOSE ASSOCIATED BY MARRIAGE, by June Lee Mefford Kinkead.
Including the lineages of **Allin, Barr, Berry, Blackburn, Bullock, Burgess, Carneal, Chrisman, Farra, Fontaine, Gay, Groff, Hart, Jouett, Lyle, McClung, Neet, Paxton, Shelby, Simpson, Terrell** and **Warfield.** Published in commemoration of the 200th Anniversary of Kentucky's Statehood, with the support of the Kentucky Genealogical Society as their Bicentennial Project. Published by Gateway Press. It contains: an index, 41 illustrations, many heretofore unpublished documents, photographs and first-hand accounts of these pioneer ancestors.
A history of the Governor Isaac and Susannah **Hart Shelby** Family.
The Descendants of Governor **Isaac** and Susannah **Hart Shelby**--three generations.
The Descendants of **Evan** and Catherine Davies Shelby--three generations. (Grandparents of Governor Isaac **Shelby**)
A history of the **Fontaine** Family (from France to Kentucky. A history of the **Warfield** Family; The English Ancestry of the **Warfields**; The **Warfields** of Maryland and the **Warfields** of Kentucky. The Descendants of Elisha and Ruth **Burgess** Warfield--four generations. Elisha **Warfield**, Jr., M.D.; Doctor, Businessman and Horseman. A history of the Ephraim and Margaret Irvine **McDowell** Family. Judge Samuel **McDowell**, Pioneer and Statesman, in Virginia and Kentucky. In Virginia, he was a member of the House of Burgesses from Augusta County. In Kentucky, he was a framer of the First State Constitution and President of the Convention which adopted it. Included are 17 letters from Judge **McDowell** to his son-in-law Andrew **Reid** in Virginia, written from 1783-1814, courtesy of the Filson Club of Louisville, Inc.--four are previously unpublished. The Descendants of Judge Samuel and Mary **McClung McDowell**--three generations. History of the **Kinkead** Family in Virginia and Kentucky including an account of Eleanor Gay Kinkead's capture by the Indians, as told by her youngest son, John, in a letter to his son George Blackburn Kinkead.
The Descendants of Eleanor Gay and William Kinkead. (Children and Grandchildren). The History of the Thomas Davis Carneal Family. He was one of the founders of Covington, Kentucky and a Kentucky Legislator from there.
Cloth--$53.00--478pp F5224

1286   - ANCESTORS OF CORA BELLE **ADAMS** 1881-1957 - MY WORKING NOTEBOOK, by William Sheperd West.
Adams family members include: John Emory, 1844-1935; Isaac, 1809-1877; Isaac, ca 1790. Related families include **Gordy, Dashiell, Jones, Magee, Mcgee, Ward, Winder, Wootten, Cordry, Cordray, Crewe, Sterling, Hearn, Jones, Carter, Walters, Cannon, Inglis, Davis, Frizzell, Southern, de Chiel, Waters, Foxcroft, Robesoume** primarily in Sussex County, Delaware and in nearby counties on Maryland's Eastern Shore.
Interesting charts, photographs, etc. planned. Your information welcome.
Cloth--$35.00--est.200p F5226

1287   - ANCESTORS OF CURTIS TURNER **DAVIDSON** 1864-1924 - MY WORKING NOTEBOOK, by William Sheperd West.
Davidson family members include: Samuel, 1817-1870; James, 1784-1854; James, 1751-1819; William, - 1779; James, -1744.
Related families include **Coffin, Joseph, Wood, Hardy, Simonton, Claypole, Claypoole** primarily in Sussex County, Delaware and in nearby counties on Maryland's Eastern Shore.
Interesting charts, photographs, etc. planned. Your information welcome.
Cloth--$30.00--est.200p F5226

1288   - ANCESTORS OF SHEPERD SALISBURY **WEST** 1876-1937 - MY WORKING
NOTEBOOK, by William Sheperd West.
     West family members include: Samuel Painter 1853- 1922; William S.,
1829-1905; Painter, -1832.
     Related families include **Moore, Timmons, Warren** primarily in Sussex County,
Delaware and in nearby counties on Maryland's Eastern Shore.
     Interesting charts, photographs, etc. planned. Your information welcome.
Cloth--$25.00--est.100p F5226

1289   - ANCESTORS OF MARGIE **WILLEY** 1877-1937 - MY WORKING NOTEBOOK,
by William Sheperd West.
     Willey family members include: James, 1836-1911, herein of three wives and
twenty-one children; John, 1806-1877.
     Related families include **Saterfield, Brown, Higman**. Primarily in Sussex County,
Delaware and in nearby counties of Maryland's Eastern Shore.
     Your information welcome. Interesting charts, photographs, etc. planned.
Cloth--$25.00--est.100p F5226

1290   - ABSTRACTS OF THE ACCOUNT BOOKS OF EDWARD **DIXON**, VOL. I,
(1743-1747),
     Edward **Dixon**, Merchant of Port Royal, Virginia in Caroline County.
Cloth--$15.00-- F5228

1291   - ABSTRACTS OF THE ACCOUNT BOOKS OF EDWARD **DIXON**, VOL. II
(1747-1752),
     Edward **Dixon**, Merchant of Port Royal, Virginia in Caroline County.
Paper--$15.00-- F5228

1292   - "**BACON'S** ADVENTURE", WITH **BACON & WOOD** GENEALOGIES., by
Herbert M. Bacon. Repr. of 1948 ed.
Cloth--$39.50--Paper--$29.50--197pp F5159

1293   - **BALCH** GENEALOGICA., by T.W. Balch. Repr. of 1907 ed.
Cloth--$61.50--Paper--$51.50--410pp F5159

1294   - **BARNHART**. THE DESCENDANTS OF JOHN & MARIAH (**HIVELEY**)
BARNHART, by James K. Raywalt. Repr. of 1990 ed.
     A genealogy of the ancestors & descendants of John **Barnhart** & Mariah **Hively** of
Eastern Ohio to the present.
Cloth--$29.00--Paper--$19.00--109pp F5159

1295   - A GENEALOGY OF THE DESCENDANTS OF JOSEPH **BARTLETT** OF
NEWTON, MASS., FOR SEVEN GENERATIONS., by Aldis E. Hibner. Repr. of 1934
ed.
Cloth--$67.00--Paper--$57.00--291+78pp F5159

1296   - **BEEBE**. GENEALOGY OF THE FAMILY OF **BEEBE**, FROM THE EARLIEST
KNOWN IMMIGRANT, JOHN **BEEBE** OF BROUGHTON, ENG., 1650., by Clifford
Beebe. Repr. of 1991 ed.
Cloth--$41.00--Paper--$31.00--217pp F5159

1297   - **BELLEVILLE**. JEAN **BELLEVILLE** THE HUGUENOT, HIS DESCENDANTS.,
by Paul Belville Taylor. Repr. of 1973 ed.
Cloth--$99.00--Paper--$89.00--610pp F5159

1298   - **BETHEA** FAMILY OF MARION CO., S.C. (EXTR. "HIST. OF MARION CO.")., by W.W. Seller. Repr. of 1902 ed.
Cloth--$6.50--Paper--$5.50--23pp F5159

1299   - **BOYD-PATTERSON** ANCESTRY., by H.M. Pitman and K.P.B. Hunt. Repr. of 1967 ed.
write for price, 6+191pp F5159

1300   - **BOYDEN**. HERE AND THERE IN THE FAMILY TREE., by Albert Boyden. Repr. of 1949 ed.
Cloth--$56.00--Paper--$46.00--294pp F5159

1301   - **BRUMFIELD**. DESCENDANTS OF THOMAS **BRUMFIELD** OF BERKS CO., PENN.: GENEALOGY & FAMILY HISTORY, 1720-1960., by Ray C. Brumfield and Blackman O. Brumfield. Repr. of 1962 ed.
Cloth--$86.00--Paper--$76.00--493pp F5159

1302   - **BRYANT** FAMILY HISTORY, ANCESTRY & DESCENDANTS OF DAVID **BRYANT** (1756) OF SPRINGFIELD, NJ, WASHINGTON CO., & WOLF LAKE, NOBLE CO., IN., by C.V. Braiden. Repr. of 1913 ed.
Cloth--$52.50--Paper--$42.50--270pp F5159

1303   - **BURGESS**. COLONISTS OF NEW ENGLAND & NOVA SCOTIA: **BURGESS** & **HECKMAN** FAMILIES., by Kenneth Farwell Burgess. Repr. of 1956 ed.
Cloth--$34.00--Paper--$24.00--134pp F5159

1304   - **BURHANS**. DESC. FROM THE FIRST ANC. IN AMER., JACOB **BURHANS**, 1660, & HIS SON, JAN **BURHANS**, 1663., by S. Burhans, Jr.. Repr. of 1894 ed.
Cloth--$124.00--Paper--$114.00--799+11pp F5159

1305   - **BURNETT**. THE FAMILY OF **BURNETT** OF LEYS, WITH COLLATERAL BRANCHES., by G. Burnett (Compiler) and J. Allardyce (Editor). Repr. of 1901 ed.
Cloth--$71.00--Paper--$61.00--xxii+367pp F5159

1306   - **CABOT**. HISTORY & GENEALOGY OF THE **CABOT** FAMILY, 1475-1927., by L. Vernon Briggs. Repr. of 1927 ed.
Cloth--$145.00--Paper--$135.00--885pp F5159

1307   - **CALHOUN**. THE STORY OF THE **CALHOUNS** OF JUDEA, CONN. (RENAMED WASHINGTON, 1779)., by M.B. Calhoun. Repr. of 1956 ed.
Cloth--$24.00--Paper--$12.00--57pp F5159

1308   - THE HOUSE OF **CESSNA**, SECOND SERIES., by H. Cessna. Repr. of 1935 ed.
Cloth--$41.00--Paper--$31.00--199pp F5159

1309   - **CLAIBORNE** PEDIGREE; A GENEALOGICAL TABLE OF THE DESCENDANTS OF SECRETARY WILLIAM **CLAIBORNE** OF THE JUNIOR BRANCH OF THE U.S., by G.M. Claiborne. Repr. of 1900 ed.
      With some tracings in the female line.
Cloth--$20.00--Paper--$10.00--51pp F5159

1310   - **COMINS**. THE **COMINS** FAMILY: DESCENDANTS OF JOHN **COMINS** OF WOBURN, MASS., by W.B. O'Connor. Repr. of 1915 ed.
Cloth--$16.00--Paper--$6.00--30pp F5159

1311   - **CONE**. SOME ACCOUNT OF THE **CONE** FAMILY IN AMERICA, PRINCIPALLY THE DESCENDANTS OF DANIEL **CONE**, WHO SETTLED IN HADDAM, CONN., IN 1662., by W.W. Cone. Repr. of 1903 ed.
Cloth--$93.00--Paper--$83.00--546pp F5159

1312   - THE **COX** FAMILIES OF HOLDERNESS, WITH PARTIAL GENEALOGIES OF THE **COX**, **RANDALL**, **NUTTER** & **PICKERING** FAMILIES, & BIOGR. SKETCHES OF FOUR BROTHERS, by L.S. Cox. Repr. of 1939 ed.
Descendants of these families.
Cloth--$47.00--Paper--$37.00--235pp F5159

1313   - ADDITIONS & CORRECTIONS FOR "THE **COX** FAMILIES OF HOLDERNESS", by Cox. Repr. of 1949 ed. 1957.
Cloth--$31.00--Paper--$21.00--58+90pp F5159

1314   - **DAGUE**. THE HISTORY & GENEALOGY OF THE **DAGUE** FAMILY., by Carrie M. Dague. Repr. of 1938 ed.
Cloth--$49.00--Paper--$39.00--253pp F5159

1315   - **DANA**. THE **DANA** SAGA: THREE CENTURIES OF THE **DANA** FAMILY IN CAMBRIDGE., by Henry Wadsworth Longfellow. Repr. of 1941 ed.
Cloth--$22.00--Paper--$12.00--61pp F5159

1316   - **DANIELS**. THE **DANIELS** FAMILY: A GENEALOGICAL HISTORY OF THE DESCENDANTS OF WILLIAM **DANIELS** OF DORCHESTER & MILTON, MASS., 1630-1951., by James Harrison Daniels, Jr.. Repr. of 1952 ed.
Cloth--$51.50--Paper--$41.50--264pp F5159

1317   - **DANIELS**. THE **DANIELS** FAMILY: A GENEALOGICAL HISTORY OF THE DESCENDANTS OF WILLIAM **DANIELS** OF DORCHESTER & MILTON, MASS., 1730-1957, VOLUME II., by James Harrison Daniels, Jr.. Repr. of 1957 ed.
Cloth--$83.00--Paper--$73.00--484pp F5159

1318   - **DINWIDDIE** FAMILY RECORDS, WITH ESPECIAL ATTENTION TO THE LINE OF WILLIAM WALTHALL **DINWIDDIE**, 1804-1882, by E.D. Holladay. Repr. of 1957 ed.
Cloth--$39.50--Paper--$29.50--191pp F5159

1319   - **DOOLITTLE**. THE **DOOLITTLE** FAMILY IN AMERICA, PART VIII., by L.S. Brown and M.R. Doolittle. Repr. of 1967 ed.
Cloth--$97.50--Paper--$87.50--619pp F5159

1320   - **DORMAN**. SOME DESCENDANTS OF JABEZ **DORMAN** OF ARUNDEL (1678-1765): TEN GENERATIONS OF **DORMANS** IN MAINE., by Franklin A. Dorman. Repr. of 1992 ed.
Cloth--$26.50--Paper--$16.50--112pp F5159

1321   - **EGE**. HISTORY & GENEALOGY OF THE **EGE** FAMILY IN THE U.S., 1738-1911., by Thompson P. Ege. Repr. of 1911 ed.
Cloth--$64.00--Paper--$54.00--281pp F5159

1322   **- FAIRFIELD.** DESCENDANTS OF JOHN **FAIRFIELD** OF WENHAM, VOL. I: FIRST FIVE GENERATIONS, WITH AN APPENDIX ON **FAIRFIELD** FAMILIES IN ENGLAND., by W.C. Fairfield. Repr. of 1953 ed.
Cloth--$26.50--Paper--$16.50--82pp F5159

1323   **- FERGUSON.** RECORDS OF THE CLAN & NAME OF **FERGUSSON, FERGUSON & FERGUS.**, by J. Fergusson and R.M. Fergusson. Repr. of 1895 ed.
Cloth--$104.00--Paper--$94.00--xxx+618p F5159

1324   **- FERGUSON.** THE **FERGUSON** FAMILY IN SCOTLAND & AMERICA., by M.L. Ferguson. Repr. of 1905 ed.
Cloth--$35.50--Paper--$25.50--142pp F5159

1325   **- FLEMING** FAMILY & ALLIED LINES: **BAIRD, BLAIR, BUTLER, COOK, CHILDS, CLARK, COLE, CRANE,** ET AL., by P.V. Lawson. Repr. of 1903 ed.
Cloth--$56.50--Paper--$46.50--304pp F5159

1326   **- FLOYD-JONES.** THOMAS **JONES,** FT. NECK, QUEENS CO., LONG ISLAND, 1695, & HIS DESCENDANTS: THE FLOYD-JONES FAMILY WITH CONNECTIONS FROM THE YEAR 1066., by T. Floyd Jones. Repr. of 1906 ed.
Cloth--$39.50--Paper--$29.50--183+11pp F5159

1327   **- FOX** COUSINS BY THE DOZENS, by Nellie Fox Adams and Bertha Fox Walton. Repr. of 1976 ed.
        Includes allied lines **Aldridge, Ballard, Berryman, Brookshire, Conkwright, Fish, Franklin, Haggard, Haley, Hughes, Parrish, Noe, Oliver, Todd, Tuttle, Vivion.**
Cloth--$69.50--Paper--$59.50--408pp F5159

1328   **- GALLEY.** HISTORY OF THE **GALLEY** FAMILY, WITH LOCAL & OLD-TIME SKETCHES IN THE YOUGH REGION., by H. Galley and J.O. Arnold. Repr. of 1908
Cloth--$63.00--Paper--$53.00--271pp F5159

1329   **- GAMBLE.** THE MOUNT DESERT WIDOW: GENEALOGY OF THE MAINE **GAMBLE** FAMILY FROM THE FIRST LANDING ON THE COAST OF MT. DESERT DOWN TO THE PRESENT DAY., by G. Cilley and J.P. Cilley. Repr. of 1896 ed.
Cloth--$40.00--Paper--$30.00--196pp F5159

1330   **- GLASSELL.** VIRGINIA GENEALOGIES: GENEALOGY OF THE **GLASSEL** FAMILY OF SCOTLAND & VA., ALSO OF THE **HOLLYDAY, LEWIS, LITTLEPAGE** & OTHERS OF VA. & MARYLAND., by H.E. Hayden. Repr. of 1891 ed.
Cloth--$59.50--Paper--$49.50--777pp F5159

1331   **- GORBY.** THE **GORBY** FAMILY ORIGIN, HISTORY & GENEALOGY; DESC. OF SAMUEL & MARY **(MAY) GORBY.**, by A. Gorby. Repr. of 1936 ed.
Cloth--$57.00--Paper--$47.00--304pp F5159

1332   **- GRANVILLE.** THE HISTORY OF THE **GRANVILLE** FAMILY, TRAVED BACK TO ROLLO, FIRST DUKE OF NORMANDY, WITH PEDIGREES, ETC., by R. Granville. Repr. of 1895 ed.
Cloth--$84.50--Paper--$74.50--489pp F5159

1333   - THE **HAVENS** FAMILY IN NEW JERSEY, WITH ADDITIONAL NOTES ON
THE **TILTON, FIELDER, HANCE, OSBORN, DAVISON, COX & GIFFORD**
FAMILIES, CONNECTED BY MARRIAGE, by Henry C. Havens. Repr. of 1933 ed.
Cloth--$32.50--Paper--$22.50--103+30pp F5159

1334   - **HAYDEN**. RECORDS OF THE CONN. LINE OF THE **HAYDEN** FAMILY., by
J.H. Hayden. Repr. of 1888 ed.
Cloth--$61.00--Paper--$51.00--329pp F5159

1335   - **HEINECKE**. THE GENEALOGY OF ADAM **HEINECKE** & HENRY
VANDERSAAL, FROM 1747-1881., by S. Heinecke. Repr. of 1881 ed.
Cloth--$26.00--Paper--$16.00--81pp F5159

1336   - **HIBBARD**. SUPPLEMENTS TO THE 1901 *"GENEALOGY OF THE **HIBBARD**
FAMILY*"., by Frederick A. Hibbard and Robert E. Patterson. Repr. of 1991 ed.
Cloth--$41.00--Paper--$31.00--209pp F5159

1337   - **HIBBARD**. GENEALOGY OF THE **HIBBARD** FAMILY, WHO ARE
DESCENDANTS OF ROBERT **HIBBARD** OF SALEM, MASS.: UPDATE OF 1901
EDITION., by Frederic A. Hibbard. Repr. of 1992 ed.
Cloth--$49.50--Paper--$39.50--268pp F5159

1338   - **HOLLOWAY**. WILLIAM **HOLLOWAY** OF TAUNTON, MASS., IN 1637, &
HIS DESCENDANTS, 1586-1949., by E.H. Pendleton. Repr. of 1950 ed.
Cloth--$65.00--Paper--$55.00--356pp F5159

1339   - **HOPKINS**. (STEPHEN) **HOPKINS** OF THE MAYFLOWER: PORTRAIT OF A
DISSENTER., by Margaret Hodges. Repr. of 1972 ed.
Cloth--$41.00--Paper--$31.00--274pp F5159

1340   - **HUMPHREYS** FAMILIES IN AMERICA (DORCHESTER & WEYMOUTH
FAMILIES)., by Gilbert Nash. Repr. of 1883 ed.
Cloth--$49.00--Paper--$39.00--275pp F5159

1341   - ABSTRACTS OF WILLS & MEMORANDA CONCERNING THE ENGLISH
HUMPHREYS, COLLECTED FROM THE...RECORD OFFICES OF GREAT
BRITAIN (ADDENDA TO **"HUMPHREYS** GEN."), by   Repr. of 1887 ed.
Cloth--$28.00--Paper--$18.00--106pp F5159

1342   - **LAYNE-LAIN-LANE** GENEALOGY, BEING A COMPILATION OF NAMES &
HISTORICAL INFORMATION OF MALE DESCENDANTS OF 16 BRANCHES OF
THE **LAYNE-LAIN-LANE** FAM IN U.S., by F.B. Layne. Repr. of 1962 ed.
Cloth--$62.00--Paper--$52.00--336pp F5159

1343   - **LANE**. ..AND A CAST OF THOUSANDS: A HISTORY OF THE **LANE**
FAMILY OF CANADA & THE U.S., FROM THEIR ARRIVAL IN 1819 TO THE
PRESENT., by James K. Raywalt. Repr. of 1989 ed.
Cloth--$99.50--Paper--$89.50--751pp F5159

1344   - **LECONTE** HISTORY & GENEALOGY, WITH PARTICULAR REFERENCE TO
GUILLAUME **LECONTE** OF NEW ROCHELLE & NEW YORK, & HIS
DESCENDANTS. 2 VOLUMES., by Richard LeConte Anderson. Repr. of 1981 ed.
Cloth--$169.00--Paper--$159.00--1350pp F5159

1345   - **LIVINGSTON** FAMILY IN AMERICA & ITS SCOTTISH ORIGINS., by Florence van Rensselaer and William Laimbeer (Editor). Repr. of 1949 ed.
Cloth--$73.00--Paper--$63.00--413pp F5159

1346   - **LOMEN**. GENEALOGIES OF THE **LOMEN (RINGSTAD), BRANDT & JOYS** FAMILIES., by G.J. Lomen. Repr. of 1929 ed.
Cloth--$65.50--Paper--$55.50--361pp F5159

1347   - **LONGYEAR**. THE DESCENDANTS OF JACOB **LONGYEAR** OF ULSTER CO., NEW YORK., by Edmund J. Longyear. Repr. of 1942 ed.
Cloth--$99.00--Paper--$89.00--622pp F5159

1348   - **LYLE**. THE **LYLES** OF PENNSYLVANIA, BEING AN ACCT. OF THE ORIGIN, MIGRATIONS & GENERATIONS OF THE FAMILY, by Alvin Dinsmore White. Repr. of 1963 ed.
Cloth--$63.00--Paper--$53.00--343pp F5159

1349   - **MALLET**. JOHN **MALLET**, THE HUGUENOT, & HIS DESCENDANTS, 1694-1894., by A.S. Mallett. Repr. of 1895 ed.
Cloth--$53.00--Paper--$43.00--342pp F5159

1350   - **MCGAVOCK** FAMILY: A GENEALOGICAL HISTORY OF JAMES **MCGAVOCK** & HIS DESCENDANTS, FROM 1760 TO 1903., by Robert Gray. Repr. of 1903 ed.
Cloth--$38.00--Paper--$28.00--175pp F5159

1351   - **MCMATH**. COLLECTIONS FOR A HISTORY OF THE ANCIENT FAMILY OF **MCMATH**., by F.M. McMath. Repr. of 1937 ed.
Cloth--$53.00--Paper--$43.00--272pp F5159

1352   - **MOELICH-MALICK-MELLICK** GENEALOGY, EXTR. FROM "*STORY OF AN OLD FARM*", by A.D. Mellick. Repr. of 1889 ed.
ALSO AVAILABLE: Complete book "*Story of an Old Farm, or Life in N.J. in the 18th Cent., with gen.*" 742pp. Hardcover, $75.00.
Cloth--$27.00--Paper--$17.00--85pp F5159

1353   - **MILK**. HISTORY & GENEALOGY OF THE **MILK-MILKS** FAMILY., by Grace Croft. Repr. of 1952 ed.
Cloth--$57.00--Paper--$47.00--308pp F5159

1354   - **MILLS**. ANDREW **MILLS** & HIS DESCENDANTS, WITH GENEALOGIES OF RELATED FAMILIES., by E.M.L. Taylor. Repr. of 1944 ed.
Cloth--$33.00--Paper--$23.00--150pp F5159

1355   - **MITCHELL**. THE **MITCHELL** RECORD., by C.B. Mitchell. Repr. of 1925 ed.
Cloth--$37.00--Paper--$27.00--183pp F5159

1356   - **MORE**. HISTORY OF THE **MORE** FAMILY, & AN ACCOUNT OF THEIR REUNION IN 1890, WITH A GENEALOGICAL RECORD., by David Fellows More. Repr. of 1893 ed.
Cloth--$73.00--Paper--$63.00--409pp F5159

1357   - **MORGAN**. A HISTORY OF THE DESCENDANTS OF HENRY OSCAR **MORGAN** & ELLEN JANE **MANDIGO**., by James K. Reywalt. Repr. of 1991 ed. Cloth--$39.00--Paper--$29.00--203pp F5159

1358   - **MORTON**. THE **MORTONS** & THEIR KIN: A GENEALOGY AND A SOURCE BOOK., by D. Morton. Repr. of 1920 ed. Cloth--$129.00--Paper--$119.00--899pp F5159

1359   - **NIVEN**. THE FAMILY OF **NIVEN**, WITH BIOGRAPHICAL SKETCHES (AND THE VOYAGES, LETTERS & DIARIES OF CAPT. JOHN **NIVEN**.), by John Niven. Repr. of 1960 ed. Cloth--$47.00--Paper--$37.00--252pp F5159

1360   - **PELT**. A GENEALOGICAL HISTORY OF THE **PELT** FAMILY BRANCH OF THE **VAN PELT** FAMILY TREE., by Chester H. Pelt, Sr.. Repr. of 1992 ed. Cloth--$32.00--Paper--$22.00--140pp F5159

1361   - **PENNOCK**. THE **PENNOCKS** OF PRIMITIVE HALL., by George Valentine Massey III. Repr. of 1951 ed. Cloth--$32.50--Paper--$22.50--139pp F5159

1362   - **PRIME**. THE AUTOBIOGRAPHY OF AN OCTOGENARIAN, WITH THE GENEALOGY OF HIS ANCESTORS & SKETCHES OF THEIR HISTORY., by Daniel N. Prime. Repr. of 1873 ed. Cloth--$54.00--Paper--$44.00--293pp F5159

1363   - **RANDALL**. GENEALOGY OF THE DESCENDANTS OF STEPHEN **RANDALL** & ELIZABETH **SWEZEY**: 1624-1668, LONDON, ENG.; 1668-1738, RI & CONN.; 1738-1906, LONG ISL., NY., by S.M. Randall. Repr. of 1906 ed. Cloth--$23.00--Paper--$13.00--64pp F5159

1364   - **RHODES** FAMILY IN AMERICA: A GENEALOGY & HISTORY, FROM 1497 TO THE PRESENT DAY., by Howard J. Rhodes. Repr. of 1959 ed. Cloth--$89.00--Paper--$79.00--525pp F5159

1365   - **ROBINSON**. DESCENDANTS OF REV. WILLIAM **ROBINSON**., by Bertha Smith Taylor. Repr. of 1936 ed. Cloth--$24.00--Paper--$14.00--71pp F5159

1366   - **ROCKEFELLER**. TRANSACTIONS OF THE **ROCKEFELLER** FAMILY ASSOC. FOR 1910-1914, WITH GENEALOGY., by H.O. Rockefeller. Repr. of 1915. Cloth--$56.50--Paper--$46.50--338pp F5159

1367   - **RYMES** GENEALOGY: SAMUEL **RYMES** OF PORTSMOUTH, NH & HIS DESCENDANTS., by C.E. Rymes. Repr. of 1897 ed. Cloth--$14.50--Paper--$4.50--13pp F5159

1368   - THE **SHARPE** FAMILY MAGAZINE, VOL. I., NOS. 1-32., by Repr. of 1893 ed. Cloth--$44.50--Paper--$34.50--212pp F5159

1369   - **SHOVE**. AN ENGLISH ANCESTRY: AN ACCT. OF THE ANCESTRY OF EDWARD MELVIN **SHOVE** & HIS SIBLINGS., by James K. Raywalt. Repr. of 1992 ed. Cloth--$31.00--Paper--$21.00--149pp F5159

1370   - **SHURTLEFF**. DESCENDANTS OF WILLIAM **SHURTLEFF** OF PLYMOUTH & MARSHFIELD, MASS. 2 VOLUMES., by B. Shurtleff. Repr. of 1912 ed.
Cloth--$175.00--Paper--$165.00--758+738p F5159

1371   - THE ANNALS OF THE FAMILIES OF CASPAR, HENRY, BALTZER & GEORGE **SPENGLER**, WHO SETTLED IN YORK CO. (PA.) RESPECTIVELY IN 1729, 1732, 1732, & 1751, by E.W. Spangler. Repr. of 1896 ed.
With biographical & historical sketches.
Cloth--$101.00--Paper--$91.00--604pp F5159

1372   - **STARBIRD**. GENEALOGY OF THE **STARBIRD-STARBARD** FAMILY., by A.A. Starbird. Repr. of 1942? ed.
Cloth--$37.00--Paper--$27.00--179pp F5159

1373   - **STARKEY**. THE **STARKEYS** OF NEW ENGLAND & ALLIED FAMILIES., by Emily Wilder Leavitt. Repr. of 1910 ed.
Cloth--$34.00--Paper--$24.00--149pp F5159

1374   - **STETSON** KINDRED OF AMERICA (BOOKLETS NOS. 3 & 4)., by G.W. Stetson and N.M. Stetson. Repr. of 1912 ed.
Cloth--$39.50--Paper--$29.50--45+147pp F5159

1375   - **STORRS**.   THE **STORRS** FAMILY: GENEALOGICAL & OTHER MEMORANDA., by C. Storrs. Repr. of 1886 ed.
Cloth--$94.00--Paper--$84.00--xv+552pp F5159

1376   - **STOUT** AND ALLIED FAMILIES., by H.F. Stout. Repr. of 1951 ed.
Cloth--$139.50--Paper--$129.50--xxii+889 .... F5159

1377   - **STRETCHER**.   ALLIED FAMILIES OF DELAWARE: **STRETCHER,** **FENWICK, DAVIS, DRAPER, KIPSHAVEN, STIDHAM.**, by E.E. Sellers. Repr. of ed.
Cloth--$38.00--Paper--$28.00--171pp F5159

1378   - A HISTORY OF THE AMERICAN & PURITANICAL FAMILY OF **SUTLIFF** OR **SUTLIFFE**, SPELLED **SUTCLIFFE** IN ENGLAND, by S.M. Sutliff, Jr. Repr. of 1909. And a genealogy of all the descendants through Nathaniel **Sutliff**, Jr.
Cloth--$41.00--Paper--$31.00--199pp F5159

1379   - **SWALLOW**. GENEALOGY OF THE **SWALLOW** FAMILY, 1666-1910, by Baker, North & Ellis. Repr. of 1910 ed.
Cloth--$44.50--Paper--$34.50--217pp F5159

1380   - **SWANDER**. HISTORY OF THE **SWANDER** FAM., by J.I. Swander. Repr. of 1899 ed.
Cloth--$33.00--Paper--$23.00--143pp F5159

1381   - **TALIAFERRO-TOLIVER** FAMILY RECORDS., by N.W. Sherman. Repr. of 1960 ed.
Cloth--$43.50--Paper--$33.50--242pp F5159

1382   - **TOLIVER** - SEE **TALIAFERRO** (#1381),
.... F5159

1383   - **TUTTLE-TUTHILL**. ONE BRANCH OF THE ELI **TUTHILL** FAMILY OF LIBERTY TWP. OF MICHIGAN, by Jean L. LaPorte.
Descendants of the **Tuthill** family of Southold & Orient, Long Isl., 1640, & of Tharston, England.
Cloth--$25.00--Paper--$15.00--107pp F5159

1384   - **UPSON** FAMILY IN AMERICA., by Upson Family Association. Repr. of 1940 ed.
Cloth--$104.00--Paper--$94.00--624pp F5159

1385   - **USHER**. A MEMORIAL SKETCH OF ROLAND GREENE **USHER**, 1823-1895, TO WHICH IS ADDED A GENEALOGY OF THE **USHER** FAMILY IN NEW ENGLAND FROM 1638 TO 1895., by E.P. Usher. Repr. of 1895 ed.
Cloth--$35.00--Paper--$25.00--160pp F5159

1386   - **VAN PELT**. SEE **PELT** (#1360),
.... F5159

1387   - **WARNER**. SIR THOMAS **WARNER**, PIONEER OF THE WEST INDIES: A CHRONICLE OF HIS FAMILY., by Aucher Warner. Repr. of 1933 ed.
174pp F5159

1388   - **WASHBURN**. THE RICHARD **WASHBURN** FAMILY GENEALOGY; A FAMILY HISTORY OF 200 YEARS, WITH SOME CONNECTED FAMILIES., by Ada C. Haight and Frank C. Lewis. Repr. of 1937 ed.
Cloth--$149.50--Paper--$139.50--1271pp F5159

1389   - **WATERHOUSE**. THE ANCESTRY OF JOSEPH **WATERHOUSE**, 1754- 1837, OF STANDISH, MAINE., by Walter G. Davis. Repr. of 1949 ed.
Write for price, 144pp F5159

1390   - **WEIMER**. BIOGRAPHICAL SKETCHES & FAMILY RECORDS OF THE GABRIEL **WEIMER** & DAVID **WEIMER** FAMILIES, by L.C. Potts. Repr. of 1936 ed.
Cloth--$52.50--Paper--$42.50--270pp F5159

1391   - **WHEELOCK** FAMILY OF CALAIS, VERMONT: THEIR AMERICAN ANCESTRY & DESCENDANTS., by M.W. Waite. Repr. of 1940 ed.
Write for price, 175pp F5159

1392   - **WHITIN** FAMILY HISTORICAL NOTES, by Katherine W. Swift. Repr. of 1955 ed.
Write for price, 216pp F5159

1393   - WILLCOX. IVY **MILLS**, 1729-1866: **WILLCOX** & ALLIED FAMILIES., by J. Willcox. Repr. of 1911 ed.
Cloth--$33.00--Paper--$23.00--139pp F5159

1394   - **WOOD**. SEE **BACON** (#1292).

1395   - **YOUNG**. OUR **YOUNG** FAMILY IN AMERICA., by Edward Hudson Young. Repr. of 1947 ed.
Cloth--$58.00--Paper--$48.00--315pp F5159

1396   - ZAHNISER. THE ZAHNISERS: A HISTORY OF THE FAMILY IN AMERICA.,
        by Kate M. Zahniser and Charles Reed Zahniser. Repr. of 1906 ed.
        Cloth--$43.00--Paper--$33.00--218pp F5159

1397   - CAPTIN JOHN MASON, FOUNDER OF NEW HAMPSHIRE, by John Ward Dean
        (Editor). Repr. of 1887 ed. 1991.
        Mason. With memoir by C.W. Tuttle.
        Paper--$49.50--492pp F5159

1398   - POCAHONTAS, by Stuart E. Brown, Jr.. 1989.
        This very valuable work is the COMPLETE story of Pocahontas' words and actions
        as recounted by her contemporaries and near-contemporaries.
        Illustrated.
        Paper--$9.95--34pp F5102

1399   - ANCESTORS AND DESCENDANTS OF FRANCIS EPES I OF VIRGINIA
        (EPES-EPPES-EPPS), by John Frederick Dorman. 1992.
        Epes-Eppes-Epps. Chronicles the family in England from Alan Epes (d. 1471)
        through the first five generations in this country. Includes color photos of Coat-of-Arms
        and churches in England associated with the family.
        Cloth--$45.00--257pp F5229

1400   - HOY FAMILY IN PLATTE COUNTY, MO, by Daisy Hoy Bell.
        Hoy family.
        Paper--$3.00--32pp F5231

1401   - AN IRISH RUDD FAMILY 1760 - 1988, RUDD ORIGINS AND OTHER IRISH
        RUDDS, by Norman N. Rudd. 1992.
        First 87 pages of interest to all with Rudd connections. Remainder covers progeny of
        Gordon Arthur Rudd and Alicia Wellwood of Rathsarn parish in Queen's Co. Ireland.
        112 pages of pictures, 27 family summaries, 3 early Rudd charts.
        Cloth--$33.30--552pp F5233

1402   - DESCENDANTS OF JOHN HOUSER (1709 - 1763), by Elmer A. Houser, Jr. and
        Nannie Ellis Houser. 1991.
        The most extensive genealogy of the Houser Family ever published, with fully
        indexed factual data on 17,000 people in 600 pages, along with stories on the life of early
        Housers. Descendants are scattered throughout the United States and Canada, with large
        groups in 160 counties in 30 states.
        Collateral families include: Austell, Bean, Borders, Cruze, Davis, Dixon, Finger,
        Goforth, Hood, Johnson, Long, Martin, Miller, Sayne, Sepaugh, Smith, Spangler
        and White.
        Paper--$40.00--600pp F5234

1403   - PHELPS FAMILY NEWS, by Dallas L. Phelps, Editor.
        .... F5179

1404   - AN ADDINGTON/CHALFANT FAMILY HISTORY WITH A HISTORY OF
        THE ADDINGTON FAMILY IN RANDOLPH COUNTY, INDIANA, by David Vern
        Addington. 1992.
        Paper--$23.50--297pp F5216

1405   - THE DESCENDANTS OF GEORGE **HOLMES** OF ROXBURY, 1594-1908/DESCENDANTS OF JOHN **HOLMES** OF WOODSTOCK, CONN., by George Arthur Gray. Repr. of 1908 ed. 1992.
Paper--$30.00--432pp F5216

1406   - A **HUFF** GENEALOGY: DESCENDANTS OF ENGLEBERT **HUFF** OF DUTCHESS COUNTY, NEW YORK, by George Lockwood Trigg. 1992.
Paper--$65.00--535pp F5216

1407   - THE DESCENDANTS OF WILLIAM & ELIZABETH **TUTTLE**, by George Frederick Tuttle. Repr. of 1883 ed. 1992.
Paper--$45.00--754pp F5216

1408   - FIVE GENERATIONS OF THE FAMILY OF BURR **HARRISON** OF VIRGINIA, 1650-1800, by John P. Alcock. 1991.
Paper--$25.00--300pp F5216

1409   - A GENEALOGICAL REGISTER OF THE DESCENDANTS IN THE MALE LINE OF DAVID **ATWATER**, ONE OF THE ORIGINAL PLANTERS OF NEW HAVEN, CT, TO 6TH GENERATION, by Edw. A. Atwater. Repr. of 1873 ed.
Paper--$8.50--66pp F5216

1410   - THE **BLAIR** MEMORIAL: WRITTEN BY, ABOUT, AND FOR **BLAIRS** AND THEIR RELATIONS, by Bob Blair. 1991.
Paper--$18.00--214pp F5216

1411   - THE **DURBIN & LOGSDON** GENEALOGY WITH RELATED FAMILIES, 1626-1991, by Betty Jewell Durbin Carson. 1991.
Paper--$36.50--597pp F5216

1412   - **WERTZ, WIRT, WUERTZ**, ETC. FAMILIES OF PENNSYLVANIA, 1400'S-1990, by Carolyn Choppin. 1990.
Paper--$30.00--435pp F5216

1413   - THE **CHURCHILL** FAMILY IN AMERICA, 2 VOLUMES, by Gardner Asaph Churchill, et al. Repr. of 1904 ed.
Paper--$43.00--707pp F5216

1414   - GENEALOGY OF THE DESCENDANTS OF NATHANIEL **CLARKE** OF NEWBURY, MASS., TEN GENERATIONS, 1642-1885, by George K. Clarke. Repr. of 1885 ed.
Paper--$17.50--216pp F5216

1415   - THE AMERICAN **CORYS**:THEIR SETTLEMENT AND DISPERSION IN THE U.S. & CANADA, by Vernon Cory and Michael R. Cory. 1991.
Paper--$17.00--98pp F5216

1416   - **WHITE** FAMILY GENEALOGICAL ABSTRACTS FROM REVOLUTIONARY WAR PENSIONS, by Elnore White Farquhar. 1991.
Paper--$17.50--93pp F5216

1417   - THE **BURNSIDE** BIOGRAPHICAL DICTIONARY, by Laverne Galeener-Moore. 1991.
Paper--$19.50--242pp F5216

1418 - DESCENDANTS OF JOSEPH **GREENE** OF WESTERLY, RI, by Frank L. Greene. Repr. of 1894 ed.
      Also other branches of **Greenes** of Quidnesset or Kingston, RI, and other lines of **Greenes** in America.
Paper--$30.00--500pp F5216

1419 - THE AUTOBIOGRAPHY OF HENRY **FOWLE** OF BOSTON (1766-1837), by Henry Fowle and David H. Kilmer. 1991.h
Paper--$20.00--248pp F5216

1420 - THE **JEWELL** REGISTER, CONTAINING A LIST OF THE DESCENDANTS OF THOMAS **JEWELL** OF BRAINTREE, NEAR BOSTON, MASS., by Pliney Jewell and Rev. Joel Jewell. Repr. of 1860 ed.
Paper--$14.50--104pp F5216

1421 - SOME DESCENDANTS OF MICHAEL & SARAH (**CATLIN**) **MITCHELL** OF CONN. & MASS., 1694-1988, by Marilyn Jordan-Solari. 1988.
Paper--$35.00--489pp F5216

1422 - **LEWIS** PATRIARCHS OF EARLY VIRGINIA & MARYLAND WITH SOME ARMS AND ORIGINS, by Robert J.C.K. Lewis. 1991.
Paper--$24.00--177pp F5216

1423 - YESTERDAY: THE **HAMPTON, MCCRACKEN, LONGWITH, MABRY & WELLS** FAMILIES, by Diana L. Mellen. 1991.
Paper--$26.00--392pp F5216

1424 - THE **MOORE** FAMILY IN AMERICA: DESCENDANTS OF SHILDES **MOORE** OF WALES FROM 1732-1891, by George L. Moore. Repr. of 1891, 1986 ed.
Paper--$20.00--175pp F5216

1425 - A HISTORY OF JAMES **MORGAN** OF NEW LONDON, CONNECTICUT, AND HIS DESCENDANTS FROM 1607-1869, by Nathaniel H. Morgan. Repr. of 1869 ed.
Paper--$22.00--282pp F5216

1426 - A MEMOIR AND GENEALOGY OF **JOHN POORE**, by Alfred Poore. Repr. of 1881 ed.
      Ten Generations: 1615-1880, Including the posterity of numerous daughters whereby pedigrees of many other families, extending through from three to six or more generations are given.
Paper--$22.50--333pp F5216

1427 - THE DESCENDANTS OF WILLIAM **BROWN** (1819-1908), ISABELLA **KENNEDY** (1820-1894) OF IRELAND, SCOTLAND & HAMPTON FALLS, NH, by Wilma T. Regan and Laird C. Towle. 1992.
Paper--$17.00--165pp F5216

1428 - THE DESCENDANTS OF JOHN **STUBBS** OF CAPPAHOSIC, GLOUCESTER COUNTY, VA, 1652, by William Carter Stubbs, Ph.D.. Repr. of 1902 ed.
Paper--$15.00--120pp F5216

1429 - THE **VIRDINS** OF DELAWARE AND RELATED FAMILIES, by Donald O. Virdin. 1991.
Paper--$21.50--147pp F5216

1430   - THE **STANLEY** FAMILIES OF AMERICA, AS DESCENDED FROM JOHN, TIMOTHY & THOMAS **STANLEY** OF HARTFORD, CT, 1636, by Israel P. Warren D.D.. Repr. of 1887 ed.
Paper--$26.00--402pp F5216

1431   - CHRONICLES OF A VIRGINIA FAMILY: THE **KLOMANS** OF WARRENTON, by Erasmus Helm Kloman, Jr.. 1991.
Cloth--$15.50--165pp F5216

1432   - **LYNN/LINN** LINEAGE QUARTERLY, by Phyllis J. Bauer, Editor.
      Surname publication. Quarterly - Spring, Summer, Fall, Winter. 30pp/issue. Features family biographicals, census, court records, abstracts, Bible records, queries, family group sheets, lineage charts, etc. $18.00 per calendar year.
      Volumes 1, 2, 3, 4, 5 available at $18.00 each postpaid.
Subscription--$18.00/yr--30pp/iss F5239

Index to Family Genealogies & Newsletters

[Numbers shown are not page numbers; they refer to the *Surname* Index # - pages 293 to 364]

Cody, 294
Coffin, 1007, 1287
Coggeshall, 295
Coggin, 431
Cogswell, 296
Colcord, 297
Cole, 39, 62, 806, 1325
Coles, 109
Colgate, 298
Colglazier, 1241
Collin, 299
Collins, 109, 300, 301
Comins, 1310
Comly, 302, 303
Compton, 81
Comstock, 304, 305
Comtes de Montgomery, 747
Conan, 1259
Conand, 1259
Conant, 1259
Cone, 1311
Conger, 306
Conings, 1259
Coningus, 1259
Conkwright, 1327
Connan, 1259
Connelly, 49
Conning, 1259
Conrad, 1277
Converse, 307, 759
Conway, 32
Conynges, 1259
Cook, 27, 30, 63, 1325
Cooke, 69, 308, 309
Cooley, 310, 311
Coolidge, 312, 313
Coon, 314
Coons, 50, 314
Cooper, 49, 88, 1061
Copeland, 315
Coppage, 316
Coppedge, 316
Corbin, 879
Cordes, 43
Cordray, 1286
Cordry, 1286
Core, 109
Corlies, 1007
Cornelius, 317
Cornell, 318
Cornwall, 319
Cornwell, 1258
Corson, 320
Cory, 1415
Cotton, 321

Covington, 66, 1245
Cowden, 322
Cowles, 323
Cowley, 1283
Cowperthwait, 109
Cox, 1312, 1313, 1333
Craig, 67
Crain, 28
Crandall, 324
Crane, 28, 81, 1325
Crawford, 96
Creighton, 1235
Crewe, 1286
Cripe, 29
Crisler, 32
Crisp, 50
Crispin, 109
Crist, 29
Critchett, 708
Crites, 1277
Crockett, 325
Crone, 326
Cronkite, 26
Crook, 57
Crouch, 49
Crow, 110, 1283
Crowe, 327
Crull, 1282
Cruze, 1402
Culberson, 328
Culbertson, 328
Culpepper, 56
Cults, 242
Culver, 56
Cummins, 28
Cumyns, 233
Cunien, 1259
Cuninges, 1259
Cuningson, 1259
Cunnane, 1259
Cunnein, 1259
Cunnieson, 1259
Cunnin, 1259
Cunning, 1259
Cunningson, 1259
Currier, 114
Curry, 4, 84
Curtis, 329, 459, 1006
Curtiss, 329, 431, 490
Curwen, 330
Cushman, 331
Cutcheon, 708
Cutter, 332

-D-

Daggett, 1277
Dague, 38, 1314
Dakin, 333
Dal Cais, 1259
Dalcassians, 1259
Dalton, 66
Damm, 66
Dana, 1315
Daniel, 1274
Daniels, 2, 1274, 1316, 1317
Darcy, 362
Dare, 108, 334
Daring, 347
Darling, 335
Darlington, 109, 336
Darnell, 108, 109
Darragh, 1281
Dashiell, 1286
Davidson, 1258, 1287
Davis, 30, 50, 101, 337, 338, 339, 479, 662, 1258, 1286, 1377, 1402
Davison, 1333
Dawes, 340, 446
Dawson, 25
Dayton, 18
de Carpentier, 344
de Chiel, 1286
De Cou, 346
de Franchimont, 350
De Hinnidal, 522
De Lannoy, 350
Deal, 62
Dean, 56, 341, 342, 519
Deane, 342
Dearing, 347
DeBorde, 48
Decamp, 343
DeCarpentier, 344
Decher, 345
Decherd, 345
Dechert, 345
Deckard, 345
Decker, 345
Deckert, 345
DeCou, 346
Deering, 347
DeGraffenried, 348
Deis, 1103
Deland, 349
Delano, 350
Demarest, 351
DeMoss, 50

Denio, 352
Denison, 353
Denniston, 1072
Denton, 1239
des Cou, 346
Des Marest, 351
Detwiller, 398
Dey, 1116
Dibble, 354
Dickerson, 25
Dickey, 355
Diedrich, 400
Dietz, 509
DiGiacomo, 1283
Dille, 356
Diller, 618
Dilling, 993
Dinwiddie, 1318
Dixon, 63, 357, 1290, 1291, 1402
Dockery, 1258
Dodd, 358
Doggett, 1277
Domingoes, 28
Dommerich, 359
Donald, 6, 360
Donaldson, 4, 6
Doolittle, 1319
Dorman, 361, 1320
Dorminy, 1274
Dorsey, 362
Doty, 81
Douglas, 363
Dow, 28
Dowse, 364
Drake, 365
Draper, 1377
Dromgold, 510
Drugan, 1026
Dryer, 366
Duckett, 95
Dudley, 109, 367, 368
Duffie, 50
Duffield, 1278
Dufour, 369
Duke, 28, 370
Dunaway, 371
Dunballoch, 434
Dunbar, 95, 1262
Dungan, 262
Dunham, 372
Dunlap, 25, 57
Dunn, 91, 556
Dunwoody, 373
Dupuy, 374, 375
Duralde, 66
Durbin, 1411

Durkee, 107
Dustin, 376
Duston, 376
Duyckinck, 377
Dwight, 378

-E-

Eager, 379
Eames, 1270
Earle, 380
Earlin, 11
Earling, 11
Early, 381
Easterday, 38
Eastlick, 25
Eastman, 26, 35, 82
Eaton, 382
Eberhart, 383
Eberly, 1284
Eck, 384
Eckman, 73
Eddy, 385, 1277
Edgerly, 386
Edwards, 50, 387, 388, 1283
Egbert, 62
Ege, 1321
Eggman, 73
Egner, 56
Eiler, 88
Elder, 34
Eldridge, 109
Eliot, 389
Elkinton, 109, 390
Eller, 391, 534
Ellerbe, 1260
Elliman, 62
Elliot, 392
Elliott, 81, 490, 1278, 1284
Ellis, 393, 895
Ellsworth, 468
Ellyson, 95
Elmore, 95
Elston, 394
Elswick, 5
Ely, 109
Emerson, 69, 395
Ensley, 61
Epes, 1399
Eppes, 96, 1399
Epps, 1399
Erb, 112
Estes, 1034
Esty, 116
Ethridge, 710

Evans, 109, 396
Eves, 109
Ewing, 397
Eyerman, 398, 399

-F-

Fahnestock, 400, 401
Fairbanks, 81
Fairfax, 230, 402
Fairfield, 1322
Falconer, 867
Falkner, 39
Fancher, 403
Farish, 48
Farley, 404, 431
Farmer, 1258
Farnum, 1250
Farr, 4
Farra, 1285
Farrington, 44
Farwell, 405, 1078
Fauconnier, 867
Fauntleroy, 96
Faust, 50
Feaster, 49
Featherstone, 406
Feero, 26
Feke, 439
Felch, 407
Felker, 49
Fellows, 710
Felton, 408, 409
Fenwick, 1377
Fergus, 1323
Ferguson, 2, 410, 1323, 1324
Fergusson, 1323
Ferris, 1277
Fessenden, 820
Fickes, 3
Field, 411
Fielder, 1333
Fielding, 96
Fields, 18
Filbrun, 29
Fillmore, 412
Fillow, 413
Finch, 519
Findlay, 1278
Finger, 1402
Finley, 556
Fischer, 414
Fish, 415, 1327
Fishback, 416
Fisher, 417

Fiskes, 438
Fissell, 326
Fitch, 418
Fite, 419
Fitts, 8, 10, 420
Fittz, 8
Fitz, 8, 10, 420
Flagg, 421, 1277
Flaherty, 82
Flanders, 422
Flaningam, 1280
Flaningham, 1280
Fleetwood, 18
Fleming, 423, 1325
Fletcher, 1274
Flickinger, 424
Flinn, 84
Flint, 425
Flippin, 762
Flora, 29
Flory, 29
Floyd, 1326
Flynn, 84
Folsom, 426
Fontaine, 1285
Foote, 34, 427, 428
Forbes, 429, 563
Ford, 81, 430, 773
Fore, 28
Forman, 84
Fosnot, 62
Foss, 69
Foster, 59, 109, 431, 895
Fountain, 111
Fowle, 432, 1419
Fowler, 108, 433
Fox, 88, 1327
Foxcroft, 1286
Franklin, 1327
Frantz, 29
Fraser, 434
Frazier, 65
Freeman, 63, 1258
Freese, 435
French, 109, 436, 437, 522
Fretwell, 28
Fricks, 1258
Friday, 50
Frisbee, 438
Frisbie, 438
Frisbye, 438
Frizzell, 1286
Frost, 439, 440
Fuller, 28, 69, 441, 442, 504

Furlong, 1281

-G-

Gade, 464
Gah, 55
Gale, 443
Galley, 1328
Gamble, 1329
Gardiner, 109
Gardner, 39, 84, 444
Garner, 49
Garnett, 57
Garrett, 88, 445, 806, 1258
Garrison, 62, 65
Garrisson, 65
Garroute, 11
Garst, 29
Gaskins, 1274
Gates, 340, 446
Gaudern, 464
Gaudie, 464
Gawdy, 464
Gay, 1285
Geib, 447
Geiger, 50
Gerber, 85
Getzendanner, 55
Gibbs, 448, 898, 1274
Giersch, 82
Giffem, 783
Giffen, 783
Gifford, 583, 1333
Gilbert, 39
Gildersleeve, 449
Gilfillan, 450
Gillespie, 56
Gilliland, 322
Gilman, 451
Gilmour, 259
Gilpin, 452
Gipson, 54
Given, 1187, 1189
Givens, 28
Gjerde, 27
Gjere, 27
Glarmorgan, 756
Glascock, 77, 78
Glassco, 77
Glasscock, 77, 78
Glassell, 1330
Glen, 453
Glenn, 11, 13
Glidden, 454
Goforth, 1402
Goldthwait, 455

Goodloe, 48
Goodwin, 258, 456, 457, 458
Gorby, 1331
Gordon, 459, 997
Gordy, 1286
Gorton, 259, 460
Goss, 4
Gould, 461, 462
Gourlay, 463
Gowdy, 49, 464
Gradick, 50
Graham, 25, 49, 465
Graichen, 1
Granger, 61
Grannis, 466
Grant, 26, 88, 258, 1274
Granville, 1332
Graves, 95, 1258
Gray, 4, 81
Graybeal, 662
Greeley, 467
Greely, 467
Green, 63, 468, 583, 1198, 1261, 1284
Greene, 2, 89, 469, 1418
Greenwood, 470, 471
Griffin, 96, 1274
Griffing, 472
Griffith, 62
Grimes, 22, 30, 473
Grimm, 38
Grisso, 29
Griswold, 474
Groff, 1285
Gros, 49
Grout, 475
Grove, 62, 1072
Guest, 1283
Gump, 1284
Gunning, 1259
Gunnison, 1259
Gustine, 476
Gysbert, 199
Göppner, 2

-H-

Hackley, 48
Haggard, 1327
Hagin, 84
Hagood, 62
Haines, 109, 477
Haldron, 52
Hale, 34, 478

Haley, 479, 1327
Hall, 49, 406, 480, 773, 898
Hallock, 481
Hamilton, 1281
Hamlin, 482, 483, 484
Hamm, 29, 48
Hampton, 485, 1423
Hanaford, 486
Hance, 1333
Hancock, 581
Haney, 487
Hannum, 488
Harbaugh, 489
Hardy, 63, 1287
Haring, 662
Harkness, 57
Harlan, 109
Harnish, 112
Harper, 1274
Harrell, 28
Harris, 39, 84, 1057, 1271
Harrison, 1408
Hart, 490, 1277, 128
Hartley, 84
Harvard, 491
Harwood, 492
Haskell, 438, 493, 642, 686
Hatch, 81, 494, 773
Hatfield, 495
Hathaway, 496
Hatter, 1278
Havard, 50
Havens, 1333
Hawkes, 498, 1256
Hawkins, 48, 583
Hawley, 497
Hay, 498
Hayden, 499, 500, 501, 1334
Hayes, 502, 503, 1185
Hayford, 504
Hayhurst, 28
Haynie, 505
Hays, 2, 14, 18
Hazard, 89, 411
Hazelton, 82
Hazen, 506
Heard, 553
Hearn, 810, 1286
Heath, 1277
Heatwole, 326
Heck, 29
Heckman, 1303
Hedgepeth, 28

Hegeman, 662
Heighe, 106
Heinecke, 1335
Heistand, 112
Heller, 398, 1277
Helm, 33
Helmer, 507
Helton, 18
Hembree, 1258
Hemenway, 508, 509
Hench, 510
Hendershot, 511
Henderson, 923, 1274
Hendry, 81
Henry, 512, 1245
Herr, 112
Herrick, 513
Hersey, 792
Hester, 514
Heulings, 109
Hewitt, 108
Hewitts, 1249
Heydon, 95
Heyl, 544
Hibbard, 1336, 1337
Hickman, 30
Hiddleston, 459
Higby, 515
Higdon, 93
Higginbotham, 62, 84
Higgins, 516, 517, 518
Higman, 1289
Hill, 519
Hillhouse, 520
Hillman, 521
Hilmer, 2
Hinsdale, 522
Hinsdill, 496
Hiscock, 108
Hitchcock, 992
Hiveley, 1294
Hoagland, 523
Hoard, 49
Hobart, 524
Hobby, 1274
Hobson, 583
Hodges, 4, 84, 525
Hoeft, 43
Hoffman, 526, 1235
Hogg, 662
Holbrook, 773
Holcomb, 527
Holcombe, 527, 528
Holdredge, 783
Holdsworth, 106
Holladay, 1260
Holland, 790

Holleman, 529
Hollimon, 30
Hollingsworth, 530
Hollis, 49
Hollon, 531
Holloway, 1338
Hollyday, 1330
Hollyman, 529
Holman, 532
Holmes, 76, 1405
Holt, 48, 107
Holtfort, 45
Hood, 3, 49, 373, 533, 1402
Hook, 534
Hooker, 30
Hoover, 28, 38
Hope, 258
Hopkins, 767, 1339
Hord, 553
Horner, 11
Hornsby, 50
Horsewell, 1277
Hostutter, 1031
Hottel, 535
Houser, 1402
Houston, 536, 537, 556
Hovey, 538
Howard, 95, 539, 540, 541
Howe, 542
Howell, 11, 96
Howes, 543
Howlett, 49
Hoy, 1400
Hoyle, 544
Huckins, 486
Hudnall, 84, 1260
Huff, 1250, 1406
Hufford, 545
Hughes, 546, 1327
Hull, 22, 81
Hume, 49, 547
Humphrey, 729
Humphreys, 50, 1340, 1341
Humphries, 57
Hungerford, 548, 549
Hunsicker, 550
Hunt, 109, 551
Hunter, 552
Huntington, 757
Hunton, 898
Hurd, 553
Hurley, 104

ORDER FROM GENEALOGICAL & LOCAL HISTORY BOOKS IN PRINT

Title: _____

_____

Author: _____ Vendor # _____ Price: $ _____
Last name sufficient

Tax, if you live in same state as the vendor: _____

Postage, if vendor specified as extra : _____

TOTAL: _____

_____ *Mailing Label - Please print or type clearly the portion that says "SHIP TO"*

From:

SHIP TO: _____

_____

_____

BOOK - SPECIAL 4TH CLASS RATE

ORDER FROM GENEALOGICAL & LOCAL HISTORY BOOKS IN PRINT

Title: _____

_____

Author: _____ Vendor # _____ Price: $ _____

Tax, if you live in same state as the vendor: _____

Postage, if vendor specified as extra: _____

TOTAL: _____

_____ *Mailing Label - Please print or type clearly the portion that says "SHIP TO"*

From:

SHIP TO: _____

_____

_____

BOOK - SPECIAL 4th CLASS RATE

ORDER FROM GENEALOGICAL & LOCAL HISTORY BOOKS IN PRINT

Title: _____

_____

Author: _____ Vendor # _____ Price: $ _____
Last name sufficient

Tax, if you live in same state as the vendor: _____

Postage, if vendor specified as extra : _____

TOTAL: _____

_____ *Mailing Label - Please print or type clearly the portion that says "SHIP TO"*

From:

SHIP TO: _____

_____

_____

BOOK - SPECIAL 4TH CLASS RATE

---✂

ORDER FROM GENEALOGICAL & LOCAL HISTORY BOOKS IN PRINT

Title: _____

_____

Author: _____ Vendor # _____ Price: $ _____

Tax, if you live in same state as the vendor: _____

Postage, if vendor specified as extra: _____

TOTAL: _____

_____ *Mailing Label - Please print or type clearly the portion that says "SHIP TO"*

From:

SHIP TO: _____

_____

_____

BOOK - SPECIAL 4th CLASS RATE